FUNDAMENTALISMS
AND SOCIETY

The Fundamentalism Project

VOLUME 2

FUNDAMENTALISMS AND SOCIETY

Reclaiming the Sciences, the Family, and Education

EDITED BY
Martin E. Marty and R. Scott Appleby

Sponsored by
The American Academy of Arts and Sciences

The University of Chicago Press
Chicago and London

MARTIN E. MARTY and R. SCOTT APPLEBY direct the Fundamentalism Project. Marty, the Fairfax M. Cone Distinguished Service Professor of the History of Modern Christianity at the University of Chicago, is senior editor of *The Christian Century* and the author of numerous books, including the multivolume *Modern American Religion,* also published by the University of Chicago Press. Appleby, a research associate at the University of Chicago, is the author of *"Church and Age Unite!" The Modernist Impulse in American Catholicism.*

The collection of essays in this volume is based on a project conducted under the auspices of the American Academy of Arts and Sciences and supported by a grant from the John D. and Catherine T. MacArthur Foundation. The opinions expressed are those of the individual authors only, and do not necessarily reflect the views of the American Academy or the supporting foundation.

The University of Chicago Press, Chicago 60637
The University of Chicago Press, Ltd., London
©1993 by The University of Chicago
All rights reserved. Published 1993
Printed in the United States of America

02 01 00 99 98 97 96 95 94 93   5 4 3 2 1

ISBN (cloth): 0-226-50880-3

Library of Congress Cataloging in Publication Data

Fundamentalisms and society : reclaiming the sciences, the family, and
    education / edited by Martin E. Marty and R. Scott Appleby.
        p.   cm.—(Fundamentalism project ; v. 2)
    "Sponsored by the American Academy of Arts and Sciences."
    Includes index.
        1. Fundamentalism.   2. Religion and sociology.   I. Marty, Martin
    E., 1928–   . II. Appleby, R. Scott, 1956–   . III. Series.
    BL238.F83   1991 vol. 2
    291′.09′04 s—dc20
    [291′.09′04]   92-10259
                                                                  CIP

CONTENTS

Part 3   Education and Media

CONTENTS
vii

ACKNOWLEDGMENTS

We thank first the advisers who began planning and conceptualizing this volume in meetings at the House of the American Academy of Arts and Sciences in Cambridge, Massachusetts. Gabriel Almond, Said A. Arjomand, Harvey Brooks, Gerhard Casper, Bruce Hoffman, Gerald Holton, Mohsin Khan, Daniel Levine, Şerif Mardin, Joel Orlen, David Rapoport, Susan Rose, Emmanuel Sivan, and Marvin Zonis participated in those sessions in November 1988.

Also contributing in significant ways to the process of identifying and recruiting scholars and clarifying themes for this volume were Nancy Ammerman, Daniel Brumberg, Stephen Graubard, Jeffrey Kaplan, Bruce Lawrence, Edward Levi, and Martin Riesebrodt. Many other scholars contributed to this volume through written responses and criticisms of particular essays after they were presented during a public conference; those not mentioned by name here are acknowledged by the authors in the endnotes.

Joel Orlen, executive officer of the American Academy of Arts and Sciences, merits another word of thanks for his leadership and encouragement in advancing the project from stage to stage.

Alan Thomas of the University of Chicago Press made valuable recommendations and supervised the various phases of volume review and production. Randolph M. Petilos, Jennie Lightner, and Kathy Gohl also contributed to the editorial process in significant ways.

We thank the University of Chicago professors W. Clark Gilpin, dean of the Divinity School, and Bernard McGinn, director of the Institute for the Advanced Study of Religion, for providing intellectual stimulus, office space, and the semi-annual use of Swift Lecture Hall. The Divinity School also hosted a graduate seminar, led by the Project directors, during which students drawn from throughout the university discussed and dissected early drafts of the essays.

We are most grateful for the tireless efforts of the Project staff, who put in many hours of "overtime." Patricia A. Mitchell shared editorial responsibilities, compiled the index, and prepared the final manuscript for publication. Barbara A. Lockwood organized the conferences, coordinated research trips, and managed the office. We are happily in their debt.

Introduction: A Sacred Cosmos, Scandalous Code, Defiant Society

Martin E. Marty and R. Scott Appleby

In the early 1990s, pondering the collapse of communism across Eastern Europe and the unraveling of Marxist ideology even in the Soviet Union, many American political commentators began to speculate: Whence will come the new enemy? Who or what will replace the "evil empire" as the focus of American reaction and enmity? What ideology, fortified by military, economic, or political power, will be virulent and contagious enough to challenge the efforts of liberal Western democracies to direct the course of global development?

"Religious fundamentalism" was the answer that came from many quarters.[1]

The delicate symbiosis by which the two great superpowers sustained their rivalry for four decades of the Cold War had produced an era of relative stability in the developed world. National borders were respected in principle, if not always in practice, as the postwar order was maintained along the NATO and Warsaw Pact axes. In the Third World, border disputes and civil wars, debilitating foreign debt, and ongoing economic crises only deepened the dependency of regimes on one of the two superpower patrons competing for global hegemony. With the diminishing of the Soviet player in this dangerous but effective game of deterrence and neutralization, political scientist John Mearsheimer warned that the era of world history dawning in the 1990s, contrary to widespread expectations, did not augur a splendid Pax Americana. The end of the Cold War would lead instead, in Europe at least, to a new factionalism, to sectarian strife and violent ethnic particularisms, to skirmishes spilling over into border disputes, civil wars, and battles of secession.[2]

In 1991, armed conflicts in "Yugoslavia," "Czechoslovakia," and the Baltic republics supported Mearsheimer's thesis, at least for the short term, while the splintering of what appeared increasingly to have been a poorly constructed national unity in India, Afghanistan, Sri Lanka, Algeria, the Sudan, Nigeria, and elsewhere suggested that in certain respects the Mearsheimer thesis may be applied beyond Europe. Once the Soviet Union was no longer able to act as a viable constructor and preserver of the (satellite) state, the full extent of the fragility and the artifice of the postwar nation-state became painfully apparent to indigenous bureaucrats in these troubled regions and to their postcolonial patrons. Factionalism and disorder seemed to mock the believers in "progress," some of whom had predicted an age of globalism, ecumenism, one-worldism. Instead the world now seemed beset by an inward turning of peoples, by antipluralist particularisms, or by the open aggrandizement of more powerful states at the expense of the newly created states. Against this chaotic background, the forging of an American-led alliance to halt and reverse Saddam Hussein's aggression against Kuwait in the Gulf Crisis of 1990–91, and the subsequent American policy of respecting Iraqi borders, even at the expense of ethnic (Kurdish) and religious (Shi'ite) claims to autonomy, seemed to have more to do with preserving the old order than with establishing a "new world order."[3]

In this context religious fundamentalisms in some nations seemed poised to inherit the mantle of failed leftist and nationalist ideologies. Elsewhere, their influence seemed to be spent or diminished. Whether or not these movements attain a greater measure of power and influence in the years ahead, an examination of their impact in the 1970s and 1980s offers important lessons for those who seek to understand the sociopolitical goals of fundamentalists in various nations, and the strategies they have successfully or unsuccessfully pursued to attain these goals. We chose to do this in two companion volumes. One, *Fundamentalisms and the State,* examines and evaluates the ways in which fundamentalists have sought to influence the course of developments in politics, law, constitutionalism, and economic planning during the past twenty-five years. Meanwhile, *Fundamentalisms and Society* assesses the progress of fundamentalist leaders and movements in their attempts to reorder scientific inquiry, to reclaim the patterns of "traditional" family life and interpersonal relations, and to reshape educational and communications systems.

One conclusion that will be immediately apparent to readers of both volumes is that "fundamentalism" has been much more in evidence in its extreme or unmodified form on certain levels of "society" than at the level of the "state." The three terms set off in quotation marks are central to this discussion and thus require early working definitions.

As a comparative construct encompassing movements within religious traditions as rich and diverse, and as different one from another, as are Islam, Judaism, Christianity, Hinduism, and Buddhism, "fundamentalism" is a useful analytical device. Objections to use of the term are discussed in the first volume of this series, *Fundamentalisms Observed.*[4] The title of that volume, as of the project itself, is not meant to indicate that every movement examined within it equally qualifies as a fundamentalism. Rather, the project tests the hypothesis that there are "family resemblances" among disparate movements of religiously inspired reaction to aspects of the global processes of modernization and secularization in the twentieth century. In the concluding chapter of *Fundamentalisms Observed* the editors note and describe a pattern of traits recurring throughout the book's fourteen separate studies of fundamentalist-like movements in seven religious traditions and five continents. From those "family traits" the editors construct a working definition of fundamentalism that we repeat here to give readers of the present volume a general idea of how the term is understood by contributors.

Religious fundamentalism has appeared in the twentieth century as a tendency, a habit of mind, found within religious communities and paradigmatically embodied in certain representative individuals and movements. It manifests itself as a strategy, or set of strategies, by which beleaguered believers attempt to preserve their distinctive identity as a people or group. Feeling this identity to be at risk in the contemporary era, these believers fortify it by a selective retrieval of doctrines, beliefs, and practices from a sacred past. These retrieved "fundamentals" are refined, modified, and sanctioned in a spirit of pragmatism: they are to serve as a bulwark against the encroachment of outsiders who threaten to draw the believers into a syncretistic, areligious, or irreligious cultural milieu. Moreover, fundamentalists present the retrieved fundamentals alongside unprecedented claims and doctrinal innovations. These innovations and supporting doctrines lend the retrieved and updated fundamentals an urgency and charismatic intensity reminiscent of the religious experiences that originally forged communal identity.

In this sense contemporary fundamentalism is at once both derivative and vitally original. In the effort to reclaim the efficacy of religious life, fundamentalists have much in common with other religious revivalists of past centuries. But fundamentalism intends neither an artificial imposition of archaic practices and lifestyles nor a simple return to a golden era, a sacred past, a bygone time of origins—although nostalgia for such an era is a hallmark of fundamentalist rhetoric. Instead, religious identity thus renewed becomes the exclusive and absolute basis for a re-created political and social order that is oriented to the future rather than the past. Selecting elements of tradition and modernity, fundamentalists seek to remake the world in the service of a dual commitment to the unfolding eschatological drama (by returning all things in submission to the divine) and to self-preservation (by neutralizing the threatening "Other"). Such an endeavor often requires charismatic and authoritarian leadership, depends upon a disciplined inner core of adherents, and promotes a rigorous sociomoral code for all followers. Boundaries are set, the enemy identified, converts sought, and institutions created and sustained in pursuit of a comprehensive reconstruction of society.

"Society" is understood here as the relationships among human beings as characterized by "the values [these relationships] embody, the individual and collective motivations they encourage, the incentives they inspire and sanction, and the ideals by which belief, attitude, and behavior are established and secured."[5] In accord with this general definition, the authors of the present volume pay special attention to the "values, motivations, incentives, and ideals" that guide fundamentalists in protecting and ordering the intimate zones of life. How best is one to marry, conduct sexual relations, order family life, raise children? How best is one to understand and teach others about creation and procreation, providence and scientific evidence, morality and spirituality? These perennial questions have generated religiolegal rulings, moral and behavioral codes, and scores of learned treatises by fundamentalist scholars and educators intent on sustaining, re-creating, or fortifying a religious enclave within a larger society that is perceived as invasive and threatening.

Because fundamentalists often live in close proximity to nonfundamentalists—or to fundamentalists of a different religious tradition—a second question is inevitably raised when one examines "fundamentalist impact," as each author in this volume does. The observer must ask not only "How effective have fundamentalist movements been in influencing their own adherents?" but also "How much impact have they exercised in the lives of nonfundamentalists?" Inevitably this second question leads to a consideration of the fundamentalist social reformer's relationship to the "state," understood here as "the supreme public power within a sovereign political entity."[6]

Fundamentalists are boundary-setters: they excel in marking themselves off from others by distinctive dress, customs, and conduct. But they are also, in most cases, eager to expand their borders by attracting outsiders who will honor fundamentalist norms or by requiring that nonfundamentalists observe fundamentalist codes. The state is the final arbiter of boundary disputes within its borders. In cases in which the state is "fundamentalist" (Iran, Sudan) or has been influenced by fundamentalist sociopolitical agendas (Pakistan, Egypt, India, and Israel), the fundamentalism of the enclave is encouraged or even empowered to spill over its natural boundaries and permeate the larger society. The impact in these instances is of a different order than in a society which successfully marginalizes fundamentalists within it, as does the scientific establishment in the United States or the political establishment in Japan.

By dividing this extensive study of "fundamentalist impact" into two volumes labeled "state" and "society," we do not mean to imply that the two realms are distinct one from the other; rather, they overlap and interact in complex ways. Because the state regulates many aspects of social existence and establishes the basic political and cultural conditions within which social life occurs, fundamentalists inevitably become involved in modern political life, even when they attempt to preserve their separateness (as in the case of the haredi Jews profiled by Michael Rosenak). In so doing they participate in a common discourse about modernization, development, political structures, and economic planning—a point made in Majid Tehranian's introduction to part 3 of this volume, which is devoted to an examination of fundamentalist educational systems. Fundamentalists may nuance and modify the terms of that discourse—they may successfully or unsuccessfully try to redirect or reinvent aspects of it—but they are contained within it and find any hope of even a partial return to a pristine premodern world, much less the construction of a purely Islamic or Christian or Jewish modern society or polity, well out of reach.

When they play politics to influence the policies of the state, fundamentalisms are thus necessarily involved in some measure of compromise and accommodation. Political involvement may alter the original exclusivist, dogmatic, and confrontational mode of the fundamentalist to such a degree that the word "fundamentalism" may no longer seem to apply. In the attempts to create alternative social and educational institutions, however, the arena of fundamentalist concern is more narrowly circumscribed for maximum effect and minimum compromise. Authors of *Fundamentalisms and Society* use words like "pragmatist" or "accommodationist" to describe their subjects less frequently than do authors of *Fundamentalisms and the State*. The authors of *Fundamentalisms and Society* discuss fundamentalist strategies designed to challenge the state selectively rather than to destroy or remake it through the proximate means of a national election, a coup, or a popular revolution. In all of the cases examined in this volume, an intense preoccupation of fundamentalists with individual conduct and interpersonal relations has had significant consequences for women in their relationship to men and to children, and for children in terms of their education and upbringing. The chapters in this volume on women, family, and education document intense and persistent efforts on the part of fundamentalists to secure what they describe as a traditional social and religious order.

Indeed, with a few important exceptions, fundamentalists have expended the greater portion of their energies, and have enjoyed the greater success, in reclaiming the intimate zones of life in their own religious communities than in remaking the political or economic order according to the revealed norms of the traditional religion. The essays in this volume suggest a number of explanations for this pattern.

A Sacred Cosmos

First, the majority of fundamentalists considered in this volume are "people of the book." It is not surprising that Christians, Muslims, and Jews garner most of the attention in a study of fundamentalist prescriptions for personal and communal life. The leaders of fundamentalist movements within these traditions were educated in seminaries, madrasas, or yeshivot in which the primary pedagogical method has involved the scrutiny of sacred texts and traditional teachings, along with their codifications in religiolegal manuals. These religious traditions have historically emphasized the regulation of personal conduct, family life, and education according to divinely revealed norms and commentary on these norms; they have been far less specific in stipulating macroeconomic policies and political structures.

These revealed and elaborated norms, taken together, establish a framework within which all fundamentalist inquiry occurs. This is a central theme in part 1 of this volume, a series of chapters examining the worldviews of various fundamentalisms, especially as these worldviews pertain to the proper role of knowledge, scientific understanding, and applied technologies. Although Muslim, Christian, and Jewish fundamentalists have different visions of the cosmos and of a just social order, they adopt similar attitudes toward secular sciences and anthropocentric notions of "progress" and "development." Fundamentalists seem to have more in common with one another across traditions than they do with their nonfundamentalist coreligionists, at least in regard to seminal questions such as the role of revealed truth in guiding human inquiry.

In part 1, "Worldviews, Science, and Technology," Everett Mendelsohn notes that Jewish, Christian, and Muslim fundamentalists alike reject the "decoupling" of religion and science by secular modernists. By elevating natural knowledge and disregarding revealed truth, they argue, secularists have disrupted the proper relationship between knowledge and wisdom. One result, fundamentalists in the three traditions contend, has been the destruction or loosening of normative restraints that would otherwise harness the dehumanizing forces of modern technology. Fundamentalists would reintroduce those restraints, thereby providing a model of behavior for other believers who would make use of modern scientific products. "Designed by God to be harmonious partners in the subordination of nature, science and religion instead enter into an inappropriate competition brought on by the secularizing trends of the early modern period and the Enlightenment," Mendelsohn writes. "Fundamentalists have made claims to be the restorers of the lost harmony."

The case studies that follow Mendelsohn's survey explore these themes in detail. James Moore examines the efforts of "a significant and growing minority" of Christian anti-evolutionists ("creationists") who maintain that the non-Christian temper of the post-Darwinian world is the result of willful disbelief in the clear teaching of the biblical book of Genesis. Moore traces the connection between "the creationist cosmos of Protestant fundamentalism" and the specific efforts of educators, parents, and creationists to recast the history and philosophy of science in public schools in the United States and, increasingly, around the world. He describes fundamentalist creationism in North America as "a well-heeled popular movement using advanced technologies—film, television, video, computerized direct-mail promotions—to commend its cosmos as genuine science to a culture still largely impressed with claims to scientificity." Activist organizations such as the Creation Social Science and Humanities Society have targeted local school boards, where they advance the argument that creationism is a genuine scientific method that commends itself on academic as well as philosophical grounds.

Similarly, the conservative and fundamentalist Sunni Muslims in Egypt, profiled in the chapter by Bassam Tibi, insist that ideas and instrumentalities adopted from Western science be interpreted and applied according to the procedures of the "Islamic methodology." This involves "accepting the text of the Qur'an as *sola scriptura*." In this view the foundational sources of Islam establish the irreducible requirements for any "authentic" scientific culture, for they provide not only specific moral injunctions but a revealed cosmology within which such moral injunctions make sense.

In surveying Sunni Arab attitudes toward scientific inquiry and technological application, Tibi makes a series of important distinctions between the different levels of the Islamic resurgence. The radical *takfir* cells that seek the violent overthrow of the Egyptian government seem little concerned with scientific questions in general and even less inclined to allow theoretical or specific theological considerations to govern their use of arms technology or other products of Western science. Philosophical-scientific considerations, discussed at length by Tibi, are the province of fundamentalist publicists and professors who are exercising an increasing influence over the mainstream conservative Muslim establishment. The impact of these internal debates on the official science and medical-technological policies of the Egyptian government seems negligible, with the possible exception of the recent debate on population control.

The issue of birth control and the proper use of reproductive technologies has also arisen in Iran. While belief in the Qur'anic cosmology is shared by all Muslims, Shi'ites in power in the Islamic Republic of Iran have enjoyed an unprecedented opportunity to control the direction and application of scientific research within a modern state. As Farhang Rajaee points out in his chapter on the construction of an "alternative science" in Iran, this "opportunity" creates considerable difficulties for those who would respect the integrity of Islamic thought while formulating workable public policies, that is, policies designed to meet the complex medical, scientific, and technological needs of a developing nation. Such considerations as population control and the exigencies of international economic competition, no less than Islamic theology and cosmology, have informed the philosophical discourse of such Muslim thinkers as Dr. Abdolkarim Soroush, who "lives in an Islamic state which has to deal with practical application of Islam to all areas of life." The Iranian ruling, discussed by Rajaee, permitting the use and distribution of contraceptive technologies is an instructive example of the compromises that may occur when a putatively fundamentalist regime attempting to legislate religious norms is faced with overwhelming material and social exigencies that render such legislation highly problematic.

A Scandalous Code

If sacred sources reveal a cosmology that makes moral claims on believers and sets absolute boundaries which society shall not transgress, there is a second reason that fundamentalists stay close to home in their most comprehensive and successful efforts to reclaim a lost "world." For it is in the realm of domestic relations that the moral injunctions are most developed, the boundaries most enforceable. This theme recurs in part 2 of *Fundamentalisms and Society,* which is devoted to a study of fundamentalist impact on women, the family, and interpersonal relations. Whereas their efforts to construct alternative sciences and to control the application of technologies are hindered by the sheer scope of the fundamentalists' ambitions, by the resolve of their opponents, or by the requirements of material prosperity, the attempt to "restore" "traditional" family structures and interpersonal relations is far more successful, precisely because the sphere of impact is self-contained. In the most intimate zones of life, fundamentalists can shape behavior according to specific norms and traditional patterns, with relatively little resistance.

In a chapter providing an overview of comparable domestic patterns within Islamic and Christian fundamentalisms, Helen Hardacre notes that for many fundamentalists the family serves as both a potent symbol of the idealized moral order and a microcosm of society. The attempt to conform daily life to this idealized order is "the highest priority of the fundamentalist social agenda." Existing social inequalities provide an inherent advantage for fundamentalists, whose efforts to order gender relations along "traditional"—that is, patriarchal—lines have met with considerable success. Hardacre suggests that fundamentalisms, with their severe restrictions of female sexual expression and autonomy outside the home, may be seen as patriarchal protest movements against the empowerment and "liberation" of women in nontraditional societies.

Hardacre explores the reasons women have for submitting to and even supporting fundamentalist prescriptions which, seen from a nonfundamentalist perspective, seem to inhibit their personal freedom.

Literature on the complex role of women in traditional societies suggests the various ways that religious ritual and myth may become means of resistance within patriarchal contexts.[7] The question of whether women are willing participants in the return to traditional norms of personal and social behavior is nuanced in several ways in the chapters of part 2. Which women in a given society are so willing? Under what circumstances do women support male-dominated fundamentalist movements? Do women assume leadership roles within fundamentalist movements, many of which seem designed to preserve and fortify patriarchal structures?

With these questions in mind, each author is careful to situate movements within their larger sociopolitical contexts. The varying contexts raise, in turn, a definitional question. Are these chapters studies of "revivalism" or "fundamentalism"? The distinctions between the two forms of religious resurgence are not always clear, either in scholarly discussions or in the behavior of the subjects themselves.[8] Crowded mosques, veiled women, and bearded men are not in themselves reliable signs that one is in the presence of Islamic fundamentalism. Indeed, some fundamentalists in Egypt and Pakistan look skeptically upon the revival of Islamic dress or Islamic preaching, in part because the revival is tolerated or even promoted by a state that is not Muslim. In this radical fundamentalist view, a controlled and co-opted revival may be a placebo that substitutes for the real medicine of structural and political reform according to the dictates of the *Shariʿa,* the Islamic law. This attitude is based on the assumption that fundamentalism, unlike many forms of revivalism, is inherently political.[9] A religious revival may involve a general cultural and social, but not explicitly political, return to Islamic paradigms and juridical sources. But fundamentalisms are totalistic: an authentic revival is safeguarded and secured by a comprehensive return to the fundamentals, the determining principles and doctrines, not only of religious belief and practice but especially of the polities in which Muslims find themselves. The chapters by Andrea B. Rugh and Shahla Haeri explore the scope of Muslim women's responses to these various expressions of the "Islamic current."

Rugh's study of Muslim women in Egypt, where the secular state attempts to contain the political expression of Islam, suggests that fundamentalism "from below" has given rise to a cultural revival permeating all levels of society and ultimately advancing the fundamentalist cause of Islamic rule. Muslim efforts to revive traditional family relations have strengthened the "Islamic alternative" to the state as the guarantor of the collective welfare. "To meet everyday needs, Egyptians now must move beyond primarily kin-centered relationships to personal relationships of broader instrumentality," Rugh explains. "In steering individuals toward loyalty to the *umma,* or community of Muslim believers, fundamentalist ideology gives direction to this tendency, and ultimately encourages a reorganization of society integrated at the suprafamilial level. Thus Islamic resurgence ideologies are reshaping the way individuals of the mainstream behave in Egyptian society, both as social beings and as family members."

Rugh notes that women today are not merely supportive sisters and wives—a role they played exclusively in the earlier stages of the Muslim Brotherhood—but are extensively involved in the Islamic movements as activists. These women represent all ages and classes, rural as well as urban, in Egyptian society; they are recruited to the cause by means of numerous independent sources of information, including sermons in the mosque, popular religious literature, television, radio and cassette exhortations, local study and prayer groups, and discussions sponsored by religious institutions. The most important source of religious influence, however, is the family itself.

In Iran and Pakistan, states which in different degrees have imposed Islamic law "from above," women who do not conform to Islamic norms are not only stigmatized by their peers but penalized by their governments. In extremist fundamentalist regimes, such as Iran under Khomeini, disobedient women may fear male reprisal. "Further restriction and seclusion, withdrawal of economic support for herself and her children, battery, and even rape are not unknown punishments within the home," Haeri writes. "Outside the home, women may fear the legal procedures that may be brought to force conformity, such as divorce, taking custody of her children, and the various physical punishments sanctioned by Islamic law." Thus it is not surprising that the attitudes of Iranian and Pakistani women reflect a full range of responses to Islamization programs that enforce veiling of women, segregation of the sexes, and Islamic marriage laws. These responses include a shrewd manipulation of the terms of the marriage contract by Muslim women who exercise a powerful measure of influence over their husbands, and the formation of small but vocal protest movements led by women who oppose fundamentalist patriarchalism.

At the same time, women in other religious traditions and contexts may view fundamentalist-like movements as vehicles for socioeconomic advancement. Jorge Maldonado finds that the new Pentecostal and fundamentalist churches in Latin America assist women in efforts to domesticate their husbands, to bring them under the discipline associated with responsible partnership in a Christian family. This is experienced as a considerable benefit to believers struggling to survive in a changing economy that offers opportunities for upward mobility to those who follow a rigorous work ethic. The importance of female leadership in the evolution of these church societies suggests that "impact" is not always in one direction. These churches, often founded by women, nonetheless espouse the biblical patriarchalism associated with other forms of contemporary fundamentalism. But they also stress that men as well as women should assume a submissive attitude before God. Maldonado's surveys of new religious communities in Venezuela, Brazil, and Ecuador, formed in part in reaction to the failures of institutional Roman Catholicism, illustrate the ways in which the new family roles of women and men stand in stark contrast to those of the previous generation. With conversion to the evangelical faith, women became more active in establishing the rules of domestic behavior and in making decisions about the use of money and time. Men became more affectionate and assumed a greater measure of responsibility for raising children, even as they demonstrated a renewed commitment to ensuring the family's economic prosperity. "If this is 'fundamentalism' of a sort in that it binds born-again believers to a close-knit moral community governed by literal biblical principles," Maldonado comments, "it is nonetheless a new variant of evangelicalism, one that is only selectively conservative of traditional patterns of behavior and is strikingly adaptive in matters of church organization and social leadership."

Because patriarchalism characterizes social and familial relations among nonfundamentalists as well as fundamentalists, it is not necessarily a distinctive or identifying mark of the latter. But the pronounced patriarchalism of religious fundamentalisms in North and South America, the Middle East, and South Asia is distinctive in terms of the level of self-awareness and intensity by which it is practiced. In these communities an insistent and at times fierce patriarchalism seems to serve as a pillar of the fundamentalist worldview. Fundamentalists are reading different signs of the times than are secularists or liberal believers; they look to heaven for their bearings and seem intent on demonstrating to outsiders that their worldview, their way of knowing, is different. If this scandalizes outsiders, so be it. The fundamentalist cosmos is not generated by the energy of post-Enlightenment Western rationalism but by the unseen but all-powerful hand of God. If the cosmos is sacred and meaningful, with its meaning revealed in doctrines and moral law, societies that modify or repeal the "irrational" aspects of that law are in disobedience. Not so the fundamentalist societies. Defiance of human norms that violate revealed norms is essential to fundamentalist identity and instrumental to fundamentalist world-construction.

D. Michael Quinn's detailed case study of Mormon fundamentalist families offers a dramatic and poignant example of this dynamic of fundamentalist enclaves. The abandonment of polygamy by mainstream Mormonism symbolizes for the fundamentalists the loss of devotion to the revealed word of the Book of Mormon. Scandalized by a practice that violated their own nineteenth-century ethical standards, non-Mormons, supported by the federal government, intimidated Mormons into abandoning the practice. In so doing, the fundamentalists believe, the mainstream Mormon community abandoned its very soul. All the more reason for fundamentalists to rally around the principle of polygamy as a non-negotiable fundamental: honoring the command of plural marriage gives witness to an untempered commitment to the unambiguous will of the Creator. The principle of plural marriage is preserved (if not the practice in all cases) and becomes a countercultural sign of defiance and allegiance at once. "A major appeal of fundamentalism is the intensity of its doctrinal emphasis compared with the primarily social emphasis of the mainstream Mormon church," Quinn explains. "Converts to Mormon fundamentalism do not hunger for polygamy—they thirst for a greater doctrinal and spiritual emphasis than they have known in the Latter-day Saints community."

In the final chapter on this topic, Helen Hardacre examines Japanese New Religions, a case that exhibits striking similarities to the relational patterns described above, but that occurs in what seems to be a nonfundamentalist religious context. In Asian religions one encounters a cosmology radically different than the one shared in general by the Abrahamic faiths. The divine is not primarily a law-giver or judge; sacred texts are not accorded the normative status that the Bible or Qur'an is in the West; and history is seen as having a cyclical rather than a progressive or evolutionary character. Nevertheless, Hardacre writes, the New Religions bear resemblances to fundamentalisms elsewhere, especially in their emphasis on male superiority and authority, supported, in this instance, by a sociobiological argument for female submission and deference. Furthermore, this assertion of female inferiority accompanies a program to reinstate the patriarchal family form of the prewar Meiji Civil Code, in which the authority of elders and the dominance of males were rigidly institutionalized and given legal force.

As in Christian and Islamic fundamentalisms, women participate vigorously in the New Religions, often taking leadership roles and in some cases founding new movements. But individual women lead in order to reaffirm traditional roles for all men and women. "The Japanese New Religions' ideologies of gender present a difficult paradox," Hardacre writes. "Their female founders typically defy social convention and achieve a public voice only by throwing off the very restrictions of marriage and motherhood that they spend their careers telling other women represent the one true path to salvation." The prewar family system favored by the New Religions restricts the woman's sphere of choice in matters of marriage, reproduction, and divorce. In the New Religions, "this older family form is imbued with religious significance so that it is not just proprietous to be a good wife and mother—it is essential to women's salvation." Women's rightful arena is the domestic sphere, while men represent the domestic sphere to the outside world. Women should not attempt to take a place alongside men in the public world, or the domestic sphere will be thrown into chaos. In this East Asian "fundamentalism" an idealized traditional Japanese society seems to stand in place of a revealed moral law as the ultimate desideratum of right-thinking Japanese.

A Defiant Society

A third explanation for the fundamentalist preoccupation with personal and family life may be found in the conviction, shared by other world-constructing ideologies in the twentieth century, that control of the moral and spiritual formation of children and young adults is the certain path to the eventual transformation of society as a whole, including the state. Intricately planned educational institutions, enhanced in their efforts and overall impact by coordinated advanced communications technologies, serve a rapidly growing number of "fundamentalists in training" around the world. Schools, day care centers, seminaries, and colleges are the local chapters of fundamentalist movements. But these movements transcend localities by virtue of the regional or universal appeal of the message and through the homogenization and marketing of that message via communications technologies that fundamentalists of every sort have harnessed to their various ends. These local products of efforts by fundamentalists to reclaim the institutional and moral foundations of society are by their scope and stability perhaps the most impressive results of fundamentalist efforts at any level and, in terms of long-term impact, likely the most important.

The linking of these local educational efforts with mass media channels in the United States, Guatemala, Iran, India, the Sunni Arab world and elsewhere places the fundamentalist message in a larger global context described by Majid Tehranian in the introduction to the third part of the volume, on "Education and the Media." By considering fundamentalist educational efforts within the larger context of global social and economic development, Tehranian's chapter provides a helpful analytical lens by which to understand themes recurring throughout the volume. He provides seven different but overlapping explanatory models for the various attempts of fundamentalists to create and sustain alternative societies. Tehranian makes the important point that the reactions to the Western secular programs that inform fundamentalist counterprograms occur within a "discourse of development" shared tacitly by secularists and fundamentalists alike. Explicit awareness of the shared goals implied in this common discourse may be a key to achieving a measure of rapprochement between the competing and conflicting worldviews of fundamentalists and secularists.

The attempt to clarify these goals and to integrate the values standing behind them into the common development discourse informs the specific social agendas of fundamentalists worldwide. Tehranian takes the antifeminist animus of fundamentalism as an example of the attempt to control the interpretation given to concepts such as "human rights" and "liberation." "A reassertion of patriarchal values in reaction to modern feminist values is reflected in the fundamentalist discourses against abortion, coeducation, unveiling, and more generally, women's full and equal participation in social, economic, and political life," he writes. "In the perceptions of fundamentalists across religious traditions the combinations of these insidious trends has led to a pervasive deterioration of the moral order and the traditional social nexus that once governed societies."

In mounting this counter-argument within the larger discourse of development and human liberation, fundamentalists eagerly and skillfully employ both traditional and modern networks of communication in the religious institutions, schools, and media. In the historical contexts in which the schools and the macromedia of communication (the national press and broadcasting) have been largely under the control of secular authorities, fundamentalist movements have relied heavily on alternative schools and media. Tehranian provides a concrete illustration in his chapter on education and communications in pre- and postrevolutionary Iran. During the last years of the shah's reign, Iranian Muslims availed themselves of the traditional educational, cultural, and communication forms and channels in conjunction with the modern micromedia (telephones, cassette recorders, copying machines, and mimeographing) to launch an effective campaign for the dissemination of their counterprograms. In the Islamic Republic of Iran, Tehranian demonstrates, the fundamentalist "development discourse" was institutionalized in madrasas, schools, university curricula, and textbooks during the decade following the revolution. Just as the exiled Ayatollah Khomeini's messages in the late 1970s were transmitted via long-distance telephone calls, recorded on audio-cassettes, and transcribed by long-hand to be mass produced by copying machines at government agencies, so today do Algerians, Egyptians, Jordanians, and West Bank Palestinians disseminate fundamentalist messages through the mosque, school, and communications networks.

Seeking access to the media, however, "seems to be a function of the strategy of social and political engagement," Tehranian writes. "The more engaged groups need and employ the media in their cause; the less engaged rely more on religious networks and schooling." Michael Rosenak's chapter on two types of Jewish fundamentalism and their different approaches to traditional education illustrates this point. The enclave of "ultra-Orthodox" haredi Jews in Israel rejects secular science and technology, and a great deal of secular learning, as being inherently and irredeemably opposed to the will of God revealed in the Torah. Thus any type of liaison with the surrounding environment of Zionists, much less any participation in a global "development discourse," is forbidden. These Jews feel themselves to be "in exile" from the world, Rosenak explains, and thus strive to create their own "total world" centered on the scholarship of Torah sages in Jewish yeshivot.

However, the socially engaged religious Zionists of Gush Emunim have no hesitation in employing the modern means of communication, education, and weaponry in their campaigns. The Gush insists that it is the only true representative of the national tradition, and that secular Zionism is bankrupt or played out. The success of the Gush in propagating this message, Rosenak states, "convinces the great majority [of Israelis] that historical Jewish culture is incorrigibly religious and therefore not for them." Here we have a case in which the consequences of fundamentalist activism are unforeseen and unintended by the activists. There is, ironically, a decreasing interest in Jewish studies on the university scene in Israel. Gush activism frightens secular Israelis away from their religious roots, for "the teaching of Judaism seemed, in the spiritual and political situation of contemporary Israel, less like a bridge between religious and secular Jews and more like a threatening beachhead of fundamentalists." Rosenak points out that this development seriously weakens the status and educational power of traditional religious Zionism.

Christian fundamentalists and conservative evangelicals in the United States and Guatemala are also occupied in the task of sustaining an alternative "total world," with its own profound social and political implications for the larger society. Susan Rose and Quentin Schultze explore these efforts in three detailed case studies.

Fundamentalist educators in the United States have made extensive use of communications media in recruiting for their schools and colleges and in spreading the message of these institutions beyond their walls. Rose and Schultze weigh the impact of North American media blitzes upon Guatemalan natives in relation to indigenous efforts to provide evangelical education and formation, and find the latter much more important in the overall scheme of things. Fundamentalist-style evangelicalism has become the sociopolitical alternative to the Catholic establishment in Guatemala, the authors contend, in part due to the cumulative impact of a wide array of educational endeavors in the 1980s, from Christian day schools to Bible institutes and seminaries that train people for the ministry, extension schools, Sunday schools, and orphanages.

Evangelicalism in Latin America has tended to promote political passivity and to legitimate capitalism. Rose and Schultze point out that successful small-scale entrepreneurship on the part of revitalized neo-Pentecostals does not necessarily portend major industrial development for the nation as a whole. Indeed, the small-scale entrepreneur is likely to be pushed aside by large-scale agriculture and industrial developers. "In this context," the authors write, "the entrepreneurial growth of evangelical churches is not eliciting a parallel development in the economy." The prospects for stability and economic growth in Guatemalan society are also threatened by the religious polarization that is one unavoidable outcome of competition between Catholics and Protestants for dominance of the culture. The impressive growth of evangelical schools and media outreach in the 1980s has guaranteed that the competition will intensify in the 1990s.

In the United States fundamentalist educators have established day schools, academies, and secondary schools whose educational methods and texts stress the mastery of basic skills and foster a fact-oriented approach designed to compartmentalize and "control" knowledge, rendering it "risk-free." Students in these schools perform quite well on the Iowa Basic, the SAT, and other standardized tests, but score poorly when evaluated on independent judgment, critical thought, and exposure to competing views on various topics. As Rose points out, these institutions are preparing their matriculants for the low-paying service jobs of the post-industrial capitalist economy of the 1990s, for employment by an elite corporate class which values punctuality, orderliness, obedience to superiors, and, in turn, frowns upon initiative, independent reasoning, and individualism.[10]

Rose reviews the recent legislative battles and lobbying efforts led by fundamentalists and evangelicals who seek both to supervise the content of textbooks and curricula in public schools, and to protect or extend the privileges enjoyed by private Christian schools. The pedagogy and curriculum of these Christian days schools and academies, which grew in numbers exponentially in the 1970s and 1980s to challenge the Catholic parochial school system as the dominant form of private education in the United States, is rooted in a biblical worldview. Fundamentalist history is *His* story; fundamentalist math, an entree to the ordered and dependable processes of creation; fundamentalist science, a lens by which to view an enchanted universe sustained at every moment by divine providence. In these systems Christian pedagogy proceeds from a biblically based view of human nature as depraved and sinful, ever in need of supervision, discipline and restraint. Knowledge is fixed and unchanging, to be accepted and internalized. The "facts" are established and verified by consultation with the sacred scriptures. In this regard the key concept is "integration": presentation of material from history, literature, the sciences, and mathematics must be integrated with the relevant biblical verses that provide the appropriate context for the material. In fundamentalist science textbooks provided to secondary schools by Bob Jones University, one finds a persistent juxtaposition of Scripture and content, a perspective informed by creationism and anti-evolutionism, and frequent recourse to pious exclamations about divine wisdom as an explanation for the complexity of organisms. Fundamentalist educators prefer texts produced by Bob Jones, because "secular textbooks are written to promulgate the secular humanist world view . . . the 'official religion' of the public school system."[11]

Bob Jones University embodies Erving Goffman's definition of a "total institution" as "a place of residence and work where a large number of like-situated individuals, cut off from the wider society for an appreciable period of time, together lead an enclosed, formally administered round of life." [12] The university exhibits a high degree of staff coordination and consensus about work goals and practices: good behavior is defined as conformity by all to the same unvarying set of moral codes, and deemed genuinely possible only in an environment free of the corrosive influences of a syncretistic culture. BJU isolates its participants in order to control the stimuli that impinge upon them. This "organizational tyranny" creates a "closed universe" and is the means to achieve its broad purpose of providing a Christian alternative to an educational system supported by a secular state.

As in the Jewish case, the Christian separatist strategy of maintaining an enclave from the world does not exhaust the possibilities of fundamentalism. Schultze examines newer institutions of evangelical higher education which participate more directly in the "development discourse" of mainstream America by preparing graduates not only for missionary work and Christian preaching, but for responsible Christian witness in all professions. By 1990, Schultze writes, "it was clear that the growth of Liberty University and Regent University, as well as the overall success of the Christian College Coalition, symbolized major changes in Protestant higher education as well as in American society. The new colleges and universities were far from bible schools or institutes, and their academic professionalism and vocationally oriented curricula reflected little direct concern with evangelization."

Schultze's comparison of these "new evangelical" institutions with the old-style separatism of Bob Jones University and numerous bible institutes provides an example of what happens when the boundaries between the fundamentalist enclave and the surrounding secular society become porous. In a pluralist society where they are in a minority, fundamentalists may find that they are the victims rather than the agents of cultural transformation. Schultze suggests that fundamentalist higher education may be significantly corrupted by its turning toward career-directed degrees and academic programs. "Higher education generally secularizes both individual students and faculty and eventually this leads to the secularization of the social institutions which the students enter upon graduation." Nonetheless the new evangelical institutions may experience difficulties entering the mainstream academic community, given accreditation requirements that could inhibit religiously inspired scholarship. Accepting public funds and following state and federal educational guidelines may also prove troublesome to many of the constituents of these institutions. This is not an important issue for the more separatist institutions, but it does affect the mission and purpose of the newer, more professional and cosmopolitan evangelical colleges and universities.

Fundamentalist access to media channels is, in most cases, a function of cost and government policy. In India, prior to independence, Hindu revivalists were unable to depend on major media channels to disseminate their message. Instead, they sustained a campaign, described in the chapter by Krishna Kumar, to develop Hindi as a medium of modern education. Seeking to establish the hegemony of a provincial upper-caste over the Westernized Indian elites who control key apparatuses of the state, Hindu activists in the twentieth century transformed Hindi "from a spoken language to a narrow dialect of educational and political communication." This political dialect, perfected in the Dayanand Anglo-Vedic (DAV) revivalist schools that adopted the syllabus and examination pattern of the state system, promotes an ethos of "Hindu nationalism" which is marked by a bias against "foreigners" (i.e., non-Hindus, including Muslims, Sikhs, and Westernized elites) and a glorification of the symbols and Vedic rituals of a mythologized Hindu past.

After independence, with open support from the Indian government, the dissemination of the revivalist consciousness of the Hindi literati accelerated. State funds supported textbook translations into Hindi by voluntary organizations dedicated to developing and propagating the language. State-controlled radio, and later television, provided another powerful channel of dissemination. Kumar notes that "the government's Hindi industry provided a means whereby the religiocultural agenda of the Hindi movement could be absorbed by the state apparatuses of formal education and broadcasting. Thus, having shaped Hindi in accordance with their ideology, the Hindu revivalists were able to develop a device uniquely suited for working within the secular state's apparatus." In the 1980s the number of DAV institutions grew dramatically throughout northern India, attracting the children of urban and small-town shopkeepers and professional families. Meanwhile, the ideology of the Hindu fundamentalist organization Rashtriya Swayamsevak Sangh (National Union of Volunteers) was conveyed to children studying in Saraswati schools that recruited exclusively from the Hindu population.

Hindi has been a major ingredient in the revivalist politics of religious and cultural separatism, which came into the visible arena of competition in the 1980s with the prominence of the Jana Sangh and Bharatiya Janata political parties and with the penetration of revivalist ideology into political organizations like the Indian National Congress and into professional and salaried urban groups. In the early 1990s this message has been translated to electoral campaigns and television shows, as the Hindu fundamentalists have found it necessary to expand and "westernize" the legend of the Hindu god Rama in order to render him as a metaphysical basis for Hindu nationalism. The televised "epics" of Rama's life, and legendary "birth" at the contested site of Ayodhya have built upon the nationalist educational programs of Hindu revivalists.

A Matter of Perspective

In a volume surveying and evaluating the impact of fundamentalists, who is doing the evaluating? The topics discussed in this volume elicit great passion both from fundamentalists and from those who would oppose them or even seek merely to understand them. The authors, many of whom hail from the nations or religious traditions about which they are writing, are nonetheless resolutely "of the Western academy." The editors asked them to put in brackets their own presuppositions, an approach which does not mean that they successfully leave them behind, but that they become aware of them, take them into consideration, and do some compensating for them. The goal in every case is to come up with essays in which the people described therein would recognize themselves in the portrait, even if they would almost inevitably disagree with the conclusions and evaluations of these nonfundamentalist authors.

The fact that nonfundamentalists do the writing guarantees that this volume, and the entire project, will reflect a particular orientation to foundational questions and will produce conclusions in keeping with that orientation. What are the sources of truth? What are the appropriate criteria for evaluating data and judging success or failure? From the perspective of a nonfundamentalist, fundamentalisms are often scandalous. They appear to stand in the way of individual self-determination, to violate basic human rights, and to impede material advancement, progress, and prosperity. But this is precisely the point of fundamentalisms: they and their God are not to be judged according to human standards. One cannot evaluate social behavior along strictly humanistic lines; behavior is good if it conforms to God's will. Thus, the reasoning goes, critics who do not share the ethical and philosophical assumptions of fundamentalists cannot hope to do them justice.

In mentioning this important matter of various perspectives on a controversial subject such as fundamentalism, it is important to state clearly that the positions or interpretations put forth in this collection of essays are those of the individual authors and do not necessarily reflect the views of the American Academy of Arts and Sciences. In undertaking this project, the principal purpose of the Academy is to bring together scholars with the best credentials in the several areas and cultures under study, and to ask them to present as inclusive and fair a presentation as possible.

By glancing at the table of contents, the reader will see that some important cases of fundamentalist influence are not examined. This is due to a number of considerations, not the least of which is the physical limitations of volumes which are already encyclopedic in length. Furthermore, the implications of recent developments such as the rapid dissolution of the Soviet Union for the spread of fundamentalisms were apparent only after these studies were commissioned, and will be treated in subsequent volumes. The project does not attempt to chase the latest headlines; most of the chapters in this volume were completed in 1991, at a time when fundamentalisms worldwide seemed to be entering a new phase of intense activism in the aftermath of the Gulf War of 1990/91 and the collapse of the Soviet Union. Thus the usefulness of these chapters lies not in up-to-the-minute reportage, but in their exemplification and analysis of patterns of fundamentalist activism that the reader may expect to discern in the headlines and news accounts for some time to come.

Even a casual sampling of the chapters in this volume will alert the reader to a number of these general patterns, discovered independently by authors studying "fundamentalisms and society" in quite different cultures, political and economic systems, and religious traditions. We have discussed some of these themes and conclusions, but the reader will also find synthetic comments in the chapters which open each of the three parts of the book. In the epilogue historian William McNeill has taken a broader synoptic view in order to assess the importance of fundamentalisms in world historical context and the prospects for their continuing influence in the 1990s and beyond.

Notes

1. See, for example, "U. S. Official Calls Muslim Militants a Threat to Africa," *New York Times*, 1 January 1992, p. 3; "Mahatma vs. Rama," *Time,* 24 June 1991, p. 35; Benjamin J. Barber, "Jihad vs. McWorld," *The Atlantic* 269, no. 3 (March 1992): 53–55, 58–62, 64–65.

2. John J. Mearsheimer, "Why We Will Soon Miss the Cold War," *The Atlantic* 266, no. 2 (August 1990): 35–50.

3. See the conclusion to Hermann Frederick Eilts, "The Persian Gulf Crisis: Perspectives and Prospects," *Middle East Journal* 45, no. 1 (Winter 1991): 22.

4. "Among the reasons for insistence on a single term are these: First, 'fundamentalism' is here to stay, since it serves to create a distinction over against cognate but not fully appropriate words such as 'traditionalism,' 'conservatism,' or 'orthodoxy' and 'orthopraxis.' If the term were to be rejected, the public would have to find some other word if it is to make sense of a set of global phenomena which urgently bid to be understood. However diverse the expressions are, they present themselves as movements which demand comparison even as they deserve fair separate treatment so that their special integrities will appear in bold relief. Second, when they must communicate across cultures, journalists, public officials, scholars, and publics in the parts of the world where these books have their first audience have settled on this term. Rather than seek an idiosyncratic and finally precious alternative, it seemed better for the team of scholars to try to inform inquiry with the word that is here to stay and to correct misuses. With those two reasons goes a third: all words have to come from somewhere and will be more appropriate in some contexts than in others. Words which have appeared in these paragraphs—'modern,' 'religious,' 'liberal,' and 'secular'—are examples. It is urgent in all cases that these terms be used in such ways that they do justice to the particularities of separate realities, something which we are confident readers will find the present authors responsibly undertaking to do. Fourth, having spent three of the five years set aside for research and study comparing 'fundamentalism' to alternatives, we have come to two conclusions. No other coordinating term was found to be as intelligible or serviceable. And attempts of particular essayists to provide distinctive but in the end confusing alternatives led to the conclusion that they were describing something similar to what are here called fundamentalisms." See Martin E. Marty and R. Scott Appleby, "The Fundamentalism Project: A User's Guide" in Marty and Appleby, eds., *Fundamentalisms Observed* (Chicago: University of Chicago Press, 1991), pp. vii–xiii.

5. Walter H. Capps, "Society and Religion," in Mircea Eliade, ed., *Encyclopedia of Religion*, vol. 13 (New York: Macmillan and Free Press), p. 375.

6. *The American Heritage Dictionary*, 2d college ed., s.v. "state."

7. See, for example, C. Nadia Seremetakis, *The Last Word: Women, Death, and Divination in Inner Mani* (Chicago: University of Chicago Press, 1991), chap. 6. Seremetakis studies Inner Mani as a cultural periphery, "a detached fragment of a global modernity" in which the construction of power by Inner Maniat women "is a ritualized process concerned with the divination of cosmological truth and the presence of fate" (p. 1). The case study offers insights concerning the way that women ritualize the pain inflicted by unjust social structures as a means of challenging and manipulating oppressive institutions. Cf. Leila Ahmed, *Women and Gender in Islam: Historical Roots of a Modern Debate* (New Haven: Yale University Press, 1992).

8. See, for example, the discussion in Shireen T. Hunter, ed., *The Politics of Islamic Revivalism: Diversity and Unity* (Indianapolis: Indiana University Press, 1988).

9. The point is made at greater length in James Piscatori, ed., *Islamic Fundamentalisms and the Gulf Crisis* (Chicago: American Academy of Arts and Sciences, 1991), pp. xiv–xvi.

10. Susan Rose, *Keeping Them Out of the Hands of Satan: Evangelical Schooling in America* (New York: Routledge, Chapman, and Hall, 1988), pp. 213–15. See also R. Scott Appleby, "Keeping Them Out of the Hands of the State: Two Critiques of Christian Schools," *American Journal of Education* 98, no. 1 (November 1989): 62–82.

11. Alan Peshkin, *God's Choice: The Total World of a Fundamentalist Christian School* (Chicago: University of Chicago Press, 1986), p. 115.

12. Erving Goffman, "On the Characteristics of Total Institutions," in idem, *Asylums: Essays on the Social Situation of Mental Patients and Other Inmates* (Garden City, N. J. : Anchor Books, 1961), p. 143.

1

Worldviews, Science, and Technology

Religious Fundamentalism and the Sciences

Everett Mendelsohn

Of all the manifestations of "modernization" or "Westernization," science is often identified as the outstanding achievement. Not only are its productions and its explanations or concepts applauded, but its approach, the "scientific way" or worldview, is celebrated as marking a distinctly higher form of human activity. From Condorcet's identification of the scientific with the civilized to the present routine teaching of "scientific method" in schools, science has emerged as almost emblematic of the "modern" in the world. What should be expected, then, when modernization and Westernization come under attack, as seems to be the case in many fundamentalist religious challenges? That social institutions, political and legal structures, and personal and family behavior should become the focus for extensive reformation comes as no surprise. But what of science? Has it achieved some privileged position that should protect it from, or make it immune to, the vigorous questioning that is part of the current movement of fundamentalist religious militancy?

One of the striking aspects of fundamentalist movements in Judaism, Christianity, and Islam[1] is the open willingness of their members, in many instances, to adopt the instrumentalities and technologies of modernity in order to "reclaim" a society that they believe has been (mis)shaped by the manner in which these modern means have been used by secularists. Given their rejection of any cultural system that marginalizes the sacred and allows or encourages pluralism, fundamentalists are neither uncritically modern nor thoroughly traditional; they are, rather, careful adaptors to modernity even as they attempt to reinterpret significant elements of the traditional.[2] Like religious modernists, fundamentalists seek in their educational and political programs to construct a viable synthesis between tradition and modernity; unlike the modernists, however, fundamentalists refuse to privilege modern (that is, secular) methods and values (including the sciences) in the course of integrating segments of the modern alongside the traditional. Fundamentalists, by and large, are not uniformly or uncritically antiscientific and often share with nonfundamentalists a sense of awe and, at times, outright admiration of the products of modern science and technology, especially those deemed useful for the program of recasting modernity in an antisecularist mode.

Indeed, in their desire to compete with secular groups for control of the cultural system (and state authority), some fundamentalists have gone so far as to make broad claims about their own special qualifications to serve as arbiters of scientific research and the application of technologies. Not surprisingly, these claims and "qualifications" are often severely challenged by the secular establishment, especially by the practitioners of modern science. Fundamentalist intellectuals (notably some among Muslim and Christian groups) may be alienated from the culture of modern universities and scientific research centers of the West, but they insist they are not strangers to science; to the contrary, they claim "modern" science and many of its basic understandings had their roots in the golden age of their religious civilization.[3] In this fashion they see themselves not simply adopting the products of modern science and technology, but rather reclaiming ownership and control of things inspired and nurtured in their traditions before the secularizing Enlightenment separated scientia from its ties to revealed religion.[4]

Among fundamentalists' claims, an additional theme has emerged—a critique of what moderns have done with, and to, science. Fundamentalists believe that the "decoupling" of science and religion, natural and revealed knowledge, has removed normative restraints against the often destructive forces of modern technology. Designed by God to be harmonious partners in the subordination of nature, science and religion instead enter into an inappropriate competition brought on by the secularizing trends of the early modern period and the Enlightenment. Fundamentalists have made claims to be the restorers of the lost harmony.

In the outlook of the fundamentalists studied in the chapters of part one, a consequence of the disruption of the premodern relationship between religion and science was the emergence of distorted notions of "freedom" and "progress." While fundamentalists believe themselves to be defenders of authentic human freedom, they give the concept a special meaning: "authentic human freedom" is rooted in the divine will; it is the freedom to realize God's purposes on earth. In *Fundamentalisms and the State*, volume 3 of the Fundamentalism Project and a companion to the present volume, legal scholar John Garvey examines this conviction, which he sees as being shared by religious fundamentalists in several traditions:

> Fundamentalists are also (like liberals) devoted to the ideal of freedom. . . . Freedom also characterizes the individual's relation to God. The godly individual is one who obeys God's commands of his own free will. Fundamentalists believe, as Calvin did, that true freedom is voluntary submission to the will of God.
>
> This is where they part ways with the liberal tradition . . . because freedom is ultimately submission, even if it is voluntary submission. Fundamentalists argue that laws which drive us toward God's will are not inconsistent with freedom; indeed, they set us free. Conversely, true freedom must not be confused with license—with actions that are inconsistent with God's will. "Free-

dom of speech," Jerry Falwell says, "does not include perverting and sickening the moral appetites of men and women. . . . Liberty cannot be represented by sexual license." In liberal theory the idea of freedom is bilateral, in the sense that it permits choices (to have an abortion/to give birth). For fundamentalists freedom is unilateral. The government must leave us free to do God's will, but it may properly close off other paths.

In some ways, then, fundamentalism is a peculiarly modern brand of religion that shares the ideals (individualism, freedom) of liberalism. But these are subordinate to a higher ideal: to get people to live as God commands. This peculiar blend of principles helps to explain various aspects of the fundamentalist political program.[5]

This ultimate subordination to sacred authority similarly marks fundamentalists' approaches to modern science and technology. Fundamentalists seek influence and control of political decisions, including the extent and direction of funding for scientific research, particularly in areas considered religiously sensitive. They also attempt to shape the discussion of science in the educational process. But fundamentalists face a vexing problem in this ambition. There is evidence to suggest that religious fundamentalism and the power to govern a modern nation-state effectively represent deeply conflicting forces. The current experience of Iran suggests that the fundamentalists who win the day and inherit the mantle of power find that it presents an uncomfortable fit with the mantle of the Prophet. Similarly in Jordan, where militant Islamic groups scored well in the 1989 elections, their leaders in Parliament were uneasy with the compromises seemingly called for by their direct participation in day-to-day governance. When once-radical or militant fundamentalists in the developing world find themselves faced with the concrete problems of health care, population growth, adequate useable water, food production, modern industries, participation in international trade, or the requirement of securing borders and maintaining modern armed forces, then science and technology become proximate means by which social problems may be effectively addressed. Their position in other more abstract or philosophical debates is largely downplayed or displaced and their pragmatic and instrumental role brought to the fore.

When this process of compromise occurs, hard-line fundamentalists—those who resist or refuse to accept secular-accommodative policies—establish and/or strengthen alternative institutions and systems to compete with the mainstream. Within these institutional havens, militants may be content to settle for a separate subculture that influences only a small portion of the population (although the numbers grow if the secular-accommodative regime fails in successfully dealing with pressing social problems). Or the hard-liners may see these alternative institutions and systems as centers from which to mount a long-term drive to repeal secular cultural influences through strengthened countercultural educational programs. This has been the case where issues of special doctrinal sensitivity are involved.

These two approaches are not exclusive. The anti-evolutionist Christian creation science movement in the United States, to take but one example from the following chapters, pursues both strategies. On the one hand, creation science has its own small but thriving subculture of research institutes, publishing houses, and professional affiliations. On the other hand, creationists' legal representatives are pursuing a strategy of direct challenge in the courts and legislatures in an attempt to introduce creation science studies into the public school curricula of several states. Similarly, among ultra-Orthodox Jews in Israel, cultural separation has become a community norm, but efforts are made to enforce the norms of Orthodoxy on the practices of the whole society.

The following three chapters provide the substance and detail of these general observations about the relationship of religious fundamentalisms to modern science. In his study of contemporary Sunni Arab thinkers influenced by Islamic fundamentalist critiques of modern culture, Bassam Tibi notes that these thinkers portray modern science as having its origins in early Islam and its first full expression in Islamic civilization. In justifying Muslim Arab acceptance of Western scientific research and technology, the fundamentalists speak of what might otherwise be called "borrowing" (from the infidel) as, rather, an act of "repossession." Tibi cites Sayyid Qutb as one among many Islamic scholars who hold that modern science and technology "originate in Qur'anic instructions." Farhang Rajaee quotes the nineteenth-century Shi'ite author Rifa'a Rafi al-Tahtawi as initiating the claim that the Arab adoption of European sources is quite simply "an act of repossession." If, in truth, the sciences originated in Islam, Islamic scholars contend it is only correct that they should be returned to the abode of Islam. Because all true knowledge comes from God—whether from the sacred Qur'an alone or from the traditions of the Prophet as well—scientific inquiry must be conducted within guidelines established by the religious belief. The claims of science must always be subsumed by, but never contradictory to, proclaimed religious truth and authority.

Tibi points out that many fundamentalist ideologues assume naively that this proposed partnership between religion and science is and will remain a viable one. Islam should decide questions of value and ensure that the technology and sciences imported (or returned) from the West are divorced from the corrupt, secularized cultural value system of the West. In a peculiar but invisible alliance, Western scientists have been equally happy with the supposed dichotomy between fact and value, instrument and belief. This view has been challenged in recent years from several sides. Herbert Marcuse, for example, in *One-Dimensional Man,* rejects the idea of the "*neutrality* of science" and technics, or the notion that "the machine is indifferent toward the social uses to which it is put" and constrained only by technical capacity. Instead, Marcuse adapts as his "purpose, to demonstrate the *internal* instrumentalist character of this scientific rationality by virtue of which it is a priori technology, and the a priori of a specific technology—namely, technology as a form of social control and domination." Other critics of the turbulent decade of the 1960s joined in challenging the idea of a science that stood outside values and beyond political debates. Lewis Mumford provoked the ire of defenders of the integrity of science in his *Pentagon of Power,* and Theodore Roszak, a voice of the counterculture, challenged not only the uses of scientific knowledge and technique but objected as well to the privileged position of scientific "objectivity" itself.[6] All the critics share a sense that science and technology do not enjoy independence from the forces of the social order and culture of which they are a part, and instead carry with them "values" and "interests" as well as the essential cognitive and technical elements of that culture.

From Tibi's report of interviews with religious thinkers across the spectrum of conservative Sunni Islam in Egypt, one may conclude with him that much of the voluminous writings on this question remain largely speculative and in the nature of theoretical concerns rather than practical advice, providing little that could actually direct science, technology, and health policy. Tibi argues that because of the urgency of economic development needs and the obvious relevance of science and technology to the development process in the Middle East, even traditionalists among the Muslim elite have been willing to appropriate aspects of the fundamentalist discourse in an attempt to establish the theoretical foundations for a working relationship between Islam and the sciences. Only the most radical fundamentalist groups have failed to produce tracts on the subject. These militant cells, working for revolution from above, acquire and use technology and modern arms without attempting elaborate theoretical justifications for this "borrowing." Because it is unlikely that these radical cells will succeed in ushering in an Islamic state in Egypt through armed revolution, Tibi points to the long-term impact of education and public discourse as the means by which a fundamentalist mentality will continue to permeate Sunni Arab society for the foreseeable future.

Farhang Rajaee discusses the case in which revolution did succeed in establishing an Islamic state, the Islamic Republic of Iran. (Pakistan has also established an Islamic state system, and other states with large Muslim populations have adopted various forms of Islamic governance and Islamic law.) In the first part of his essay, Rajaee reviews the work of the major modernist and fundamentalist Shi'ite thinkers who wrote on Islam, science, and technology preceding the revolution of 1979. The reader will notice that the basic themes of repossession and antisecularism are similar to those sketched by Tibi in the Sunni case. But when Rajaee discusses fundamentalism in control of actual state power, the reader is struck by the accommodative spirit of even the revolution's most famous ideologue, the Ayatollah Khomeini. Faced with the need for advanced Western technology in order to conduct the war with Iraq (1980–88), the fundamentalist leader took the supremely pragmatic step of suspending Islamic injunctions for the sake of the survival of the Islamic Republic. Rajaee quotes Khomeini's retort to the traditional *ulama* (religious scholars) in Iran who objected to such innovative and adaptive rulings: "The way you interpret the traditions, the new civilization should be destroyed and the people should live in shackles or live forever in the desert."[7] Rajaee continues:

[Khomeini] addressed the problems of interpretation raised by scientific and technological innovations. Many contemporary areas of concern had little relevance in the past; accordingly, previous jurisconsults did not provide any injunctions for them. But, Khomeini acknowledged, these questions are pressing and must be dealt with today. The Islamic government and "the nature of the revolution and its regime warns it that the doors to ijtihad [independent reasoning] be opened and that several juridical viewpoints be expressed even if they seem to be contradictory."[8]

Khomeini apparently invoked other juridical maxims, discussed by Rajaee, in the effort to support the one non-negotiable "fundamental"—an Islamic government. To implement this, Rajaee explains, Shi'ite leaders felt it necessary to take advantage of many "worldly means." In this decision was implied "an agreed-upon need for accommodation based on expediency and realism." This attitude of compromise made it possible for the Islamic Republic "to follow certain courses of action and make certain adaptations which, by traditional criteria, would have constituted 'forbidden innovations.'" Khomeini even argued that, because the intention of the Islamic Republic is righteous, it can perform acts that would otherwise be considered unlawful. Such notions, Rajaee concludes, "paved the way for the adoption of modern ways and the acceptance of modern products in postrevolutionary Iran." The essay goes on to consider areas in which the government has had to modify its stand, based on the dictates of expediency and realism. These include the issue of population growth and reproduction (the regime approved and distributed birth control pills and IUDs) and medical training and experimentation.

Clearly, Iran under the fundamentalists seeks to move away from a traditional way of life. One technocrat, quoted by Rajaee, expressed the meaning directly: "We have to change our pattern to that of a modern technical society." In this appropriation of modern science, medicine, and technology, Islamic religious leaders rely on casuistic reasoning and subtle adjustments in traditional teaching to achieve a pragmatic balance between religious absolutism and modern knowledge and practice. The question still remains, however, whether modern science and technology can be reconciled with the religious imperative. History will have to provide the answer.

James Moore's insightful essay raises the issue of a fundamentalism that has created alternative scientific institutions that nonetheless imitate secular scientific practice and form. Christian fundamentalism in North America emerged in the context of a society where modern science was fully established, modern medicine practiced very widely, and modern technology almost ubiquitous. The idea of a frontal attack on, or rejection of, these realms is clearly out of the question, even if fundamentalists had desired it. Instead, most of science and technology have been adopted and fully practiced. Where possible, they have been "Christianized"; where not, they have been instrumentalized. In those several sensitive areas where religious doctrine and scientific theory collide, fundamentalists have moved to assert the primacy of religious claims. The creation story has been forcefully advanced as either an alternative to biological evolution (the preferred option) or at least an equally accepted interpretation (the fallback position). Early in the century, attempts were made to ban evolution from the schoolroom and criminalize its teaching. In the post–World War II period, efforts through state and local legislation have been to gain "equal time" in the classroom for Christian creationist theories.[9]

What has marked the creationist efforts in recent decades has been the establishment of a parallel Christian-based "science" of creation. It has adopted many of the structures of scientific explanation and practice and has challenged as "unscientific" the probability-based concepts of evolution. In this latter move, Creation Scientists have cited the strong criticisms of the epistemologic bases of evolution by philosophers of science such as Sir Karl Popper. In adapting elements of modern science as their own and turning these against biological evolution, and especially human evolution, they have developed novel forms of the fundamentalistic critique of modernity, without giving up crucial elements of the modern. But their "bottom line" is clear: the biblical account of creation must take precedence over the merely scientific theory.

The creationist cosmos of Christian fundamentalism, an amalgam of traditional Christian theism and anti-Darwinian positivistic "science," should not in itself be surprising. It is rather a reflection of the complex relationship between science and religion in the post-Enlightenment world. This often problematic relationship sets the context for the chapters to follow.

Religion and Science: Intermingling of Myth and Reality

History provides some important clues to the location and interaction of science and religion in the European tradition, and these in turn provide elements of a framework for viewing comparatively the science-religion nexus.[10]

There are two parallel histories of religion-science interaction—one antagonistic, the other congenial. Even as science made its entrance as a new force in European life, it was negotiating its place and status. When the Royal Society of London was being established in 1663, the curator, Robert Hooke, prepared a draft of its statutes. One excerpt from this document is worth noting: "The business and design of the Royal Society is To improve the knowledge of natural things, and all useful Arts, Manufactures, Mechanick practices, Engynes and Inventions by Experiments (not meddling with Divinity, Metaphysics, Moralls, Politicks, Grammar, Rhetorick, or Logick)."[11] While by no means an accurate description of how the society's members might actually behave, it directly addressed the condition of science and its relationships in seventeenth-century England, and to some extent reflected its status in much of Europe. Organized science was attempting to define a secure, social, and cognitive space. Whether the activity was occurring in Restoration England, where Crown and Church had only recently reestablished their authority, or in Counter-Reformation Italy, where the reinvigorated Church was reclaiming its power and restating its doctrinal supremacy, science was anxious to avoid direct challenge to either of these two strong institutions.[12]

Scientists were aware of and had already constructed a mythology around the condemnation of Galileo.[13] They knew that René Descartes had sequestered his *Traité du monde* (published posthumously) and sought refuge under the protection of Protestant nobility of northern Europe. Almost by way of response, science self-consciously attempted to create an image of religious and normative neutrality. Experiment, not theory, was proclaimed as the guide to science in both the introductory notes of the *saggi* of the Academia del Cimento and the long "apologia" for science set down in

Thomas Sprat's *History of the Royal Society,* written just five years after the society's actual formation.[14]

Science was to be viewed explicitly as instrumental knowledge, connotive of no religious or metaphysical position. The historical contexts of the establishment of this position notwithstanding, the arrangement served science well and probably was equally valuable for state and religious authority. It is also true that science, at least from the period of its cognitive and organizational reconstruction in the seventeenth century, was in actuality becoming a significant alternative explanatory system to those systems held and defended by traditional authority, both religious and secular. Even if its specific theories or formulations could be criticized or cast aside, its epistemology, or way of knowing, gained increasing strength and posed increasing challenge. "Not by revelation but by experience and reason shall things, shall truth be known," science seemed to proclaim. In Enlightenment Europe this became a battle cry. Science, in spite of any self-proclaimed neutrality, was one of the strong forces supporting the increasing secularization of both worldview and social order. In a probably apocryphal, but nevertheless widely repeated story, Napoleon, after hearing Laplace's description of his new system of the world, was supposed to have queried the great scientist, "Where in your system is the place of God?" to which Laplace is said to have replied, "Sire, I have no need of that hypothesis."[15]

The myth of separation and even antagonism between science and religion can be found even more strongly stated in the nineteenth century. The increasing popularity of materialist philosophies, both scientific and political, and advances in sciences dealing with the origins and other aspects of life, seemed to create an even wider gap between the profane and the sacred.[16] Darwinian evolution, though variously interpreted by contemporaries, became a symbolic site of "battle" between science and religion. The rich symbolism of the largely mythical characterization of the public debate between Thomas Henry Huxley (Darwin's "bulldog") and Bishop Samuel Wilberforce at the 1860 Oxford meeting of the British Association for the Advancement of Science has often been brought as testimony of the antithetical character of religion and science. While women in the audience were reported to have swooned, the bishop and the scientist were reported to have exchanged barbed comments about descent from the ape and ignorance hidden behind the cloth.[17]

The point of this recitation is to indicate that there is both myth and reality behind the story of the increasing separation of religion and science in the period of Europe's (and North America's) modernization. The context for this, however, was the obvious successful growth of industrial and technological activity and the imputed important role that science played in those successes. Science became increasingly and inextricably linked to the modernizing process—instrumentally for sure, but also I would contend as a very significant part of the worldview (perhaps the defining part) of modern industrial societies. The scientific way of knowing increased its explanatory—and epistemological—domains from the physical through the behavioral, economic, political, and social realms. Any challenge to the project of modernity would, therefore, at least seem to involve a challenge to science. This certainly is a core feature of science's self-constructed worldview, persistent claims to the contrary notwithstanding.[18]

There is, of course, a second, not quite parallel but overlapping history. Its symbols are everywhere visible: Charles Darwin lies buried in Westminster Abbey (the focal center of the Anglican Church) a few yards from Isaac Newton. This second history includes elements of a congenial or at least accommodating relationship between religion and science. It too has roots in the seventeenth century, involving many of the same actors visible in the antagonistic history.

Francis Bacon articulated one view which gained wide currency. God, he claimed, had written two books: one, of course, the Word, the Bible; the second was the Book of Nature, God's handiwork displayed on earth. God's will therefore could be learned through study of the Word, but also by examining the structures of his earthly productions. So important a task was this that Bacon believed if humans could so thoroughly understand God's material productions that they could extend them by human artifice, might not humans through this effort be able to reachieve the state of Grace from which they fell in the Garden of Eden? [19] Science in this account joined in a form of common cause with religion. In the hands of others such as John Ray, a full-blown *natural* theology was elaborated. God was the creator of natural laws which were discoverable by human effort; nature was informed by God's design. Particularly in England this Christian form of natural explanation remained active well into the nineteenth century, although the established scientific community had abandoned it somewhat earlier.

Another dimension of the religion-science relationship was charted by the sociologist Robert K. Merton in his classic study *Science, Technology and Society in 17th-Century England* (1938). He makes the claim that not only was religion not detrimental to scientific practice but, in the case of British Puritanism (and by extension other forms of radical or ascetic Protestantism), served as an actual spur to involvement in the sciences. His explanation closely parallels the theories of Weber or Tawney about the positive relation between Protestantism and the emergence of capitalism. Merton added strength to his claim through an extensive empirical examination of the religious affiliations of identifiable seventeenth-century British scientists. The core of Merton's thesis was the existence of an overlapping value structure or ethos behind both Puritan religious activity and scientific practice.[20] Religious fundamentalisms raise this question of religious commitment as a potential impediment to involvement in the sciences as differentiated from attitudes toward specific scientific beliefs or practices.

History gives us some important examples of individuals who at one and the same time were active and significant contributors to science and deeply committed practitioners of fundamentalist forms of Christianity. Michael Faraday, a major English scientist of the first half of the nineteenth century, was a firm believing member and elder of the Sandemanian sect, a group committed to minute scrutiny of the Bible and rigid adherence to a code of Christian behavior. His science took the very specific form of elevating experiment to the exclusion of speculation. His biographers suggest it was probably this single-mindedness which permitted him to avoid the controversy over Darwinian evolution; he might also have practiced a compartmentalizing of his thoughts. He believed that his scientific researches revealed God's rules and creations in nature, adopting elements of the natural theology tradition.[21] While Faraday may illustrate an extreme case, there were numerous examples through the nineteenth century of individual scientists who succeeded in consciously adapting their religious and scientific beliefs and practices to each other. By the mid and late twentieth century, however, it is rare to find active scientists who engaged in forms of explicit integration of their professional life with vigorous religious activity. If scientists were adherents to religious groups, a comfortable bifurcation marked these two spheres. Religion, if it provided any guide, was limited to moral questions about the use and application of knowledge and technique.

The Fundamentalist Reassertion of Religious Primacy

If there is a single theme uniting militant or revived religious fundamentalisms, it is the primacy of religious belief and authority in all spheres of human life. Beyond that, "understanding lies in the details." The special cases and variations seem as interesting and important as the broad similarities and generalizations.

Is opposition to modern science and technology a characteristic of religious fundamentalisms as we know them today? In any simple or general form the answer must be no. But the observation that Aviezer Ravitzky makes concerning the Lubavitch Hasidic movement of Jewish ultra-Orthodoxy would seem to be true for many forms of religious fundamentalism: "It condemns any trace of modern epistemological skepticism." Hasidic leaders made clear, "Whenever any contradiction is to be found [between the literal meaning of the biblical text and scientific conceptions], the scriptural passage should be read in its clear, literal fashion."[22] The ambiguity arises in the extent to which science and technology in their separate, specific forms and manifestations are used, accepted, or at least tolerated. Most fundamentalists (tacitly at least) agree to live and operate within a world significantly informed and influenced by modern science and technologies. Some, such as Abdul Latif Arabayyat, the Muslim Brotherhood political leader and Speaker of the Jordanian Parliament, refer to the use of "scientific methodology," to "experiments and tests," when dealing with social and material problems. But for this Texas-trained Ph.D. in engineering there is a concomitant (contradictory?) sharp criticism of the overwhelming materialism which has come to the Orient through Westernization.[23]

Which leads to a second focused question: how shall we, in summary, characterize fundamentalisms' attitudes toward science and technology? In a word, the answer is mixed. The attitudes are nuanced, selectively hostile, widely accepting, with some important boundaries and limitations imposed. Problems emerge most clearly at the epistemological level, especially where those things to be known are at the border, or interface, of the religious and the secular. The most striking, of course, involve life and the living, both at the explanatory and active level. But the points of contest have changed and been sharpened with the growth of scientific ability to intervene and with militant religions' attempts to reassert control or hegemony over areas ceded by default or defeat in earlier contests. But the circumstances and conditions vary widely: from the Protestant revolts against some forms of scientific and medical incursion in the highly modernized context of North America to the fundamentalist challenges in mixed or traditional societies of the Islamic Middle East.

The extensive establishment of a creation science in the United States to reexplain human origins or the building of a movement to oppose the use of fetal tissue in medical experimentation is partly shaped by the immediate social and scientific history and context of the United States. The attempt to adapt the creationist argument to the context of ultra-Orthodox Judaism in Israel in the late 1980s met with singular failure, despite the fact that there were some active local advocates and that one of the strong American proponents, Duane T. Gish, was invited to speak at an important meeting where the project was launched.[24]

While many of those involved in the Christian creation science controversy have training in modern science, it is probably true to claim that for many, if not all, of the Jewish practitioners of fundamentalist religion, science is just not important. As Michael Rosenak puts it concerning ultra-Orthodox Jews, the haredi "learner" had a "studied disregard for the surrounding reality."[25] Perhaps even more important, in their education "there is almost no teaching for deliberation," no dealing with inconsistencies or historical influences. Members of fundamentalist groups are not drawn into careers in the theoretical sciences; the schools established by the religious communities do not teach science, but give attention to the sacred not the secular, to religious text and practice, not to things scientific and material. Indeed the scientist is seen as the "victim of illusion." Some analysts like Rosenak consider Jewish fundamentalism as a "counterculture" which is antagonistic to scientific method albeit generally comfortable with modern technology.

Another element worth noting is that there is a strong gender differentiation, at least among Jewish fundamentalists. Women are not included in the formal education system of the Orthodox, a system devoted only to Torah learning. Because they are considered spiritually less talented, girls from ultra-Orthodox families receive a humanistic education and have traditionally served as a bridge between the profane and holy communities; women keep house, perhaps run a store, teach in a school, or even operate a computer.[26]

But if women in ultra-Orthodox Judaism are destined to receive a secular education and work in the world, for the believing man study of the Torah is preeminent and any scientific endeavors are consequently diminished. Even if women were not excluded from scientific practice by religious precept, there is no indication that women from the Jewish fundamentalist tradition are drawn to science. The surrounding attitudes certainly give no encouragement.

An equally strong claim about the negative impact of fundamentalism in Islam was made by the Pakistani-born Nobel Prize–winning physicist Mohammad Abdus Salam: "There is no question but today, of all civilizations on this planet, science is weakest in the lands of Islam. . . . Science only prospers provided there are sufficient practitioners to constitute a community which can work with serenity, with fullest support in terms of the necessary experimental and library infrastructure, and with the ability to criticize openly each other's work. These conditions are not satisfied in contemporary Islam."[27] Salam's point is explored in detail by a younger Pakistani physicist, Pervez Hoodbhoy, in a recent study, *Islam and Science*. The impoverished state of science and technology in Islamic countries is documented by a range of statistical data. Hoodbhoy tells the story of the Islamic modernist movement, which had emphasized Islam's compatibility with modern science and technology, being overwhelmed by fundamentalist movements which have come to dominate intellectual discourse in the Muslim world. This has led to the disinterest in, and low state of, scientific activity in many Islamic countries. But with Salam, he notes that the Islamic world is not monolithic, and differential patterns and practices may emerge. Both these physicists agree that "pragmatism may provide the one modality through which real science in Muslim countries may be regenerated."[28]

As mentioned above, opposition to science and criticism of its major forms, objectivity and normative neutrality, have other, nonreligious proponents in the late twentieth century. The counterculture of the 1970s in North America and Western Europe took direct aim at science not only as practice, especially in its links to the military and to "oppressive" industry, but also as a way of knowing. Scientific objectivity as a guide to human action was rejected, and the scientific way of knowing was challenged as inadequate.[29] The cry was for reintegration of normative considerations into the canons of science; ethics and values became a focus for a reconstructed science, and as one author put it, it was time for a "reenchantment of the world." The new left, epitomized by the writings of Marcuse and his disciples, engaged in a sharp critique of domination where science was seen as providing the voice and vocabulary for the domination of nature and consequently of people.[30]

The challenge to the adequacy of scientific epistemology and the primacy of fact continues into the 1990s in the texts of postmodernism and deconstructionism on the literary and philosophical front, while feminist scholars reexamine the foundations of all knowledge and practice. Science as privileged knowledge is clearly a thing of the past as the continuing activities of science and scientists come under the same scrutiny as all other forms of social action.[31]

Complete rejection of science by fundamentalist religious groups is, however, limited to small sectors of religious militants; more common have been forms of adaptation and accommodation. Several strategies have been utilized either explicitly or tacitly to allow an integration of science into the daily life of fundamentalist communities. The boundaries and modes differ and continually shift, but there has been some uniformity in practice, as noted above and made apparent in the studies that follow. One mode has been to segregate those special areas where religious considerations have explicit meaning, primarily those dealing with the human body, life, and reproduction. Here the battle for the primacy of religious authority is engaged. In all other areas the assumption is made that religious primacy is unchallenged.

It is in this decoupling of several controversial areas of scientific activity from the broadly accepted realms that religious fundamentalists and scientists accept a common explanation: Scientific knowledge in most realms is instrumental knowledge connotive of no normative intent or interest. It is in this context of knowledge as mere instrument, given guidance by other more authoritative sources for the achievement of religious ends, that most technology has been easily adapted. The well-known image of the sermons of the Iranian religious leader Ayatollah Khomeini being smuggled into Iran as cassette recordings and disseminated throughout the country for rebroadcast to a restive population seems to clearly link militant Islam and modern communications technology. Technology served the ends of militant and revolutionary religion. Even at the height of religious militancy, the Islamic government of Iran made every effort to secure from the West the latest technologies of war to pursue its battles against Iraq.

That moves of this sort are, however, not wholly unproblematic for some forms of religious fundamentalism is made clear in a study by Aviezer Ravitzky which shows one leader of Hasidic Judaism vigorously condemning another for using the radio to broadcast basic religious texts and lessons. The radio was an "abominable vehicle—'an act of Satan,'" normally used for the communication of heresies. The defense offered by the Hasidic user against this total "demonization of modernity" went beyond the mere instrumental argument that broadcasting was a neutral tool, to praise radio waves in terms normally reserved for the holy: "It was a tremendous power implanted by the Creator within nature so that, by means of an appropriate instrument, the voice of the speaker may be heard from one corner of the world to the other—at the very moment of speech. In radio, there is reflected a sublime spiritual matter."[32] The underlying argument which is repeated in many other religious contexts involves praise for those things that extend religious knowledge and authority. Tibi and Rajaee examine this point in the context of Islamic responses to and adaptations of modern science and technique; both doctrine and practice provide ample evidence of successful adaptation and uneasy alliance. There is evidence in the attempts to instrumentalize science and technology of something of the same ambivalence faced by China during the closing years of the nineteenth century and opening years of the twentieth. The motto which was repeated there with frequency during the meeting of Western science and traditional Chinese culture was heard also in the Middle East as Islam engaged modern science: to become Western in technique but remain Eastern in essence.[33] Tibi points directly to the efforts of the Egyptian fundamentalist Imaduldin Khalil to mediate the interaction. Science is a neutral instrument; it is not heretical. It can be used in the service of Islam; the technologies can be Islamicized and separated from their norms and values.[34]

But beyond instrumentalization and utility as the bases for adaptation of science and technology, some Islamic fundamentalists add an additional, critical element—the history of modern science itself. As Khalil forcefully notes, "modern science is not only the achievement of Western civilization. . . . The civilization of Islam essentially contributed to establishing its underpinnings."[35] This theme of an Arabic and Islamic role in the building of modern science is repeated in numerous sources. The history of the Arabic-Islamic role in the construction of "Western" science is still being written and reinterpreted. The early descriptions of Islam as merely a site for the "incubation" of Greek science before its absorption in late medieval Europe have now been significantly supplemented with accounts of important contributions to the corpus of science. The relevance of the fundamentalists' justification for utilizing elements of science and technology is based on strong historical grounds. The key point of contention will almost certainly continue to be the instrumental-value dichotomy advanced by religious advocates. At times this issue becomes confused with the existence of a distinct "Islamic science" or "Islamic technology."[36]

While historical antecedent and theoretical discourse can provide one level of understanding of the fundamentalism-science exchange, the outstanding question comes in the realm of current action. Where contemporary religious fundamentalisms have achieved power over the apparatus of the state or other forms of authority over social institutions, what has been the outcome in the interaction between science and religion? That state authority can be used to impose an "orthodoxy" on science comes as no revelation to those who watched the creation of "Nazi sciences" in the Germany of the 1930s and 1940s: relativity was banned and racial and genetic theories were introduced and put into practice to take but a few of the examples.[37] Similar attempts to construct an ideologically acceptable science in the late Stalin years of Soviet history also involved the rewriting of several basic sciences to bring them into conformity with state and Communist party orthodoxy.[38] In both cases scientific institutions were reorganized, individual scientists lost jobs (and even their lives), and the educational and research systems were brought into conformity with the new ideology. Scientific truths were proclaimed, and practicing scientists had no choice but to accept. The coercive use of state power to structure or limit intellectual activity has unfortunately been used all too often in history. Nonetheless, in neither the Soviet Union nor Nazi Germany was the whole enterprise of science and technology compromised, albeit significant segments were weakened. Institutionalized science proved to have a certain resilience and viability in both of these modernized societies.

In the United States, efforts have been made on several occasions to bring scientific concept and practice into conformity with religious belief. Because of the state structure this has most often occurred at the local (state or municipal) level. From the Scopes trial of the early twentieth century in Tennessee to the more recent efforts in several midwestern states, attempts have been made by Christian fundamentalists to control the teaching in biology classes (and in others on some occasions) of theories dealing with evolution, most particularly human origins. Laws were passed in state legislatures mandating the content of textbooks and classroom instruction to bring it into adherence with what the advocates believed was basic Christian teaching. That the laws were ultimately ruled unconstitutional in federal court does not take away from the intent of the fundamentalist activists: to impose their system of beliefs about creation on the public-at-large through the public school system. Their efforts, however, have been unsuccessful in a society where church and state are separated by both constitution and tradition.

On other questions success might be closer at hand as conservative jurists become more numerous in the federal courts, including the Supreme Court. Debates about the use of fetal tissue in medical experimentation become more urgent, and restricting abortion has become the focus of a mixed religious and secular conservative movement. Thus even in a modern secular society such as the United States, where science is largely celebrated, attempts to limit or shape scientific and medical theory and practice using the apparatus of the state are enduring and in some cases may succeed. But beyond these controversial areas concerning life and reproduction, science as a whole flourishes. It may be criticized and chided for its arrogance, for its failures to respond to ethical and normative concerns, but by and large it receives broad public approbation. It has become institutionally embedded in the social order and has largely worked out a modus operandi with the society at large.

But what about countries where religious fundamentalism actually has state authority, as in Iran? Rajaee's examination of the interaction of Shi'a Islam in Iran and the modern sciences is instructive. A prominent figure in defining what the relations between science and an Islamic state should look like was the medically trained Dr. Abdulkarim Soroush. The task he set himself after returning to Iran in 1979, following the successful overthrow of the shah, was to elaborate an "Islamic alternative worldview to that of modernity." Science, in its proper place, had to be maintained. No one should suffer the fate of Galileo under the rule of an Islamic Republic, and religion should not become a hindrance to science—the two should be closely linked. Thus, Rajaee claims, following the establishment of the Islamic Republic in April 1979, the philosophical debates were pushed to the background and the immediate questions facing a state came forward: the tension between Islamic ideals of little restraint on human reproduction and population control; the gender-related issue of education of women in a modern society and the Islamic injunction of segregation of the sexes; the touchy issue of archaeological exploration and the rules forbidding the disturbing of graves; the appearance of women on television and other modern media. In the latter case, Ayatollah Khomeini himself reversed tradition and approved women's participation on radio and television. Similarly, in the face of an excessively high population growth rate (4 percent per year) by 1987, the Islamic Republic took steps to convince the public of the virtues of smaller families and to introduce various methods of birth control and family planning; birth control devices were widely distributed at government expense. In like manner the injunction against using human cadavers in medical school training was reversed with the explanation that it served the cause of Islam by making sure that Islamic physicians would be fully trained. While other injunctions are being preserved (e.g., sex-segregated classrooms), it is clear that a form of social adaptation is under way. An Islamic state has to find the means in real time to meet the dual demands of fealty to religious commitment and life in a modern world system.[39]

Tibi points forcefully to another area, warfare, where Islamic militants have urged adaptation of the most modern technologies to defend their culture and states and to permit the practice of jihad. Japan and China, in the nineteenth century, as they came to terms with the military power of the West, similarly modified their attitude toward the adoption of Western technology.

But even in instances where fundamentalist religions have not gained full state authority, they have often been able to exert substantial power. In Israel, the ultra-Orthodox have had significant influence, beyond their actual numbers, because of the special characteristics of the Israeli electoral system and the need to form complicated coalitions with small parties, including the ultra-Orthodox, in order to govern. In this instance, Jewish fundamentalists have not been able to carry out the full imposition of "universalistic obligations" on the whole society as would be required of them had they achieved political power; instead they have "negotiated" or coerced an increased adherence to religious rules and observances. Most apparent are those cases dealing with the human body (sharp curtailment of archaeological exploration and restrictions on autopsy, etc.), reproduction, abortion, and, of course, stricter adherence to Sabbath observance with its restrictions on operating technologies. But there is an underside to the technology issue: there is intense research into technologies which will permit Sabbath observance (e.g., voice-activated microphones for use in the synagogue).

Clearly the one area where the fundamentalist state and science will have profound interaction is in the schools. The question is not only what will be taught and how (this battle has been fought on many fronts already), but what attitudes will be developed toward knowledge and practice, toward how things will be known and how "truths" will be established. A state may put few impediments in the way of the practice of science and its teaching, but may at the same time provide little incentive to adopt science as a career and to enable participation in its creative activities. If students of the sociology of science are correct, some balance must be achieved between serving the needs of a society and an ability to challenge its authority. Areas of Soviet science clearly suffered under ideological constraints and reluctance to challenge them. It certainly can be no different where religion replaces Marxism-Leninism as the authoritative voice.

Notes

1. Limiting this discussion to Judaism, Christianity, and Islam is partly dictated by the availability of scholarly study and research directly linking fundamentalist religious movements and modern science. Other papers in this volume and the companion volumes demonstrate the richness of the field still to be explored. See also Martin E. Marty and R. Scott Appleby, eds., *Fundamentalisms Observed* (Chicago: University of Chicago Press, 1991).

2. See "Conclusion: An Interim Report on a Hypothetical Family," in Marty and Appleby, *Fundamentalisms Observed*, pp. 814–42.

3. "Science and theology were never more closely interrelated than during the Latin Middle Ages in Western Europe," writes historian of medieval science Edward Grant in "Science and Theology in the Middle Ages," in David C. Lindberg and Ronald L. Numbers, eds., *God and Nature: Historical Essays on the Encounter between Christianity and Science* (Berkeley: University of California Press, 1986), pp. 49–75. Other scholars have pointed to the roots of science as located in the conjunction of "Athens and Jerusalem," Greek philosophy and Judeo-Christian religion; see David Lindberg's discussion in "Science and the Early Church," in Lindberg and Numbers, *God and Nature*, esp. pp. 22–29. The rich legacy of science in the Muslim Arab world was first significantly plotted by George Sarton, *From Omer*

to *Omar Khayyam,* vol. 1, and *From Rabbi Ezra to Roger Bacon,* vol. 2, pt.1, of *Introduction to the History of Science* (Baltimore: Williams and Wilkins, 1927 and 1931). The special claim for the flourishing of science in medieval Islam is made with great clarity in several books by Seyed Hussein Nasr, including *Science and Civilization in Islam,* 2d ed. (Cambridge: Islamic Texts Society, 1987).

4. A whole new historical tradition has emerged in which the secularization "thesis" is reanalyzed and much more deeply contextualized and placed firmly in the variety of national contexts. For an introduction to this literature, see the relevant chapters from John Hedley Brooke, *Science and Religion: Some Historical Perspectives* (Cambridge: Cambridge University Press, 1991).

5. John Garvey, "Fundamentalism and American Law," in Martin E. Marty and R. Scott Appleby, eds., *Fundamentalisms and the State* (Chicago: University of Chicago Press, 1992).

6. Herbert Marcuse, *One-Dimensional Man: Studies in the Ideology of Advanced Industrial Society* (Boston: Beacon Press, 1964), esp. pp. 157–58. Jürgen Habermas has provided a detailed commentary on this theme in "Technology and Science as 'Ideology,'" in his collection *Toward a Rational Society: Student Protest, Science and Politics,* trans. Jeremy J. Shapiro (Boston: Beacon Press, 1970), pp. 81–122. Lewis Mumford, *The Pentagon of Power,* published as part 2 of *The Myth of the Machine* (New York: Harcourt, Brace and Jovanovich, 1970), esp. chap. 5. Theodore Roszak, *Where the Wasteland Ends: Politics and Transcendence in Postindustrial Society* (New York: Doubleday, 1972).

7. Answer to a letter questioning the validity of declaring chess and trade in musical instruments lawful acts. For the text of the letter, see *Sahifeye Nur,* vol. 21 (Tehran: Sazemane Madareke Engelabe Eslami, 1369/1990), pp. 34–35.

8. See Rajaee's essay in this volume, "Islam and Modernity."

9. In addition to the fine essays by Moore cited in his notes, there have been several other valuable studies of the "creation controversy." See Edward T. Larson, *Trial and Error: The American Controversy over Creation and Evolution* (New York: Oxford University Press, 1985); Dorothy Nelkin, *The Creation Controversy: Science as Scripture in the Schools* (New York: Norton, 1982); Marcel C. LaFollette, ed., *Creationism, Science and the Law: The Arkansas Case* (Cambridge: MIT Press, 1983); Raymond A. Eve and Francis B. Harrold, *The Creationist Movement in Modern America* (Boston: Twayne, 1991).

10. See Brooke, *Science and Religion,* for a recent historical overview and introduction to the literature.

11. Quoted from C. R. Weld, *A History of the Royal Society with Memoirs of the Presidents, compiled from Authentic Documents* (London: 1848), in Martha Ornstein, *The Role of Scientific Societies in the Seventeenth Century,* 3d ed. (Chicago: University of Chicago Press, 1938), pp. 108–9.

12. See Everett Mendelsohn, "The Social Construction of Scientific Knowledge," in Everett Mendelsohn, Peter Weingart, and Richard Whitley, eds., *The Social Production of Scientific Knowledge: Sociology of the Sciences, Yearbook 1977* (Dordrecht: D. Reidel, 1977), pp. 3–26.

13. The classic story as told in Giorgio de Santillana, *The Crime of Galileo* (Chicago: University of Chicago Press, 1955); a revisionist version in Pietro Redondi, *Galileo Heretic,* trans. by Raymond Rosenthal (Princeton: Princeton University Press, 1987). Key documents have recently been reproduced in Maurice A. Finocchiaro, ed. and trans., *The Galileo Affair: A Documentary History* (Berkeley: University of California Press, 1989).

14. Thomas Sprat, *History of the Royal Society* (1967), ed. with critical apparatus by Jackson I. Cope and Harold Whitmore Jones (St. Louis: Washington University Studies, and London: Routledge and Kegan Paul, 1959).

15. Roger Hahn has examined the sources and meaning in "Laplace and the Vanishing Role of God in the Physical Universe," in Harry Woolf, ed., *The Analytic Spirit* (Ithaca, N.Y.: Cornell University Press, 1981), pp. 85–95; and idem, "La-

place and the Mechanistic Universe," in Lindberg and Numbers, *God and Nature,* pp. 256–76.

16. See Frederick Gregory, *Scientific Materialism in Nineteenth Century Germany* (Dordrecht: D. Reidel, 1977); and idem, "The Impact of Darwinian Evolution on Protestant Theology in the Nineteenth Century," in Lindberg and Numbers, *God and Nature,* pp. 369–90; see also Everett Mendelsohn, "The Origin of Life and the Materialism Problem," *Revue Metaphysique et de Morale* 90, no. 1 (1985): 15–29.

17. See the stunning new biography by Adrian Desmond and James Moore, *Darwin* (London: Michael Joseph, 1991), pp. 494–98; see also James Moore, *The Post-Darwinian Controversies: A Study of the Protestant Struggle to Come to Terms with Darwin in Great Britain and America, 1870–1900* (Cambridge: Cambridge University Press, 1991).

18. See Frank Miller Turner, *Between Science and Religion: The Reaction to Scientific Naturalism in Late Victorian England* (New Haven: Yale University Press, 1974); Owen Chadwick, *The Secularization of the European Mind in the Nineteenth Century* (Cambridge: Cambridge University Press, 1975).

19. See James R. Moore, "Geologists and Interpreters of Genesis in the Nineteenth Century," in Lindberg and Numbers, *God and Nature,* pp. 322–24.

20. Robert K. Merton, "Science, Technology and Society in Seventeenth Century England," *Osiris,* vol. 4, pt. 2 (1938): 360–632. Responses to the "Merton thesis" have been charted in I. Bernard Cohen, ed., with the assistance of K. E. Duffin and Stuart Strickland, *Puritanism and the Rise of Modern Science* (New Brunswick, N.J.: Rutgers University Press, 1990).

21. See the recent biography of Faraday by G. N. Cantor, *Michael Faraday: Sandemanian and Scientist: A Study of Science and Religion in the Nineteenth Century* (Basingstoke, England: Macmillan, 1991).

22. Aviezer Ravitzky, "Habad Ideology: Continuity and Change in the Contemporary Lubavitch Hasidic Movement," in Marty and Appleby, eds., *Accounting for Funda-*

mentalisms (Chicago: University of Chicago Press, forthcoming).

23. Abdul Latif Arabayyat, interview, Parliament Building, Amman, Jordan, 20 July 1991.

24. Israeli geneticist Professor Raphael Falk, interview, 20 March 1991, at Harvard University, where he recounted his participation in a conference in 1986 organized under the auspices of the Israeli Ministry of Education and Israel Academy of Sciences by a group of anti-Darwinist scientists.

25. Michael Rosenak, "Jewish Fundamentalism in Israeli Education," in this volume.

26. Ibid.

27. Mohammed Abdus Salam, "Foreword," in Pervez Hoodbhoy, *Islam and Science: Religious Orthodoxy and the Battle for Rationality* (London: Zed Books, 1991), p. ix.

28. See Hoodbhoy, *Islam and Science,* pp. 28–49, ix.

29. See note 6 above.

30. The theme is explored in depth in William Leiss, *The Domination of Nature* (New York: George Braziller, 1972).

31. See, for example, Donna J. Haraway, *Simians, Cyborgs and Women: The Reinvention of Nature* (New York: Routledge, 1991); Sandra Harding, *The Science Question in Feminism* (Ithaca, N.Y.: Cornell University Press, 1986).

32. Ravitzky, "Habad Ideology," in *Accounting for Fundamentalisms.*

33. See Peter Buck, *American Science in China, 1876–1936* (Cambridge: Cambridge University Press, 1980).

34. See Tibi's essay in this volume, "The Worldview of Sunni Arab Fundamentalists."

35. Ibid.

36. See, for example, Ahmad Yusuf Hasan and Donald R. Hill, *Islamic Technology: An Illustrated History* (Cambridge: Cambridge University Press, 1986); Nasr, *Science and Civilization in Islam.*

37. Serious scholarship on this question is fairly recent. See Herbert Mehrtens and Steffen Richter, eds., *Naturwissenschaft, Technik*

und NS-Ideologie: Beiträge zur Wissenschafts-geschichte des Dritten Reiches (Frankfurt: Suhrkamp, 1980); Jörg Tröger, ed., *Hochschule und Wissenschaft im Dritten Reich* (Frankfurt: Campus, 1984).

38. See Loren R. Graham, *Science, Philosophy and Human Behavior in the Soviet Union* (New York: Columbia University Press, 1987).

39. Salam, "Foreword"; Hoodbhoy, *Islam and Science.* Both make secularist recommendations for improving the position of science in Islamic countries; see pp. xii and 134–39, respectively.

The Creationist Cosmos of Protestant Fundamentalism

James Moore

Origins

Creation is the Christian answer to the mystery of existence.[1] Why is there something rather than nothing? Because God so willed it and brought something into existence *ex nihilo*. This reply, breathtaking in its simplicity and generality, has come down the centuries in various dogmatic forms. None has stanched the native inquisitiveness of the human mind. People have wanted to know not merely why there is something rather than nothing, but why particular things—notably themselves—exist and how these things came to be. Answers to this problem necessarily take the form of stories. For the origin of every thing is ultimately inscrutable, lost in the mists of time or of impalpable events, and an exercise of imagination is needed to fill in the details.[2]

Creation stories throughout the ages have had diverse actors, animate or inanimate, and plots dramatic, narrative, and naturalistic. Astrophysicists and paleoanthropologists, no less than priests, shamans, and necromancers, have invented and embellished such accounts. The Christian creation story, dating from Jewish antiquity, is inscribed in the early chapters of the Book of Genesis. Like other creation stories, it has attracted a vast number of interpretations.[3] What these interpretations have in common is the understanding that every thing in particular as well as all things generally have been brought into existence by the one true God. This Creator is the prime actor in the Christian account of origins, and those who so believe have been known historically as creationists. What interpretations of the Genesis story do *not* have in common is an understanding of the manner in which God has brought particular things into existence. The Creator is held to have acted in different ways that are variously scrutable by human beings. Creationists, therefore, are distinguished by their belief that God created each and every thing *rather than* by any contingent statement as to how, in particular cases, this was achieved.

For statements about the manner in which God originated particular things, creationists have invariably looked beyond the Book of Genesis. They have depended largely if not exclusively on the existing state of natural knowledge. (Indeed, without investigating the world they would not have known what things had been created.) Natural knowledge, then, is sometimes shown to elucidate the creation story in Genesis. The stories told by interpreters of nature are used to interpret phrases such as "let there be," "let the earth bring forth," and "after its kind." It follows that, for creationists, the changing body of natural knowledge has, to a large extent, given the interpretation of the Genesis story its historical character.[4] The unwisdom of absolutizing a single interpretation, of clinging to a passing state of natural knowledge for an authoritative account of the divine creation method, is also generally admitted. To do so would bring creationism into disrepute and open it to refutation.

History bears this out. Although the concept of nature as a static hierarchy of beings had long been implicit in Platonic and Aristotelian philosophic traditions, it was nevertheless recognized that species might originate in the ordinary course of events. From Augustine through Thomas Aquinas to Francis Bacon and beyond, different "kinds" of plants and animals could be naturally generated; one kind could give rise spontaneously to another; and these kinds were by no means necessarily identical with those of the Book of Genesis.[5] But in the late seventeenth and eighteenth centuries, a new natural knowledge came into existence. In 1686 the Cambridge botanical divine John Ray offered a bulwark against contemporary atheism by asserting the fixity of species, on high philosophical authority, over against what he called "spontaneous generation" and "transmutation." Fifty years later, the great taxonomist Carolus Linnaeus added his own unrivaled authority to the doctrine, declaring that there were now only as many species as had been created at the beginning.[6] Meanwhile, in the most memorable evocation of the Edenic miracle ever penned, the Christian world learned from John Milton how "let the earth bring forth" might be construed:

> The grassy clods now calved; now half appeared
> The tawny lion, pawing to get free
> His hinder parts, then springs as broke from bonds
> And rampant shakes his brinded mane.

The literalism of *Paradise Lost,* together with the almost unquestioned dogma of fixity, was disseminated through the vast literature of natural theology and held sway over the imaginations of ordinary Christians, in the English-speaking world at least, until the middle decades of the nineteenth century. Whatever else the Genesis story was taken to mean, the plant and animal "kinds" described there were believed to be both miraculously created and essentially fixed. The license of a Puritan poet and the metaphysics of a Latitudinarian divine and a Swedish taxonomist (reinforced, it must be said, by the strict empiricism of a nineteenth-century French paleontologist named

Georges Cuvier) set the terms for a prevailing orthodoxy. A view with neither biblical nor patristic nor medieval authority, the belief in the "special creation" of permanent biological species, became practically synonymous with creationism.[7]

The result was a blow from which creationists have never recovered. While a few Christian naturalists had begun to question the dogma of fixity by the mid-nineteenth century (proposing instead that species originated as extraordinary births according to a divine creative "plan"), it was the massive dual alliance of creationism with the fixity of species, and of species with the kinds of Genesis, that Charles Darwin confronted in 1859. The *Origin of Species* published in that year did not once use the word "evolution," but "creation" and its cognate terms appeared in the text over one hundred times. Darwin aimed his shrewd polemic at the "ordinary view" of "special" or "miraculous" acts of creation.[8] The effect he produced is well known and need not be detailed here. Briefly, creationists were forced to decide whether their fundamental belief in God as the Creator of all things had become too closely tied to a particular scientific statement of the manner in which living species originated. Within twenty or thirty years, most informed creationists held that this was indeed the case, and many of them—especially liberal Protestants—embraced theories of creative evolution.[9] When some of these theories, in turn, began to be discredited, those creationists who had held out against Darwin, in favor of interpretations of Genesis informed by the older natural knowledge, warned earnestly about "the tendency of theology to conform itself to the philosophical and scientific hypotheses which are ever cropping up and disappearing." "For a time such conformity carries all before it," wrote J. W. Dawson, the last major nineteenth-century naturalist to defend the doctrine of special creation, "but it incurs the danger that when the false and partial hypotheses have been discarded the higher truths imprudently connected with them may be discarded also."[10]

This, however, was precisely what happened to creationism in the aftermath of Darwin. The "higher truth" that God had created all things was discarded along with the "false and partial hypotheses" respecting the origin of living species, with which it had been imprudently connected for over one hundred years. People domiciled themselves in a non-Christian cosmos. In the twentieth century, with the consolidation of Darwin's hold on the life sciences, those who would call themselves creationists have had to struggle with this legacy. A sizable majority of educated Christians have simply accepted the new Darwinian natural knowledge as a statement of the divine method of creation; they seldom use the "evolutionary epic" to interpret the creation story in Genesis. At the same time, however, a significant and growing minority of Christians have stayed estranged from this new consensus. They maintain that the non-Christian temper of the post-Darwinian world—Christian evolutionists notwithstanding—far from owing anything to the imprudent connection of creationism with the science of the eighteenth century, has been the necessary consequence of willful disbelief in the clear teaching of the early chapters of Genesis. Creationism, according to these Christians, is to be equated with certain interpretations of the manner in which God originated living species—and, indeed, annihilated them in Noah's Flood—which were widely accepted up to the time of Darwin and have lately been confirmed by their own researches. The creationist cosmos is thus held to be at daggers-drawn not only with scientific modernity, but with the theology of the majority of those who call themselves creationists. This is the creationist cosmos of Protestant fundamentalism.[11]

Creativity

The world from which Protestant fundamentalism emerged in the early twentieth century was, in many respects, a world turned upside down, a chaos rather than a cosmos. In the industrial cities of the northern and eastern United States, indigenous Protestants were outnumbered by immigrant Jews and Catholics; Christianity was openly attacked by infidels, socialists, or worse; and the great denominations, once the mainstay of evangelical civilization, were riddled with doctrinal controversy and increasingly powerless to resist the storm of religious indifferentism and immorality into which (as cultural traditionalists saw it) Christian America had veered.[12] Under these circumstances, the majestic vision of a fixed natural order summoned into existence immediately by God and subject to unswerving moral judgment had obvious appeal. Just as liberal Protestants found justification in evolution for functional social relationships that would foster industrial progress without revolution, so those who became fundamentalists found in Genesis a sanction for stable social forms that would conserve eternal values. On either hand, creationism had ideological consequences.[13]

But it would be wrong to suppose that fundamentalists simply opted for the security of an ancient creed. Contrary to their stated aim of restoring the "fundamentals" of Christian doctrine to preeminence in national life, they became architects of innovation. Three chief ingredients of fundamentalist ideology as it emerged in the 1920s—premillennial dispensationalism, the Hodge-Warfield defense of biblical inerrancy, and Scottish commonsense realism—were distinctly modern doctrines. None of them was held, or even formulated, two centuries before.[14] The belief in the special creation of fixed biological kinds according to the Book of Genesis, as explained above, dates from the same period, and the first fundamentalists relied heavily on nineteenth-century naturalists such as Dawson for expert arguments on its behalf. Indeed, the very lack of contemporary scientific authority for fundamentalist creationism in the 1920s was itself a new departure. For the first time, in the cause of biblical truth, masses of ordinary Christians stood up to the combined arrogance of the established sciences with no one better to represent their interests than a superannuated populist politician named William Jennings Bryan.[15]

The Scopes trial of 1925 was the last time this happened. Protestant fundamentalism, born of evangelical zeal to confront the world in its strongholds and take captives for the cause of truth, has remained creative in the face of cultural adversity ever since. Over sixty-odd years its creationist cosmos has evolved. It has shared fully in the social fortunes of fundamentalist constituencies, from Bryan's moral defeat in Dayton, Tennessee, to the moral rearmament of the 1980s, when another superannuated politician, of the opposing party, uttered creationist sentiments on the way to the White

House. Today fundamentalists may have fair claim that up to a quarter of the population of the United States, and a rapidly increasing number of converts worldwide, live in a universe created miraculously only a few thousand years ago, and on an earth tenanted only by those fixed organic kinds that survived a global Flood. The Book of Genesis and its interpreters now command an audience unknown since before the time of Darwin. The creationist cosmos of Protestant fundamentalism has acquired an authority rivaling that of the established sciences.[16]

This reversal of fundamentalist fortunes in the fields of hermeneutics, hydraulics, and geochronology has come about largely through innovative management, charismatic leadership, and sophisticated promotional techniques. To the extent that mainstream biblical scholarship and academic science lack these characteristics, they have suffered by comparison in the eyes of the American churchgoing public. With the collapse of the nineteenth-century evangelical academy and the failure of efforts in the late 1920s to stem the tide of modernism in religion and science, fundamentalists set about cultivating a dynamic institutional subculture. Bible institutes flourished alongside the few but influential colleges and seminaries under fundamentalist control. Bible conferences brought the classrooms to the untutored each summer, a sort of adult extension program that burst the bounds of time and space as fundamentalist preachers took enthusiastically to the airwaves. Publishing houses meanwhile expanded and diversified to serve the information needs of all these enterprises, so that slowly but surely new personalities, new leaders, new authorities impressed themselves on the movement.[17] Scientists were not at first among them, although like successful exemplars elsewhere in American culture, their style and strategy were emulated.

At the time of the Scopes trial, fundamentalist scientists could be numbered on a single hand. Except for a physician or two, none had achieved the least professional distinction, and they differed categorically among themselves over the detailed interpretation of Genesis. (Indeed, Bryan himself believed in an ancient earth and allowed for the possibility of "evolution before man.")[18] What united these individuals was their hostility toward evolution, taught at the expense of Bible-believing taxpayers as the scientific alternative to special creation; but by the early 1930s, after the general collapse of legislative efforts to exclude evolution from public school science curricula, they sought to organize themselves on a more permanent basis. Despite several creative attempts, this proved impossible for a generation. The Religion and Science Association lasted only from 1935 to 1937. The Society for the Study of Deluge Geology and Related Sciences, set up in 1938 by Seventh Day Adventists, attracted interest outside its denomination before expiring in 1945. The American Scientific Affiliation (ASA), organized in 1941 by an emerging new breed of scientifically trained evangelicals, ran into troubled waters after the war but held intact for over two decades. Then it hit the selfsame rocks on which its predecessors had foundered. These were real rocks: the stratigraphic record as interpreted by a self-taught, armchair geologist named George McCready Price.[19]

Price was the common factor in each of the failed attempts to unite fundamentalists in a scientific organization. Although himself a miscellaneous science instructor in

Seventh Day Adventist colleges, he gained a high reputation in fundamentalist circles for his uncompromising attacks on evolution. These appeared chiefly in the movement's periodicals and in numerous books, especially an imposing seven-hundred-page college textbook entitled *The New Geology* (1923). Here Price's view that there is no natural historical order to the fossil-bearing rocks, that a worldwide catastrophic Deluge caused all the geological strata, and that the earth in consequence is very young became the surd problem for fundamentalist creationism. How could so-called Deluge geology, with its corollary of a creation in six solar days, be squared with older evangelical views—such as Dawson's—of geological progression, age-long creative days, and a limited, tranquil Flood? How, in other words, could fundamentalists be brought to agree not merely on special creation and the fixity of species, but on a radical revision of earth history based on the Book of Genesis? Until a virtue could be made out of this apparent vice, until a new and authoritative natural knowledge was produced to buttress Price's interpretation, the creationist cosmos of Protestant fundamentalism lacked the coherence it would need to become an intellectual force in American culture.[20]

Success

What changed the fortunes of fundamentalist creationism almost overnight was the publication in 1961 of another imposing text, a five-hundred-page work of apparent scholarship entitled *The Genesis Flood*. Its authors were Henry M. Morris, a distinguished hydraulic engineer at Virginia Polytechnic Institute, who had been smitten with Price since university days in the early 1940s, and John C. Whitcomb, Jr., an Old Testament professor at the Grace Brethren theological seminary in the Bible conference center of Winona Lake, Indiana, who had recently completed a doctoral dissertation there on the Deluge. Morris and Whitcomb began collaborating in 1957. Both of them had been dismayed at the ASA's postwar drift toward evolution. Both were galvanized by the evangelical apologist Bernard Ramm's *The Christian View of Science and Scripture* (1955) and the praise it received from ASA members for adopting "progressive" creationist views.[21]

In 1959, as if to confirm Morris and Whitcomb's worst fears, evolutionary biologists gathered at the University of Chicago for the Darwin centennial celebration and made a show of force. Chicago in the 1950s was a unique evangelical stronghold, the headquarters of over one hundred different agencies and educational institutions, most of which had been set up, staffed, or otherwise supported by fundamentalists.[22] When Julian Huxley, the guest of honor at the Chicago event, informed the media that "there is no longer need or room for the supernatural," that "the earth was not created; it evolved," the message struck home. Theistic evolution was impossible. Morris and Whitcomb therefore put the finishing touches to *The Genesis Flood* in the white heat of conviction: the sole, self-consistent biblical cosmology is one in which the earth and its inhabitants were created in six, twenty-four-hour days, with the appearance of age, no more than about ten thousand years ago; the data of historical geology and paleontology are explained by the year-long universal Flood; and neither pain nor death nor the Second Law of Thermodynamics was operative in the world until after Adam's fall.[23]

Since 1961 the narrowing of fundamentalist creationism to this updated version of Price's Deluge geology and the broadening of its basis of support, both in the United States and worldwide, have gone hand in hand. This is one of the great ironies of the late twentieth century. It may, however, be at least partially explained by a single consideration. *The Genesis Flood* provoked an intense debate among evangelicals not in the depressed 1930s or the war-torn 1940s, but at a period when the offspring of the first fundamentalists had benefited from stable economic growth and possessed the resources to organize themselves effectively and impressively. These resources were not only financial, but educational. Wartime needs and the Cold War campaign for scientists and engineers to counter the Soviet threat meant that quite suddenly, by the early 1960s, fundamentalist constituencies had acquired vastly more members with accredited scientific and technical backgrounds than ever before. Most of these individuals possessed knowledge or skills essential for the national effort in physical science and technology; few were naturalists trained in geology and the life sciences.

Although scientific recruitment among fundamentalists has not been studied systematically, the experience of the ASA from 1956 to 1958 may be taken as symptomatic. In these two years the organization added approximately one hundred new members who had at least a first degree in science, medicine, or engineering and who were not in full-time Christian service. Some 42 percent of such new members were established in business and industry, or served in a branch of government or the armed forces. Over half of them worked in the physical sciences, engineering, or mathematics; almost 30 percent of this latter group came from industry or military research. Only 11 percent of the new membership were in the life sciences, including biochemistry; only 5 percent were in geology. If these figures are indicative, there is good reason for supposing that fundamentalist creationism à la Morris and Whitcomb found a ready-made basis of support among believers who routinely concerned themselves with optimal design, binary logic, thermodynamics, and precision testing of theories. To fundamentalist technicians, engineers, and military personnel, the notion of creation as a fiat command structure in which all the "bugs" are the result of sin must have had obvious appeal.[24]

But until further studies have been carried out, all such conclusions deserve to rank as fruitful speculation only. For now, what can be known with much greater certainty than the cultural affinities of the new fundamentalist creationism is the social form it assumed. It was only to be expected that when individuals such as the ASA's Cold War recruits—Morris, a young hydraulic engineer, chief among them—wished to accredit a cosmology based on the Book of Genesis, they would organize themselves, as other scientists did, to formulate and defend a natural knowledge conducive to their views. This had of course been attempted repeatedly before, following the pattern of the fundamentalist institutional subculture, but never by a large number of relatively affluent individuals with respectable scientific credentials, nor at a propitious historical moment, when the dominant culture bowed to the forms as well as the pronouncements of scientific expertise.[25]

In 1963, when Morris and a team of like-minded men—most of them physical scientists or engineers, including seceders from the ASA and refugees from the old Deluge Geology Society—organized the Creation Research Society, they hit on a formula for success beyond most fundamentalists' wildest dreams. Make it a scientific society, for research and publication; make it strictly nonpolitical; make full voting membership open only to individuals with postgraduate degrees in the natural sciences, medicine, and engineering; make membership contingent on subscription to a cast-iron "statement of faith" avowing the simple historicity of Genesis, the fixity of created kinds, and the universality of the Flood. Within a few years there were hundreds of voting members—seven hundred by 1982—or about one quarter of the total membership at any time. Morris and his partners made sure these scientists felt professionally at home. They started the *Creation Research Society Quarterly,* since 1964 the academic flagship of fundamentalist creationism; they formed a textbook committee that in 1971 brought out yet another imposing volume, this one for use in high schools, *Biology: A Search for Order in Complexity;* and in 1972 Morris himself set up the Institute for Creation Research (ICR).[26]

Located on the campus of the right-wing Christian Heritage College, a fundamentalist liberal arts school in San Diego, California, this low-cost, high-commitment think tank rapidly established itself as the magisterium of fundamentalist creationism worldwide. Fiercely independent, the ICR did not seek funding from government bodies such as the National Science Foundation. It bankrolled a growing annual budget—$545,000 by 1979, $1.2 million in 1984—chiefly by soliciting contributions from individuals and local churches. Three-quarters of ICR income was eventually to come from such sources, and by 1984 the biennially updated ICR mailing list held some seventy-five thousand names. The majority were college graduates drawn about equally from business and the professions; 20 percent were clergymen or Christian workers. No other creationist organization had a list even half this size. The ICR was regularly in touch with more individuals through its monthly newsletter *Acts & Facts* than all other major creationist organizations combined.[27]

Publishing *Acts & Facts* was from the start one of the main responsibilities of the ICR's full-time "staff scientists." Then as the team expanded—from three members in 1972 to thirty or more a decade later—the activities proliferated. By 1984 the ICR had brought out no less than fifty-five creationist books and monographs written in-house. These sold over one million copies, yielding royalties to make up the balance of ICR annual income. Meanwhile the scientists were constantly on the move. They ran summer institutes, a graduate school, a library, a museum, and a press. They gave hundreds of public lectures, participated in scores of sensational debates, and made expeditions in search of fossil anomalies, geological discontinuities, and Noah's Ark.[28]

All the ICR's many impressive achievements have been linked to a single objective, similar to one that animates other scientific professionals, namely, the demarcation of science from nonscience. But the "boundary work" that the ICR engages in is intended to reinforce its own home-grown distinction between "scientific creationism" and "biblical creationism."[29] Scientific creationism is what the creation scientists of the ICR devote themselves, as scientists, to researching. It is the new natural knowledge required to validate biblical creationism. Biblical creationism is the six-day, young earth, global Flood cosmology that, as fundamentalists, they believed in all along. This distinction was enshrined, notoriously, in the two versions of the ICR's own textbook, *Scientific Creationism* (1974), edited by Morris—the "Public School Edition," dealing with "the creation-evolution question from a strictly scientific point of view," and the "General Edition," placing "the scientific evidence in its proper Biblical and theological context."[30]

The notion that objective, empirical research necessarily yields results in accord with the self-evident cosmological claims of Genesis had scarcely been entertained by Christian scientists since the 1830s, when the Anglican geologist William Buckland repented of his view that science could prove the universality of the Flood "had we never heard of such an event from Scripture, or any other authority."[31] But in the United States 150 years later, where no religion may be established by law, fundamentalist and right-wing activists reverted to Reverend Buckland's first view. Their aim was to get creationism into public school science curricula not at the expense of evolution, but alongside it. Creationism for them, thanks to Morris and his associates, had been made as scientific as evolution—"scientific creationism" and "creation science" were now interchangeable terms. Who, after all, could object to teaching more science in schools? The argument was refined, the protagonists politicized; and in the early 1980s, when laws favoring the fundamentalists were passed in Arkansas and Louisiana, the issue inevitably wound up in court.[32]

Dozens of campaigning creationist groups—local, regional, and national—supported the cause. The oldest and largest of these was the Bible-Science Association, founded in 1964 by a Missouri Synod Lutheran pastor named Walter Lang. The most litigious was the Creation Science Research Center, headed by Morris's former colleagues, Nell and Kelly Segraves. Neither organization placed a premium on scientific expertise, and the Segraves pair had proved too political for Morris during his brief association with them in California. Their break in 1972, and the founding of the ICR, clearly evinced Morris's concern that creation science should be a professional undertaking.[33] When, therefore, a federal judge in 1981 declared the Arkansas "balanced treatment" law unconstitutional, repeatedly citing ICR publications as evidence that creation science was only disingenuous fundamentalism, Morris felt aggrieved. "Neither I nor any other ICR scientist was a witness (I would have declined even if asked)," he protested innocently, "but we were somehow very much present in influence" (which is rather like Darwin complaining that his name got dragged into the famous debate between T. H. Huxley and Bishop Wilberforce at Oxford in 1860). In the case of the Louisiana law, Morris pinned his hopes on fellow-creationist professionals Wendell Bird and John Whitehead, attorneys for the Creation Science Legal Defense Fund. But even their arguments on behalf of a law "more independent of Biblically-oriented connotations" (as Morris put it) were to no avail. In 1985 a federal judge ruled that whatever else creation science might be, it certainly involved religion, and therefore teaching it in public schools, even as a "theory," was tantamount to teaching the principles of "a particular religious sect or group of sects." Repeated appeals against this ruling were unsuccessful, and in 1987 the U.S. Supreme Court struck down the Louisiana statute once and for all.[34]

But despite the failure, to date, to achieve legislative sanction, fundamentalist creationism in North America retains all the vitality of a well-heeled popular movement using advanced technologies—film, television, video, computerized direct-mail promotions—to commend its cosmos as genuine science to a culture still largely impressed with claims to scientificity.[35] From being anti-evolution sixty years ago, Protestant fundamentalists have become pro-creation. From basing their creationism on biblical arguments, they have endeavored to make their arguments scientific. From lacking scientific credentials or having amateur status at best, they have acquired the insignia of professionalism and, with these, the poise and self-esteem to pursue their politico-religious aims regardless of temporary setbacks. Already, for example, in the wake of the Louisiana ruling, fundamentalist experts have been hard at work in the history and philosophy of science, seeking to strip creationism of its religious connotations by classifying it among theories of "abrupt appearance" or by distinguishing it as "origin science" as opposed to "operation science."[36] Activists, meanwhile, have turned their attentions on local school boards, more easily swayed than federal judges by the plausibility of creationist arguments. Among academics, the Creation Social Science and Humanities Society, organized in 1977, continues to enlarge the hard-science territory claimed by Morris and his colleagues, publishing its own journal; and in Canada, where "creationists have been more active and productive than in probably any country except the United States," the Creation Science Association subsumes all these interests, with branches in most provinces.[37]

Indeed, the international upsurge of fundamentalist creationism in the last twenty years is a singular witness to the institutional prestige and the personal fortitude of its U.S. evangelists. Almost everywhere, it seems, *The Genesis Flood* or personal visitations by Morris, Whitcomb, and the ICR staff scientists have been decisive. In Britain the elderly Evolution Protest Movement, founded in 1932, reconstituted itself in 1980 as the Creation Science Movement, although another organization, the Biblical Creation Society, started two years earlier, gives evidence by its name and in its official publication, *Biblical Creation* (later renamed *Origins*), that the scientificity of creationism is a more typical American preoccupation. On the Continent, the Dutch took the lead in promoting creationism as early as 1974; creationist organizations or periodicals have also been established in Germany, France, Spain, Sweden, and—on a smaller scale—in Italy and Portugal. Where U.S. global power has, in recent decades, been exercised more decisively than in Europe, the influence of fundamentalist creationism seems to have been commensurately greater. In Asia and the South Pacific, the creationist movement thrives. Australia has its own vigorous Creation Science Association, founded in 1978, with a slick quarterly magazine, *Creation Ex Nihilo*. The Creation Scientists' Forum of India was set up in the same year. The Korean Association of Creation Research, organized in 1980, rapidly added scores of scientist-members, while in Japan, Taiwan, Sri Lanka, and Hong Kong smaller creationist groups began to flourish. There are also embryonic creationist societies in the United States' own "backyard"—in Puerto Rico, Mexico, El Salvador, the Dominican Republic, and Brazil—leaving only the former Soviet Republics, the Chinese mainland, the Islamic world, and black Africa to be reached. None of these groups has yet mounted an effective challenge to established science in its country, but together they represent a potential upheaval of epochal proportions. On past performance, fundamentalist creationism in North America will lack neither the resilience nor the resourcefulness to pursue its global objectives. The movement is here to stay.[38]

Dilemmas

The creationist cosmos of Protestant fundamentalism is not only one in which a vast number of educated Christians around the world now believe, as a matter of respect for scientific authority; it is also the biblical cosmos in which they live and move and have their being, from childhood to the grave. For them, *The Genesis Solution* (1988)—to use a book and film title by an ICR staff member—is the comprehensive corrective to *The Lie: Evolution* (1987), another title by the same author. Every aspect of existence in the late twentieth century is ordered and commanded by the six-day, young-earth, global Flood interpretation of the Genesis creation story made normative by creation science. Philosophic, economic, political, and social doctrines each have their appropriate texts.[39]

The uniqueness of human beings (Gen. 1:26–27; 2:7, 21–23), their warrant to populate and dominate the earth (1:28; 9:1–2), their disobedience as the source of natural and moral evil (3:1–22), and their obligation to labor hard as the penalty for sin (3:17–19)—these are the fundamental doctrines. Then on this basis of Creation and Fall an entire polity takes shape: marriage and the family (2:24; 4:1–25; 5:1–5), sexual modesty (2:25; 3:7, 11, 20; 9:22–27), subordination of women (2:18; 3:16), Sabbath day observance (2:1–3), retributive justice (3:14–19; 4:11–12; 6:7, 12–13), and capital punishment (9:5–6), all within a promised secure natural order (8:21–22; 9:11–17). For fundamentalists, the legitimating power of the Genesis texts depends squarely on the literal historicity of the events to which they refer, not simply because creation scientists demand it but because the New Testament takes these events as precedents for God's further historic dealings with humanity in redemption (Rom. 5:12–17) and final judgment (Matt. 24:37–39; 2 Pet. 3:5–13). Once admit allegory, once allow a naturalistic assumption to condition the literal meaning of God's words, and the whole fabric of Christianity (on the fundamentalist view) begins to collapse.[40]

Here, then, is why evolution is like a dagger pointed at the fundamentalist's throat. At stake are not merely the findings of creation science or a passing interpretation of Genesis, but nothing less than the fundamentalist's religious way of life—a cosmos rather than chaos. Sensitive outsiders have always recognized this agonizing dilemma, beginning with Walter Lippmann in the 1920s, whose canny "fundamentalist" rebuffs the "modernist's" request that he should be "tolerant and amiable" as "a suggestion that I submit the foundation of my life to the destructive effects of your skepticism, your indifference, and your good nature. You ask me to smile and to commit suicide."[41] But the stark choice between evolution and Christianity is only the most conspicuous dilemma posed within the fundamentalist cosmos. There are a range of lesser but similarly portentous choices to be made, on which fundamentalists, by and large, have failed to agree. These dilemmas impinge closer and closer, in turn, on the everyday life of ordinary believers. How they are resolved may significantly affect the future of fundamentalist creationism at the end of this millennium.

The first dilemma is an epistemological one. It has been widely felt among fundamentalists, especially in the mid-1980s, although naturally enough only their creationist cognoscenti have sensed its implications. The dilemma may be put simply thus: *Is creation science religion or science?* In Arkansas and Louisiana the courts replied unequivocally—it is religion—which is perhaps why, for the first time, fundamentalists have lately begun to realize that selling their cosmology to the American public may require more than scientific prestige, pedagogic ingenuity, and juridical sophistication.

Those who have maintained that creation science is veritable science have, indeed, been led and instructed by natural scientists, educationalists, and lawyers. Their views were formulated in response to the 1968 ruling in *Epperson v. Arkansas,* which struck down an anti-evolution law of the 1920s. Departing from the older "democratic epistemology" of the first fundamentalists, a synthesis of Baconian empiricism and commonsense realism, they evolved a strategy based loosely on the then-ascendant philosophies of Karl Popper and Thomas Kuhn, a strategy not for excluding evolution from public school science curricula, but for introducing creationism there.[42] Creation science and evolution science, according to this strategy, are to be seen as alternative "metaphysical research programs" or paradigms, which, though unfalsifiable, can be assessed more or less objectively by their congruence with the facts. These "two models," then, should be introduced into schools with the eminently respectable aim of encouraging students to become critical thinkers. "Students should be cautioned to hold their theories with a light hand and thus spare themselves the agony of seeing these theories fall apart before their eyes," wrote ICR staff member Richard Bliss, who devised the two-models approach.[43] The creation-science-as-science strategy had its apotheosis in 1974, in the two editions of the ICR's textbook *Scientific Creationism;* in 1978 the strategy was expounded at length by Wendell Bird in a noted *Yale Law Review* article, which furnished the legal platform for fundamentalist attempts at "neutralization" of public school instruction in the biological sciences during the 1980s.[44]

But even before the failure of such attempts, other voices were being heard. A handful of fundamentalist theologians, social scientists, and philosophers had realized that the two models, paradigms, or metaphysical research programs were not simply two sciences on an equal footing, between which it was possible to adjudicate "objectively" on the basis of the "facts." All facts, they argued, are theory-laden; all theories are value-laden; and therefore scientific inquiry is a moral enterprise—a branch of religion. As between creationists and evolutionists, there is no neutral methodology by which the facts of nature can be objectively known. To hold otherwise, or to pretend to do so with the two-models strategists, is to compromise the "strictly Baconian" methodology of the first fundamentalists with the secular notion of conceptual relativity, a component doctrine of evolutionary pragmatism.[45] In 1983 this view of creation-science-as-religion, or religious science, came to the fore dramatically in a review by Whitcomb of an ICR publication with Morris's name on it, *What Is Creation Science?* (1982). So far had creation science become professionalized that the co-authors of *The Genesis Flood* now publicly disagreed. Whitcomb praised the book's unanswerable scientific erudition but objected categorically to its presentation of creationism as a "mere scientific theory," devoid of "theological identity" and "ultimately authoritative answers." In this way, he warned, "we may be able to gain equal time in some public school classrooms. But the cost would seem to be exceedingly high, for absolute certainty is lost. . . . Science and divinely-revealed religion/ethics cannot be isolated without inviting long-range disaster."[46]

The implications of the fundamentalists' dilemma over creation science are clearly profound. Not only is their academy touched by C. P. Snow's "two cultures"—a reassuring prospect for pluralist outsiders—but their strategy for supplanting the evolutionary worldview of "secular humanism" would appear to be deeply torn. The creation-science-as-science strategy says, "Teach more science in our schools and neutralize the teaching of evolution science alone." The creation-science-as-religion strategy tends toward the proposition, "Teach less religion in our schools by eliminating evolution science or, since this is now impossible, teach creationism as religious science in separate fundamentalist schools." These strategies may subsist together for a time, as indeed they have until the late-1980s, but in the end they are mutually exclusive. Convince people that creation science is religion, on the one hand, and a large number of influential fundamentalists lose the basis of their claim to cultural ascendancy. The ICR and its creation scientists sacrifice the status and emoluments attaching to scientific professionalism; the creationist lawyers must give up their ambitious constitutional battle to teach creationism in public schools. Convince people that creation science is science, on the other hand, and a much larger, nonscientific group of fundamentalists loses its prerogative to furnish what fundamentalists believe to be the essential biblical basis for natural knowledge. Creationism may now be insinuated into public schools, but only, it will be said, at the expense of fundamentalism's sole source of "final authority, power, and victory," the very revelation which distinguishes its creationist cosmos from that of Judaism or Islam, or indeed from any other merely human attempt to interpret the world.[47]

In raising the question of the Bible's place in creation science strategies, the second dilemma confronting fundamentalists is posed. And it does impinge more directly on their religious life at-large for the simple reason that, being Protestants, they hold by the indefeasible right of every believer to make private interpretations of Scripture. The first dilemma posed the problem of the epistemological status of the natural knowledge formulated by creation scientists. The second dilemma is a related, hermeneutic one, which may be stated briefly thus: *Must the Bible always take priority in interpreting nature or may natural knowledge have priority in interpreting the Bible?* Now from one standpoint it is difficult to see how this problem could ever arise. The very existence of the Bible is contingent on a range of empirical sciences—paleography, lexicography, textual criticism—that have already assessed its constitutive documents in the light of extrinsic, natural, and historical knowledge before the fundamentalist interpreter gets to work. If scientific reason must learn its rightful function only from biblical texts, how could rational interpretation of the Bible *or* of nature ever begin? Fundamentalists seldom ask themselves such questions, but their hermeneutic dilemma looks at least plausible from another standpoint. It would appear to arise because fundamentalist creationism has always insisted—chiefly in the person of Whitcomb—that biblical statements must always take priority when they conflict with purported natural knowledge, never the reverse, *and yet* creation scientists have differed notoriously about what biblical statements mean.[48]

The hard case for creation science—the most difficult piece of natural knowledge to disregard in interpreting the literal historical sense of inerrant biblical statements—is the modern scientific notion that the earth moves around the sun. Geocentrism has not, so far as is known, made inroads at the ICR, but elsewhere in recent years there has been a minor groundswell of support. Walter Lang of the Bible-Science Association is reportedly sympathetic, and the subject was formally debated at the association's national conference in 1985 before a "solemn and demure" audience.[49] The Creation Research Society has also been willing to countenance geocentrist views. As early as 1973 the tolerant, if dissenting, voice of a physicist was raised in its quarterly journal, stating that Christians might at least agree that "the earth is at the geometric center of the visible universe," although to concede more, he said, would call into question "the entire framework of celestial mechanics created by Newton, Kepler, and others."[50] Then in 1978 the journal began to publish the intricate mathematical arguments of James N. Hanson, professor of computer science at Cleveland State University. Hanson claimed to base his work on "the simple literal narrative of the Bible." "The earth does not spin nor does it translate through space but is at the center of Creation just where the Bible puts it." "Cosmologies, which happen to be favorable to geocentricity," he suggested, echoing the standard creationist line, "have been neglected or suppressed on evolutionary bases."[51]

Critics of geocentrism, like critics of creation science a quarter century ago, have been slow off the mark, thinking no doubt that this eccentricity would soon disappear. In 1982 Hanson was answered briefly by a fellow creationist who, having made the obvious point that "Copernicanism is not basically Darwinian," asserted with remarkable detachment, that "many aspects of the geocentricity/heliocentricity issue seem open to question; nevertheless, my personal favorite is a sun-centered system."[52] Recently, however, creation scientists seem to have become more concerned. In 1988 the editors of *Creation Ex Nihilo,* which circulates widely in both Australia and North America, chose the geocentrism debate as the feature of their tenth anniversary issue. The lead article was written by Whitcomb's colleague at Grace College in Winona Lake, Indiana, the physicist Donald DeYoung, a member of the Creation Research Society's board. DeYoung first offered six scientific arguments against geocentrism, which he called "harmful" and "misguided"; then, in conclusion, he explained that when the Bible says, "the sun stood still," it speaks in "the language of *appearance,* the only way it could be understood." This thought, so often urged upon the entire creation science movement, was embellished in the accompanying editorial:

> We must be careful not to ignore that the inspired writers of God's Word were led to speak in understandable terms; they employed literary devices such as figures of speech. . . . By denying figures of speech in the Bible, people at one time insisted the world is flat. . . . If one is determined to restrict one's thinking by denying figures of speech in the Bible, one is likely to land in trouble quickly.[53]

But how is one to decide whether or not a biblical statement about the natural world is a figure of speech—unless by referring to extrabiblical natural knowledge to find out what it might be a figure *for*? A *tu quoque* is sorely tempting.

The reason why fundamentalists cannot see that they are in fact, and have always been, dependent on extrabiblical knowledge in constructing their cosmology—which remains, for that reason, conventionally heliocentric—is, at root, the same reason why most of them labor under the illusion that creationism can be made into something like a positive science. It is hardcore epistemological dualism. Protestant fundamentalists, as a whole, are innocents abroad in a post-Kantian, relativistic, cybernetic world. Suggest the social conditioning of perception—broach the sociology of knowledge—and their absolutes begin to shake. Certitude vanishes; either-or reasoning is out; the cosmos disintegrates.[54] Moreover, a deep critique of technology—particularly high-tech communications—becomes possible. And nothing speaks more eloquently of the epistemology of Protestant fundamentalists (let alone their modernity) than their resounding silence on this point. With the partial exception of children's toys—fantasy creatures, video games, Dungeons and Dragons—they fail as completely to recognize the constitutive relations of technology and society as they fail to analyze the creative nexus of text and interpreter. Only a fundamentalist magazine could overlook the irony of printing adjacent articles, as one did in 1984, the first given to a glowing inventory of "our growing electronic arsenal" and entitled "What Hath God Wrought?" the latter unmasking "moral and political bias" in the electronic media and headed "The Distortion of Network Television." Indeed, anyone who would recognize, in a coherent manner, a problem with the medium-message distinction or with the divorce between technical artifacts and social values could scarcely remain a fundamentalist.[55]

None of this is meant to suggest that fundamentalists neglect to concern themselves with ideology. They merely discuss it in different terms. It is perhaps no coincidence that the two magazine articles on the electronic media were immediately preceded by an offering entitled "Demons: Our Invisible Enemies." For all the evil in the cosmos, according to fundamentalists, all the misuse of technology, all the lies and disinformation leading to immorality, suffering, and death, is to be explained by the actions of innumerable wonder-working personal spirits who conspire with their leader, the fallen angel Satan, and with free human subjects to subvert God's purposes for a creation that originally was "good." Evolution, indeed, is the satanically inspired ideology of this cosmic insurrection, as Morris and other fundamentalist leaders have often urged; UFOs are the avant-garde of Satan's final assault on the earth.[56] The whole sorry, sinful business got started in the Garden of Eden, when the serpent said to Eve, "Ye shall not surely die. . . . ye shall be as gods, knowing good and evil" (Gen. 3:4). This was the first ideological statement ever uttered. Eve was deceived, then Adam; they sinned, and for their Fall the entire creation was supernaturally cursed. Now, for the first time, a few thousand years ago, plants and animals began to die. Populations began to exceed their food supplies; there was a struggle for existence. The carnivores acquired their fangs and began feeding on the herbivores and each other. The herbivores began eating plants instead of fruit. Accidents began to happen. Adam first trod on an ant. And the whole vast creation began to decay, to degenerate, to run down into a state of disorder that one day would be formalized in the Second Law of Thermodynamics. Satan, by his deception, brought Adam and Eve to a knowledge of good and evil, but with this knowledge came death.[57]

Leaving aside the question of whether the fundamentalist account of evil is a theodicy or merely a demonology, there can be no doubt that it is as much an ideological representation of the world—a value-laden version of reality—as the serpent's remark to Eve, "Ye shall not surely die." In the creationist cosmos, things die because of sin; the "balance of nature" is providential retribution. Things come into and go out of existence in their appointed times and ways. Satan has scope for maneuver, but God is still in control. Paleontology becomes a moral science not only by testifying to God's cataclysmic judgment in the global Flood, but by witnessing to the Edenic curse. The fossilized remains in the earth's crust furnish sobering evidence that the cosmos is ruled by a righteous Creator.

If such evidence is to be taken into account, however, then fundamentalists are faced with a further dilemma. It is an ideological dilemma because it involves the moral economy of the world; it is simultaneously a deeply personal dilemma because fundamentalists feel, perhaps more strongly than do other Christians, that their individual life spans are ordained. To ask, Does death result from natural necessity or from a supernatural curse? of course broadens the issue to take in plants and animals, but it is here that evidence for God's providential care exists on a scale unimaginable for human beings. Morris and Whitcomb have argued repeatedly that, if humans had been on the earth for millions of years, thousands of billions of people would have lived and died, and an incredible number would still be alive today; yet only a few billion remain, and scarcely a trace of the rest has been found. They conclude that the present population is consistent with multiplication at usual rates over less than five thousand years from the family of eight who survived the Flood.[58] But consider the case of an animal type of which it can safely be said that thousands of billions have lived and died, an incalculable number survive today, and evidence of its past and present existence is available in superabundance. Ironically, this evidence was the subject of Darwin's first successful scientific theory, in 1835, and its significance for geochronology was first established by core drilling in preparation for U.S. atom bomb tests between 1946 and 1952. A creation scientist named Daniel Wonderly first alerted his colleagues to its implications in the early 1970s, but to date it appears that the dilemma to which it points is unresolved.

Corallines are marine animals that, with other lime-secreting species, leave their skeletons to deposit and fossilize, generation upon generation, in formations known as reefs. Wonderly calls these creatures God's "time-keepers of the past." The thickest reefs yet discovered are in the Marshall Islands, where at Eniwetok Atoll one drilling passed through 4,610 feet of reef deposit before striking the volcanic base. At observed growth rates, and leaving aside numerous retarding factors, the total length of time required for forming this reef deposit is approximately 176,000 years. Allow for the retarding factors, Wonderly says, and the period is "undoubtedly many times" greater, although even the lower figure lies far beyond the bounds to which the most daring creation scientist would stretch the biblical chronology. Equally important, this dating refers to a natural formation made up of the skeletons of animals that, according to creation scientists, could not have begun to die until after the Fall, a few thousand years ago. The rocks were *"biologically produced."*[59]

Now creation scientists (including Wonderly) take it as axiomatic that the earth and all its inhabitants were brought into existence miraculously with the appearance of age—the doctrine of a "mature creation." But no one so far has seriously maintained that God planted evidence in the world of things that never lived. A righteous Creator cannot simulate the effects of sin. Fossils are supposed to be the remains of living things that perished since the Fall, especially in the Flood. Three avenues, therefore, are open to creation scientists in dealing with the evidence from coral reefs. The first involves a procedure analogous to the one followed in creationist astronomy, where the proposal that God created the light from distant galaxies in transit, because they appear to be more than about ten thousand light-years away, has been superseded by the theory that the speed of light was much higher at the creation and has since been slowing down.[60] Coral reefs must have been built up more rapidly in ancient times than at present, leaving them with the appearance of great age. Death was not simulated by the Creator; life was merely abridged. Wonderly anticipates this response, arguing that it would make a nonsense of metabolic processes, but creation scientists could still invoke a local miracle. This miracle, however, would involve a suspension of the Second Law of Thermodynamics, which applies to metabolic processes as much as anything else, and thus an abrogation of the Edenic curse. It would also fail to relieve God of responsibility for arranging fossil evidence in the world, which He knew would be misinterpreted. Deception is another word for it, and fundamentalists find this more becoming in Satan than in a righteous Creator.[61]

The second avenue open to creation scientists is to concede that, although the creation was recent and mature, the death of at least some kinds of animals did take place before the Fall. Coral reefs have been forming ever since the day on which the first coralline was created. The problem with this response is twofold. It allows only a few more thousand years, at most, in which reef deposits could have accumulated, thereby solving practically nothing, and it entails construction of a "harmonistic theodicy" in which the presence of death is somehow made compatible with the purposes of a righteous Creator, who saw that His work was "good." Neither prospect would seem likely to find favor in fundamentalist circles, which leaves only one avenue of escape from the evidence of coral reefs: ignore or suppress it.[62]

In a recent lengthy survey of "evangelical positions" on the age of the earth, Wonderly's "careful work" is mentioned in passing without comment. In a specially commissioned "in-depth literature review" of dating methods, published in 1987 in the journal of the Creation Research Society, nothing is said at all.[63] Wonderly himself formerly served as head of the biology department at Grace College in Winona Lake, Indiana, the sister institution of Whitcomb's seminary. As a creation scientist, he much regretted that "fundamentalist teachers" had adopted the young-earth view: "This very often closes the door to their being able to help the science-oriented public." Yet his efforts to enlighten men "honest in their ignorance" with the evidence from coral reefs and other nonradiometric sources led to accusations of infidelity. By early 1972 his work had been "brought to a standstill." "The Seminary"—by which Wonderly seems to have meant Whitcomb—had sealed his mouth and pen. In August 1973 he broke silence in a "bland" survey of nonradiometric dating methods delivered at the annual meeting of the American Scientific Affiliation. Within months he was out of a job. "So many Christians (in many institutions and churches throughout the United States)," he observed sadly, "are just accepting the young earth view because men of seemingly high educational stature are telling them that 'science has now shown that the earth is probably very young,' 'the Bible says it is young,' etc. This wouldn't be so bad except that along with it goes the claim that any other view is to be avoided—and the people who believe it avoided."[64]

But the ideological dilemma over the origin of death cannot be resolved by making Velikovsky-like victims. Sooner or later Protestant fundamentalists must choose the kind of Creator in whom they want to believe. Either it will be a God who has left the world full of illusions and enigmas as a way of testing human willingness to believe in the "infallible Book" where they are decoded, or it will be a God for whom struggle and death are somehow unavoidable—perhaps even necessary—ingredients in the moral order of the world.[65] Whichever choice is made, it will require a fundamentalist theodicy, and this theodicy will express normative concerns that make it ideological. The lack of evidence to date that fundamentalists, or their creation science elite, are capable of the sustained reflection needed to construct such a theodicy is not only a further indication that epistemological self-criticism may be impossible in the fundamentalist cosmos; it also suggests an explanation for the creation scientists' resounding silence on another point of recent cultural debate.

The most prominent, well-formulated, and authoritative ideological competitor of fundamentalist creationism in contemporary America is human sociobiology—the study of the biological evolutionary basis of social behavior. Both movements burst onto the public scene in the later 1970s. Both are likely to remain buoyant for decades. But although their metaphysical assumptions are diametrically opposed, fundamentalist creationism and human sociobiology appear to offer demonstrable transformations of the same set of normative concerns: in short, that "the American way of life is founded on eternal [i.e., permanent] values which are best inculcated by the traditional family, and alternative lifestyles threaten to destroy this way of life."[66] If this is so, the failure of creation scientists to tackle their chief competitor may evince something more than their inability to formulate a coherent ideological alternative. It suggests the possibility of blind collusion in the work of social legitimation, a de facto this-worldliness profoundly at odds with the belief that the creation—presumably including American culture—is under the spell of demons and evolution is satanically inspired. Fundamentalists may not be as incorruptible as they suppose in their self-appointed task of remaking the evolutionary worldview.

Futures

As the second millennium of the Christian era draws to a close, the creationist cosmos of Protestant fundamentalism is confronted with urgent, practical challenges that throw its internal dilemmas into stark relief. Epistemological, hermeneutic, and ideological choices are rapidly becoming political ones. The struggle for respectability and "balanced treatment" is giving way to a battle to save the world. For the first time since the Flood (as fundamentalists see it), life on earth faces annihilation. Toxic radiation levels are on the rise. Ozone depletion and global warming portend fatal climatic changes. Human populations are ravaged by sexually transmitted diseases, particularly AIDS, and efforts to contain or reverse the consequences of sin through genetic engineering risk perpetrating worse evils in their stead. "Unless mankind discovers an adequate reason why he should not destroy himself," warned one fundamentalist divine in 1984, "he conceivably could before the light dawns upon the twenty-first century. . . . Seeking to save the world, both spiritually *and* temporally . . . is acknowledging with the Creator that what He has made is good and worth keeping."[67]

How, then, will the fundamentalist salvage operation be mounted? Who should lead the campaign and what might they expect to achieve? Secular society regards its own scientists, engineers, and technocrats as the ones best qualified to preserve the biosphere from irreversible degradation; the same cannot be said of many fundamentalists. Members of the Creation Research Society may boast an impressive record of publication, but much of it consists of individual, hobbylike efforts funded on a shoestring and based on library work or desultory field observations. These efforts are descriptive and historical rather than predictive and experimental. Rather than try to falsify evolution by proving creationism true, they contrive to undermine evolution by recycling its data in support of the "creation model." ("An experimental measurement or an observed fact," according to Morris, "should be the same whether obtained by an evolutionist or a creationist.")[68] More to the point, all the work of creation scientists is geared to the production of a natural knowledge relevant not for the urgent amelioration of the created order today, but for the support of foregone conclusions about the ancient created order as inferred from biblical texts. And such will doubtless remain the pattern in the foreseeable future.[69] Creation scientists will not appear as such on blue ribbon panels examining the ethics of fetal brain cell transplants, on commissions of inquiry into the destruction of the tropical rain forests, or on advisory bodies concerned with the storage of high-level radioactive waste. None of them has shown the aptitude to serve in such ways; few if any have the qualifications. Instead, the Creation Research Society has proposed to set up a "research laboratory" where diluvial "cave formation," "rapid deposition of sedimentary strata," and "natural regulation of animal populations" will be investigated. And at the Thomas G. Barnes Institute of Physics efforts will continue to return modern physical theory to the concepts of absolute space and time, thereby pursuing the interests of the eponymous former president of the Creation Research Society, who laments that the distorted "philosophy of relativism" has become "evident in the ills of society today."[70]

If, therefore, creation scientists are not to be counted at the forefront of the fundamentalist crusade to save the world, who will take the initiative? If creation science does not mix with politics, what does? The answer in late twentieth-century America is, clearly, religion. It is from the preachers and pundits of fundamentalism, the Protestant moralists and mullahs, that salvation will be dispensed. Already these shapers of opinion in churchgoing America—Jerry Falwell, Pat Robertson, the disgraced Jimmy Swaggert and Jim Bakker, D. James Kennedy, and many others—have become the most visible and influential defenders of the creationist cosmos. They are the vanguard who would roll back the frontiers of "secular humanism" by exposing its satanic ideology. They are the prophets of doom or deliverance whose electronic evangel and paperback nostrums set the political agenda for millions. With aid from their private educational trusts, and abetted by an array of right-wing religious think-tanks, these arbiters of the fundamentalist conscience lay claim to the entire moral world. They seek to return sinful society to the biblical bedrock of right conduct and belief. Chaos is to be averted, the cosmos preserved, on the firm foundation of the Book of Genesis. The fact that none of them has yet directly influenced the pattern of federal funding for science or the research priorities of the major foundations must not be taken to rule out any long-term indirect effects owing to pressure from the political grass roots.

But all is not well among the fundamentalist ideologues, even disregarding the tarnished reputations. They may agree that secular humanism is to be blamed for the state of the world, that the philosophy of a "struggle for existence" rather than the Genesis creation mandate has plunged the biosphere into crisis, but they are by no means united about what the future holds.[71] Their eschatologies diverge. The historic mainstream of fundamentalism has adhered to the ultimately enervating belief that the creation will be restored in a literal millennial kingdom only *after* the earth and its inhabitants have become degraded to such an extent that God has had to remove all true believers and intervene directly to smash the hosts of Satan. "Premillennialism" makes history into a holding operation; a better world is the sovereign gift of God. "Until Satan himself is destroyed," Morris has declared, echoing the sentiments of the fundamentalist majority to date, "we have no hope of defeating the theory of evolution, except intermittently and locally and temporarily."[72]

Alongside premillennialism, however, an older evangelical doctrine has persisted, waiting in the wings; with the accession of fundamentalists to power and respectability in the later 1970s, it began to share the political limelight. This is the ultimately galvanizing belief that the creation will be restored in a literal millennial kingdom *before* God intervenes in final judgment; the earth and its inhabitants will be perfected, and Satan will be defeated by the triumphant progress of Christian civilization. "Postmillennialism" makes history since the Resurrection into a mopping-up operation; a better world is God's gift to those who help themselves. "The general advance of creationist thinking," as one preacher put it in the U.S. bicentennial year, 1976, "seems to have reached the point where proponents must now come to grips with certain political implications . . . already being skirted in efforts to force state schools to present the teaching of creation with equal fairness alongside the teaching of evolution. . . . The school question is little more than a scouting expedition to test the strength of evolutionary forces. . . . For politics is dominion. . . . He who believes in the truth of creation is bound to devote himself to the enforcement of God's Law."[73]

Dominion, indeed, is what postmillennial fundamentalist creationism is all about, the final fulfillment of the mandate given to Adam before the Fall and to Noah after the Flood to take charge of the earth and its inhabitants on God's behalf. Forget about "two models," "balanced treatment," and scientific objectivity. These are compromises with secular humanism. Postmillennial fundamentalist creationism demands a return to Old Testament law—it is unabashedly totalitarian and theocratic. There is no concept of "natural law" in Genesis; no scope for "the philosophy that all people have a right to their own opinions." Humans are "essentially different from and superior to nature," but true Christians are better than the rest. In their coming commonwealth, slavery will be reinstituted and the death penalty restored for a variety of moral offences. Believers will "be fruitful and multiply" and displace God's enemies from the earth. Every institution, every department of thought and human conduct, will be brought into captivity to creationist norms, so that at last the dominion mandate will be fulfilled, the cosmos will be complete. Religious liberty will be impossible.[74]

Although postmillennial fundamentalist creationism—Christian reconstructionism, to use the generic term—is as yet a minority movement within Protestant fundamentalism, its advocates are erudite, self-assured, and adamant: Rousas Rushdoony, the chief theoretician, with his Chalcedon Foundation; Gary North, Rushdoony's son-in-law, with his Institute of Christian Economics; and several other influential leaders such as Gary DeMar and John Whitehead, each with his own nonprofit organization or think tank, and each a strict creationist. These men appeal as activist scholars rather than as abstracted scientists. Theocrats by conviction, they nonetheless belong to the democracy of the text rather than the aristocracy of the lab. Their efforts to erect a counterhegemonic worldview for an expanding fundamentalist subculture are deadly serious and cannot be ignored. If the creationist cosmos begins to fragment over the dilemmas that all fundamentalists sooner or later must face, it is entirely possible that such reconstructionists among them, true to their name, will be able to weld the pieces back together and make creationism into something like a coherent ideology for the first time.[75]

For there is no doubt that reconstructionists already have the dilemmas well in hand: creation science is a fraud—it is religion through and through; the Bible takes priority in interpreting nature or anything else, even if this requires all science and history to be rewritten; death in nature results from a supernatural curse, just as the Bible says, and appearances to the contrary need not detain the true believer. In *Is the World Running Down?* (1988) Gary North throws down the gauntlet to his rivals in the Creation Research Society and the Institute for Creation Research:

> Scientific creationists have been too soft and academically gracious in their dealings with God-hating Darwinian scientists. These defenders of the faith have not "gone for the jugular" of their opponents, for they have accepted too many of their opponents' illegitimate ground rules in the debate. . . . Scientific creationists have not yet successfully attacked the soft underbelly of Darwinism: historical despair. Scientific creationists, by proclaiming the sovereignty of the entropy process, have also immersed their own worldview in historical despair. . . . Christians need a better alternative than historical despair, both for themselves and for their presentation of Christ's gospel of redemption. We are at war with post-Darwinian evolutionism, and this war encompasses every area of life. . . . Scientific creationists have written virtually nothing on how and why the doctrine of the six-day creation must reshape all of modern Christian theology and the entire Christian way of life. Christians have not been shown clearly and decisively that Darwinism is a total worldview, and that by accepting any aspect of this worldview, Christians compromise and weaken the presentation of the Christian worldview as well as risk disobeying God. They have not been shown how evolutionism spreads like cancer from the geology or history textbook to every area of personal ethics and public policy. To win the battle with Darwinism, which is above all a comprehensive worldview justifying comprehensive power, six-day creationists must believe that the stakes are far larger than mere laboratory experiments or one-evening debates. Creation scientists must demonstrate that six-day creationism really makes a difference in every area of life.[76]

All that is lacking for this new and more nearly self-consistent version of fundamentalist creationism to emerge as a major intellectual force is removal of the countervailing force of premillennialism, coupled perhaps with serious defections among creation scientists in the interests of accommodating Genesis to their researches. The closing years of the millennium, with the opportunity they afford for prophetic conjecture of the premillennial variety, may have to pass uneventfully before the final shape of the creationist cosmos will be known.

Whether the creationist cosmos of Protestant fundamentalism will go on evolving, as it has throughout the twentieth century, is not, however, merely an academic point. The intractable problems of life and death that confront the fundamentalists necessarily face us all. And it is by no means certain that "secular humanist" science, any more than creation science, will unravel the skein of causes and put the world aright before profound and far-reaching changes in the biosphere threaten chaos on planet Earth. In this case, the cosmos of fin-de-siècle fundamentalism will not be the only one affected; the reigning assumptions of liberal, evolutionary enlightenment—naturalism, reductionism, materialism—will also be sorely tried. A Kulturkampf may well take place in which rival totalitarianisms clash, violently perhaps, to mobilize consent and enforce political order.[77] Under less dire circumstances, after all, as it was predicted a decade ago, "Christian doctrine, made an adjunct to right-wing and capitalist policies, could provide the necessary self-imposed order that a fascist movement in America would require to maintain control over the country." And more recently, "a state religion, compulsory in character, authoritarian in tone, 'traditional' in outlook," has been seriously foreseen. "America would be 'socialized' not in the name of Marx but of Jesus, not in the name of communism but of Christian republicanism."[78]

None of these possibilities is inevitable, of course, or even likely. But one thing at any rate seems certain. Whatever shape the creationist cosmos may take at the hands of Protestant fundamentalists, it will break free from its flourishing subculture and hold sway over peoples and nations only when it is commended in its integrity: not as a mere science among sciences, but as the one religious answer, among uniquely religious answers, to the unfathomable mystery of existence.

Notes

1. This essay is the immediate outgrowth of discussions with members of the Fundamentalism Project team and separate conversations with Joel Carpenter, Mark Noll, and Ron Numbers. It has also been informed by correspondence with Dick Aulie, Paul Fayter, Langdon Gilkey, John Greene, George Marsden, and Dan Wonderly. I am especially grateful to Tom McIver, who sent me timely information about the creationist movement, and to David Livingstone for constructive criticism. None of these individuals should be held responsible for my interpretations. The libraries of Moody Bible Institute and Wheaton College yielded up many of the sources on which the essay is based, including four periodicals that were consulted systematically. These are abbreviated in the notes as follows: *CEN* equals *Creation Ex Nihilo*; *CRSQ* equals *Creation Research Society Quarterly*; *CSSHQ* equals *Creation Social Science and Humanities Quarterly*; *FJ* equals *Fundamentalist Journal*.

2. Milton K. Munitz, *The Mystery of Existence: An Essay in Philosophical Cosmology* (New York: Appleton-Century-Crofts, 1965); Peter A. Bertocci, "Creation in Religion," in Philip P. Wiener, ed., *Dictionary of the History of Ideas*, vol. 1 (New York:

Charles Scribner's Sons, 1968), pp. 571–77; Langdon Gilkey, *Maker of Heaven and Earth: A Study of the Christian Doctrine of Creation* (Garden City, N.Y.: Doubleday, 1959); David B. Burrell and Bernard McGinn, eds., *God and Creation: An Ecumenical Symposium* (Notre Dame, Ind.: University of Notre Dame Press, 1990).

3. E.g., see Misia Landau, "Human Evolution as Narrative," *American Scientist* 72 (1984): 262–68; Robin W. Lovin and Frank E. Reynolds, eds., *Cosmogony and Ethical Order: New Studies in Comparative Ethics* (Chicago: University of Chicago Press, 1985); Jeffery Burton Russell, *The Devil: Perceptions of Evil from Antiquity to Primitive Christianity* (Ithaca, N.Y.: Cornell University Press, 1977); Eric Smith, *Some Versions of the Fall: The Myth of the Fall of Man in English Literature* (London: Croom Helm, 1973); and William E. Phipps, *Genesis and Gender: Biblical Myths and Their Cultural Impact* (London: Greenwood Press, 1989).

4. Roland Mushat Frye, "The Two Books of God," *Theology Today* 39 (1982): 260–66; James R. Moore, "Geologists and Interpreters of Genesis in the Nineteenth Century," in David C. Lindberg and Ronald L. Numbers, eds., *God and Nature: His-*

torical Essays on the Encounter between Christianity and Science (Berkeley: University of California Press, 1986), pp. 322–50; Langdon Gilkey, "Cosmology, Ontology, and the Travail of Biblical Language," Journal of Religion 41 (1961): 194–205.

5. Cf. Aubrey L. Moore, Science and the Faith: Essays on Apologetic Subjects (London: Kegan Paul, Trench, Trübner and Co., 1889), pp. 173–80; and Richard P. Aulie, "Evolution and Special Creation: Historical Aspects of the Controversy," Proceedings of the American Philosophical Society 127 (1983): 432–39.

6. John Ray, The Wisdom of God Manifested in the Works of Creation, 7th ed. (London: printed by R. Harbin for William Innys, 1717), p. 321; Linnaeus, in Etienne Gilson, From Aristotle to Darwin and Back Again: A Journey in Final Causality, Species, and Evolution, trans. John Lyon (Notre Dame, Ind.: University of Notre Dame Press, 1981), pp. 35, 135–38. On Ray's ideology, see Neal C. Gillespie, "Natural History, Natural Theology, and Social Order: John Ray and the 'Newtonian Ideology,'" Journal of the History of Biology 20 (1987): 38ff. Linnaeus subsequently modified his views, but the technique he continued to use to describe or define species was "adequate only to his early belief that the elements of order consist of the fixed, discrete 'natural' kinds created by God": James L. Larson, Reason and Experience: The Representation of Natural Order in the Work of Carl von Linné (Berkeley: University of California Press, 1971), p. 121.

7. A. L. Moore, Science and the Faith, p. 180; Aulie, "Evolution and Special Creation," pp. 438–39.

8. Paul H. Barrett, Donald J. Weinshank, and Timothy T. Gottleber, A Concordance to Darwin's "Origin of Species," First Edition (Ithaca, N.Y.: Cornell University Press, 1981); Charles Darwin, On the Origin of Species, or the Preservation of Favoured Races in the Struggle for Life (London: John Murray, 1859), pp. 185, 394, 398, 469, 482, etc.

9. James R. Moore, The Post-Darwinian Controversies: A Study of the Protestant Struggle to Come to Terms with Darwin in Great Britain and America, 1870–1900 (Cambridge: Cambridge University Press, 1979); idem, "Herbert Spencer's Henchmen: The Evolution of Protestant Liberals in Late Nineteenth-Century America," in John R. Durant, ed., Darwinism and Divinity: Essays on Evolution and Religious Belief (Oxford: Basil Blackwell, 1985); Jon H. Roberts, Darwinism and the Divine in America: Protestant Intellectuals and Organic Evolution, 1859–1900 (Madison: University of Wisconsin Press, 1988).

10. John William Dawson, Modern Ideas of Evolution as Related to Revelation and Science, rev. ed. (London: Religious Tract Society, 1890), p. 182.

11. The "creationist cosmos" as described in this essay is characteristic of Protestant fundamentalism, but there are many nonfundamentalists—evangelicals, sectarians, Roman Catholics—who inhabit it as well. And some Protestant fundamentalists of course may not adhere to every tenet of my description. For bibliography, see Arnold D. Ehlert, "The Literature of Scientific Creationism and Anti-evolution Polemic," Proceedings of the American Theological Library Association 31 (1977): 151–72, and James H. Shea, "A List of Selected References on Creationism," Journal of Geological Education 32 (1984): 43–49, which have been largely superseded by Ernie Lazar, The Creation/Evolution Bibliography and Directory, 3d ed. (Sacramento, Calif.: privately printed, 1987), and by the comprehensive work of Tom McIver, Anti-Evolution: An Annotated Bibliography (Jefferson, N.C.: McFarland and Co., 1988). For a wider view, see James R. Moore, "Evolutionary Theory and Christian Faith: A Bibliographical Guide to the Post-Darwinian Controversies," Christian Scholar's Review 4 (1975): 211–30; Paul Fayter, "Scientific Creationism and Its Critics," Journal of the American Scientific Affiliation 37 (1985): 104–8; and David N. Livingstone, "Evangelicals and the Darwinian Controversies," Evangelical Studies Bulletin, November 1987, pp. 1–6.

12. Nancy T. Ammerman, "North American Protestant Fundamentalism," in Martin

E. Marty and R. Scott Appleby, eds., *Fundamentalisms Observed* (Chicago: University of Chicago Press, 1991). Cf. George M. Marsden, *Fundamentalism and American Culture: The Shaping of Twentieth-Century Evangelicalism, 1870–1925* (New York: Oxford University Press, 1980), pp. 11–39, 102–7; and James Davison Hunter, *American Evangelicalism: Conservative Religion and the Quandary of Modernity* (New Brunswick, N.J.: Rutgers University Press, 1983), chap. 3.

13. Moore, "Herbert Spencer's Henchmen," pp. 90–97.

14. Ernest R. Sandeen, *The Roots of Fundamentalism: British and American Millenarianism, 1800–1930* (Chicago: University of Chicago Press, 1970); Marsden, *Fundamentalism and American Culture*, pp. 48–71, 109–18, 212–21; idem, "Understanding Fundamentalist Views of Science," in Ashley Montagu, ed., *Science and Creationism* (New York: Oxford University Press, 1984), pp. 109–12.

15. Ferenc Morton Szasz, *The Divided Mind of Protestant America, 1880–1930* (University of Alabama Press, 1982), chaps. 9–10; Marsden, *Fundamentalism and American Culture*, pp. 184–91. Cf. William H. Ellis, "Evolution, Fundamentalism, and the Historians: An Historiographical Review," *The Historian* 14 (1981): 15–32; and Paul M. Waggoner, "The Historiography of the Scopes Trial: A Critical Re-evaluation," *Trinity Journal*, n.s., 5 (1984): 155–74.

16. See William Sims Bainbridge and Rodney Stark, "Superstitions: Old and New," *Skeptical Inquirer* 4 (1980): 18–31; and the statistics in Roger Handberg, "Creationism, Conservatism, and Ideology: Fringe Issues in American Politics," *Social Science Journal* 21 (1984): 37–51; Douglas Lee Eckberg and Alexander Nesterenko, "For and against Evolution: Religion, Social Class, and the Symbolic Universe," *Social Science Journal* 22 (1985): 1–17; Richard John Neuhaus, ed., *Unsecular America: Essays* (Grand Rapids, Mich.: Wm. B. Eerdmans Publishing Co., 1986), pp. 134–35, 143; and Eugenie C. Scott, "Antievolution-ism, Scientific Creationism, and Physical Anthropology," *American Journal of Physical Anthropology* 30, supp. 8, (1987): 21–39.

17. George M. Marsden, "The Collapse of American Evangelical Academia," in Alvin Plantinga and Nicholas Wolterstorff, eds., *Faith and Rationality: Reason and Belief in God* (Notre Dame, Ind.: University of Notre Dame Press, 1983), pp. 219–64; Joel A. Carpenter, "Fundamentalist Institutions and the Rise of Evangelical Protestantism, 1929–1942," *Church History* 49 (1980): 62–75; idem, "From Fundamentalism to the New Evangelical Coalition," in George M. Marsden, ed., *Evangelicalism in Modern America* (Grand Rapids, Mich.: Wm. B. Eerdmans Publishing Co., 1984), pp. 3–16; Quentin J. Schultze, "The Wireless Gospel," *Christianity Today*, 15 January 1988, pp. 18–23.

18. Ronald L. Numbers, "The Creationists," in Lindberg and Numbers, *God and Nature*, p. 402.

19. Ibid., pp. 404–6; Henry M. Morris, *A History of Modern Creationism* (San Diego, Calif.: Master Books, 1984), chaps. 3–4.

20. George McCready Price, *The New Geology: A Textbook for Colleges, Normal Schools, and Training Schools; and for the General Reader* (Mountain View, Calif.: Pacific Press Publishing Association, 1923), chaps. 38–41. See Ronald L. Numbers, "The Dilemma of Evangelical Scientists," in Marsden, *Evangelicalism in Modern America*, pp. 150–60; and cf. V. Elving Anderson, "Evangelicals and Science: Fifty Years after the Scopes Trial (1925–75)," in David F. Wells and John D. Woodbridge, eds., *The Evangelicals: What They Believe, Who They Are, Where They Are Changing* (Nashville, Tenn.: Abingdon Press, 1975), pp. 249–68.

21. Morris, *History of Modern Creationism*, chap. 5.

22. Carpenter, "Fundamentalist Institutions," pp. 62–63.

23. Morris, *History of Modern Creationism*, pp. 69ff. and the title of chap. 4, "Creationist Associations before the Centennial"; Morris and John C. Whitcomb, Jr., *The Genesis Flood: The Biblical Record and Its Scientific Implications* (Philadelphia: Presbyte-

rian and Reformed Publishing Co., 1961), pp. 442–43.

24. "Supplement to 1956 Directory— New Members," *Journal of the American Scientific Affiliation* 10 (1958): 26–28. See the suggestive remarks in Christopher Paul Toumey, "The Social Context of Scientific Creationism" (Ph.D. diss., University of North Carolina at Chapel Hill, 1987), chap. 11.

25. Morris, *History of Modern Creationism,* pp. 57–70. For the social context, see Robert Wuthnow, *The Restructuring of American Religion: Society and Faith since World War II* (Princeton, N.J.: Princeton University Press, 1988). See also Eileen Barker, "In the Beginning: The Battle of Creationist Science against Evolutionism," in Roy Wallis, ed., *On the Margins of Science: The Social Construction of Rejected Knowledge,* Sociological Review Monograph 27 (University of Keele, 1979), pp. 179–200; Dorothy Nelkin, *The Creation Controversy: Science or Scripture in the Schools* (New York: Norton, 1982); and James R. Moore, "Interpreting the New Creationism," *Michigan Quarterly Review* 22 (1983): 321–34.

26. Morris, *History of Modern Creationism,* chap. 6, App. B. See also William J. Tinkle, "Creationism in the Twentieth Century," *CRSQ* 10 (1973): 44–47; Walter E. Lammerts, "Early Steps in Formation of Creation Research Society," *CRSQ* 12 (1976): 213; Wilbert H. Rusch, Sr., "A Brief Statement of the History and Aims of the CRS," *CRSQ* 19 (1982): 149–50; idem, "Recollections in My Final Year as President of the Society," *CRSQ* 24 (1987): 71–75; and "Institute for Creation Research Established at Christian Heritage College," *CRSQ* 9 (1972): 87.

27. Toumey, "Social Context of Scientific Creationism," pp. 78, 111–25; Morris, *History of Modern Creationism,* pp. 237–38.

28. Morris, *History of Modern Creationism,* chap. 8. For the Noah's Ark expeditions, see John D. Morris, *Adventure on Ararat* (San Diego, Calif.: Creation-Life Publishers, 1973); and Tim F. LaHaye and John D. Morris, *The Ark on Ararat* (Nashville, Tenn.: Thomas Nelson Publishers/ Creation-Life Publishers, 1976).

29. Thomas F. Gieryn, "Boundary-work and the Demarcation of Science from Nonscience: Strains and Interests in Professional Ideologies of Scientists," *American Sociological Review* 48 (1983): 781–95; Gieryn, George M. Bevins, and Stephen C. Zehr, "Professionalization of American Scientists: Public Science in the Creation/Evolution Trials," *American Sociological Review* 50 (1985): 392–409.

30. Henry M. Morris, ed., *Scientific Creationism,* general ed. (San Diego, Calif.: Creation-Life Publishers, 1974), p. iv.

31. William Buckland, *Vindiciae Geologicae; or, The Connexion of Geology with Religion Explained* (Oxford: at the University Press for the author, 1820), p. 23. Cf. idem, *Geology and Mineralogy Considered with Reference to Natural Theology,* vol. 1 (London: William Pickering, 1836), pp. 94–95n.

32. Toumey, "Social Context of Scientific Creationism," pp. 57–65. Cf. Donald Heinz, "The Struggle to Define America," in Robert C. Liebman and Robert Wuthnow, eds., *The New Christian Right: Mobilization and Legitimation* (New York: Aldine Publishing Co., 1983), p. 140.

33. Toumey, "Social Context of Scientific Creationism," pp. 91ff.; Morris, *History of Modern Creationism,* pp. 212–19, 230–34. Cf. Frank Viviano's sympathetic but chilling account of interviews at the Institute for Creation Research and with Nell Segraves, in "The Crucifixion of Evolution," *Mother Jones,* September–October 1981, pp. 22ff.

34. Morris, *History of Modern Creationism,* pp. 291–92; "Supreme Court Strikes Down 'Creation Science' Statute," *Congressional Quarterly Weekly Report* 45 (1987): 1303. Cf. Wayne Frair, "Remarks by the President," *CRSQ* 24 (1987): 109.

35. E.g., the ministry of Jerry Falwell (Morris, *History of Modern Creationism,* p. 304) and the Liberty University School of Lifelong Learning, begun in 1985, the year after the parent organization, Liberty Baptist College, received accreditation for its biology education program. See A. Pierre Guillermin, "LBC Biology Accreditation," *FJ,* October 1982, pp. 63–65; idem, "Creationism and Biology at LBC," *FJ,* October

1984, p. 12; and Frank C. Nelsen, "When Christian Parents Meet the Public School," *FJ,* September 1988, pp. 12–13, 64.

36. Wendell Bird, *The Origin of Species Revisited: The Theories of Evolution and of Abrupt Appearance,* 2 vols. (New York: Philosophical Library, 1989); Norman L. Geisler and J. Kerby Anderson, *Origin Science: A Proposal for the Creation-Evolution Controversy* (Grand Rapids, Mich.: Baker Book House, 1987).

37. Morris, *History of Modern Creationism,* pp. 277–79, 302; "Ten Years of the CSSHS," *CSSHQ* 10 (1988): 1ff.

38. Morris, *History of Modern Creationism,* pp. 293–304, 332–35, App. C; David J. Tyler, "Creationism in Japan," *Biblical Creation* 7 (1985): 35–37; John Mackay, "An Interview with God's Smuggler," *CEN,* March 1987, pp. 21–24. On the openness of black Africa, see the first-person testimony by Ross Jones, "Genesis in the Jungle," *CEN,* March 1987, p. 25.

39. Ken Ham and Paul Taylor, *The Genesis Solution* (Grand Rapids, Mich.: Baker Book House, 1988); Ken Ham, *The Lie: Evolution* (El Cajon, Calif.: Master Books, 1987). For a brilliant evocation, see the account based on a week's diary kept by an Australian mother of four, Marie Ishahon, "A Crash Course in Coping with Anti-Creation Society," *CEN,* June 1986, pp. 27–32.

40. See Henry M. Morris, *The Genesis Record: A Scientific and Devotional Commentary on the Book of Beginnings* (Grand Rapids, Mich.: Baker Book House, 1976), pp. 30–32, passim. For a wider sampling of ideology, see Ian Hodge, "Creation Economics: The Economics of Reality," *CEN,* March 1986, pp. 43–48; Ellen Myers, "Biblical Creation as the Foundation of Sound Economics (A Bibliographic Essay)," *CSSHQ* 9 (1987): 13–19; William Stroud, "Creation and the Origin of Sex," *CRSQ* 7 (1970): 104ff.; John Mackay, "Creation and Marriage: For Women—The Price of True Love?" *CEN,* March 1986, pp. 25–28; Lance Box, "Genesis and Child-rearing," *CEN,* March 1987, p. 38; Jerry Falwell, "Capital Punishment for Capital Crimes,"

FJ, November 1982, pp. 8–9; "Capital Punishment," *CEN,* March 1986, p. 2; William H. Baker, "Capital Punishment: Vengeful Satisfaction or Judicial Necessity?" *FJ,* March 1988, pp. 18–21; Ellen Myers, "God's Sabbath Rest—Man's Created Destiny," *CSSHQ* 7 (1985): 11–14; and V. Wright, "Why We Need a Day of Rest: A Medical Point of View," *CEN,* December 1986, pp. 35–36.

41. Walter Lippmann, *American Inquisitors: A Commentary on Dayton and Chicago* (New York: Macmillan, 1928), p. 66. See also Alan Peshkin, *God's Choice: The Total World of a Fundamentalist Christian School* (Chicago: University of Chicago Press, 1986), p. 291.

42. See Edward J. Larson, *Trial and Error: The American Controversy over Creation and Evolution,* rev. ed. (New York: Oxford University Press, 1989); and, on "democratic epistemology," Logie Barrow, *Independent Spirits: Spiritualism and English Plebians, 1850–1910* (London: Routledge and Kegan Paul, 1986), chap. 6.

43. Richard Bliss, "A Two-Model Approach to Origins: A Curriculum Imperative" (1976), in Duane T. Gish and Donald H. Rohrer, eds., *Up with Creation! ICR Acts/Facts/Impacts 1976–1977* (San Diego, Calif.: Creation-Life Publishers, 1978), pp. 208–9. See also idem, "One Man's View on the Teaching of Origins in the Public School Science Classroom," *CRSQ* 8 (1971): 185–87; and "Testimony of an Ex-evolutionist: An Interview with Dr. Richard Bliss," *CEN,* December 1987–February 1988, pp. 28–30. For other exemplary statements, see John N. Moore, "Some Definitional Formulations," *CRSQ* 11 (1974): 3–5; idem, "On Methods of Teaching Origins: A Progress Report," *CRSQ* 13 (1976): 46–49; Robert F. Kofahl, "Correctly Defining Distorted Science: A Most Essential Task," *CRSQ* 23 (1986): 112–14, which provoked controversy in subsequent issues; and Henry M. Morris, "Science on Origins," *FJ,* March 1987, pp. 19ff.

44. Wendell Bird, "Freedom of Religion and Science Instruction in Public Schools," *Yale Law Review* 87 (1978): 515–70, esp.

550ff. Cf. Arthur O. Lovejoy, "Anti-Evolution Laws and the Principle of Religious Neutrality," *School and Society* 29 (1929): 133–38, a conclusive argument against neutralization by abridgement that, in effect, demanded that fundamentalists find a new strategy.

45. Barry Ferst, "What Bible-Scientists Can Learn from Bible Science," *CRSQ* 20 (1983): 119. See also the philosophical reflections of Ralph E. Ancil, "The Limits of Human Thought and the Creation Model," *CRSQ* 20 (1983): 30–39; and idem, "On the Importance of Philosophy in the Origins Debate," *CRSQ* 22 (1985): 114–23. For other exemplary statements, see Gary L. Schoepflin, "On Assumptions and Their Relation to Science," *CRSQ* 9 (1972): 125–29; T. Robert Ingram, "Can There Be True Science without True Religion?" *CRSQ* 11 (1974): 6–13; Randall Hedtke, "The Episteme Is the Theory," *CRSQ* 18 (1981): 8–26; Lawrence A. McGhee, "Gracious Science and Interfering Science," *CRSQ* 17 (1980): 10–11; and idem, "The Metaphysics of Modern Science," *CRSQ* 24 (1987): 138–41.

46. John C. Whitcomb, "Creation Science and the Physical Universe," *Grace Theological Journal* 4 (1983): 293–96. Cf. Robert Charles Williams, "Scientific Creationism: An Exegesis for a Religious Doctrine," *American Anthropologist* 85 (1983): 92–102, which demonstrates from Morris's publications that he and Whitcomb still fundamentally agree.

47. Whitcomb, "Creation Science and the Physical Universe," p. 296.

48. John C. Whitcomb, Jr., *The Origin of the Solar System: Biblical Inerrancy and the Double-Revelation Theory* (Philadelphia, Pa.: Presbyterian and Reformed Publishing Co., 1964); idem, *The Early Earth, 1972*, rev. ed. (Grand Rapids, Mich.: Baker Book House, 1986); idem, *The World That Perished*, 1973; rev. ed. (Grand Rapids, Mich.: Baker Book House, 1988); idem, "The Science of Historical Geology in the Light of the Biblical Doctrine of a Mature Creation," *Westminster Theological Journal* 36 (1973–74): 65–77; idem, "Contemporary Apologetics

and the Christian Faith," *Bibliotheca Sacra* 134 (1977): 99–106, 195–202, 291–98; idem, "The Limitations and Values of Christian Evidences," *Bibliotheca Sacra* 135 (1978): 25–33. For other exemplary statements, see Charles A. Clough and Louis E. Fredericks, "Creationist Science: A Challenge from Professor Young," *CRSQ* 15 (1978): 47–52; Richard Niessen, "A Biblical Approach to Dating the Earth: A Case for the Use of Genesis 5 and 11 as an Exact Chronology," *CRSQ* 19 (1982): 60–66; Richard L. Mayhue, "Scripture on Origins," *FJ*, March 1987, pp. 14ff.; Stephen R. Spencer, "Is Natural Theology Biblical?" *Grace Theological Journal* 9 (1988): 59–72; and, on the controversy, Bill Durbin, Jr., "How It All Began: Why Can't Evangelical Scientists Agree?" *Christianity Today*, 12 August 1988, pp. 31–46.

49. Toumey, "Social Context of Scientific Creationism," pp. 146–48.

50. George Mulfinger, Jr., "Review of Creationist Astronomy," *CRSQ* 10 (1973): 175.

51. James N. Hanson, "Against Catastrophic Rationalism: Gravitational Attitude Deflections of the Earth's Axis," *CRSQ* 15 (1978): 55–72; idem, "Reply to Akers' Letter," *CRSQ* 16 (1979): 83. See also idem, "The Sun's Luminosity and Age," *CRSQ* 18 (1981): 27–29. Cf. Robert J. Schadewald, "The Evolution of Bible-Science," in Laurie R. Godfrey, ed., *Scientists Confront Creationism* (New York: W. W. Norton and Co., 1983), pp. 283–99.

52. Jay Hall, "Defense of Copernicus," *CRSQ* 19 (1982): 80.

53. Don DeYoung, "Does the Earth Really Move? A Look at Geocentrism," *CEN*, June–August 1988, pp. 8–13; "Editorial: The Shoes of Ptolemy," *CEN*, June–August 1988, p. 2. See Donald B. DeYoung and John C. Whitcomb, "The Origin of the Universe," *CRSQ* 18 (1981): 84–90.

54. For a rare attempt to address this issue, cf. Jerry Bergman, "Reality: Real or Conventional?" *CRSQ* 19 (1982): 67ff., with idem, "What Is Science?" *CRSQ* 20 (1983): 39–42. See also the important discussion in Mark A. Noll, *Between Faith and*

Criticism: Evangelicals, Scholarship, and the Bible in America (San Francisco, Calif.: Harper and Row, 1986), pp. 145ff.

55. "Toys with Christian Values," and Zed Daniels, "Evaluating Toys and Cartoons," *FJ*, November 1987, pp. 47–48; Deborah Huff, "Video Games Invade U.S.," *FJ*, December 1982, pp. 57–59; Michael R. Smith, "Dungeons and Dragons: Confessions of a Former Dungeon Master," *FJ*, October 1985, pp. 36ff.; Carl D. Windsor, "'What Hath God Wrought?' Our Growing Electronic Arsenal," *FJ*, October 1984, pp. 24–25; Marc E. Harris, "The Distortion of Network Television," *FJ*, October 1984, pp. 26ff.

56. C. Fred Dickason, "Demons: Our Invisible Enemies," *FJ*, October 1984, pp. 21–23; Norman Geisler, *Signs and Wonders* (Wheaton, Ill.: Tyndale House, 1988), chap. 7; idem, *Miracles and Modern Thought* (Dallas, Tex.: Probe Ministries/Zondervan Publishing House, 1982), pp. 121–22; Henry M. Morris, "The Spirit of Compromise" (1964), in idem, *Studies in the Bible and Science; or, Christ and Creation* (Grand Rapids, Mich.: Baker Book House, 1966), pp. 98–102. On UFOs, see idem, "Foreword," in Sidney J. Jansma, Sr., *UFO's and Evolution* (privately printed, 1980); Norman L. Geisler et al., *The Creator in the Courtroom, "Scopes II": The 1981 Arkansas Creation-Evolution Trial* (Mott Media, 1982), p. 118; and Langdon Gilkey, *Creationism on Trial: Evolution and God at Little Rock* (Minneapolis, Minn.: Winston Press, 1985), pp. 76–77.

57. Morris and Whitcomb, *Genesis Flood*, pp. 224–27, App. 1; Morris, *Genesis Record*, pp. 112–28; Norman L. Geisler, *The Roots of Evil* (Grand Rapids, Mich.: Zondervan Publishing House, 1978), pp. 68ff.; E. Norbert Smith, "Population Control: Evidence of a Perfect Creation," *CRSQ* 7 (1970): 91–96; William J. Tinkle, "Is Nature Cruel?" *CRSQ* 9 (1972): 44–46; Richard Rice, "Natural Selection and the Christian View of Redemption," *CRSQ* 19 (1983): 212ff.; Ham, *The Lie*, chap. 7. For provisos, see John W. Klotz, "Is Destruction of Plants Death in the Biblical Sense?" *CRSQ* 16

(1980): 202–3; and Robert E. Kofahl, "Entropy Prior to the Fall," *CRSQ* 10 (1973): 154–56.

58. Whitcomb, *Early Earth,* pp. 128–29.

59. Dan Wonderly, *God's Time-Records in Ancient Sediments* (Flint, Mich.: Crystal Press, 1977), pp. 23–33.

60. Cf. Toumey, "Social Context of Scientific Creationism," pp. 150–51. On the speed of light, see G. Russell Akridge, "The Mature Creation: More Than a Possibility," *CRSQ* 16 (1979): 68–72, 83; Paul M. Steidl, *The Earth, the Stars, and the Bible* (Phillipsburg, N.J.: Presbyterian and Reformed Publishing Co., 1979), chap. 12; and Carl Wieland, "Has the Speed of Light Slowed Down?" *CEN*, December 1987–February 1988, pp. 12–14. For exemplary statements on apparent age, see Morris and Whitcomb, *Genesis Flood*, pp. 232–39, 344–46, 355–57; Lewis H. Worrad, Jr., "God Does Not Deceive Men," *CRSQ* 13 (1977): 199–201; and Frank L. Marsh, "On Creation with an Appearance of Age," *CRSQ* 14 (1978): 187–88.

61. Wonderly, *God's Time-Records,* pp. 33–34; cf. 231–32.

62. Morris and Whitcomb, *Genesis Flood,* pp. 468ff. (on coral reefs, see pp. 408–9); Wonderly, *God's Time-Records,* pp. 61–62. Cf. Geisler, *Roots of Evil,* pp. 70–74.

63. Frederic R. Howe, "The Age of the Earth: An Appraisal of Some Current Evangelical Positions," *Biblotheca Sacra* 142 (1985): 23–37, 114–29; Eugene F. Chaffin, "A Young Earth?—A Survey of Dating Methods," *CRSQ* 24 (1987): 109–17.

64. Correspondence with the author, January 1971–September 1975; Daniel E. Wonderly, "Non-Radiometric Data Relevant to the Question of Age," *Journal of the American Scientific Affiliation* 27 (1975): 145–52. See also idem, "Critique of 'Is the Capitan Limestone a Fossil Reef?' by Stuart Nevins, *Christian Research Science Quarterly* 8: 231–248, March 1972," *CRSQ* 10 (1974): 237–44, to which Wonderly was obliged to prefix a statement of personal belief in special creation, the divine inspiration of Genesis, and a global Flood. For the Grace institutions, see "Universities and Col-

leges Having the Creationist Point of View: Grace College," *CRSQ* 7 (1971): 229–30, and "Seminary Adopts Position Statement," *CRSQ* 17 (1980): 74.

65. Whitcomb, *Early Earth*, p. 45.

66. J. Patrick Gray and Linda D. Wolfe, "Sociobiology and Creationism: Two Ethnosociologies of American Culture," *American Anthropologist* 84 (1982): 591.

67. Dennis R. Mitchell, "Man: On the Eve of Destruction," *FJ*, December 1984, pp. 23, 26. For exemplary statements, see Paul D. Feinberg, "Homosexuality and the Bible," *FJ*, March 1985, pp. 17–19; Edward Dobson, "AIDS: Looking for the Cure," *FJ*, October 1985, p. 14; Duane T. Gish, "Genetic Engineering: A Biological Time Bomb," *CRSQ* 10 (1973): 10–17; Kerby Anderson and Raymond G. Bohlin, "Genetic Engineering: The Evolutionary Link," *CRSQ* 19 (1983): 217–19; Chris Darnbrough, "Genetic Engineering: Monster or Miracle?" in David C. Watts, ed., *Creation and the Christian Response to Warnock: A Symposium Sponsored by the Biblical Creation Society and Evangelicals for Life* (Rugby, Warwicks): Biblical Creation Society, 1985), pp. 13–30; and Carl Wieland, "Of Lettuces and Cow-Humans," *CEN*, September–December 1987, pp. 27–30.

68. Morris, *History of Modern Creationism*, p. 254.

69. See Duane T. Gish, "A Decade of Creationist Research," *CRSQ* 12 (1975): 34–46; idem, "More Creationist Research (14 years)—Part 1: Geological Research," *CRSQ* 25 (1989): 161ff.; and "Creation Research Society Research Committee (RC) Activities: A Decade Review including Philosophy and Purpose," *CRSQ* 20 (1983): 125ff.

70. "Creation Research Society Laboratory Project," *CRSQ* 18 (1981): 181–82; "Report on the Search for a Site for Our Research Laboratory," *CRSQ* 20 (1983): 68–69; Max W. Cullen, "Thomas G. Barnes Institute of Physics," *CRSQ* 24 (1988): 216; Thomas G. Barnes and Francisco S. Ramirez IV, "Velocity Effects on Atomic Clocks and the Time Question," *CRSQ* 18 (1982): 200. See also Barnes, "Decay of the Earth's

Magnetic Moment and the Geochronological Implications," *CRSQ* 8 (1971): 24ff.; Barnes and Raymond J. Upham, Jr., "Another Theory of Gravitation: An Alternative to Einstein's General Theory of Relativity," *CRSQ* 12 (1976): 194–97; Barnes, Richard R. Pemper, and Harold L. Armstrong, "A Classical Foundation for Electrodynamics," *CRSQ* 14 (1977): 38–45; and Barnes, "Electric Explanation of Inertial Mass," *CRSQ* 19 (1983): 208ff. For a biographical portrait, see "Thomas G. Barnes," *CRSQ* 9 (1972): 3–4.

71. John W. Klotz, "Creationism and Our Ecological Crisis," *CRSQ* 8 (1971): 13ff.; idem, "A Creationist Environmental Ethic," *CRSQ* 21 (1984): 6–8.

72. Henry M. Morris, *The Twilight of Evolution* (Grand Rapids, Mich.: Baker Book House, 1963), p. 93. Cf. idem, *History of Modern Creationism*, pp. 332ff.

73. T. Robert Ingram, "A Most Urgent Job for Creationists in 1976," *CRSQ* 13 (1976): 23–25.

74. Tom McIver, "Christian Reconstructionism, Post-Millennialism, and Creationism," *Creation/Evolution Newsletter*, January–February 1988, pp. 10–16. See Ham and Taylor, *Genesis Solution*, pp. 50–51; Ellen Myers, "Does Man Have 'Natural Rights'?" *CSSHQ* 6 (1983): 10–13; idem, "Monistic Evolutionism as a Pseudo-Paradigm for Theories of Human Action," *CSSHQ* 5 (1982): 25; idem, "Population, Resources, and Ecology: A Bibliographical Essay," *CSSHQ* 6 (1984): 10–16; Colin G. Clark, "Faith and Population in a Declining Civilization," *CRSQ* 18 (1981): 117–18; and Gary DeMar, "Developing a Biblical World View," in Richie Martin, ed., *Judgment in the Gate: A Call to Awaken the Church* (Westchester, Ill.: Crossways Books, 1986), pp. 19–33.

75. Ammerman, "North American Protestant Fundamentalism." In this respect the reconstructionists have been far more active and ambitious than another fundamentalist minority which has played a leading role in the creation science movement, the amillennial Missouri Synod Lutherans.

76. North, quoted in Thomas Allen Mc-

Iver, "Creationism: Intellectual Origins, Cultural Context, and Theoretical Diversity" (Ph.D. diss., University of California at Los Angeles, 1989), pp. 564–66. See idem, *Anti-Evolution,* pp. 197–99.

77. See Richard John Neuhaus, "From Providence to Privacy: Religion and the Redefinition of America," in idem, *Unsecular America,* pp. 60ff.; and cf. Anson Shupe and David G. Bromley, "Interpreting the New Christian Right: A Commentary on the Substance and Process of Knowledge Creation," in idem, eds., *New Christian Politics* (Macon, Ga.: Mercer University Press, 1984), pp. 10–11.

78. Jeremy Rifkin and Ted Howard, *The Emerging Order: God in the Age of Scarcity* (New York: G. P. Putnam's Sons, 1979), p. 239; Martin E. Marty, "Fundamentalism as a Social Phenomenon," in Marsden, *Evangelicalism in Modern America,* p. 67. Cf. James R. Moore, *The Future of Science and Belief: Theological Views in the Twentieth Century* (Milton Keynes: Open University Press, 1981), pp. 53–55.

The Worldview of Sunni Arab Fundamentalists: Attitudes toward Modern Science and Technology

Bassam Tibi

Islam is a thirteen-centuries-old religion-based civilization.[1] Modern science and technology are secular achievements culturally based on the tradition of the European Enlightenment.[2] The term "religious fundamentalism" refers in this essay to the revival—under the conditions of modernity—of a cosmological worldview embraced in its various particulars by different monotheist religions.[3] Can we relate these divergent issues to one another and discuss them under the heading of Sunni Arab fundamentalism? Is this an appropriate framework for a study of certain contemporary efforts to remake the world of Islam?

Notwithstanding the fact that fundamentalism, as a religious response to modernity, first emerged in the context of Western Christianity, the expression itself has become global through the globalization of modernity. As Lionel Caplan tells us, "The most prolific rhetoric of fundamentalism . . . is reserved for Islam, and especially for the depiction of contemporary events in the Middle East."[4] Contemporary Muslim thinkers have accepted a recently coined term in modern Arabic, *uṣūliyya* ("fundamentalism"), based on the concept of *uṣūl* ("fundamentals," roots or principles), which is as old as Islam. For every Muslim, the pious and unquestioned submission to the uṣūl of Islam is the essential part of Islamic religious conviction.

If one agrees that the term "Islamic fundamentalism" denotes a real social phenomenon in the contemporary Middle East, two basic questions arise. What underlies this phenomenon? Why do modern science and technology constitute core issues for the fundamentalists? These questions reflect the substance of this inquiry. Behind these two questions stands the cultural dimension of the modern globalization process which has impinged on Islam. Accompanying this process is the assumption that Western science possesses a universal status. But in recent decades Muslim fundamentalists have vehemently challenged this assumption.

Science is a cultural product,[5] and the modern world, despite all of its structurally unifying elements, is a culturally plural world. This raises the significant question of whether the revolt of non-Western peoples against cultural impositions[6] is also a revolt against modern science and technology in themselves. Muslim fundamentalists adopt favorable attitudes toward science and technology even as they demand "the de-Westernization of knowledge."[7] This would seem to indicate that the protest against Western cultural hegemony does not necessarily include a wholesale rejection of the scientific and technological achievements of the West. Muslim fundamentalists acknowledge that the modern European conquest of the abode of Islam has been based on techno-scientific achievements, and they argue accordingly that Islam must focus attention on modern science and technology. Yet they seek to construct alternative formulas, and even to inspire a countermovement in the sciences. They seek to adopt modern science and technology as instrumentalities while de-coupling them from their underlying norms and values.

The Islamic quest to construct alternative formulas begins with a searing examination of the epistemological assumptions understood to be at the root of Western science. Sayed Muhammad Naquib al-Attas, author of recent treatises on this topic, articulates a view shared by many fundamentalist Muslims. Western science has long accepted the Cartesian principle by which "doubt and conjecture," as al-Attas puts it, are seen as essential ingredients of scientific methodology. This perspective "regards doubt as an eminently valid epistemological tool in the pursuit of truth." Yet scientists who hold the Islamic worldview with full integrity must, he argues, reject this "epistemological tool" on the grounds that "the Holy Qur'an is the complete and final revelation . . . and there is no other knowledge—except based upon it and pointing to it—that can guide and save man."[8] Islamic knowledge is absolute and not subject to revision, as is scientific knowledge.

To say the least, validating scientific research on the basis of the revelation of the Qur'an poses unique methodological problems for Islamic science. But closing the gap between Euro-American techno-scientific modernity and the Muslim world is important to fundamentalist thinkers, who selectively adopt accomplishments alien to their culture even as they reject the worldview associated with these accomplishments. As secular, strictly human, and thus revisable accomplishments, modern science and technology embrace a socially formed fundamental methodology. The question, then, is whether scientific products are congenial to a theocentric worldview in which divine revelation is considered to be the ultimate source of knowledge and not subject to any doubt or conjecture.

The prominent Pakistani fundamentalist Hussein al-Sadr is one of several Islamic apologists to address this "problem" directly. He underlines the distinction between science and technology per se (the acknowledged means of Western hegemony) and the Western worldview and epistemological presuppositions that have been barnacled to modern science (and that serve as the inspiration and source of Western hegemony). On these grounds he denies the existence of any fundamental conflict between Islam and science—as long as a hierarchy of knowledge is respected in which Islam is at the pinnacle: "The pursuit of knowledge in Islam is not an end in itself; it is only a means of acquiring an understanding of God and of solving the problems of the Muslim community. . . . Reason and the pursuit of knowledge has a very important place in Islamic society, but it is subservient to Qur'anic values and ethics. In this framework reason and revelation go hand in hand. Modern science, on the other hand, considers reason to be supreme."[9]

In this view, similar in important respects to the approach of Christian fundamentalists to the question of the relationship between reason and revelation, the knowledge of the world attained by human reason must be informed by sacred knowledge and must ultimately be placed in its service. Modern Muslims like Hussein al-Sadr seek to combine the instrumentally adopted techno-scientific products with the Islamic uṣūl. This is an uneasy synthesis fraught with methodological difficulties. In attempting to create this synthesis, their retrieval and "application" of both the uṣūl and the techno-scientific accomplishments of the alien culture are highly selective. Although the fundamentalist enterprise recalls that of Islamic modernists in certain important respects, the symbiotic relationship between the fundamentals and modernity is significantly different. In the case of fundamentalism, the retrieved fundamentals are interpreted in such a way as to yield a field of possible inquiry for scientific research, while that research is limited in such a way as to protect the integrity of the retrieved fundamentals. In short, Muslim fundamentalists reject cultural modernity as a holistic, integrated civilizational project even as they remain cautiously enthusiastic about aspects of modernization.[10]

For example, Adel Husain, the prominent Egyptian fundamentalist, rejects the application of the methodology of natural sciences, with its emphasis on experiment and observation, to the realm of social behavior. This is, he argues, an example of Western cultural imperialism. Muslim social behavior enacts a worldview drawn exclusively from "the doctrine of Islamic civilization and its core issue, monotheism." Thus it may not be evaluted according to the norms established for the study of nature.[11] Adel Husain nonetheless affirms the endeavor to adopt modern science and technological means in service of "Islamic" ends.

In a similar vein Yusuf al-Qaradawi, a leading ideologue of the Egyptian Muslim Brotherhood,[12] emphasizes the distinction between "modernity" and "Westernization" in cautioning against the view that the present modern civilization is a universal one. For him modern civilization is indisputably Western, but it is not the only modern civilization possible or desirable. In the present situation, to accept modernity is to accept Westernization. Yet "if modernization [*tahdith*] and modernity [*mu'asara*] can be restricted to making use of the achievements of modern science and of its technological applications, then Islam . . . is favorable to such efforts."[13] In this context, al-Qaradawi revives the concept of authenticity (*al-asalah*) as a basic component of a distinctly Islamic modernization. That which is adopted from modern science must be subordinated to the "Islamic methodology" (*al-manhaj al-Islami*). The substance of this methodology lies in accepting the text of the Qur'an as *sola scriptura*. In this view the foundational sources of Islam provide the irreducible foundations for the desired holistic, integrated culture.

But can one pick and choose from the Western techno-scientific repertoire and then provide proper epistemological foundations for the instrumentalities selected? Can modernity be torn apart, broken down—"deconstructed," as it were—yielding instruments that can selectively be adopted while the worldview incorporated into them is dismissed? Muslim fundamentalists believe that the aspects of modern sciences they are willing to adopt from the West in fact originated in Islam. Their "adoptions" are thus not viewed as cultural borrowing, but rather as an act of repossession. Given the hostile attitudes of the Enlightenment toward religion, this argument raises the following questions: Did science as a discipline free of religion and as a revisable form of knowledge ever exist in Islam? Does science, conceived in a secular framework, run counter to Islam, insofar as Islamic revelation as absolute knowledge leaves no room for the autonomy of human reason?

The Islamic concept of the universe is theocentric in that the world is viewed as governed by God in a nonfinite way. The broadly disseminated formulas among Sunni Arab fundamentalists are those coined by their foremost ideological authority, Sayyid Qutb. The world is, in a manichaeistic way, split between a domain of *jahiliyya* (ignorance) and a domain in which God's method prevails. Both wage war against one another.[14] Human beings are receivers of God's commands, obedient servants in relation to God. God's will is the law of the universe. In the pursuit of knowledge man can discover this will by studying God's revelation in order to act in line with it. In this view Islamic science basically consists of the textual study of this revelation: man has no ability to produce knowledge, since only God is The Knowledgeable *(Allah al-ʿalim)*.

Most Islamic fundamentalists whom I read or interviewed lack familiarity with the history of science, even of Islamic science. In particular, they seem to overlook the distinction between two different traditions of knowledge in Islam: Islamic religious sciences and rational sciences (philosophy and natural sciences). A classical distinction in medieval Islam between the "Islamic sciences" and the "foreign sciences" held that the former are, in contrast to the latter, "closely bound together . . . the unity of sciences being based on their service to religion . . . the interrelations among scope, method, and worldview were firmly embedded in their intellectual structures and remained functionally operative."[15]

The cosmological doctrine that man through his own reason cannot discover the facts determining the structure of the universe is a basic tenet of Islamic science. The basic belief of Islamic sciences lies in the subordination of man to God, whose omniscience has been verbally revealed to the Prophet Muhammad. God's revelation is His law for the universe which Muslims comprehend in legal-substantive terms. The Qur'an is the textually fixed form of this revelation. Thus, the Qur'an is for Muslims the ultimate source of all knowledge. For them it incorporates the highest rank of *ʿilm* and thus science per se. "Allah brought you out of your mothers' womb devoid of all knowledge, and gave you ears and hearts so that you may give thanks" (16: 78).

The standard Islamic interpretation of this revelation is that man, without God, is unable to create knowledge. God provides the human beings whom He has created with "instruments" (i.e., ears, eyes, and hearts) which they can use as means for obtaining knowledge originating in God. Because the cognitive capability of man's reason is limited, the knowledge obtained with the help of these instruments can be true or false. Knowledge is true only if it is in line with God's revelation, for only God is omniscient. Islamic sciences are, therefore, composed of textual methods of studying God's revelation, as fixed in the Qur'an and the transmitted tradition of sayings and deeds of the Prophet *(hadith)*, the messenger of God. In contrast to the philosophical knowledge acquired from Greek sources, Islamic sciences were generally Qur'anic exegesis *('ilm al-tafsīr)*, the reading of the Qur'an *('ilm al-qirā'a)*, hadith sciences (tradition of the Prophet), and theory and methodology of sacred law *(uṣūl al-fiqh)*. In addition, there were ancillary sciences related to the study of Arabic as the language of the Qur'an. Foreign sciences were considered to be "godless sciences" and thus were excluded from the curriculum.[16]

The shared assumption of contemporary Islamic fundamentalists is that modern science and technology, as Qutb held, "originate in Qur'anic instructions."[17] Max Weber argued that the science recognized as valid by Western standards only exists in the Occident, even though some elements in the process of the development of this science were not derived exclusively from the Greek legacy and the Enlightenment. Weber conceded that some elements of this scientific tradition existed in medieval Islam and in classical China.[18] His argument nonetheless characterizes science as a secular product of human reason. The anthropocentric Enlightenment continued the classical Greek tradition of relating the skills *(techne)* of man to his knowledge *(episteme)*.[19] Elements of this scientific tradition also existed in Islam insofar as Muslim rational philosophers adopted the Greek legacy.[20]

In the view of Enlightenment figures such as Condorcet, *l'intolerance religieuse* is shared by all religions and is an impediment to the rise of sciences. Thus the necessary prerequisite for *la marche des sciences* was the breaking of the *privilege exclusif* of the religious scholars, who monopolized the function of interpreting and judging knowledge. In place of transrational revelation, human reason became the hallmark of modern inquiry.[21] The progress of science was therefore predicated on the disentanglement of human reason from the sacred.

This type of reasoning troubles Muslim fundamentalists and creates the major source of their dilemma with modern science. For they hold that "the problem of the progress of science in Islamic society is not how far can that society liberate itself from the clutches of its religion, but how more truly Islamic can it make its educational program."[22]

In the same year that Ismail al-Farnqi advanced this view, 1969, it was rebutted by the Damascene philosopher Sadiq Jalal al-'Azm in his book *Critique of Religious Thought*. Al-'Azm, a philosopher with a degree from Yale and a descendant of a notable family of Damascus, espoused the secular Enlightenment tradition of Condorcet. Against the prevailing view among Muslims, he wrote: "The conflict between both Islam and science is far-reaching. It concerns the method which we employ in order to arrive at our insights and convictions. . . . In this respect there is a fundamental contradiction between Islam and science. For Islam . . . the correct method consists in referring to certain revealed religious texts. . . . It is superfluous to mention that the scientific method stands in complete contradiction to this religious . . .

method."[23] Although the current wave of Islamic fundamentalism was still in its formative period in 1969, the statement aroused intense indignation among Muslim intellectuals in the Arab Middle East. The book was promptly banned, leading Swiss and French newspapers to join the Middle Eastern press in reporting the story of the "heretic of Damascus." [24] Sadiq al-'Azm was briefly imprisoned in Beirut, but later, under pressure by secular intellectuals in Lebanon, he was acquitted of blasphemy. He did, however, lose his job at the American University of Beirut.

In 1969 it was still possible for the free-minded secular intellectuals convened in the Beirut-based Arab Cultural Club to protest the oppression of al-'Azm. In a published statement these secular intellectuals argued that such censure lent credence to a stereotype of Arabs as people "who reject intellectual freedom and who despise human reason." Such action would only serve to "isolate the Arabs in suffocating darkness."[25] A few years later a protest of this kind was no longer conceivable. The imprint of Islamic fundamentalism has become the salient feature of public life in the Middle East. Islamic fundamentalist thought, based on the foundational principles sketched above, has become a widespread intellectual approach to all major issues, including the question of the appropriation of modern science and technology. The prevailing argument is that Islam is not only compatible with modern science and technology; rather, it is the *ultimate source* of modern science and technology.[26]

Islamic Fundamentalism as a Medieval-Modern Worldview

Religious fundamentalism is not an unspecific pattern that always occurs when religious fundamentals are called on; it is related to the cultural system from which it evolves and to the structures of society in which it occurs.[27] To Muslim fundamentalists, Islam is a cultural system which provides a model for reality, guidance for remaking the world. Thus in contemporary Islamic societies in which anthropocentric science and technology are not yet fully institutionalized, the problem of human knowledge of the cosmos must be seen differently than it is in industrial societies based on secular techno-scientific culture. Muslims are at pains to separate "science" from "secularism." [28] Fundamentalist intellectuals find the "model for reality" appropriate to their societies in the writings of the Islamic classical thinkers, but seek to forge a modern worldview by plumbing these writings for epistemological principles by which scientific research and technological development may proceed.

Islamic fundamentalists view their efforts at reviving the Islamic uṣūl as first a battle against secularism. To them the revival of Islam ensures the defeat of secular outlooks. From the Latin *saeculum* (generation, age) nineteenth-century Arab Christians coined the Arabic term *'alamaniyya* (worldly). However, because Muslims conceive Islam as religion and world *(dīn wa dunya),* there may be no form of separation between the worldly and the religious. This is a theme retrieved from medieval times by contemporary Muslim polemicists.[29]

If, as Franz Borkenau contends, "the development of modern natural science has been the most important single component in the formation process of the modern worldview,"[30] then it is important to note the inextricable binding of the modern scientific mathematical-mechanical worldview to Cartesian epistemology.[31] In classical Islam there was a similar religiocultural adjustment which contemporary fundamentalists reject. Hellenized Muslim philosophers disentangled epistemology from religious belief. Contemporary secular Muslims such as Syrian philosopher Tayyib Tizini argue that these philosophers placed human polity and nature within a rationalized cosmos that was nonetheless consistent with Islam.[32] But Westernized Muslim intellectuals of the liberal period pursued this line of thought without preserving the delicate but central role of religious belief. For example, the prominent Egyptian liberal Taha Husayn (1889–1973), who was educated at the Sorbonne and absorbed the Comtean positivism in fashion at the time, wrote that "the aim of human life is civilization, and that means the control of nature and life by reason. The attainment of this is a gradual process divided into several phases. In the early ones, religion and blind faith dominate the whole man's life; later, reason asserts its independence from religion."[33] In Egypt, "religion cannot be the guide to political life or the touchstone of national policy."[34] After his death Taha Husayn became one of the targets of fierce indictments by Muslim fundamentalists.[35]

Indeed, the recent retreat of Muslim intellectuals from a secular orientation must be seen in the light of earlier processes of acculturation by which European-educated Muslims adopted Western colonial-era attitudes to modern science and technology. This attempted acculturation was in a double sense unsatisfactory. On the one hand, these intellectuals did not make any substantial effort at introducing cultural innovations into Islam that could have been functionally similar to those of the Christian Reformation. Instead, they simply discarded religion as a meaningful element in their worldview. On the other hand, they failed to realize that secularism, as an attitude of mind, cannot thrive if unaccompanied by the secularization of societal structures and institutions.[36] Cultural and socioeconomic change sustain one another.[37] Westernization, as pursued in the early acculturation process, was thus an unsuccessful and unsatisfactory effort to superficially adopt, but not to culturally accommodate, modern science or technology. Viewed from this perspective, contemporary Islamic fundamentalism represents a *counteracculturation*, a revolt against Westernization. It marks an effort to establish one's own "Islamic science" against the one perceived as alien. In this sense Islamic fundamentalists are neither religious traditionalists nor modernists. They have their own version of modernity as well as their own troubles with its civilizational project.

But have Muslim fundamentalists been able to achieve what Muslim liberals have failed to realize? If not, will they be able to achieve this? Robert Wuthnow has observed that "fundamentalism, although rooted in traditional communities, is rapidly accommodating to modernity itself, gaining resources in the process, but losing many of its distinctive qualities."[38] In the case of Islam, the explanation of the fundamentalists' ability to reconcile traditional religion with modernity lies in the relatively low correlations between fundamentalist beliefs and many other attitudes, and the diversity of ways in which the core tenets of fundamentalism mesh with other beliefs and attitudes. Fundamentalism has, for example, demonstrated remarkable resilience in the face of processes such as urbanization and industrialization, but it has struggled in its relation to "cultural processes of rationalization."[39]

This "resilience of fundamentalism," whatever its source, makes possible the acceptance of cultural borrowing and use of items of modernity including science and technology as produced in other cultures and societies. But this process of appropriation is hindered by an absence of an accompanying cultural accommodation. This problem of the "cultural accommodation of social change"[40] manifests itself throughout the Islamic world. A liberal market economy is simply introduced as Islamic economics without much nuance; non-Islamic approaches to science are ushered in under the banner of authentic Islamic science.[41] In particular, modern technology is generally viewed as a technicality; it is not seen as inherently accompanied and buttressed by a radically different and new (and potentially anti-Islamic) worldview, but simply rather as a neutral instrument. Some Islamic fundamentalists have advocated the unfolding of an Islamic technology *(teknologia Islamiyya)*.[42] However, the program of this Islamic technology remains sketchy and appears to be little more than Western technology placed in the service of Islam.

An Islamic Technology?

The Egyptian writer Imaduldin Khalil adopts what may be called a fundamentalist line on the question of an Islamic technology by first citing *Surat al-Hadid* (Qur'an, 57th sura), in which God credits iron as "the most important and most influential raw material on earth."[43] Applying this verse to the contemporary concern for the military defense of Islamic lands, Khalil writes that "iron is the basis of armament and military equipment. . . . In our age, iron is the most important instrument of international forces in war and peace. Those states who dispose of the raw material for producing steel are capable of threatening their enemies in view of the fact that iron smoothes the way for heavy armament."[44] The reference to the Qur'anic sura is meant to lend legitimacy to Khalil's call for an appropriation of modern military technology: "The call for modern technology-based Islamic society is in continuity with the substance of Islam and with its open-mindedness toward all givens of science in all horizons."[45] This heretofore Western technology can be considered "an Islamic technology" in that "modern science is a neutral instrument. Modern science is not a heretic giant of which we ought to distance ourselves and to wage war against it, but rather a neutral instrument which we can employ in the service of our religion and to support our belief. For modern science is not only the achievement of Western civilization. . . . The civilization of Islam essentially contributed to establishing its underpinnings."[46] This is virtually the meaning of the formula "Islamization of technology": Muslims ought to separate modern technology from its norms and values so as to handle it as Western in technique, but Eastern in spirit. But the formula "Eastern in spirit" remains, to this date, an extremely vague notion devoid of substance.[47]

Nonetheless, Islamic fundamentalists want to provide an alternative to the present situation of Islamic societies. This vision is, however, not restricted to Islamic societies themselves. Contemporary ideologues have retained the seminal argument of Qutb, who portrayed the Islamic option as an alternative to the present world order. Thus Jarisha and Zaibaq indict the "civilizations of the twentieth century or rather of those of ignorance [*jahiliyya*] which rely on the machine and on the factory and thus put man in the second rank. Contrary to this, Islam puts man in the first place."[48]

This is not a diatribe, however, against modern technology. The need to develop or apply technology—in particular military technology—is a recurring theme in current Islamic fundamentalism. In fact, fundamentalist Muslims are dramatically exposed to modernity in the guise of arms technology and see it as both the symbol and substance of the threatening modern. Thus Islamic fundamentalists seek to harness technology's power and turn it against the oppressor. During the Gulf War of 1991, Saddam Hussein's slogan, "Islamic belief against technology" (*al-iman did al-teknologia*), designed to win fundamentalist support, fell on deaf ears. The Iraqi failure to master modern technology was duly noted.

It must be remembered that since the Ottoman period, war has been a central context in which Islam confronted the European project of modernity.[49] The current wave of Islamic fundamentalism has been in part a repercussion of the crushing Arab defeat in the Arab-Israeli 1967 War.[50] The defeat was interpreted as punishment from God because Muslims have deviated from the path of God in turning to non-Islamic systems. Yet others saw it as a failure of the Muslim Arabs to master modern technology. Islamic fundamentalists were uniquely poised to respond to this seemingly paradoxical reading of the military defeat. When they joined the chorus demanding the acquisition of modern technology in general, and arms technology in particular, they employed a form of thought steeped in the Islamic worldview.[51]

The encounter with militarily superior techno-scientific modernity generated a conflict among Muslims which split them into traditionalist and modernist camps even as it provoked new skirmishes between the secularists and the fundamentalists. Muslim fundamentalists adopted a stance on this issue that incorporated elements from both the traditionalists and the modernists. The traditionalists consider technological appropriation from the West as a *bid'a*, or innovation, a notion loaded with the negative cultural meaning of deviating from the path of the righteous ancestors (*salaf*).[52] Modernists sought to avoid this reproach by imparting to their technological adoptions from the enemy an Islamic character.[53] The traditionalists called for a return to true and pure Islam, while Islamic modernists envisaged military reform as one among other reforms (e.g., legal reform)[54] as the best way to rescue Islam. In their view military reform included borrowing from the enemy, that is, from the infidels. Fundamentalists also called for a return to Islam, even as they developed a school of thought which defined this act of borrowing as instead an act of repossession. They did not eschew technological appropriation as bid'a, but they worked more systematically than did the modernists to link the appropriations to the Islamic worldview, even to specific Qur'anic verses.

Each of these Islamic "schools" was reacting, of course, to the crisis of modern

Islam brought about by the discrepancy between the claim of Islam to be in possession of the perfect and final knowledge (revelation) and the concrete reality of the "backward" abode of Islam as existentially challenged by the modern and militarily superior Euro-American powers. There is something unique in this superiority. Unlike classical conquests (Greek, Phoenician) in which the stress was on the heroic and aesthetic aspects, modern Europeans see the superiority of their endeavors in their demonstrably scientific character.[55] The rector spiritus of nineteenth-century Islamic modernism, Jamāl ad-dīn al-Afghānī (1839–1897), employed a similar argument: the Europeans were superior to Muslims basically due to their mastery over science. "Colonialism is basically the dominance of states and peoples disposing of science over weak and ignorant people. The superiority is based on power and science, which always win against weakness and poverty. That is a law of the cosmos."[56] The interplay between Muslims and infidel Europeans was no exception. Afghānī frankly acknowledged the weakness and ignorance of Muslims in modern times due to their lack of science.[57]

On this point the arguments of early Muslim modernists are strikingly similar to those of the contemporary fundamentalists. Afghānī's "stress on Islam as a force to ward off the West and to strengthen Muslim peoples . . . his call for reforms and changes under the banner of Islam . . . are all themes that found a long and continued success after him."[58] Contemporary Muslim intellectuals have also relied on the analysis of a later prominent Islamic modernist, Shakib Arslan (1869–1946), who published *Treatise on Why the Muslims Are Backward While Others Have Developed* (1930). Arslan argued that Muslims failed to understand their own Islamic culture and thus too easily discarded it in the drive to imitate the West.

> Except the Muslims, all other peoples stand by their own religion, respect the tenets of their community and honor their own heritage. If one asks the Muslims to act in line with their Qur'an and their religion . . . then one collides head-on with those whose heart is sick and who scream "down with the reaction" and who argue "How do you want to adapt to higher standards of development while sticking to outdated outlooks of the Middle Ages in the modern times we are living in?" My question to them is, why did all those other people succeed to develop and to prosper while they, be they Christians or Jews, have kept to stand by their religion? And why must the sad Muslim throw away his Qur'an and his religion . . . to get his share of modernity?[59]

This early indictment against superficial and self-renouncing Westernization reappeared in the 1970s and 1980s; Arslan was cited prominently in field interviews I conducted for this essay.[60] In this view, scientific achievements cannot be properly assessed on the grounds of their own merits since they are "in reality only offshoots and nothing original; they are products and not initiations. Sacrifice [*tadhīya*] or exertion [*jihad*] are the highest kinds of knowledge and tower over all other forms of knowledge."[61] In the 1970s, Islamic fundamentalists argued that, because liberal and secular Westernized Muslim elites had failed to adopt modernity successfully, the only acceptable path to modernity is the "Islamic solution" (*hall Islami*). It is a "duty and necessity" *(farida wa darūra)*. These are the terms coined by al-Qaradawi in the early 1970s.

Fundamentalist Impact at Various Levels of Society

What is the impact of this fundamentalist worldview on the Sunni Muslim societies in which it is disseminated? Does it affect techno-scientific adoptions in the Muslim world?

The drive to obtain arms technology has been a central concern of fundamentalists as "Islamic" defeats, in past and in present, have revealed the military superiority of the industrialized West. The 1991 Gulf War has been embedded in this chainlink. Islamic fundamentalist underground groups, known under the collective noun *al-Jama'at al-Islamiyya* (Islamic Societies), combine a strident verbal rejection of everything coming from the West with use of bombs, dynamite, machine guns, and other small arms supplied by Western merchants. This articulation of "Islamic violence" with Western means does not seem incongruous to them.

Of course we have to be wary of any superficial reduction of Islamic fundamentalism to these minority militant groups. The Islamic fundamentalist worldview in its broad strokes embraces many million more Muslims than represented by these extremist groups. To accept the Qur'anic text as *sola scriptura,* to view its revelation as infallible and wholly and literally binding, and to combine these attitudes with an effort to adopt instrumental achievements of modernity (while rejecting the rational worldview related to it) are elements of fundamentalism characteristic not only of the Islamic militants but also of a much larger community of thought in the Sunni Arab world. This larger community of thought, representatives of which I quote frequently in this chapter, also displays a tendency toward fundamentalism even as it seeks to influence Sunni Arab societies from within.

However, the argument is sometimes made that in describing contemporary Islamic resurgence as an expression of religious fundamentalism, we must narrow the scope of our analysis to the militant groups. This leads to the perhaps comforting conclusion that fundamentalist pronouncements and attitudes are fully contained within the rhetoric, polemics, and apologetics of a vocal minority whose words fall on deaf ears outside a small circle of militants. The fact that these radical fundamentalists have exercised no direct, significant impact on governmental policies on scientific research, health care, or population control, for example, does not mean that they have been without influence regarding mainstream attitudes toward techno-scientific adoptions in Sunni Arab societies. Based on his fieldwork in Morocco, John Waterbury speaks, for example, of a behavioral lag of Muslims.[62]

It is also important, at this point, to draw a distinction between official mainstream government policy and the activities of radical Islamic groups. Governmental policies related to scientific research and technological appropriations are mostly pragmatic, even though government spokesmen regularly exploit the Islamic conceptual and symbolic repertoire. The evidence of the past decade is by no means conclusive, but there are signs suggesting that the articulations of radical fundamentalists are filtering into the commentaries and treatises of sympathetic Muslim intellectuals as the expression of collective choices.[63] In addition, the 1991 Gulf War contributed to strengthening the collective Islamic choices which are most congenial to fundamentalism.

We must bear in mind the historical fact that Muslim reformers failed to achieve a better Islamic society and gave way to secular Westernized Muslim intellectuals. In the course of Euro-American penetration of Islamic and other non-Western societies, a system of secular-modern education was imposed within which Western values and norms were transmitted but not institutionalized due to the lack of corresponding structures for their appropriation. This penetration did not, therefore, result in cultural uniformity consonant with modernity. It rather contributed to further cultural fragmentation of which current varieties of Islamic fundamentalism are a distinctive outgrowth.

Thus one would not expect and indeed does not find a sustained and detailed program and explication of "Islamic science" or "Islamic technology" even in the writings of leading intellectuals who sympathize with the fundamentalists, much less in the tracts and publications of the major fundamentalist groups themselves. Indeed the Muslim fundamentalist critique has not affected the actual adoptions of Western techniques and technologies themselves—nor has it affected the statements of the traditional Sunni establishment in Egypt, which has rejected employing the traditional Islamic term *bid'a* (innovation) as a reference to forbidden things. On this particular point laymen fundamentalists, who are generally in opposition to this traditional religious establishment, have not even challenged it.

The impact of fundamentalist thought in contemporary Sunni Arab Islam shows itself not in particular state policies or societal predispostions on the questions of modern technologies. Rather, genuine impact, limited still though it is, is exercised in the realm of education. In daily practice, Muslims import techno-scientific products from the West; they hire scientists and technologists and even send their children to study in the West. But, as we have seen, they are hostile to adopting the worldview related to these products and achievements. It is no wonder, then, that Sunni fundamentalist ideologues tend to focus on education rather than on research or on methods of scientific inquiry in the process of techno-scientific development.[64] The fundamentalist worldview requires students to memorize scientific findings but inhibits them from learning how to collect data or conduct experiments. Accordingly, its impact on the system of education lies in impeding the unfolding of human creative activities: God is the only Creator.[65]

In the history of Islam a secular scientific spirit developed as epistemological philosophy and natural sciences became known to Muslims in the course of the Hellenization of Islamic civilizations. Islamic philosophy "developed out of and around the nonreligious practical and theoretical sciences; it recognized no theoretical limits other than those of human reason itself. . . . Islamic philosophy was not a handmaid of theology."[66] But this strain did not transform the "Islamic sciences." That the rationalist line of Islamic philosophy and sciences did not determine the Islamic worldview consistently is due in part to the lack of institutionalization. The rationalist line was

kept out of the curriculum and was restricted to the realm of noninstitutional learning. Yet science can only become rooted when it "ceases to be merely a set of ideas
and becomes a social institution."[67] In modern Europe, science gained predominance
only through the process of becoming a social institution; the basic four aspects of
this institutionalization are autonomy, resources, legitimacy, and internal communication and organization.[68] These elements of the institutionalization of science were
lacking in medieval Islam and have been slow to develop in the modern era. The
tension between Islam as a religion and modern science is clear despite the Islamic
fundamentalist assurance that only the enemies of Islam proclaim an "invented tension
between Islam and science."[69] Interviews conducted in Cairo in fall 1989 contribute
to a further elaboration of this interpretation.

Attitudes toward Modern Science and Technology: A Cairo Survey

The Islamic thinker Hasan Hanafi argues that "it is difficult to find a more appropriate
term than the one recently used in the West, 'fundamentalism,' to cover the meaning
of what we name Islamic awakening or Islamic revival."[70] Furthermore, the term has
taken on a different meaning from the one traditional Muslims impute to uṣūl in their
study of Islamic jurisprudence (fiqh). Hanafi points out:

> The Islamic state is grounded on an understanding of the Islamic legitimacy.
> The term "Islamic fundamentalism" means, among others, that this legitimacy
> should be reformulated and realized in establishing the Islamic system (nizam
> al-Islami). The notion "Islamic fundamentalism" defends this system regardless
> of the other existing systems and of their achievements. . . . Islamic fundamen-
> talism does not necessarily mean conservatism, backwardness, or an enmity
> against modern civilization. Among Muslim fundamentalists there are those
> who are enlightened and progressive and who adhere to methods of progress
> and of modern civilization. Among them are also those who call for an adop-
> tion of modern science and technology, as well as of the systems of freedom
> and democracy.[71]

In recognizing the modernizing drive of Islamic fundamentalists, one can hardly
find today any "mere" traditionalists, as were the Wahhabi Ikhwan[72] of nineteenth-
and early twentieth-century Arabia or the Sanūsī of Libya. I contend that fundamentalist patterns of thought have indeed become so prevalent that even the religious
establishment of al-Azhar University in Cairo can no longer be viewed as merely
traditionalist.[73] There are rather several variants of Islamic fundamentalism. The militant fundamentalists form but one pattern. While insisting that the ultimate and
prime source of knowledge is God, the adherents of the different streams of Muslim
fundamentalism vary when it comes to a closer determination of modern science and
technology. The groups may be divided as follows:

1. A close reading of al-Azhar publications, and interviews I conducted with al-
Azhar professional authorities, makes it difficult for me to view them as mere tradi-

tionalists. Al-Azhar professors, many of whom hold Ph.D.s from Western universities, represent conservative institutional fundamentalism in Egypt. They are, of course, closer to the governmental establishment than the laymen and the militant fundamentalists of the Islamic Societies. In noting this conservative fundamentalism I argue that Islamic fundamentalism is not tantamount to the ideologies and activities of the Islamic underground.[74]

The conservative fundamentalism of al-Azhar proceeds from the assertion that knowledge comes only from God. The Azhar scholars place traditional Islamic symbols at the service of modern needs. Science and technology are neutral—"They have no nationality nor do they have a religion" *(Jad ul-Haq)*—and may thus be adopted from non-Muslims and harnessed for the benefit of Muslims.[75] In this view the Qur'an is not considered a scholarly book of knowledge but, as both the shaykh of al-Azhar and the mufti of Egypt told me, a "book of orientation" *(kitab hidaya)*. This is not a modernist worldview, nor is it simply traditionalist. On one hand the retrieved "fundamentals" insisted upon are not conspicuously selected and elevated, as they are by the radical fundamentalist groups. Yet unlike Islamic traditionalists, the scholars of al-Azhar do not incriminate innovations.[76] Scientific or technological achievements are thus not bid'as: "Science comprises every knowledge that leads to the benefit of man. Only within the boundaries of the Islamic concept of *ḥalāl* and *ḥaram* [the not-forbidden and the forbidden] can scientific achievement be rejected." Yet the conservatives reject the drive of lay-group fundamentalists to derive modern science from the Qur'an:

> The Qur'an includes references to science, though it is not a handbook of sciences. The truth of scientific theories can be approved or disproved experimentally. This is not a concern of the Qur'an, which only includes the absolute truth and which is *mu'jiza* [miraculous]. But the Qur'an is not a set of rules for scientific research.
>
> Modern scientific and technological innovations can be harnessed for the welfare of Muslims, but science and technology have no home and no religion [*la watan wa la din*]. However, the distinction between good and bad [*khair* and *sharr*] must be the binding criterion while adopting modern sciences.[77]

In this view the adoption of innovations must be in line with the fundamentals; violations of the fundamentals must lead to a clear rejection of such sciences or scientific achievements. This means that certain sciences, such as molecular biology, are in principle off-limits. Shaykh al-Azhar used the formula that if the results of rational inquiry are bound to the theological fundamentals *(uṣūl al-'aqaidiyya)* of Islam, no contradiction will arise between the two. From the point of view of the Enlightenment, this is of course the imposition of fundamentalist limits on science. From the point of view of al-Azhar, there are no such restrictions since "the progress in science consistently proves the miraculous character of the Qur'an and of the truth of the revelation included in it."[78]

The publications of al-Azhar elaborate the notion that the "bond between science and religion" belongs to the "fundamentals" of Islam.[79] Basic to this worldview is the "comprehensive character of Islam." Since secularization leads to a separation between worldly and divine issues, it runs counter "to the all-embracing Islam. . . . Secularism rejects the substance of Islam. Moreover, it is one of the instruments of the colonial and intellectual invasion."[80] Western scientific discourse is, to this school of thought, limited if compared with comprehensive Islamic thought. Thus, Islam is against the "Western scientific methodology," but not against science.[81] To Anwar al-Jundi, Islam is also against the distinction between "science and the philosophy of science."[82] While the Western mind splits the view of the world, Islamic *tawhid* (theocentrism) restores in the Islamic worldview the unity of the world as governed by God.

The cosmological worldview of the Azhar establishment does not differ substantially from other fundamentalist groups, nor from Qutb's original determination of Islam as a cosmological law *(shari'a kawniyya)*. Yet there is great enmity between the Azhar establishment and the laymen fundamentalists on one hand and the dissident militant fundamentalists on the other. In part this is because the Azhar remains one of the institutional mainstays of the Sunni tradition of religious establishment which has always been an instrumental legitimizer for the existing elites. One would never expect al-Azhar to play a dramatic oppositional role. During the Gulf Crisis of 1990–91 the Azhar supported the deployment of U.S. troops in Saudi Arabia through a *fatwa* issued by Shaykh Jad ul-Haq, while the laymen fundamentalists viewed this as a new crusade against Islam. Thus al-Azhar may be said to be further from a pure or extreme manifestation of fundamentalism than are the other varieties of Islamic fundamentalism which do subscribe to political opposition, be they "rational-enlightened" like Hanafi's school, or extremist like the Jama'at. The latter subscribe to the political rule of Islam *(hakimiyat al-Islam)* which makes them collide head-on with the existing political regimes. Al-Azhar has always been at the service of these regimes and has played a considerable role in legitimizing the introduction of some aspects of science and technology into Egyptian society. To explore further this double function of Islam as a legitimizing ideology of incumbent regimes and as an increasingly useful instrument for opposition movements lies beyond the scope of this chapter. It must suffice here to show that the difference between the legitimizing *conservative fundamentalism* of al-Azhar and the oppositional *radical fundamentalism* of the laymen and even the Jama'at Islamiyya is not due to specific differences in the cosmological worldview.[83]

2. The second category pertains to those Islamic fundamentalists who believe that the Qur'an includes all sciences. The most prominent example is the work of 'Abulhalim al-Jundi, though this notion can be found in numerous other works. These individuals seek to derive natural sciences and modern medicine from the Qur'an. Unlike the reserved fundamentalism of al-Azhar, the fundamentalism of these contemporary Islamic laymen authors is unrestrained with regard to the claim of Islamic origins of modern science. Shaykh al-Azhar cautiously drew a clear distinction between revelation and science, noting that scientific findings can be falsified in the course of scientific progress, whereas the truth of the Qur'an is not subject to any

experiment. Yet laymen fundamentalists read every scientific achievement into the Qur'an. The "modern reading of the Qur'an" is thus the first step in their endeavor.[84] Every page of the Qur'an "is an instrument of science that the human being receives from the teachings of God." Islamic fiqh, the Islamic science of sacred law, is the supreme science since it facilitates the proper understanding of the Qur'an as the prime source of all science. To 'Abulhalim al-Jundi the transfer of this methodology to other sciences, including natural sciences and rational philosophy, provides evidence for the contention that all origins of science also lie in the Qur'an.[85] The terms *din* (religion) and *'ilm* (science) are thus used synonymously.[86]

Al-Jundi recognizes no distinction between religious sciences and natural sciences/rational philosophy in Islamic history. In this presentation, the faqih Ibn Taymiyya and his declared enemies, the Hellenized Islamic philosophers, stand on equal footing; the impact of the Islamic sciences on Europe is interpreted as an intellectual influence of the Qur'an; Descartes's and Bacon's writings are based on "almost literary copying" of the Islamic heritage. Al-Jundi's conclusion is that Islamic scientific methodology was transmitted to the West and became the major source of European civilization. Muslim adoptions are thus an act of repossession.

> Bacon's *Novum Organon* did not include anything new. The Qur'an preceded him and provided the grounds for Arab scientists to work in all branches of science. . . . This present book addresses at the same time the past and the present while dealing with the capacity of the Qur'an to bring human reason to the highest ranks. It is time for those Muslims who aim at progress and who aspire for science to realize that they dispose of the keys required for the pursuit of these ends. If they did, then they may repossess, but not import, the progress needed.[87]

Al-Jundi appeals to the need for self-assertion. To boast against the West by arguing that it would not have developed as it did had it not appropriated Muslim sciences, and, at the same time, to remind fellow Muslims that they were once prosperous, is a major ploy for Muslim fundamentalists currently reviving Islam and at the same time recognizing Muslim backwardness in modern sciences.[88] In a way, this is no more than a continuation of previous Islamic apologetics. This view is widespread among the supporters of the "Islamic solution." Most of them are aware of the fact that the "Islamic awakening" cannot thrive without modern science and technology. The claim of being the first community from which science has evolved renders more palatable the "repossession" of techno-scientific achievements.

3. The third category encompasses the most intolerant stream among contemporary Muslim fundamentalists. These fundamentalists want to Islamize science by imparting to it an Islamic character. The adherents of this stream have coined the term "Islamization of science" and have conducted the search for an "Islamic technology."[89] This group is quite small, and their formulas, which represent more an educational plan for action than a polemic, are imported from the Washington-based and Saudi-supported International Institute of Islamic Thought. Saudi funding may render this plan viable. At stake is replacement of "Westernization" and "modernization" with

"Islamization." The book *Islamization of Knowledge*[90] is a Washington product, published in Arabic by a prominent press in Cairo, al-Ahram. Unlike the polemical fundamentalists of the second category who subsume Hellenized Islamic sciences and philosophy under the general Islamic, predominantly religious sciences, the adherents of the "Islamization of sciences" are very clear about ruling out rational sciences from their program. The "Islamization of knowledge" means "to reformulate knowledge on Islamic grounds." This plan includes "the effort to determine and to classify the available information and to reconsider the ways in which they were acquired and how they are linked to one another. Furthermore, the findings ought to be reassessed and the goals reviewed."[91]

The classificatory rules along which knowledge ought to be Islamized are "the basic principles of Islamic methodology." They can be summarized under the headings theocentrism, unity, and comprehensiveness of Islamic knowledge, and the complementarity of revelation and human reason.[92] This "Islamization program" encompasses all scientific disciplines and repudiates the achievements of the Enlightenment.[93] It is aimed at establishing "Islamic sciences" within the framework of the two principles: "1. Islam is the religion of science. . . . 2. The necessity of linking all sciences to religion. To separate science from Islam is a crime."[94] Yet the reader of this genre of Islamic literature can hardly find out what exactly is meant by the "Islamization" of natural sciences. Except for the imposition of limitations related to the *ḥalāl-ḥaram* concept, one can barely distinguish between general medicine and what is named "Islamic medicine."[95] In consequence, the impositions alluded to render "Islamic medicine" a censored medicine.

In addition to the Saudi-funded efforts, there are other efforts in this line. It is obvious that the formula "Islamic physics" is nothing else than physics in general, even though it is introduced by some Qur'anic verses. Saifuldin 'Abdulfattah Ismail's claim to establish an Islamic political science may be taken more seriously than the claim of an "Islamic physics." By the same token, the efforts of the influential Egyptian fundamentalist publisher 'Adel Husain to lay foundations for an Islamic sociology based on the Islamic doctrine have to be taken into consideration.[96] The impact of these efforts lies in establishing unbridgeable gulfs between one's own worldview and that of others—a tendency that results in what Fouad Ajami describes as an imaginary "self-completed world." Western social-scientific knowledge is "malicious" (*mu'adiya*) to all Muslims and must be replaced by truly Islamic knowledge. Were this position to become generally accepted, Muslims might ghettoize themselves by disentangling from global commmunication networks.[97]

Egypt is, in educational terms, the most modernized Arab-Islamic country. Egypt has exported high school teachers and in particular university professors to other Arab-Islamic countries. The unbiased observer of the most industrious fundamentalist authors in Cairo may ask why the name of Islam is inserted in all kinds of writings. The answer is simple: the Islamic reputation of such authors improves their stakes for getting a teaching position in the Islamic oil-producing countries, given the low pay of teachers and professors in Egypt and in the other poor Muslim countries. The Saudi-funded Islamization of knowledge in Arabic (Arab Middle East) and English (the broader world of Islam) decisively affects the contents of education. In Sudan, for example, only those institutions which subscribe to Muslim education have been eligible to receive Saudi funding, and only those teachers and professors with fundamentalist outlooks have access to Saudi-funded positions.[98]

4. "Enlightenment fundamentalists" wish to retrieve the fundamentals within a broader conceptual framework consonant with the Enlightenment. It is for this reason that I refer to them as "enlightened"; they refer to themselves as fundamentalists. Hasan Hanafi and his followers exemplify this minority option by drawing on the tradition of Islamic Hellenized rationalism. Hanafi clearly distinguishes between theological sciences and rational philosophy in Islam:

> In our days there is much talk about science and technology as if they were magic keys with which we can enter another world and so add a new myth to our rich mythology. The truth is that science follows from human reason, which is principally based on the autonomy from all other things. To characterize our crisis in a few words is to say that we lack the rational method which constitutes the frame for a scientific view of the world. The unscientific character of our life [*al-laʿilmaniyya*] is the result of the prevailing irrationalism [*la-ʿaqlaniyya*]. Our ancient scientists were able to establish science due to their awareness of the function of human reason.[99]

Hanafi calls for a "revolutionary fundamentalism" which is based on his selective view of "Islamic fundamentals," but not on the scripture. He dismisses scripturalism and asks his fellow Muslims to rely on reason instead of the authority of the text.[100] Instead of adding to the literature of Islamic rebuttals of secularism and Westernization, Hanafi regrets that no serious innovation of religious dogma has been undertaken and that no serious dialogue between fundamentalists and secularists has taken place. "I am interested," he writes, "in the innovation of the religious doctrine to smooth the way for a revolutionary Islamic ideology which accommodates all contemporary revolutionary ideologies."[101]

Hanafi's "fundamentalism" has been questioned.[102] Nonetheless he uses the term *uṣūliyya* to describe his convictions and his work, which is also disseminated among scriptural fundamentalists.[103] However, his fundamentals are much different from those of others known as fundamentalists. Rationalism is among them. "Hanafi acknowledges the crisis of current Islamic thought which can only be overcome if enlightened Islam [becomes] the framework for the interests of the Islamic *ummah* . . . Secular ideologies may only affect a minority of intellectuals, but it could never enter the ears of the masses. . . . It is only Islam which is able to mobilize the masses and let them sacrifice for its ends."[104]

5. Most of the concerns of the militant fundamentalists have little to do with the substance of theology or with the religious doctrine of Islam; these groups are political in nature. Nonetheless, the members of these groups perceive themselves to be the only true Muslims. Moreover, they raise the reproach of jahiliyya (ignorance) against the majority of Muslims, thus declaring them unbelievers to be opposed. These Jamaʿat Islamiyya groups are peripheral in comparison to mainstream fundamentalism

in contemporary Islam. It is true that the Egyptian variety of these groups—al-Jihad, Takfir wa Hijra, and so forth—are at the hub of these militant fundamentalists, and they are uppermost in an American audience's mind when it comes to Islamic fundamentalism in general. However, the Jama'at al-Islamiyya are a regional phenomenon[105] not restricted to Egypt or to any one Middle Eastern country.

Due to the lack of a cultural tradition of political opposition and existing institutional outlets to express and practice oppositional concerns, Islam, as a cultural system, is the last resort for opposition political groups. Most of the existing underground Islamic-militant groups like al-Jihad or Najun mina al-Nar, in Egypt, al-Da'wa in Iraq, al-Tabligh in Morocco, among others, have produced relatively little literature on their concerns. These groups include activists and practitioners, and may not cite their own theorists or political ideologues. This does not mean they lack a political ideology or a comprehensive worldview. Indeed, they have both. However, they tend to rely on existing patterns of fundamentalist ideology and related worldview. The writings of Sayyid Qutb, highly disseminated in illegal or legal "printings" published by the Cairo press Dar al-Shuruq, remain influential with these groups; indeed, I would venture that militant fundamentalists are more familiar with the major writings of Qutb than with the Qur'an itself.[106] Another source is the Pakistani ideologue Maulana Maududi. Hasan al-Banna, the founder of the Muslim Brotherhood, is also among their authorities. From Qutb and Maududi they borrow the idea that modern societies are returning to jahiliyya. From al-Banna militant fundamentalists borrow the idea of jihad in its contemporary expression of soldiery *(al-jundiyya)*. Muslims have to fight for Islam and are thus, as believers, soldiers.

The raison d'être of these groups is to practice violence to achieve the ends they perceive as Islamic: the commitment to violence is fully conscious. To legitimize their violation of the existing laws, they draw a distinction between *qanun* (law) and *Shari'a* (divine law of Islam).[107] Under the present global conditions in jahiliyya societies the rule of qanun is not the rule of Islam. Only when the Shari'a is applied is Islam present. To hasten the return of Islam requires the defeat of the jahiliyya. Modern means of violence are clearly technological tools: to practice jihad, interpreted as armed struggle against the jahiliyya, the most effective weaponry available provides the means. Not surprisingly, in the practice of the militant group al-Jihad, the holy book (as a source of indoctrination) held the same ranking as did bombs and dynamite. 'Adel Hammuda summarizes the story of al-Jihad as "Bombs and Holy Books" *(Qanabil wa masahif)*.[108] In Hasan al-Banna's legacy is the call "from the Holy Book to dynamite" *(mina al-mishaf ila al-dinamit)* as an expression for jihad.

Needless to say, in the primeval period of Islam, which is the model for these militant Islamic fundamentalists, neither machine guns nor dynamite existed. These industrial commodities are based on technological innovations—that is, on bid'as developed by non-Muslims which nonetheless constitute the tools militant fundamentalists require. Thus they regard modern technology as selectively and instrumentally valuable to Islam and do not object, or even make reference to, the cultural origin of these tools. On this question the Moroccan philosopher al-Jabiri explains the stance of the Jama'at al-Islamiyya–Morocco as a case in point: "The Jama'at al-Islamiyya aspire to establish an Islamic state, thus to seize power. They, however, will not be successful as long as they fail to accommodate political and social needs. . . . Consequently, their success will depend upon their ability to adjust religion to politics, which, in return, depends upon their ability to introduce those innovations to religion that are required by the needs of our age. The innovations are needed to the extent of making the religious discourse encompass modern political and social substances."[109]

A closer look at the ideology and worldview of militant fundamentalists discloses the narrow scope of their options for the future of Islam. They seldom go beyond the catchwords of Qutb, Maududi, and Hasan al-Banna: "Islamic rule," "the jahiliyya of the modern age," and "Muslims as soldiers of Islamic jihad." They cite Yusuf al-Qaradawi's formula, "the Islamic solution," as intending the establishment of the "Islamic state," which can only be achieved by true Muslims. These are the "obedient soldiers" who perform the "Islamic collective action based on planning and organization." There are only two options for Muslims: "either belief moves into the hearts of the rulers or the political rule moves into the hands of the believers. The first option refers to an illusory dream . . . those rulers have grown as secularists and they will get old as such. . . . There only remains the option that political rule moves into the hands of the young Muslim generation."[110]

For al-Qaradawi, guidance for the proper use of science and technology is included in the same Qur'anic instructions upon which the Prophet Muhammad acted. For this reason the messenger of Islam was the foremost scientist in the entire history of mankind.[111] Although Qaradawi's books make no explicit mention of specific weapons to be employed in the war against the jahiliyya, the "young Muslim generation," possessed of the ambition to become believer-rulers, perceives "Islamic collective action" as requiring their appropriation. Islambuli, Sadat's murderer, has been advanced to the status of "Islamic legend," and his story now serves as a narrative of al-Jihad itself.[112]

Conclusion

Fundamentalists justify the appropriation of Western technology under the banner of "repossession." But this act of "repossession" may also be seen simply as an act of imitation and reproduction. It has yet to be demonstrated that a fundamentalist variant of Islam is able to inspire anything more than the mere instrumental borrowing dictated by the theocentric worldview; at this stage it seems doubtful that the range of diverse, loosely organized, and uncoordinated groups that manifest essential characteristics of Islamic fundamentalism will be able themselves to acquire the ability to produce a viable Islamic science yielding innovative technological applications.

The fundamentalist worldview will continue to prevail, but without substantially affecting the ongoing adoptions from techno-scientific modernity. The substance of the Islamic religious doctrine (i.e., the immutability of Islamic revelation) compels Muslims to interpret any adaptations to historical circumstances as being in strict compliance with Islamic precepts. This worldview may not have direct impact on scientific research in the Arab world or on applications of technology, but it has a broader impact on the future of Muslims. It may in fact impede Arab Muslim cultural innovation. The mixture of futurism and a retrospective orientation opens the way for an instrumental handling and adoption of techno-scientific advancements achieved by others, but seems less effective in the task of creatively constructing an Islamic way to modernity because, as Antoine Zahlan points out, "science and technology in their modern meaning are relatively recent in the Arab homeland. . . . There exists no relationship between modern science in the Arab world and Arab sciences in the classical Islamic age."[113]

The preponderant concern of fundamentalist ideologues is in locating science culturally. The challenge posed by Western civilization "is the challenge of knowledge . . . which is productive of confusion and skepticism, which elevated doubt and conjecture to the 'scientific' rank in methodology."[114] The subsequent impulse—the "de-Westernization of knowledge"—amounts to suspending the "reliance upon the powers of human reason alone to guide man throughout life."[115]

Muslim fundamentalists thereby aim at establishing the priority of revelation against the superiority of human reason. The question is then: Is there an Islamic anthropology of knowledge?[116]

In an effort to locate science in cultural space, Muslim fundamentalists question the universal validity of Western science and indict the "epistemological imperialism"[117] of the West. Yet they claim to rediscover "the epistemology of Islam,"[118] which for them is no less universal than Western science. To be sure, they do not reject the products of techno-scientific modernity as much as they focus on the methodology of acquiring knowledge. Fundamentalists object to the disentanglement of secular knowledge from religious belief and reject the replacement of the truth gained by authority and revelation with truth gained by reason and experience. This stance makes difficult the creative accommodation to techno-scientific modernity. The formulas "de-Westernization of knowledge," "epistemology of Islam" and "Islamization of sciences" are in fact ideological cover for imitative instrumental and selective adoptions of techno-scientific items of modernity. Modern Muslim "de-Westernized" sciences clearly bear a Western imprint, inasmuch as they are imported from the West and not produced by Muslims.

The intended impact of Islamic fundamentalism is to establish authenticity and to reestablish the superiority of Islam. Needless to say, this intended impact is perceptual and, under the present structural givens, beyond reach. More important is the unintended impact. Creating impediments toward the cultural accommodation of techno-scientific modernity is the most significant unintended impact of fundamentalist Islam.

Islamic fundamentalism in the Middle East is neither a political fashion nor a passing phenomenon since it is rooted in the culture of Islam and underlaid by the present structural crisis of the Middle Eastern nation-state. Despite rhetoric, polemics, and apologetics to the contrary, Muslims will continue to instrumentally adopt techno-scientific products. Structural constraints coupled with the prevailing fundamentalist worldview will also continue to be crucial impediments hindering Muslims in the effort to accommodate modern science and technology in a creative manner. Medieval Islamic philosophers failed to institutionalize their rationalization of the cosmos. In this respect, modern Muslim secularists failed as well.

Acknowledgments

I am most grateful and deeply indebted to Scott Appleby for his close and critical reading of the many drafts which preceded this version and foremost for his most valuable comments and suggestions for further revisions. I am also grateful for my colleagues of the science-technology group of the Fundamentalism Project, in particular to Professor Everett Mendelsohn and Mary Douglas for their valuable comments on an early draft of this paper presented in London and Chicago. The Fundamentalism Project provided me with the needed grant for fieldwork in Cairo, without which the survey included in section 5 of this chapter could not have been completed.

Notes

1. The most comprehensive survey of this thirteen-century history of Islam is Marshall G. S. Hodgson, *The Venture of Islam,* 3 vols. (Chicago: University of Chicago Press, 1974).

2. For a constructive recent discussion of this issue, see Steven Yearley, *Science Technology and Social Change* (London: Unwin Hyman, 1988). Also see Edward Zilsel, *Die sozialen Ursprünge der neuzeitlichen Wissenschaft,* 2d ed. (Frankfurt: Suhrkamp-Verlag, 1985).

3. Cf. Thomas Meyer, *Fundamentalismus: Aufstand gegen die Moderne* (Reinbeck bei Hamburg: Rowohlt-Verlag, 1989), pp. 15–50; and Thomas Meyer, ed., *Fundamentalismus in der modernen Welt* (Frankfurt: Suhrkamp-Verlag, 1989), pp. 13–22.

4. Lionel Caplan, ed., *Studies in Religious Fundamentalism* (London: Macmillan, 1987), p. 1.

5. Robert Wuthnow, *Meaning and Moral Order: Explorations in Cultural Analysis* (Berkeley: University of California Press, 1987), pp. 265–98.

6. In his seminal work, *The Anarchic Society: A Study of Order in World Politics* (New York: Columbia University Press, 1977), Hedley Bull observed that the techno-scientifically induced "shrinking of the globe, while it has brought societies to a degree of mutual awareness and interaction that they have not had before does not in itself create a unity of outlook and has not in fact done so" (p. 273). The result is then a simultaneity of unifying political and economic structures and of cultural fragmentation. In applying this observation to Islam, we can state that the stronger the techno-scientific unifying challenge is, the more defensive cultural Islamic fundamentalism reacts. The universalization of modern science and technology coincides with the revival of local cultural outlooks contrary to them. The fact that the modern techno-scientific discourse is Western in nature and origin is the ground of the argument that this discourse has been "imposed" on non-Western cultures. The argument is elaborated by R. B. J. Walker, ed., *Culture Ideology and World Order* (Boulder, Colo.: Westview Press, 1987), pp. 182ff.

7. This formula is articulated by the fundamentalist al-Attas, who states: "Today's challenge posed by Western civilization . . . is the challenge of knowledge." Sayed Mu-

hammad Naquib al-Attas, *Islam, Secularism and the Philosophy of the Future* (London: Mansell Publications Ltd., 1985), p. 127.

8. Ibid., p. 138.

9. Husain Sadr, "Science and Islam: Is There a Conflict?" in Ziauddin Sardar, ed., *The Touch of Midas: Science, Values and Environment in Islam and the West* (Manchester: Manchester University Press, 1984), pp. 22–23.

10. I draw here on Jürgen Habermas's concept of modernity as elaborated in *Der Philosophische Diskurs der Moderne*, 2nd ed. (Frankfurt: Suhrkamp-Verlag, 1985). Also see Richard J. Bernstein, ed., *Habermas and Modernity* (Cambridge: Polity Press, 1986).

11. 'Adel Husain, *Nahwa fikr 'arabi jadid* (Cairo: Dar al-Mustaqbal al-'Arabi, 1985), p. 30, see also p. 17.

12. At this writing, al-Qaradawi is a dean at al-Ain University of the United Arab Emirates.

13. Yusuf al-Qaradawi, *Bayinat al-Hall al-Islami* (Cairo: Maktabat Wahba, 1988), pp. 137–38. In my view, this is a textbook-like definition of fundamentalism provided by a leading Muslim fundamentalist.

14. Sayyid Qutb, *Al-Islam wa mushkilat al-hadarah,* 9th "legal" ed. (Cairo: Dar al-Shuruq, 1988), p. 110. The result of this separation has been the "modern global society of *jahiliyya*" (p. 196), from which Qutb seeks to free Muslims. The impact of the two years Qutb spent in New York (1948–50) on his fundamentalist approach is dealt with in the fundamentalist book by Salah A. al-Khalidi, *Amerika min al-dakhil bi minzar Sayyid Qutb,* 3d ed. (al-Mansura/Egypt and Jeddahs Dar al-Wafa' and Dar al-Manarah, 1987).

15. Gustave von Grunebaum, in George Hourani, ed., *Essays on Islamic Philosophy and Science* (Albany: State University of New York, 1975), p. 4.

16. Two tendencies developed in the history of Islamic education: institutionalized learning, which followed traditionalist lines, and non-institutionalized learning, which followed rationalist lines. Before the eleventh century the institutions of learning were totally dominated by Islamic sciences: "The sciences of the Ancients, that is of the Greek . . . were studied in private, and were excluded from the regular courses of Muslim institutions. The religious sciences were at the forefront of education." George Makdisi, *The Rise of Colleges: Institutions of Learning in Islam and the West* (Edinburgh: Edinburgh University Press, 1981), pp. 75ff., p. 79.

17. Qutb, *Mushkilat,* p.110.

18. Max Weber, *Soziologie, Weltgeschichtliche Analysen, Politik* (Stuttgart: Kroener-Verlag, 1984), p. 340; see p. 342 on Islam.

19. The classical Greek concepts of *techne* (skills) and *episteme* (knowledge) which culminated in the man-centered worldview of the European Enlightenment illustrate the tension between Islamic fundamentalism and the Enlightenment. The basic idea of the Enlightenment can be traced back to the Greek political philosophy which in medieval times also affected rational sciences and philosophy in Islam. This basic idea revolves around the view that man is able to conduct knowledge and to pursue action based on it to determine human life. In his valuable essay on the Greek origins of the modern notion of progress and on the distinctions between the Greek concept and the modern one, the historian of ideas Christian Meier suggests that the belief in a *Können-Bewusstsein* is the hallmark of both. See Meier, *Die Entstehung des Politischen bei den Griechen* (Frankfurt: Suhrkamp-Verlag, 1980), pp. 435–99. This *Bewusstsein* (awareness, consciousness) is based on the assumption of the ability of man *(Können)* to autonomously acquire knowledge and to act in the pursuit of his prosperity along lines of this knowledge. Meier draws on the Greek concept of *techne:* "Techne is the common concept which covers all meaning included in arts, science, and craft, etc. It denotes the ability and skills of man for which we use the German word *Können.* . . . Through *techne* man is able to be the master of all things that affect his life. . . . The *Können-Bewusstsein* integrates all expressions of knowledge. It

is the culmination of knowledge which—in the classical Greek view—leads to the proper action. In this manner *techne* and *episteme* are linked to the Greek concept of *arete* in its abstract and general meaning" (pp. 472–73). This Greek concept is a basic idea of the Enlightenment and denotes *that man is able to construct his existence through human knowledge and to perform action based on it.* This view is not acceptable for Islamic fundamentalists insofar as knowledge is, in their view, derived from the revelation *(wahi)* as verbally fixed in the Qur'an (See Section 4). Based on this historical reference I qualify Islamic fundamentalism as a drive toward anti-Enlightenment with regard to science and technology.

20. See George Hourani, ed., *Essays on Islamic Philosophy and Science* (Albany: State University of New York, 1975).

21. The statement of Condorcet that man is "capable de former des raisonnements et d'acquerir des idées morales" is a historical highlight of European Enlightenment and its modernization project. The statement is included in the chapter "Depuis Descartes jusqu'à la formation de la Republique francaise" of Condorcet's *Tableau historique* (1794), a new printing of the complete French original with a German translation: *Entwurf einer historischen Darstellung der Fortschritte des menschlichen Geistes* (Frankfurt: Europaische Verlagsanstalt, 1963), p. 258 (French); p. 259 (German).

22. Isma'il R. al-Farnqi, "Science and Traditional Values in Islamic Society," *Zygon* 2 (1969): 231–46, here p. 241.

23. Sadiq Jalal al-'Azm, *Naqd al-fikr al-dini* (Beirut: Dar al-Tali'a, 1969), p. 22.

24. See the survey by Stefan Wild, "Gott und Mensch im Libanon: Die Affäre Sadiq al-'Azm," *Der Islam,* 48 (1972): 206–53.

25. The statement was published in the Beirut daily *al-Nahar,* 31 December 1969.

26. Islamic fundamentalists reject human reason as a source of knowledge and, consequently, reject any interpretation based on the autonomy of human reason while they simultaneously attempt to accommodate modern science in Islam. For fundamentalists, who competed among themselves to publish rebuttals against al-'Azm, the Qur'an is the source of all knowledge. The source of the contradiction pointed at by al'Azm, they contend, is found in the author's Western-American education—not in Islam.

27. Religion is conceived of here along lines of Clifford Geertz's essay "Religion as a Cultural System," in idem, *The Interpretation of Cultures* (New York: Basic Books, 1973), pp. 87–125. By the same token religion can be a source of religious ideology which is also conceived of here as a cultural system. See Clifford Geertz, "Ideology as a Cultural System," in David Apter, ed., *Ideology and Discontent* (London: Macmillan, 1964), pp. 47–76.

28. For example, the Arabic word for science is *'ilm.* "Secularism" has been translated into modern Arabic with the word *'ilmaniyya* and has become an established term. The Islamic rebuttals directed against secularism and secular worldviews are numerous, be these writings by fundamentalists of the religious establishment or by fundamentalist laymen. See 'Imaduldin Khalil, *Tahafut al-'Ilmaniyya* (Beirut: Mu'assasat al-Risalah, 1979); Zakariyya Fayid, *Al-'Ilmaniyya, al-nash'a wa al-athar* (Cairo: al-Zahra', 1988), and Yahya H. S. Farghal, *Haqiqat al-'ilmaniyya* (Cairo: al-Azhar Press, 1989).

In one of the most prominent contributions to the increasing literature of Islamic fundamentalism on this subject, published in Arabic by two professors of the Saudi University of Medina, 'Ali Jarisha and Muhammad Sh. Zaibaq, *Asalib al-ghazu al-fikri li al-'alam al-Islami,* 2d ed. (Cairo: Dar al-I'tisam, 1978), the authors contend that this translation into Arabic is misleading if *'il-maniyya* merely "give[s] the impression that the promotion of science is the goal [of secularism] . . . [this leads to the impression that] secularism may be seen as one of the instruments of Islam." For the authors, however, secularism is more than an appropriation of science; it is also a conspiracy against Islam insofar as it aims to separate religion from science. Thus, they argue, the translation of "secularism" should be *al-lad-*

iniyya (the irreligious) insofar as "secular" and "nonreligious" are synonymous in Western languages (p. 59). Also, see B. Tibi, "Islam and Secularization," in *Proceedings of the First International Islamic Philosophy Conference* (Cairo: Ain Shams University Press, 1982), pp. 65–79. On this issue, see also the final part in B. Tibi, *The Crisis in Modern Islam* (Salt Lake City: University of Utah Press, 1988).

29. For example, the classical texts on moral conduct by a Muslim jurist of the eleventh century, al-Mawardi (d. 1058), focus on *kitab adab al-dunya wa al-din*, a concern that formed the central theme of the 1986 work by Hisham Qablan, *Ma'a al Qur'an fi al-din wa al-dunya* (Beirut: Uwaidat Press, 1986). Also see Abu al-Hasan al-Mawardi, *Adab al-dunya wa al-din* (Cairo, 1955). Both books emphasize the inextricable link between *al-din* (religion) and *al-dunya (saeculum)* in Islam.

30. Franz Borkenau, *Der Uebergang vom feudalen zum buergerlichen Weltbild* (Darmstadt: Wissenschaftliche Buchgesellschaft, 1980), p. viii.

31. Ibid., pp. 268–383.

32. Tayyib Tizini, *Mashru' ru'ya jadidah li al-fikr al-'Arabi al-wasit* (Damascus: Dar Dimashq, 1971), in particular pp. 405–10.

33. Taha Husayn as interpreted by Albert Hourani, *Arabic Thought in the Liberal Age* (London: Oxford University Press, 1962), p. 328.

34. Quoted by Hourani, ibid., p. 334.

35. Cf. the fundamentalist attack on Taha Husayn by Anwar al-Jundi, *Taha Husayn: Hayatuhu wa fikruhu fi mizan al-Islam* (Cairo: Dar al-I'tisam, 1977).

36. In my book, *Crisis of Modern Islam*, I draw a distinction between normative and structural Westernization. Westernization, as merely transmitted by educational means, is normative devoid of the structural underpinning (industrial society) needed for its establishment.

37. Cf. B. Tibi, "The Interplay between Social and Cultural Change," in George Atiyeh and Ibrahim Oweiss, eds., *Arab Civilization: Challenges and Responses* (Albany: State University of New York Press, 1988), pp. 166–82.

38. Wuthnow, *Meaning and Moral Order*, p. 193.

39. Ibid.

40. B. Tibi, *Islam and the Cultural Accommodation of Social Change* (Boulder, Colo. Westview Press, 1990), pp. 31–55.

41. For examples, see 'Abdulhalim al-Jundi, *Al-Qur'an wa al-manhaj al-'ilmi* (Cairo: Dar al-Ma'arif, 1984), pp. 30ff.; and 'Abdulrazzaq Nawfal, *Al-Muslimun wa al-'ilm al-hadith,* 3d ed. (Cairo: Dar al-Shruruq, 1988), pp. 21ff.

42. 'Imaduldin Khalil, *Al-'Aql al-Muslim wa al-ru'ya al-hadariyya* (Cairo: Dar al-Haramayin, 1983), pp. 43–53.

43. Ibid.

44. Ibid., p. 49.

45. Ibid., p. 51.

46. Ibid., p. 45.

47. Sociologically this is nothing else than an example for a selective adoption of items of modernity which takes place without substantive modernization. See the conceptualization of this phenomenon by the late Reinhard Bendix. I draw here on Habermas's concept of modernity in his *Der Philosophische Diskurs der Moderne.* For a valuable debate on the concept which includes Habermas himself, see Bernstein, *Habermas and Modernity.* The application of the concept of postmodernity to the issue of Islam and modernity goes beyond the confines of this chapter. See J. F. Lyotard, *La Condition postmoderne* (Paris, 1979); and an essay by Richard Rorty, "Habermas and Lyotard on Postmodernity," in Bernstein, *Habermas and Modernity,* pp. 161–75. Also see Reinhard Bendix's distinction between *modernization* and *modernity* in his essay "Tradition and Modernity Reconsidered," in idem, *Nation Building and Citizenship: Studies of Our Changing Social Order,* 2d enlarged ed. (Berkeley: University of California Press, 1977), pp. 361–434. Bendix is of the view that modernization in some spheres of life may occur without resulting in "modernity" (p. 411). Bendix also deals with "the gap created between advanced and

follower societies," and he comes to the conclusion that "the efforts to close it by more or less *ad hoc* adoptions of items of modernity produce obstacles standing in the way of successful modernization" (p. 416). This observation is most important for understanding Islam and the modern sciences.

48. Jarisha and Zaibaq, p. 211. The term neo-ignorance (*al-jahiliyya al-jadida,* "ignorance of modernity") was originally coined by Sayyid Qutb; see Qutb, *Ma'alim fi al-Tariq,* 13th "legal" ed. (Cairo, Dar al-Shuruq, 1989) and *al-Islam wa Mushkilat al-hadarah,* 9th "legal" ed. (Cairo: Dar al-Shruq, 1988).

49. Historically, the military revolution in Europe was based on the development of machines. The technology of instruments was replaced by the technology of machines; see M. van Creveld, "The Age of Machines 1500–1830," *Technology and War,* (New York: Free Press, 1989), pp. 81ff. This age coincides with the "Rise of the West," according to Geoffrey Parker. Europe's military revolution facilitated the European superiority. See Geoffrey Parker, *The Military Revolution: Military Innovation and the Rise of the West, 1500–1800* (Cambridge: Cambridge University Press, 1989). The highlight of this development has been "the industrialization of war" as described in A. Giddens, *The Nation-State and Violence* (Berkeley: University of California Press, 1987), pp. 222–54.

50. Cf. B. Tibi, "Structural and Ideological Change in the Arab Subsystem since the Six Day War," in Yehuda Lukacs and Abdalla Battah, eds., *The Arab-Israeli Conflict: Two Decades of Change* (Boulder, Colo.: Westview Press, 1988), pp. 147–63. Yvonne Haddad argues on safe grounds that the rise of Islamic fundamentalism is "in no small part the result of the Arab-Israeli wars of 1967 and 1973." Haddad, "The Arab-Israeli Wars, Nasserism, and the Affirmation of Islamic Identity," in John Esposito, ed., *Islam and Development* (Syracuse: University of Syracuse Press, 1980), p. 121.

51. Cf. Yusuf al-Qaradawi, *Al-Hulul al-mustawradah* (The imported solution), vol. 1 of *Hatmiyat al-hall al-Islami,* reprint (Beirut: Mu'assasat al-Risalah, 1980). In al-

Qaradawi's view, the defeat of June 1967 was the defeat of these "imported solutions." In 1988 Qaradawi published his third volume of *Hatmiyat al-hall al-Islami—Bayyinat al-Hall al-Islami wa shabahat al-'ilmaniyyin wa al-mutagharribin* (Cairo: Maktabat Wahba, 1988). In this book Qaradawi indicts the secularists and the Westernized, and also provides "evidence" that Islam, if understood well, is the "source of science." For him this is true even in "the age of science" (p. 86); see also part 3, "Authenticity . . . but Not Westernization," pp. 107–55.

52. According to Bernard Lewis, *bid'a* is a novelty which "denotes a departure from the sacred precept." In contrast to a bid'a, tradition is viewed to be "good and enshrines God's message to mankind. Departure from tradition is therefore bad . . . bid'ah among Muslims came to have approximately the same connotation as heresy in Christendom," *The Muslim Discovery of Europe* (New York: W. Norton Co., 1982), p. 224.

53. The paramount issue in the eighteenth-century Ottoman Empire was how to respond to the threat to Islam posed by the military superiority of the European armies; therefore, reform meant military reform. See the chapter on the Ottoman Empire in Ralston, *Importing the European Army* (Chicago: University of Chicago Press, 1990). At present, the Middle East is according to *SIPRI Yearbook,* the world's major market for conventional arms. Cf. Tibi, "Structural and Ideological Change in the Arab Subsystem since the Six Day War," pp. 147–63.

54. Cf. Malcolm Kerr, *Islamic Reform* (Berkeley: University of California Press, 1966).

55. More about this by Gerard Leclerc, *Anthropologie und Kolonialismus* (Munich: Hanser-Verlag, 1973), pp. 23–26.

56. Jamal al-Din al-Afghani, *Al-A'mal al-Kamiliah,* ed. Muhammad 'Imara (Cairo: Dar al-Kitab al-Arabi, 1968), p. 448.

57. Surprisingly, Afghani addresses in this quote the Muslims and not the Westerners as *juhala'* (ignorants). In current Islamic fundamentalism, the jahiliyya is attributed to Western modernity from which Muslim

fundamentalists want to acquire the instruments, and free themselves from its "ignorant spirit" (worldview). Those Muslims who subscribe to modernity are denounced as juhala'. See Jarisha and Zaibaq, p. 211.

58. Nikki Keddie, ed., *An Islamic Response to Imperialism* 2d ed. (Berkeley: University of California Press, 1983), p. xxi.

59. Shakib Arslan, *Limadha ta'akhara al-Muslimun wa Tagaddam ghairuhum* (Beirut: Maktabat al-Hayat, reprint 1965), p. 102.

60. A prominent example of the Islamic fundamentalist ideological indictment against Westernization is Anwar al-Jundi, *Ahdaf al-taghrib fi al-ʿalam al-Islami* (Cairo: al-Azhar Press, 1987)

61. "If a community [*umma*] has complete command of this knowledge and acts accordingly, then it can master all other sciences, including their branches, and can appropriate all conceivable fruits and achievements from them. . . . The Muslims have to, if they choose to, strive and behave as the Holy Scripture commands them to. Then they [will be able to] reach the ranks of the Europeans, Americans and Japanese in both science and prosperity, while still preserving Islam" (Arslan, *Limadha,* p. 176). On Arslan, see William Cleveland, *Islam against the West: Shakib Arslan and the Campaign for Islamic Nationalism* (London: al-Saqi Books, 1985).

62. Insofar as it is more important to understand what they do and why they do it than to deal with what they think they are doing. John Waterbury, *The Commander of the Faithful: The Moroccan Political Elite* (New York: Columbia University Press, 1970), p. 5.

63. The results of the June 1990 communal elections in Algeria, during which the fundamentalist Front Islamique du Salut won the majority of the votes (55.4 percent), support this observation. The favorable responses of most Muslims to the fundamentalist formulas employed by Saddam Hussein during the Gulf War provided strong evidence of these collective choices.

64. The major part of Jawdat Muhammad ʿAwwad's *The Islamization of Sciences,* for example, is described as a teaching of

the sciences *(taʿlim al-ʾulum),* but not as the production of them. Jawdat Muhammad ʿAwwad, *Haul aslamat al-ʿulum* (Cairo: al-Mukhtar al-Islami, 1987), p. 55.

65. In Islam there exists to date no tradition of *Können-Bewusstsein* (see n. 19 above). This statement refers to a cultural legacy of rote memorization in Islam and not to a characteristic of the fundamentalist worldview. As the historian of Islamic institutions of learning George Makdisi and prominent Islamic authors like al-Jabiri and Hanafi have shown, the problem of *text (and not reason) focused learning* lies far deeper in Islamic history than the concept of modern Islamic fundamentalism would imply. The classical well-known enmity in Islam between the text-oriented *fiqh* (sacred jurisprudence) and *falasafa* (philosophy) reveals that inductive reasoning has always been denounced in Islam as a source of heresy.

66. Muhsen Mahdi, "Islamic Philosophy and Theology," in *Encyclopaedia Britannica,* vol. 9, pp. 1012–25, here p. 1012.

67. Wuthnow, *Meaning and Social Order,* p. 265.

68. Ibid., pp. 275–93.

69. Muhammad Ali Yusuf, *Al-Jafwa al-muftaʿala bain al-ʿilm wa al-din* (Beirut: Dar al-Hayat, 1966).

70. The survey on which this section is based was conducted in Cairo with a grant of the Fundamentalism Project (September–October 1989). My research in Cairo consisted of informal interviews and collection of primary materials. During my fieldwork a closed dialogue, organized by the Beirut-based Centre of Arab Unity Studies, between Arab secularists and fundamentalists *(al-hiwar al-qawmi al-dini)* took place. I was admitted and attended the three-day meeting. Most leading Middle Eastern fundamentalists (Muhammad ʿImara, Muhammad al-Gazali, Muhammad Salim al-ʿAwwa, Fahmi Huwaidi, etc.) as well as intellectually prominent secularists (Muhammad Abid al-Jabiri, Hisham Djait, Sayyid Yasin, etc.) were in attendance. While in Cairo, I interviewed representatives of all five groups listed and surveyed in this section. Among the persons I interviewed were the leading

scholars of the religious establishment. The latter are named in the text, but not the laymen, who wish not to be named. For this reason I resort to the published primary literature whenever I need to support my findings with formal evidence. In fact, without formal interviews as a basic source for quantitative data, no quantitative research can be run. The Iraqi sociologist Ali al-Wardi discusses the problem of the impediment of running such formal interviews in the Middle East in his book *Tabi'at al-mujtama' al-Iraqi* (Baghdad, 1965): "The Iraqi society is much different from the American one in which people could simply knock on the door and ask for an interview. . . . In Iraq people get scared as soon as they see a well-dressed person with a pen and a note pad in his hands. They believe his target is to find out the amount of unpaid taxes due or to check that a person is deserting the military service. They also may think he simply wants to find reasons for putting them in jail. For these reasons they are already prepared to lie in a variety of ways when asked by a stranger, just to keep the so-called interviewer, whom they are afraid of, aloof." Ali al-Wardi, *Soziologie des Nomadentums: Studie über die irakische Gesellschaft* (Darmstadt: Luchterhand-Verlag, 1972), p. 25. In the course of my two decades of research in the Middle East, I have repeatedly had this experience.

71. Hasan Hanafi, *Al-Usuliyya al-Islamiyya*, vol. 6 of *Al-din wa al-Thawra fir Misr,* 8 vols. (Cairo: Maktabat Madbuli, 1988–89), pp. 4–7.

72. Cf. John Habib, *The Warriors of Islam: The Ikhwan of Najd and Their Role in the Creation of the Sa'udi Kingdom* (Leiden: E. J. Brill, 1978).

73. The scholars of this establishment no longer view innovations as bid'a as traditional Muslims commonly do. My interviews in Cairo with the shaykh of al-Azhar, Jadul-Haq (28 September 1989), with the mufti of Egypt, Tantawi (24 September 1989), and with the dean of the al-Azhar faculty of Usul al-din, Professor Zaqzuq (20 September 1989), support the view that these leading personalities of the religious establishments are open-minded toward innovations, and thus, in a way, modernists, and by no means can be viewed as traditionalists, as some students of modern Islam suggest.

74. Barry Rubin, *Islamic Fundamentalism in Egyptian Politics* (New York: St. Martin's Press, 1990), presents an interesting current-historical overview of fundamentalism in Egypt. Rubin observes that the fundamentalist worldview is shared by the majority of the Muslim population insofar as Islam "has a powerful resonance in Egypt as the well-spring of popular identity and worldview" (p. 61). He states that "Islam offers a message of certainty and hope in a world marked by military defeats, confusion over identity, and economic hardship" (p. 6). Most interesting is Rubin's typology in which underground fundamentalists (the Jama'at Islamiyya), legal fundamentalists (Muslim Brotherhood), and the religious establishment (al-Azhar) are presented as fundamentalist without distinction in terms of their worldview and identity (pp. 80–92). (Rubin overlooks, however, both the Ahrar and the Amal parties.) This is also done in the present chapter. The distinction between the militants and the Azhar scholars is not in their fundamentalist worldview, but in the political concept related to the *Weltanschauung* shared by both. Only a minority of Muslim fundamentalists subscribe to violence as a means to achieve the goals of Islam, but the majority of Muslims share the same fundamentalist patterns for determining the Islamic view of the world and the identity related to it.

75. See the authoritative handbook of al-Azhar : Jad ul-Haq 'Ali Jad ul-Haq, ed., *Bayan lil-nas min al-Azhar al-sharif* (Declaration to the people), 2 vols. (Cairo: al-Azhar Press, 1984 and 1988). This authoritative two-volume publication reflects a worldview which combines both revivalist and futurist elements.

76. "We should not invoke the name of bid'a for qualifying every new addition which can be, individually or collectively, a blessing" (ibid., vol. 2, p. 180).

77. Jad ul-Haq, as Shaykh al-Azhar told

me in our interview, 28 September 1989. On the one hand this statement reaffirms the Islamic doctrine of *haram-halal* as a yardstick for determining what is admissable and what is not. On the other, it opens the door to innovations on the grounds that not every innovation is bid'a, and thus that innovations as such are not *haram* (forbidden). This argumentation is obviously inconsistent and reveals an oxymoron. In the Islamic doctrine, bid'a has no meaning other than innovation. It is clear that the inconsistency in the argumentation is a result of an oscillation between the old and the new, which is characteristic of all fundamentalist thought.

78. *Bayan lil-nas*, vol. 1, p. 76.

79. Farghal, *Haqiqat al-'ilmaniyya*, p. 163.

80. Ibid., p. 199.

81. Anwar Al-Jundi, *Ahdaf al-taghrib*, p. 82.

82. Ibid., p. 136.

83. The idea of *"Shari'a kawniyya/*cosmological law" and of Hakimiyat al-Islam in Qutb, *Al-Islam wa mushkilat*, pp. 185ff. The reference is to Michael Hudson (the double/dual function of Islam opposition/legitimacy), in John Esposito, ed., *Islam and Development* (Syracuse: Syracuse University Press, 1988), pp. 1–24, in particular pp. 16ff.

84. Mustafa Mahmud, *Al-Qur'an: Muhawala li fahm 'asri*, 5th ed. (Cairo: Dar al-Ma'arif, 1987), pp. 6ff.; and also Qablan, *Ma'a al-Qur'an*, pp. 22ff.

85. Abdulhalim Al-Jundi, *Al-Quran wa al-manhaj al-'ilmi*, p. 31, and pt. 3, pp. 105ff.

86. Hasan al-Sharqawi, *Al-Muslimun 'ulama' wa hukama'* (Cairo: Mu'assasat Mukhtar, 1987), pp. 85ff.

87. Al-Jundi, *Al-Qur'an*, p. 238. A reference to Roger Bacon can be found in Qutb's *Al-Islam wa mushkilat al-Hadara* (p. 35), where Bacon is qualified as "a messenger of Islamic science and methodology to Christian Europe." In my interviews in Cairo I heard this view repeated many times. Many of the interviewees, when asked for a specification of their claims, confused Roger Bacon (1214–1294) and Francis Bacon (1561–1626). The source of confusion is probably Qutb himself, who credits Roger Bacon with having established modern science in Europe. In fact, historians of science (see Zilsel, *Die sozialen Ursprünge*, pp. 61–62) think that Francis Bacon "was the first in the history of humanity who recognized the decisive meaning of the methodologically grounded research for the advancement of human civilization."

88. Nawfal, p. 45f.; Qablan, pp. 35ff.; al-Sharqawi, pp. 9–11.

89. Khalil, *Al-'Aql al-Muslim wa al-ru'ya al-hadariyya;* and 'Awwad, *Haul Aslamat al-'ulum*, pp. 128ff.

90. *Islamiyyat al-ma'rifah*, International Institute of Islamic Thought (Cairo: al-Ahram li al-Tawz', 1986). The English original of this booklet is *The Islamization of Knowledge: General Principles and Work Plan*, reprint (Herndon, Va.: International Institute of Islamic Thought, 1989). For, however, not always reliable information about the Saudi funding of the *al-hall al-Islami/*Islamic solution, see Muhammad Jalal Kishk, *Al-Sa'udiyyun wa al-Hall al-Islami* (Cairo: al-Matba'a al-Faniyya, 1984).

91. *Islamiyyat al-ma'rifah*, p. 54.

92. Ibid., pp. 87–117.

93. *Toward Islamization of Disciplines* (Herndon, Va.: International Institute of Islamic Thought, 1989).

94. 'Awwad, *Haul Aslamat*, p. 103.

95. Ibid., pp. 84–89.

96. Saifuldin 'Abdulfattah Ismail, *Al-Tajdid al-siyasi wa al-waqi' al-'arabi al-Mu'asir. Ru'ya Islamiyya* (Cairo: al-Nahda Press, 1989), in particular pp. 12–134. 'Adel Husain, *Nahwa fikr 'arabi jadid* (Cairo: Dar al-Mustqba al'Arabi, 1985), pp. 9–37.

97. Fouad Ajami, *The Arab Predicament: Arab Political Thought and Practice since 1967* (Cambridge: Cambridge University Press, 1981), p. 117.

98. Sa'id Ismail 'Ali, *Dirasat fi al-Tarbiya al-Islamiyya* (Cairo: 'Alam al-Kutub, 1982); and idem, *Usul al-Tarbiya al-Islamiyya* (Cairo: Dar al-Thaqafa, 1978).

99. Hasan Hanafi, *Al-Yasar al-Islami wa al-wihda al-wataniyya,* vol. 8 of *Al-din wa al-Thawra fir Misr,* p. 319.

100. Ibid., pp. 46 and 265.

101. Ibid., p. 310.

102. Rudi Matthee, "The Egyptian Opposition on the Iranian Revolution," in Nikki Keddie and Juan Cole, eds., *Shi'ism and Social Protest* (New Haven: Yale University Press, 1986), pp. 247–74. Mathee argues that "the circumspection with which Hanafi discusses the role of Islam . . . reflects . . . instrumentalist view of religion" (p. 251).

103. Hanafi, *Al-Usuliyya al-Islamiyya,* p. 197. In Cairo I had the chance to witness the great appeal and dissemination of his work among young fundamentalists. To be sure, Hanafi is not inclined toward any secular orientation. To him the fundamentals of Islam are beyond question.

104. Ibid., p. 319.

105. Nabil 'Abdulfattah, *Al-mishaf wa al-saif* (Cairo: Maktabat Madbuli, 1984), pp. 54–59.

106. The most influential pamphlets of Qutb are *Ma'alim fi al- tariq,* 13th "legal" ed. (Cairo: Dar al-Surhuq, 1989), and *Al-Islam wa mushkilat al-hadarah,* 9th "legal" ed. (Cairo: Dar al-Shuruq, 1988). On Qutb's impact on the Islamic movements, see Gilles Kepel, *Le Prophete et Pharaon: Les mouvements islamistes dans l'Egypte contemporaine* (Paris: Editions la Decouverte, 1984), pp. 39–70.

107. See Rif'at al-Sa'id, *Hasan al-Banna: Mata? kaif wa limadha?* (Cairo: Madbuli, 1977), pp. 122–24.

108. 'Adel Hammuda, *Qanabil wa masa- hif: Qissat tanzim al-Jihad,* 3d ed. (Cairo: Dar Sina, 1989).

109. Muhammad 'Abd al-Jabiri's paper is published in the proceedings of *al-Harakat al-Islamiyya al-Mu'asira,* pp., 189–235; see p. 210. Al-Jabiri is professor of philosophy at Muhammad-V-Universite, Rabat, Morocco.

110. Yusuf al-Qaradawi, *Hatmiyat al-hall al-Islami,* vol. 2, pp. 88–89, 229–30, 224, 240.

111. Yusuf al-Qaradawi, *al-Rasul wa al-'Ilm,* 3d ed. (Beirut: Mu'assasat al-Rislah, 1985). On Qaradawi's impact on Jama'at al-Islamiyya in Egypt see the chapter by Muhammad Ahmad Khalafallah in *Al-Harakat al-Islamiyya,* pp. 37–98, here pp. 71–80.

112. See Rif'at Sayid Ahmad, *Al-Islambuli: Ru'yah jadidat li tanzim al-Jihad* (Cairo: Madbuli, 1988).

113. Antoine Zahlan, *Al-'Ilm wa al-siyasa al-'ilimiyya fi al-watan al-'Arabi,* 4th ed. (Beirut: Markaz Dirasat al-Wihda al-'arabiyya, 1984), p. 14.

114. Syed Muhammad Naquib al-Attas, *Islam, Secularism and the Philosophy of Future* (London: Mansell Publishing Ltd., 1985), p. 127.

115. Ibid., p. 131.

116. Everett Mendelsohn has urged historians of science to consider not only a sociology of knowledge, but also an anthropology of science. Everett Mendelsohn et al., eds., *Sciences and Cultures* (London: Reidel Publishing, 1981), p. viii.

117. Ziauddin Sardar, *Islamic Futures: The Shape of Ideas to Come* (London: Mansell Publishing Ltd., 1985), p. 91.

118. Ibid., pp. 85–116.

Islam and Modernity:
The Reconstruction of an Alternative Shi'ite Islamic Worldview in Iran

Farhang Rajaee

Modernity emerged from and blossomed within the context of Christianity,[1] and presented the greatest ideological challenge to the Christian worldview.[2] Islam encountered modernity indirectly. The Islamic world responded to the *consequences* of modernity—to its political (i.e., colonialism), educational (i.e., new school systems and modern institutions of learning), and ideological (i.e., the ideologies of nationalism, democracy, and socialism) by-products.[3] Islamic thinkers, then, often reacted to, rather than shaped, the complex philosophical and ideological presuppositions which dominated the worldview of modernity. These very presuppositions went unattended for a long time. Instead, it was assumed within the Islamic world that simply by acquiring the instrumentalities that had enabled the West to gain economic and political ascendancy, Muslims could overcome their weaknesses and shortcomings. Thus, as we saw in the previous chapter, Muslims emulated the West and justified it by Islamic principles.

However, the more Muslims of the late nineteenth and early twentieth centuries emulated the West, the less they were able, paradoxically, to free themselves from a "state of backwardness." By the mid-twentieth century Muslim intellectuals began questioning the validity of the assumption that imitating the West would lead to prosperity. Such reevaluation gave rise to the notion of the "return to the self." Yet how were Muslims to preserve their distinctive identity in the face of an increasingly pervasive world culture sustained and driven by a universalizing and expansionist technological and scientific system?

This chapter considers the ways in which the movement for the return to the self manifested itself within the Shi'ite context. The direct interaction of modernity and Shi'ite fundamentals, on the one hand, and with the realities of modern life, on the other hand, has necessitated mutual modifications and adjustment. This chapter outlines and analyzes the evolving story of this encounter within the Shi'ite world, particularly within Iran, in the areas of science, industry, and technology, within the framework of the evolution mentioned above. I have analyzed the views of those thinkers who are seen as the heroes of the present resurgence of Islam within the Shi'ite context and who have either constructed an alternative Shi'ite worldview or have worked toward the reconstruction of an Islamic worldview in light of the exigencies of the modern world.

The emergence of the Islamic revolution provides a comprehensive test of the degree to which such a reconstruction of the Islamic worldview could be achieved. The institutionalization of the Islamic fundamentalist framework itself went through phases. During the revolutionary years (mid-1970s to February 1979), competing ideologies contended to impose their preferred political order; in the second phase (1979 to October 1983), the accepted view was that the future order would be an Islamic government; and finally in the third phase, continuing at this writing, Imam Khomeini's interpretation of Shi'ite political thought is the dominant view. In this third phase, categories such as "radical" and "moderate" or "pragmatist" are often applied to various figures in Iran. But these categories are irrelevant to my discussion; whether one is a radical or a moderate in approach, each is attempting to live within the boundaries of Islamic teaching. In this chapter, therefore, I draw a general picture, including all of the debates that contribute to the encounter of Islam with modernity. Thus the chapter considers areas in which Shi'ism had to accommodate modernity as well as areas in which Shi'ism resisted modifications despite the demands of modernity. The guiding questions throughout the discussion include the following: How have Shi'ite thinkers reacted to modern sciences, modern worldviews, and their by-product, technology? Do they define science differently from the way it is perceived in the West? Have they attempted to explain science in terms of their religious faith and tenets or, on the contrary, have they tried to explain their religious principles in terms of modernity? Are they selective in their application of sciences? If so, which aspects of the sciences do they welcome and which do they reject? How do they justify their preferences?

Religious Conformity: Shi'ism and Modernity

The Safavids (1502–1736) made Shi'ism the official religion of their state, and thus identified it with Iran as an independent political entity. This has meant that, to a significant degree, social, political, and economic changes affecting Iran have been instrumental in changes, modifications, or reformulations of Shi'ism. In the aftermath of the Iranian defeat in wars with Russia in 1813 and 1828, for example,[4] Shi'ite sentiment figured prominently in the Iranian reaction. A declaration of *jihad* (holy war) on Russia by a contemporary Shi'i leader did not help and only made the religious leaders appear responsible for the consequent disaster.[5]

The immediate reaction to these defeats was an attempt to reform Iran according to the model of the West. Successive reformist ministers—Haj Mirza Abbas Aqasi

(1834–48),[6] Mirza Taqi Khan Amir Kabir (1848–51),[7] and Mirza Hossein Khan Mushir ud-Dawlah known as Sepahsalar[8]—paved the way for the Constitutional Revolution of 1905–11, which attempted to establish a new order modeled after modern Western societies not only politically, but also socially, economically, and even intellectually.[9] The new reform was approved by the majority of the Shi'ite religious establishment, and two prominent Shi'ite religious leaders became known as important leaders of the revolution.[10] One major religious leader, Ayatollah Mirza Hossein Na'ini, wrote a treatise in defense of constitutionalism and treated it as the next best thing to an ideal Shi'i polity ruled by the infallible Imam.[11]

In terms of our own discussion of modernity, the guiding question for reformers in Iran at the time, whether religionist or otherwise, was, How do we become like the West? This was the overriding concern of Muslim thinkers and religious-minded Iranians until the death in 1961 of Shi'ite religious leader Muhammad Hossein Tabataba'i Borujerdi, the last senior marja' al-taqlid to be recognized as preeminent by the ulama, the public, and by the secular ruler. This first phase of the direct encounter with and imitation of modernity featured apologetic defenses of Islam as thoroughly modern, expositions of Islamic views in terms of modernity, and refutations of competing ideologies. Very little opportunity was provided in this phase for presenting an alternative worldview. There was, however, one notable exception to this rule.

The protagonists of the first phase included Jamal ad-Din Asadabadi (d. 1892), better known as al-Afghani, and Mahdi Bazargan (b. 1904), a prominent Muslim thinker and the first prime minister of the Islamic Republic of Iran. Afghani is known as the founder of the pan-Islamic movement and claimed by many as a Sunni Muslim. Regardless of his religion, nationality, or ethnicity, he is of particular importance for my discussion, because he is considered by contemporary Shi'ite intellectuals as the founder of modern Islamic movements in the sense that his views are often taken as the conceptual paradigm for the reconstruction of their belief system. Afghani's lectures, treatise, and books—particularly his response to a lecture by the French philosopher Ernest Renan, published in *Journal de Debat* in 1883, and his treatise *The Refutation of the Materialists*—formed the basis of an Islamic alternative to the modern worldview.[12]

Afghani wrote for two different audiences. On the one hand, he invited his co-religionists to be mindful of the new sciences; on the other, he defended Islam before his Western readers as a religion compatible with the sciences. On the compatibility of religion and science he held as axiomatic that "religious beliefs, whether true or false, are in no way incompatible with civilization and worldly progress. . . . I do not believe that there is a religion in the world that forbids these things."[13] Throughout history, Hindus, Christians, and Muslims have progressed in the spheres of science, knowledge, and industry. Afghani set out to correct the perception that Islam and its followers were hostile to the scientific and philosophical spirit. As an authentic guide to human nature, Islam holds that "no nation at its origin is capable of letting itself be guided by pure reason."[14] Thus a people must "look outside itself for a place of refuge" in religion, which history has demonstrated to be a civilizing force: "One cannot deny that it is by this religious education, whether it be Muslim, Christian, or pagan, that all nations have emerged from barbarism and marched toward a more advanced civilization."[15]

Afghani admitted with Renan, however, that religion has at times attempted to halt philosophical movement. "In truth, Muslim religion has tried to stifle science and stop its progress. . . . A similar attempt, if I am not mistaken, was made by Christian religion, and the venerated leaders of the Catholic church have not yet disarmed so far as I know."[16] But this attempt, he held, was related to the attitude of the guardians of the religions and had nothing to do with the *founding principles* of religion. This point emerges clearly in a lecture Afghani delivered in Calcutta in 1882. He complains that the religious scholars *(ulama),* by dividing sciences into Islamic and European sciences, forbid others to learn the new sciences. How very strange it is that the Muslims study those sciences that are "ascribed to Aristotle with greatest delight, as if Aristotle were one of the pillars of Muslims." However, Afghani continues, if the discussion turns to Galileo, Newton, and Kepler, these same Muslims might consider them infidels. "The father and mother of science is proof, and proof is neither Aristotle nor Galileo."[17] The ulama "have not understood that science is that noble thing that has no connection with any nation, and is not distinguished by anything but itself."[18] Afghani urged Muslims to treat the new sciences as tools for the betterment of their temporal as well as religious life, much as the early Muslims did with the Greek heritage. This basic argument constitutes an important aspect of Muslims' attitude toward sciences today.

Refutation of the Materialists was the first attempt at the reformulation of modern Islamic ideology. Departing from the traditional approach of emphasizing the Qur'an and the traditions of the Islamic divines, Afghani constructed a more utilitarian argument for modern audiences. But his medium of discourse remained Islamic, that is, he used concepts which are recognized categories within Islamic theology, jurisprudence, and related disciplines.[19] The *Refutation,* written "to expose the corruption that has come into the sphere of civilization from the materialist or *neicheri* sect . . . and to explain and elucidate the virtues, advantages and benefits of religions, especially the Islamic religion,"[20] begins with a summary of the views of the materialists from the time of the Greeks to the present "leader of the group," Darwin.[21] In opposing the materialists, Afghani reviews three important beliefs which "mankind from ancient times has attained from religion," namely, that "man is the noblest of creatures," that "the community is the noblest one," and that "man has come into the world in order to acquire accomplishments worthy of transforming him to a world more excellent."[22] (These formulations were based on Qur'anic verses or on the traditions of the Islamic divines.)

Out of these emerge three qualities which, according to Afghani, serve as the firm pillars for "the existence of nations and permanence of all social order." They include shame, trustworthiness, and truthfulness or honesty.[23] The materialists deny the existence of these principles and thereby "extirpate the six-sided castle of human happiness that is built of these three noble beliefs and three great qualities."[24] The treatise then dwells upon the "treachery and falsehood" which emanate from the teachings of the materialists. Afghani concludes that "the Islamic religion is the only religion that censures beliefs without proof . . . and sets up proofs for each fundamental belief in such a way that it will be useful to all people."[25] His closing, a verse from the Qur'an, has since become the motto of self-consciously Muslim thinkers : "Verily never will God change the condition of a people until they change it themselves" (13:11; Yusuf Ali's translation).

This verse seemed particularly appropriate to Mahdi Bazargan's experience. From Afghani's death until the 1930s, political and administrative reforms modeled after the West were tacitly approved by the religious establishment with little effort to develop theoretical justifications. Returning from France in 1934, Bazargan noted that his religious beliefs were under attack not only from Westernizing reformers, but also the leftists at the newly established universities.[26] Yet he believed that science and technology are human achievements to which Islam is in no way opposed. Like Afghani, Bazargan distinguished between science and technology as instruments for the bettering of material well-being, and religion as the way for spiritual salvation. But the spread of the leftist notion that "religion is the opiate of the masses" made his task doubly difficult. His first book, on religion in Europe, tried to refute the notion that Western advancement and progress are the product of secularism and modernity.[27] In this effort he echoed the dual message of Afghani. To his coreligionists he gave assurance that being modern does not necessarily mean being secular and to the materialists he proved the compatibility of religion with modernity.

Insofar as the discussion here is concerned, Bazargan authored two kinds of works: books or pamphlets which refute modern thinking and modern ideologies, and those which prove that Islam conforms with a modern scientific worldview.[28] The second set of works constitutes a more positive statement of an Islamic worldview in light of modernity as he understood it. In *Atmospheric Phenomena* and *Wind and Rain in the Qur'an,* Bazargan elevates the practice of the sciences and new learning from the status of simply a good thing to an accepted religious behavior dealt with by the Qur'an. "God with his high position," he writes, "feels no embarrassment to refer to a small insect as an evidence and even calls one chapter of the Qur'an Scorpions."[29] Whatever modernists read in modern scientific books is also referred to in the Qur'an, he declares. The following passage is exemplary: "What we want to show here is that the basic [modern scientific] principles related to the atmosphere, wind, and rain are reflected in the concepts and expressions of the Qur'an."[30]

By his own lifestyle Bazargan demonstrated to many of his contemporaries that it is possible to be pious while adhering to the principles of science and conforming to the demands of modernity. A modern man in the sense of having a progressive outlook and using both the material and the conceptual tools of modernity, he is also unswervingly religious and implements the required principles of his religious conviction. Perhaps more than his writing, Bazargan's example as statesman and educator has influenced the contemporary generation of Iranian Muslims, including those referred to here as fundamentalists, to believe that Islam can be observed and preserved within a thoroughly modern society.[31]

Other contemporary Iranian educators and scientists are less significant but worth mentioning. Some wrote treatises along the line of Afghani. Muhammad Taqi Mazinani Shari'ati (b. 1910), the late Dr. Ali Shari'ati's father, was a teacher in Mashhad and established the Society for the Dissemination of Islamic Truth.[32] He published a book which argued that Islam is compatible with modern sciences and, moreover, that the sciences and technology of the modern West emerged under the influences of the Islamic heritage.[33] Similarly, the author of a novel entitled *The Glittering Sun (of Islamic Miracles Today)* wanted to attract youth to their heritage and stop them from thinking that "the sun of science is shining from Western Europe."[34] The story revolves around two young men, one a modernist type with confidence in European sciences and the other a believer in the universality of Islamic imperatives in all aspects of life. In each topic of discussion, the first young man presents a scientific explanation and the second presents an Islamic justification for it, proving that Islam comprehensively encompasses everything including modernity.

Whether the arguments of Afghani, Bazargan, and their imitators can withstand vigorous scientific evaluation is irrelevant to the story of the development of a coherent Muslim fundamentalist worldview. The fact is that this thinking was widely influential: Muslim youth were the final judges, and they were the ones who accepted these arguments. By the late 1950s and early 1960s, Afghani's view that "science . . . has no connection with any nation" and Bazargan's model of a devout Muslim scientist were playing an important role in the development of a new generation of Muslim thinkers who were primarily concerned with the question of how one remains Muslim in the face of modernity.

Religious Identity: A Distinction between Modernity and the West

A number of developments in the 1950s and 1960s led to an intellectual reawakening in Iran and to the articulation of a distinctively Iranian Shi'ite worldview in the decades following. In the late 1960s concerned Iranian Muslims established new educational, cultural, recreational, economic, and even training centers designed to inculcate in professional Iranians a degree of devotion to the fundamentals of Shi'ite Islam. The most notable of these were Hosseiniye Ershad, a center for lectures and studies on Islam, and the Alavi High School system of private schools and high schools. These schools became the centers of intellectual reform in Iran.

Following the death of Ayatollah Borujerdi, a book appeared in Qum, entitled *A Discussion of Leadership and Religious Establishment,* ·in which a group of prominent Shi'ite leaders treated pressing issues faced by the religious community.[35] The book called on the religious establishment in Qum to be more responsive to contemporary demands and more forthcoming in finding ways for the preservation of the religious identity of the younger generation. At the same time, the essayist and social critic Jalal al-Ahmad wrote a book entitled *Westamination,* possibly the most controversial and the most widely read essay in twentieth-century Iran.[36] The main thesis of the book is that the West has never been a panacea, but instead is a terrible disease which has contaminated Iranian society.

Changes in the Muslim political arena also contributed to the momentum toward intellectual reform. The nationalization of the oil industry in Iran, the nationalization of the Suez Canal in Egypt, and the Algerian resistance against France had broken the myth of Western power. In the wake of these self-assertions against Western power, Muslims began to ponder how to remain Muslim in the face of the aggressive challenge of modernity. The reconstruction and reassertion of the faith and its central tenets became the preoccupation of Shi'ite thinkers. Central among the new generation of thinkers was Dr. Ali Shari'ati (1933–1977), "the martyred teacher of the revolution," Ayatollah Murtaza Mutahari (assassinated in 1981), "the martyred philosopher of the revolution," and Dr. Abdolkarim Soroush (b. 1945), the most articulate and influential of the present thinkers in Iran. Shari'ati and Mutahari operated within the framework of concerns set by Afghani and Bazargan, whereas Soroush, prominent in the years after the 1979 revolution, works and writes in a different political and social milieu. Living under the monarchical system of government, Shari'ati and Mutahari expended their energy in the political sphere defending Islam in the face of antagonistic views and approaches. Soroush lives in an Islamic state which has to deal with practical application of Islam to all areas of life. He no longer feels the need to justify himself as a Muslim thinker; instead, he devotes his career to developing an alternative Islamic view on sciences and modernity. Moreover, he has inherited the tradition of the previous thinkers whom he himself calls "the early revivalists of the past century."

Ali Shari'ati sought to refamiliarize his fellow Muslims with their heritage so that they may "return to their true self." Pointing out the fallacies of Western schools of thought, he constructed, in his teaching and writing, his own theory of Islam which would accommodate modernity while avoiding these fallacies. Shari'ati's sytem of thought was based on the assertion that the era of the view that "religion and science contradict . . . and or religion is the opiate of the masses has passed."[37] Religion and science should not be compared. "Science means awareness about the outside world, the discovery of a relation or an attribute which exists in man or in nature. . . . Thus, science is essentially passive," he wrote. "[But] ideology means a creative belief about values and objective materials . . . [and is] the way in which one should change ideals."[38]

Because religion and science have different functions to perform, the two should not be confused. According to Shari'ati, reconstructed Islam, whose formulation began with Muhammad Iqbal (1875–1938), the intellectual father of Pakistan, is an ideology which is in no way "threatened by science, technology, and the fast modern changes of life."[39]

Shari'ati saw two problems with the prevalent views on science and technology. On the one hand, scholars had evaluated the relation of religion and science according to the norms of the Christian church and even then had only offered general observations. On the other hand, due to its remarkable achievements, modern science had become for many a cult of scientism. Shari'ati argued that Islamic ideology avoided these extremes. His interpretation of Islam accorded science, technology, and modernity their proper place alongside such modern concepts as freedom of the individual and equality.

Mutahari saw his task differently. On the one hand, he sought to encourage the members of the religious establishment to adapt themselves and their teaching in order to address the more pressing issues of the day; on the other hand, he sought to mobilize the Muslim public to take a more active role in social life. Regarding science and technology, Mutahari echoed Shari'ati's respect and commitment. Those who propagate the incompatibility of religion and sciences, Mutahari wrote, are either ignorant traditionalists or Iranians with a modern education who have turned away from their own tradition. "Two classes of people have tried to show sciences and religion as opposites. The first group are those who pretend to be religious . . . and make their living of it but are [in fact] ignorant. . . . The other is the new educated class who has turned away from human and cultural commitments. . . . Then there is a third class of people who are both religious and educated and see no contradiction between these two."[40] Mutahari, of course, considered himself one of the third class, whose main task should be "to cleanse the ambiguities and distortions which have been inflicted upon these sacred principles."[41] To that end, Mutahari constructed his argument along the following lines. First, he brought all scientific investigation within the realm of Islam, criticizing the division of sciences into "religious sciences and nonreligious ones." By such a distinction "the so-called nonreligious science is alienated in Islam. The all-comprehensive nature of Islam allows us to call any necessary science for the Islamic community as a religious science."[42] "Believers and religious-minded [people] should not be threatened by science and new schools and imagine that if science comes, religion vanishes. This means misunderstanding Islam, because the latter is a religion which flourishes in a scientific atmosphere."[43]

In defining science from "the Islamic point of view," Mutahari stood in the line of Afghani and Bazargan: science itself is an instrument for higher ends, including the propagation of Islam.[44] Muslims should thus pay close attention to sciences and modernity, as four famous Islamic aphorisms counsel: "Obtaining science/knowledge is incumbent upon all Muslims"; "Seek science/knowledge from birth till death"; "Seek science/knowledge even if you have to go to China"; and finally, "Wisdom is the lost commodity of Muslims [who should look for it always]."[45] To this folk wisdom Mutahari added a utilitarian and sociological argument, summarized in his three principles for an Islamic community: (1) Muslims should be independent and accept no mastery or superiority of others, as taught by the Qur'an; (2) the contemporary world is undeniably based on sciences and scientific method; and (3) for the "satisfaction of any human needs, science and technology are the key."[46] Obtaining new sciences and technology becomes in this scheme tantamount to performing a religious obligation. Mutahari sounded a ringing call for his fellow Muslims to "turn [scientific education] into a sacred jihad . . . under the command of religion and with religious coloring."[47]

To Iranians, Mutahari's popularization of the definition of sciences and technology as means to material and spiritual ends brought about a revolution within the more traditional Islamic families. The influential Iranian families embraced two precepts from Mutahari's teaching. First, they accepted a distinction between sciences, technology, and their products, on the one hand, and the West as a cultural value system on the other.[48] Second, they accepted the notion that the corrupting effects of modernity lie in the evil intentions of the various doctrines originating from materialistic philosophy that have set the Western objectives for science and technology. The obvious implication of this notion was that a different intention—a rightly guided Islamic intent—will lead to a different result.[49]

Further elaboration of the notion of the distinction between the products of science and the cultural value system of the West was left to Dr. Abdolkarim Soroush. After finishing his studies in Iran, Soroush went to England to study philosophy of science and Islamic studies. He recognized better than anyone else the necessity of formulating a modern Islamic worldview as an alternative to the value system of the West. His work in the 1980s may well be considered the conclusion of the second phase of the encounter of Islam and modernity. During the first phase, people explained Islam in terms of modernity and, in Soroush's term, they extracted an "ethics of science" from the Qur'an. The second phase began with the questioning of that approach. Soroush notes that in practice, however, he still has to deal with two kinds of skeptics Mutahari opposed—traditionalist Muslims who think that the reformulation of an Islamic worldview constitutes an innovation, and the modernists who think that such a reformulation is a new and hidden apologia for a strictly religious worldview.[50]

Soroush, who remains vitally active in the Islamic Republic of Iran at this writing, is distinctive from his predecessors in terms of his qualifications as a thinker and his methodology. First and foremost, he is not a political figure. A graduate of Alavi High School, he is, however, very influential among those in power. Second, Soroush is one of the most prominent speakers in Iran in the 1990s. He lectures both in traditional forums such as mosques and in modern universities; his Friday mosque lectures are broadcast regularly on the radio. Third, he takes a multidisciplinary approach to the study of Islam and science. Whereas Bazargan was a man of science, Shari'ati a social scientist, and Mutahari a philosopher, Soroush attempts to draw upon each of these disciplines. Unlike his predecessors, he avoids generalities or sweeping statements, and focuses instead upon specific questions.

In his debate with the modernists in Iran, Soroush elaborated the "fundamentalist distinction"[51] and established the foundation for the reconstruction of a revived Islamic ideology. In his book against the modernists, *Danesh va Arzesh* (Science and value), Soroush employed the terminology of his opponents to examine the relations between "fact and value," "end and means," and "is and ought to be" in Western philosophy and in Islam. In so doing, he explored science's limitations in dealing with questions of value and human subjectivity and thus mounted a sustained attack against the modernist confidence that science provides a comprehensive alternative worldview to that of Islam (or religion in general).[52] Soroush subtly was reframing the basic question of modernity and challenging the assumption that religion and science alike may serve as equally compelling and viable worldviews.

The purpose of this book, he writes, "is to show analytically that a deadly plague has inflicted the famous schools of ethics . . . namely, the enormous fallacy of deducting 'ought to be' from 'is,' 'values' from 'realities,' and 'ethics' from 'sciences.'"[53] The rapid advance of knowledge and technology has created the (erroneous) impression that society should be ordered and governed by the laws which apparently govern the natural world. Soroush's specific referent was evolution. If Darwin teaches us many realities about the evolution of the physical aspects of our existence as human beings—a statement Soroush accepted as true—this does not imply that we should formulate our social norms and conduct accordingly. The Islamic modernists, following the capitalists of the West and the Marxists of the East, have accepted a type of social Darwinism, an "ethics of positivism" in society and economy. "The dawn of Marxism," Soroush writes, "in the nineteenth century along with publication of Darwin's *Origin of Species* and the evolutionary view of the appearance of animals, and then the joining of these two schools, have given rise to a new ethical system which should be called the 'ethics of evolutionism.'"[54] This is accompanied by an "ethics of science" by which moral obligations are deduced from empirical models of human development.

Soroush's analysis of Darwin is a clever argument designed to appeal to the faithful in that Darwinian theory is never considered as a worldview in competition with religion. Such an approach—viewing Darwinism as a possible substitute for religion—would violate the fundamentalist distinction and separation of "ought" from "is." Darwin's theory is simply a scientific proposition which presented a new way of explaining the origin of species. The conclusion that only the fittest will survive should remain within the constraints built by Darwin himself, who did not apply this axiom to human social life, but only to biological evolution.[55] By dethroning Darwinism from the status of an ideology and refusing to compare or even contrast it with a religious worldview, Soroush took an important first step among Iranian intellectuals toward an eventual demystification of the materialistic *Weltanschauung*.

Yet Soroush's evaluation of Darwin's science was even more devastating to the latter's would-be followers. Soroush utilized the two criteria set out by Karl Popper to test the scientific nature of Darwin's proposition: refutability (Can the hypothesis be falsified by the introduction of additional data or evidence to the contrary?) and predictability (Is the hypothesis useful in predicting future patterns?). The essence of Darwinian theory, Soroush writes, is that "a group of species which are fit to survive will live and those which are not fit will vanish. . . . Now, if one asks which one is the fittest, he would say the one which survives" and vice versa.[56] This makes prediction impossible, thus making it "an irrefutable proposition that constitutes nothing but a tautology."[57] Soroush emphasizes that this tautology gained such a backing because people linked the concept of evolution with an invention of the modern age— "time"—and thus equated evolution with progress. "Evolution should not be taken as progress. Not every evolutionary move constitutes progress. . . . It is one thing to say that man is the result of apes and quite another to say he has sprung out of (evolved from) of apes [*baramadan*]."[58]

For Soroush this distinction is not a matter of semantics. When taken as "the result of apes," man becomes a materialistic being in need of a materialistic explanation for his existence. The result, according to Soroush, has been the emergence of "satanic ideologies."[59] Freud introduced a Satan called "id," Marx introduced another called "class," and Hegel talked about "the spirit."[60] But these constructs, Soroush maintains, are the unfortunate products of the confusion between fact and value. If one understands the fundamentalist distinction accurately, then one realizes the place of science and religion in man's existence. On the issue of the nature of science, Soroush marshals the opinions of such philosophers of science as Popper, Julian Huxley, and even David Hume to establish that science can only discover and describe the principles governing the complex interactions between the particles of the material world. Thus science has no way of predicting any future event. Sciences can indeed make us understand our limitations and point out the areas where we cannot perform certain tasks; but people have confused this ability of the sciences with that of formulating positive norms. "Science can show us which tasks we cannot perform, and when one cannot perform a task, one can find no value in it," Soroush writes. "In other words, we cannot expect positive commandments from philosophical and scientific explanations of nature and existence."[61]

Once the status and position of science are properly construed, one should explore its relation to Islam and an Islamic order. This is the task Soroush has conceived for himself since his return to Iran in 1979.[62] The Islamic worldview he has articulated is based on the Islamic belief in the oneness of God, the "Tawhidi ideology" which aims at "seeing the world through God and living for the satisfaction of His will."[63] But this ideology contains a role for the sciences among Muslims, for "we do not want the fate of Galileo to be repeated in this land under the rule of the Islamic Republic. We do not want religion to become an impediment of science. We want religion and science to be closely linked, and the former to act as the lights do in a car and not as the brakes do."[64]

Considering the power and pervasiveness of technological advancement and the new sciences, how do the two relate to one another? Soroush is aware of the remarkable status of the sciences. The "automatism, self-augmentation, universalism, autonomy and monism"[65] of the new technological achievements have taken science beyond a discipline which "will help us to realize our weaknesses"; rather, with its robots and microprocessors, science has imposed itself within the realm of creation. In the face of the unbridled acceleration of technological achievements leading to immediate material gratification, Soroush has advocated a degree of moderation and preservation of traditional lifestyles, which some would see as a form of (Islamic) asceticism in the current climate. This is a cultural as well as a spiritual prescription because, as he put it, "we should learn from our past that the more we have tried to reach others, the more we have stayed behind. We should try to be ourselves."[66] Having said that, Soroush falls back on the notion of distinction.

Nonetheless Soroush has pursued a constructive task of establishing guidelines for the Iranian acceptance of technologies from the West. What I have called the "fundamentalist distinction" is invoked in this effort. When one looks at the West, one is either factual or judgmental. Those who look at the West with the distinction between the products and values of Western modernity in mind will inevitably become pragmatic and experimental, whereas those who do not understand such a distinction will fall into the trap of talking about the West as an "essence" or a "totality" which should either be accepted or rejected.[67] Ignited by the notion of *Westamination,* which as we have seen gained greater currency in Iran after the revolution, opponents of the West[68] denounce "the imperialistic West, Westamination, the homocentric philosophy of the West, or the capitalist West as though there is an essential totality of which people of the West are its manifestation."[69] This demonization has had the effect at times of discouraging Muslim scientists and scholars from "daring any inquiry" about the West. Ironically, he notes, this demonization has led to either subjugation to the West or isolation from the international political, business, and scientific communities. What Soroush proposes is "distinction and selection" to guide the adoptive process which has been practiced, in the absence of any theory, by Muslims for decades. By the concept of selection, "we mean that the West is neither a unit nor unique. Even if all its parts comprise one organic whole, that does not mean they do not fit any other system. We should not assume that by accepting one of these parts, we have accepted the whole. We should be daring in selection."[70]

In Soroush's approach, particular selections are made on the basis of the distinction between fact and value. The Islamic value system dictates the selection process. Islamic Tawhidi ideology should guide life in "Islamic Iran," he argues. Within this comprehensive unity of God *(tawhid),* how should religious tradition, comprised of unchanging principles, deal with the changing world?[71] Soroush summarized the essence of his argument with the traditionalist ulama as follows:

> In one way or another, the revivalists before me wanted to reconcile tradition with change. [Muhammad] Iqbal wanted to establish a peaceful coexistence between them. Mutahari and [Allameh Muhammad Hossein] Tabatab'i said that we should identify the unchanging principles of religion with its changing ones and then allow for the modification of the second based on time and place. Shari'ati considered the tenets of religion unchanging, but argued that it takes different forms in different places. The Sunni Muslims try to open the gate of *ijtihad* [individual reasoning]. I argue that, in order to solve the problem of the relation between tradition and change, we should separate *religion* from the *understanding of religion.* The first is unchanging, but the second changes. In fact, we should try to establish constant exchange and interaction between the second and other branches of human knowledge and understanding such as sociology, anthropology, philosophy, history, and so on. [Emphasis added][72]

This statement of intent does not, however, clarify the criteria by which the selection should be made or has been made. Religion in this formulation remains the special prerogative of those divines who understand and convey the message. The sciences and philosophy can guide our changing interpretations of the message, as long as the traditional ulama remain in place as final arbiters of the negotiation between religion and scientific practice. How has this worked in practice in the Islamic Republic of Iran? Has Soroush's vision been implemented by government officials?

To understand how Soroush's process defines the Islamic nature of a decision or an act, one should consider the practices of the Islamic Republic of Iran during the past decade.

Before examining the practical areas in which the Islamic Republic of Iran has had to negotiate the relationship between Islam and the sciences, brief mention must be made of another organ of dissemination of the the "Islamic position" on this issue. The religious and social monthly *Maktabe Eslam* (Islamic creed) began publication in 1958 in Qum and remains today the organ of the religious establishment in Qum. It has played an important role in making the traditional religious establishment more relevant to the modern life of Iran. Many of the contributors to the journal have been those who were very active during the revolution and achieved high status afterward. Mutahari and Imam Musa Sadr, the vanished leader of the Lebanese Shi'ites, were among the prominent contributors to the journal.

The journal deals with any conceivable problem that Muslims face today, ranging from the quality and orthodoxy of cinema, theater, and magazines, to rules governing marriage with foreign nationals. The main task of the contributors is to simplify Islamic teachings and help the new generation live in accordance with them. This is in line with Mutahari's concern that the Islamic way of life extend to all aspects of Iranian society. At the same time, as the founder of the journal puts it, the journal is "to awaken Easterners from their benumbing sleep to their heritage and show them the vital but apparently silent civilization of the East."[73] Many essays deal with Islam as "a modern, scientific, and accommodating ideology." Imam Musa Sadr summarized the general tendency of the journal when he wrote that "the truth is that science has committed no sin save the discovery of the truth. A faithful [Muslim] who opposes sciences and is threatened by them should revise his own views and doubt them. Fearing the truth means nothing but that one is afraid of the encounter of one's religion with realities, while true belief in fact causes a scientific renaissance."[74]

Iranian Shi'ism and Sciences in Practice

By the time the revolutionaries established an Islamic Republic in Iran following the referendum of April 1979, the notion of "distinction" had already entered philosophical and general intellectual discourse in Iran and had made possible the acceptance of almost a century of modernization. This modernization was also justified in terms of Islamic jurisprudence. The notions of "distinction" and "selection" proved adequate as long as religion was not directly accountable to the complex process of running a modern state. Since Islam was not responsible for the running of the state before 1979, the religious leaders could be selective about, or ignore, or be unaware of, the great number of detailed decisions required by and stemming from modernity. Their occasional encounters with the complex realities of the functions of a modern nation-state led Islamic leaders to invoke jurisprudential maxims. For example, a faqih might invoke the principle of the lesser evil, or, in the parlance of jurisprudence, "preventing the bigger corruption with the smaller one" *(daf'e afsad be fased)*. The principle of the lesser evil was used by the religious leaders of the constitutional period to defend constitutionalism.[75]

Having an Islamic state raised more pressing practical questions and forced the question of the philosophical conformity of religion and sciences into the background or, at most, into academic debates. But pressing questions, answers for which are still forthcoming in many cases, were nonetheless immediately raised once the banner of Islam was hoisted over Iran. How may the state uphold Islamic injunctions in areas of reproduction while population control is kept in balance? How may the modern demand for the education of women be met while the Islamic "fundamental" of segregation of the sexes is respected? Is archaeological excavation possible while Islamic jurisprudence forbids the digging of any grave? How may the Islamic Republic deal with the issue of music or the appearance of women singers on the public media?

There are many important areas for which the Islamic injunctions have no clear ruling, partly because these areas represent the demands of the modern age. And a great number of areas have emerged only recently through technology and scientific innovations. The interesting paradox is that the Islamic Republic, which by conventional expectation is expected, as a fundamentalist state, to be virulently antimodern, has shown a remarkable degree of adaptability to modern ways. At the same time, in many areas the leaders of the Islamic Republic have found it impossible to modify Islamic injunctions.

In an astonishing religious ruling *(fatwa),* Ayatollah Khomeini, the late leader of the revolution, approved the appearance of women on radio and television. Women's voices could be heard as part of a singing group. In another fatwa, he permitted the playing of chess and the trading of musical instruments. Not surprisingly, shortly thereafter he received a letter from the more traditional religious leaders about the validity of such rulings. Imam Khomeini's answer to this objection is fascinating. "I feel it necessary," he wrote, "to express my despair about your understanding of the divine injunctions and that of the [Shi'ite] traditions. . . . The way you interpret the traditions, the new civilization should be destroyed and the people should live in shackles or live forever in the desert."[76] He thereby addressed the problems of interpretation raised by scientific and technological innovations. Many contemporary areas of concern had little relevance in the past; accordingly, previous jurisconsults provided no injunctions for them. But, Khomeini acknowledged, these questions are pressing and must be dealt with today. The Islamic government and "the nature of the revolution and its regime warns that the doors to *ijtihad* [independent reasoning] be opened and that several juridical viewpoints be expressed even if they seem contradictory."[77]

When pressed for an explanation of his position, Khomeini invoked another juridical maxim, namely, the concept of the "secondary apparent rules" *(ahkame sanaviyeye zaheriye)*. These rules in Shi'ite jurisprudence govern the details of the application of religious injunctions to worldly affairs. Specifically, these rules govern the arrangements that must be made for an Islamic principle to be implemented. The rules are not part of the principle, but govern the implementation of the principle and thereby are of determinative weight in coming to any decision regarding state policy on matters of science and the application of technology.

For example, suppose the accepted Islamic principle is that there should be an Islamic government. To implement this, one needs to take advantage of many worldly means which necessitate the efficient operation of such a government. They fall within the scope of the secondary apparent rule and thus become lawful and even mandatory within the framework of Islamic jurisprudence. Added to this is the agreed-upon need for accommodation based on expediency and realism. A combination of these forces made it possible for the Islamic Republic to follow certain courses of action and make certain adaptations which, by traditional criteria, would have constituted forbidden "innovations." The more pressing the need, the more the principle of the secondary apparent rule is invoked, and vice versa.[78]

Interestingly, Khomeini also spoke of the role of intention. Invoking the Prophetic tradition that "Lo! an act is not but its intention," he argued that, because the intention of the Islamic Republic is righteous, it can perform acts that would otherwise be considered unlawful. When asked about music, for example, he said that Iranian music broadcast in "other, so-called Islamic, states" would be unlawful because their intention is not righteous.[79]

These notions—that is, the notions of "distinction," "selection," "apparent rule," and "having the proper intention"—paved the way for the adoption of modern ways and the acceptance of modern products in postrevolutionary Iran. But the process is neither uniform nor without opposition. Domestic, regional, and international contexts affect the momentum of the process of adoption. Internally, factors such as the "revolutionary passion" of the society and various intellectual approaches among the "men of power and authority" play an important role. Regionally and internationally, the growth of an "open society" throughout the world has also made its mark on Iran.

For our purposes, however, we must concentrate on the internal factors and processes. The first of these factors relates to the revolutionary passion that had radicalized and polarized Iranian society, making it possible for extremism to rule with little opposition. "Fundamentalist" measures were carried out either with the full support of the people or with their tacit approval. As revolutionary zeal subsided, support for radical measures decreased. More people questioned things with their head rather than their heart. The notion that the revolution would create an ideal society isolated from any interaction with the outside world has been modified with the realization that the Iranian people's very survival requires interdependence with others, even with those who appear to have an opposite worldview. In turn this realization has paved the way for freer "selection."

The second factor relates to what is referred to in the West as the division of radical and pragmatic groups within Iranian politics. I prefer to refer to these cleavages as simply various intellectual approaches because, although their proponents may disagree with one another, they are united by a common worldview and by a shared ideology based on the attempt to live life according to Islamic rules and regulations, while still remaining modern and powerful. The difference among these groups is a matter of degree rather than kind. The approaches range from a "pragmatic funda-mentalist" position to a more "revolutionary fundamentalist" position. But an inter-esting third position has also emerged, which may be referred to as "traditional pragmatist." This position is represented by traditional Muslims who have always been apolitical and have objected only to the radical adaptation of any foreign ele-ments. As revolutionary zeal subsides, the traditional pragmatist position grows and in fact serves as a moderating force.

This situation frames the debate regarding the degree to which the Islamic Repub-lic of Iran should adopt modern ways, acquire new technologies, and pursue scientific research. The stand each group takes depends on the issue at hand. For example, when President Rafsanjani, during Friday prayer in October 1990, advised Iranian Muslims to try to live well and even urged that "Friday prayer is an occasion for Muslims to display their wealth," *Bayan,* the organ of the more revolutionary ulamas, carried the most radical attacks on him. It accused the president of becoming the spokesman for the trend that "not only does not condemn direct negotiation with America, but sees it as diplomatic dynamism and innovation."[80] Later, when it appeared that the more relaxed and nonrestricted approach was gaining currency with regard to economic, social, and cultural policies, a campaign against "cultural imperialism" and "indirect cultural influence of the West" began. The debate was triggered by a letter that ap-peared in one of the daily papers signed by thirty-five scholars and scientists from the most technical university in Iran. Claiming affiliation with no group in particular, these scholars and scientists, most of whom hold advanced degrees from abroad, stated that their main concern was with the "expansion of cultural liberalism."[81]

These incidents show that it is incorrect to identify the so-called radicals with opposition to the adoption of modern technologies, scientific research, participation in the international system, global trade, and so forth. Nor is it correct to assume that the so-called moderates or pragmatists will in every case support such measures and policies. The reality is far more complex.

Let us first examine the areas in which the government has had to modify its stand, based on the dictates of expediency and realism. One such case is the issue of popu-lation increase and reproduction. From 1980 to 1988 Iran was involved in a costly and disastrous war with the regime of Saddam Hussein in neighboring Iraq. Until 1987, relatively little attention was paid by Iran to its enormous rate of population increase, which had reached 4 percent annually and had begun to drain the already weakened Iranian economy. But as the war with Iraq wound down, a campaign began against the evil of disproportionate population increase; government officials in the Ministry of Health publicized the damage that unchecked population growth would do to the family and lauded the virtues of the small family and its quality of life. The final step in this campaign was the announcement of various methods of population control and family planning. Due to Islamic injunctions which had been interpreted as prohibiting birth control, this serious measure, although taken gradually, could not have been implemented without considerable debate on the issue. A report given to the Majlis (Parliament) on 14 January 1991 by the minister of hygiene stated that "the distribution of the means for controlling reproduction in the year 1367 [1988–89] reached 4.3 million people and was increased to 6.8 million for the year 1368 [1989–90]. . . . the IUD was distributed even in the remote corners of the country, free of charge."[82] A later report documented that "8,079,993 packs of pills, 37,938,343 condoms, and 133,121 IUDs have been distributed" in the Iranian year 1396 (1990–91).[83] In 1991 in any Iranian clinic or hospital, one could see posters advertising free contraceptives.

A debate about these practices continues in Iran at this writing. It is conducted in the media, with the various parties to it presenting utilitarian or sociological justification for the encouragement of birth control measures. One proponent of the measures argued, for example, that "the population growth of our society is still patterned after a traditional way of life. We have to change our pattern to that of a modern technical society." Only a traditional mode of economic production requires a large number of children.[84]

If one looks for an Islamic justification for the policy of birth control, one must search beyond the daily papers. Citing the Qur'anic verse that "No soul shall have a burden laid on it greater than it can bear. No mother shall be treated unfairly on account of her child" (2:233), the religious leaders in Iran under Khomeini ruled that "using preventive measures against pregnancy is lawful so long as it does not cause the woman to lose her fertility."[85] While accepting this ruling, Khomeini added that such measures should not cause major medical consequences.[86]

Another area in which the demands of modernity necessitate a radical departure from traditional norms is experimentation and use of the human body for the study of anatomy in Iranian medical schools. In the early days of the revolution, it was forbidden to use the body of a Muslim for such a purpose, and thus Iran had to import bodies from non-Muslim countries. But as the demand grew and as the economic pressure of the war and the various sanctions made their impact felt, the secondary apparent rule was invoked to pave the way for the use of Iranian bodies. The use of the human body for "scientific purposes" is serving the cause of Islam by helping to train better Muslim doctors—thus ran the argument of the invokers of the rule.[87]

Perhaps the most important area in which leading pragmatic ulama have invoked the secondary apparent rule has been over, as suggested above, the issue of mass computerization and the acquisition of sophisticated technology. It is "apparent" and "obvious" that running a modern state requires sophisticated machinery and mechanisms; accordingly, it is not only proper but necessary for Iran to be a full participant in the international system of commerce and communications. There has been no hesitation in obtaining sophisticated arms and other technological products.[88] Indeed, the government of the Islamic Republic of Iran is in a better position than its predecessor in this regard, precisely because "the intention of the state" is Islamic and its functions are seen popularly as being at the service of the Islamic cause. In an astonishing response to the president of the republic, the late Imam Khomeini wrote that the preservation of the government "takes precedence over other injunctions such as praying and fasting. . . . Government can prevent temporarily the pilgrimage to Mecca if it contradicts the interest of the Islamic country."[89] How enduring this impression will be is a matter of speculation beyond the scope of this chapter.

There are areas in which the government does not apply these accommodating jurisprudential principles, the most notable area being the Islamic criminal code. The Iranian legal code had combined Islamic law and European legal principles, directly translated, but the criminal codes were almost completely Westernized. When the "modernist" Iranians reorganized the entire legal system in the first quarter of this century, they had considered Islamic penal codes backward and inhumane. The most controversial piece of legislation after the revolution, thus, has been the introduction of the Islamic criminal code. Opposition to these *hudud* (penal) laws did not get very far, and the government stood upon "fundamental" principle and would not back off at all. At first the general public, radicalized by the revolution, accepted the severe punishment of "stoning to death" or "cutting off the hands of a robber" or even the "death penalty for adultery."[90] This was the functional code of the Ministry of Justice. When I attended some trials in 1991, however, in order to observe the actual implementation of the code, I noted that, as society had recently modified its revolutionary adventurism, the application of the law had also lost its intransigency. The judge went out of his way to show that the case was not so clear as to require the death penalty. Even in cases in which there was a great possibility that the death penalty was appropriate by law, the judge would assign extra investigation and inquiry.[91]

Another area in which the government was intransigent is the issue of sex segregation and "veiling" (women's wearing of prescribed clothing and keeping their distance from nonkin men). Since it is the dictate of a clear injunction in the Qur'an that women should cover themselves from all men save their close kin by blood or marriage, leading ulama argued that it cannot be compromised in any form. These were the areas in which the traditional ulama had customarily been in control; they enjoyed far less experience in pronouncing upon the intricacies of international arms networks, telecommunications, or geopolitics. Thus strict rules and regulations were formulated for the observation of the principle of sex segregation. In university classrooms, women were made to use one side of the room and men the other; institutions specifically dealing with women were run by them; stores selling specific female commodities were administered only by women, and so forth.

Even here, however, the power of accommodation has left its mark. A poster issued by the Department of Traffic hung on many governmental walls in 1991 and made the general point well. The poster depicts a woman dressed in the required Islamic (dark) garb and warns that "crossing the street at night in dark color dresses will cause accidents." Also, there are many male gynecologists practicing in Iran today, despite the government's conscious effort to encourage female doctors to take on this specialty and its elevation of midwives to positions as independent practitioners through special training courses.[92]

Finally, in contemporary Iran there are cases in which practical needs take precedence over the articles of Islamic jurisprudence demanding the observance of Islamic tenets. The most interesting such case is that of the media, particularly television. As Majid Tehranian points out in chapter 17 of this volume, the revolutionaries understand the power of the media very well: many still talk of the media as one of the major contributors to the downfall of the Pahlavi dynasty. Imam Khomeini characterized television as a big university. Thus, from the first days of the revolution an attempt has been made to "Islamize" television. The law which approved the constitution of the organization of the Iranian radio and television in 1982 states that "mass media, radio and television, must be at the service of . . . the dissemination of Islamic culture."[93] In the early days of the revolution, therefore, the majority of programs were "educational." But the public demand for entertainment and comedies gradually expressed itself in a very interesting way. First, a children's program became the most popular show because it showed cartoons and entertainment. Second, despite the aforementioned ban on the sale of video machines, the number of video dealers and unofficial video distributors skyrocketed. The policy on television gradually shifted toward a balancing between the "mundane and temporal" demands with those of the "immortal and sublime."

Conclusion

This chapter portrays the fate of those traditional Shi'ites who try to preserve their heritage and survive in light of, in Soroush's words, the "universalism, autonomy and holism" of the changing modern world. The essence of their trial is captured in the fact that they can only succeed insofar as they can accommodate to the forces of reality and pragmatic needs. The struggle to preserve Islamic principles and at the same time to become modern continues. Islam and modernity, or, in Soroush's words, tradition and change, are unfolding in parallel lines. Those who have resolutely decided to revive their tradition in its full medieval strength have been made aware by their pragmatic coreligionists that the management of a modern state requires jurisprudential flexibility and pragmatic reasoning. The efforts of the traditionalists in the Rafsanjani administration seem to have been concentrated on identifying the areas in which flexibility is not required in such abundance.

The tension between the traditionalists and the more adaptive fundamentalists will likely continue. It is no wonder that the late leader of the Islamic Republic adamantly attacked those who advocated wholesale adoption of new and Western ways and, with the same vigor, the "stone-headed" (motahajer) Muslims who were not prepared to accommodate themselves to the demands of modernity. Those resisting accommodation seem to have the harder road in the long run. The following account of a passenger who had bought a music keyboard for his child illustrates the essence of the challenge before them. Told that he could not take the keyboard into Iran because it had been declared unacceptable, he objected: "But I have seen many like it in Tehran's market." The official responded: "We can only regulate those areas over which we have control."

Notes

1. The research for this chapter was conducted in Tehran. The Iranian Scholar Fellowship at St. Antony's College, Oxford, provided me with serenity and the scholarly environment in which to write it. I hereby acknowledge the help extended to me by friends and colleagues in both places. The librarians at my home institution, the Cultural Studies and Research Institute, in Tehran, were very cooperative. The Persian collection in Wadham College at Oxford University made the task of finding some contemporary material extremely easy. The comments of my friends and colleagues—Dr. John Gurney, Professor James Piscatori, Dr. Fatemeh Givechian, and Professor Everett Mendelsohn—were insightful. In Iran, I learned a great deal from my talks with M. M. Shabestari. Above all, Dr. A. Soroush was generous and forthcoming in giving me time and elaborating his views. Ahmad Jalali gave me some of the Persian sources. The Fundamentalism Project's support for my travel to Iran while I was a fellow at St. Antony's College of Oxford University greatly facilitated the work.

2. See Jürgen Habermas, *The Philosophical Discourse on Modernity* (Oxford: Polity Press, 1987).

3. There are excellent works available in English on Islam's encounter with the West. See, for example, the works of Albert Hourani and Edward Said. Hamid Enayat, in a short but concise essay, outlines the recurring resurgence of Islam in modern times as a result of Islam's encounter with the West. See Enayat, "Resurgence of Islam," *History Today,* February 1980, pp. 16–27.

4. Cf. Hafez Farman-Farmayan, "The Forces of Modernization in Nineteenth Century Iran," in W. Polk and R. Chambers, eds., *The Beginning of Modernization in the Middle East* (Chicago: University of Chicago Press, 1968).

5. Tracing the active role of the ulama in Iranian politics, Ali Davani portrays the contemporary religious leader Muhammad Mujahid as an important player during the Russo-Iranian wars. See Davani, *Nahzate Rohaniyune Iran,* vol. 2 (Tehran: Bonyade Imam Reza, 1360/1981), pp. 56–67.

6. Considering Aqasi a reformer contradicts the conventional wisdom on modern Iranian historiography. I was convinced, however, to count him as a reformer after reading Homa Nateq's recent book on the period of Aqasi's premiership. See Nateq, *Iran dar Rahyabiye Farhangi* (London: Payam Publishing and Distribution Center, 1988).

7. The classic work on Amir Kabir is Fereydun Adamiyat's *Amir Kabir ya Iran* (Tehran: Kharazmi, 1361/1982). Interesting is the work of the present president of Iran on Amir Kabir. See Ali Akbar Hashemi Rafsanjani, *Amir Kabir va Qahremane Mobareze ba Este'mar* (Teheran: Farahani, 1346/1957).

8. See Fereydun Adamiyat, *Andisheye Taraqi va Hokumate Qanun* (Tehran: Kharazmi, 1352/1973).

9. The classic on this revolution is Ahmad Kasravi, *Tarikhe Mashrutiyate Iran* (Tehran: Amir Kabir, 1356/1977).

10. Ibid., p. 49.

11. Mirsa Hossein Na'ini, *Tanbih al-Umma va Tanzih al-Mella,* ann. and ed. M. Taleghani (Tehran: Ferdousi, 1955). For an English treatment of the same work, see Abdolhadi Ha'iri, *Shi'ism and Constitutionalism in Iran* (Leiden: Edinborough University Press, 1977).

12. Both works are translated into English and published in Nikki Keddie, ed., *An Islamic Response to Imperialism: Political and Religious Writings of Sayyid Jamal ad-Din al-Afghani* (Berkeley: University of California Press, 1968). Rendering of the works into English is done in collaboration with Hamid Algar.

13. Lecture by Afghani entitled "Commentary on the Commentator," in Keddie, *An Islamic Response to Imperialism,* p. 128.

14. Afghani, "Answer of Jamal ad-Din to Renan," in Keddie, *An Islamic Response to Imperialism,* p. 182.

15. Ibid., p. 183.

16. Ibid.

17. Afghani, "Lecture on Teaching and Learning," in Keddie, *An Islamic Response to Imperialism*, p. 107.

18. Ibid.

19. The emphasis on the Islamic quality of Afghani's argument is necessary because of the views put forward about the unorthodoxy of Afghani in Ellie Kedourie, *Afghani and Abduh: An Essay on Religious Unbelief and Political Activism in Modern Islam* (London, 1966), and Keddie, *Islamic Response to Imperialism*.

20. Afghani, "Refutation of the Materialists," in Keddie, *Islamic Response to Imperialism*, p. 140.

21. Afghani, "The Truth about the Neicheri Sect and an Explanation of the Neicheris," in Keddie, *Islamic Response to Imperialism*, pp. 132–39.

22. Ibid., p. 141.

23. Ibid., pp. 144–47.

24. Ibid., p. 148.

25. Ibid., p. 172.

26. Bazargan's life and political activism are captured in Hooshang Chehabi, *Iranian Politics and Religious Modernism: The Liberation Movement of Iran under the Shah and Khomeini* (London: I. B. Tauris, 1990).

27. Mahdi Bazargan, *Mazhab dar Europa* (Houston: Book Distribution Center, 1978).

28. Among the first group is *A Review of Erich Fromm's Works*, in which Bazargan takes on liberal and secular views of man and society, as well as *How Scientific Is Marxism*, in which he questions the validity of the scientific claim of historical materialism.

29. M. Bazargan, *Bad va Baran dar Qur'an* (Tehran: Enteshar, 1343/1965), p. 5.

30. Ibid., p. 91.

31. Many of the protagonists of the revolution, including the founder-members of the various Islamic associations as well as radical Islamic groups such as the People's Mujahidin of Iran, were either his colleagues or former students and followers.

32. The following comprehensive interview with him is both informative about his life and insightful about his views: "Muhammad Taqi Shari'ati, the Defender of the Shari'a in the Face of Unbelief and Oppression," *Kayhan Farhangi*, Bahman 1363/February 1985, pp. 5–19.

33. In his interview (ibid.), Muhammad Taqi Shariati refers to the book: *Ta'sir Danesh va Honarhaye Moslemin dar Sanaye' va 'ulume Orupa* (The influence of Muslim art and knowledge on European technology and sciences). In the famous collection of Persian books in print, by Khanbaba Moshar, this book is recorded as follows: Mohammad Hossein Zaki, *Ta'sire Honarhaye Moslemin bevizhe Iranian dar Orupa* (The impact of Muslim arts, particularly [that of] Iranians on Europe) (Mashhad: Bastan, n.d.).

34. Mu'ayyed al-Islam Haj Shaykh Mirza [Muhammad] Hassan Jaberi Ansari Isfahani, *Aftabe Derakhshandeh (Az Mojezate Emruzeye Islamiye* (Tehran: n.p., 1302/1923), p. 4. I came to know about this work after reading the dissertation by Ali Gheissari, "Ideological Formation of Iranian Intelligentsia" (Ph.D. diss., Oxford University, 1989). My quotation from this novel is from Gheissari's work and his treatment of the novel in part 2.

35. *Bahsi darbareye Marja'eyat va Rouhaniyat* (Tehran: Enreshar, 1341/1962). Among observers of Iranian society, Professor Ann Lambton was the one who, at the time, recognized the importance of the book. See Lambton, "A Reconstruction of the Position of Marja' al-Taqlid and the Religious Institutions," *Studia Islamica* 20 (1964): 115–36.

36. Even in Persian the word *Gharbzadegi* is a neologism coined by Seyyed Ahmade Fardid. Since the revolution there have been many translations of it into English.

37. Ali Shari'ati, *Majmu'eye Asar* (The collection of works), vol. 27 (Tehran: Daftar Tadvine Asar, Dr. Shari'ati, 1360/1981), p. 233.

38. Ali Shari'ati, *Ensan va Islam* (Tehran: n.p., 1975), pp. 187–88.

39. Shari'ati, *Majmu'eye Asar*, vol. 27, p. 233.

40. Murtaza Mutahari, "Nazare Eslam Darbareye 'Elm," in a collection of his lectures entitled *Bist Goftar* (Twenty lectures) (Qum: Entesharate Eslami, 1361/1983).

41. Ibid.

42. M. Mutahari, "Farizeye 'Elm," in a collection of his lectures entitled *Dah Goftar* (Ten lectures) (Tehran: Sadra, 1356/1977), pp. 146–247.

43. Ibid., p. 151.

44. He portrays sciences as a means for achieving higher ends. "Without any doubt," he argues, some sciences, such as the sciences related to God and theology, are ends in themselves. . . . Other than these, sciences are means and not ends, in the sense that they are of preparatory use for something else." Mutahari, "Nazare Eslam," pp. 177–78.

45. Mutahari, "Farizeye 'Elm," pp. 129–35.

46. Ibid., pp. 142–44.

47. Ibid., p. 151.

48. To justify and explicate his position he referred to two historical cases. One was the reaction of Muslim thinkers to Greek philosophy, which Muslims adopted with no difficulty by distinguishing between the philosophical genius of Greek philosophers and their pagan religious practices; he also cited the case of Iranian thinkers who accepted Islam and contributed to its development by distinguishing between the Islamic message and the practices of Arabism and tribal tradition "of the time of ignorance."

49. For justification of this position Mutahari invoked the Prophetic tradition: "Lo! an act is not but its intention." One result of the acceptance of Mutahari's distinctions was the increasing adaptation of modern facilities and accessories by the more traditional families in Iran. But this adaptation has been governed by the interpretations of leading ulama. For example, the banning of the sale of video recorders after the revolution was based directly on Mutahari's principles.

50. Like Mutahari, Soroush considers himself one of the third group (in the former's categorization) who wants to continue the traditions of Mutahari and Shari'ati. See Soroush, *Roshanfekri va Dindari* (Tehran: Poyeh, 1367/1988), pp. 13–15.

51. This is my term, not Soroush's.

52. Abdolkarim Soroush, *Danesh va Arzesh* (Science and value), 8th ed. (Tehran: Yaran 1361/1983).

53. Ibid., p. 8.

54. Ibid., p. 6.

55. In details and with long quotation from the original works, Soroush presents Darwin's theory for his readers, before he evaluates it. See ibid., pp. 55–95.

56. Ibid., p. 112.

57. Ibid., p. 114.

58. Ibid., pp. 59–60.

59. See Abdolkarim Soroush, *Eideologye Sheitani* (Satanic ideology), 4th ed. (Tehran: Yaran, 1362/1983).

60. Ibid., p. 26.

61. Abdolkarim Soroush, *Danesh*, p. 290.

62. See, for example Abdolkarim Soroush, *Naqdi va daramadi bar Tazade Dialektiki* (A critique and introduction of dialectical contradiction), 2d ed. (Tehran: Yaran, 1361/1982).

63. See Abdolkarim Soroush, *Eideologye*, p. 145.

64. See Abdolkarim Soroush, *Tafaroje Son'* (A panorama on technique) (Tehran: Soroush, 1368/1990), p. 196.

65. He explains what he means by each, ibid., pp. 291–93.

66. Ibid., p. 39.

67. Abdolkarim Soroush, *Tafaroj*, p. 228.

68. He is referring to Reza Davari, the professor of philosophy at Tehran University who is known as following the views of Martin Heidegger. For the view of the former see his important book, *Waz' Kununiye Tafakor dar Iran* (The present state of thinking in Iran) (Tehran: Soroush, 1357/1978).

69. Abdolkarim Soroush, *Tafaroj*, p. 239.

70. Ibid., pp. 234–35.

71. The debate was covered by the monthly magazine *Kayhan-i Farhangi*, which first appeared in 1363/1984 and

stopped publication in early 1990. So-roush's first essay appeared in vol. 5, no. 2 (Ordibehesht 1367/April–May 1988) and the last in December 1989. In fact, many argue that the magazine had to stop publishing altogether because of these essays.

72. Author's interview with Abdolkarim Soroush, Tehran, 4 January 1991.

73. Nasir Makrem, "Tamadone Khire-konandeye Sharq" (The shining civilization of the East), *Maktabe Eslam* 8, no. 4 (1345/1967): 240.

74. Musa Sadr, "Khutute Asasiye Far-hange Eslami" (The basic features of Islamic culture), *Maktabe Eslam* 9, no. 13 (1347/1969): 65.

75. Na'ini, *Tanbih al-Umma va Tanzih al-Mella;* Ha'iri, *Shi'ism and Constitutionalism in Iran.*

76. Answer to the letter questioning the validity of declaring chess and the trade of musical instruments to be lawful acts. For the text of the letter, see *Sahifeye Nur*, vol. 21 (Tehran: Sazemane Madareke Enqelabe Eslami, 1369/1990), pp. 34–35.

77. See ibid., p. 46.

78. The secondary apparent rule was first used in the twentieth century by Haj Shaykh Abdulkarim Ha'iri Yazdi (d. 1937), the leader of the religious establishment in Qum at the time. When military conscription was instituted, religious leaders and students were exempted, provided they would be identified and obtain a picture identity card. When the issue of taking a picture was put to Ha'iri, he declared that it was permitted and justified on the basis of the principle of secondary apparent rules. (Interview with Ali Asghar Faqihi in Tehran, 15 April 1990. He is one of the prominent scholars on the history of Qum.)

79. This was reported to me by a close associate of Khomeini who wishes to remain anonymous. Tehran, 25 August 1991.

80. Hojjatoleslam Azizollah Bayat, "Mo-lahezati darbareye Sokhanane Riyasate Jom-huri," *Bayan,* no. 7 (Azar 1369/October 1990): 12.

81. "Nameye Sargoshadeye 35 Tan az Asatide Daneshgahe San'atiye Sharief dar morede Khatare Gostareshe Liberalism Fa-hangi," *Keyhan,* Tir 6, 1370/27 June 1991, p. 18.

82. *Ettela'at,* 15 January 1991, p. 14.

83. *Keyhan,* 28 Shahrivar 1370/19 September 1991, p. 5.

84. Quoted in Minoo Badi'i, "Roshde Jam'iyat" (Population growth), *Keyhan,* 27 Shahrivar 1370/ 18 September 1991), p. 5.

85. Fatwa of Ayatollah Golpayegani. See "Tanzime Khanevadeh dar Islam," Report by Research Group for Muslim Women's Issues in Cultural Studies and Research Institute, (manuscript), p. 11.

86. Ibid.

87. Problem number 2858 in Imam Khomeini, *Resaleye Towziolmasa'el* (Qum: Jame'eye Modaresin, n.d.), p. 556.

88. When I asked the head of the acquisitions department in the Ministry of Commerce about the decision process and the Islamic justification for it, he told me that I need only explain the reasons necessitating the purchase of a commodity, and he will obtain the proper justification later.

89. See Ruhollah Khomeini, *Sahifeye Nur,* vol. 20 (Tehran: Sazemane Madareke Engelabe Eslami, 1369/1990), pp. 171–72.

90. The text of the Islamic criminal codes can be found in *Majmu'eye Qavanine Avvalin Doureye Qanungozari* (Tehran: Majlise Shou-raye Eslami, 1363/1984), pp. 235, 263, 273, 302, 494.

91. A review of the files of two law firms in Tehran confirms my conclusion. The closer in time the case is to the revolution, the more radical is the decision.

92. Interview with Dr. Najmabadi, Tehran, December 1990.

93. See Khomeini, *Sahifeye Nur,* vol. 20, p. 190.

2

Family and Interpersonal Relationships

The Impact of Fundamentalisms on Women, the Family, and Interpersonal Relations

Helen Hardacre

Religions worldwide invest the family with sacred significance, and this extends to gender and interpersonal relations. The family is a primary unit for ritual observance as well as an influential site of religious education and the transmission of religious knowledge from one generation to the next. It embodies primary relationships in which religious values are expressed, and in this sense it is frequently taken as a microcosm of a universal moral order. Its relationships (parent/child, husband/wife) are frequently used as models of the relations ideally pertaining between divinity and humanity.

The family is so basic to religious thought and behavior that in eras of social, political, and economic change affecting the family, religions are liable to perceive that they and their view of the world are being undermined at their very foundations. This would seem to be the situation fundamentalists in various religious traditions now face. Their particular responses differ widely, but they share the perception of a threat to values "traditionally" associated with the family. Many fundamentalist movements, and each of those examined in these pages, pursue social programs designed to re-shape the family in accord with these values. These programs in turn share another trait: they define the role of women and children quite narrowly and often place severe restrictions on these family members.

The primary focus of the essays in part 2 of this volume is on Christian and Muslim fundamentalisms. (Buddhism and Japanese New Religions also receive attention in chapter 11). In this section the editors have focused on the two religious traditions that have produced major fundamentalist movements in many countries and regions of the world, rather than extend the scope of the comparison to fundamentalist movements in Judaism, Hinduism, and Sikhism. Thus it is left to other scholars to raise similar questions about other fundamentalisms. The conclusions drawn in this section do not necessarily apply to those movements.

Contributors dealing with Islam have studied the effects on family life of state-sponsored Islamic fundamentalism in Iran and Pakistan (Shahla Haeri, chapter 8) and what we might call a diffuse cultural fundamentalism in Egypt (Andrea Rugh, chapter 7). In preparing this introductory chapter I have also drawn on previously published case studies of fundamentalist practices in Morocco, the Sudan, and sub-Saharan Africa. Jorge Maldonado, in chapter 9, examines the ways in which strategies for building strong family structures contribute to the rapid growth of contemporary Latin American evangelicalism. Michael Quinn, in chapter 10, has examined a group marginal to mainstream Christianity, polygamous Mormons, as a fascinating example of extremist-fundamentalist movements' insistence on patriarchy as essential to the "authentic" religious tradition.

The essays of part 2, along with other studies in the project, demonstrate clearly that fundamentalist movements are in many respects uncoordinated, locally specific, and starkly diverse. This being the case, it would be highly misleading to give the impression that fundamentalism, as some monolithic entity, has a blueprint for the family, gender roles, and interpersonal relations which it seeks always and everywhere to implement. This is not the case, by any means. Nevertheless, comparing within Islam or Christianity, or even across these two traditions, it seems clear that analysis of the *consequences* or *impact* of both diffuse fundamentalisms and specific fundamentalist movements on the family, gender roles, and interpersonal relations reveals an identifiable pattern. That is, the picture drawn from data on women and family life in fundamentalist-influenced communities within the Sudan, Iran, Pakistan, Egypt, and elsewhere in the Islamic world seems to support the hypothesis that Islamic fundamentalism—here understood as a selective retrieval and imposition of Islamic law and sacred texts as the basis for a modern sociopolitical order—is, among other things, a patriarchal protest movement against selected aspects of secularized modernity. In their approach to women and family, Christian fundamentalisms are incomparable to Islam in terms of ontology, specific religious beliefs, or specific sociomoral norms and practices. But there is sufficient evidence to warrant a comparison of the impact of the two fundamentalisms in terms of basic attitudes and understandings of women's roles and the function of the "traditional family" within a hierarchical and divinely sanctioned social order.

Because the primary focus of part 2 is on fundamentalism within Christianity and Islam, this introductory essay is limited to comments on those two traditions. In the final chapter of this section I have explored similar patterns of male-female interaction within Japanese society, and in particular within Japan's New Religions, which acutely reflect the larger cultural struggle between tradition and modernity within Japanese society. Although I conclude that "fundamentalism" does not apply on many points, it does provide part of an explanatory model for the attitudes on abortion and other issues related to women and family as they are articulated in the New Religions.

Issues and Themes in American Protestant Fundamentalism

For American Protestant fundamentalism, the family has become a potent symbol of an idealized moral order, and the imperative to "return" to an idealized form of the family is perhaps the highest priority of the fundamentalist social agenda. That much energy has been devoted to the family may be seen from the plethora of fundamentalist projects and organizations founded in the last thirty years to uphold the family: seminars and workshops such as Family Life Seminars, the Institute of Basic Youth Conflict, political organizations such as the Moral Majority, the Coalition for Better Television, Christian Family Renewal, United Families of America, Pro-Family Forum, Pro-Family United, Family Protection Lobby, National Pro-Family Coalition, Family America, and Christian Action Council. The fundamentalist media have produced such films as "Focus on the Family," "Maximum Marriage," "Marriage Enrichment," "Crisis in the Homes," "The Family: God's Pattern for Living Series," and "The Family Gone Wild."

These many initiatives are united by a belief in a divinely ordained and unchanging family pattern. The following statements by fundamentalist leaders, quoted by James Davison Hunter, illustrate the perception that society is threatened by changes in family life: "The family is that basic institution of society which undergirds all else. . . . If the family fails, then all the other institutions of society will fail." "The hope of America today is strong Christian families. Determine to make your family a fortress of spiritual and moral strength against the shifting tides of moral change." "America is in trouble today because the home is in trouble." "If we are to rebuild our nation we must first strengthen our homes and make sure they are Christ-centered. Husbands and wives must assume the full responsibilities of Christian parents so that children may walk in the ways of the Lord."[1] The implied remedy is a "restoration" of the ideal form of the family, seen as a panacea for a variety of social ills.

American Protestant fundamentalists champion the "traditional family." Inasmuch as American family patterns have changed markedly over the nation's history, however, and because in all periods the practice of various ethnic groups has shown extreme variation, it is by no means obvious what is meant by this expression. This being the case, it is appropriate to examine representative statements by influential fundamentalist leaders on the proper constitution of the family. According to Jerry Falwell,

God Almighty created men and women biologically different and with differing needs and roles. He made men and women to complement each other and to love each other. . . . Scripture declares that God has called the father to be the spiritual leader in his family. . . . Their wives and children want to follow them and be under their protection. The husband is to be the decision-maker and the one who motivates his family with love. . . . He is to be a protector.[2]

Speaking at the Family Forum conference "The New Traditional Woman," Connie Marshner explained women's role: "A woman's nature is, simply, other-oriented. . . .

To the traditional woman self-centeredness remains as ugly and sinful as ever. The less time women spend thinking about themselves, the happier they are. . . . Women are ordained by their nature to spend themselves in meeting the needs of others."[3]

The ideal family pattern advocated by these two leaders stresses the complementarity of male and female roles. Both are necessary, but not interchangeable or equivalent. A hallmark of the pattern is an insistence on hierarchical relations between women and men.[4] Authority rests with men, and it is women's role to obey and to submit to male authority. Furthermore, women are to submerge their own aspirations in the service of others.

The fulfillment of this ideal pattern is regarded as essential to the achievement of divine will: "The family belongs to God. He created it. He determined its inner structure. He appointed it for its purpose and goal . . . to bring glory and honor to God."[5] The family is thus not only efficient in the functions of reproduction or child rearing, it is divinely ordained.

The family idealized here is the nuclear family, a coresidential group basically consisting of a married female and male and their minor children. The husband is ideally the sole breadwinner who exercises final authority in all matters affecting the group. He is the disciplinarian and spiritual leader. He is expected to direct his children's moral development and to spend time with them. He should not abuse the authority he holds over his wife and children, but neither are any limits on that authority specified clearly.

The fundamentalist prescription for family life typically elaborates the wife/mother role in far greater detail than the roles of men and children. The wife's role is to assist the husband in the exercise of his God-given authority, first by submitting to it herself, and also by training her children to respect and obey it. She is to consider that her principal responsibility is in the domestic realm, for this is the site where she will achieve spiritual fulfillment. She need not venture outside: "What is the key to success for a married woman? First it is constantly seeking God's perspective on life. Secondly it is modeling a personal plan for utilizing herself and serving her husband, children, and home. At last it is allowing God to meet her needs through her husband, children, and opportunities found through the home."[6]

Women are to find their greatest fulfillment in motherhood, and the maternal role is regarded as ground zero of the family as a whole: "[The] maternal role is more than just one component in the patterns of complementary roles. It is the crucial pivot—the foundation—upon which both family and society revolve. How women fill that role determines the potential happiness and fulfillment of all of us."[7] There are two crucial elements in this conception of motherhood. First, the correct performance of motherhood implies withdrawal from paid employment, staying at home to be available to husband and children. Second, mothers should not be permissive with children, but should lay down clear rules and enforce obedience. In connection with these elements, fundamentalists tend to distrust independent intellectual or political activities by women.[8]

The family as a whole should provide a haven from a harsh world. It is ideally an arena where emotion can be expressed, where one can feel loved, secure, and sheltered, "a Christian oasis far from the maddening throng and godless currents and pressures."[9] It is the realm of succor and sentiment. Its members can find peace of mind there as nowhere else, because it can be modeled according to a template of divine origin. No other sphere of life can be so closely controlled.

The so-called traditional family described here is largely an ideal that has taken on mythic proportions in fundamentalist discourse. There is, however, no widespread historical reality to which the ideal corresponds. Until relatively recently in Western history, sentiment and emotional sustenance have not been the main preoccupation of family life. Instead, the family was primarily defined as a common economic enterprise in which privacy was virtually nonexistent. In the Middle Ages, for example, marriages were contracted not by the principals but by their parents, and hence there was little expectation of romance or affection. Childhood was not recognized as a period of life requiring specialized guidance and nurture. The major concern of the family group was survival, not nurture or sentiment, and this extended to the parent/child relationship, a trend continuing for centuries.

Changes in the seventeenth century introduced a greater preoccupation with children and with privacy, although these interests were limited to the upper classes. "I cannot abide that passion for caressing newborn children, which have neither mental activities nor recognizable bodily shape by which to make themselves lovable," Montaigne wrote, "and I have never willingly suffered them to be fed in my presence."[10] By the eighteenth and nineteenth centuries, however, this trend began to take hold in the bourgeois family in both Europe and America. Privatization was, in the first instance, constituted by larger and more intricately partitioned dwellings that literally created private spaces for children and their parents, while serving as physical testaments to the economic power of the bourgeoisie. Romance and affection came to be viewed as central to married life, and children became objects of affection and specialized nurturing. Because this family type was formed in the wake of industrialization and an increased primacy of commerce, it came increasingly to be seen as a retreat from the alienation accompanying this transformation of society. Women acquired the central responsibility for creating an atmosphere that could provide respite from the world of commerce. "Good mothering" became a single, absolute standard by which to evaluate women.[11] These trends evolved further in the twentieth century: "The main features of the bourgeois pattern of family life spread to all classes of Western society. Lower-class but upwardly mobile women, in fact, came to regard the attainment of this family arrangement as the height of liberation and fulfillment." In the post–World War II era, however, the family underwent "a further intensification and radicalization of the tendencies predominant in the bourgeois family model. Hyperindividuation and hypersentimentalization became particularly prominent."[12]

When American fundamentalists refer to the traditional family, they have in mind the bourgeois nuclear family.[13] They elevate this model to a supernatural plane, believing it to be divinely ordained and timeless, and all variation from it to be morally reprehensible. The social history of the family is not relevant to this idealization. Rather, as a sacred archetype, the family cannot have a variegated history in which each episode is equally weighted or valued, as that would imply that a divine creation is subject to change by the vagaries of politics, economics, and society. Hunter concludes: "The ideal Christian family is, in fact, novel inasmuch as it is related to the process of national development itself; structurally, a precondition and product of modernity; culturally, a reflection of its symbolic realities."[14]

Yet fundamentalist rhetoric claims that the traditional family is historically typical as well as divinely ordained and calls upon society to "return" to it. Ronald Godwin, vice-president of the now-defunct Moral Majority, exemplified the Christian fundamentalist's denial of the significance of variant patterns of the family by attacking them on moral grounds:

> You'll hear many, many feminists and anti-family spokesmen today talking about history. . . . They'll tell you that down in the Fiji Islands, somewhere down on an island of Uwunga-Bunga, there's a tribe of people who have never practiced family life as we know it. But they also have bones in their nose and file their front teeth. And they eat raw meat for breakfast. They're some fairly strange, non-representative people. But they'll tell you about all the strange aberrations that have popped up in the human family over the centuries in various strange geographical locations. They'll tell you that in the nineteenth century in the backside of Europe such and such a thing went on. . . . They'll try to build a historical case for the proposition that the traditional family never really was traditional and never really was a dominant force in all civilized societies.[15]

In this way of thinking the supposed dominance of the bourgeois nuclear family invalidates whatever alternative patterns may exist or have existed, and its absence in any particular society or the failure of any individual to adhere to it becomes ipso facto proof that the society or individual in question is not "civilized."

Since about 1960, however, the gap between the fundamentalists' family ideal and the realities of American life has become increasingly conspicuous. Since that time the nuclear family has ceased to be statistically typical in the United States.[16] By 1980 "only 7 to 15 percent of American families fit into the nuclear family norm of father at work and mother at home with the children." Divorce ended one in three marriages and half of all first marriages. As of 1976, 37 percent of the mothers of pre-school-age children were employed outside the home, and women constituted half of the United States work force, a dramatic rise caused by an increase of married women working. "Half of all mothers of school-age children are wage earners in the United States today."[17] These trends were found in far advanced forms in some regions of the country. For example, in 1990 only 22 percent of households in Los Angeles were composed of a heterosexual couple and children, according to the city's Task Force on Family Diversity.[18] In the face of such mounting statistics, Christian fundamentalists were faced with the argument that the much-touted "traditional family" had little basis in either history or contemporary American society.

There is, however, one important thread of continuity between the historical family (in the West) and the fundamentalist ideal: "a strong form of patriarchal rule."[19] Even with bourgeois privatization and sentimentalization of the family, patriarchal authority was preserved, and romantic love embodied different meanings for women and men. In the nineteenth-century bourgeois family, the husband's first duty continued to be providing a good living. According to Hunter, "By virtue of having to leave home in order to work, he was necessarily removed from the routines of everyday life. Thus, his authority became more abstract and symbolic. Still, his influence in the affairs of the family remained virtually incontestable. Family hierarchy remained resolutely patriarchal though not always or necessarily tyrannical. . . . Over all, however, the image of the bourgeois father and husband continued to be one of autocratic dominance, paternal severity, and moral and religious authority."[20]

In the late twentieth century a weakening of the insistence on absolute distinctions between female and male roles, growing pressure on married women to enter the paid work force, the rise of feminism, and a diminution of male monopoly on cash income contrived to challenge the legitimacy of patriarchal authority. This became the battleground on which the fundamentalist agenda on the family centered. In this context Martin Riesebrodt has interpreted fundamentalism as "a protest movement that reacts primarily to the replacement of patriarchal structures and social morals by modern depersonalized, bureaucratic structures and social morals." In this view fundamentalists initially oppose "the agents, representatives, and intellectuals of the modern order; all institutions which are structured on bureaucratic principles, such as 'big business,' 'big labor,' and 'big government'; and above all feminism, which is most explicitly opposed to the patriarchal ideal."[21]

Support for this interpretation is found in the fact that fundamentalists focus on gender as the pivotal issue in their attempt to establish a moral order with the family as its center. Rendered symbolically, "gender" encompasses issues of privacy, family, domesticity, patriarchy, and sexuality. This focus on gender subsumes a variety of issues perceived as tied to the threat to the family: opposition to the legalization of abortion, the "threat" of homosexuality, the busing issue, and the desire to establish Christian schools outside the supervision of public school systems. Given this emphasis it is hardly surprising that the large majority of fundamentalist leaders are "marginalized male elites, co-opting women by claiming to protect them as custodians of domestic space."[22] Such marginalized male elites, "extolling women as mothers and custodians of family values but never recognizing an individual woman as an authoritative teacher," have provided Protestant fundamentalism with its leaders.[23]

The management of gender relations is indeed an area in which Christian fundamentalists have enjoyed success within their own ranks. Fundamentalist ideologues have been able to take existing social inequalities in the larger society for granted. They do not need to overturn basic social structures to achieve their ends. Instead, their efforts are designed further to enhance the power of males within these structures.

In addition to preoccupation with gender in the sense outlined above, fundamentalists also are concerned to create an environment for their children which reflects their understanding of the family. The general style of child rearing favored by American Protestant fundamentalists is antipermissive, favoring the establishment of clear rules for all aspects of life. Inasmuch as the fundamentalist worldview rejects many aspects of contemporary American life, there is an impetus to keep children away from influences deemed unwholesome, including much of the media (especially film) and such youth-oriented genres of music as rock, hard rock, punk, and other types which glamorize promiscuous sexuality and rejection of authority.[24]

Fundamentalist parents themselves, however, reject in large numbers a basic social institution—the public school. Many Christian academies were founded in the 1970s as a response to what fundamentalists saw as excessive interference by government, to the detriment of parental authority. In many cases the immediate stimulus to found an alternative school that could inculcate religious values was the advent of busing to achieve racial balance. For many parents Christian academies were seen as "havens from the racial desegregation of public schools."[25] The Christian academy monitors closely all aspects of pupils' behavior and extends supervision, through close cooperation with parents, well beyond school hours and the school grounds, creating what Alan Peshkin calls a "total world."[26] As Susan Rose points out in this volume, students are encouraged to confine their friendships, dating partners, and spouses to persons within the church. The scope of regimentation at Christian academies is sweeping by the standards of contemporary American life, but it would be misleading to suggest that the products of the schools conform in all aspects to the intended ideal.[27]

Fundamentalisms and Families within the Context of Economic Development

Fundamentalists have been described as antimodernists who "rely on modern instrumentalities while rejecting the goals of modernism."[28] Regarding the family, gender roles, and interpersonal relations, this antimodernism assumes a characteristic constellation of positions and attitudes closely linked to the circumstances in which such movements typically arise—circumstances characterized by the weakening of traditional controls, kinship loyalties, and traditional forms of patronage and paternalism. There is often a reaction of shock at the confrontation of new values encountered in adapting to an urban environment or to an industrial workplace, coupled with a sense of loss of community.[29]

We have examined those dynamics as they have informed American Protestant fundamentalism. Analogous changes can be seen at work in other types of fundamentalism. Sometimes these changes have coincided with anticolonial movements and the rise of nationalism. This would seem to be the case in many expressions of Islamic fundamentalism.[30] Fundamentalism arises not only in conjunction with modernization, the formation of the nation-state, and nationalism, however, but also can appear, as in the contemporary United States, in a crisis of capitalism, when older ideologies of gender are disrupted by economic imperatives forcing the great majority of women into the workplace and when those ideologies are challenged intellectually, morally, and philosophically by powerful feminist and homosexual movements.

These global changes are mirrored within the family. Industrialization entails broad shifts to wage labor and an accelerating dependency of family units upon cash income. As an industrial work force is accumulated through migration to the cities, younger workers and their families move from the countryside to reside near urban factories in smaller, sometimes nuclear family units. In so doing, their ties to wider kinship units in rural areas are changed and the authority of elders attenuated. Nucleation of the family or other shifts to greater dependence upon the conjugal unit, in conjunction with a shift to wage labor, have special implications for women. Where women have been admitted to the paid work force, it has generally been for considerably less remuneration than men, so much less that women have generally been able to live at a higher standard by accepting a position of economic dependence on a man than by relying solely upon their own earnings. The vulnerability inherent in a situation of economic dependence can be significantly ameliorated if a woman has around her a network of kin who can be called on to restrain a man's exploitation of that vulnerability. Similarly, in agrarian economies the value of women's work in the production of goods, crops, and food is recognized, but when a household is principally dependent on cash for the purchase of goods and food that women would have produced in rural areas, then women's unpaid labor in maintaining a household is disvalued, because it does not produce cash.[31] Thus industrialization, urbanization, a shift to wage labor, and nucleation of the family are intimately related phenomena which tend to enhance male dominance, bring about a lowering of women's status, and entrench women ever deeper in economic dependence upon men, with decreasing support from wider kinship networks.[32]

As the family shrinks, its ability to provide for the wide range of human needs associated with extended kinship networks decreases markedly. Childcare, for example, is a task routinely shared among multiple individuals in an extended family, but one which tends increasingly to fall exclusively upon the mother in the nuclear family. Similarly, care for the sick and the aged can be shared among a large network of kin living in close proximity, but when nuclear families are living in isolation from larger networks of kin, this burden tends to fall exclusively upon women. In the same way, small families strain under the burden of absorbing the divorced, the widowed, the disabled, and the unemployed.[33]

In the face of the family's shrinking ability to provide for all the needs of all of its members, the state may assume many of the family's former functions. Welfare nets are created that provide more or less comprehensive coverage for the sick, the injured, the divorced, the widowed, the disabled, and the unemployed. A by-product of this expansion of the functions of the state, however, is an extension of its supervisory role into virtually all areas of human life. In many regions of the developing world, fundamentalist movements provide their own social care programs in the absence or inefficiency of programs provided by the secular state. In this effort both the secular state and fundamentalist organizations have attempted to regulate the behavior of women so as to make them more accountable for the welfare of all members of a family. Thus a common phenomenon among nation-states and fundamentalist movements alike at different periods of development has been a sustained attention to "women's education." This has often amounted to the inculcation of a gender ideology that situated women's work and life within the scope of the family and systematically discouraged them from seeking alternative ways of life or the skills and education which could equip them to live independently of the family or to become economically independent of men.[34]

Those who feel most deprived of the privileges, wealth, and opportunity associated with the advent of modernity—those least able to realize anticipated ways of life idealized by the parental generation—are ripe for conversion to fundamentalist creeds.[35] Fundamentalism promises to restore the family, to put the nation on a course that aligns it with divine purpose, and to establish a social order in which life can be lived morally, meaningfully, and in accord with divine will.[36] Fundamentalist groups have not, however, been in a position to reverse urbanization, industrialization, the immiseration of the countryside, the creation of an urban proletariat, or the nucleation of the family. Neither have they been in a position to attempt to restore the wealth and privilege that disappear as a result of such macro-level change. Neither have they succeeded in eradicating the appeal of Western material culture or the values of societies based on consumerism.

In the face of these frustrations in dealing with external forces beyond their control, fundamentalists have found themselves most able to effect significant change in interpersonal relations, especially within the family. Building upon existing inequalities between women and men, patterns of discrimination against women, and the exclusion of women from positions of power, fundamentalists call for a strengthening of prerogatives for males and elders in the name of a return to "tradition," sanctified as the expression of God's will on earth. Given their greater exclusion from the benefits of colonialism, modernization and development,[37] women in developing countries have not been in a position to chart their own path to development independent of the plans of their menfolk.

While fundamentalism has many varieties, the doctrines of which have little or nothing in common with each other, we can nevertheless isolate elements of a common "message" on women, the family, and interpersonal relations shared by Christian and Muslim fundamentalists. First, the message may be chronologically quite "new," but it is invariably presented as the distillation of timeless "tradition."[38] The essence of the message is a strengthening of patriarchy in all its forms, but calling especially for an increase in men's power and authority in the home and over women and children. Islamic fundamentalist movements emphasize in particular that women should be subordinate to men, and that men should rule over women in all things; this is not just the prevailing social order, but represents the heart of the religion, the best of the people.[39] A new social order should be constructed around the mirror-image principles of male dominance and female submission. Thus one of the first acts of the Khomeini regime was to repeal the Family Protection Act of 1967, which granted women access to divorce, child custody, and alimony.[40] Such restrictions are presented as central keys to remedying the ills of modernization, the first step to throwing out the colonial overlord, and the sine qua non in realizing the highest destiny of the nation.

When we analyze fundamentalist ideologies in terms of their posited ideal social order, we find a consistent emphasis on patriarchal structures. The ideal family is the patriarchal family where the father is responsible for the public sphere (economy, politics) and the women for the private sphere (home, children). The economic ideal extols family enterprise and a religious integration of "capital" and "labor" instead of institutionalized class-conflict, "big business," and "big labor." The political ideal ascribes to the state primarily the role of a protector of the moral order, but otherwise eschews intervention into people's affairs. Private charity based on social, moral, and religious control constitutes the fundamentalist idea of brotherhood. It is distinctly opposed to the depersonalized structures of the welfare state. Therefore, in my view, fundamentalism is primarily a radical patriarchalism.[41]

The details in which this message is further specified differ widely, as the following case studies imply. A full, empirical description of these messages is beyond the scope of this chapter, but a few comments on some of the more serious consequences for women within fundamentalist spheres of influence are appropriate.

The Impact of Fundamentalist Worldviews upon Women

As we have seen, fundamentalism requires reform of the family in the image of an idealized tradition. In general, however, it is striking that women are called upon to embody and represent tradition.[42] The ways in which women are urged to personify tradition vary widely within different fundamentalisms, but have historically included the following tendencies, documented in the practice of fundamentalist communities. These tendencies are not found in all such communities, nor is there a doctrinal or logical requirement for their connection. These tendencies do, however, appear repeatedly in quite different circumstances and movements, and configure to illustrate a loose coherence of ideas and practices relating to the family, gender roles, and interpersonal relations.

Across movements and traditions a "common" gender ideology places women in charge of the home, responsible for the happiness and well-being of everyone in it. By this ideology men live the greater part of their lives outside the home. The home becomes for men the sanctified, privatized retreat from the world of work, where they may relax and exercise authority. Women's personification of tradition also takes the form of (often explicit) restrictions on their physical movements away from the home. Women should use whatever economic power they have solely in service to the family.[43] Closely linked to restriction of physical movement are codes regulating dress and sexual conduct, bringing these matters under male control. Dress codes and veiling are pervasive requirements in the Islamic world, though they are enforced with acute attention in fundamentalist contexts, as Haeri demonstrates. As Rugh shows, the specifications of dress and veil vary widely. The underlying concern is that women should not, by their dress or exposure of their bodies, excite men's sexuality.[44] In Islamic fundamentalisms the sexual conduct of males is not to be dependent upon that of females: sexual relations are at the male's discretion. Female sexuality exists in service to male sexuality and for the reproduction of the family. These various specifications are seen as central to a return to "tradition" in family life.[45]

In fact, as much as possible, fundamentalisms seek to elide women's sexuality and reproductive power, stigmatizing nonreproductive sex of any kind. A corollary requirement of diverse Christian and Islamic fundamentalisms is that women should reject contraceptive technologies, have children by the will of the male (and God), and take primary responsibility for raising these children. Radical fundamentalists have sometimes resorted to coercion and violence to enforce these norms. One is reminded here of Khomeini's retrieval of the Shari'a's corporal punishment for adultery and immodesty. An extreme example is that, Muslim women in sub-Saharan Africa have endured genital mutilation in such forms as infibulation and clitoridectomy. This curbs female sexuality by making heterosexual intercourse painful and orgasm impossible.[46]

Additional consequences of women's symbolization of "tradition" have included the requirement that women forego such benefits of modernity as the franchise, education beyond basic literacy, and employment in most of the professions and in the leading sectors of the economy. Post-revolution Iran has ejected women from public service, and Pakistan ousted Benazir Bhutto from elected office, in part, apparently, because of strong Islamic resentment in Pakistan against a woman prime minister. Here American Christian fundamentalists, in calls for women to return to kitchen, church, and children, seem to share Islamic wariness about the full participation of women in the benefits of modernity.[47] Processes of exclusion and marginalization in politics and the labor force have occurred in varying configurations in relation to the other methods of control mentioned here.

The Persuasive Power of the Fundamentalist Message

The persuasive power of the fundamentalist message for men seems obvious. Men are provided with a divine mandate to exercise authority over women and children with little interference or restraint. They are told that God commands them to exact obedience and submission from women and children. They can fulfill the search for authenticity and moral rectitude without relinquishing personal independence or autonomy. Men experience a restoration of the power and authority that they may feel has been illegitimately stolen from them in the outside world. Power and privilege are comfortable and pleasurable, especially when they are assured that women's happiness, indeed, their entire existence, lies in serving men. Michael Quinn's essay (chapter 10) provides eloquent testimony to the satisfactions polygamous Mormon men derive from the enhancement of status which having several wives confers upon them. Quinn shows how men's status among other men and within fundamentalist hierarchies is enhanced by plural marriage.

Another factor in fundamentalism's appeal to men lies in a correlation sometimes found between membership in such groups and upward mobility. Jorge Maldonado, in chapter 9, contends that membership in Pentecostal and fundamentalist churches and organizations is associated, in a spectrum of Latin American societies, with eco-nomic stability across social classes. Maldonado points out that men are "restored" to a position of leadership and authority within the family, and within the socioeco-nomic community, by their participation in Pentecostal and fundamentalist churches. Ironically, their participation is often inspired by their wives, who are the actual leaders and founders of many of the new evangelical communities. The appeal of these new communities, in which wife and husband share in decision making within an overarching ideology that remains "traditional" (i.e., patriarchal), is apparently very strong, for large numbers are converting from Catholicism to Protestant evangelical-ism. In the Latin American ethos, Maldonado writes, conversion to a fundamentalist-like evangelical religion leads to the curbing of some of the more extreme aspects of machismo, in favor of stabilizing attitudes of thrift and hard work.

Whereas women's duties toward men are diffuse and unbounded, men's duties toward women in fundamentalist creeds are typically clearly demarcated and nar-rowly specified, centering on the provision of material support as long as a marriage lasts. Typically in Islam, for example, the husband can initiate divorce on trifling grounds. He can compel a wife to render sexual service, but she does not have the same claim, nor in all cases an exclusive claim, to his sexuality or to his reproductive potential. Shahla Haeri's essay (chapter 8) on the themes of contract and obedience details the ways in which Islamic marriage law in Iran and Pakistan is applied to limit men's responsibilities toward their wives and to enforce their power in legal, eco-nomic, and sexual modes.[48]

It is little wonder, then, that men are attracted to fundamentalist creeds, but the persuasive power of such creeds for women is much more difficult to comprehend. Why do women become such staunch advocates of fundamentalist creeds, when those same creeds seem to deepen their subordination to men and require them to relin-quish power and authority to men? This is perhaps the most difficult of all questions concerned with fundamentalism, the family, and interpersonal relations. There are a number of possible explanations, not all of which are relevant to every fundamentalist movement.

Women involved in Islamic fundamentalist movements inspired by anticolonialist or nationalist sentiments share much of men's alienation and deprivation arising from urbanization, industrialization, immiseration of rural areas, colonization, and nation-alist appeals. They are as fearful of change as men, and they stand to lose more than men in the loss of the security of wide kinship links in the social changes that fre-quently accompany the growth of fundamentalist movements. Women are thus pow-erfully attracted by fundamentalism's interpersonal networks that invoke the language of kinship and in which the religion itself is portrayed as a "family." The general message of a return to "tradition" as the key to the ills of dislocation and disempow-erment is as readily accepted by women as by men. Fundamentalist movements in both Islam and Christianity also strike a responsive chord in many women who wish to be recognized as morally upright members of their religion seriously engaged in addressing contemporary social problems.

Second, the fact that women are either excluded from the labor force or relegated to lower-status jobs means that in most cases they can live at a higher standard when coupled with a man than they could on their own earnings. Thus the fundamentalist injunctions by which women remain peripheral to advanced economic sectors are perceived as having an element of economic realism, that is, legitimating and sanctifying an economic inevitability. Because fundamentalists tend to restrict women's rights to own property, women lack economic resources that they can control independently. Hence they are seldom able to establish independent lives, especially if they have children. It is true that fundamentalism frequently provides extensive networks of patronage and economic support, but these are not always available to women except in support of projects that confirm the overall fundamentalist program. There is no doubt that, faced with a no-win game in the labor market, many women make conscious decisions to use the fundamentalist message to secure the husband's loyalty to and support of them and their children. Fundamentalism offers a different standard of value to apply to women exclusively: "Women can and ought to be judged by the criteria of femininity," says Elizabeth Elliot, author of *Let Me Be a Woman*.[49] Women are confirmed in these decisions by media messages from both secular and religious sources. "Let's face it: we have a desire for 'husbanding,'" conservative evangelical Maxine Hancock told her audience, "for someone big enough and strong enough to be more than just a partner, someone to take the leadership in every essential way."[50]

Fundamentalist networks also frequently assist women in their efforts to domesticate men, to bring them under the realm of life defined by the family. Fundamentalists often, for example, expound a religious meaning in parents taking responsibility for their children's spiritual development and stress that men as well as women should assume a submissive attitude before God.[51] In the perception of many women fundamentalists, including Hancock, many men are weak and passive husbands, failing to provide the leadership women seek.

Third, the idea that women do not require education as a necessity, as men do, has inhibited women raised in fundamentalist creeds from discovering and exploring alternative values and ways of life. Because movement is restricted, women, especially in Islamic fundamentalisms, have few outside contacts of any depth, a situation that increases with time and number of children borne. In many cases neither they nor their societies have any tradition of placing value on equality, and certainly not between the sexes.[52] Elizabeth Elliot makes a similar point for Christian fundamentalists: "Equality is not a Christian ideal . . . it is the nature of the woman to submit."[53]

Fourth, in extremist fundamentalist regimes, such as Iran under Khomeini, women may in certain contexts fear male reprisal for nonconformity and disobedience. Further restriction and seclusion, withdrawal of economic support for herself and her children, battery, and even rape are not unknown punishments within the home. Outside the home, women may fear the legal procedures that may be brought to force conformity, such as divorce, taking away custody of her children, and the various physical punishments sanctioned by Islamic law.[54] In addition, outside the household she is further subject to stigmatization, battery, and rape.

Fifth, women in fundamentalist communities or cultures may fear divine disapproval, excommunication by the earthly church or religious community, and super natural punishments. This is the threat of spiritual ostracization and banishment to outer darkness, accompanied by guilt and fear that the punishments for their own transgressions will be visited on their children and other kin. In the case of Mormon fundamentalism, for example, women idealize obedience and submissiveness. Questioning these values does not immediately overcome decades of socialization in them, nor does its automatically give women alternative values or patterns of thought.[55] Women receive little support for either their questioning or the development of alternatives.

Finally, many women find that modernity presents them with difficult choices to make about things they were raised to believe inevitable. For example, American women can economically support themselves by their own labor, though this is not to deny that most could live at a higher level when solely supported by a male. If this is so, then women do not have to marry to secure their basic economic support, and marriage changes from a compulsory to an optional institution. Similarly, married or not, a woman involved in a heterosexual relationship, for the first time in human history, can control her own fertility and choose not only when but whether to have children. Contraceptive technologies have ended exclusive reliance on abstinence and late marriage. Crude and dangerous as many of these technologies are, they have been enthusiastically adopted by American women. Thus within a remarkably short time, marriage, self-support, and control of fertility have become matters of choice, representing a complex of revolutionary change for women, for the character of their relations with men, and for the course of the female life cycle.

These rapid changes have precipitated a moral crisis in conceptions of marriage. Fundamentalism's assertions of marriage's divine origins and its significance as the nexus in which women's salvation is achieved have presented an answer to the crisis. Fundamentalism's call for renewed dedication to the institution in absolutist terms gives such women a program of moral action that imparts religious meaning to the choices they have made about how to support themselves, whether to marry, and how to conduct their reproductive lives. The assurance that this program of action accords with divine will removes the fear associated with such basic and highly consequential choices. Many fundamentalist women freely and knowingly decide to relinquish power and autonomy in favor of men in order to fulfill a pattern of moral action which they believe is key to the achievement of personal salvation.[56]

Islamic Fundamentalism and the Battle for Liberation

In Iran and other Islamic regions where fundamentalism has prospered, fundamentalism has frequently arisen in conjunction with nationalism, anticolonialism, and anti-Westernism. Women have been expected to join in the battle for liberation. Both sexes attribute sacred significance to the struggle for liberation from foreign domination, and they saturate their ideals for the newly independent nation with religious meaning. Men have expected that women will support the struggle for liberation.[57] Fundamentalist women typically see the priority of solidarity with men in service to national liberation as having far greater preeminence than any other claims, including the enhancement of women's rights. They see the oppression of a colonizer or a despot ruling as the client of Western powers as a much greater source of oppression than anything inflicted upon them by their own menfolk.[58]

Fundamentalist women tend to analyze male violence against women as rooted in the greater evil of Western imperialism or colonialism, and, when challenged by Western feminists to create bonds of solidarity with other women, they have rejected that call. Women who have rejected fundamentalism in favor of global feminism have been attacked as "dupes of imperialism," stigmatized not only on all the religious grounds brought to bear on women who violate fundamentalism's codes, but as traitors to the cause of national liberation as well.[59] However, fundamentalist men expect that once the battle has been won, women will return to "traditional lifestyles," that is, that women will return to childbearing, traditional dress, respect for men, and traditional marriage practices. This the men view as putting the world back into its rightful order.[60]

The Contest for Control of Female Sexuality

As we have seen, fundamentalist movements have paid special attention to questions of sexuality, especially female sexuality. Female sexuality tends to be seen as hindering male spiritual perfection, an idea which also finds support historically in certain non-fundamentalist expressions of Christianity, Islam, and Buddhism. Female sexuality is in some contexts viewed as dangerous: polluting, liable to bewitch men, causing them to lose all dignity, reason, and self-respect, and thus leading to the ruin of the family and the downfall of the nation.

These ideas take on a new semiological dimension for fundamentalist movements formed in a society's encounter with the cultural and economic hegemony of the West in its own struggle to modernize. The powerful image of the Western woman, supposedly the incarnation of sexual liberty and licentiousness, has alternately been a potent inducement toward, and has also provoked reactions of revulsion against, the transformation of power and authority occurring in the central government of a nation and within communities and families in the course of fundamental social change. Achieving stronger control over indigenous women's sexuality is, in the eyes of some fundamentalist ideologues, an indispensable key to preserving the spiritual integrity of the nation and of the religion.

In relation to the West or to former colonial overlords, men may experience themselves as unfairly "feminized," rendered passive and powerless. A struggle to overcome those conditions ensues through an exaggerated masculinism, manifested by rituals of male bonding and by highlighting such marks of male gender as beards, and restricting the wearing of trousers or other types of male dress to men.[61] Strict boundaries are drawn between appropriate male and female behavior in all areas, thus aiding men in casting off all taint of the feminine. In this struggle against spiritual emasculation, woman is cast as the immediate and proximate "other" over and against whom men must define themselves, whose domination men must assure, even by force, even though for the most part the men remain powerless to confront a colonial or imperialist power.

In nationalist, anticolonialist, or anti-Western wars of liberation, the struggle to masculinize male patriots is coextensive with the effort to legitimize local "tradition" against the powerful appeals of Western rationalism and materialism. We have seen how women are closely aligned with tradition and how they become its custodians and embodiments. One of the ways in which they mold themselves and are molded for this role is through distinctive constructions of female sexuality that restrict its legitimacy to reproductive service to communal liberation and which subordinate aspects of female sexuality which do not make such a contribution, such as pleasure and play. The coercive means of exercising this control are coextensive with the sanctions discussed above. Equally important, however, are women's own constructions of the religious meaning of their sexuality in light of the imperative of communal liberation. While these vary widely, they share the belief that improvement of their condition as women must await the achievement of communal freedom from oppression.

Haeri's essay shows, for example, how fundamentalist readings of Islamic (principally Shi'ite) law use sexuality to epitomize women's entire being. Women's sexuality in this discourse is only imperfectly separated from their persons. Since marriage asymmetrically assigns to men rights in women's sexual and reproductive potential, these potentials become commoditized and fetishized. Female sexuality becomes objectified, as the object of male control, which enhances "men's sense of power and virility" through being made a commodity to be wielded, desired, controlled, accumulated (through polygamy), secluded, and (in divorce) repudiated and discarded.

Throughout the Islamic world, the veil has been an especially potent symbol. During the early twentieth century, the period of Westernizing reforms in many Islamic nations, the veil was to be discarded: "The modernists saw the veil as a mark of women's seclusion and backwardness; Jamal Sudki Azza Khawy who, in Iraq in 1911, advocated doing away with the veil, was imprisoned for sedition. The act of throwing off the veil, regarded as a symbol of feudalism, was given great significance, and occasions when prominent women appeared unveiled became dramatic moments of defiance of the old order."[62]

In the 1980s, however, veiling was increasingly strictly required, the more so the stronger fundamentalism's influence, and the minutiae of its application subjected to increasingly thorough scrutiny, so that to "well veil" or to "bad veil" became a sign of a woman's degree of compliance with the Iranian regime as a whole.[63] In spite of tightening controls, Haeri shows, women continued to use the veil as a form of covert resistance, asserting their autonomy through such mildly seductive variations as the use of colored scarves, veils with gold and silver threads, and veils wrapped to display a few strands of platinum hair. Nevertheless, the penalties for going too far under the Iranian regime were set in a 1989 law at seventy-four lashes and incarceration.

Andrea Rugh's essay includes a remarkable survey of advice columns from contemporary Egyptian newspapers. This wide-ranging survey shows a persistent concern with women's correct behavior. This is in fact the area attracting the largest volume of letters from the perplexed to Islamic advisers. Husbands inquiring how to handle a wife's "disobedience" are told first to withhold sexual contact, and to beat them if the problem persists. This recommendation is justified because of Allah's creation of men as superior to women. A woman inquiring whether she may refuse the sexual advances of her drug-addicted husband is told that "she must fulfill her husband's desires whenever they occur." Women must have male approval for employment. A woman whose perfume excites a male is herself guilty of adultery. A woman's entire body except for the hands and face is genital—all of it must be covered. In one case genital mutilation is affirmed as a practice which decreases female sexual desire.

Haeri and Rugh discuss Islamic fundamentalist movements arising within the larger phenomenon of Islamic resurgence. These movements have one important source in the desire of Islamic societies to establish their own cultural and political authority by throwing off the cultural and political imperialism of the West. It is not the case, however, that all fundamentalist groups arise in such a matrix.

In Latin America, as Jorge Maldonado explains, Pentecostal churches do not link the restoration of the family and the ordering of personal lives with the reform of larger social and political structures. These structures are, in the Pentecostal view, not able to inhibit the real work of religion, which is the saving of souls and the rebuilding of individual lives. If Pentecostals are in the business of "remaking" more than personal lives and family structures, Maldonado suggests, it may be said that they are remaking religion itself in Latin America. The oppositional character of these movements, which provides their few analogues to fundamentalist movements elsewhere, seems to turn on the relationship between the newly converted evangelical Christians and their erstwhile religious home, Roman Catholicism. Maldonado describes the new converts as having been spiritually and socially malnourished in an institutional setting that preached "traditional values" but did relatively little to help (a nonrevolutionary) people adjust, on the mundane level, to changing economic conditions, including the opportunity for upward social mobility. Sensing the need and moving into the gap, evangelical preachers offer a program for socioeconomic and religious mobilization that weds traditional verities to an egalitarian work ethic.

Contemporary Mormon fundamentalism, identified with pockets of diehard polygamists living in small communities in the American West, seem to be among those who have profited least from the ethic of mainstream Mormonism, which has been so successful in facilitating upward mobility through individual abstemiousness and tight-knit networks of mutual support. The fundamentalist polygamists are marginalized from such networks, and Quinn describes most of them as poor. Ostracized from the church by excommunication, Mormon polygamists nevertheless attempt to extend mutual support and patronage among themselves. Plural wives are a necessity for status among the men; says one polygamist who has five wives, "Some of the groups kind of have the idea that the more wives you have the more power, authority, whatever," while another says that some groups of polygamists, "figure that anybody who's the head of a group ought to have seven wives."

Marriage is frequently arranged by the male elders of these groups, with little scope for youth, especially girls, to reject a match planned for them. Women's authority in marriage is further undermined by the practice of arranging marriages for women with husbands much older than themselves. Since contraceptive use is disapproved, women are further deprived of control over reproduction.

Surrounded by American culture's obsession with sexual jealousy, this topic provides a major dynamic of family life. Only women are called upon to accept a partner's multiple sexual relationships, and Mormon polygamous women are called upon to sublimate this emotion, to transform it into a deeper attachment to the man. A byproduct of enhanced ties to her fellow plural wives sometimes emerges, but these are inevitably premised on the stronger attachment to the man.

As these brief previews suggest, the essays in part 2 allow us to make provisional assessments of fundamentalism's impact to date upon family, gender roles, and interpersonal relations. As noted at the outset, the movements themselves are highly diverse, their doctrines bearing little commonality, and their origins having few if any meaningful points of contact. On the basis of the studies presented here, however, it seems clear that the impact of fundamentalist beliefs, practices, and policies regarding gender roles and family relations is comprehensive and dramatic across the board. In the majority of cases, fundamentalist influence in its severest form is felt primarily by those who adhere to the movement and thus "choose" the accompanying lifestyle. The important exception to this generalization, of course, is Iran, the case in which "fundamentalism" has come to power over the security mechanisms of the state. There, the impact of fundamentalist gender and family prescriptions at every level of society is considerable and has inspired an increasingly vocal protest movement, as Haeri documents.

Within fundamentalist enclaves in Islam, and among Christian fundamentalists in the Americas, resistance to dominant secular models of family and interpersonal relations extends to the construction and strengthening of countercultural movements in which authority of men over women is enhanced, and patriarchal gender structures are sanctified and sanctioned. Indeed in these growing fundamentalist cultures the mission of establishing a divinely ordained social order takes the program of "restoring the traditional family" as its microcosmic blueprint. And it is in this "private" zone of secularized societies that fundamentalists have enjoyed their greatest success in reclaiming the world they suppose to have existed before the troubling advent of secular modernity.

Notes

1. Quoted in James Davison Hunter, *Evangelicalism: The Coming Generation* (Chicago: University of Chicago Press, 1987), p. 82.

2. Jerry Falwell, *Listen, America!* (Bantam Books: New York, 1981), pp. 110–11.

3. Quoted in Rebecca Klatsch, *Women of the New Right* (Philadelphia: Temple University Press, 1987), pp. 44–45.

4. Susan Rose, "Women Warriors: The

Negotiation of Gender in a Charismatic Community," *Sociological Analysis* 48 (1987): 245–58.

5. Quoted in Hunter, *Evangelicalism,* p. 78.

6. Ibid., p. 80.

7. Ibid.

8. See, for example, Amy L. Bentley, "Comforting the Motherless Children: The Alice Louise Reynolds Women's Forum," *Dialogue* 23 (1990): 39–61.

9. Quoted in Hunter, *Evangelicalism,* p. 82.

10. Ibid., p. 85.

11. Ibid., pp. 89–90.

12. Ibid., p. 90.

13. "[When] contemporary Evangelicals (preachers, spokesmen, family experts, lobbyists, and politicians) speak of the Christian family, the traditional family, or traditional values, they are really referring to the prototypical nineteenth-century bourgeois family. Its structure of relationships (nuclear), its quality of relationships (the place of intimacy and sentiment), and even its place and function in the modern world (family as utopian retreat) are all idealized in similar ways" (ibid., p. 92).

14. Ibid.

15. Quoted in Klatsch, *Women of the New Right,* p. 126.

16. It had been the pattern among (mostly Caucasian) "higher-paid skilled workers and professionals," and even there women's employment helped support the family, so that the economic dependence of women and children on men obscured the dependence of men on women's work. Around 1900 in New York City only about half the total number of households were composed of nuclear families. In lower-class families children's labor helped support the family, and in immigrant, black, and Hispanic families married women typically worked outside the home. Cf. Amy Swerdlow et al., *Household and Kin: Families in Flux* (New York: Feminist Press, 1981), p. 34.

17. Ibid.

18. Laurie Becklund, "The Word Family Gains New Meaning," *Los Angeles Times,* 13 December 1990, pp. A3, A34.

19. "The only . . . quality which comes close to transcending the vagaries of historical change in the past two millennia has been [the family's] hierarchal nature. An intractable form of patriarchy has characterized family organization for virtually all of this time" (Hunter, *Evangelicalism,* p. 113). "A strong form of patriarchal rule . . . typified the preindustrial family type, requiring total submission from children and wife" (ibid., p. 84). Children in the Middle Ages viewed their father with fear and respect and were taught to behave with such formality and awe that the familiarity often experienced in the twentieth century would have been unimaginable. The pattern persisted in the American Puritan family of the seventeenth century.

20. Ibid., p. 89.

21. Martin Riesebrodt, "Fundamentalism and the Political Mobilization of Women" (Paper presented at the 85th Annual Meeting of the American Sociological Association, Washington, D.C., 11-15 August 1990).

22. Bruce Lawrence, *Defenders of God: The Fundamentalist Revolt against the Modern Age* (San Francisco: Harper and Row, 1989), p. 236.

23. Ibid., p. 230. In the case of Islamic fundamentalism, he writes, male leaders build upon preexisting gender asymmetry, "using tradition as an excuse to exclude women from the public sphere even though it is the prevalence of unemployed men vying with one another for the few available jobs that reinforces the need to curtail women's professional horizons" (p. 237).

24. For a detailed discussion of fundamentalist child-rearing by a social critic of the movement, see Philip Greven, *Spare the Child: The Religious Roots of Punishment and the Psychological Impact of Physical Abuse* (New York: Alfred A. Knopf, 1991), pp. 46–96. Also, see Alan Peshkin, *God's Choice: The Total World of a Fundamentalist Christian School* (Chicago: University of Chicago Press, 1986); also, Tim Heaton,

"Four Characteristics of the Mormon Family: Contemporary Research on Chastity, Conjugality, Children, and Chauvinism," *Dialogue* 20 (1987): 101–14.

25. Donald G. Matthews and Jane Sherron DeHart, *Sex, Gender, and the Politics of the ERA* (New York: Oxford University Press, 1990), p. 176.

26. See Peshkin, *God's Choice*.

27. See Hunter, *Evangelicalism*. Hunter found considerable deviation in student opinion on a variety of family-related issues from the rigid ideals expressed by fundamentalist leaders. Thus it is not the case that young fundamentalists are necessarily molded precisely in the image of their religious leaders and spokespersons.

28. Lawrence, *Defenders of God*, p. 232.

29. Martin E. Marty and R. Scott Appleby, "Conclusion: An Interim Report on a Hypothetical Family," in Marty and Appleby, eds., *Fundamentalisms Observed* (Chicago: University of Chicago Press, 1991).

30. See Lawrence, *Defenders of God*, chap. 8.

31. Ester Boserup, *Women's Role in Economic Development* (New York: St. Martin's Press, 1970).

32. See Frederick Engels, *The Origin of the Family, Private Property, and the State*, ed. E. B. Leacock (New York: International Publishers, 1972), pp. 123, 137–38; also, Boserup, *Women's Role*.

33. Engels, *Origin of the Family*, p. 137.

34. Kumari Jayawardena, *Feminism and Nationalism in the Third World* (London: Zed Books, Ltd., 1986), pp. 15–17.

35. Lawrence, *Defenders of God*.

36. Marty and Appleby, "An Interim Report."

37. See Boserup, *Women's Role*.

38. Eric Hobsbawm and Terence Ranger, *The Invention of Tradition* (New York: Cambridge University Press, 1983), pp. 1–14.

39. Andrea B. Rugh, "Reshaping Personal Relations: Islamic Resurgence in Egypt," in this volume.

40. See Adele K. Ferdows, "Women and the Islamic Revolution," *International Journal of Middle Eastern Studies* 15 (1983): 283–98.

41. Riesebrodt, "Fundamentalism and the Political Mobilization of Women."

42. Jayawardena, *Feminism and Nationalism*, pp. 14–15.

43. See Leila Ahmed, "Western Ethnocentrism and Perceptions of the Harem," *Feminist Studies* 8 (1982): 521–34; also, Richard T. Antoun, "On the Modesty of Women in Arab Muslim Villages: A Study in the Accommodation of Traditions," *American Anthropologist* 70 (1968): 67–97; also, Marlene Dobkin, "Social Ranking in the Woman's World of Purdah: A Turkish Example," *Anthropological Quarterly* 40 (1967): 65–72; also, Hannah Papanek, "Purdah: Separate Worlds and Symbolic Shelter," *Comparative Studies in Society and History* 15 (1973): 289–325; also, Carrol Pastner, "Accommodations to Purdah: The Female Perspective," *Journal of Marriage and the Family* 36 (1974): 408–14; Nadia H. Youseff, "The Status and Fertility Pattern of Muslim Women," in Lois Beck and Nikki Keddie, eds., *Women in the Muslim World* (Cambridge: Harvard University Press, 1978); also, M. Abu-Zahra, "On the Modesty of Women in Arab Muslim Villages: A Reply," *American Anthropoligist* 72 (1970): 1079–92.

44. See Ferdows, "Women and the Islamic Revolution"; also, Patricia J. Higgens, "Women in the Islamic Republic of Iran: Legal, Social, and Ideological Changes," *Signs: Journal of Women in Culture and Society* 10 (1985): 477–94.

45. See Vern L. Bullough, *The Subordinate Sex* (Baltimore: Penquin Books, 1973); also, Nawal el Saadawi, *Women and Sex* (Beruit, 1972); also, Nazirah Zein Ed-Din, "Removing the Veil and Veiling," trans. Salah-Dine Hammoud, reprinted in *Women's Studies International Forum* 5 (1982): 221–26; also, Andrea Rugh, *Reveal and Conceal: Dress in Contemporary Egypt* (Syracuse: Syracuse University Press, 1984).

46. See Kathleen Barry, *Female Sexual Slavery* (Englewood Cliffs, N.J.: Prentice-Hall, 1979); also, Rose D. Hayes, "Female Genital Mutilation, Fertility Control, Women's Role and the Patrilineage in Modern

Sudan," *American Ethnologist* 2 (1975): 617–33; also, Nawal el Saadawi, *The Hidden Face of Eve: Women in the Arab World*, trans. Sherif Hetata (Boston: Beacon Press, 1980); also, Fran P. Hosken, *The Hoskin Report: Genital/Sexual Mutilation of Females* (Boston: Women's International Network News, 1978); also, Lillian Passmore Sanderson, *Against the Mutilation of Women* (London: Ithaca Press, 1981).

47. Thus fundamentalism restricts women's access to occupations that can be expected to produce high income and hence create the condition in which women could become economically independent and reject the role of personifier of tradition. See Lawrence, *Defenders of God*, p. 237.

48. See also Abdul Fadl Mohsin Ebrahim, "Islamic Teachings and Surrogate Motherhood," *Journal for the Study of Religion* 3 (1990): 35–45.

49. Elizabeth Elliot, *Let Me Be a Woman*.

50. Quoted in Fowler, p. 206.

51. Hunter, *Evangelicalism*, pp. 91–106; Rose, "Women Warriors."

52. Higgens, "Women in the Islamic Republic," pp. 492–94.

53. Quoted in Fowler, pp. 207–8.

54. See Guity Nashat, *Women and Revolution in Iran* (Boulder, Colo.: Westview Press, 1983); also, Farah Azari, *Women of Iran: The Conflict with Fundamentalist Islam* (London: Ithaca Press, 1983).

55. See Martha S. Bradley, "The Women of Fundamentalism: Short Creek, 1953," *Dialogue* 23 (1990): 14–37.

56. See Rose, "Women Warriors"; also, Alison Walker, "Theological Foundations of Patriarchy," *Dialogue* 23 (1990): 77–89.

57. Jayawardena, *Feminism and Nationalism*, pp. 12–13.

58. Amal Jou'beh, "Women and Politics: Reflections from Nairobi," in Miranda Davies, ed., *Third World, Second Sex* (London: Zed Books, Ltd., 1987), p. 53.

59. Ibid.

60. Omani Women's Organization, "Women and Revolution in Oman," in Davies, *Third World, Second Sex*, p. 119; also, Jayawardena, *Feminism and Nationalism*.

61. See Higgens, "Women in the Islamic Republic," p. 490.

62. Jayawardena, *Feminism and Nationalism*, p. 13.

63. See Valerie J. Hoffman-Ladd, "Polemics on the Modesty and Segregation of Women in Contemporary Egypt," *International Journal of Middle East Studies* 19 (1987): 23–50.

Reshaping Personal Relations in Egypt

Andrea B. Rugh

A central issue for all cultures is defining how individuals should relate to one another in society. Eastern and Western cultures have come to fundamentally dissimilar resolutions of this issue, the West stressing individual rights and independence and the East stressing obligation and incorporation in cooperative groups.

The thesis of this chapter is that resurgent Islam,[1] in pursuing its goals of an Islamic society, is drawing upon a tendency already present in contemporary Egypt in which individuals operate more independently from their families than has been the custom in the past. To meet everyday needs, Egyptians now must move beyond primarily kin-centered relationships to personal relationships of broader instrumentality. In steering individuals toward loyalty to the *umma,* or community of Muslim believers, fundamentalist ideology gives direction to this tendency, and ultimately encourages a reorganization of society integrated at the suprafamilial level.

Egypt's particular history has tended to strengthen family units at the expense of efficient organization at other levels. Religious movements are uniquely equipped in this respect to redefine personal loyalties toward the higher entity of community without destroying the stability that comes from strong family institutions. This process works better under two conditions: if adherents become convinced of the higher morality that accompanies personal loyalty to the wider religious community, and if, on the practical level, that loyalty is rewarded with greater access to goods and services the individual needs to survive and prosper. When these two conditions are met, families are also indirectly compensated for the weakening that occurs when members devote more of their energies to outside loyalties. Thus Islamic resurgence ideologies are reshaping the way individuals of the mainstream behave in Egyptian society, both as social beings and as family members. This chapter is divided into three parts: a section detailing the historical and structural antecedents of contemporary personal and family relations in Egypt; a section describing Islamic resurgence views of personal relations as seen through one channel for communicating these ideas—the answers by religious and moral authorities to readers' letters in newspapers; and a conclusion summarizing themes concerning the impact of the Islamic resurgence on social relations. Ultimately, these new behaviors may profoundly change the character of Egyptian society. In such a study, however, it is difficult to know how much the ideas of the movement are a reflection of contemporary thinking and how much they influence it.

Islamic Resurgence in Egypt

The following event occurred in 1990. A man mistakenly entered the less crowded women's car of the Cairo metro. A woman shouted at him to leave and continued to grumble about the evils of men, including their desire to take more than one wife. "If the Prophet were alive today," she declared, "he would prohibit men from marrying more than one at a time." Several women exchanged comments about her remarks, and one muttered angrily that she was being blasphemous and should be quiet, "especially since it's Friday." Others shook their heads in agreement. "Just look at the Christians," she continued, "they are better people than we are because they only marry one in their lives." A university student, dressed in Islamic style, leapt to her feet trembling and declared that she would not tolerate any more of this kind of talk. The student's sister led her weeping to the other end of the car. Another young woman shouted that no one can be a true Muslim who talks in this way. The infuriated speaker charged down the aisle and yanked the young woman from her seat: "Look at this whore who says I am not a Muslim; look at her!" The speaker then pointed out, one after another, discrepancies between her own modest attire and that of the young woman: the knee-length dress, high-heeled shoes, uncovered head and made-up face. The young woman sheepishly replied that her dress had nothing to do with the extent of her faith and got off at the next stop, continuing to defend her position to another passenger who also got off at that stop. The car remained in an uproar until the crowd gradually dispersed at their various stops.

The story illustrates how close religion is to the surface in present-day Egypt. For the vast majority of Egyptians, it is not a question of whether a person is seriously committed to religion but rather the degree of that commitment and how it is expressed. The late 1980s and early 1990s provided insurmountable evidence of that preoccupation: attempts to return the country to full Islamic law; repeal of the liberalizing 1979 law of personal status; the effort to legislate Islam as the major basis for the Constitution; laws proposed in the People's Assembly relating to the early retirement of women government workers, to the imprisonment of those who publicly broke the Ramadan fast, and many other Islamic practices; greater emphasis on Islamic studies in public school curricula; lively discussion of religious issues in books and periodicals; and the growing strength of religious candidates in elections. Recognizably "religious dress" could be seen everywhere, and special places (prayer areas, sex-segregated classroom spaces) and times (for prayers and religious meetings) became such an integral part of public life that they were no longer noticed. On the way to work men and women read the Qur'an, and in the market the fez makers converted some of their business to making fashionable pill box hats to serve as a base for anchoring veils. More ominous were the increasing clashes between Muslims and Christians, leading to deep rifts between the communities. The ubiquitous reminders of religion made it uncomfortable, if not unwise, for anyone to flaunt antireligious practices in public at any time.

Members of militant Islamic groups in Egypt have been characterized as young people from the lower middle classes, often students—especially those who temporarily or permanently reside away from their families and study in the elite faculties of medicine and engineering. Young women are extensively involved in the movements in activist positions different from the supportive roles they played as sisters and wives of the earlier Muslim Brotherhood. In Egypt, though core members tend to be urbanites, many have rural backgrounds, and disproportionately large numbers come from Upper Egypt. The age factor reveals a "youth revolt" and "a profound mood of disillusionment and frustration," while the rural-urban factor "points to a development crisis and to the tensions and pressures of recent immigration into decaying cities that have serious and escalating problems."[2] These militants engage the debate about the present failings of government and generate many of the understandings about Islam that eventually filter into mainstream thinking. Though they are a minority, they nonetheless keep the pot boiling with acts of violence against government authorities and Christians.[3]

Individuals appear to find Islamic movements most compelling for psychosocial reasons.[4] Young people feel that modern society ignores their economic and cultural interests: they have difficulty finding appropriate employment, and their success tends to be measured in terms of Western values and lifestyles. Islam provides a non-Western alternative for them, and generally for a society seeking an indigenous solution to local social ills. These messages particularly appeal to students of science and math who have been most subjected to Western culture and education without opportunity for criticism and evaluation. As in most Arab countries, these and other subjects are taught by rote, a method which prepares students to accept without question the literal messages of religion. Young people of modest backgrounds aspiring to higher levels in the class hierarchy and those dislocated from rural backgrounds face moral temptation and loneliness as they shift between two worlds within their own society. Religion offers an approved way to satisfy the need for moral certitude and belonging. Also the Islamic movements provide women who wear the prescribed dress and behave in the approved manner a sense of security against censure, and a ready-made circle of male and female acquaintances with similarly professed norms of behavior.[5]

Beyond the radical militant members, a mainstream comprising the majority of Egyptians espouses more moderate fundamentalist views of religion. This mainstream comprises elements ranging all the way from the now moderate Muslim Brotherhood, who, though proponents of political change and critical of the religious establishment, are no longer radical in their activities, through non-organized individuals, to the passive Sufi Orders who carry on popular traditions through *tariqah* (path) organizations, most active in the Egyptian countryside.[6] For the most part the mainstream is apolitical, committed to individual salvation through personal deeds rather than political activities. Its predisposition toward religion, however, means that when circumstances are right—if conditions worsen socially, economically, or politically—the mainstream becomes easier to mobilize. The members are attracted by an issue which has religious overtones and may find appealing persons who commit radical acts in pursuit of their convictions, even though the members themselves might not become involved in such acts. Politicians have learned this lesson and consequently dress all issues in religious rationales. For a politician to be perceived as antireligious, whether true or not, is tantamount to political suicide.[7]

If the numbers of women who don Islamic garb are any indication of those who have at least some nominal attachment to Islamic resurgence ideologies, then the mainstream includes Egyptians of all ages, all classes, and rural as well as urban areas, although one observer[8] identified the middle class as the core group. Developed as a class only recently, largely through education, the middle class in the 1980s found many of its members frustrated by poor pay and uninspiring work, while others became powerful through jobs in oil-rich countries. A number in both groups lost money in housing and investment swindles. Many found themselves unable to provide the same opportunities for their children that they enjoyed during the socially mobile period of the 1970s and early 1980s. Simply to remain in the middle class, the rising generation must complete long years of education, and when they emerge, it is difficult for them to find jobs that pay enough to sustain a family. The class order no longer fits older definitions, and people now speak of class on two scales—social and economic. Many with educations are socially middle class and economically lower class, or socially lower class and economically middle or upper class.

A television program which aired in January 1990, "The White Flag," presented this issue as a crisis of culture. The drama portrayed an "uncultured" but rich woman coffee-shop owner who wanted to buy the ancestral home of a "cultured" retired ambassador. She resorted to underhanded methods including bribes and bulldozers to obtain the house. In the last scene the ambassador calls on those in the audience who love culture to stand up with him and defend themselves from the encroachment of the uncultured.

The shaping of the religious perspectives of the mainstream is most interesting because it reveals the extent to which new ways of thinking can be swiftly assimilated and eventually internalized in a reorganized worldview by a large number of Egyptians. Where do those who espouse the current purist views but do not belong to formal groups obtain their guidance? Individual experience seems to vary a great deal; however, some sources for the current views are clear. At an early age, all Muslim children study religion in school, in addition, often, to religious study in mosques. They are taught by specially trained teachers, usually graduates from the parallel al-Azhar religious system. In recent years these conservative teachers have gone far beyond a rote memorization of the Qur'an that was once considered sufficient, to lectures on the correct behavior of a good Muslim. Children invariably observe the discrepancies between what the teacher says is correct behavior for a Muslim and the behavior of their parents at home, even when the parents see themselves as fully observant Muslims. In the early years the children may do no more than comment on these differences, but by the time they reach adolescence, many begin to take religion more seriously. At that age they may be attracted by the experience of an older sibling or a friend who has undergone a religious transformation. These peer leaders become informal tutors in correct religious attitudes and behaviors. At this age, the individual moves more freely through the society and finds more independent sources of information from which to form opinions. These sources include, besides the continuing discussions with peers, sermons in the mosque, religious literature (of which there is an explosion in the popular book stalls), print media articles on religion and morality, television, radio and cassette exhortations on proper religious practices, study and prayer groups, and discussions sponsored by religious institutions.

Islamic movements in Egypt in the early 1990s are rooted in the deep-seated discontent that exists in Egyptian society. At the personal level, there are numerous individual reasons for discontent, but perhaps these reasons can be summarized as converging in a climate where young people are seeking "authenticity," a search for cultural self-assertion and identity, and "participation" in the political process.[9] They not only want to be involved in changes in social life that relieve their discontents, but they want to be assured that the directions they take are "correct" by a higher moral standard. On the personal level, they want to take control of, or at least ascribe meaning to, their own lives in an atmosphere where the average individual is restricted on all sides. Many find in religion a way of making the intolerable conditions of everyday life more liveable. Institutions such as the family that previously served the major needs of young adults no longer are capable of providing comprehensive solutions to all or even many of their problems.

Resurgence movements grow out of such a social and economic context—one that for various reasons has become intolerable to many people. By drawing on familiar symbols and values, such movements are capable of mobilizing a consensus among their followers to move in what appear to be new and promising directions, offering potential solutions to the ills that affect individual lives. The process is made easier by an encapsulating ideology which clarifies and identifies approved directions for the changes.

The Shape of Family and Interpersonal Relations in Egypt

Historic Antecedents

In Egypt, the institution of the family developed a strength it might not have possessed had its history been different. Comparatively speaking, the principles and laws which governed family and personal life were left relatively untouched by the powers that ruled Egypt in the last several centuries. During this period, the state apparatus was controlled by foreigners with centralized governments much more comprehensive and impersonal than the smaller face-to-face community-based states of early Islam.

Foreign rulers were less interested in Egyptian personal family life and religion, and more interested in ways they could exert control over local populations and extract labor and taxes from them. During this period a split occurred in Egyptian society: personal life came to be controlled from within the community by institutions with a basis in Muslim law, while public life was controlled by outsiders using laws based on imported, usually Western values.

While this pattern was reasonably consistent during both Ottoman and British rule, the basis for ignoring private life, except when it converged with state interests, was different. In the Ottoman period, a convergence of religious belief between ruler and ruled saw no reason to disrupt family law and family institutions based on the same religious foundations, while in the British period, these institutions were left intact primarily because they did not challenge the basis for control of the region. The British occupiers hesitated to do anything which might affect the stability of family life, sensing that to do so might aggravate the conditions of their occupation. Consequently they modified civil, commercial, and criminal law, but left family law intact under the jurisdiction of the religious authorities.

For most Egyptians, immersion in family was a means of passive withdrawal from events over which there was, in any case, little control. Cut off from access to economic and political power and with most of daily life narrowly circumscribed by family relations, the common man came to see the fulfillment of family duties as the highest form of social and moral good. Those sycophants, on the other hand, who accommodated the rulers in exchange for influence and wealth were people known to imitate the non-Islamic dress, manners, and customs of the foreigners. It was with some pride that the term *ibn al-balad* (authentic countryman) came to denote the genuine Egyptian who remained true to his origins, a person usually from the powerless lower social classes.

There was another reason that family life flourished during this period. While governments could be expected to provide little for the masses or, at best, certain minimum services and resources, family proved a mechanism whereby the utmost good, emotional and material, might be extracted from a difficult situation. Even such seemingly finite resources as the amount of water released from government-controlled floodgates could be increased substantially through use of jointly owned pumps or cooperative efforts to keep canals clean and flowing freely. Thus, individuals cooperating, usually through close relatives where trust was greatest, were able to expand the otherwise finite inputs controlled by the government.

As part of this renascence, families took almost exclusive control over what happened to their members: marriage, employment choices, security in old age, and psychological and moral support. Because members were dependent on their families for these social goods, they were also subject to their control in moral matters. Families determined the codes of behavior for their members, based on prevailing social norms as interpreted by the older generation, especially the male patriarch, who guided the relations between family members and the outside world. Families competed with each other for moral perfection in anticipation of the rewards—marriage and power connections—which accrued to families with unblemished reputation. In this way they developed instrumentally valuable relationships to extend influence over wider areas of social and economic life.

To all intents and purposes, the growing strength of family was a pragmatic reaction during a period of foreign rule and limited access to power and resources, and had little to do with religious ideology. However, there were two ways these events affected views about religion: First, religion and religious rationales became the essential basis for the conduct of personal life, synonymous with authentic indigenous culture and opposed to establishment forces which were seen as alien. Second, neglect of the state-solidifying ideals of Islam left the community open to criticism by the purists who saw in that retreat a serious weakening in the moral bases of society. This criticism became relevant after independence, when there was no longer an alien power to provide the excuse for public resistance to the state.

At that point, the established strength of family institutions compromised efforts to build a unified nation. Individuals focusing on narrow family interests were accustomed to selfishly taking from the public offerings without returning or enhancing the welfare of the society as a whole. The self-interest of one family competing with the self-interest of other families made it impossible to come to agreement on issues which concerned them all, and therefore made it difficult to develop the cooperative modes at the extrafamilial level that are required if an economically poor country is to use its limited resources efficiently.

According to the Islamic ideal, cohesive families provide the bedrock of the society, but their strength should contribute to, rather than conflict with, the interests of the larger community of Muslims. The Prophet Muhammad frequently made this point in the sayings ascribed to him. One *hadith* reports him to have said that the blood of a Muslim can be spilt only in three instances: adultery, murder, and forsaking one's religion and abandoning the community. Membership in the religion and the community should be synonymous.

The Structure of Family and Personal Relations

As family structures provided increasingly important ways for Egyptians to cope with daily life, so, too, did the customs and practices supporting family solidarity. Though many of these customs are essentially an elaboration of culture, most are compatible with tenets of Islam supporting family roles and responsibilities. In almost every instance, these structures contrive to build a solidly corporate structure for family by reinforcing the sense of interdependence among members. Islam plays an important role in this conception because it describes in detail family roles and obligations, and because it provides a widely accepted irrefutable authority for continuing the practices that support connection between kin. More than those of other religions, Islamic truths serve as the basis for everyday cultural truths.

A group holds together better when its members feel a strong need for one another based on functional interdependence. Western societies discovered the negative of this fact when they attempted through the pursuit of equality to reduce the differences among family members so that everyone, male and female, old and young, was expected to become functionally interchangeable. Egyptian families, to the contrary, encourage difference among their members in a number of ways: by firmly believing in the complementarity of roles, including, for example, what is appropriate for males and females to do; by assigning authority differentially; and by establishing hierarchies of age and function. People depend upon others for the services they themselves cannot perform because of the unique roles each plays in the context of the family group. Family—not the individual—becomes the lowest common denominator of functional survival: physical, social, economic, and psychological. Individuals, of course, exist with their own special needs and contributions, but they exist in an implied relationship as mothers, fathers, sons, daughters, sisters, and brothers—each role with its functional requirements, and not in isolation as separated beings with needs that supersede the interests of the groups to which they belong.

Because each person's position in the Egyptian household is unique, any one individual does not expect the same treatment as that received by any other individual. The uniqueness of each person's contribution to family, and the clearly understood orders of precedence by which resources and power are distributed, works to reduce internal conflict within the family circle. Members are patient with this system because they know that by the end of the life cycle, each in turn will assume most of the roles and positions and receive appropriate shares in the resources of the group. In that respect, the system is equitable to its members and efficient in its distribution of resources. Instead of assuming that each individual should have equal access to the collective resources at any time, the system conserves these assets and distributes them unequally to members (for example, when marrying children one by one in specific order) by conditions affecting group good at the given time.

The one crosscutting characteristic that prevents the principles of hierarchy and relationship from being internally uniform for every family member is gender. The accident of a person's gender, in Egypt as elsewhere, prescribes that a person move along one ladder or the other and not both in the life cycle. Of all the social principles that reinforce the solidarity of family, however, the complementarity of sex roles is perhaps the most crucial. Women do not do men's work without some justifying rationale,[10] and men do not do women's work without risking ridicule or disrespect. As a consequence, each sex depends heavily on the other to carry out the functions he or she is not permitted to do. This fact of life even in the modern world might be rationalized as an adaptive practice in countries of limited resources and massive under- and unemployment. Investing members of one gender of the family with income-generating responsibilities serves to distribute resources to more family units and thus to more people, while the dual nature of sex roles prevents the income earners from using their economic independence to desert the family unit.

The basic differences expected of women and men in Egypt may be summarized as the classic difference between nurturing and support. Implied in this distinction is the difference between inside the family/outside the family, private/public, protected/protector. In certain respects, the distinction also includes the difference between quality and quantity. While men satisfy masculine roles to the extent that they bring in the material wherewithal for the family to survive, women gain their rewards from the way they form those offerings into a shape that makes family life pleasant. Women's relationships with others are often marked by personal services, with the emphasis on the quality with which the service is performed; men's exchanges are often more material, with an emphasis on the worth or quantity of items given.

Many societies create rules like these that integrate the group. But Egyptians, perhaps more than others, have an elaborate system of exchanges that reinforces the inequalities in close relationships. The exchanges consist of small tangible gifts, visits, services, and efforts at keeping in touch. Where groups need to be cohesive—families for example—the exchanges are complementary and unequal, subject to degree of relationship, sex, age, and other characteristics. The point in these arrangements is that no relationship is the same—each is a unique piece of the puzzle that is required for the total picture to emerge. As is true for age hierarchies, the fairness in the system comes through completing the life cycle with the full complement of relatives available so that the rights and obligations of a single individual are balanced. Variation in the way people perceive their obligations to others keeps these arrangements from becoming too static.

Relationships with persons outside the family are more fluid in the sense that they can be turned on and off and do not hold the same kind of permanence as kin relations. Unless the persons involved are of distinctly different status, these exchanges with friends are more likely than those with kin to be fairly equal in nature (cakes for cakes among office colleagues). Since the exchanges are equal, or accelerating at approximately equal rates, the net advantage would appear to be zero. However, in the strictest utilitarian sense, individual A may have access to the services of a doctor which he or she can pass on to B, while B knows someone who can obtain rationed goods without standing in long lines. By exchanging influence, both friends come off better in the long run. A strong social sense encourages people to build relationships on all fronts, even when it is not immediately clear what instrumental roles people might play for each other in the future.

The "traditional" mode of implementing relationships rests heavily on ensuring that kin connections—both close and not so close—are kept sufficiently strong to ensure the instrumental needs of families. In rural areas, where the major bulk of the Egyptian population lived until recently, farming families relied on household work groups for most of their needs and on extended kin when a larger work force or more capital was required. Other relationships, of a marketing or business nature, were limited to a few trusted individuals. The full complement of relatives was present locally to allow exchanges to be carried out continuously and according to expectation.

In the contemporary world, conditions which reinforce the solidarity of families are either absent or confined to family units of very narrow circumference. Extended kin may no longer live in physical proximity with other family members, and may no longer feel that they share overlapping social, economic, and political interests. Moreover, virtually all the activities required for a normal urban existence in the modern world—preparing official documents, finding housing and employment, locating reasonably priced doctors or plumbers, and so forth—are often not easily accomplished through kin connections. It may prove more convenient to establish relationships with friends who have access to the needed services. Friends tend to be located close by, and the favors extended to them are finite and equally returned, whereas relatives may be cultivated for years without making any substantial contribution to a person's daily needs. Compounding the weakening of family ties are the potentially individu-alizing effects of education, conditions of urban housing and employment, and tem-porary or permanent migration away from family members and communities of origin.

If much of the strength of family relationships depends on mechanisms which create an interdependence of family members, then circumstances of contemporary life which have weakened the effects of these mechanisms have also weakened familial relationships and have not replaced them with relationships that command the same kind of moral force. The old equity in unbalanced exchanges that depended on a complete network of relatives participating in exchanges has been lost to the prohibi-tive costs of time, distance, and energy. In this confusion all generations feel like losers—older people because they no longer receive the respect due them under the earlier rules, and younger people because of insecurity about futures their parents can no longer guarantee. In the way the society, including most importantly the education system, is constructed, the younger generation still expects to look to "authorities" for answers. Who are these authorities in contemporary Egypt who have the answers? Who can establish a new moral order for what is right and wrong in a complicated world where families no longer solve all the problems of their members?

These developments set the stage for leaders who express strong moral positions to appear and reorganize social relations on a more promising footing. Leaders of Islamic movements, as well as others who attempt to set the moral tone for contem-porary Egypt, are aware of these conditions and make use of this knowledge when appealing to and holding their audiences.

Reshaping Personal Relations through Islam

Emphasis on an Islamic Model

Islamic resurgence is not new to Egypt. Over the last century it has proved a recurring theme as Muslim writers and scholars have tried to reconcile deeply held Islamic cul-tural values with secular values encroaching from other sources. Muslims consider the Qur'an (the holy word of Allah) and the Sunna (the conduct of the Prophet) the perfect model for society and the conduct of personal affairs. Over time, societies introduce corruptions into the model that need to be rooted out. "Revitalization movements were necessary to bring communal and individual realities into line with the basic norms and values of the belief system," to bring them back, in other words, to a more authentic and genuine Islam.[11] The present resurgence of Islam in Egypt should not be construed, therefore, as an attempt to re-create the conditions of an earlier period; rather, it should be seen as using the important mechanism for social change, *ijtihad* (interpretation), to apply the perfect model to existing conditions.[12] Thus the core issue at stake in the movements is not resistance to social change, but rather the identification of a course in the modern world compatible with Islamic values and models.

Hasan al-Banna founded the Muslim Brotherhood organization in 1928. The Brotherhood advocated a return to a stricter interpretation of the Qur'an, and though they did not reject modernization, they were against the Westernization and seculari-zation of Muslim society. The Brotherhood was officially disbanded and many of its leaders jailed under the Nasser regime; it only reemerged in the 1970s when Sadat saw in the movement a way to offset leftist and Nasserist political trends in the coun-try. When members of the Brotherhood emerged from prison, they had split into a moderate group willing to accommodate the established government and a group that rejected as true Muslims all those associated with the persecution of fellow Muslims in jail. Many of the anti-establishment group went to the oil states to earn money that later funded some of the present militant groups of the movement. As the most recent antecedents of present-day Islamic resurgence (and still part of it), the Muslim Broth-erhood was important in setting precedent for practices still at the top of the agenda in the 1990s: an emphasis on living a personal life of faith and Islamic practice, a sense of broad community among Muslims, political efforts to establish an Islamic state, and the provision through mosques of a network of social services.

In helping contemporary Egyptians sort out their lives, Islamic ideologies serve a mediating role at three levels: they redefine and set priorities for people's relationship to the Muslim community, to family members, and, finally, to God.

Creating Muslim Community

Perhaps the most significant influence of contemporary Islamic resurgence movements is the guidance they provide to individuals seeking to establish a different relationship with society.[13] It would be inaccurate to characterize all aspects of this change as intended. Rather, many are by-products of activities aimed at creating a model Islamic society. To provide the consensus and coordination required for such a society re-quires redirecting personal loyalties from family to the larger entity of Muslim com-munity. It is convenient for those who are motivated toward political change in the movements that the concept of umma is so central to Islamic philosophy and can be seized upon as an issue that was ignored during the period of foreign rule. This gives an irrefutable moral base for the call to community as well as an acceptable scapegoat for earlier deviations from the model.

There are three ways that fundamentalist thought and practice support a change in the relationship of individuals to society: first, by stressing the individual's obliga-tion to the umma; second, by providing activities and services whereby members come to depend upon each other and see their interests overlapping; and, third, by defining the boundaries of community, that is, identifying the "external enemy" or those who are different from "us." While continuing to reinforce the importance of family roles—being a good wife, husband, parent, and child according to Islamic prescriptions—religious spokespersons also encourage followers to feel the special relationship that exists between themselves and Muslims everywhere. The important question is how successful this transfer of individual loyalties will be, or whether it may ultimately result in the kind of Islamic society and state envisioned by the fundamentalists.

An example of how fundamentalist groups ease this transformation from kin-based to religious-based social groupings is found in the way some of the groups are organized. Single cells of the organization are built around a core of individuals possessing traditional ties of kinship, while other members are recruited to the group on the basis of friendship and student acquaintance. To cement the sense of trust and mutual connection, these organizations are called brotherhoods and sisterhoods, drawing on the warmth of the family image that is so pervasive in Egyptian life. Sadat and other politicians also employed similar analogies: "I am the Father of the Country and you are my children. Would a father do anything to harm his children?"

El Guindi says of the resurgence that there exists "a social cultural collectivity of active Muslim women and men manifesting characteristics of a community within society at large." [14] She points out that the term *al-jama'a*—appearing synonymously in the hadith with the term *umma*—means "wife, family, or home" in the vernacular. Islamic groups are blurring the distinction between jama'a and umma, in some contexts using the first to mean "representatives" and the second to mean "the entire community of believers." [15] The general use of the word in 1990 to mean "family" is one evidence of the extent to which, in recent history, small kin units have usurped the role of community in Egypt. Reverting to an older meaning of a word with such positive contemporary meanings has advantages: "community" members invest their extrafamilial relationships with the sense of solidarity and mutual interest expected among family members and at the same time preserve a proper family atmosphere for activities where both sexes commingle.

How does one join this larger Muslim community? Membership does not necessarily require active participation in organized groups. El Guindi distinguishes between the mainstream, which is invisibly bounded by its ideology without physical isolation, and militant groups, which physically retreat from both mainstream society and the mainstream movement. [16] "One 'joins' . . . via internal transformation which occurs spontaneously to individuals, removing them spiritually, intellectually, and ideologically from mainstream society, even as they remain in it physically. A person continues to live at home with the family but lives 'beyond' with other Muslims in the wider community of Islam. Once an individual by volition or analytic thought, has reached a state of *iqtina* (conviction), he/she is then *multazim(a)* . . . a member. As a member one adheres to ritual rigidity, behavioral, verbal and dress prescription, and to the strict avoidance taboo between the sexes." [17] A woman usually signifies this crossing over by donning the *zey il-islami,* the recognized religious dress, and, as her states of conviction intensify, the changes may be made visible through additions to the dress—a longer skirt, a looser fit, a covered head and throat, subdued colors, gloves, face covering, and so forth. [18]

Removal from family life may be actual as well as metaphysical. In an example from the central Delta, young people from the four main families in the town organized their own mosque in competition with the four mosques which were supported individually by their own families. The youth behave as though they comprise one family and set rigid rules about who can join their mosque. They help each other marry, sometimes without the approval of their parents, and set limits on the amounts that need to be paid for marriage. The mosque contains rooms that can be rented inexpensively for marriage. This example illustrates the importance of peer groups in drawing individuals of the younger generation away from the exclusive control of parents. Parents no longer hold the rewards—marriage, money, and employment— that once encouraged compliance with their moral authority.

There is an element of generational rebellion in the removal from family, whether spiritual or actual. Rebellious young people have the choice of carrying out in secret activities disapproved by their parents, or they can openly pursue a religious life as a sign of their disapproval of the secular lives of their parents. Both choices preserve the relationship, however tenuously, since neither puts the child in a position where parents can easily disapprove the behavior. It sets the young people apart from the views of their parents, however, and prepares them for further removal to groups more compatible with their own way of thinking. It is ironic that parents who grew up in the prefundamentalist era are more liberal and pragmatic in their views than their children. Many are of a generation when women were coming out of seclusion and considered the removal of the veil liberating;[19] they are unhappy to see their daughters "undoing" their gains. Others, feeling guilty about their possible failings in religion and wanting to keep in touch with their children, open themselves to direction in religious matters. It is not unusual, for example, for mothers who dress in the Islamic style to say they adopted this practice at the urging of their daughters. In such cases, a reversal of the usual parent-child roles occurs where children become the models for proper religious observance.[20]

Fundamentalists have institutionalized a number of public practices which encourage a conformity of view and in many cases an identity with Muslim community. While fifteen years ago it was a conscious and courageous decision to demonstrate fundamentalist views openly, in 1990 those who refrain from demonstrating commitment are considered rebellious. Parental resistance to "radicalism" has lessened, and many now encourage children to conform to what have become public norms in Islamic dress and behavior. Similarly, young people who adopted resurgent values in the 1970s out of strong conviction and sometimes at great personal sacrifice have now become parents themselves and are consciously raising their children to hold fundamentalist views. The practices these young people established in pursuit of their beliefs have become a regular part of daily life: separately designated spaces and facilities for males and females in public places at the university and in schools; the cessation of classes at prayer times; and since October 1989, one car per train of the metro for the exclusive use of women.

Internal migrations of rural populations to urban areas, which infused Egyptian cities from the 1940s through the 1960s with the comparatively gentle traditionalism of the peasant, were replaced during the 1970s and 1980s with the influences of the more austere Wahhabi fundamentalism brought by Egyptians returning from work in Saudi Arabia. The visible economic successes of the religiously conservative Saudis contributed to Egyptian belief that the problems at home were a reflection of Allah's displeasure with a nation weak in faith. This early admiration for the Saudis recently has been waning as people come to believe that the ostentatious observance of religion in public may mask immoral behaviors carried out in private.

On their side, Saudis, fearful of the extremism of Middle Eastern militants, support establishment groups like al-Azhar, allowing them to flourish on their own in the climate of fundamentalism. As a result, in the first half of the 1980s, while the modern primary system in Egypt expanded by 26 percent, the al-Azhar primary system of education, though still small by comparison, increased by 65 percent. The system is expected to feel even greater demand as regular universities limit their expansion, and al-Azhar University guarantees exclusive and automatic admission to those who come up through its primary and secondary systems. This expansion may have far-reaching effects on the education of the next generation. Al-Azhar University, where students after the 1967 war were said to have initiated the present wave of fundamentalism, has been receptive to some of the most extreme effects of fundamentalist views on educational programs, such as the debate over whether female doctors should be able to study the reproductive system, and the requirement that postdoctoral students demonstrate an ability to recite the Qur'an from memory before admission.[21] Overall, fundamentalist views are spreading rather than abating, producing an identity of view, even within the moderating ranks of the mainstream, that makes the creation of Muslim community easier.

The second way loyalty to Muslim community is fostered is through activities which bring individuals into contact with other Muslims, and give them a sense that their interests and the interests of the community are synonymous. Increasingly, private mosques are providing this focus for the community. Estimates vary widely, but most observers believe that between two-thirds and three-quarters of the mosques in Egypt today are supported by private funds,[22] many by money earned in the oil-rich states, others by the growing tendency to contribute *zakat* (alms) directly to religious establishments (rather than privately to a needy *booāb*—gatekeeper—or a poor widow with children), and some by owners who construct the mosques as parts of new buildings to take advantage of tax breaks given by the government. Some of these mosques confine their activities to routine religious services, while a few others (such as the famous complex of Mustafa Mahmud, and the much longer service of a private mosque in Maadi) have histories of providing other kinds of services to their members over several decades. Many private mosques have expanded into services that compete directly with less efficient and lower quality public services. Services may include the provision of subsidized clothing and food, health care, regular educational programs (usually at the preprimary or primary level), after-school tutoring for children, religious instruction, subsidies for students, evening courses, social group activities, Qur'an reading sessions, and special programs for religious holidays. In poor areas, mosque representatives hand out free food, clothing, and money in exchange, as one poor woman put it, "for our wearing proper Islamic dress." Money can also be borrowed through Islamic banks in the approved "profit sharing" way where a fixed interest is not required. These banks have prospered in the fundamentalist period.

People usually find the religious community's services more dependable than those marshaled through the influence of extended family and friends, and definitely better than services provided by the government. They claim the services themselves are qualitatively better, usually do not require such long waits, and the specialists who perform them—at least partially if not wholly out of a sense of religious conviction, take the service seriously and treat the customers with respect. The issue of dignity has become important in the general climate of rudeness that often accompanies public services. People usually pay for the regular services and goods in the mosques unless they are given special dispensation for reasons of poverty, and the price is reasonable compared to equivalent public and private services, if the required gratuities are taken into consideration.

The services of the private mosques contribute to the sense of a "community within a community." They attract nominal as well as active Muslims into connection with religious institutions, and some even permit Christians to use their facilities. Some Christians disapprove of using these services, seeing them as a device to attract and convert them. The popularity of the private mosques puts pressure on government mosques by comparison. When asked by a reader in a letter to the *Islamic Banner*, a periodical put out by the government's party, about the propriety of using mosques for many purposes and the practice of using zakat money to create such services, Shaykh Mahmud Bassyuni Fawdah, representing an establishment view, replied that money intended for the poor should be kept in custody until it is given to the poor and should not be used to build mosques or clinics, or disposed of in any other way; similarly, money intended for the construction of mosques should not be used for any other purpose such as the subsidization of students. A mosque is a place of worship and any other use for it is unlawful.[23] The minister of *waqf* (religious endowments), in statements appearing in *Al-Ahram*, argued the contrary—that the public mosques should become more active in providing services for Muslims.

The concept that institutions of the Muslim community should actively work toward satisfying the needs of the membership was not new in the 1970s and 1980s.[24] However, the idea spread rapidly during this period to create a proliferation of services and a significant expansion in the number of clients who could be helped. In addition to serving the needs of the community, the practice, by comparison, undermined government credibility by demonstrating its impotence to solve the daily problems that effect Egyptians. Individuals found compensation for the inability of their families to provide the resources and services required to live at even the most modest standard of living. By taking advantage of the services, the individual developed greater freedom to operate outside the exclusive control of family. The more comprehensive the service organization, the more individuals found their personal interests overlapping with the economic, social and religious interests of other Muslims, until they found they had become a de facto "community within a community."

The third way to deepen a feeling of community is through marking clear boundaries around those who are members and those who are not. The contrast can be intensified by identifying nonmembers as in some way hostile or antithetical to the core beliefs of members. Who are these "external enemies" of the Muslim community and how are clear lines drawn between them and community members?

At various times in the recent past, the enemy has shifted. Hasan al-Banna was opposed to the Westernization and secularization of Egyptian society. After the 1967 war, Egyptians emphasized the "enemy within," the lack of individual faith, and the retreat from their indigenous cultural base—Egyptians in the movement at that time turned to a preoccupation with personal salvation. As the belief grew, however, that the problem was greater than the personal salvation of individual Egyptians, involving also the need for reform of the entire state and society, the concept of Muslim community grew along with the need to define who was within and who outside the boundaries of right thinking. Muslim Brothers emerging from jail in the Sadat period were unable to agree on who should be considered a Muslim—one who simply claimed belief in Islam, or one who stood up and supported fellow Muslims working toward an Islamic state. As a result, it was easier to identify who was clearly not a Muslim. Westerners provided a convenient target when the main issues were foreign occupation[25] and war with Israel, but were not as convenient when the issue became the internal transformation of the society. Instead, Christians, who comprise anywhere from 10 percent to 16 percent of the Egyptian population, became a much clearer "obstacle" to the Islamization of Egyptian society.

The comparative tolerance toward Christians in the early 1970s, evidenced in Muslim participation in the sightings of the Virgin seen at Zeitoun,[26] eroded over the 1970s to produce such events as church burnings in Minya and elsewhere, and the religious riots of Zawya il-Hamra. The 1990s also began with serious disturbances in Upper Egypt between Christians and Muslims, sparked by pamphlets and a mosque sermon in the small town of Abu Qus alleging an affair of honor between a Christian boy and a Muslim girl. During the 1970s and 1980s, Christians had become more visible and therefore more vulnerable, as much of the female Muslim population took up the new styles in Islamic dress.

Though Westerners and Christians over this period have been perceived as the main enemy to the Islamization of the state, recently there has been a subtle shift from this external enemy to an internal enemy in Muslims of other-nuanced belief. In 1990 the enemies, taken from most offensive to least offensive, were Muslims with a difference, Egyptian Copts, non-Egyptian Christians, Zionists and Jews—a neat progression from those most liable to undermine the purity of the ideal to those who may be inimical to it, but have less influence in changing it.[27]

The Islamic concept of *jihad,* which implies an "external enemy," includes actions to spread the principles of Islam, defend the religion, and right the injustice of Muslims persecuted by non-Muslims. As long as the enemy was Russian, Egyptian fundamentalists considered Afghanistan the only true jihad in the Islamic world. However, as various Afghani factions began battling each other, Muslim against Muslim, the status of the war changed in many Egyptians' minds. According to their rationale, the Palestinian uprising cannot be considered a jihad because some of the Palestinians involved are Christians. A true jihad requires Muslim against Jew or Muslim against Christian.

Egyptian Christians have reacted defensively to the increasing public presence of Islam. They became most angry when the media, which could be controlled by the government, allows editorials and commentaries disrespectful of Christianity and Christians. After attacks on Christians in Upper Egypt in 1990, one columnist in *Al-Ahram* demanded that Christians accept the fact of an Islamic state and work toward it, since it was going to happen anyway. On his regular Friday television show, the charismatic Shaykh Muhammad Mitwalli Sharawi, on occasion, interprets passages from the Bible in a way that holds Christian practices up to ridicule. Christians say he was becoming more aggressive toward them until a visit to the United States made him moderate his comments. Another reflection of the Christian state of siege is found in the present proliferation of conversion stories. One of these, which turned out to be false, was that Mustafa Mahmud, the organizer of the largest and most well-known mosque service organization, had recognized the truth about Christianity and had converted.

Survival as an entity is easier when there is the juxtaposition of another entity. For fundamentalists, Christians are a particularly convenient target for several reasons. They profess beliefs that differ in many respects from Islam; there is a residue of ill feeling toward them for the special relationship they enjoyed under the British (where they were favored for employment and followed a lifestyle generally closer to that of foreigners). They are still associated with outside influences in the West and are generally vulnerable within the country. The government is so anxious to appear balanced and not to offend Muslim elements that it treats even those incidents clearly instigated by Muslims as though the blame should be evenly shared. Provoking incidents with Christians has the added benefit for the fundamentalists of destabilizing social life and showing the present government's inability to maintain control.

Reshaping Individual Lives and Personal Relations

One psychiatrist[28] in 1990 saw the trend toward religion as the result of an internal war waged by individuals' consciences against the temptations that prevail in daily life. Young people, especially, face the temptations of corruption and sex, and, because of the difficult times at present, have few of the normal defenses that are found in sufficient income and early marriage. There is no way condoned by religion to satisfy these temptations. By visibly submerging themselves in religion, young people preserve themselves both from temptation and from efforts by others to tempt them. The society is turning, in effect, from external means of controlling individual morality to internal self-monitoring controls. Where women were once controlled by keeping them home, or providing them protectors who accompanied them in public, or permitting them only certain activities (or the lower-class equivalents of these controlling behaviors), now, because of education and employment, they can no longer be subjected to the same controls. Parents have to rely on their children's own desires to be "good" people. In turn, young people are looking for a ready-made morality, independent of their parents, that will make them acceptable to their peers and offer some hope of solving their personal problems. Religion provides them an ideology which helps them feel in control again; it helps them cope with poverty by renouncing worldly need and by tolerating suffering. Piety has the other advantage of being looked upon favorably. Where once social class and wealth were emphasized, now an individual can compensate for the lack of these qualities by demonstrating personal piety.

One entry point to an understanding of the Islamic resurgence in its impact upon personal relations is through readers' letters published in the explicitly religious and secular columns of major daily and periodic newspapers.[29] The letters give an idea of some of the personal concerns of readers, while simultaneously demonstrating "correct" views that established religious and other moral authorities feel are important to convey in the current social climate. In the late 1980s and early 1990s, religious shaykhs who were largely ignored during the fifties and sixties became spokespersons for "right thinking" in religious matters for mainstream readers.[30]

The regular and invited writers of the religious pages are well-known religious shaykhs, including the mufti of Egypt, shaykhs from al-Azhar or from private mosques, and religious scholars from the universities. Most of these writers, in one capacity or another, are associated with establishment views, since radical organizations are not permitted to publish openly in Egypt. Despite this fact, fundamentalist views have colored the views of mainstream authorities in recent years, just as they have colored the perspectives of members of the People's Assembly and even the behaviors of recent presidents of Egypt. The most extreme answers are found in the weekly *Islamic Banner*, put out by President Mubarak's National party. The editor responsible for the "Letters to the Editor" column in the Friday *Al-Ahram* newspaper, taken here as an example of secular approaches, is Abdul Wahhab Mutawwa'. Abdul Wahhab has been a journalist since the age of eighteen and has edited the letters column since 1982.

Because they illuminate the problem from different sides, it is useful to look at both religious and secular letters. The religious letters narrowly focus on legalistic applications of religious interpretations to specific questions, keeping the discourse at an impersonal level.[31] When a large number of these letters are examined, themes begin to appear. The secular letters, by comparison, usually consist of a detailed description of a real-life personal problem either presented to solicit advice from Abdul Wahhab or offered as an exemplary commentary on life.[32] The secular letters, which have no obligation to produce answers in a religious framework, are useful in assessing the extent to which religious interpretations have worked their way into mainstream morality.[33]

Religious Views of Correct Personal Behavior

On the religious pages, from the relative volume of letters, the most troubling issue for individuals appears to be anxiety over the proper observances of religion—what are obligatory, prohibited, and forbidden activities in Islam and of how these activities should be carried out. Next most common are questions about family relations: most prominently, husband-wife relationships, followed by those of parents and children. Surpassing these three, if the letters are sorted differently, are questions concerning the proper roles and responsibilities of women in contemporary life. A final major area of concern is the relationship of Muslims to other religious groups and cultures. Noteworthy by their absence (except in questions about inheritance rules) are questions about extended kin relations. It appears that these relationships have little instrumental value in present-day life and therefore can be abandoned if they prove difficult.

As noted earlier, mainstream practitioners of fundamentalist Islam seek personal salvation through efforts to conduct their lives in ways that conform as closely as possible with religious models found in the Qur'an and Sunna. The dilemma for the individual is to know what constitutes correct behavior. Many of the practices cannot be simply referred to a general principle, but require knowledge of what the Prophet found acceptable. Contradictions in some of the sources make it difficult for the layperson to know which practices to adopt. Consequently, religious writers in newspapers are commonly asked to comment definitively on the appropriateness in Islam of specific practices. The answers suggest one of the ways that public opinion is shaped—in the revitalization mode—to bring the "corrupt" practices of modern life in line with the ideal models found in the Qur'an and the Sunna. Below, examples of answers provided by the religious authorities are organized by theme. Only those topics have been included which relate to the personal themes of this chapter.

Several writers described for their readers what are serious[34] crimes in Islam. One writer listed the seven deadly sins: denying the oneness of Allah, black magic, murder, usury, taking the money of orphans, neglecting jihad, and accusing women falsely of adultery.[35] Another explained that since man is a creation of Allah, the Prophet generally condemns destroying human beings, except in one hadith where he urges believers to kill anyone who commits the most heinous crime of abandoning Islam. Murder should be punished by death unless blood money is given to relatives. Adultery requires stoning a married man to death and giving a single man one hundred strokes.[36] A person has committed a crime from the time he conceives of it, whether he carries it out or not, except when he does not carry it out from fear of Allah.[37]

A number of activities were forbidden or not recommended. Hunger strikes are contrary to Allah's will if the purpose is suicide, but fasting is recommended to purify the body.[38] Working in a bar where alcoholic beverages are served and taking drugs which may affect the mind are forbidden; smoking is harmful because of its addictive quality, but it is not forbidden.[39] A Muslim youth who does not have the means to marry must remain chaste.[40]

Concern was expressed in a number of columns about the correct observance of prayer, including especially the proper way to carry out ritual ablutions. A column in *Al-Ahram* interviewing the then mufti of Egypt responded to questions about unusual conditions: when traveling or when no water is available, stones or soil may be used by beating the hands first on the stones and then on the face. If one-quarter of a person's garment is dirty, it must be changed before prayer, and if a man accidentally touches a woman after washing, there was disagreement on whether he must wash again.[41]

Permitted under certain conditions are music and singing, if they are not carried out in an improper way.[42] Family photos may be displayed as long as they are not sexually stimulating, or shown for purposes of vanity, or represent a specific personality or occasion which might be venerated out of proportion to its significance.[43]

Questions were asked about earning a livelihood and the use of money. One writer supported the view of the ex-mufti of Egypt (against the present mufti) who said the only permitted investment certificates were those with no fixed monthly or yearly interest, but rather a profit-sharing arrangement.[44] A person whose income is not sufficient for himself is not required to pay alms tax and is himself entitled to the tax.[45] Money earned illegally may be given in alms, but will carry no reward for the one who offers it.[46] Lotteries are a form of gambling and are therefore prohibited.[47] A person should depend on Allah for a livelihood only after exerting strong efforts to earn his own living.[48] Wages are collected fraudulently if a worker fakes an illness or pays a bribe for a sick leave.[49] Money to which a worker is entitled is his right, and an employer who refuses to give it to him refuses him his right.[50]

The shaykhs vigorously supported traditional family roles, most importantly those of husband and wife and parents and children, after acknowledging that new factors enter the equation. Many of the questions to the religious leaders concerned the relationship between husband and wife, and the obligations and the rights each has to the other. Since marriage is a contract under Islam, the marriage bond of Muslims is only as strong as the desire of the spouses to honor the details of the contract. Because men have demonstrated their commitment financially to the relationship, they have greater flexibility in instituting divorce proceedings, and as a consequence, in practice, women often feel an anxiety about the possibility of divorce.

In speaking about the husband-wife relationship, one writer said, a husband and wife have the right to mutual enjoyment in each other's company, as long as there is no sinful purpose in what they do. They should be pleasant, compassionate, understanding, and kind to one another. Though it is permitted for them to dance and do other such leisure activities, they are advised to sit together and serenely read the Qur'an aloud so they may attain the peace of soul and tranquillity of mind recommended by Allah. A man who follows all the Islamic rites is not a good Muslim if he abuses his wife, for there are hadith about the importance of having a good relationship with a wife and seeing that she is well taken care of.[51] The fact that in Islam a husband is a grade above his wife doubles the burden of responsibilities and duties he carries; manhood is concerned with ethics and morals, not physical strength and masculinity.[52] One writer warned that a wife and children are enemies of a man when they cause him to do a wrong, but in such cases a man must be forgiving and merciful.[53]

As for rights and obligations, a woman should be obedient to her husband in all that is not contrary to the teachings of the Qur'an. If she is disobedient, Allah recommends that the husband first appeal to her good sense, and if she does not improve, then he may abandon her in her marital bed. Thereafter it is permissible for him to give her a good, but gentle, beating. In short, Allah says that men are in charge of women, because Allah made him to excel her and because men support women. Good women are obedient and guard in secret that which Allah asks them to guard.

The letters reveal that husbands have the indisputable right to sex in the marriage relation. A writer explained to a reader that the Qur'an says women are a tilth for you to cultivate, so go to your tilth as ye will; in sum it is forbidden for a man to copulate with his wife during menstruation, but apart from that it is his right and privilege to penetrate her as long as it occurs through the proper channel.[54] Another writer commenting on an otherwise pious wife who refused bodily contact with a husband who used drugs, ruled that she must be obedient to her husband in all matters, except in what Allah forbids, and accordingly she must fulfill her husband's desires whenever they occur. It is her duty to bring him back to the right path by advice, talk, and warning of the consequences of his behavior, hoping he will come to his senses and put his life in order.[55]

The columns concerning women emphasized their obligations to others; few mentioned their rights. However, one writer, in answering a contemporary problem, claimed that a husband does not have the right to take his wife abroad without her consent. Nor has a husband the right to manage the money of his wife without her permission, and she has the right to leave the house without his permission to manage her money.[56]

In the matter of faith, a husband has no right to demand of his wife that she take off her ḥijāb (Islamic covering), because she is fulfilling the Qur'anic injunction to conceal her attractions from all but those men permitted to see them. She should convince her husband gently that the ḥijāb stands for the family honor, dignity, and reputation.[57] Another writer on the same point taught that Allah requires wives' obedience to their husbands except when there is a contradiction with what Allah has commanded. In general a woman's duty to her creator is deficient until she fulfills her duties to her husband.[58]

As for specific conditions in which divorce is possible, one shaykh permitted a woman to seek divorce if her husband is absent abroad for more than a year without contact, even though he has left money sufficient for her needs.[59] Another writer, however, rejected the idea of divorce for a woman without sufficient resources who wanted to remarry and whose husband was in a mental asylum.[60] Another writer cautioned a husband against divorcing a wife who claimed she was virtuous, but whose hymen was found not intact on the wedding night, because scientists in the field say that a missing hymen may have several causes and not just sexual intercourse.[61]

The bond between parents and children is expected to be strong. You should not disinherit a son who is difficult because he may change and because the Qur'an says, according to the writer, that one should stay close to both parents and children because one cannot know which will be more useful to you.[62] Allah shows more concern for mothers than fathers because of the greater time and effort a mother puts into raising children.[63] The father who abandons work and neglects his family has committed an evil act toward himself, his offspring, and society.[64] A son who feels it his duty as a Muslim to fight with the Palestinians should not do so against the wishes of his father; obedience to parents is a personal duty, but in carrying out his personal duty he should not neglect his duty to society. The Prophet said the best deeds were prayer at the proper time, and after that, reverence to parents, and third, jihad for the sake of Allah.[65] The Qur'an says that possessions and children are a test; this means that both are good if they come from a good source and are used in a good way, and both harmful if they come from a bad source and are used in a bad way. Allah warns about being too fond of either, for in that way it may be difficult to attain salvation and nearness to Allah.[66]

The conduct of women was one of the main concerns of the religious writers. The propriety of their working outside the home, their proper role in the household, and their potential for sexual misbehavior dominated the discussions in print. Whereas men are generally supposed to show greater responsibility than women because of their natural superiority, in matters of sex the writers seemed to hold women responsible for immoral behavior, which results from their presence in public places.

Islam is not opposed to a woman working outside the home as long as that work is adapted to her natural qualities, as in nursing, teaching, or doctoring (her own sex). If the work requires mingling with male co-workers, the important requirement is to avoid loose conduct and irresponsible behavior. It goes without saying that her father, husband, or male relative responsible for her must be willing that she work. Generally it is better if she gives her time, energy, and devotion to maintaining a healthy, sane, and well-organized household.[67] One writer ruled that as long as the husband provides sufficient income to live on, a wife must have his approval to work if she wants to safeguard the equanimity of their marital life.[68] Islam does not require that a wife pay for household expenses, but to preserve family harmony it may be better for her to share this burden.[69]

The modesty of women was also a major issue. Shaykh Sharawi said in one of his weekly Friday television programs that it was not necessary for unattractive women to cover themselves, because the injunction to hide one's charms was only intended for those with such attractive attributes they might cause men immoral thoughts. A writer in the religious letters told a reader that she need not take off her covering (*ḥijāb*) on the eve of her wedding since she need not uncover what Allah recommended to cover, which includes everything but the face and hands; women should not start their married life disobedient to Allah.[70] The whole of a woman's body is a pudendum except her face and hands; accordingly if any part of her shows during prayer, then the prayer is not valid. A woman who prays in short skirts is exposing her secondary pudendum.[71] Good Muslims should not look overly long at the forbidden parts of men or women—if the glance is inadvertent and not intended, it is forgiven; if it is repeated on purpose then it is sinful.[72] A woman should not be treated by a male gynecologist except in extreme emergency; in any case, according to the writer, the issue should not arise since there are now enough trained women in the field to avoid consulting a male.[73]

Some writers required a higher standard of morality for women. A wife who encourages her husband to commit sinful activities, such as dealing in drugs, commits a compound sin because of the danger she has placed on him, on her family, on her children, and on the nation.[74] A veiled woman observing all the teachings of Islam, asking if she could wear a light perfume when she goes on errands, was told she should only wear perfume in her home, for the Prophet said that a pungently perfumed woman passing a group of men who cannot help smelling the odor is quasi-adulterous since it is a rare group of men that does not contain one or more persons with sickly souls, and thus their lust will be aroused. Hence adultery is almost established even if only in their minds.[75] Two writers commented rather weakly on the circumcision of girls. One said it is not forbidden because it does a good thing by lowering the sexual desires; the other ruled there is no misdeed in omitting it.[76]

The writers spent considerable space on appropriate relations between Muslims and foreigners, and between Muslims and those of other religious faiths. Because most writers represented government or establishment institutions in some respect, they generally took a much more conciliatory approach to the issue than members of radical Muslim groups might have.[77]

A Secular View of Personal Behavior

Since the secular letters appeared in smaller numbers and each was chosen to represent an important problem, it is more difficult to judge by sheer volume alone what the major problems were as the 1990s began in Egypt. However, the letters generally dealt with personal relationships, specifically those between actual or potential husbands and wives, and parents and children, and sometimes relationships with those who control major aspects of an individual's life: an employer, in-laws, and so forth. The specific problems that complicate relationships are poverty, death, disease, and the disappointment in or difficult behavior of a "significant other."

Abdul Wahhab mentioned in an interview that the details of problems have changed since 1982 when he started the column. During the early years, before the liberalizing personal status laws were changed, men wrote to complain about the difficulties they faced in giving up the family apartment in the case of divorce. During that period also, social and economic problems arose from *infitah*—or "the opening to outside economic influences" when a class of nouveau riche appeared and the gap between the rich and poor widened to change the social order of Egypt. This period was followed by the problems of family disruption, outside cultural influence (including more conservative religious perspectives), and rapid inflation resulting from the large number of Egyptians going for long periods to work in the Arab oil countries. The main problems in 1990, however, involved young people's difficulties in finding jobs and marriage partners. Abdul Wahhab believes that the age of marriage among the educated has increased significantly, to perhaps twenty-seven or older, largely because of economic problems. When young people are physically ready to marry and meet "the right kinds of people" at the university, the young men have no money; ten years later, when they are financially ready to marry, it is difficult to find the right person. Abdul Wahhab finds the religious attitude today having a positive effect on people and marriage. It encourages them, he says, "to find their happiness in marriage and family life, yet gives them greater freedom to manage their own lives." Most marriages are love matches now, rather than arranged marriages, and most of the failed marriages are those not built on love. He says, "Even though there are many factors in successful marriage, the most important of these is love." Abdul Wahhab enjoys what may be called a cult following of avid readers from all walks of life. One night a week he opens his office to those with problems, and in a number of cases has linked benefactors to people with problems, to effect actual solutions.

The problems addressed to Abdul Wahhab in the Friday *Al-Ahram* reflect more realistically, than do the narrow "points of law" letters addressed to the shaykhs, the kinds of complicated problems confronting Egyptians. What does the woman whose husband dies abroad do when she is told by a potential suitor that he will marry her but she cannot bring her young daughter into the new home? What should a young man do whose education is interrupted and whose life is on hold as he takes care of his senile, incontinent mother?[78] What does a woman do when she marries a respectable man and her first love for whom she still pines reappears again and wants to claim her, even though on the earlier marriage date at the behest of his mother he rejected her? What is the proper emotion for children to feel toward a mother who has left them with relatives and shows no interest in them when she remarries?[79] How can a man salvage his life after rejecting his parents and finding that the woman he married against their warning turns out to be the wrong one for him?[80] Must the young woman who struggles out of drug addiction tell her fiancé about her past?[81] What does the poor man do who has debts and a pregnant wife and who, when he accepts a menial job beneath his station, is fired because he refuses the immoral propositions of the boss's wife?[82]

A point of Islamic law interpretation would not suffice for these writers who want to feel good about themselves, want reassurance about the right way to lead a moral life, and want practical advice about solving their problems. Abdul Wahhab is a master at satisfying the needs of the letter writers, while at the same time preserving a strong moral tone in his answers. While the details of the answers change, the overall message has a strongly religious flavor: Happiness is the product of effort; work toward your goals, but in the end accept what happens as Allah's will. Goodness and correct behavior will be rewarded in heaven if not on earth. Immoral behavior will also find its own reward: the sins of the fathers will be visited on the children. Sorrow and difficulties will be compensated by better times. What happens in the end comes from Allah.

The assumptions that underlie his arguments are that husband and wife should accommodate any personality difficulties of the other, but that women have a greater responsibility to see that a pleasant atmosphere is created in the house. A woman should bear the responsibilities of her role: if she is working and her husband complains about neglect of the household, she is responsible for solving the problem if she wants to continue working. A mother cannot/should not under most circumstances leave her children. Children must fulfill their duty to their parents, even if doing so is difficult. In general, he encourages people to fulfill their traditional duties to close family members, but gives them more flexibility in dealing with those outside the family. In marriage, matching such characteristics as age, social class, and economic level of partners may or may not be important in themselves, and their importance may vary from case to case. Individuals should have a chance for their own happiness, after doing their utmost to fulfill traditional obligations. For example, after trying once more to obtain the consent of the father whose daughter he wants to marry and explaining what he will do if not given that consent, a young man is told to marry the girl without the father's consent. Abdul Wahhab thus attempts to balance obligations to families while tacitly underlining the new reality, that individuals have their own lives to consider, independent of their families.

This kind of reassurance from a moral authority is what people are looking for in a world where traditional relationships still bear the weight of moral sanction, and many are uncertain which new behaviors will satisfy the scrutiny of the current morality. In answering questions, Abdul Wahhab often uses a standard pattern: first, he reaffirms the good behavior of an individual, sometimes quoting, in the same way that shaykhs quote the Sunna, a famous person who has either commented on something relevant to the behavior or who has himself or herself illustrated a similar behavior. The people he cites include, among others, Shakespeare, Balzac, Saint Francis, Einstein, Helen Keller, Dante, Naguib Makfouz, and Francisco Xavier. Then he comments on the bad behavior, or the "incorrect thinking," of the letter writer and says what he thinks would have been better under the circumstances. Next, he provides some mode of action that will atone for, or correct, the situation; finally he may provide a general moral message from unspecified religious sources or from those authorities mentioned above. In general his messages encourage peace and accommodation, and the satisfaction of behaving toward others in proper ways.

Abdul Wahhab's interest is in a moral world, whether that world is based on religious or secular principles. In that respect he is more broad-minded than the religious writers, who see the only source of moral authority in Islam. His perspectives are also more sympathetic to the frailties of human beings and less inclined to rigidly prescriptive solutions which can be generalized to every case of the same kind. Not surprisingly, many of his assumptions about personal relationships and the sources of rewards in life are similar to those of the religious writers. Allah to both is the ultimate source of approval. The important difference between Abdul Wahhab and the religious leaders is in Wahhab's references to those from other religious backgrounds. While the religious writers generally promote peaceful coexistence between people of different religious backgrounds, the fact that they highlight differences between Islam and other religions reinforces a sense of boundary between the groups. Abdul Wahhab, on the other hand, never refers to religious differences; on the contrary, he masks the differences with references from moral authorities of all groups. If the reference is to an overtly Christian source, such as Saint Francis, he may quote the individual without revealing the name. At other times he may refer to the piety of individuals who, the reader knows through other signs, are Christian. The sensitivity to religious issues in Egypt today, may prevent him from overtly promoting the integration of religious groups, but the implicit references he provides are enough for many readers, who are used to reading between the lines, to grasp the message.

Conclusion

Underlying the current emphasis on Islamic models is a consensus forming around new social norms, with a potential for moving the society in important new directions. At least five "new tendencies" in the late 1980s and early 1990s can be identified which, when promoted, either consciously or not, by mainstream and radical fundamentalist Islamic groups, move society in directions more amenable to the formation of an Islamic state. Some are tendencies, already at work in Egyptian society, which may have prospered without the advent of Islamic resurgence, but which fundamentalist encouragement has given added urgency. The first stresses individual, personal responsibility and accountability in realizing the values of Islamic society. This "new" idea modifies the cultural values which tended to locate responsibility for individuals' behavior in the primary groups of which they were a part. As family institutions strengthened in recent history, individuals submerged their own concerns in those of the group and came to accept ultimate moral guidance from authority figures in their own households. Now the movements assert explicitly that the higher authority to which the individual is accountable is Allah, even when compliance with that authority requires that individuals take actions which contradict the guidance of mundane authorities. In essence, the individual is asked to exhibit a sense of individual conscience—shaped by the values and norms of the movement.

The second "new" idea endorses the continuing importance of the specialized roles of husband, wife, mother, father, child, and so forth, but balances the requirements of these roles against obligations to the extrafamilial interests of the larger community of believers. Islam is in the unique position of being able to reaffirm the essential relationships of family while demanding that new relationships be established with "close strangers," based on a common religious affiliation. While Allah replaces the father as the ultimate authority for individuals, the Muslim community replaces family as the ultimate group to which the individual is responsible. Through the mechanism of a society organized at the extrafamilial level, there is greater potential to accomplish larger social, political, and economic goals than existed in the fragmented Egyptian society of the past.

Third, and a derivative of the second, is that Muslim institutions are taking on the responsibility of solving the problems and satisfying the needs of the larger membership of Muslims. In much the same way as families once were able to do, Muslim communities are now providing opportunities for the social, economic, and cultural needs of their members. The more comprehensive the services they offer, the more potential there is for religious communities to command the loyalty of people pursuing their overlapping interests through community membership. Private mosques, sponsored largely through the community, have become the locus for providing such goods and services.

Fourth, the movements have given tacit recognition to the fact that women's roles are now different—that women will take a more active, even though still secondary, role in formal religious and public life. Women have been given the major share in the burden of maintaining public morality, much as if they constituted a time bomb which needs to be defused before it goes off. The movement articulates proper ways for them to deal with their new roles to allow them to feel they are "good people." Women are active participants in the movements; they both support community services and help to socialize the rising generation in personal commitment toward "correct" Islamic values.

Finally, the movements draw conspicuous boundaries around the Islamic community, against other religions and other cultures. This phenomenon may be the "natural" reaction of a community in the throes of redefining its own boundaries from internally fragmented entities to integration on the broader scale. In these circumstances it can be helpful to direct attention to the "outsider" against whom the entire membership can unite. The mechanism is one familiar to the experience of Egyptian families—identifying and uniting against external competitors.

Notes

1. There are objectionable nuances of meaning in almost any word that has been used to stand for the recent preoccupation with Islamic ideologies in modern Arab societies: fundamentalist, revivalist, revitalization, resurgence, renewal, conservative, orthodox, etc. Even the word "movement" carries with it the implication of organized activity that is stronger than the reality for most of those involved in the phenomenon. In this chapter "resurgence" is used as the least objectionable term, implying that the phenomenon is not new, has an iterative aspect about it, and has positive if not joyous qualities about it to believers. The word "movement" is used sometimes in its broader sense to connote those with generally similar directions or tendencies in belief. The single theme which comes closest to linking the various participants is the belief that society should return to the "fundamental" ideals described in the Qur'an and the Sunna.

2. Nazih Ayoubi, "The Politics of Militant Islamic Movements in the Middle East," *Journal of International Affairs* 36, no. 2 (Fall/Winter 1982–83): 271–83; quotation from p. 280.

3. One example occurred in March 1990 when preachers in two mosques in Abu Qurqas and Minya incited their congregations to go on a rampage burning and looting churches, Christian organizations, pharmacies, hospitals, shops, and cars. The purported offense was a love affair between a Christian boy and Muslim girl.

4. S. Waltz, "Islamist Appeal in Tunisia," *Middle East Journal* 40, no. 4 (Autumn 1986): 651–70.

5. Ibid.

6. Interview with Saad Eddin Ibrahim, February 1990.

7. The most open attempt to provide an explicitly secular political alternative is the party proposed by Farag Fouda, which until now has been refused legal status. He accepts the idea of personal faith, but feels that religion and politics should be separated; all other parties in Egypt have as their main goal the installation of Islamic law. One observer who prefers to remain anonymous commented, "He says what we all want to say but are afraid to say openly. Many people would vote for his party if it came on the ballot." Fouda has already had three attempts made on his life and now is guarded twenty-four hours a day.

8. Interview with Muhammad Shaalan.

9. Ayoubi, "Politics of Militant Islamic Movements," p. 281.

10. Married women who work outside the home frequently use the excuse that they do so to provide "extras" for the family, and rarely because they see themselves as a major support of the family or define themselves in terms of the work.

11. John O. Voll, "Renewal and Reform in Islamic History: Tajdid and Islah," in John L. Esposito, *Voices of Resurgent Islam* (New York: Oxford University Press, 1983), p. 33.

12. Ibid., p. 40.

13. The concept of umma was even more revolutionary in seventh-century Arabia when it was first introduced by the Prophet Muhammad. The idea was that membership in the Islamic community *(umma)* should take precedence over the strong tribal loyalties then prevailing in the region. Tribal leaders were expected to submit to the

higher authority of Allah and follow the codes of conduct found in the sacred writings of the Qur'an. The concept of umma was an important one in laying the foundations for an Islamic state that transcended the petty interests of smaller groups in the society.

14. Fadwa El Guindi, "The Emerging Islamic Order: The Case of Egypt's Contemporary Islamic Movement," in T. Farah, ed., *Political Behavior in the Arab States* (Boulder, Colo.: Westview Press, 1983), pp. 55–65; quotation from p. 59.

15. Ibid., p. 59.

16. Ibid., p. 58.

17. Ibid., p. 60.

18. This donning of the garb has unique features that contrast with the previous use of dress by Egyptians. First, it is a conscious adoption and not automatically handed down through the generations, as is the traditional dress of peasants. A woman may choose not to wear it at the moment, but know that when she comes to the proper "state of grace" it will be worn. Second, the implications, whether real or manifest, are religious and not intended to signify the previously more important secular symbols of dress—geographical location, wealth, status, class, and level of sophistication. Andrea Rugh, *Reveal and Conceal: Dress in Contemporary Egypt* (Syracuse: Syracuse University Press, 1984). Third, it is a largely invented style, which, though possessing overtones of earlier styles, has appeared without the usual long period of slow adaptation.

19. Now young women say that wearing the veil in public places "liberates" them from, in this case, unwanted attentions.

20. This phenomenon parallels what has happened with almost universal education in Egypt. Family work groups no longer center around adult activities, but rather around the study needs of children.

21. Because all knowledge is available in that document anyway. A conference on "Science and the Qur'an," which attracted scientists from around the world, concluded that there were no new scientific discoveries

that had not been described previously in the Qur'an.

22. By one estimate, private mosques now number more than forty thousand against six thousand public mosques controlled by the Ministry of Religious Endowments. H. Ansari, "The Islamic Militants in Egyptian Politics," *International Journal of Middle East Studies* 16 (1984): 123–44, p. 129; S. Ibrahim, "Egypt's Islamic Activism in the 1980s," *Third World Quarterly* 10, no. 2 (April 1988): 642–43, says there are more than nongovernmental mosques.

23. *Islamic Banner,* 7 December 1989.

24. In the 1930s, Hasan al-Banna and his Muslim Brotherhood established a number of similar social service institutions at a time when such services were not provided by either Sufi Brotherhoods or government agencies. See John O. Voll, "Fundamentalism In the Sunni Arab World: Egypt and the Sudan," in Martin E. Marty and R. Scott Appleby, eds., *Fundamentalisms Observed* (Chicago: University of Chicago Press, 1991).

25. The high point of Christian-Muslim cooperation came in the 1940s when both groups combined to oppose British occupation under the banner of the Wafd party.

26. Voll, "Fundamentalism in the Sunni Arab World."

27. Interview (interviewee prefers to remain anonymous).

28. Interview with Muhammad Shaalan.

29. The periodicals from which the letters to religious authorities were chosen include the *Islamic Banner (IB),* a National party weekly; *Al-Mujahid (M),* an army monthly; *Islamic Mysticism (IM); Al-Messa (ME),* a mainstream evening paper; *Minbar al-Islami (MI);* al-Azhar monthly; *Al-Nur (N)* weekly; and *Tasawif (T),* a Sufi orders monthly. The issues were collected from October 1989 to the end of January 1990. The secular letters were collected from the Friday *Al-Ahram* for the month of January back to the time the column began in 1982, along with a random group collected over other months during that period.

30. Radicals revile them for representing accommodation with the establishment,

and intellectuals ridicule them as ignorant and barely literate in the sacred texts they interpret.

31. Some of the columns are probably instigated by the shaykhs themselves without benefit of letters from readers.

32. Abdul Wahhab reorganizes the letters sent by readers to give them a more powerful story line and more appealing style. Each Friday he chooses one, two, or three letters to represent problems common to a number of the approximately two hundred letters he receives each week. Abdul Wahhab says he tries to avoid giving specific advice on religion, ethics, and law, though there are elements of each of these in the column. He describes his approach as humanistic.

33. Another reason to include the secular letters is their mass appeal. Whereas the religious letters are "hard sell" morality, and probably of interest mainly to the most literal of those wanting to follow correct observances of Islam, the secular letters enjoy an enormous popularity among educated readers from all walks of life in Egypt. They use one of the most common forms for conveying moral values: the personal narrative—found elsewhere in the way people explain themselves, and in the way popular television serials and films are dramatized. The messages are conveyed clearly, yet with some complexity, and the audience becomes deeply involved in the resolution of the problems concerned.

34. Islam classifies activities into those that are required *(wajib)*, forbidden *(mahzur)*, recommended *(mandub)*, disapproved *(makruh)*, or permitted *(mubah)*. The religious writers do not follow these distinctions rigorously.

35. *IB*, 26 October 1989. The initials standing for the various periodicals can be identified by referring to n. 29.

36. *IB*, 23 November 1989.

37. *MI*, December 1989.

38. *IB*, 14 December 1989.

39. *IB*, 9 November 1989.

40. *IB*, 2 November 1989.

41. 18 January 1985.

42. *MI*, December 1989.

43. *IB*, 4 January 1990. As far as personal appearance is concerned, a beard is recommended but not required, but it is hypocrisy if used to attract the attention of others (*MI*, December 1989). Women are permitted to remove unwanted facial hair, as well as to decorate themselves with gold and silks (*IB*, 30 November 1989). The Prophet looked favorably upon men who dye their hair with henna to hide white hair, but not those who dye it black because, says one writer, "Jews and Christians use it, and we are different from them" (*IB*, 11 January 1990).

44. *M*, November 1989.

45. *IB*, 7 December 1989.

46. *IB*, 2 November 1989.

47. *IB*, 7 December 1989.

48. Ibid.

49. *MI*, December 1989.

50. *IB*, 7 December 1989.

51. *IB*, 16 November 1989.

52. *IB*, 11 January 1989.

53. *IB*, 26 October 1989.

54. *IB*, 30 November 1989.

55. *IB*, 21 December 1989.

56. *IB*, 4 January 1989; *IB*, 30 November 1989.

57. *IB*, 16 November 1989.

58. *IB*, 18 January 1990.

59. *IB*, 16 November 1989.

60. *IB*, 30 November 1989.

61. *IB*, 25 January 1990.

62. *IB*, 16 November 1989.

63. *IM*, November 1989.

64. *ME*, 21 November 1989.

65. *IB*, 14 December 1989.

66. *IB*, 21 December 1989.

67. *IB*, 25 January 1990.

68. *IB*, 26 October 1989.

69. Ibid.

70. *IB*, 7 December 1989.

71. *MI*, December 1989.

72. Ibid.

73. *IB*, 7 December 1989.

74. *IB*, 9 November 1989.

75. *IB,* 25 January 1990.

76. *IB,* 30 November 1989; *IB,* 21 December 1989.

77. In answer to one question, a writer assured his readers that wearing a hat to protect oneself from the elements does not imply a drawing away from Islam or show an intention to follow another religion; also meat slaughtered by "persons of the book" is lawful to Muslims according to the Qur'an (*IB,* 26 October 1989). Another less tolerant writer warned that Allah has told believers to keep away from close contact with unbelievers and those of other religions. A person's intimates are those who know his secrets, and therefore it is dangerous to become close with such people. These people will never spare an effort to deceive you even if they do not fight you openly; they hide their hostility toward Muslims and refuse to speak openly about it (*IB,* 23 November 1989). On whether children of unbelievers, polytheists, and those who do not believe in Islam go to Paradise, Muslim scholars differ, says one writer. The Prophet said that only God knows their destiny; however, Aisha, the wife of the Prophet, quoted him as saying that the children of unbelievers go to hell. One hadith says that the children of polytheists are servants in Paradise. Another says that those who willingly enter fire will be purified, while those unwilling to submit to this test will go to hell. The writer prefers the belief that all who die before puberty will go to Paradise because they are too young to understand the meaning of sin (*IB,*

30 November 1989). Different peoples embrace different religions because they exercise their Allah-given choice; difference of opinion is produced by the struggle between the mind and the instincts (*MI,* December 1989). Several columns address the question of how to treat "people of the book" (people from the revealed religions, which includes Christians and Jews). The Prophet warned Muslims about the rights given to the "people of the book" by Allah. First, Muslims should not harm them in their persons or their wealth; second, they should protect and defend, in the case of war, those who happen to live among Muslims. The "people of the book," on their side, should pay their dues and follow Islamic rules; they should refrain from speaking out against Islamic teachings and from committing any deeds forbidden under Islam, and should abstain from acts harmful to Muslims (*MI,* December 1989). A clearer definition of the relationship is provided by the writer who clarified how alms should be distributed among poor neighbors. A Muslim kinsman living nearby is entitled to three shares of the usual alms tax, a Muslim neighbor who is not a kinsman is entitled to two shares, and a neighbor who is a person of the book should get one share only (*IB,* 28 December 1989).

78. 6 January 1989.

79. 13 January 1989.

80. 5 May 1989.

81. 27 January 1989.

82. 26 January 1990.

Obedience versus Autonomy: Women and Fundamentalism in Iran and Pakistan

Shahla Haeri

Since the Islamic regime of the Ayatollah Khomeini, Woman's Day has been celebrated on the occasion of the birth of Fatimah, the Prophet Muhammad's daughter.[1] On that day in February 1989, two producers of a radio show interviewed women regarding their choice of role models. A young woman identified Oshin, the heroine of a Japanese television serial popular in Iran, as her ideal woman. When asked why she did not prefer Fatimah, the young woman explained that Fatimah had lived many centuries ago (and, by implication, is not a suitable role model for contemporary Iranian women). This insolent expression of individual will, coming as it did from a woman, provoked the Ayatollah Khomeini's wrath. Unceremoniously and without further provocation, he called for the producers' heads.[2] The crisis was averted only through the intense mediation of the Ayatollah Montazeri, then successor to the Ayatollah Khomeini, and Mrs. Zahra Mustafavi, Ayatollah Khomeini's daughter.[3]

On 26 February 1989, the first democratically elected woman prime minister in Pakistan, Benazir Bhutto, left Pakistan to attend the funeral of the late Japanese emperor Hirohito. Bhutto's political opponents used the publication of *The Satanic Verses* by Salman Rushdie as a pretext to stage a rally against her government. Five men were killed and scores of others were injured, but the rally failed to bring down her government—in this instance. Some of Bhutto's opponents contested her legitimacy as leader on the grounds that women are not suited to govern an Islamic state.[4]

In these cases, Islamic religiopolitical leaders in Iran and Pakistan were reacting to what they interpreted as the manifest autonomy—hence, disobedience—of women, a trend they and their followers found alarming. The young Iranian woman rejected the saintly Fatimah, the traditionally revered ideal model for women,[5] despite a decade of intensive Islamization and enculturation in Iran. And Benazir Bhutto, as politician, appropriated a hitherto exclusively male domain of activity and thereby introduced a "gender" dimension to the religious and political discourse in Pakistan.

Such behavior posed a challenge to the perceived traditional Islamic ideal of feminine modesty (veiled and silent) and obedience (sacrificing and selfless) and, consequently, to the set of expectations men hold for women in Islamic society. Not only did these women consider alternative models for woman's role in society, they expressed these publicly and acted on them.[6] Their "disobedience" and "willfulness" was perceived, by a significant segment of the population, as disrupting the "natural" order of reciprocal male-female duties and obligations in the family, and transgressing the greater boundaries between leader/follower, male/female, and private/public functions and domains.

The actions of these women, at the same time, highlight the intricately interconnected dual crises of *identity* of an Islamic society and the *legitimacy* of competing political discourses ("reformists," "modernists," "traditionalists," "revivalists") vying for power and political constituencies in Islamic societies. Within this context, the "women's issue" emerged as one of the most dramatic dilemmas of the 1980s and promises to remain vital in the 1990s. Given the belief in the divine nature of the Islamic law, and hence the assumption of its immutability, a fundamental issue facing Islamic societies is how to respond to the questions raised by women about their status, role, and function in the context of a "modern" Islamic state. How should a woman's role and social position as an individual and then in relation to men be defined or redefined, especially regarding issues such as polygamy, divorce, and child custody? And, above all, who has the legitimacy to do so?

Islamic societies from Morocco to Indonesia were radically affected in the 1980s and early 1990s by movements advocating a return to the Islamic ideals, to the fundamentals, particularly in the area of family relations, marriage, and divorce. This chapter is set, however, within the broader context of an ongoing dialectical relationship between Islamic secular reformers of the 1950s and 1960s, and Islamic fundamentalists[7] of the late 1970s and 1980s in Iran and Pakistan. The former, who initiated legal and social reforms, came under strong criticism by the latter who have argued that the laws and the ensuing reforms are un-Islamic and hence illegal. The fundamentalists contested the legitimacy of these reforms, claiming them to be inspired (or imposed) by the West rather than guided by Islamic law. The tension between the secularist governments and fundamentalists has mirrored the alienation from and disillusionment with ideals and promises of "modernity" in many Muslim societies.

Much of the debate between fundamentalists and secularists has centered on the issues of status of women, marriage, and family law. Islamic laws and commandments are spelled out in the Qur'an, the hadith, and other classical legal sources. They are believed to be divine and unchanging, and are understood to be central to the texture of social life in an Islamic society. Changes in Islamic marriage law were initiated by the colonial powers in the late nineteenth century in India and Egypt,[8] setting the stage for later protests by Islamic groups, including the fundamentalists in Iran and

Pakistan. On the whole, however, Islamic family law itself remained unchanged well into the twentieth century, and relative unanimity has existed among different schools of Islamic law regarding the contractual form of marriage *(nikah)*, the reciprocal rights and obligations of the spouses, divorce, and child custody.[9]

Ironically, after centuries of resistance to changing Islamic family law, the Muslim reformers of the 1950s and 1960s adopted elements of Western law and applied them within an Islamic framework. They referred to the sources, to the Qur'an and Sunna of the Prophet Muhammad, to find an "Islamic rationale" for such adoptions, and an "Islamic methodology" to implement them.[10] Nonetheless, a number of the ulama and their followers, including Maulana Maududi[11] in Pakistan and Ayatollah Khomeini in Iran, perceived such "reforms" as a form of capitulation to the West, as a thinly veiled apologetic, and as an all too eager attempt to find an "Islamic justification" for an essentially Western approach to the issue of interpersonal relations.[12]

Within this context I discuss the interaction and exchange between fundamentalists, who continue to advocate structured gender relations, and Iranian and Pakistani urban middle-class women, who are articulating their own interpretations of personal laws as their knowledge of religious, legal, and political discourses grows. In the 1980s these women added a new voice to the decades-old debates between the fundamentalists and secularists.

The theoretical concepts underpinning my argument are those of *obedience* and *autonomy*, both of which are inextricably associated with the reciprocal rights of the spouses and derived from the contractual form of marriage in Islam.[13] Though seminal to the historically dominant worldview of Islamic countries, both concepts are subject to new interpretations due to a heightened tension between secularists and fundamentalists. Whereas the former are more inclined to break through or improvise on the predetermined boundaries of the marriage contract,[14] the latter are determined to return to a literal meaning of such concepts.

We must look to the broader logic of an Islamic marriage contract, and the historically maintained perception of its immutability, to understand some of the specificities of gender relations in Iran and Pakistan, historical resistance to the reform of personal laws, and hence the basis for the fundamentalists' objection to women's legal autonomy. Contracts constitute the dominant metaphor, or model, for marital relations in Islamic societies[15] and belong to that category of concepts referred to as "root paradigms," that is, "as distinct from what is probably in each culture a wide range of quotidian or situational models for behavior under the sign of self or factual interest," and are "concerned with fundamental assumptions underlying the human bonds."[16] Root paradigms provide people with "cultural maps" that can guide them through specific social "territories."[17] Accordingly, the logic of a marriage contract necessitates a woman's obedience to her husband, while limiting her autonomy.

My concern is with the legal structure of the Islamic marriage contract. Wedding rituals, of course, vary greatly from one Islamic society to another. They take on local coloring and flavor, but the legal form of the Islamic marriage contract, nikah, is the same in almost all Islamic cultures. Moreover, although my focus is on women in Iran and Pakistan, the model of contractual marriage I am proposing is theoretically relevant to other Islamic cultures. Although both are Muslim societies, Pakistan is predominantly a Sunni and Iran mainly a Shi'ite society. Whereas Pakistan is within the South Asian cultural sphere, Iran shares the cultural area of the Middle East. Unlike the fundamentalists who represent the state in Iran and have appeared to be omnipotent within their domain, Pakistani fundamentalists are only a part of the ruling coalition and must compete for political and electoral power with other parties and interest groups. Their interpretation of the role and status of women, marriage, and family law is more contested than that of their counterparts in Iran, at least publicly. Despite years of apparent prosperity under Zia ul-Haq and their renewed prominence in the early 1990s, the fundamentalists' impact in Pakistan has been more limited, indirect, selective, and uneven than the Shi'ite fundamentalists' impact in Iran.[18]

Obedience is a cornerstone of the Islamic vision of a just social order; the term "Islam" means, among other things, submission and obedience. The Qur'an enjoins believers to "Obey God, His Prophet, and those in authority among you."[19] Like the concept of contract, the concept of obedience is paradigmatic in an Islamic culture. Obedience maintains the status quo, making the hierarchy of social relations culturally meaningful. In the context of family life and marriage, the observance of obedience (*tamkin*), and avoidance of disobedience (*nushuz*), are not just obligations with far-reaching legal and social ramifications for women; they are also a wife's divine obligation.[20] A disobedient wife is known as *nashizih*, a rebellious one, who should be admonished[21] because her action transgresses the divine command, and brings about discomfort to the husband and disorder to the family. She also sets a bad example for her own children and others. Within such a worldview, a wife cannot legally be autonomous; a man cannot be obedient to a woman; a woman cannot be the leader of a Muslim state.

Islamic Worldview: The Marriage Contract

The marriage contract maintained its legal form until the passage of the Family Law Ordinance (1961) in Pakistan and the Family Protection Law (1967) in Iran.[22] These acts were intended to give women some judicial relief by granting them certain rights and minimizing a man's unilateral right to divorce. In legal form, an Islamic marriage is a contract of sale (*'aqd*), although contemporary Islamic legal scholars generally shy away from specifying the category of contracts to which it actually belongs. Such reluctance, or "misrecognition,"[23] is more pronounced in the case of the contemporary ulama, who have become increasingly conscious of the implications of the concepts of ownership and purchase that are embedded in a contract of marriage. There are nonetheless significant similarities between a contract of marriage and a contract of sale.[24]

Like a contract of sale, an Islamic marriage involves an exchange of goods and services, each meticulously tied in with the proper functioning of the other. In exchange for brideprice (*mahr*) and daily maintenance (*nafaqih*), which the wife receives, the husband gains exclusive ownership right *(tamlik)*, over his wife's sexuality and reproductive activities and, by extension, over her person.[25] Significantly, Islamic marriage does not involve the purchase or exchange of women, at least not in the sense conceptualized by Lévi-Strauss.[26] Initially, Islamic law upholds the right of a woman as partner, albeit an unequal one, to the marriage contract; this provision assumes she has some degree of autonomy and volition. According to Islamic law, the woman is to give her consent, however nominally, and it is the woman, not her father, who is to receive the full amount of brideprice (custom aside). However, the moment a woman agrees to a marriage contract, she is understood to relinquish "voluntarily" all control and autonomy she may have had over her own legal and social persona. Prior to signing the contract of marriage, an adult Muslim woman is accorded a degree of legal autonomy (though the extent differs among the Sunnis and the Shi'ites), but after the conclusion of the contract she is legally and conceptually associated with the object of exchange, and hence she comes under the jural authority of her husband.

Conceptually, within the structure of a marriage contract, a woman's sexual and reproductive organs are viewed as an object, a fetishized "commodity"—actually and/or symbolically—that is separated from her person and is at the core of an individual, social, and economic transaction. Though conceptually isolated from a woman's body, a woman's sexuality is in practice identified with her whole being. In this gender ideology, woman as person is conflated with woman as object. Furthermore, women are perceived not only as sexual beings but as the very embodiment of sex itself. In this sense veiling is an expression of the concealment of sexuality itself. This cultural/religious ideology leads to a particular pattern of interpersonal relations. Men view women as objects to be owned and jealously controlled; as objects of desire to seclude, to veil, and to discard; and, at the same time, as objects of indispensable value to men's sense of power and virility. This association of women with objects of exchange is at the heart of an ideological ambivalence toward women, inspiring a sustained resistance against granting women independent rights.

Within this ideological scheme, a man is legally empowered to engage in a dual relationship with his wife; in the one she is considered a person, and in the other a sexual and reproductive object. The woman, too, assumes the dual characteristics of a person and an object—characteristics that, though often subjectively blurred, nonetheless color her sense of self-perception. Theoretically, the relationship between husband and wife is mediated through the object of exchange, an object that has become a highly charged cultural symbol, a gift that bestows power on the woman who has it and authority on the man who has legal control over it.[27]

The logic of this particular form of contract dictates a wife's obedience to her husband, while limiting her autonomy. The legal structure of a marriage contract obliges a wife to be obedient, while the divine verses in the Qur'an[28] and the sociocultural beliefs regarding the "nature" of man and woman further entangle a wife in a web of obedience and surrender.[29]

The comments of Ayatollah Khomeini and his Sunni counterparts in Pakistan are indicative of shared legal conceptualizations of the sexes, and the reciprocal rights and obligations of the spouses. "A permanent wife," argued Ayatollah Khomeini, "must not leave the house without her husband's permission, and must submit *(taslim)* herself for whatever pleasure he wants. . . . In this case her maintenance is incumbent upon her husband. If she does not obey him, she is a sinner *(gunahkar)* and has no right to clothing, housing, or sleeping." [30] Similarly, citing a hadith, Maulana Maududi (1903–79), the founder of the most vocal fundamentalist movement in Pakistan and a renowned Sunni scholar, wrote: "When a woman steps out of her house against the will of her husband, she is cursed by every angel in the heavens and by everything other than men and jinn by which she passes, till she returns." [31] Citing Bukhari and Muslim (two major sources of Sunni collections of hadith), Muhammad Imran, a member of the Jamaat-i-Islami, wrote in a similar vein: "As a rule, no wife should refuse her husband what he wants from her except on legitimate grounds, i.e., at the time of menstrual flow or fasting. Some theologians regard even this refusal unlawful as the husband may get enjoyment from his wife in other ways—embracing, kissing, etc. The duty of the wife to her husband is to give him pleasure in his bed whenever he wants her. . . . No woman should, therefore, cause anxiety or give trouble to her husband. If she acts otherwise, she will not be able to be his mate in Paradise. There the pure-eyed virgin maids will be his consorts." [32]

The general secretary for the women's division of the Jamaat-i-Islami in Lahore, though not expressing her interpretation of marital obligations in exactly the same terms, reflected on the issue from a broader perspective shared by the public: "A man's primary duty is to 'provide' (or 'protect') for his family, and that of the wife's is to raise children, take care of her husband, and be obedient to him at all times." [33]

A woman's obedience to her husband and to the larger social order is reciprocated with financial security in the family and prestige in society. A wife's disobedience, however, has legal ramifications that may lead to a severing of her daily support and maintenance, if not to her repudiation. "Women are sometimes murdered by their husbands," wrote Justice Javid Iqbal from Pakistan, "for being rude or disobedient. In such cases the man is not sentenced to death, he usually gets off with a sentence of ten years or life imprisonment." [34] A disobedient wife is guilty of a double violation: reneging on her contractual promise by denying her husband access to that which he legally possesses, and transgressing God's will.

The underlying assumption here is twofold. First, as "purchasers" in a contract of marriage, men are "in charge" of their wives because they pay for them, [35] and naturally they ought to be able to control their wives' activities. Second, women are required to submit that for which they have been paid—or promised to be paid. It follows, therefore, that women ought to be obedient to their husbands. The issue of child custody and the expectation of their unquestioned obedience to their father should be seen within this context as well. Given that a contract of marriage creates "some sort of ownership," [36] it follows that any issue of this contract should automatically belong to the father. Although different schools of Islamic law have different minimum-age requirements, the custody of children is nonetheless a legal/divine right of a father. [37]

By the same rationale, it is woman's autonomy and independence that pose a "problem" for the status quo within the family and the proper functioning of marital relations, and ultimately a challenge to the social order. Any expression of female autonomy can be construed as disobedience and an infringement on male prerogative, and by extension a deviation from the divinely ordained, legally upheld, and historically enforced duties of a wife. The ulama's fierce resistance to any legal/political changes in the status of women in Islamic societies and the moral and cultural ambivalence felt toward empowering women proceed from the assumptions undergirding the logic of the marriage contract.

Of course the legal requirement and cultural expectation that women obey their husbands does not mean that women always do so. Nor does it mean that marital relations necessarily lack partnership and romance. They do mean, however, that the contractual form of marriage provides the basis for a range of specific patterns of gender relations and expectations in Islamic societies. For example, the preoccupation with virginity and the obsession with veiling[38] assume a certain coherence within the framework of the marriage contract and the worldview it enacts. And the potential insecurity embedded in marital relations, which can be manipulated at the moment of conflict, also stems from the set of rights and assumptions on which the contract rests. Recent ethnographic data emerging from the Middle East underscore the often subtle forms through which many women negotiate their wants and desires. Using the potential power that is tacitly perceived to be inherent in their being in possession of the object of desire, women exercise a degree of autonomy and self-assertion.[39] The logic of the marriage contract sets the context, framing the outer boundaries for marital obligations and duties. Having contained the boundaries of marital relations accordingly, this same structure allows for a range of negotiated and improvisational social behavior by means of which both husband and wife, though departing from different junctures, can exercise control, negotiate power, "bargain reality,"[40] use or abuse each other.

Muslim women are intimately aware of the reciprocal implications of obedience and financial support: if they do not oblige their husbands' wishes, their very livelihood is in danger. At the same time they are aware, however vaguely at times, of the potential power inherent in their possession of an object that is tied to a man's sense of history and continuity, honor and virility. Theoretically, therefore, women have the power to be obedient (or disobedient) to their husbands; they can use that power judiciously, situationally, and strategically as leverage. A woman has little authority to force her husband to support her, however, should he decide to punish her for insubordination.

Fundamentalism Consolidated: The Case of Iran

The decade of the 1970s was a period of dramatic change and restlessness in Iran and Pakistan. Even though they were following different historical paths, both societies seemed poised for an upheaval. In the end, the financial deluge of the petro-dollar brought about more destruction than development in Iran.[41] It widened the gap between the haves and have-nots; disrupted the traditional patterns of social relation, expectation, and propriety; distorted the fabric of moral order; and created crises of identity. Personal privileges were abused and public trust was betrayed. The economic, political, and moral corruption that followed in the wake of the economic boom and development left many citizens disoriented, dislodged many from their physical environment and ideological beliefs, and perplexed others as to where the nation was heading and where they stood in the overall scheme of things. A sense of moral chaos prevailed, particularly in cities and urban centers.[42]

As confusion and uncertainty in all spheres of public and private life intensified, the need to reassert oneself and hang on to the familiar also increased. Many Iranians were unable to internalize the "unveiling" of gender relations, or to tolerate the vagaries associated with modern life in Iran, or to focus on any one of the many voices that dictated new directions and orientations for citizens almost daily. An overwhelming majority of Iranians took a collective plunge into an idealized past, hoping to retrieve what they thought they could agree on, namely, an Islamic identity. The stunning victory of Ayatollah Khomeini is attributed, among other causes, to his unambiguous call for an Islamic identity that presumably once existed but had been seriously undermined by the policies of successive ruling monarchies, particularly by Muhammad Reza Pahlavi (1941–79).

Ayatollah Khomeini portrayed the latter as a usurper, an impostor, and a "false god," a *taghut,* who sold his soul and that of his nation to the "Great Satan." Khomeini regarded the shah's policies as inimical to a "genuine" Islamic society, and contrary to "God's purposeful creation to further the establishment of ethical order on earth."[43] In the area of family and personal law Khomeini objected in particular to the Unveiling Act of 1936 and the Family Protection Law of 1967 that granted women some autonomy and rights in the family.[44]

The most immediate and noticeable change in the status of women after the revolution was the requirement of veiling. The Islamic regime made wearing a veil (optional since 1941) mandatory and required all women to wear an "Islamic veil" while appearing in public.[45] Despite this, however, a significant degree of continuity in the legal status of women and in the social beliefs associated with their role and status endured the revolutionary changes.[46] What changed significantly was the rhetoric of the Islamic regime (matched at times by the "emancipation" rhetoric of the Pahlavi regime) regarding the high status accorded veiled women in an Islamic society. Caught in the exuberance of the moment, women initially donned the veil and participated en masse in the anti-shah demonstrations. Many women's reason's for wearing the veil were symbolic (a protest against its forced removal in the 1930s) or pragmatic (fear of recognition by the SAVAK, the shah's secret police) rather than motivated by religious conviction.

In response, the fundamentalists encouraged women to participate in demonstrations against the Pahlavi regime, to fight against oppression and demand justice in the spirit of Zainab, the Prophet Muhammad's granddaughter who defended her martyred brother, Imam Husain, in the aftermath of the tragedy of Karbala in 680 C.E. The Iranian revolution thus ushered in a new role model for women, one that proved to have widespread appeal to urban women, and also one that the regime began to retract soon after consolidating its power.[47] Although for political purposes the Zainab model is still publicly supported, in the privacy of marital relations and in relation to men, the Fatimah model is the privileged one and the one encouraged by the government. However, the representation of Zainab as a patron saint of women sowed the seed of a new consciousness in the minds of many urban Iranian women. Here lies a locus of tension between the Islamic regime and women.

The Islamic fundamentalist regime found itself challenged to fulfill its revolutionary promises, made during the mobilization of 1978–79, to provide social justice, welfare, equal access to education, jobs, and other resources to women.[48] For their part, with increasing sophistication, Iranian women have engaged the fundamentalist regime in frequent dialogues and debates during the 1980s and early 1990s, articulating their own interpretations of various Qur'anic commandments and injunctions, and sayings of the Prophet Muhammad. Individually and collectively, be they women leaders such as Mrs. Zahra Rahnavard and Azam-i Taliqani (discussed later in this chapter) or members of the editorial board of a popular weekly magazine (such as *Zan-i Ruz*), women have criticized and even scolded the regime, demanding that it live up to its promises and allow Iranian Muslim women to develop their full potential in a just and equitable Islamic state.[49] They call for full participation of women in the public sphere and in education, demand the creation of opportunities for divorced and widowed women, and seek to curb men's unilateral right to divorce and polygamy.

The fundamentalists thus have been confronted with an unintended consequence of their success as revolutionaries—the heightened awareness and increased expectations of small but vocal segments of the urban female population. The fundamentalists responded by attempting to negotiate "new" boundaries of male-female relationships, rights, reciprocal obligations, and duties with an old "adversary" who is determined to assert herself—to be the Zainab of her time—and take her place on the sociopolitical hierarchy. The fundamentalists' dilemma has been how to deal with this "new woman" without themselves being dislodged from their traditional position of power and privilege, yet without appearing to undermine their own revolutionary Islamic rhetoric.[50]

Although disgruntled women have not been able to challenge the legitimacy of the regime, they have endeavored to counter the cultural images and perceptions detrimental to its view of women in family and society. Having acquired knowledge of the Shi'ite Islamic discourse, educated urban Iranian women have engaged the fundamentalists in frequent debates, questioning publicly the images of "nagging," "weak," or "dependent" women portrayed on Iranian National Television.[51] For example, a public debate occurred in 1989 between the editorial board of *Zan-i Ruz* (Modern woman)[52] and Hashemi Rafsanjani (the present Iranian president and then Speaker of the Parliament). Mr. Rafsanjani apparently feared popular discontent with the high casualty rate of young men in the Iran-Iraq War, and the consequent frustration of many families with delays in arranging suitable marriages for their children. In one of his Friday sermons, Rafsanjani called on men to marry several wives (permanently or temporarily), telling women to put aside their inhibitions and selfishness. His recommendations prompted swift response from the editorial board of *Zan-i Ruz,* leading him to revise and modify his comments. "Only in a true Islamic society," argued the editorial board of *Zan-i Ruz,* "can a man be a good enough Muslim to maintain justice between his wives. Until then, polygamy leads to more misery for women. That is why we object to polygamy [and recommend monogamy]."[53]

The tension between the fundamentalist regime in Iran and the women who helped bring them to power is exacerbated by a number of issues affecting daily life, some of which are discussed below.

Veiling

Veiling in the Islamic world is not monolithic and uniform, even within individual Islamic societies. Rather, veiling is a multifaceted and polysemic institution, involving a multiplicity of forms and meanings both domestically and internationally. Unlike in Iran, veiling is not universally prescribed in Pakistan. It is much more diverse in Pakistan than in Iran, ranging from the very thin and attractive scarf casually worn by female television newscasters (under Zia ul-Haq's regime, use of the scarf became mandatory for them), to the facial veils worn by some, to the *burqa* which covers all parts of the body except for a narrow rectangular "window" over the eyes (particularly worn by female beggars in urban areas). The particular garment prescribed for women in Iran after the revolution came to be known as "Islamic veiling" *(hijab-i Islami).*

Despite the Islamic regime's attempt at uniformity, many urban women have learned to assert their "individuality" by improvising on the theme of Islamic veiling. Some reverted to wearing the traditional long black veil *(chador)* because underneath they can dress anyway they like.[54] Others, rather than using the dull colors of black, brown, maroon, or gray prescribed by the government, use colorful scarfs interwoven with gold and silver threads;[55] some wrap their scarves differently, and others show a few strands of highlighted hair. These variations of veiling have consistently provoked the ire of the more radical elements within the Islamic regime, toward whom the "moderates," such as President Rafsanjani, have had to defer.

Notwithstanding the differences of perception on veiling among the ruling fundamentalists themselves, the issue in Iran is no longer to veil or not to veil. It is, rather, to "veil well" or to "veil bad" *(bad hijabi),* the former a sign of a good woman, one who obeys the regime's teachings and directives, and the latter a sign of a bad (autonomous) woman, one who holds on to the remnants of the old "decadent" and "Westoxicated" Pahlavi regime. In April 1989 the regime passed laws forbidding once again the "bad veiling" of women and threatening disobedient women with seventy-four lashes and internment for "rehabilitation." A woman's family would also be punished by being forced to pay all her expenses during internment.[56]

That the Islamic regime found it necessary to pass yet another set of directives with harsh punishments is indicative of the regime's continued intolerance of any expressions of autonomy by women.[57] It also indicates that there is a relentless, though submerged, struggle against the veiling directives of the Islamic regime. Although the veil itself is not subject to negotiation, what emerges from this continuous and subtle subversion of authority is a public and highly politicized debate about the particular way the veil is worn, the specific colors chosen, or the arena within which women can appear and work.[58]

Iranian history is replete with unilateral orders and edicts issued by autocratic rulers. In 1936 Reza Shah Pahlavi (1925–41), responding to a growing ideology of modernity that was rapidly spreading across the globe, dramatically ordered Iranian women to appear in public unveiled. Any form of veiling was banned. Women caught disobeying the law were severely punished.[59] The impact of law was felt strongly in the Iranian urban centers where traditionally women wore a chador, or long black veil.[60]

Then as now some women obeyed the law. Some, though resenting it, did not take any action, but others felt obliged to challenge such unilateral laws. Many refused to leave their homes, not even to go to the public bath; some defied the regime and paid a heavy price for their insubordination. Only women who obeyed the law and packed their veils in their trunks could hope for any public recognition in the form of access to education, professional training, and employment. Similarly, after the Islamic revolution, only women who wore the veil were permitted to leave their homes, to enter government premises and agencies, and to have limited access to sociopolitical and economic resources.

In both situations obedience to the authorities was the key to access. The relationship between the dominant regime (in its autocratic as well as theocratic form) and women operates on two interconnected levels. On a more obvious level, women who obey the law are accorded certain concessions and given limited privileges. On a more subtle level, however, women quietly yet consistently challenge the premises of their oppression, while asserting a degree of their own will, however minimal, at times. In the early 1980s some women were openly defiant, which led to their punishment or incarceration. Later they changed their tactics to quiet resistance: while wearing the veil they attempted to subvert the law. Women disobey the law not only to defy the male authority, but also to protest their exclusion from decision-making processes, from having a choice in a matter so directly involving their lives.

Plural Marriages and Divorce

In 1967 when the Family Protection Law (FPL) was passed, many of the ulama, including the Ayatollah Khomeini, protested vehemently.[61] The new FPL restricted (but did not abrogate) men's unilateral right to divorce and to a second marriage, and left child custody to the court's discretion.[62] Despite the initial slow pace of enforcement and implementation, the FPL incrementally enhanced women's position, primarily in the urban centers, where knowledge of the law, and hence its use, was greater.[63]

In the ulama's view, however, the law transgressed the limits of the divinely predetermined boundaries of Islamic law of the marriage contract by making a man's right to a second marriage conditional upon court permission and allowing both man and wife to sue for a divorce. The FPL required that such conditions be included in all marriage contracts irrespective of a husband's wishes. Because a Muslim man's rights to divorce or plural marriage are perceived to be divine, such restrictions or limitations are considered illegitimate. (This argument is consistently maintained by the ulama in both Iran and Pakistan.) The Ayatollah Khomeini declared that "the Family Protection Law which has been recently passed by the illegal parliament is against the tenets of Islam. Those who implement this law are guilty of an irreligious act. Women who have been divorced through this mechanism are still considered married, and their divorces remain annulled. If they remarry, they are committing adultery."[64]

The Family Protection Law was challenged soon after the Islamic regime came to power, although it was not legally abolished until 1982–83. Minimum age for a first marriage was changed from fifteen to thirteen for woman, and from eighteen to fifteen for men; polygamy and divorce were no longer subject to restrictions. In the 1980s a woman's most frequent complaint was of her husband's plural marriages or her own unfair divorce.[65] A woman who sued for divorce because her husband had married three other women, each without knowledge of the other, was told by the court that polygamy is a man's right: "He can have ten wives if he can support them financially; four permanently and the rest temporarily."[66]

Divorce is the unilateral right of the husband.[67] In 1985–86 the Islamic regime replaced the FPL with a new set of directives known as "conditions at the time of marriage contract" *(shurut-i zimn-i 'aqd).*[68] Improvising on the theme of contract, the Islamic regime proposed a set of twelve conditions to be included in the marriage contract. These conditions are to be read to the husband and wife at the time of signing the marriage contract. Only those conditions signed by both spouses have the force of law.

The first condition merits attention, for it is the most controversial and misleading. It reads: "In a marriage contract if divorce is not requested by the wife, and if in the court's judgment the request for divorce is not due to her ill temper and behavior, then the husband is required to pay her up to half of his income earned during the time they have been married together, or something equivalent to it as deemed appropriate by the court."[69]

Note that the divorce must not come from the wife. That falls under the category of *khul'* divorce, in which case the wife receives nothing and must even pay something to her husband to secure her freedom.[70] Also, the divorce must not be due to her "ill temper and behavior." The interpretation of good or bad behavior is of course subjective. Potentially a wife is always in perilous state of being accused of disobedience.[71] Assuming that she "qualifies" for such a divorce, a wife may receive up to half her husband's income earned during their married life. This provision is somewhat ambiguous in that it does not require the husband to give his wife half of his income; the judge could order a lesser amount or determine some equivalent award. In cases in which a husband is unemployed or poor, the court may defer such payments. And the whole affair would be null and void if the husband refuses to sign each of these conditions to begin with.

During the month preceding Ramadan (the fasting month) in 1986, more than one hundred marriage engagements were broken off at the last minute when the man's family came to learn of the implications of these conditions.[72] This confusion was partly due to the fact that the law was relatively new and that no concerted effort had been made to educate the public. Aware that other women will agree to contract a marriage without these conditions, and fearful of losing their opportunity to marry, some women still agree to waive these conditions, thereby leaving themselves vulnerable to the built-in insecurities of a marriage contract and the whims of a capricious spouse.

Here the paradigmatic significance of the concept of contract emerges in a new light. Utilizing the concept of contract, the Islamic regime set out to reform male-female relations,[73] but the new law was short-circuited by implementation within the very same rigid boundaries that had created the marital problems in the first place. Having introduced a proper legal channel, or an "Islamic rationale," for initiating possible improvements in the status of women and changes in marital relations, the regime burdened the process with qualifications and conditions, and failed to educate men and women regarding its possibilities. Moreover, men were not required to sign these conditions and have been provided with little incentive to do so. A marriage contract without these conditions remains licit and valid. The ambivalence of the fundamentalist regime in Iran has effectively nullified any potential of the law to inspire reform in marital relations. While the Islamic state supports the negotiation of every aspect of the marriage contract, the leading clerics have been ambivalent about the possible outcomes of the situation—about how far, or how well, women can or should actually use the law to negotiate on their own behalf.

Moreover, in these new directives, the issue of child custody is no longer subject to negotiation (the FPL left the matter to the court's discretion). Based on the traditional Shi'ite Islamic law,[74] custody of boys over two years of age and of girls over seven years of age automatically passes to the father. In cases of the husband's absence or death, his father has legal rights over the grandchildren. Only in the absence of the father or his father is a mother given the right to custody of her children. Fear of separation from their children keeps many women in bad marriages and prohibits them from initiating a divorce.[75]

Access to Resources

As soon as the Islamic regime consolidated its power, it embarked on a massive purge of female workers, terminating their services with either some financial compensation or a simple dismissal. The realities of modern life, the requirements of the market, and the labor shortage created as a result of the Iran-Iraq War, however, obliged the regime to acknowledge its needs and to bring some women back to the labor market very quickly.[76] Iranian women, on the whole, worked under adverse situations and, despite a real need for their labor, were encouraged to stay within areas traditionally preserved for women, such as teaching and nursing.[77]

Taking issue with the regime's policies toward employed women, Azam-i Taliqani, president of the Institute for Muslim Women, a representative in the first revolutionary parliament, and daughter of the late Ayatollah Taliqani (d. 1981),[78] argued:

> No attention has been paid to women after the revolution, and indeed, rather than progressing, women have regressed. Unfortunately, after the revolution the government representatives, members of Parliament, and even the ulama have not paid attention to woman's role as a human being [*insan*] . . . that is, they fail to view her as a person. . . . When I ask a working woman to tell me of her views regarding Islamic issues, the only answer she gives is, "with the things [posters and slogans] they have put on the walls, and the way they have treated me I feel so humiliated. My understanding is that they consider me only as an object that is to be used. They have reduced me to the level of an animal [*hayvan*]. No self-respect [*shakhsiyyat*] is left for me."[79]

Similarly, Zahra Rahnavard,[80] a supporter of the Islamic regime, director of the Committee for Higher Education, a prolific writer, and wife of ex–Prime Minister Husain Musavi (1980–89), argued that "It is shameful for a Muslim man to prevent his wife from serving Islam, the Qur'an, and the Islamic Republic [of Iran]; to confine educated women within the four walls of the home with the excuse that 'I don't want her to work.'"[81]

Since the revolution of 1979, women's participation in agriculture, mechanical and electronic engineering, metallurgy, chemistry, computer programming, civil engineering, accounting, and commerce has been restricted.[82] Where women had gained access to jobs, often they have been pressured to vacate their positions. The comments of the political/ideological officer of the defense industry are indicative of such policies: "In order to make the work environment healthy, we cooperate fully with women who want to terminate their position. Instead of them, we use the active energy of young and interested men."[83] Rahnavard points to men's fear of being replaced by women or seduced by them: "In fields such as engineering where the number of male students overwhelms that of women, men feel uncomfortable in women's presence. . . . They feel that if they allow it, women will fill all the spots in the universities and so no room is left for [them]."[84]

State planners contend that they lack the means to invest equally in men and women and must spend limited resources on those who provide a higher return for society. Since women's domestic obligations mean they do less work at their jobs, planners "cannot allocate too great a portion of our scarce resources to them." Rahnavard responds that

> this is the wrong approach since Islam demands education for all and does not discriminate in learning. . . . Scientific training is of the essence and there should be no barriers on this path. It is true that an educated woman may choose to stay home for a time to raise her children, but she may choose to work outside her home at another time. . . . In our society the Muslim woman is perceived as a consumer. That is, she represents consumption in every one of

its dimensions. Not only in economic terms, but also in intellectual and emotional ones, in terms of choices and decisions and determination. Our women are not seen as people with independent and creative minds capable of making logical decisions. A creative, free, independent, and determined woman who makes her own choices is denigrated for being unfeminine and unwomanly.[85]

Mrs. Rahnavard concludes that the absence of women in top social and political positions is "indicative of a social disaster or an unresolved fundamental ambivalence, *ibham-i buzurg* [toward women]."[86]

In these passages the tension between the regime's reluctance to provide public opportunities for women and women's determination to demand their rights is revealed. Rahnavard and Taliqani emphasize the right of a woman to be a relatively autonomous individual, and her inherent right to an education and career, which in their view are not specifically prohibited in the Qur'an, but have come (through historical practices) to be acknowledged as prohibited. The fundamentalists, on the other hand, continue to define woman's role and function in terms of the "rights" and privileges of men; accordingly, the clerics-turned-bureaucrats who administer goods and services evaluate women's capacities for participating in the job market in relation to their responsibilities toward their husbands and children, their traditional household duties, and their influence on men.[87]

Social Welfare for Divorced and Widowed Women

In the late 1960s, a prominent and socially aware female member of the Iranian Parliament, Senator Mihrangiz Manuchihrian, wrote a series of articles in which she objected to the fact that Islamic family law made no financial provision for a widow, although three months' alimony was given to a woman after divorce.[88] The Ayatollah Mutahari (d. 1979), a leading religious scholar, responded:

The criterion for giving *nafaqih* [financial support] is not woman's need. According to Islamic law a wife has a right to her own property. If this was not the case, then it would be correct to claim that immediately after a husband's death a wife's life would be ruined. But the law has given women an ownership right, and because women are also supported by their husbands[89] they can always save up their own wealth. Why should it be necessary to support a wife once their mutual life is over? *Nafaqih* is for ornamenting a man's nest. After this nest is destroyed [by death] then there is no point to continue this right for a wife.[90]

Muslim women do have a right to own property. But to deduce from this that all women in Iran, irrespective of class, age, and profession, have saved enough money to support themselves during their widowhood is to confuse boundaries of the ideal and the real. Providing for the well-being of widowed women was an unresolved issue a decade after the Islamic revolution and continues in 1991 to be a social problem in Iran.

In accordance with clause 4 of article 21 of the Constitution of the Islamic Republic of Iran, in 1983 the Majlis (Parliament) mandated the government to draw up a plan of action for the welfare of widowed and elderly women, and abandoned children. The result was to be submitted to the Majlis within three months. However, such a plan of action had not been submitted to the Majlis by early 1991. Justifications for the delay included, among other things, lack of budgetary resources for a problem that is not "fundamental" *(bunyadi)*.[91]

In the meantime the number of widowed women increased due to the Iran-Iraq War. No long-term help has been forthcoming, and the problem persists years after the war's end. Not all widows, of course, share the same fate. The well-being of widows depends on their age, the age of their surviving children, and their own and their husbands' economic, professional, class, and ethnic backgrounds. The war, however, accelerated migration to the cities, minimized or eroded traditional family networks, and loosened family ties and mutual responsibilities. To help ease the pain of the war victims, the Islamic regime established the Martyrs' Foundation to assist families in need. Although the foundation has provided real assistance to many families, mismanagement and abuse of the funds mar its efforts.

Much has been written on the stigmatized, vulnerable, and ambiguous status of divorced women in Iran. In 1988 the Office of Social Welfare and Insurance in Iran proposed a comprehensive plan to meet the financial needs of such women and their children. This proposal was an elaboration of the one originally designed in 1975 and included only those women whose husbands had insurance policies. Article 6 read: "To use the benefits of Social Welfare in case of divorce, one-third of the amount accrued on the basis of the time the husband has worked and for which he has paid a premium will be transferred to his wife. This applies only to the period they have been married together."[92] This bill was welcomed enthusiastically by women, but created consternation among some men as well as a few of the ulama. The ulama objected to the bill's conflict with the contractual form of marriage and hence with the divine right of the husband: "A man is the sole owner [*malik*] of his work [and whatever benefit that is drawn from it]. Therefore it cannot be transferred to a woman after a divorce."[93]

Couching his argument within the logic of the marriage contract, Ayatollah Sayyid Muhammad Bujnurdi, a member of the Supreme Judicial Council affirmed that a man's permission was needed in order to transfer one-third of the amount he had earned to his wife after the divorce; "however, if this is made into a condition written into his job contract, then there is no religious/legal problem with it." That is to say, it cannot automatically pass on to his wife. It must be agreed upon at the time of signing the marriage contract or his job contract. "The money," the ayatollah reiterated, "belongs to the man; it is the result of his work. That a man is responsible to support his family is another matter. This duty should not be confused with the money that is saved in the name of the husband." The reporter interviewing him countered: "This would have been fair if the wife would be also paid a salary for the work she does at home. But no one acknowledges any rights for a wife working in the house. Unlike her husband, she doesn't even have the weekends off. If Friday is a rest day for the man, all the household chores are still left for the woman to do. There is no resting, no retirement for a woman at any age. Is it fair then to allocate only to the man an insurance that has been made possible by his wife's [work at home]?" "Look," said the ayatollah, "A man has certain obligations toward his wife and we are not denying it. A woman can tell a man to pay her 10,000 *tuman* monthly for the work she does at home."[94] "But will our women ever ask for something like that from their husbands?" "Now, if women don't ask and men don't pay that is something else," reasoned the ayatollah. "Assume that I have some money at a bank. That is my money. Now if I owe my wife some money, that is no reason to give my savings to her. I have to perform my duty toward my family, but this should not interfere with my savings." "Then who is to defend a wife's right," he was asked, "because a women herself will not ask for such salary for the work she does with love. If women insist on receiving a salary, then the whole fabric of family life will come undone." The Ayatollah Bujnurdi answered, "If an Islamic culture prevails and if a man is a true Muslim, he should know that a wife has no compulsion to carry out household chores.[95] We pay a stranger [i.e., a domestic] and are duty bound to compensate her. For our wives, too, we should take this issue into consideration. If we can make people understand that a man has no right to expect his wife to work at home, but that she can even get paid for it, then be sure that this problem will not remain in the form it is today. Everyone knows that if they hire a cook they have to pay five thousand tuman monthly. I have calculated that if women want to get money from their husbands for the work they do, men would have to pay them 10,000 tuman per month."[96]

The logic of marriage contract, as I have argued, provides a metaphor for male-female relationships, responsibilities, and reciprocal obligations in Muslim Iran. The legal form of this particular contract tends to create a fundamental ambiguity in the minds of both men and women, but particularly in that of men, by conveying a double image of woman: as a person and an object. So long as women remain obedient they are provided for financially and afforded social prestige. It is woman as an autonomous individual that is ideologically an ambiguous being, and potentially a source of temptation, a locus of conflict.

With increasing articulateness, middle-class urban Iranian women have engaged the fundamentalists in frequent debates and dialogue. The more women try to engage the fundamentalists in their own discourse, negotiating and bargaining over their rights (Islamic or otherwise), the more frequently has the Islamic regime emphasized the ideal, the Fatimah model, the quintessential obedient woman. The fundamentalist regime in Iran has yet to resolve its central dilemma regarding the role of women and male-female relationships: should women emulate a Zainab—autonomous and assertive—or a Fatimah—obedient and submissive? Given the logic of an Islamic marriage contract and the worldview it implies, the fundamentalist regime has shown a marked preference for the latter. Thus Woman's Day and Mother's Day in Iran are celebrated on the occasion of Fatimah's birth.

Further, the fundamentalist regime's apparent unwillingness or inability to reconcile its promises of an improved life for Iranian women with their actual life experiences lies in its advocacy of a return to the sacred and immutable marital law. By the logic of fundamentalists' beliefs, any legal change in the marital relation becomes nearly impossible, because it challenges the perception of the divine and predetermined boundaries of the marriage contract. Paradoxically, having identified the form of the contract itself as a possible venue for change, one that has potentially an "Islamic rationale," the Islamic regime exhibited uncertainty as to how far negotiation and bargaining over the marriage contract can or should be extended.

Fundamentalism in Flux: The Case of Pakistan

As inhabitants of greater India, and as Sunni Muslims (Hanafi school), Pakistanis' experience of secularization differs from that of Iranians. To begin with, Muslims were a minority in India, but, like the Hindu majority, they came increasingly under colonial rule and subject to direct imposition of an alien way of life. Although for the most part the British government left the Hindus and Muslims free to carry on their own family laws and obligations,[97] in relation to Iranians the Indo-Pakistani Muslims have experienced a greater sense of diversity, plurality, and longer exposure to secularism. The partition of 1947, however, set off an intense debate and political and moral conflict regarding the legitimacy and raison d'être of the state of Pakistan. A key issue was whether Pakistan should be a secular state in which a Muslim majority would live side by side with members of other faiths (as was the intention of Jinnah, Pakistan's founder), or whether it should be an Islamic state where Islamic law is the basis of the constitution. The debate over the "true" identity of Pakistan has not abated; it intensified under General Zia ul-Haq (1977–88) with the apparent rise to prominence of fundamentalists, adherents of the latter position. Culturally too, it has been argued that "Pakistan does not any longer know whether it is a part of South Asia or a part of the Middle East" because of its loss of economic ties with Bangladesh after the bloody war with Pakistan in 1971, and subsequently closer economic and political alliance with the Arab Gulf states.[98]

After coming to power by military coup in 1977, General Zia promulgated the "Islamization" plans in 1979. The perception of a relatively powerful public image of the fundamentalists in Pakistan is well known, but there is little consensus as to either the degree of the implementation of the Islamic reform, or the extent of fundamentalists' influence on social life in general and on women and family in particular.[99] The organization most closely associated with fundamentalism in Pakistan is that of the Jamaat-i-Islami,[100] and its affiliated student wing, Jamiyat-i-Tulaba. The Jamaat-i-Islami was founded in 1941 by Maulana Abul Ala Maududi (1903–79), who, though a controversial figure, is nonetheless recognized as "one of the most important thinkers of twentieth-century Islam" and a "charismatic leader."[101] The party's "support base consists mainly of educated, lower-middle-class Muslims from both the traditional and modern sectors of society."[102]

Reacting against years of British rule and colonization as well as cultural, political, and administrative domination by the West, Maududi systematically voiced his displeasure with the West and its "corrupting" influence on Islamic societies, particularly on women and the family. He objected strongly to the "free" relations between the sexes in the West and derided Muslim "apologists," "reformists," and "modernists" who attempted to find justifications in the Qur'an for promoting monogamy or abandoning veiling, for example. Instead, he called for observation of veiling and strict segregation of the sexes in public.[103] In the area of family and interpersonal relations, Pakistani fundamentalists have taken strong positions on the issue of women's garments and compulsory veiling, and on legal reforms that aimed to "modernize" women's status after the independence of 1947, which was consolidated with passage of the Family Law Ordinance in 1961.

Historically, the relationship between the Jamaat-i-Islami and the central government in Pakistan has been complex and generally adversarial. Having taken an aloof and critical stance toward earlier regimes in Pakistan because of their leanings toward secular ideology, the Jamaat supported the military regimes of Yahya Khan and General Zia because it feared the spread of socialism.[104] The Jamaat-i-Islami, suspicious of Zulfikar Bhutto's political maneuvering and his program of "Islam and socialism," intensified its opposition to his regime. Its leadership welcomed Zia's coup d'etat of 1977, perceiving it to be in line with their ideological thinking. Having come to power through a military coup, the general in turn relied heavily on the Jamaat for legitimacy.

Feeling more secure after several years in power, Zia distanced himself from the fundamentalists. Further, the Jamaat lost much of its formal yet relatively tenuous grip on the state apparatus after the 1985 election and Zia's death in August 1988. In the wake of Benazir Bhutto's ouster as prime minister in August of 1990 and the fundamentalists' reentry into the Pakistani political structure (in alliance with the ruling party), an examination of various perceptions of the fundamentalists' impact on Pakistani women and family suggests that the relationship between fundamentalists, the regime, and women remains complex, elusive, and often uneasy.

A politically puzzling but sociologically significant point in the arena of power politics in Pakistan has been the voters' mercurial behavior toward Jamaat-i-Islami. The Jamaat appeared to be a formidable force throughout the 1970 campaign, for example, but the election results were disastrous for the party: only four out of the three hundred seats in the National Assembly were won by Jamaat candidates. Consequently, the Jamaat-i-Islami adopted a new political strategy of street power and sought influence through nondemocratic means, including intimidation of their opponents and collaboration with the military regimes. Similar patterns of electorate change of heart were manifested in 1985, despite the fact that the Jamaat had virtually the entire field open to them.[105]

Likewise, the tumultuous popular welcome Benazir Bhutto received upon her return to Pakistan from exile in 1986 was in part an expression of discontent with Zia's Islamization policies and with the fundamentalists' involvement in the affairs of the state. The voters translated their discontent into a November 1988 election victory, enabling Bhutto to become the first woman prime minister of Pakistan. The election of Benazir Bhutto initially seemed to shift the balance of power in favor of secularists, marginalizing the fundamentalists and throwing into doubt the perception of the fundamentalists' strength in Pakistan.

Within two years, however, Benazir Bhutto was ousted from power, fighting charges of corruption and nepotism. Her husband, Asif Ali Zardari, was in jail charged with massive corruption in the awarding of state contracts. This dramatic fall from grace offers some insight into the changing yet still ambiguous status of women in the Islamic world. Committed to the goals of development, democracy, and advances in the status of Pakistani women and children, particularly in the area of child labor, Benazir Bhutto was also committed, with equal if not greater fervor, to the legacy of her father, the hereditary position of her family, and the traditional ties of clan and region. As prime minister she was unable fully to resolve this conflict.

At a time when the state was virtually bankrupt, she promised an extensive program of social welfare and public works. She criticized the injustice and abuses, borne largely by women, of President Zia's Islamization campaign, but some Pakistani women's groups noted at the time that she tended to shy away from women's issues for fear of being labeled a Western-style feminist, and in any case, the Islamic parties had already turned against Zia, making her caution unnecessary from an electoral standpoint.[106] This seems to have been borne out by the 16 November 1988 elections, which gave her Pakistan People's Party (PPP) 92 of 215 seats, against her arch-rival Nawaz Sharif's Islamic Democratic Alliance's showing of only 54 seats.[107]

The election and its aftermath marked the high point of Benazir Bhutto's popularity. However, it soon became clear that the new head of government was frustrated in her efforts to alter substantively the Islamizing legislation of the Zia years; she even hesitated to submit a bill to repeal the Islamization decree on adultery.

By the time of her ouster from power in a "constitutional coup" executed by President Ishaq Khan in August 1990, the most vocal of her opponents were the fundamentalists, particularly those grouped under the Jamaat-i-Islami banner, who would never be reconciled to a woman leading an Islamic nation. The events that eventually led to her ouster were at the same time expressions of an ongoing and intense power struggle between the "fundamentalists" and "secularists." From the beginning, Benazir Bhutto's prime ministership was opposed by the ulama, who perceived her public role as contrary to the ideal of statesmanship, detrimental to society at large, and particularly damaging to the Islamic ideal of the family.[108]

While the Benazir Bhutto administration apparently failed to address the terrible problems of her country, and while unable to redress even the most egregious of abuses arising from the Islamization campaign of Zia, her brief prime ministerial reign may be given a wider interpretation. In the words of Prime Minister Bhutto herself: "It meant a lot not only to Pakistani women, but to women the world over. It has given women a role model and an example. And it also upheld something that many Muslims believe in: that men and women are equal in the eyes of God."[109]

The Family Law Ordinance

The "modernist" fervor that had led many Islamic states to initiate changes in the legal and political status of women in the mid-twentieth century set off similar responses in Pakistan. The Islamic marriage contract was modified with the passage of the Family Law Ordinance in 1961. On 4 August 1955, eight years after the creation of the state of Pakistan, the Commission on Marriage and Family Law was established to determine whether changes were necessary in Muslim family law. Consisting of four men, including a religious scholar, and three women, the commission submitted its report in June 1956. The report represented the recommendations of the six laymen. In August, however, the "traditionalist" religious scholar published a vigorous dissenting report taking issue with virtually every major recommendation of his colleagues on the commission. "There then ensued an extended debate between modernists and traditionalists."[110]

It was not until March 1961 that many of the recommendations of the Commission on Marriage and Family Law were embodied in the Family Law Ordinance (FLO) of 1961. The law was intended to initiate liberalization of marriage, divorce, maintenance, and succession. By the time the law was actually approved and put to the test, however, "the effect of conservative opposition to reforms [could] be seen in certain provisions or qualifications that weakened the effect of the reforms."[111] In the area of marriage and divorce, as was the case in Iran, the law sought to limit a man's unilateral rights by requiring a written notice to the Arbitration Council (and to the wife) for a divorce or a second marriage. In both cases, failure to follow the guidelines would bring about punishment of up to one year in prison and a fine of up to five thousand rupees for the husband. But in either case, despite the breach, the new marriage or divorce would still be considered valid; these provisions limited a genuine application of the law even further.[112]

Maulana Maududi and Jamaat-i-Islami perceived the changes intended by the FLO as contrary to the divine law of marriage contract, and thus un-Islamic. They pursued an intense policy of agitation for its repeal. The law was not repealed, but their agitation against the regime's modernization policies eventually led to the resignation of President Ayub Khan in 1969. On the whole, the law encouraged a trend toward nuclear families in the big cities, but had little effect in small towns, and was "simply ignored" in rural areas.[113]

With Zulfikar Bhutto in power (1969–77), the prospects of an improved life for women and family seemed more attainable than ever before. The Constitution of 1973 granted the women of Pakistan further opportunities by maintaining that "there shall be no discrimination on the basis of sex alone," and that "steps shall be taken to ensure full participation of women in all spheres of national life."[114] Early in 1976, Zulfikar Bhutto set up a Pakistan Women's Rights Committee to "consider and formulate proposals for law reforms, with a view to improve the social, legal, and economic conditions of the women of Pakistan and to provide for speedier legal remedies for obtaining relief in matters like maintenance, custody of children, etc."[115] The committee recommended that women be provided with education, employment in all occupations, and encouraged to partipate in sports, culture, and the media.[116] Pakistan National Television showed a series of plays whose positive images depicted the "new" woman as an independent and articulate human being.[117] "All this was to be accomplished," wrote Neghat Said Khan, "by a massive women's mobilization programme; encouragement was to be given to women to form national women's rights organizations, and grass-roots committees were to be formed to raise awareness among women of their legal and social rights."[118] Female literacy reached its peak in the mid-1970s, and "women were just beginning to participate in larger numbers in both general elections and labor politics."[119]

The Family Law Ordinance, like its Iranian counterpart, the Family Protection Law, aimed at limiting men's unilateral right to plural marriages and divorce, in order to grant women limited autonomy and enable them to make certain decisions regarding their lives. The Pakistani fundamentalists' objections, similar to those of their Iranian counterparts, were to the deviation of this law from the contractual form of marriage, the changed reciprocal obligations and duties of the spouses, and thus the predetermined divine boundaries of male-female relationships. From the fundamentalists' point of view the changes brought about by the FLO and FPL were incompatible with Islamic ideology of obedience to the divine law.

The Family Law Ordinance continues to be a major point of debate between the fundamentalist ulama and the regime in Pakistan, which remains vulnerable to charges of being "anti-Islamic."[120] Believing that the general political climate had been further "Islamized" by the upsurge of popular sentiment during the Gulf Crisis and fearing a massive onslaught by the newly formed United Shari'a Front—a coalition of religious parties—with its demand for the radical Shari'a Bill, Nawaz Sharif introduced in Parliament on 10 April 1991 his own moderate version of the bill—a package of legislative and administrative measures to Islamize education, the mass media, the economy, the bureaucracy, and the legal system.

Pakistani women's groups expressed alarm. Benazir Bhutto, who was under a legal cloud and leading only 49 members of the PPP in a 217-seat chamber, gave a cautious endorsement to the proposals despite her record of strong opposition to the Islamization program of Zia. Senator Qazi Hussain Ahmad of the Jamaat-i-Islami, on the other hand, warned that "we need many, many, many explanations" before endorsing the proposal.[121] The full text of the Islamization bill was published in the leading Pakistani daily newspapers shortly after its submission to Parliament.[122]

Hudood Ordinance

With General Zia's military coup d'etat of 1977, policies to Islamicize the nation began. Plans for the political and economic empowerment of women were shelved. Events in Pakistan took a dramatic turn; Zulfikar Bhutto was hanged in 1979, and a revival of Islamic criminal law under the Hudood (punishment) Ordinance was reinstated in the same year. The new law included punishments for theft, drunkenness, adultery, rape, and bearing false witness. The most noteworthy article in the Hudood Ordinance, and hazardous for women, was the treatment of rape as adultery (*zina*).

Under the Hudood Ordinance it became virtually impossible for women to press charges against rapists, for the plaintiff was required to provide four men who would testify on her behalf; otherwise, the woman would likely be accused of adultery. Under Islamic law adultery is punishable by death. So, theoretically, the Hudood Ordinance left many women in the perilous situation of being accused of adultery even if they were raped.[123] The law remained in effect under Benazir Bhutto's government; her efforts to change the law were frustrated by the Combined Opposition party, a loose coalition of several parties, including those of the fundamentalist ulama.

The irony of this unique interpretation of "Islamic law" focussed public attention in 1983 on an eighteen-year-old half blind servant girl. She had become pregnant after being raped by her employer and his son and was subsequently convicted of adultery. The presiding judge decided the case was based on "circumstantial evidence," and acquitted the landowning father and son of wrongdoing, while dismissing the girl's father's complaint of rape. The girl was sentenced to fifteen lashes, three years' imprisonment, and a fine of one thousand rupees.[124] Another case involved a Pakistani woman who fled to England in 1985 after being raped. She was about to be deported to Pakistan in March of 1990 when her attorney convinced the British Home Office that her return would mean "up to 10 years in jail and 40 lashes for alleged 'adultery.'"[125]

After the passage of the Hudood Ordinance, in Justice Javid Iqbal's view, women were no longer provided "special legal protection" because of their "oppressed class," despite the fact that "they are still the most victimized and oppressed segment of society." "Now if a woman leaves her house in order to escape the cruelty of her stepmother or husband and takes refuge in her sister's house, the woman and her brother-in-law can be accused of zina and abduction, and they can both be arrested and punished."[126]

Urban middle-class women, like other Pakistanis, are divided between those sympathetic to the Jamaat-i-Islami (or other like-minded parties) and those drawn to the secular parties and organizations. Women followers and sympathizers of the fundamentalists have generally obeyed and followed the directives of their male leaders, adhering strictly to the ideological positions and policies advocated by the party. Unlike their sisters in Iran, supporters of the Jamaat-i-Islami do not seem to have engaged the party leaders in debates on different issues of relevance to them. They have not, to my knowledge, developed their own interpretations on women's status, marriage, and family law.

Independent women's organizations and supporters of secular parties include the All-Pakistani Women's Association (APWA), Women's Action Forum (WAF), Aurat Foundation, and Simorgh. In the 1980s WAF—an umbrella organization created in 1981 in response to General Zia's Islamization policies, most specifically to the Hudood Ordinance—was the most vocal and noted of women's organizations. WAF members agitated against the ordinance and have been vigilant regarding existing rights such as the Family Law Ordinance.[127] Their interactions with the fundamentalists and the state in the 1980s led them more toward a rereading of their own history, religious precepts, and indigenous discourses. They add their own articulations of marriage and family laws to the gamut of existing ones, and are determined to safe-guard their existing rights and to negotiate their wants and needs, rights and obliga-tions with the fundamentalists and the ruling regimes. Women's Action Forum, for example, holds Arabic classes to "counter charges by fundamentalists that its members are a small minority of Westernized women who don't understand or care about Is-lam."[128] Likewise, Shirkat Gah, an affiliate of WAF, arranges meetings and confer-ences on women and the law in Muslim societies. It collects detailed interpretations of Islamic law—highlighting the plurality of Islamic legal practices and interpreta-tions of Islamic family law in different Islamic societies, including among those who follow the Hanafi school of Islamic law.[129]

The passage of the Hudood Ordinance, given the legal assumption of its "inten-tion of universal application,"[130] has had a direct impact on the texture and quality of social life in Pakistan. Implementation of the law, however, has been less universal and certain. Its application has varied with such indexes as class, educational level, professional background and connections, and above all, the policies of implementa-tion pursued by the regime itself. Being a pragmatic politician, Zia could not afford to alienate the elite, the military, or his huge bureaucracy for very long.[131] Discretely, he mediated between fundamentalists and those opposing his Islamization pro-grams.[132] He did little to counter the charges of "antifemale" bias, for example, of the Islamization program.[133] He "was trapped in a dilemma of his own making. If he argued that the pace of reform was prudent, he would leave his administration open to the countercharges from the opposition that *Nizam-i Mustapha* [the Islamization program] was merely a sham. Accordingly, he adopted a policy of restraint, and in-structed relevant institutions not to enter into public debate with the opposition on matters pertaining to the Islamic reforms."[134]

Public perception of the issue of women's rights in Pakistan fluctuates widely; in the eyes of many women and men struggling for their rights, the influence of the fundamentalists waxes and wanes, from being almost overwhelming to almost negli-gible. Bushra Rahman, a woman MP from the Muslim League, observed, "Outside of their own households, the fundamentalists have virtually no impact on families in Pakistan."[135] Given the diversity of religious devotion to a gamut of Sufi orders and saints, she argued, a desire to bring them all under a dominant and austere ideology such as that of the Jamaat-i-Islami is nearly impossible. This sentiment was repeated by the chairman of the Senate, who objected to the concept of fundamentalism and said he did not think there is a "revival" of Islam in Pakistan. Rather, he saw the increase in religious activities as politically motivated: "Within a particular time pe-riod a particular regime found it particularly expedient to include the ulama in the government. Otherwise they have no impact on the family or society."[136]

Zia's own assessment of the impact and future of Islamization in Pakistan adds an ambiguous dimension to the whole issue. Asked about the success of his Islamization policies, he initially responded, "It has been a failure," then modified it by saying, "It has not entirely been a success."[137] The problem, in Zia's view, "lay in persuading other Pakistanis who did not see the issue as he did."[138] The Jamaat has little impact on the way of life of upper- and middle-class Pakistanis; it has also made little headway with peasants in the countryside.[139] On the other hand, the Jamaat-i-Islami has maintained a strong presence in other spheres of social life in Pakistan, such as in the universities, though the degree of its impact and influence has been less obvious and more disputed.[140] As one observer has noted, "Islamization in Pakistan has been less thoroughgoing in practice than in rhetoric."[141]

Conclusion

Veiling of women, segregation of the sexes, control of female sexuality, and opposition to women's autonomy have been subject to fundamentalists' reforms and pressures in Iran and Pakistan in the 1980s and early 1990s. In both nations, fundamentalist leaders emphasize a literal interpretation of marriage and divorce law, maintaining a more "objectified" perception of women. They react against the autonomy and liberties gained by women (in fact or in theory) in the postcolonial era, viewing these gains as a result of the Western hegemony in these societies, and as a deviation from the sacred rights and obligations conferred upon men and women within the contract of marriage. The fundamentalists attribute the ills of their societies to these "un-Islamic" changes in the male-female relationships, which they perceive as against the divine and natural laws. In their opposition to a trend they regard as secularization in the guise of modernization, fundamentalist clerics have reaffirmed the reciprocal obligations and duties of man and wife within the logic of the marriage contract. Their characteristic demand for a return to the Islamic sources is justified rhetorically by the appearance of "autonomous" "Westoxicated" women. Yet the irony of the situation, especially in Iran, is that the fundamentalist revolution helped spur the emergence of vocal factions of urban middle-class women determined to reinterpret Islam as empowering rather than restricting.

Acknowledgments

I would thank Kaveh Safa-Isfahani, R. Scott Appleby, Helen Hardacre, Rita Wright, Mary Hebert, John L. Esposito, Seyyed Vali Reza Nasr, Mohamad Tavakoli Targhi, Charles H. Kennedy, Mumtaz Ahmad, and Afsaneh Najmabadi, for their comments on earlier drafts of this chapter.

Notes

1. Prior to the Islamic revolution, it was celebrated on the anniversary of the Unveiling Act, on 4 January.

2. Apparently women were interviewed anonymously, and for that reason this particular young woman could not be located.

3. *The Muslim,* 28 January 1989; Mrs. Zahra Mustafavi is director of the Society of Women of the Islamic Republic. She is vocal on certain women's rights issues in Iran,

such as the right to equal education but under strict segregation.

4. Using a hadith attributed to the Prophet Muhammad ("Never will suceed such a nation as makes a woman their ruler" [Sahih al-Bukhari, vol. 9. chap. 18, pp. 170–71]) they warned that catastrophes befall a people who leave their affairs in the hands of a woman. In the view of the founder of Jamaat-i-Islami, Maulana Maududi: "Some nations have given women the position of governor over man. But no instance is found of a nation that raised its womanhood to such a status and then attained any high position on the ladder of progress and civilization. History does not present the record of any nation which made the women the ruler of its affairs, and won honor and glory, or performed a work of distinction." Maududi, *Purdah and the Status of Women in Islam* (Lahore: Islamic Publications Ltd., 1987), p. 111. After arguing that all over the world man is the "governor over woman," Maududi goes on to argue how men have abused their "higher position." Dr. Israr Ahmad, a one-time member of the Jamaat-i-Islami, claims that it is "better to embrace death than live in an age when women [are] running the affairs of State." Cited by K. Mumtaz and F. Shaheed, eds., *Women of Pakistan: Two Steps Forward, One Step Back?* (London: Zed Books, Ltd., 1987), p. 85. See also Muhammad Samiullah, *Muslims in Alien Society* (Lahore: Islamic Publications, 1982), p. 34.

5. The Prophet's daughter, Fatimah, is revered among all Muslims, Sunnis and Shi'ites alike. She is held to be an ever favorite ideal model of femininity for all times. Muhammad Iqbal (1873–1938), the most renowned Indo-Pakistani poet, has composed the following poem in her honor in which the themes of obedience and submission are recurring.

The Chaste Fatimah is the harvest of the field of submission,
The Chaste Fatimah is a perfect model for mothers.
So touched was her heart for the poor, that she sold her own wrap.
She who might command the spirits of heaven and hell

Merged her own will in the will of her husband.
Her upbringing was in courtesy and forbearance;
And, murmuring the Qur'an, she ground corn.
Cited by W. C. Smith, *Islam* (1979), p. 165–66.

6. Mrs. Nisar Fatima (d. 1991), a member of National Parliament (reserved seat), objected to the prime ministership of Benazir Bhutto on the basis of her being a woman. Her reasoning was that Bhutto's primary obligation and duty is to her husband and children; therefore, because she has given priority to her job, she is neglecting her duties, and is setting a bad example for young impressionable women. Personal communication, Lahore, 18 March 1990.

7. This term is used here bearing the following points in mind. The fundamentalists are no longer an adversarial oppositional movement in Iran; they form the regime, and as such they differ from other movements in that they are in a position to implement their policies. However, a discussion of whether or not revivalist movements that gain state power should be still categorized "fundamentalist" or "revivalist" is beyond the scope of this paper. Nonetheless, there are aspects shared by various revivalist movements: that fundamentalism is a "reactive" force against an "enemy" ("relativism," "pluralism," "modernism," "uncertainty," etc.) with whom presumably no compromise is tolerated; that fundamentalists selectively "retrieve" aspects of a glorious past, reinterpreting it in light of a different situation. Further, fundamentalists are highly politicized, taking a more "instrumental" and less spiritual view of religion. See Mumtaz Ahmad, "Islamic Fundamentalism in South Asia: The Jamaat-i-Islami and the Tablighi Jamaat," in Martin E. Marty and R. Scott Appleby, eds., *Fundamentalisms Observed* (Chicago: University of Chicago Press, 1991), pp. 457–530.

8. The first change in Muslim family law was introduced by the colonial powers in India and Egypt, including the Indian Evidence Act of 1872. See John L. Esposito, *Women in Muslim Family Law* (Syracuse: Syracuse University Press, 1982), p. 76.

9. In 1988, while conducting archival re-

search on the concepts of contract, marital relations, child custody, property, and the like, using Persian manuscripts, in Pakistan and North India (primarily Hanafi Islam), I discovered that relative ideological uniformity exists between different schools of Sunni and Shi'ite law regarding family, marriage, and women. See also J. Minces, *The House of Obedience: Women in Arab Society* (London: Zed Press, 1982), p. 23.

10. Esposito, *Women in Muslim Family Law;* J. N. D. Anderson, *Law Reform in the Muslim World* (London: Athlone, 1976).

11. Maududi, *Status of Women in Islam.*

12. In a rebuttal to the "Modernist Majority Report" on marriage and family law in Pakistan in 1956, the dissenting minority report charged the "West-ridden sahibs" with ignorance of the divine nature of Islamic law. It also accused them of an "inferiority complex against the West and the desire to copy it blindly." See John J. Donohue and John L. Esposito, eds., *Islam in Transition: Muslim Perspectives* (New York: Oxford University Press, 1982), pp. 206–7. I am grateful to John L. Esposito for drawing my attention to this particular source.

13. I am not setting these concepts as mutually exclusive, nor am I considering them devoid of history and context. These concepts are polysemic and ought to be understood within the context of the history of legal and social changes in the status of women in the past few decades in Iran and Pakistan.

14. Witness the case of Tunisia where the legislature has categorically banned polygamy. See Esposito, *Women in Muslim Family Law,* p. 92. Changes in the family law of Egypt, Syria, Turkey, Pakistan, and Iran in the fifties and sixties also provide examples of the reformists' and secularists' attempt to minimize a man's absolute rights in polygamy and divorce. See also J. N. D. Anderson, "Law Reform in the Middle East," *International Affairs* 43 (1956); and idem, "The Role of Personal Statutes in Social Development in Islamic Countries," *Comparative Studies in Society and History* 13, no. 1 (1971).

15. See Shahla Haeri, *Law of Desire:*

Temporary Marriage in Shi'i Iran (Syracuse: Syracuse University Press, 1989), pp. 28–32; see also Noel Coulson, *A History of Islamic Law* (Irkley, Yorkshire: Scholar Press, 1964).

16. Victor Turner, *Dramas, Fields, and Metaphors: Symbolic Action in Human Society* (Ithaca: Cornell University Press, 1974), p. 68.

17. G. Bateson, *Steps to an Ecology of Mind* (New York: Ballantine Books, 1972), p. 180.

18. C. H. Kennedy, "Islamization and Legal Reform in Pakistan, 1979–1989," *Pacific Affairs* 63, no. 1 (Spring 1990): 62–77, and idem, "The Implementation of the Hudood Ordinances in Pakistan," *Islamic Studies* 26, no. 4 (Winter 1987): 307–19; Aijaz Ahmad, "The Counterpoint of Pakistan," *Mainstream,* 13 February 1988, pp. 11–15; H. Alavi, "Pakistan and Islam," in H. Alavi and F. Halliday, eds., *The State and Ideology in the Middle East* (London: Macmillan, 1988); W. Richter, "The Political Meaning of Islamization in Pakistan: Prognosis, Implications, and Questions," in A. Weiss, ed., (Syracuse: Syracuse University Press, 1987), pp. 129–40; R. Kurin, "Islamization: A View from the Countryside," in Weiss, *Islamic Reassertion in Pakistan,* pp. 115–28.

19. Qur'an 4:62. All references to the Qur'an in this chapter are from the translation by M. M. Pickthall, *The Meaning of Glorious Qur'an* (New York: Mentor).

20. "It is related," writes Ghazali Tusi, "if prostration were permitted to any one but God, women were required to prostrate before their husbands." Imam Abu Hamid Muhammad Ghazlai Tusi, *Kimiya-yi Sa'adat* (The alchemy of happiness), ed. Husayn Khadivjam, 2 vols. (Tehran: Franklin Press, 1975), p. 322.

21. Qur'an 4:34.

22. Esposito, *Women in Muslim Family Law,* p. 76; D. Hinchcliffe, "The Iranian Family Protection Act," *International and Comparative Law Quarterly* 17, no. 2 (1968): 516–21.

23. "The lapse of time," writes P.

Bourdieu, "separating the gift from the counter-gift is what authorizes the deliberate oversight, the collectively maintained and approved self-deception without which symbolic exchange, a fake circulation of fake coin, would not operate. If the system is to work, the agents must not be entirely unaware of the truth of their exchange . . . which at the same time they must refuse to know and above all to recognize." *Outline of a Theory of Practice* (Cambridge: Cambridge University Press, 1977), p. 6.

24. Haeri, *Law of Desire*, pp. 23–72.

25. Ibid., pp. 30–32.

26. "The reciprocal bond basic to marriage," writes Lévi-Strauss, "is not set up between men and women, but between men and men by means of women, who are only the principal occasion for it." Quoted by E. Leacock, *Myths of Male Dominance* (New York: Monthly Review Press, 1981), p. 245.

27. Haeri, *Law of Desire*, pp. 66–67.

28. Qur'an 2:228, 3:14, 4:34.

29. S. Haeri, "Divorce in Contemporary Iran: A Male Prerogative in Self-Will," in C. Mallat and J. Connors, eds., *Islamic Family Law* (London: Graham and Trotman, 1990), pp. 55–69.

30. Ayatollah Ruhallah Khomeini, *Tuzih al-Masa'il* (Book of exegesis), nos. 2412–20 (Mashhad: Kanun-i Nashr-i Kitab, 1977).

31. Maududi, *Status of Women in Islam,* pp. 144–45.

32. Muhammad Imran, *Ideal Woman in Islam* (Lahore: Islamic Publications Ltd., 1989), p. 37.

33. Personal communication, Mansura Complex, Lahore, 28 March 1990.

34. Javid Iqbal, "Crime against Women in Pakistan" (Paper presented at Triennial Conference of APWA, Karachi, 9 April 1988), p. 9.

35. Qur'an 4:34.

36. Muhaqqiq Najm al-Din Abu al-Qasim Ja'far Hilli, *Sharay' al-Islam* (Islamic law), vol. 2, trans. from Arabic to Persian by A. Ahmad Yazdi and M. T. Danish Pazhuh (Tehran: University of Tehran Press, 1968), p. 508.

37. Esposito, *Women in Muslim Family Law,* pp. 37–38; Hilli, *Sharay' al-Islam,* vol. 2, p. 508.

38. Haeri, *Law of Desire,* p. 222, n. 23.

39. Fatima Mernissi, *Beyond the Veil: Male-Female Dynamics in a Modern Muslim Society* (New York: John Wiley and Sons, 1975); Daisy H. Dwyer, "Law Actual and Perceived: The Sexual Politics of Law in Morocco," *Law and Society Review* 3 (1979): 739–56; idem, *Images and Self-Images: Male and Female in Morocco* (New York: Columbia University Press, 1978); Mona N. Mikhail, "Images of Women in North African Literature: Myth or Reality?" *American Journal of Arabic Studies* 3 (1975): 37–47; L. Rosen, "Negotiation of Reality: Male-Female Relations in Sefru, Morocco," in L. Beck and N. Keddie, eds., *Women in the Muslim World* (Cambridge: Harvard University Press, 1978), pp. 561–84; Kaveh Safa-Isfahani, "Concepts of Feminine Sexuality and Female Centered World Views in Iran: Symbolic Representations and Dramatic Games," *Signs* 6, no. 11 (1980): 33–53; J. Minces, *The House of Obedience: Women in Arab Society* (1982).

40. L. Rosen, *Bargaining for Reality: The Construction of Social Relations in a Muslim Community* (Chicago: University of Chicago Press, 1984).

41. I do not wish to minimize the importance of legal or economic developments that took place in Iran in those days. However, what eventually prepared the way for the overthrow of the Pahlavi regime and the coming to power of the fundamentalists were the uninhibited abuses of power and national wealth by the ruling regime.

42. For general reading on the Iranian Revolution of 1979, see N. Keddie, ed., *Religion and Politics in Iran* (New Haven: Yale University Press, 1983); and idem, *Roots of Revolution* (New Haven: Yale University Press, 1981); E. Abrahamian, *Iran between Two Revolutions* (Princeton: Princeton University Press, 1982); M. Fischer, *Iran: From Religious Dispute to Revolution* (Cambridge: Harvard University Press, 1980); F. Kazemi, *Poverty and Revolution in Iran* (New

York: New York University Press, 1981);
S. Bakhash, *The Reign of the Ayatollahs* (New York: Basic Books, 1984).

43. A. Sachedina, "Activist Shi'ism in Iran, Iraq, and Lebanon," in Marty and Appleby, *Fundamentalisms Observed,* p. 407.

44. A. Tabari, "The Role of the Clergy in Modern Iranian Politics," in Keddie, ed., *Religion and Politics in Iran,* p. 67.

45. An Islamic veil in present-day Iran involves a long overcoat, pants, and a dark-colored scarf.

46. P. J. Higgins, "Women in the Islamic Republic of Iran: Legal, Social, and Ideological Changes," *Signs* 10, no. 3 (Spring 1985).

47. "As the new leaders see it, while it was the religious duty of both men and women to rise up against oppression under the Shah, now that the 'right type' of government is in power, women's religious duty requires that they concentrate on fulfilling their real task of taking care of their husbands and children, and that they allow the men to run the affairs of government. Therefore, while extolling the role women played in overthrowing the Shah, the government is urging women to resume their traditional duties as wives and mothers." G. Nashat, quoted by V. Moghadam, "Women, Work, and Ideology in the Islamic Republic," *International Journal of Middle East Studies* 20, no. 2 (May 1988): 223.

48. The Ayatollah Khomeini frequently referred to Iranian women's contribution to the success of the revolution. See *Zan* (Woman) (Tehran: Amir Kabir, 1982), a collection of lectures and slogans from 1962–82. Subsequently, however, women were neglected and relegated to the fringes of politics and public life. Drawing legitimacy from Ayatollah Khomeini's comments, a contributor to *Zan-i Ruz* writes: "[Iranian] women constitute half of the population. Is it right to have only four women representatives in the Parliament (Majlis)? If we cannot have equal numbers of representatives (i.e., half), at least one-third of them should be women. If the present Islamic regime really wants to improve

women's position it should not merely talk. It should prove it through action" (no. 1154 [1987]: 9).

49. Although many Iranian women are genuinely interested in creating a "true" Islamic society, others may be using the same discourse as a political strategem.

50. See various issues of *Zan-i Ruz* since the revolution. Not all women at all times, of course, fit these descriptions. Women from all classes and backgrounds continue to obey and follow the directives set by the regime; there is greater security in obedience. My interest lies with urban-educated and middle-class women who have been involved in a dynamic dialogue with the fundamentalists. Here is where I believe changes will eventually emerge.

51. See *Zan-i Ruz,* no. 1216 (1989): 34; no. 1225 (1989): 32; no. 1226 (1989): 34–37; no. 1229 (1989): 36–37, for a critique and discussion on the portrayal of negative images of women on Iranian National Television and cinema. See *Zan-i Ruz,* no. 1159 (1987): 6–9, for criticism on the inactivity of women representatives in the Parliament on matters related to women.

52. This magazine, under a different editorial board after the revolution, is one of the most popular journals among women in Iran at the present time. It is the only "feminist" magazine presently published in Iran. According to Dr. Shokouh Navabinejad, a psychologist, member of the Women's Cultural and Revolutionary Council, and producer of a daily radio program on women in Iran, the members of the editorial board of *Zan-i Ruz* are highly educated and respected professionals and journalists. Personal communication, 6 July 1990, Boston.

53. See *Zan-i Ruz,* nos. 1044, 1045, 1046, 1047 (1985): 3; and Mr. Rafsanjani's response, no. 1045 (1985): 4–5, 52, 58. Note these women's knowledge and use of the Shi'ite political/religious discourse. Their demand for a moratorium on polygamy is couched within an Islamic framework. Reinterpreting the Qur'anic verse 4:34, they conclude that monogamy is the recommended form of marriage.

54. *Iran Times,* no. 947 (1990): 6, 14. Veiling is symptomatic of a way of life in Iran. It finds another symbolic expression in the form of walls that surround the courtyard of private houses in Iran. See S. Haeri, " Women, Law, and Social Change in Iran," in J. I. Smith, ed., *Women in Contemporary Muslim Countries* (Lewisburg, Pa.: Bucknell University Press, 1981), pp. 215–16.

55. The extent of using colorful scarfs became so "blatant" and widespread that President Rafsanjani is said to have stated in one of his Friday sermons: "It is true that we said bright colors are okay. But we did not say then go and use chandeliers (*chilchiragh*) on your heads!"

56. *Itila'at* (Tehran), 16 April 1989, p. 2.

57. The war against "bad" veiling is reaching new heights. Feeling frustrated at their inability to eradicate bad veiling, the regime has assigned undercover revolutionary guards to frequent parks, restaurants, cinemas, and the like and to arrest "bad veiled" women. *Iran Times,* 13 July 1990, p. 5.

58. *Iran Times,* 4 May 1990, p. 1.

59. O. Suratgar, *I Sing in the Wilderness* (London: E. Stanford, 1951), p. 132.

60. Village and tribal women do not wear the traditional black veil. Their costumes, however, are modest and all covering.

61. Tabari, "Role of the Clergy in Modern Iranian Politics," p. 67.

62. For a description of the Family Protection Law, see D. Hinchcliffe, "The Iranian Family Protection Act," *International and Comparative Law Quarterly* 17, no. 2 (1968): 516–21; F. R. C. Bagley, "The Iranian Family Protection Law of 1967: A Milestone in the Advance of Women's Rights," in C. E. Bosworth, ed., *Iran and Islam* (1971), pp. 47–64; F. Mirvahabi, "The Status of Women in Iran," *Journal of Family Law* 14, no. 3 (1975); and Haeri, "Women, Law, and Social Change in Iran," pp. 209–34.

63. S. K. Mirani, "Social and Economic Change in the Role of Women, 1956–1978," in G. Nashat, ed., *Women and Revo-*lution in Iran (Boulder, Colo.: Westview Press, 1983), pp. 74–75.

64. Cited by Y. L. Mossavar-Rahmani, "Family Planning in Post Revolutionary Iran," in Nashat, *Women and Revolution in Iran,* pp. 257–58.

65. See *Zan-i Ruz's* weekly column "Consult with Us"; specifically see the following issues: no. 1055 (1985): 56; no. 1087 (1986): 35; no. 1103 (1986): 34–36; no. 1151 (1987): 24–25, 42; no. 1155 (1987): 25; no. 1183 (1987): 24–25; no. 1186 (1987): 14–15; no. 1211 (1989): 48, 52; no. 1216 (1989): 20–21, 52.

66. *Zan-i Ruz,* no. 1131 (1987): 22–23.

67. Divorce is morally discouraged and culturally frowned upon. It is reported that the Prophet Muhammad said: "Of all things permissible, divorce is the most blameworthy."

68. *Iran Times,* 3 June 1986, pp. 1, 11; A. Sadiqi Guldar, "Shurut va Shurut-i Zimn-i 'Aqd" (Conditions, and conditions at the time of marriage contract) in *Faslnamih-i Haqq,* December–March 1986, pp. 704–10. See also, *Zan-i Ruz,* no. 1178 (1989): 18–19, and no. 1179 (1989): 18–19, 47.

69. *Iran Times,* 3 June 1986, pp. 1, 11; Guldar, "Shurut va Shurut-i Zimn-i 'Aqd."

70. Properly speaking, *khul'* means to take off, for example, one's clothes. In metaphoric language the Qur'an refers to man and wife as each other's "wear," that clothes and covers one another (2:187). A divorce of the *khul'* kind is usually initiated by a woman who feels repugnance toward her husband and is no longer willing to "wear" him, as it were. Because marriage is a contract, and because some money in the form of brideprice has been exchanged, actually or symbolically, the wife may obtain her divorce in exchange for some money equal, more or less, to her brideprice. Unlike divorce (*talaq*)—which is a unilateral right of the husband—khul' is a contract and is ineffective unless the husband agrees to it.

71. The case of Tuba, whose husband had a preference for sodomy, provides a telling example. When she refused to accede to

his wishes, he stopped paying her daily maintenance. She sued her husband in court, requesting a resumption of her daily support. Her husband, however, accused her of disobedience. She felt too embarrassed to tell the court the real reason for the conflict. The court decided in his favor (Haeri, *Law of Desire*, pp. 132–40).

72. *Iran Times,* 3 June 1986, p. 1.

73. The idea of using a marriage contract to safeguard a woman's right is not new, but only a few farsighted and wealthy parents actually took advantage of it. What is unique presently is the official publicity accorded such arrangements.

74. Muhaqqiq Ja'far Hilli, *Sharay' al-Islam* (Islamic law); see also Ayatollah R. Khomeini, *The Practical Laws of Islam* (Tehran: Islamic Propagation Organization, 1983), p. 118.

75. The issue of child custody is emotionally charged, and recently Ayatollah Muhammad Bujnurdi and others have devoted extensive comments to it in the pages of *Zan-i-Ruz.* See no. 1370 (1990): 6–9, 54–55.

76. V. Moghadam, "Women, Work, and Ideology in the Islamic Republic," *International Journal of Middle East Studies* 20, no. 2 (May 1988): 221–43; see also *Iran Times,* 4 May 1990, for a report of the decrease of women in the labor force from 1976 to 1986.

77. Haleh Afshar, quoted in V. Moghadam, "Women, Work, and Ideology," p. 228. At the same time it must be mentioned that some women have made exceptional progress in Iran today. Rakhshan Bani I'timad, a young woman film producer, is a good example.

78. Azam-i Taliqani was very active in politics before the revolution. Despite her initial support for the Islamic regime, she has been an outspoken critic of its policies and attitudes toward women. She was elected to Parliament after the revolution, but has subsequently been disqualified to run for a seat.

79. "In the Islamic Republic of Iran Women Have Regressed Rather Than Progressing," *Iran Times,* 27 January 1989, pp.

5, 11; see also the interview with Mrs. Mansurah Tabibzadih Nuri, member of the Women's Cultural and Revolutionary Council, "The Islamic Rights of Women Is Still Hidden behind a Curtain," *Zan-i Ruz,* no. 1164 (1988): 6–9, 51–55.

80. Zahra Rahnavard is a member of the Women's Cultural and Revolutionary Council. Ahmad Ashraf, a well-known Iranian sociologist, has referred to her as a prototype of an "Islamic feminist," cited by Moghadam, "Women, Work, and Ideology," p. 227.

81. *Zan-i Ruz,* no. 1221 (1989): 55.

82. *Zan-i Ruz,* no. 1131 (1988): 9, 41.

83. Ibid., pp. 6–9.

84. *Zan-i Ruz,* no. 1221 (1989): 55.

85. Cited by Afshar, 1990, pp. 10–11.

86. *Zan-i Ruz,* no. 1221 (1989): 55; see also *Zan-i Ruz,* no. 1224 (1989), pp. 18–19. In Rahnavard's opinion, however, it is not enough to criticize men: "It is better to criticize [i.e., to address] this fundamental ambivalence that is prevailing in every aspect of women's life." She does not elaborate on her notion of "fundamental ambivalence," nor does she suggest ways of addressing this problem.

87. It is worth noting that, while both these women wear the veil, neither calls for the segregation of the sexes in public, unlike their Pakistani counterparts.

88. This article and a few others were later published as *Nabarabariha-yi huquq-i zan va mard dar Iran va rah-i islah-i an* (Legal inequalities between men and women in Iran) (Tehran: Penguin Press, 1978).

89. A Muslim man is legally obliged to provide financial support for his wife (or wives) regardless of whether the woman works outside the home or is independently wealthy.

90. M. Mutahhari, *Nizam-i huquq-i zan dar Islam* (Women's legal rights in Islam) (Qum: Sadra Press, 1974), pp. 227–28.

91. *Zan-i Ruz,* nos. 1216–1220 (1989).

92. *Zan-i Ruz,* no. 1218 (1989): 56.

93. Ibid.

94. The *tuman* is the Iranian monetary unit. Before the revolution there were approximately 8 tumans to every dollar. The rate of inflation has presently pushed the rate of exchange to 140 tumans to a dollar.

95. In this context, it is interesting to note that his reasoning assumes that the brideprice and the daily financial support a woman receives are not geared to her performance of household chores but, in keeping with the logic of marital exhange, are exclusively in exchange for the sexual function she is to perform.

96. *Zan-i Ruz*, no. 1220 (1989): 15, 52–53. That this interview and others like it are taking place at all and are printed in such a popular magazine is by itself remarkable. It indicates the level of awareness women have reached, the sophistication of their argument, their willingness to engage authorities, and their determination in making their voices heard. See also *Zan-i Ruz*, no. 1195 (1988): 8–9, 59; no. 1221 (1989): 10–13, 56–57.

97. Anderson, *Law Reform in the Muslim World*, p. 21; Esposito, *Women in Muslim Family Law*, p. 75.

98. A. Ahmad, "Counterpoint of Pakistan," pp. 13–14.

99. Kennedy, "Islamization and Legal Reform in Pakistan"; Weiss, *Islamic Reassertion in Pakistan;* Mumtaz and Shaheed, *Women of Pakistan;* and M. Ahmad, "Islamic Fundamentalism in South Asia."

100. Mumtaz Ahmad categorizes both the Jamaat-i-Islami and Tablighi Jamaat as fundamentalist, though one is highly politicized and the other is not. This basic difference in their approaches to politics and the central government disqualifies the Tablighi from Mumtaz Ahmad's own definition of fundamentalism. In his categorization, Alavi proposes the Jamaat-i-Islami as fundamentalists only. See also Alavi, "Pakistan and Islam."

101. M. Ahmad, "Islamic Fundamentalism in South Asia," p. 464.

102. Ibid., p. 458.

103. Maududi, *Status of Women in Islam,* pp. 18–25.

104. M. Ahmad, "Islamic Fundamentalism in South Asia"; Alavi, "Pakistan and Islam," p. 21.

105. M. Ahmad, "Islamic Fundamentalism in South Asia"; Alavi, "Pakistan and Islam," p. 22; Iqbal Ahmad, personal communication.

106. "Pakistani Women Take Lead in Drive against Islamization," *New York Times,* 17 June 1988, p. 10.

107. "Bhutto Says Vote Gave Her Mandate," *New York Times,* 18 November 1988, p. 1.

108. Maududi, *Status of Women in Islam;* Imran, *Ideal Woman in Islam;* Nisar Fatima, personal communication.

109. "Bhutto Blames The Pakistani Military For Her Dismissal As Prime Minister," p. 4.

110. Esposito, *Women in Muslim Family Law,* p. 83.

111. Ibid.

112. Ibid.

113. D. Pearl, "Family Law in Pakistan," *Journal of Family Law* 9, no. 2 (1969): 187; Esposito, *Women in Muslim Family Law,* p. 101.

114. Cited by N. Said Khan, "Women in Pakistan: A New Era?" a publication of *Change: International Reports: Women and Society* (1988), p. 5.

115. Ibid.

116. These activities, particularly sports, were opposed by the fundamentalists; see Mumtaz and Shaheed, *Women of Pakistan,* pp. 90–96.

117. Changes often are immediately reflected on Pakistan National Television, which is generally controlled by the ruling regime. After Zia's death, I noticed an increase in variety shows, dance, music, and plays, but some restrictions have returned.

118. Said Khan, "Women in Pakistan," p. 5.

119. Weiss, *Islamic Reassertion in Pakistan,* p. 97.

120. Esposito, *Women in Muslim Family Law,* pp. 96–101.

121. "Pakistan's Premier Proposes Mak-

ing Islamic Law Supreme," *New York Times,* 11 April 1991, p. 4.

122. "Text of Shariat Bill," *Dawn,* 12 April 1991, p. 5; "Text of Shariat Bill," *Pakistan Times,* 14 April 1991, p. 3. Its preamble states the document's intent, tellingly, in the most general terms, identifying five major principles: (1) sovereignty belongs solely to God, but authority is to be exercised by the people through their chosen representatives "within the limits defined by Him as a sacred trust" (in effect, a limited democracy much as currently exists in Pakistan); (2) Islam is declared the state religion, and all Muslims must live according to the Holy Qur'an and Sunna; (3) the protection of life, property, and justice is guaranteed in "accordance with the moral values of an Islamic state"; (4) obscenity, gambling and prostitution, "and other moral vices" are proscribed; and, (5) future laws are to be enacted in "consonance with the injunctions of the Holy Qur'an and Sunna through a recognized mode." The specific clauses of the bill, called "Explanations," are not much more specific than is the preamble. The enabling legislation subsequent to the preamble excludes the personal status laws of non-Muslim citizens from the effects of the law. Explanation 2 cedes the interpretation of Qur'an and Sunna in cases of dispute to "any Muslim sect" presumably acting for its own members. It is precisely this mixture of ambiguity and lofty generalities which allows a Benazir Bhutto to support the bill, but which will largely alienate the Islamic parties.

123. Iqbal, "Crime against Women in Pakistan," p. 1.

124. With the agitation of Women's Action Forum and some other organizations, her case attracted international attention and was becoming embarrassing to General Zia's government. He intervened personally, asking for an immediate transfer of the case. Mumtaz and Shaheed, *Women of Pakistan,*

pp. 103–5; see also Weiss, *Islamic Reassertion in Pakistan,* p. 101.

125. *Friday Times,* 15–21 March 1990, p. 7.

126. Iqbal, "Crime against Women in Pakistan," p. 13.

127. Mumtaz and Shaheed, *Women of Pakistan,* pp. 71–72.

128. Weiss, *Islamic Reassertion in Pakistan,* p. 106.

129. See *Newsheet for Women Living under Muslim Laws* 2, 1990, pp. 4–5; personal communication.

130. L. Pospisil, "The Ethnology of Law," Addison-Wesley Module in Anthropology, module 12 (1972): 21.

131. Eqbal Ahmad, personal communication; Kennedy, "Islamization and Legal Reform in Pakistan," pp. 74–75.

132. W. L. Richter, "The Political Meaning of Islamization in Pakistan: Prognosis, Implications, and Questions," in Weiss, *Islamic Reassertion in Pakistan,* p. 137; also Begum Ispahani, personal communication.

133. Kennedy, "Islamization and Legal Reform in Pakistan," p. 76.

134. Ibid.

135. Bushra Rahman, personal communication, Lahore, 15 March 1990.

136. Wasim Sajad, personal communication, 17 March 1990, Lahore.

137. Cited in Richter, "Political Meaning of Islamization in Pakistan," p. 135.

138. Ibid.

139. Eqbal Ahmad and Chudrey Anwar Aziz, personal communication, 21 March 1990; see also Richard Kurin, "Islamization: A View from the Countryside," in Weiss, *Islamic Reassertion in Pakistan,* pp. 115–28.

140. Alavi, "Pakistan and Islam," p. 21.

141. Richter, "Political Meaning of Islamization in Pakistan," p. 137; Kennedy, "Islamization and Legal Reform in Pakistan," pp. 74–75.

Building "Fundamentalism" from the Family in Latin America

Jorge E. Maldonado

Why have persons, families, villages, and peoples in Latin America been turning to conservative evangelical movements in the last decades? What is the particular appeal of hundreds—if not thousands—of such groups which are threatening the Roman Catholic church's five hundred years of presence and are competing with governmental policies aimed at attracting popular support? Are there specific socioeconomic and cultural combinations that favor this process? Are there some features in the social structure of Latin America that make families of the various strata more or less receptive to this kind of message? What changes have occurred in human relationships both within families and in society at large as a result of this conversion? What are the implications for the future of Latin American society? These questions motivate the present work.

There are, however, several limitations to this study. First, it is impossible to generalize accurately about a vast region of more than four hundred million people with an immense variety of sociocultural expressions. Second, "family" is an elusive term which describes extended three-generational households as well as nuclear and single-parent groups. Third, there are few studies on families in Latin America upon which to draw, and even fewer on family life as it relates to religious movements. The present study attempts to examine some of the themes and assess the conclusions of the extant literature through original field research in three Latin American communities. The data collected for the present study are not sufficient to overturn the conclusions of more extensive studies, but they do suggest certain subtle modifications of the current thinking on Protestantism in Latin America, especially in regard to the impact that Pentecostal and fundamentalist-like churches are having on family and interpersonal relations.

This claim leads to a final, but perhaps most important, point. There is a terminological difficulty in speaking of "fundamentalism" in Latin America, especially if one imposes the North American meaning of that term on the Latin American scene. In the first volume in this series, Pablo Deiros discussed an impulse toward fundamentalism within Latin American Protestant evangelicalism. As he pointed out, conservative evangelicalism and tendencies toward fundamentalism exist in a rapidly changing religious landscape in Latin America in which the vigorous Pentecostal movement has in the last decade transformed the patterns of Protestant penetration in the region. Beyond the churches planted by North American fundamentalist faith missions, however, it is difficult to isolate "fundamentalism" in the sense of the word as it is accepted by and applied to ten to twelve million North American Protestants. Furthermore, indigenous Latin American churches that do in fact exhibit "family resemblances" to North American fundamentalism do not generally use that term to identify themselves. Many of these churches are Pentecostal in orientation, meaning that their emphasis on a "born-again" experience and immediate contact with the Holy Spirit exists in a dynamic relationship with biblical literalism in their churches. These distinctions must be kept in mind in what follows.

Nonetheless the Pentecostal and evangelical churches discussed in this chapter do share what may be called a "fundamentalist orientation" in that their members believe the Bible is literally true in all respects and is the authoritative guide to Christian life; they have developed a strict moral code; and most (but not all) believe in a separatist attitude toward the public order, which Christ himself will transform in the Second Coming. However, the operative beliefs of these communities are somewhat more flexible in that they share a commitment to rebuilding family life in communities shattered by social and economic dislocations, and fundamentalist doctrines and eschatological schemes are secondary to, and are meant to serve, these more immediate purposes. In what follows I also use the term the "new evangelicalism" to refer to the patterns of belief and practice that characterize the charismatic, Pentecostal, and fundamentalist communities in Brazil, Venezuela, and Ecuador that led me to this conclusion.[1]

Due to the complexity of the theme, this chapter provides a succinct sociopolitical and religious picture of the region within the last three decades (1960–90)[2] as the larger context in which the new evangelicalism has flourished. Special consideration is given to the Pentecostal phenomenon. Responses by families of different class strata to the message of the new evangelicalism are analyzed as a prelude to three case studies illustrating the impact of the message on the family life of different Protestant groups in Brazil, Venezuela, and Ecuador.

The Latin American Context

The sustained growth of Protestant evangelical groups in Latin America has taken place in a context of generalized economic, political, and ideological crisis. Since the end of World War II, an increasing economic, political, and cultural dependency on global capitalism, exacerbated by administrative corruption, has led many national economies into bankruptcy or near-bankruptcy. Some 200 million Latin Americans—almost half the population—live below the poverty line; 140 million have no access to health care; hundreds of thousands die yearly from diseases that could be prevented. These circumstances have turned Latin America into a volcano ready to erupt.[3]

Between 1960 and 1990, military regimes, some of them extremely repressive, ruled in the nations of the region. During the 1980s military dictatorships began to give way to formal democratic governments, but social and economic conditions did not change for the majority of the population. The burden of a disproportionate external debt (estimated at more than $420 billion for the region), the accumulation of wealth in fewer hands, and the deterioration of the public administrative apparatus were the most visible signs of the crisis by the early 1990s. A growing gulf between states and social movements called the legitimacy of every political system into question. Political parties lost credibility as mediators between the established order and the civil society. Moreover, the collapse of socialist economies in Eastern Europe left many radical movements in Latin America without a theoretical frame of reference and without significant international support. At the same time the impression was growing that the Roman Catholic Church was no longer capable of articulating the religious aspirations and symbols of millions of dispossessed urban migrants. In times of abrupt sociopolitical change in Latin America, new religious movements tend to emerge in rapid and unpredictable ways.[4] The recent period has seen no exception to this rule.

This generalized situation of crisis in Latin America has affected the region at all levels, but is felt primarily within the family. Unemployment, hunger, and deficient educational and health services experienced within the family have taken the form of malnutrition, illnesses, hopelessness, domestic violence, loss of moral values, uprooting, and despair. The family is not a passive nucleus limited to the reproduction of labor and predominant values of society. Research carried out in Latin America in the last twenty years on population, migrations, strategies of survival among the poor, and the domestic work of women and children has brought to light the centrality of the family as the nucleus of culture, meaning, and ideology. Thus the family may become a privileged vantage from which to observe how persons, groups, and social classes respond to a particular kind of message and live out a particular kind of faith: "In the family all institutions of a community project themselves with their failures and virtues."[5]

Until recently Protestants were restricted from full participation in the public life of the predominantly Roman Catholic societies in Latin America. As a result of this restriction, coupled with the evangelicals' belief that their message is directed first to individuals and families rather than to social and political institutions, the family has been the main level of evangelical impact.[6]

Colonized in the sixteenth century by Spain and Portugal, Latin America remained almost exclusively Roman Catholic up to the mid-twentieth century. Protestants found it difficult to penetrate those colonies, except for sporadic attempts to establish English, German, Dutch, and French (Huguenot) settlements and merchant outposts during the seventeenth and eighteenth centuries.[7] After the wars of independence, and especially with the rise of liberal regimes in the region at the end of the nineteenth century, Protestants were welcomed. The Protestant ethic was seen to be the basis of material progress, and the Protestant form of Christianity seemed to ruling elites more amenable to the secularization processes attendant upon modernization. Thus Protestantism would counterbalance the social and economic hegemony of Roman Catholicism, which was seen by many of the modernizers as a traditional force that stood in the way of development. Protestant missionaries, of course, had a somewhat different view of matters. They were convinced of the support of a special providence for their self-proclaimed role as reformers of a society in need of the benefits of liberal democracy, including education and freedoms of speech and assembly, which they saw as the authentic sociopolitical expression of the Gospel.

Methodists and other historical churches appeared on the landscape at the end of the nineteenth century. Missionary societies established small Protestant churches—sometimes in connection with European ethnic Protestant groups already in the colonies, sometimes apart. The consolidation of an identifiable fundamentalist presence followed in a second wave of missionary work at the turn of this century, with the advent of North American faith missions and revivals. Foreign missions were a prominent focus of North American fundamentalists, whose choice and training of missionaries were characterized by a determination to convey evangelical doctrine in its purest and most authoritative expression.[8] The third wave of Protestant missionaries washed over the continent after World War II. In 1949 China expelled thousands of missionaries, many of whom wound up in Latin America. In 1958, out of a total of 20,970 Protestant missionaries serving around the world, one-fourth were placed in Latin America, 87 percent of them representing fundamentalist faith missions.[9]

Despite the differences among various missionary groups, it may be said that Protestant missionary activity imported a specific type of Christian faith to Latin America in this century. As it took root, this faith developed not as an extension of the official North Atlantic churches or the religious and political powers, but as the expression of ordinary churchgoers who belonged to Methodist or Anabaptist groups, new revivalist churches, or Pentecostal movements. Alongside the message of eternal salvation, the emissaries of this kind of faith brought an experience of voluntary, lay, participatory, and enthusiastic communities and held these in association with the symbols of progress, development, and egalitarianism.[10] That this occurred in an epoch of rapid social, political, and economic dislocation, increasing anonymity in growing urban centers, and the search for more formal education and upper mobility made the evangelical message all the more powerful.

As the 1960s began, the Protestant presence—the fruit of northern European migration and the work of mainline missionary societies and faith missions—remained modest in scope. But that decade saw the proliferation of atomized groups and churches throughout the region, the rise of Pentecostalism, and the self-definition of churches by ideological markers (e.g., the "ecumenical" churches in solidarity with the struggles of the poor versus the "evangelical" churches which emphasized the comprehensive authority of the Bible, the experience of personal conversion, and the practice of evangelization).[11] Today the nearly synonymous terms "Protestant" and "evangelical" describe in Latin America the historical mainline churches, the new denominations, and the vast majority of Pentecostals.

Pentecostals by 1985 constituted approximately 66 percent of the Protestant population in Latin America and around 80 percent of the Protestant population in Central America alone.[12] These churches continue to grow more rapidly by far than any others. It is not completely accurate, however, to associate fundamentalism or fundamentalist leanings exclusively with Pentecostals of popular sectors.[13] Non-Pentecostal fundamentalist denominations (some of them explicitly anti-Pentecostal) are also growing rapidly in Latin America among urban middle-class people, rural villagers, and native Indians.[14]

Theologically, Pentecostalism shares some defining characteristics with North American Protestant fundamentalism, including a marked emphasis on personal salvation by faith, a "subjectivizing hermeneutics," and a way of being a Christian in the modern world. Both interpret the Bible literally, find in its passages a normative attitude of obedience toward the sociopolitical status quo, and are fervent anticommunists. There is, however, an important distinction. Whereas classical North American fundamentalism provides a rationalistic model that interprets the supernatural acts of the Holy Spirit as restricted to the New Testament era, Pentecostals break the dispensationalist scheme by affirming the action of the Spirit today in the lives of believers and in the church by signs, wonders, and supernatural gifts as in the biblical times. In addition, Latin American Pentecostalism—born in the streets, among dispossessed, politically marginal minorities—is less established and more flexible and adaptive religiously than fundamentalism and even conservative evangelicalism in North America.

Furthermore, Latin American Pentecostalism is in no sense a uniform or monolithic movement. On the question of involvement in politics, for example, there is a range of attitudes. Political withdrawal or passivity seems more characteristic of Pentecostals converted by missionaries than of those who have an autochthonous or indigenous origin. In my research among "home-grown" Pentecostals in three regions, 69 percent of those surveyed affirmed that "evangelical Christians should become involved in politics" despite the respondents' strongly pessimistic view of politics. Nor are all Pentecostals exclusivist in their dealings with non-Pentecostals. In 1990, for example, four national Pentecostal churches (in Venezuela, Argentina, Chile, and Cuba) defined themselves as "evangelical" and "ecumenical" at the same time. "It is clear that the Pentecostal movement (in Latin America) has been deeply marked by a conservative and fundamentalist heritage," Carmelo Alvarez writes. "It is not possible to deny that, historically speaking, it meant taking positions of antagonism and rejection of the world, society, and the sociopolitical arena. However [there is evidence to suggest] . . . the overcoming of this antagonism."[15]

Three gatherings of Latin American Pentecostals[16] in the late 1980s and 1990 underscored elements of diversity between churches of indigenous origin and those of foreign missionary work; between churches closely identified with the popular culture of each country and those more dependent on Western cultural patterns; and between churches emphasizing the baptism in the Holy Spirit on the experiential level and those emphasizing a doctrinal analysis to explain the experience.[17]

These meetings also issued reports pointing out how indigenous Pentecostals resisted, with different degrees of success, the theological influence of "missionary Pentecostalism" and its tendencies toward individualism, the establishment of massive "super churches," and withdrawal from issues that demand social action. One report concluded that "attempts to doctrinally systematize the Pentecostal experience risk forgetting . . . what is essential [to Pentecostalism]: the primacy of the experience over doctrinal statements, of relationships over beliefs. The opportunity for salvation is specially for here and now, an experience within the framework of a community."[18] In my own research, newly converted Pentecostals affirmed this sense of "experience" and "relationships" as key dimensions in their commitment to Pentecostal communities.

The firsthand experience of the divine and the presence of a welcoming community to affirm and share the experience make Pentecostalism attractive to the uprooted masses whose forebears were nurtured in the symbolic and the supernatural by both the Roman Catholic tradition and the animism of native Indian cultures. Indigenous Pentecostalist churches have experienced sustained growth in the past thirty years and have proven themselves adept at organizing people at the grass-roots level. These churches have become target groups for ambitious politicians and a motive for concern for representatives of the "official" churches, Protestant and Catholic alike, as well as for social scientists and governments.[19] A Pentecostal leader commented:

> We have become—sociologically and politically—a community that oscillates between being a substitutory or compensatory group and a group of social protest against the established order. . . . Being in the social and theological periphery and belonging to the popular social classes, we Pentecostals have been seen in this situation only as "sects" that are blocking social change . . . [as places] where marginal people get shelter to avoid overcoming their prostration . . . and as objects of study. But now we are crossing the line, becoming subjects of our own history, and, therefore, generating our own reflection. We are an alternative for change, and our "social protest" could become revolutionary—a hope for the liberation of Latin America.[20]

These recent shifts in attitude among certain Pentecostal groups warrant new studies of the political behavior of evangelical groups especially in Brazil, Peru, Nicaragua, Guatemala, Venezuela, and Puerto Rico. The new evangelicals (Pentecostals included) are playing a new and growing role not only as active members of the electorate, but also as mobilizers of a population more numerous than their own. At the same time, other Pentecostals seem to retain the older patterns of political passivity. In short, the religious landscape is varied and complex, and does not admit of easy categorization.

Types of Responses: Social Strata

Regardless of the theoretical frame of reference to define social classes, the upper strata in Latin America consist of elites who hold wealth and power in close connection with the interests of international capitalism. These groups usually coincide with the landowner aristocracy established in colonial times, and the commercial and industrial bourgeoisie established during the nineteenth century and reinforced during the oligarchical state in more recent times. Powerful extended families with strong blood and marriage links, making up for approximately 5 percent of the population, hold most of the wealth.

Historically there has been an alliance of sorts between the upper classes, the political power, and the Roman Catholic Church in Latin America since colonial times. "Colonial Christendom" entered a period of crisis during the nineteenth century as new national states achieved their political independence from Spain. The crisis deepened at the end of the century as the new liberal oligarchical states in Latin America became part of the international capitalist system. Faced with liberal and anticlerical opposition, however, the church managed to survive and gain strength by standing up to governments in the social realm of family and education. This was a most effective way of forming the conscience of new generations of Catholic elites who would defend the rights of the Church and enhance its influence in society.[21]

Throughout its history in Latin America the Catholic hierarchy has never broken with the classes in power. On the contrary, it has provided pastoral care for families of the aristocracy and the industrial and commercial bourgeoisie. The most meaningful events in an upper-class family are structured by the Church: baptism, confirmation, education, marriage, sickness, burial. The advent of liberation theology and the subsequent surge of Christian base communities in the wake of the Second Vatican Council and especially the Medellin conference of Catholic bishops in 1968 may have inspired the rise or growth of Catholic countermovements such as Opus Dei and Tradition, Family, and Property. These Catholic traditionalist movements appeal to the aristocracy to overcome the threat to "Christendom" in Latin America and to resist threats to traditional Roman Catholic doctrines, values, and privileges. These countermovements have influence with the Catholic hierarchy and are controlled by an extended network of relatives that shapes the ideology of significant portions of the Catholic elite.[22] Protestantism has scarcely penetrated those circles, and the impact of Protestant evangelicalism on the upper class remains insignificant.[23]

The middle class as such appeared in the history of Latin America only with the rise of liberalism, late in the nineteenth century, without drawing the sustained attention of the Catholic Church. "As long as the liberal oligarchies were not in crisis and the popular classes were not on the rise, the social and political movements of the middle classes remained very weak and were not able to set up any alternative to the dominant system," Pablo Richard has written. "That is why . . . the church did not open itself to the middle strata before 1930 or even 1950, depending on the country."[24] While progressive bishops and priests took stands with the poor during the 1960s, participation of the emerging Catholic middle classes was nominal. While the culture remained pervasively religious, the middle class found the church an existential vacuum and no place to express their concerns. This situation provided "the optimum chances for Protestantism."[25] Protestant witnesses found a receptive audience among first-generation urban dwellers who felt themselves neglected by the Catholic Church. Educated in state schools and influenced by liberal ideas, these Catholics found the antihierarchical, anticlerical, and democratic ethos of evangelicalism worthy of a hearing.

In spite of emotional distance from and disenchantment with their native Catholicism, however, the new middle class has retained a profound spirituality. Field research[26] for this chapter done in Brazil, Venezuela, and Ecuador among three fast-growing conservative Protestant congregationsconcentrated on whether the growth of these groups was proportionally related to (1) the intensity and speed of socioeconomic changes in the region; (2) the presence or absence of the traditional Roman Catholic Church in the life of the different social strata; and (3) ideological, ethical, and religious "vacuums" in families facing processes of modernization and secularization. In my sample of these congregations, 63 percent declared that "fulfillment of spiritual needs"—a longing for "a relationship with the living God," a search for "meaning in life"—was the primary motive for their conversion to Protestantism. Of those sampled, 89 percent were first-generation converts, almost all of them from the Roman Catholic Church.

The role of the mass media seems secondary in the ongoing transference of middle-class allegiance from Catholic to Protestant churches. Again, the responses in the three communities I surveyed confirm the conclusions of other researchers that the impact of televangelism and North American "prosperity theology"—a unique mix of consumerism, biblical imagery, and propaganda about the materialistic rewards of freedom and democracy—is quite limited in the middle class. The testimony of members of the nuclear family, of other relatives, and of friends and acquaintances was more influential (in 75 percent of the cases) than the messages of preachers or televangelists.[27]

When the Spanish and Portuguese conquerors took over the American continent, they did not bring European women with them. They took advantage of the native and, later, the black women. The abuse did not stop with the arrival of European women. In the houses of the Spanish and Portuguese families, Indian and black servants gave birth to children fathered by their white masters, giving rise to the mestizo population which is predominant in some countries. The degree of *mestizaje* varies from country to country. In countries like Argentina, where Indians were less present, a predominantly European society was developed. In Brazil the conquerors had to compete for the geographical space with the Indians, and a major ethnic and cultural integration occurred as a result. In Mexico, Guatemala, the Andean countries, and Paraguay there was greater conflict between the European and the more organized Indian societies, resulting in a European superstructure over a very strong Indian base. In places like Haiti, and the Dominican Republic, the European element is merely a thin layer covering a black and mulatto population. This history determined the formation and structuring of the family in lower strata. It also provides us a key in understanding why lower-class families in the 1980s switched church loyalties in the search for other models of family relationships.

The problems of uprooting, isolation, and anonymity of people in the lower classes (about 75 percent of the Latin American population) are also a result of migration, social alienation, and economic exploitation. In turn these conditions lead to personal and familial upheaval, symptomized by sexual abuse of women and children, alcoholism, homelessness and low self-esteem. However, the lower-class poor have developed extraordinary strategies for survival so that an income far below the level of the work force can support a family. At the level of survival subsistence, children have no childhood nor youth any adolescence. They work hard from childhood with no benefit to themselves and generally under conditions of permanent exploitation. Millions of children live on the streets in order to survive. Couples are not formed through the warmth of romance, but by the need for economic survival. The longing for intellectual, social, or cultural achievement is subordinated to the ever precarious economic conditions. The lives of family members in popular sectors revolve around the task of acquiring daily bread. Men often find themselves ferociously competing—even without training or specialization—in a labor market cheapened by the dominant classes, or fighting their way through the labyrinth of unemployment. Unemployment strikes at the root of personality and family life: self-esteem deteriorates, domestic violence increases, alcoholism finds a fertile ground, family and social relations are destroyed. The most frequent channels men choose for overcoming their frustration or for affirming their masculinity seem to be alcohol, sexual adventures, or, in the best of cases, political activity, trade-union involvement, or religious experience.[28]

The new evangelical communities offer hope and a positive solution to some of these problems. Among believers the terms "brother" and "sister" are not empty words. A lifestyle "different from the world" as evidence of conversion and new life is reinforced by a strong sense of communal belonging and networks of mutual support. In conservative evangelical and fundamentalist church communities, family life is the primary focus of sustained concern—the raison d'être of the church community itself. The "fundamentalist" message is one of family as defined by love, responsibility, commitment to the education of children, abstinence from alcohol, and marital fidelity. The community, most often represented by lay church members, is the living assurance to believers that they have someone on whom they can count when financial, personal, or emotional needs plague the family. "At any difficult time of the believer's life (sickness, loss, unemployment, familial crisis), the community will reaffirm its embracing and solidary presence, that is, its healing potential. This characteristic of the Pentecostal churches is one of the main keys for understanding the receptiveness that Pentecostalism has in popular sectors, constantly threatened by meaninglessness of life, [an existential condition] caused by a life of need and loss."[29]

There is considerable debate about the extent and influence of Catholic liberationists in their attempts to address these conditions and serve the masses, but at this writing, in late 1991, there seems to be a growing consensus among observers that the liberationists, who emphasize sociopolitical activism and corporate solidarity against unjust institutions and structures, have not been able to effectively counterbalance or compete with Pentecostals who tow a firm doctrinal line and construct social networks of support for born-again Christians. The growth of Christian base communities or CEBs (from the Spanish *comunidades eclesiales de base*)[30] declined in the late 1980s after an initial surge in the 1970s. After success in increasing levels of awareness of oppression and the need for political responsibility, leaders are leaving the CEBs and turning to political parties and unions.[31] Liberation theology has remained as a parcel of radical intellectuals who are not perceived as being "of the people."[32] Furthermore, progressive priests and bishops who embraced liberationism were systematically restricted by the Vatican in the late 1980s.[33] The penetration of liberation ideology to the masses is limited for these reasons, and the CEBs did and do provide for many Latin Americans closely knit, innovative, Bible-centered communities that, in these characteristics at least, resemble the new Pentecostal church communities.[34] However, most Catholic poor continue to rely not on systematic pastoral attention but on their own popular religiosity, in which ancient Amerindian or African beliefs lay deep beneath the symbolic surface of Christianity.

In the 1980s the poor in certain regions seemed to become not only disenchanted with but increasingly suspicious of political parties, trade unions, demagogic political promises, developmental policies, and the official religion.[35] Pentecostalism came to represent one alternative for expressing popular aspirations as well as a hope for salvation. The stronger the malaise, however, the more severe was the religious remedy for the proletariat and subproletariat. Pentecostals built communities that feature strong leadership, encourage full participation of women and men in the higher calling of church, and perhaps most important, inculcate an ethic of work suitable to the economic system. The hope of personal salvation, the forgiveness of guilt, the affirmation of personal worth, the provision of an encompassing surrogate family to serve as a Christian model for the nuclear family—these elements of a fundamentalist message are communicated in the common language of the people, but also in a mode that bespeaks a familiarity with success and an ease in the face of the challenges of modernization. "Transformation," "new life," and "power"—over one's personal and familial life and destiny—are the key words in the discourse of those who convey the message.

The Appeal to Families: Case Studies

The first case study is of a charismatic[36] congregation in Brazil—the largest Latin American country, with about 150 million inhabitants. Almost one-fifth of its population is actively involved with one Protestant church or another.[37] The second case study, of a Pentecostal church in Venezuela (where the Protestant population is relatively small), illustrates how Pentecostal groups move to the city, experience upward mobility, and reach out to middle- and upper-class people. A Quichua[38] group in rural Ecuador is the third case study. Ecuador, one of the smallest countries in South

America, has a high percentage (about 40 percent) of native Indian population. This study demonstrates the impact on indigenous peasants of the fundamentalist message about the family.

Brazil

Goiania, the capital city of the state of Goias, is not well known outside of Brazil, although its population totals more than a million. Situated 235 kilometers southwest of Brazilia, the thirty-year-old capital city of Brazil, Goiania and its inhabitants are often the subject of jokes in that its citizens are regarded as "hicks" by those living in Sao Paulo, Rio de Janeiro, or Porto Alegre. The Comunidade Evangélica is a congregation of about four thousand members built from scratch in Goiania since 1976, when two lay people were ordained to serve twenty young persons committed to God. In this way an informal group became a church.[39] The initial group was made up of young people converted in the early 1970s by the evangelistic work of Youth for Christ, a North American missionary organization that flourished in the wake of World War II and "borrowed techniques and images from consumer culture to make fundamentalist religion appeal to a wider audience."[40]

"Most of us came from broken homes and held a very negative concept of family," recalled Francisco and Ana-Maria Almeida, one of the five pastoral couples of the church. "So, we escaped 'to the Mount' [of transfiguration] and became kinds of mystics. Then we learned that God wanted us to go down to the valley where there were people as hurt as we were. When we realized that we had to heal first, we started looking for help. Small prayer groups transformed themselves into mutual help communities. As we realized how deficient our family models were, we kept looking for better ones in books and in other Christians."

The Almeidas belong to the generation that experienced vividly the effects of the modernization of Brazil initiated in 1930 with the populist government of Getulio Vargas. During the 1950s the industrialization of the country was intensified and was accompanied by an explosive urban growth, increasing dependency on foreign capital, concentration of the land in few hands, and inflation.[41] Traditional families were uprooted in this period of drastic social, political, and economic changes. Children of this era grew to adulthood and formed the Comunidade Evangélica (CE), in large part to restore broken family structures and provide a model for family life for the displaced. A majority of CE members (69 percent) today describe their pastors and leaders as the conveyors of models of "love, care, and mutual respect among spouses," "stability in relationships," "adequate raising of children," "sharing their home with others," and so forth. These pastors and leaders promote study and reading among the congregants and make available a spate of evangelical-fundamentalist sources on family life and community living. Among the books read or consulted by CE members in 1989–90, the Bible ranked first, followed by *God's Plan for Your Family*, written by CE pastor Robson Rodovalho. North American authors such as Jaime Kemps (who lives in Brazil), Tim and Beverly Lahaye, Larry Christenson, James Dobson, and others were also frequently mentioned as influential.

The Comunidade Evangélica church in Goiania sees itself as part of a national network of similar groups that are growing rapidly among middle-class young professionals. Every year this local congregation sponsors a national convention which attracts five thousand delegates, who meet during one week to sing joyfully, listen to teachers, and participate in a variety of workshops, many of them on the family. The leadership is composed of pastors, deacons, and their spouses. In most cases, a married couple works together to form one ministerial team.[42] Most of the delegates/church leaders and pastors run their own small business or are privately or publicly employed. "Tent-making" (self-supporting) missionaries with a trade or profession of their own are sent in couples. Agronomist Carlos Oliviera and his wife, psychologist Martha Oliviera, were in 1990 finishing their preparation as missionaries to Portugal. Another missionary couple was sent to Cincinnati, Ohio. "The Comunidad will initially support us [economically]. Later on we will work in our own professions or in any other job," the Olivieras explained. This arrangement is typical of husband-wife missionary/leadership teams that minister as a family to families.

A departure from former patterns of predominantly male, professional Christian ministry, this practice of couples ministry adopted by CE and other groups in Brazil has begun to challenge the traditional Catholic symbol of female piety centered on the cult of the Virgin Mary. The empowerment of couples in the leadership of the church and the recognition of women as partners in the ministry have been of paramount importance in a country where Catholicism traditionally requires that only celibate men and celibate women reach the status of sanctity, piety, and ministry through life based in a religious community or a monastery. CE ministries are built through notices and "advertisements" promising that pastoral couples will build Christian family groups in neighborhoods and provide pastoral counseling, inner healing cells, and marriage growth groups.[43] One CE member, Ana-María, resigned a teaching post at the State University of Goias to devote full time to counseling and family ministries in the church. Participation of women as teachers, evangelists, pastors, and organizers is remarkably high, and occurs regardless of their age, formal education, or married status.

In spite of the emphasis on marriage and family, the community also publicized its openness to single and divorced people. "When I was feeling depressed after my divorce, they believed in me more than I did in myself," said Esly Carvalho, a psychotherapist. "They invited me to start a 'ministry of reconciliation' in the Comunidade. Now they have started an open discussion on sexual matters, including homosexuality and the sexual abuse of children, which has been a taboo topic in Brazilian life."

CE thus presents itself as more pastorally sensitive and adaptive than the Catholic Church. CE members, however, do not directly challenge, or even seek to usurp, the traditional patriarchal structure of Latino families. In many ways, in fact, the ministry seeks to reinforce those structures by calling men back to positions of responsibility, including headship of the nuclear family. CE members also share many of the convictions of Roman Catholics—80 percent oppose abortion, for example, and 90 percent believe that homosexuality and extramarital sex are morally wrong—although they do not excommunicate or otherwise exclude people who fall short of their moral standards. Indeed, in the CE branches of Brazil it seems that a sui generis combination of conservative theological convictions and adaptive social practices has produced a form of fundamentalistic Christianity that is appealing to many erstwhile Roman Catholics.

The Comunidade Evangélica is not related to the mainline Protestant churches or directly to the Pentecostal ones. Even though members believe in the unity of the church and pray for it, their networks are among the charismatics, organized in independent congregations under local leadership. Since they have actually created their own social space, they are proudly self-governing—a symbol of their capacity to repudiate previous religious loyalties and to choose their own ties.

One important area in which CE differs from Pentecostals is in its appreciation of theological—and secular—training for its leaders. They run their own bible institute where ordinary believers who feel the calling of the Lord and demonstrate the gifts for the pastorate are candidates for the ministry. They ordain their own pastors, usually as couples, and send them throughout Brazil and abroad to start new comunidades. Access to God is not, however, mediated solely by those who go through biblical studies. On the contrary, as in Pentecostalism, men, women, and children have direct access to God, through a personal experience of love and power. This egalitarian emphasis is in part an act of protest in a region where access to the Divine has been mediated traditionally by a exclusive caste. In CE each believer exercises a "gift." Since congregations are built at least in part upon subjective experience, believers are encouraged to share and proclaim this experience as Christian witness. In that way, the distinction between those who produce the religious goods and discourses and those who participate only as passive consumers has been eradicated in CE and in like-minded evangelical groups in Brazil.

This emphasis on couple-oriented work is extremely attractive to Brazilians who are aware of the increasing divorce rate in their country. "As a general rule for all couples in the church," explained Lucía Rodovalho, one of the pastors and wife of the senior pastor:

> We have established that one night in the week should be devoted to the couple as such and another night to the children. No one among the leaders and church workers is allowed to have more than three nights engaged in church business. We all suffered in our families of origin the affective distance between spouses and between parents and children. The entire society around us is suffering of the same. That is even worse among the poor, where we started working three years ago with assistance programs and evangelization. Lack of affection and communication is astonishing.

Rodovalho is a former Catholic nurtured in the traditional Marian piety that idealized motherhood (and virginity)—and undergirded the hierarchical and patriarchal structure of "Christendom"—for almost five centuries in Latin America. Officials of the Catholic Church have resisted innovative interpretations of Mary that would transform her into a courageous protofeminist or a model for the independent woman integrated into the industrialized work force. CE members are willing to discuss the changing status and role of women. But neither do they adopt a feminist model of women's participation in society. In the wake of the massive and unavoidable incorporation of women into the labor market, the cultural separation of sexuality and reproduction, and the urgent demand that families be based on partnership, mutuality, and cooperation between the sexes, CE has developed sophisticated ministries to couples caught up in these cultural shifts. Because devotion to the Virgin Mary has placed virginity and motherhood on cultural pedestals, being a parent—particularly a mother—enjoys a high status. The openness of Protestant groups to the right of a couple to exist independently of child-bearing has provided space for the development of the couple in an environment not hierarchically controlled—but nonetheless sanctioned as truly Christian. This development seems to be welcomed by families long nurtured by spiritual values and symbols but confronted by contemporary demands.

CE continues to convey a message that insists upon the integrity of a nuclear family headed by a man, but it is a message that has been adapted to the exigencies of the contemporary social situation. The transformation of larger political structures in Brazil is not a concern of the community. Rather, families are to be "healed" and strengthened in a Spirit-inspired and Bible-based community dedicated to the survival of the family in a time of economic crisis that may also be a time of socioeconomic opportunity. But it also appears to be a time of loss for the Roman Catholic Church, whose members are leaving to join communities like CE.

Venezuela

The Iglesia Pentecostal Las Acacias is located in a lower-middle-class neighborhood of Caracas. Its building, an old huge cinema that the church bought and remodeled in 1980 when the membership was 450 people,[44] takes up the whole block. It is surrounded by a series of small shops adapted by the church to provide social services to the community, such as clothing and food for the poor, medical and dental attention, adult education, and family counseling, among others. The sanctuary seats more than two thousand people, but it is not sufficient for Sunday worshipers. Three services are held each Sunday, each fully attended, and there are additional services during the week. On the outskirts of this capital city of three million people, the church founded Hogar Vida Nueva (New Life Home) devoted to rehabilitating chemically dependent youths. Claiming a success rate of 80 percent—with most of them actively integrated in the church—the institution has gained recognition from the community and support from the state.

The Iglesia Pentecostal Las Acacias is representative of hundreds of first-generation Pentecostal churches in Venezuela (and thousands in all of Latin America) that function in part as vehicles of upward social mobility. The church was founded in 1940 in Barquisimeto, a city in the interior of Venezuela, by a Canadian Assemblies of God missionary couple. In 1942 those missionaries moved to Caracas and, with a small group of believers, opened a church in the Cerro de Belén, a poor neighborhood.[45] In 1954, after breaking apart from the Assemblies of God, the community took the name Las Acacias and held services in a rented house. Over time the congregants gained higher social status in the community, and eventually the church itself moved to a middle-class neighborhood. By the late 1980s the modality for extending the church into new neighborhoods, both rich and poor, was formation of home groups.

In 1990, in the church's board room, a big map of Caracas hangs on the wall, like those used by city authorities. Each member church is marked, each home group highlighted, and each service to the community underlined. The board of directors is formed of professional men and women of different ages. The pastor Samuel Olson, son of the missionary founders, is a Princeton graduate with a Master of Divinity degree. Among the leaders, he is not the only one with a graduate degree obtained in the United States. Other members of the board and the administrative staff are as highly qualified as the top management of any transnational corporation. They project an image of success, efficiency, honesty, and hard work in the service of the church and the community in general.

Santiago Montero, a former drug addict who was rehabilitated in Hogar Vida Nueva, is one of the pastors of Las Acacias. "I come from a large family of twelve siblings," he says. "My father, a mason, used to drink a lot. He did not have much formal education and practically did not give us any kind of orientation. There was no communication between parents and children in my family of origin. When I got married, at the age of thirty, I chose my family models from Christian couples in the church. I had to learn a lot about communication and mutual acceptance in marriage." Santiago and his wife, together with fifty other couples of the church, have participated in Marriage Enrichment programs sponsored by Las Acacias and other evangelical churches in Caracas. In 1990 that program was being reproduced by couples in workshops and weekend retreats as an effort to reinforce marriage and family relationships. The Marriage Enrichment manual covers themes such as the new roles of men and women in an evangelical community and in contemporary society, management of time and money, and "techniques for sexual fulfillment."

Open discussion of topics related to modern living and sexuality seems appealing to couples raised in the Roman Catholic Church in which traditional roles of men and women tend to be maintained. Out of my sample, 52 percent of the members of the Las Acacias congregation are married, 29 percent are single, 9 percent are widows, and 10 percent are divorced. "I knew the Lord after my divorce from my first husband," said Ana Lucía, forty-three, in one of the prayer groups linked to Las Acacias meeting in one of the exclusive upper-class neighborhoods of Caracas. "I had rejected my Catholic tradition because I was not convinced at all of the punishing God presented by the Church. My new marriage came into existence 'in the Lord,'" she said. Her marriage is sustained, she said, by the values she has found in the Bible.

> I really apply all the teachings of the Lord to my life. I took classes on Marriage and Family Relations in the Theological Seminary [sponsored also by Las Acacias]. Today I know that "love covers over a multitude of sins"—as St. Peter says—which is helping me a lot in my new relationship. My ideal of married life is a couple united in love and freedom; each one keeping his and her individuality and sharing each other in intimacy. I have my circle of friends, artists, very sensitive people with a great spiritual need, to whom I want to witness opening my home for a prayer group.

Ana Lucía has managed to combine in her own life a peculiar set of biblical principles for interpersonal relationships with the aspirations of a contemporary artist. That kind of blend is possible in a Protestant church, and especially in a Pentecostal one where each believer, after showing evidence of conversion, is encouraged to read, study, interpret, and apply the Bible to his or her own needs, in line with the notion of the universal priesthood of all believers.

Ana Lucía and Santiago are at the extremes of the social class spectrum of Venezuela, where the minority which constitutes the upper class holds most of the wealth and power. The country ranks second on the continent in oil exports, and about half of the population struggles for survival.[46] Ana Lucía lives in the modern and sophisticated eastern part of Caracas, served by wide highways and luxurious shopping centers, while Santiago comes from a shantytown like those multiplying around the city. Besides their common new faith and their common interest in learning new ways of relating with their spouses, they also share a common religious background: Catholicism. Eighty-nine percent of the members of Las Acacias in 1990 were former Roman Catholics, while only 8 percent were second-generation evangelicals. Three percent did not profess any religion before. Congregants from Catholic backgrounds shared a list of common complaints about the Church: its priests were foreign-born and did not express the faith in culturally sensitive ways; the Church was not responding to their spiritual needs; and rites and rituals were found meaningless. The new evangelicalism provided expressive participatory forms of worship, a sense of empowerment and belonging, and, most important, guidance in "translating" the traditional Catholic symbols into a nonhierarchical, nonsacramental religious mode.

Many women today have to raise their children without the support of a man, and often these children develop ambivalent feelings toward their absent progenitors. Boys, on the one hand, are emotionally distant from their fathers; on the other, they emulate male behaviors as symbols of power and prestige. This has developed a particular type of family: affectionately organized around the mother, with the "macho"[47] in a peripheral role. "I had to learn the roles of a man and a husband," said Freddy Salas, thirty-three, a small business administrator:

> I did not have an adequate model in my family of origin. In my early experience, the woman was the head of the household since my father was mostly absent. When he was at home, he did not allow us to play, to cry, much less to help our mother in her domestic tasks. To show up his *hombría* [maleness] he did not file his fingernails, he scratched the walls. I also grew up defending myself with my fists. I had to fight and drink to demonstrate that I was a macho. My fiancé left me because of my fighting and my drinking.

Salas is describing a typical Venezuelan home of the lower-class mestizo and mulatto population. In the Caribbean, northern Colombia, the coast of Venezuela, and in northern Brazil, where black settlements were numerically important, families tend to be even more strongly organized around a dominant feminine figure. Males do not remain physically at home in a regular and permanent manner.[48] In this sense the fundamentalistic message about the role of the man as father and husband, with its emphasis on the domestic submission of the wife, concretely expressed in the teach ings of Las Acacias and their readings,[49] seems attractive to both women and men. The traditional patriarchal ideology of family relations is a welcome corrective to the problem of male absence from the family. Teaching men about family management includes a new discipline, an emphasis on seriousness, cooperation, demonstration of affection, compassion, and above all "responsibility"—meaning economic support and fidelity. In a region where machismo has been part of the fabric of the culture, the "headship" ideology may be perceived as protection of women and children and the attempted easing of a heavy burden from the shoulders of proletariat and subproletariat women. Other studies[50] reveal that when men are converted, they reduce their drinking, fighting, and womanizing and increase their concern for the home and the family. "Evangelical religion literally restores the breadwinner to the home and restores the primacy of bread in the home. . . . Above all it renews the innermost cell of the family, and protects the woman from the ravages of male desertion and violence."[51]

The majority of those surveyed (60 percent) converted in the company of relatives or close family members. "My sister, who was attending a Protestant church, invited me to a service where I got converted after a deep, internal struggle," one interviewee explained. "The day I got converted I really cried with physical tears. The Holy Spirit made me a therapy. Now I can kiss a baby, I can make home chores . . . and keep being a man! I am not ashamed of crying, it is part of my healing process."

Venezuela benefited from a prosperous oil economy from the 1950s to the 1970s. Women were allowed to integrate into the labor market during the boom. Many others attended secondary schools and universities. Men were no longer the exclusive breadwinners, families became fewer in number, women enjoyed economic independence: in a sense, the country crossed the threshold of contemporary history. New ideological paradigms were needed to explain and justify the social transformation, and the new evangelical churches have been providing and articulating values and behaviors appropriate for a developing urban society—all the while retaining the conviction that these adaptations are in keeping with Christian norms and values.

In Las Acacias, conversion changed men and women's roles in household management. These new roles departed from patterns of behavior in the previous generation (mostly non-Protestant): men were—or were supposed to be—the main providers, were to define the rules in their homes and decide on financial matters; women were in charge of maintaining and cleaning the home and raising and educating the children. Women were to be the providers of affection and spiritual guidance. With conversion to the evangelical faith, women became more actively involved in establishing the home rules, and assumed a greater role in determining the use of money and time, while men became more affectionate and domestic. Sixty-five percent believed that men and women should work together for the economic supply of the family, spiritual leadership, and taking of decisions. This pattern occurred, and these convictions were voiced, however, alongside a competing rhetoric of patriarchalism reinforced by a biblical literalism and strident moral code. In this sense there seems to be a gap between professed belief and operative belief, that is, between the ideal and the actual. Autonomy for women "in the Lord" is encouraged in Las Acacias, while dependence on men—even on born-again husbands—is questioned. Alongside reaffirmations of the Christian family as led by the father and husband, there is a growing awareness that women are and have been the builders of the new evangelical and Pentecostal congregations; that while male missionaries and indigenous pastors still tend to predominate in local communities, women increasingly take on leadership roles in these communities; and that men are often drawn into active membership by their wives. Many Pentecostal churches in Latin America that experience upward mobility evince a similar pattern. If this is "fundamentalism" of a sort in that it binds born-again believers to a close-knit moral community governed by literal biblical principles, it is nonetheless a new variant of evangelicalism, one that is only selectively conservative of traditional patterns of behavior and is strikingly adaptive in matters of family life, church organization, and leadership.

Ecuador

Ecuador is one of the smallest countries in South America. Forty percent of the population is native Indian. Semi-feudal societal conditions existed in Ecuador which kept its markets out of the world economy until the 1970s. With oil exportation beginning in 1974, Ecuador experienced a brief period of rapid growth of its national product and its public expenditure. An equally rapid decline in the 1980s placed Ecuador among the rest of indebted countries of the region, struggling to maintain itself.[52]

Protestant penetration of Ecuador was successfully resisted until the late 1800s by the Roman Catholic Church, which was tied to the landowning elite and controlled education and public opinion. Incipient Protestant presence was only possible with the liberal revolution of 1895. In the early twentieth century, lay fundamentalist faith missions from North America, such as the Gospel Missionary Union and the Christian and Missionary Alliance, began to work in the coastal areas, which were more liberal politically and less tied to the landowning aristocracy.[53] Historical or mainline churches were absent. By 1950 the total Protestant population had reached only a few thousand. After World War II, with the closing of the missionary fields in China, an avalanche of North American fundamentalist and conservative missionaries arrived in Ecuador, including Pentecostals, Baptists, Evangelical Covenant, and Church of Christ missionaries. Nonetheless, only a moderate (3 percent annual) rate of Protestant growth is found in Ecuador in 1990. The exception to this rate of growth is found in the province of Chimborazo in the central highlands, where massive native Indian conversions to Protestantism occurred after agrarian reform was proclaimed in 1964, and especially after the new Reform Law passed in 1973.[54] Chimborazo became the most Protestant province in the Ecuadorian highlands by 1976, when evangelical missionaries claimed 10 percent of its two hundred thousand Quichuas. By 1986 Quichua pastors said they were shepherding fifty thousand people. Catholic opponents credited them with 30 percent of the Indian population, and World Vision's evangelical directory claimed even more.[55]

Amerindian groups have stubbornly survived under severe conditions of exploitation, genocide, and discrimination during the last five hundred years after America was "discovered" by the Europeans. It is precisely among these groups, threatened with extermination of their ethnic identity by assimilation into the main culture, that the fundamentalist message is being spread fast and vigorously (and not only in Ecuador, but also in Bolivia, Peru, Guatemala, and Mexico).

The Gospel Missionary Union (GMU), a North American fundamentalist faith mission working among the Quichuas since 1902, had only 330 baptized members in 1966. The Indigenous Association of Quichua Churches claims now to be growing at the rate of 33 percent annually.[56] The presence of North American missionaries since the turn of the century is not sufficient explanation for that growth in a place where a "holy alliance" of landowners, state authorities, and the Roman Catholic Church kept ideological and economic control over the Indians for centuries. There are two important historical events that should be taken into account. First, the new social doctrine of the Catholic Church after Vatican II helped break the role of the Church as a traditional legitimizer of the hacienda system, which weakened the control of the landowner class and established an official and effective separation of church and state. Second, governmental programs of agrarian reform carried out in the 1960s and 1970s released Indian labor for the needs of the growing capitalist farming along the coastal area and the urban construction industry in the cities. It also allowed peasants to establish a more fluid exchange with the national society and a monetary economy.

It was at this juncture that GMU, already present in the area with clinics, schools, radio stations, and the New Testament translated into the native language, Quichua, reaped a harvest. One of the few scientific studies of rural Protestantism in Latin America shows,[57] in contradiction to those who assert the overwhelming disruptive effect of dominant ideologies on the indigenous consciousness, that the Indian communities of the region have reaffirmed their ethnic identity and their creative capacity by adapting fundamentalist Christianity to their own reality. It asserts that through forms and rituals of their own version of Protestantism they have maintained and even revived a great deal of their reciprocal family and social relations, in opposition to individualism and competitiveness characteristic of most Protestant groups.

Indian groups have strongly resisted social relations and ideological practices which have gone against their own identity. "Their great flexibility and creative capacity have permitted them to adapt and transform their own traditions in order to give new answers, sometimes in conciliatory ways, sometimes in willful opposition, but always keeping or recovering their dignity as unique cultural groups."[58]

Evangelical "Quichuas"—the name they prefer as an affirmation of their own language—in the 1980s showed a new outward appearance characterized by abstinence from alcohol, neat attire, a desire for education, a new role and status for women, and a sense of belonging to a worldwide Christian family. This new image has served also as a form of protest against a long history of exploitation. For centuries Indians in Ecuador have been treated literally as beasts of burden and subhuman beings. "When I myself, a woman, approached an Indian woman to start a conversation, she avoided me and tried to fuse herself with the wall," said Blanca Muratorio, after months of doing research in Chimborazo. "But when I met an evangelical woman she related to me as a person and spoke to me with a language saturated with Bible verses."[59]

This new faith has helped the Indians restructure their family practices. Evangelicalism, with its emphasis on individual conversion, is nonetheless growing through the channels of the kinship system. Nuclear families are usually converted as a group and then convince the rest of their relatives. Testimonies about restored family relations and kinship ties are very common in their worship services. Muratorio comments:

> Protestantism has had a decisive influence in the Quichua family, mainly because it has reduced the level of violence among its members. All the evangelical informers mention the fact that they used to beat each other and neglect their children, especially when they were drunk. The more pacific family relations have led the peasant couple to a more equal participation in domestic labor and in agricultural work. Husbands who teach their wives to read and do arithmetic can often be found now. Women assert that this knowledge has given them more independence, permitting them to go to the market on their own and to have more confidence in themselves when they confront the mestizo merchants.[60]

Worship services take place not only in churches or sanctuaries, but very frequently in homes. *Culto familiar* (family worship) services take place once a week and include songs, prayers, and Bible study. They are a family event, including relatives and close neighbors, led by the male head of the household in a dialogical fashion so that all may participate. This worship service transforms the peasant home into a "sacred" place, in contrast with the hierarchical space created by Catholicism where the temple is the main worship place and where all sacred things are under control of the priest.

The ambiguity between the acceptance of the status quo promoted by the fundamentalist ideology and the struggle of the Quichua people against segregation and exploitation is a topic to be further studied. Is this kind of Protestantism a vehicle for the assertion of aboriginal Indian rights in a society dominated by whites and mestizos? Is it going to limit itself to express a form of ethnic and spiritual liberation? Is it going to be manipulated by the political establishment or is it going to be part of a joint adventure with other workers and peasants? Meanwhile, Protestant Quichua families are obviously on the road to prosperity. Their houses are bigger and better looking, the women are reading and writing, the children go to the university, the men are sober. And their awareness of their political potential is growing: in 1984 Manuel Naula, a member of the Protestant Quichua community of Chimborazo, became the first elected Indian congressman.[61]

Conclusion

Conservative Protestantism—whether called by its adherents "evangelicalism," "fundamentalism," or "Pentecostalism"—is increasingly present in Latin America, both in private and public spheres, and seems destined to endure. This "new" evangelization of Latin America may in fact be a stage in an ongoing, irreversible, and universal process of secularization in which the intimate details of family religious life are relegated to the margins of public concern but nonetheless play a vital role in shaping an ethos that empowers lower- and middle-class people to become part of the small businesses and industries that are attempting to transform these regions into players in the modern pluralistic world. The new evangelicalism may also be seen as a process of differentiation from monopolistic systems of belief—a process that occurred much earlier in the Anglo society on both sides of the Atlantic—and as a religious movement of the dispossessed seeking upward mobility. Less central to my presentation has been a theme that runs through other analyses of Latin American evangelicalism, namely, that it is the long arm of North American fundamentalists aimed at undermining progressive forces, popular organization, and revolutionary movements.

In fact, conservative evangelicalism is shaping the lives of millions of Latin Americans and is organizing and training the poor in alternative ways of surviving in the midst of chaotic, strangled economies. At the same time, it is "conserving" the family by providing creative models of family relations resistant both to the roles assigned the sexes by tradition and culture as well as to the competitive stereotypes of modernity. Evangelicalism is also providing for the uprooted and alienated a new set of relationships and networks based on a common faith, a common book, and a common destiny.

Spreading mainly among the poor and middle classes, whose impoverishment deepens in a climate of general crisis, the new faith organizes the lives of believers at three levels: as individuals, as members of a given family, and as social beings. At the individual level, every convert is expected to experience a personal conversion that transforms faith from a conglomerated cultural affair to a differentiated individual asset that is personally owned, valued, developed, and shared. The "fundamentalist" message for the family offers alternative models of relationship as well as new roles for women and men that are adjusted to the exigencies of contemporary society. At the same time, the emphasis placed on the role of the man as chief of the household is often unquestioningly accepted as a counter-balance to abandonment of families by males. Many of these people themselves have, after all, suffered the deterioration of family life. This theologically informed domestic conservatism provides a greater measure of security to women and children and establishes new guidelines of affection, responsibility, and leadership for men.

The fundamentalist message has made its impact at a moment when there has been a void of voices, models, and proposals regarding family life. The Roman Catholic teaching on family life was and remains conservative, but has been less adaptive to new social and economic circumstances. Proponents of liberation theology, though progressive in social matters, are concerned primarily with macroanalysis and social structural changes. Mainline Protestant denominations in Latin America are pursuing family policies from the perspective of a liberal Protestantism of post-Christian Europe. Finally, governmental bureaucracies in Latin America have always been slow in taking initiatives, and political parties are preoccupied with other issues. Into this vacuum a legion of fundamentalist and conservative evangelical groups has moved, armed with concise proposals for family life, with literature and preaching, and with a convincing fervor.

The void being filled is not only at the ideological level. Pentecostals at the grass-roots level are experimenting with "economies of solidarity" among families of their congregations by exchanging goods and services as a means of survival. Such alternative ways of interacting economically, marked by reciprocity networking, personal relationships, and community values, seem essential for the survival of the poor and even the middle class.

At the community level, the new evangelicalism is creating its own autonomously governed spaces where believers encounter new and significant nets of relationships—which may evoke the kin, the fictive kin, or the extended family ties—and where they are able to exercise new values, behaviors, and acquired skills, apart from the outside world. These new networks lend to the labor market elements of respect, honesty, responsibility, and loyalty that are not commonplace. In that respect the new faith functions as an important socializing factor of the lower strata into the values of the dominant society. Latin American evangelicals, then, fulfill a double (and ambiguous) role. On the one hand, they are instrumental in the trend toward consolidation of the bourgeoise democracy. On the other hand, they also provide room for one of the few forms of popular organization by providing answers to the immediate needs of the dispossessed and uprooted.[62]

Latin Americans from middle- and lower-classes may have learned in the last part of this century what aboriginal peoples have been doing for centuries: adopting a faith, worldview, and ideology in order to assure their survival, reaffirm their identity, and organize their immediate future. As people have migrated from the countryside into the city looking for better jobs and educational opportunities for their children, Pentecostal communities have become havens and way stations in the journey up the socioeconomic ladder. They teach empowerment, a sense of worth, new meaning for life, new disciplines for work, new models for family life, new skills for articulate communication and group organization, and last but not least, "the command of the new technology of conversion,"[63] which combines the pre-literate and the post-literate, the vocal and the tactile, words and symbols, the personal contact and the mass media. Pentecostal churches are now reaching the middle class and shaping their message even to the upper class, as was clearly the case of the Pentecostal church in Venezuela visited for this study.

Women, "the oppressed of the oppressed" and the voiceless group in the region, find in evangelical and Pentecostal communities the space and the opportunity to exercise their gifts. In practice if not in theory, women participate as equals in the governing of their homes, their time, their gifts, and their future; their husbands are encouraged to encounter a relational and affective part of themselves denied by the traditional macho culture.

The cultural impact of the new evangelicalism is unquestionable. What remains in question is the future scope of its influence. In the highly differentiated societies of North America and Europe, a social movement of this magnitude may remain apolitical or withdrawn from the public arena. But in Latin America, where politics and religion have been traditionally and inextricably linked, there is no guarantee that the new evangelicalism will remain isolated from the mainstream of political life.

The political impact of evangelical Protestantism in Latin America was marginal until the 1960s. It was a miniscule part of the liberal political movement which promoted democracy, modernization, and anti-oligarchic and anti-Catholic thinking. With the decline of the liberal political project in the region and the growth of Pentecostalism in the 1970s and 1980s, Latin American Protestantism developed new forms of political participation. Some groups reproduced the hacienda system with authoritarian chiefs (*caudillos*) wielding power over the oppressed and marginalized. Members of other groups became chaplains to populist politicians, dictators, or members of the military. Still others withdrew into millenarian, apocalyptic, or sectarian movements.[64]

By 1990 signs abounded that the evangelical presence was already being felt on the political level as an emerging electorate. Chapter 15 in this volume by Susan Rose and Quentin Schultze demonstrates this tendency in Guatemala, where in 1990 two presidential candidates were evangelicals. That year evangelical Venezuelans also formed a political party and ran fourth in the national elections. In Peru the presidential campaign of Alberto Fujimori was supported and in areas conducted by evangelicals of different denominations.

At this writing, however, the influence of the new evangelicalism is felt primarily in the family and in interpersonal relations, and it does not yet seem strong, articulate, or aware enough to compete consistently on a national level with the Roman Catholic Church or the state in the implementation of public policies, even those affecting the family. But this, too, may change as religious fundamentalists and Latin American families alike gain strength as a result of the processes of conversion taking place in the 1990s.

Notes

1. The term "new evangelicalism" is also used to refer to the progressive wing of evangelicalism in the United States, but I do not mean to equate or even directly compare these two recent manifestations of evangelicalism. The "new evangelicalism" in Latin America is progressive in that it facilitates the adaptation of first-generation Protestant families to the social and economic environment, but it also strives to preserve a traditional family pattern and religiopolitical conservatism. I also use the term to distinguish these new churches from traditional Protestantism.

2. The 1960s represent an important divide in the political and religious history of Latin America. Its landmark events include the following: the Cuban revolution, which was declared a Marxist model for

the proletariat in the region; the avalanche of North American missionaries, mostly fundamentalists, invading the region after China closed its doors; the convening of the Second Vatican Council and the Medellin Latin American Bishops Conference, followed by the articulation of liberation theology; the rise of military dictatorships; the growth of evangelicalism and Pentecostalism; and so on.

3. "A Decade of Challenges, Latin America in the 90s," *Latin American Press* 22, no. 27 (19 July 1990). Samuel Blixen, "Latin Americans Live with Economic 'Shock,'" *Latin American Press* 22, no. 41 (8 November 1990).

4. Christian Lalive d'Epinay, *Haven of the Masses: A Study the Pentecostal Movement in Chile* (London: Lutterworth Press, 1966);

Sinais dos tempos, diversidade religiosa no Brasil (Rio de Janeiro: ISER, 1990); Francisco C. Rolim, *Pentecostais no Brasil, uma interpretação socio-religiosa* (Petropolis: Vozes, 1985).

5. UNESCO, *Familia y desarrollo en América Latina y el Caribe* (Estudios y Documentos URCHSLAC, 1988), p. 11.

6. David Martin, *Tongues of Fire: The Explosion of Protestantism in Latin America* (Oxford: Basil Blackwell, 1990), p. 181.

7. Jean-Pierre Bastian, *Historia del Protestantismo en América Latina* (Mexico: CUPSA, 1990), pp. 43–96.

8. George M. Marsden, *Fundamentalism and American Culture: The Shaping of Twentieth Century Evangelicalism, 1870–1925* (Oxford: Oxford University Press, 1980), pp. 128, 165, 182.

9. William Read, Victor M. Monterroso, and Harmon A. Johnson, *Latin American Church Growth* (Grand Rapids, Mich.: Wm. B. Eerdmans, 1969), p. 47.

10. Martin, *Tongues of Fire,* pp. 14–23.

11. Orlando E. Costas, *Theology of the Crossroads in Contemporary Latin America* (Amsterdam: Rapodi, 1975).

12. José Valderrey, *Sects in Central America: A Pastoral Problem,* Bulletin No. 100 (Brussels: Pro Mundi Vita, 1985), p. 9. Pentecostals are often referred to as "sects" by the mass media, the Roman Catholic Church, and the occasional sociological study. See Franz Damen, *El desafío de las sectas* (La Paz, Bolivia: Secretariado Nacional de Ecumenismo, 1988); *Right-Wing Religious Sects* (Rome: IDOC, 1988); Tomas Bamat, *¿Salvación o dominación? Las sectas religiosas en el Ecuador* (Quito: Editorial el Conejo, 1986); and Abelino Martínez, *Las sectas en Nicaragua* (San José, Costa Rica: Editorial DEI, 1989).

13. The term "popular" connected with population, education, and such, is used in Latin America in a definite historical context. It is used in contradistinction to the elite, and to describe a movement from the bottom to the top, from the periphery to the center, from powerlessness to empowerment. It refers to the people as the subject and not as the object of history and to a process of organization of the dispossessed toward social change. *Pro Mundi Vita Studies,* no. 4 (1988): 13–14.

14. The Christian Missionary Alliance in Lima and other capital cities is growing among middle-class people. The Gospel Missionary Union has had an impact among native Andean Indians in central Ecuador. Seventh Day Adventists are increasingly present in rural and urban areas of almost every country.

15. Carmelo Alvarez, "Los Pentecostales en América Latina: ¿Ecuménicos o evangélicos?" *Kairos,* no. 1 (México, December 1988): 12.

16. December 1990 in Santiago, Chile; January 1988 in Salvador, Bahia, Brazil; and April 1989 in Buenos Aires, Argentina.

17. Encuentro de Pentecostales Latinoamericanos (Meeting of Latin American Pentecostals), "Documento de síntesis" (Salvador, Bahia, Brazil, January 1988), pp. 1–2.

18. Juan Sepúlveda, "Reflexiones sobre el aporte Pentecostal a la misión de la Iglesia en América Latin" (Paper presented to the Encuentro de Pentecostales Latinoamericanos, Buenos Aires, April 1989), p. 11.

19. Martínez, *Las sectas en Nicaragua,* carried out a study in Nicaragua in 1988 in an attempt to clarify why Pentecostals appealed primarily to the rural and urban poor, precisely the same base the Sandinistas claimed as their own.

20. Bernardo L. Campos, "De la experiencia a la teología Pentecostal" (Paper presented to the Encuentro de Pentecostales Latinoamericanos, Buenos Aires, April 1989), p. 6.

21. Pablo Richard, *Death of Christendom, Birth of the Church* (Maryknoll, New York: Orbis Books, 1989), p. 71.

22. Zelia Seiblitz, "Sociedade Brasileira de defesa da tradiçao, família e propriedade," in *Sinais dos tempos, Diversidade religiosa no Brazil* (Rio de Janeiro: Instituto de Estudos da Religiao, 1990).

23. Although Susan D. Rose asserts that "Guatemalan Upper Classes Join the Evan-

gelicals" (Paper presented at the American Sociological Association and Association for the Sociology of Religion, Atlanta, August 1988), what she describes is the petit bourgeoisie. My case study of Venezuela shows initial responses in those circles, but this phenomenon by no means seems a massive movement.

24. Richard, *Death of Christendom,* p. 67.

25. Martin, *Tongues of Fire,* pp. 58 and 106.

26. Research was done by personally interviewing pastors and lay leaders, and asking a selected sample in each area to fill in questionnaires. Throughout this chapter I have quoted freely from these interviews and the statistics gathered from the questionnaires. Supplementary bibliographical research was necessary for all three. Questionnaires were assigned in equal numbers to men and women of different social strata, in five different age-groups. Out of 416 questionnaires distributed, 235 were returned: 98 (42 percent) men and 137 (58 percent) women with a fair distribution among age-groups. Responses were processed by country to make comparisons.

27. The percentage converted by family members or relatives is 74.6 percent. Fifteen percent reported being converted by the preaching of the church, and only 1.2 percent by radio or television.

28. These patterns were examined by Oscar Lewis, "La cultura de la pobreza," *Mundo Nuevo,* no. 5 (Paris, November 1966): 36–42. A more recent description is found in Joyce Dickey, *Peregrinaje de esperanza: La vida de la madre de una guerrillera* (Quito: Editorial el Conejo, 1989).

29. Sepúlveda, "Reflexiones sobre el aporte Pentecostal," p. 12.

30. Christian base communities are a grass-roots movement within the Roman Catholic Church, where reading of the Bible, analysis of the social reality, and projection to the community are the main features. "The two axes—Christian community and solidarity *(comunidad)* and social commitment and solidarity *(de base)*—converge in the church *(eclesial).*" Guillermo Cook, *The Expectation of the Poor: Latin American*

Basic Ecclesial Communities in Protestant Perspective (Maryknoll, N.Y.: Orbis Books, 1985), p. 70.

31. Jose Bittencourt Filho, "Las iglesias brasileñas: Un breve diagnostico," Focus (Guatemala), CELEP, no. 97, Julio–Agosto 1990.

32. Martin, *Tongues of Fire,* p. 290.

33. Some examples of public domain are Leonardo Boff, Bishop Casaldaliga, and Cardinal Paulo Evaristo Arns in Brazil.

34. On the dynamics of Catholic base communties, see Daniel H. Levine, *Religion and Political Conflict in Latin America* (Chapel Hill: University of North Carolina Press, 1986); Scott Mainwaring, *The Catholic Church and Politics in Brazil, 1916–1985* (Stanford: Stanford University Press, 1986); and W. E. Hewitt, *Basic Christian Communities and Social Change in Brazil* (Lincoln: University of Nebraska Press, 1991).

35. UNESCO, *Familia y desarrollo,* pp. 3–15.

36. Charismatic groups in Latin America exist among Roman Catholics and Protestants. They are distinguished by their emphasis on the work and gifts of the Holy Spirit in ordinary believers. Even though charismatic manifestations are also a central part of Pentecostals, charismatic groups are newer, coming into existence in the 1960s, and especially successful in urban middle-class strata.

37. David Stoll, *Is Latin America Turning Protestant?* (Berkeley: University of California Press, 1990), pp. 8, 333. Vittorio Bacchette, "Brazil: Roman Catholic Leaders Alarmed by Pentecostal Growth," *Ecumenical Press Service,* World Council of Churches, Geneva, (October 1990), p. 45.

38. Quichua or Quechua is the language of the descendants of the Incas in the Andes. Protestant native Indians of Ecuador have chosen the name of their language—revitalized by Protestant translations of the Bible and abundant production of hymns—to describe themselves.

39. La Comunidade Evangélica de Goiania, *Comunidade evangélica, historia, visão,*

ministério, liderança, declaracão de fé (brochure, June 1986), p. 1.

40. Stoll, *Is Latin America Turning Protestant?* p. 71.

41. Helga Iracema Landgraf Piccolo, "Um esboço da historia do Brasil," in *Presença Luterana 1990* (San Leopoldo: Editora Sinodal, 1989), p. 17.

42. Their presentation brochure lists five couples as pastors and five couples as deacons.

43. Ibid., pp. 11–12.

44. "Resumen de la evolución histórica de la Iglesia Evangélica Las Acacias: Hitos destacados en sus 35 años (A summary of the history of the evangelical church 'Las Acacias': Landmarks in its thirty-five year existence)," (Report to the assembly by the elders and the board, 17 February 1990).

45. Ramón Castillo, "La UEPV, una iglesia con vocación solidaria," *El Informador Pentecostal,* vol. 3, no. 5 (August 1989).

46. Vanessa Cartaya and Yolanda D'Elía, *Pobreza en Venezuela: Realidad y políticas* (Caracas: ESAP-CISOR, 1991), pp. 5, 48.

47. Machismo could be described objectively and subjectively. Objectively, it consists of a series of social regulations, customs, and laws which discriminate against women. Subjectively, it is a series of ideas present both in men and women which regard men as superior to women. As compensation for the ruling role of the male, women tend to make an affectionate circle with their children, leaving men outside, who in turn look for other women with whom the vicious circle keeps reproducing itself. Machism and matrifocality seem to coexist in a complementary way.

48. William L. Visser, "The Dominant Family Structure in the Caribbean," in Masamba Mampolo and Cecile de Sweemer, eds., *Families in Transition* (Geneva: World Council of Churches, 1987), p. 10.

49. Their favorite authors read in 1990 on the topic of the family are in this order (besides the Bible, which is in first place): Tim and Beverly Lahaye, Larry Christenson, and James Dobson.

50. Elizabeth E. Brusco, "The Household Basis of Evangelical Religion and the Reformation of Machismo in Colombia" (Ph.D. diss., New York University, 1986).

51. Martin, *Tongues of Fire,* pp. 181–82, 284.

52. Lucía Carrión, "Ecuador: La familia del sector popular urbano," in UNESCO, *Familia y desarrollo en América Latina y el Caribe.*

53. Padilla J. Washington, *La iglesia y los dioses modernos: Historia del Protestantismo en el Ecuador* (Quito: Corporación Editora Nacional, 1989).

54. Blanca Muratorio, "Protestantism and Capitalism Revisited in the Rural Highlands of Ecuador," *Journal of Peasant Studies* 8, no. 1 (October 1980): 41.

55. Stoll, *Is Latin America Turning Protestant?* p. 273.

56. Tomás Bamat, *¿Salvación o dominación?* pp. 32, 109.

57. Blanca Muratorio, *Etnicidad, evangelización y protesta en el Ecuador* (Quito: Ediciones CIESE, 1982), p. 82, published in English as "Protestantism, Ethnicity and Class in Chimborazo," in Norman E. Whitten Jr., ed., *Cultural Transformation and Ethnicity in Modern Ecuador* (Urbana: University of Illinois Press, 1981).

58. Ibid., p. 12.

59. Part of a 1977 conversation with Blanca Muratorio in Quito, Ecuador, where she was doing research among Protestant Indians.

60. Muratorio, *Etnicidad, evangelización y protesta,* p. 91.

61. Stoll, *Is Latin America Turning Protestant?,* p. 301.

62. Jean-Pierre Bastian, *Historia del Protestantismo en America Latina,* p. 12.

63. Martin, *Tongues of Fire,* p. 108.

64. Jean-Pierre Bastian, *Historia del Protestantismo en America Latina,* pp. 261–73, provides an overall historical interpretation of this phenomenon.

Plural Marriage and Mormon Fundamentalism

D. Michael Quinn

In one sense, it is curious that there is such a thing as Mormon fundamentalism. Only 160 years have passed since the religiously "burned-over district" of New York state gave birth to the *Book of Mormon* in 1830. Despite its youth, Mormonism is to mainline Christianity what early Christianity was to Judaism—a separatist Judeo-Christian movement of extraordinary growth.[1] The principal organization of Mormonism is the Church of Jesus Christ of Latter-day Saints (LDS church), which has worldwide membership of more than eight million people who look to Salt Lake City, Utah, with the reverence usually given to Rome, Jerusalem, and Mecca.

Because LDS membership has doubled every fifteen years or less since 1945, a non-LDS sociologist projects Mormonism will be a world religion of 265 million members within ninety years.[2] For more than a century, the LDS church has dominated the Mountain West of America so completely that the area is known to geographers as the "Mormon cultural region." Mormonism is the first or second largest church in nine western states, the fifth largest in the United States, and presently fields nearly forty-five thousand full-time proselytizing missionaries throughout the world.[3] This Mormon-dominated West is also the home of Mormon fundamentalism, a twentieth-century response to changes in the LDS church that began with public abandonment of the practice of "plural marriage" (polygamy) by a 1890 Manifesto from the church president.

Mormon fundamentalists have embraced the term "fundamentalist,"[4] but generally dislike the word "polygamy." Many regard it as the disbeliever's way of mocking their faith that God sanctions and commands that righteous men of a divine latter-day Covenant marry more than one wife. Some object that "polygamy" could also refer to multiple husbands, and therefore "polygyny" (more than one wife) is the only outsider's term that is accurate. Mormon fundamentalists refer to their practice of multiple marriage as "the Principle," or "Celestial Marriage," or the "New and Ever-lasting Covenant," or the "Priesthood Work," or (most commonly) as "plural marriage." Outside anthropology, even most academics are unfamiliar with the term "polygyny," and this essay therefore uses the general term "polygamy" because it is universally understood to refer to the marriage of a man to more than one living wife at a time. The author hopes this study demonstrates there is no disrespect in his use of "polygamy" and "polygamist."

Like other fundamentalist movements, Mormon fundamentalism suffers from stereotypes fostered by the mainstream religious tradition and by the secular media. The most prevalent stereotype is that all adult Mormon fundamentalists are practicing polygamists, with the obligatory illustration of a bearded man surrounded by a bevy of young wives.[5] Another common image in the popular mind is of Mormon fundamentalist females wearing their hair in long braids, dresses to the ankle, and long-sleeved blouses buttoned to the neck.[6] Non-Mormons and mainstream Mormons often accept the view of the 1981 television drama "Child Bride of Short Creek" that a polygamist's teenage son may have to make a desperate escape to save his girlfriend from the matrimonial clutches of the young man's own father.[7] Like all stereotypes, these distort our understanding of a diverse and complex people.

The 1988 Charles Bronson movie *Messenger of Death* used those polygamy stereotypes in a kinder way but then portrayed the more recent image of wild-eyed Mormon fundamentalists engaging in murder and gun battles over rival claims to authority. This perception of Mormon fundamentalists as sectarian murderers is only twenty years old and is based on the acts of a handful of deranged individuals.[8] Even though the largest Mormon fundamentalist group, at Colorado City, Arizona, prohibits possession of firearms "as a matter of religious faith," the equation of violence and fundamentalism is powerful enough to crop up in a 1987 scholarly examination of Mormon polygamous families.[9]

Numbers

There is a problem in counting Mormon fundamentalists. The LDS church, the news media, and fundamentalists themselves have not always been helpful in giving accurate estimates.

Part of the LDS church's campaign for acceptance by non-Mormons has been to grossly underestimate the number of Mormon polygamists, both before and after the 1890 Manifesto declared an end to polygamous marriages. Church leaders and members usually claim that nineteenth-century polygamous practice was no more than 2–3 percent of the Mormon population in Utah, when it was ten times that rate.[10] During a transitional period of fourteen years after the 1890 Manifesto, LDS leaders secretly authorized and performed about 250 new polygamous marriages, yet only acknowledged the occurrence of "a few," despite disclosures of the larger numbers by a muckraking press and a three-year investigation by the U.S. Senate.[11] After 1906 the LDS church's consistent battle against the performance of new polygamous marriages was characterized by similar distortion. LDS leaders publicly dismissed renegade plural marriages as few in number, whereas privately they exhibited a paranoia that new polygamous marriages were spreading like wildfire.[12]

On the other hand, the news media and some fundamentalists have joined in inflating the numbers of twentieth-century Mormon polygamists. To embarrass the LDS church as well as sell newspapers, early in this century the *Salt Lake Tribune* made the sensational claim that there were "thousands" of new polygamous marriages after the 1890 Manifesto.[13] In like manner, the fundamentalist publication *Truth* later claimed that about twenty-two hundred men entered polygamy after the 1890 prohibition "through the blessings of the Authorities of the Church [i.e., to 1904]."[14] This was ten times higher than the actual numbers.

In recent years, promotional exaggeration has merged with the perceptions of outsiders. In 1974 one fundamentalist wrote that "no less than fifty thousand individuals are personally involved in the living of this law today."[15] That figure is still easy to dismiss as inflated, yet law enforcement officials were soon stunned at the extent of polygamous practice in Utah. Solving the murder of fundamentalist leader Rulon C. Allred in 1977 required close cooperation with fundamentalists of various persuasions who gladly distanced themselves from the aberrant fundamentalists who committed the murder. The Utah attorney general said he was "astonished at the scope of the practice of polygamy" which involved tens of thousands. The Salt Lake County attorney said: "I think that the immensity of the numbers of people right there in Salt Lake County that were practicing polygamy really did shock me. I didn't think that there were that many people that were committed to the fundamentalist ideas and actually actively practicing the fundamentalist theories."[16]

By the late 1980s it was customary to claim a minimum of thirty thousand people living in polygamy.[17] That figure is still a third too high. Even after accepting higher-end estimates on a group-by-group basis, this study finds that, from northern Mexico through the far western United States into southern Canada, about twenty-one thousand men, women, and children are Mormon fundamentalists. These numbers do not include members of the LDS church who accept fundamentalist doctrines without giving allegiance to the movement. Fundamentalist publisher Ogden Kraut observed that there are "professors of religion that I'm acquainted with who believe all the doctrines of fundamentalism, and yet they're teaching at BYU, seminaries, and institutes" of the LDS church. These fundamentalist sympathizers include "high councilmen, bishops, and in some cases stake [diocese] presidents."[18] That may be so, but this study restricts the scope of Mormon fundamentalism to those who demonstrate actual commitment.[19] Contrary to common assumptions, many of these committed fundamentalists are living in monogamous relationships, and about three-fourths of Mormon fundamentalists today have never been members of the LDS church.

The Mormon Mainstream and Plural Marriage

If living in polygamy is not necessary to be a Mormon fundamentalist, how are Mormon fundamentalists different from the currently nonpolygamist Mormon mainstream? That definition requires some discussion of Mormon theology, practice, and history.

Basic theology evolved during the fourteen-year leadership of Mormon founder Joseph Smith, Jr. (1805–1844), but the single most important characteristic of Mormonism has been its claim to the Old Testament tradition of prophetic leadership within an apostolic church of Christ. The LDS church claimed to have living apostles like those of the New Testament, but more important was the church president's claim to be a prophet like Moses—able (if called upon by God) to challenge the authority of any secular pharaoh, to reveal new commandments, to announce new words of God as revelation and scripture, to hold priesthood that bridged the authority of Old and New Testaments, and to lead His people as a self-sustaining, theocratic community. This reinvoking of Old Testament norms within a Christian context alienated Mormonism from traditional Christianity and from Protestant-dominated American society.[20]

In the mid-nineteenth century, Mormonism became "Uncle Sam's abscess," as one book title put it. Using biblical references to a premillennial "restoration of all things," Joseph Smith restored in practice (sometimes secretly) Old Testament forms, and Brigham Young institutionalized them after the founding prophet's murder by a mob in 1844. Polygamy was the most sensational, but equally disturbing to outsiders were Mormon migration to a central place, political hegemony, theocratic ideals and practices, economic cooperation and communalism, antipluralism, and speculative theology that included doctrines that Adam was God, that Christ was married, and that both God and Christ were polygamists.[21] These were flashpoints in the conflict between Mormonism and American society, and from 1862 to 1890 the federal government waged a judicial campaign against Mormonism through antipolygamy legislation. Polygamy was the easiest weapon for the nineteenth-century anti-Mormons to use in attacking everything else they abhorred about Mormonism.[22]

As the government increased its antipolygamy crusade, Mormon leaders defensively countered that the abandonment of plural marriage was theologically impossible. Jan Shipps, the preeminent non-Mormon interpreter of the Mormon experience, has observed that because polygamy alienated Mormons from mainstream America for decades, "the practice of plural marriage gave the Latter-day Saints time to gain an ethnocultural identity that did not entirely rest on corporate [church membership] peculiarity."[23] Mormon leaders gave many rationales for practicing polygamy (including its role in producing a larger number of righteous children), but always subordinated those explanations to the affirmation that revelations of God required the Latter-day Saints to live this "Holy Principle." A frequent advocate of that theme was Apostle Wilford Woodruff, who sermonized on one occasion that if Mormons gave up polygamy, "then we must do away with prophets and Apostles," and told the Mormons a decade later, "Were we to compromise this principle by saying, we will renounce it, we would then have to renounce our belief in revelation from God."[24] Nevertheless, because of the LDS church's official defiance of federal antipolygamy laws since 1862, its very existence hung in the balance by the summer of 1890. To survive, the church either abandoned or redefined all of these radicalisms, beginning with polygamy. Wilford Woodruff himself, as recently sustained LDS church president, announced the Manifesto in September 1890 to end the practice of plural marriage.[25]

Fundamentalist Origins and Definitions

During a forty-year transition after 1890, many LDS church members looked wistfully back at Mormonism's old-time religion. The reasons were larger than polygamy: "The political, social, religious, and economic world [of Mormonism] that emerged after the Manifesto of September 1890 was vastly different from the one that had existed before."[26] Nevertheless, only a few Mormons concluded that the church had corrupted itself in the process of accommodating to American society. Those who regarded these beliefs and practices as non-negotiable merely had to read the pre-1890 published statements of the church leader who issued the 1890 Manifesto. These Latter-day Saints regarded pre-1890 Mormonism as pristine and defined the post-Manifesto church as compromised in theology and authority. By the 1930s, Mormonism's fundamentalist movement resulted from those perceptions.[27]

Mormon fundamentalists believe that the LDS church is "out of order"—in other words, it has strayed off its divinely instituted path by abandoning or changing various practices and beliefs. They are also convinced that plural marriage is a divine revelation and commandment that should be practiced today by those who are willing and worthy. Finally, Mormon fundamentalists accept priesthood authority and officiators not sanctioned by the LDS church. These convictions are the three pillars of Mormon fundamentalism.[28]

But nearly all fundamentalists retained the essential Mormon views of prophetic leadership and authority, and could not simply advocate as a matter of conscience the return to practices and beliefs abandoned by the LDS church. Thus they needed a claim of authority that could counter the fact that LDS president Heber J. Grant— as acknowledged prophet, seer, and revelator in the 1920s—was leading a full-scale retreat from the radical past. Plural marriage was the foundation for fundamentalist authority claims. According to excommunicant Lorin C. Woolley, the main fundamentalist exponent in the 1920s, the president of the church who was living in 1886 had conferred special priesthood authority upon Woolley and others to continue performing plural marriages even if the church abandoned "the Principle." As the last survivor of those men, Woolley in 1929 conferred that apostleship upon others, a Council of Friends or Priesthood Council (most of whom had already been excommunicated from the LDS church). More than 90 percent of fundamentalists center their authority on Lorin Woolley's Council of Friends.[29] The fundamentalists who do not trace their authority through Lorin Woolley claim either the charismatic authority of a vision or a "patriarchal priesthood" traced in some way to Joseph Smith.

The easiest division among Mormon fundamentalists to understand is the split between "groups" and "independents." About 90 percent of fundamentalists belong to organized groups. This study identifies their numbers after inquiries on a group-by-group basis. Each has a history and character of its own.[30]

The Groups

Fundamentalist Church (Colorado City)

The small town of Short Creek (now Colorado City), Arizona, is the home of the largest fundamentalist group. The town was the focus of an unprecedented effort by American law enforcement to destroy a peaceful community, eradicate family relationships, and scatter a people to the winds. This effort is reminiscent of the federal actions against Native Americans in the nineteenth century.[31]

For thirty years after Leroy S. Johnson and other polygamists settled at Short Creek in the late 1920s, the community was the target of outside repression. First, the LDS church conducted wholesale excommunications of Short Creek residents in 1935, the same year the church's behind-the-scenes encouragement resulted in a Utah law defining unlawful cohabitation as a felony. This law exceeded the federal government's definition of polygamous cohabitation as a misdemeanor. Later that year Arizona convicted two "Short Creekers" of polygamy. In 1944, federal and local officers conducted early morning arrests of fifty people from Arizona and Utah. This resulted in the imprisonment of more than twenty men, including Short Creek's leader John Y. Barlow, a member of Woolley's Priesthood Council. In 1953 the Arizona police and the national guard made a predawn raid on Short Creek to arrest its entire population of four hundred.[32] Arizona's governor "said that they intended to put the men in prison, put the women in detention homes, take our children and adopt them out and destroy the records so that no stigma would ever be on our children, and take our lands and use them to pay for the costs of the raid."[33] Arresting officers segregated the older teenage boys, told them to scatter, and then left the unattended youths in a town of empty houses that had been ransacked without search warrants for evidence. Leroy Johnson eventually sought out and returned nearly all of these dispossessed youths to the community.[34]

Arizona made the children wards of the state and placed them in foster homes.[35] Utah authorities defined polygamists' children as neglected and abused, and sent police cars to take them from their parents. The LDS church's newspaper applauded that action and encouraged government seizure of every polygamist's child who could be found. It was two years before 161 young children were allowed to return to their mothers and fathers at Short Creek. Polygamists elsewhere hid their children and lived in dread of having them "taken" on any pretext.[36]

Although the shocks of 1953 reverberated among polygamists of every persuasion, the raid encouraged understandable clannishness in the people of Short Creek (now incorporated as Colorado City, Arizona, and its cross-border "twin city" of Hildale, Utah). In 1977 Leroy Johnson cataloged the collective memory and heritage that bind his group together: "I have been through the '34 raid, raid of '41, when they had Uncle Rich and Uncle Fred arrested, the raid of '44, and the raid of '53. We are still fighting for our liberty." Colorado City's mayor commented, "When people are under persecution from the outside, they always stick tight. They always hold way better together."[37] Often called Short Creekers no matter where they live, this group's economic cooperative was incorporated as the United Effort Plan in 1942. Incorporated by Johnson's successor, Rulon Jeffs, the Fundamentalist Church of Jesus Christ of Latter-day Saints is also called the Johnson-Jeffs group.[38]

The Colorado City group has grown in numbers and geographic distribution since the attempted destruction of its small community in 1953. Born as a polygamous child in 1958 and raised in the group's Salt Lake Valley community, one woman observes: "The Johnson group is very low profile" and therefore difficult to count.[39] Recent court documents list 4,600 beneficiaries of the United Effort Plan in Colorado City–Hildale, which corresponds to the population reported for the school board. The Colorado City group has its only foreign settlement in the farming community of Lister, Canada (near Creston, British Columbia). One Colorado City leader says that 500 to 600 persons in Lister are fundamentalists. Inside sources agree on an estimate of 2,000 Johnson group members in the Salt Lake Valley. There are also multiple-family dwellings of group members in Cedar City and Manti, Utah, and scattered families and individuals elsewhere, which probably add no more than 400 men, women, and children. This adds up to a total of about 7,600 people in the Johnson-Jeffs group.[40]

These numbers include a recent split from the Colorado City group—amounting to 20 percent of the total—originally led by Marion Hammond and Alma Timpson from the Priesthood Council. The Hammond-Timpson group (also called The Second Ward) often lives in coresidence with the main body of Short Creekers, and is difficult to identify in statistics such as the beneficiaries of the United Effort Plan and the Colorado City's school board records of community population. The split has resulted in on-going lawsuits between the two groups.[41]

Apostolic United Brethren

Of comparable size is the Allred group (Apostolic United Brethren). After a stroke, Joseph W. Musser (a member of Lorin Woolley's Priesthood Council) put his physician Rulon C. Allred onto the Council in 1951, which its other members resisted. In January 1952 the Short Creek members of the Council repudiated Allred's position, which split the movement into two groups, each with a rival Council of Friends. This schism has always been peaceful, but it divided families. Allred's group tended to be urban-oriented and more easygoing than the Johnson group, whose population is primarily centered in an isolated commune. Allred and other Salt Lake men had spent seven months in jail in 1945, and he and his families frequently moved out of state in the 1950s to avoid arrest. Still, the Allred group did not directly experience Short Creek's sense of trauma until 1977, when Rulon Allred was murdered and became a martyr for his people, as Short Creekers of 1953 are for the Johnson group. Attendance at his funeral was the largest ever in Utah up to that time.[42]

The Allred group has about 7,200 total members. In 1989 its presiding elder, Owen Allred, reported 700 adults in the Salt Lake Valley, 200 adults in Cedar City, Utah, 500 adults in its commune at Pinesdale, Montana, as well as 300 Mexican fundamentalists in Ozumba, D.F., Mexico, and scattered families in England, Germany, and the Netherlands. Figures are not available for the total number of children in the Allred group, but it is safe to assume that three-quarters of the 1,700 adults are married, and of that number more than half are women with children. Interviews with group members, as well as other sources, indicate that these women have an average of seven children. This yields an estimated 5,500 children or a total of approximately 7,200 members in the Allred group.[43]

Church of the Firstborn

Next in size is a combination of various LeBaron churches. These organized Mormon fundamentalists bypass Woolley's Council of Friends and instead claim authority through a patriarchal priesthood conferred from Joseph Smith to his polygamous brother-in-law,[44] Benjamin F. Johnson, to Johnson's grandson, Alma Dayer LeBaron, through to one of LeBaron's sons. Until 1955, most of the LeBaron family did not discuss the significance of the family's blessings and instead divided their loyalties between the LDS church, the Allred group, and two LeBaron brothers who had unsuccessfully claimed for twenty years to be the prophetic "One Mighty and Strong" of Mormonism.

When Joel F. LeBaron suddenly incorporated the Church of the Firstborn of the Fullness of Times in 1955, his brother Verlan (before converting) was "convinced that we had another false prophet loose in the family." However, most of Joel's immediate family converted after the formal organization of the Church of the Firstborn on 3 April 1956. Joel was First Grand Head, even though he was a monogamist at the time and in temporary violation of the traditional Mormon fundamentalist requirement of polygamy for leadership. He turned his family's ranch in the state of Chihuahua, Mexico, into Colonia LeBaron, a fundamentalist haven with communal laundry, kitchen, and dining area.[45]

Subsequent activities of LeBaron churches seized the attention of other fundamentalists, the LDS church, and eventually the nation itself. Unlike other Mormon fundamentalist groups, the LeBarons sent missionaries to proselytize. They shoved pamphlets under dormitory doors at Brigham Young University and passed them out at the gates of Temple Square in Salt Lake City. They made inroads on other fundamentalist groups which responded with published arguments. After the conversion of a dozen LDS missionaries in 1958, followed by defections of local LDS leaders throughout the West, the LDS church began its first publishing crusade against fundamentalists.[46] Then a schismatic group—the Church of the Lamb of God, led by Joel's brother Ervil LeBaron—murdered Joel in 1972, fire-bombed the LeBaron colony at Los Molinos, killed about twenty other family members and dissident followers, threatened the U.S. and LDS presidents, and then assassinated Rulon C. Allred at his Salt Lake office in 1977. In the decade since Ervil LeBaron's death in the Utah penitentiary, some of his family and followers have committed another twelve sectarian murders within the LeBaron groups. These incredible events reversed the momentum of the Church of the Firstborn and disenchanted all but the most devout.[47]

This murderous violence has stigmatized the Mormon fundamentalists generally, and also stigmatized the overwhelmingly nonviolent fundamentalists who still traced their authority through Alma Dayer LeBaron. One of the principal law enforcement investigators of the LeBaron murderers affirms that there are fewer than fifty persons responsible for this sectarian violence.[48] In 1990 a telejournalist spent two weeks in the polygamous commune of Colonia LeBaron and reported that its population of about one thousand is divided among the Church of the Firstborn and other LeBaron churches, with an additional three hundred LeBaron followers in another location. Followers of LeBaron's patriarchal authority are also scattered from San Diego throughout the West and in Central America. The LeBaron churches now have about seventeen hundred people as the third largest organized form of Mormon fundamentalism.[49]

Davis County Cooperative

One fundamentalist described the financially diversified Kingston group, incorporated as the Davis County Cooperative, as "the most outstanding example in all Mormondom of patriarchal family effort to establish [an economic] united order."[50] Outsiders know a general outline of the Kingston group. Charles W. Kingston was initially aligned with Lorin C. Woolley's fundamentalist authority, but in 1935 his son Eldon Kingston received an angelic commission to begin strict economic communalism with the Kingston family and their followers in Davis County, Utah, immediately north of Salt Lake City. In the early years, these ascetic people wore a uniform: blue bib-overalls for males and blue dresses for females, with no pockets and tied at the waist with string.

Fifty years later outsiders knew the Kingstons had given up uniforms, still lived austerely as individuals, were led by Eldon's much-married brother John Ortell Kingston, and had financial holdings in Utah that attracted front-page attention of the *Wall Street Journal:* a three-hundred-acre dairy farm in Davis County, a cattle ranch and coal mine in Emery County, the Bobco Discount Store, the United Bank, a restaurant equipment business, a clothing factory, wholesale distributors, shoe-repair stores, as well as a one-thousand-acre farm in Idaho.[51] Beyond that, the Kingston group is so secretive that even other Mormon fundamentalists regard it as virtually impenetrable.[52]

More details about the Kingstons have come from a plural wife within its inner circle and a man involved in the economic operation of the Davis County Cooperative.[53] Among the faithful it was first known as the New Order, and each of its male heads of household was identified by number, with Number One for the descendant of Jesus Christ, who leads the group—initially Eldon Kingston and later Ortell Kingston. "What Ortell Kingston said, went. He was a very wise economic manager. Although there was a Priesthood Council, there wasn't any council that he needed to meet with. Whatever decision he made, it happened." After Ortell's death his sister provided functional direction for the Cooperative, in concert with Merlin Kingston as religious leader.

Nonfundamentalists and even the Allred group's presiding elder have assumed that the Kingstons have also abandoned plural marriage along with distinctive dress and unusual dietary rules.[54] However, polygamy is still alive within the inner circle, but restricted primarily to the Kingstons and their kin. "However, there are a lot of interests that draw away from the interest toward plural marriage, especially the emphasis on economic success."

In fact, the Davis County Cooperative is far more extensive than previously understood. In addition to the already identified holdings, the Kingston group owned Murray First Thrift until it was absorbed by another bank. Through a variety of wholly owned subsidiaries and maze of company names, the Davis County Cooperative publishes telephone directories, screen prints T-shirts and sports shirts, owns a trucking company, hardware stores, pawn shops, and clothing stores in Utah, and distributes a variety of products (including video games) to local chain stores and other businesses. In addition, this Mormon fundamentalist organization became the exclusive distributor to stores throughout the United States of work gloves and clothing manufactured in the People's Republic of China.

Without stating the full extent of the Kingston group's revenues, the source for this economic information indicated that the Cooperative's income is far more than a million dollars a month. Until recently computerized, the accounting for these businesses and their thousands of employees was done by hand in a warehouse-size office staffed by women, primarily plural wives: "Now, the women that did all of this accounting brought all of their kids and they took turns babysitting."

The far-flung economic empire of the Davis County Cooperative creates problems for numbering membership in the Kingston group because there are various levels of participation. Those at the lowest level of trust—numbering in the thousands—are employees who may not even realize they are employed by a Mormon fundamentalist organization. In the second level, employees agree with the Cooperative to reduce their paychecks to the amount necessary to pay for such things as rent, mortgage, utilities, taxes, and so forth. At this level, the Cooperative withholds the balance of salary and each month gives the employee a special card redeemable for all goods and services in Cooperative enterprises, with discounts from 10 percent to 50 percent or more. The discounts are calculated monthly according to the Cooperative's profit margin for each item or service and applied to the next month's card.

The Kingston inner circle refuses to discuss religion with those at this second level, even if the special cardholders are polygamists from other fundamentalist groups. At the third level of trust in the Davis County Cooperative, the participant receives an even smaller paycheck, but now receives an apartment or house from among the Cooperative's widely dispersed real estate holdings. Some participants at this third level become assistant managers or managers of Kingston enterprises, and because of this trust, religion may enter the relationship at last, but not necessarily, because "the only people they trusted to really know what was going on were those that were in the family." The Kingston group's children move through the second and third levels with inside knowledge and equal unwillingness to discuss religion with outsiders in those levels of the Cooperative.

Once the Davis County Cooperative became successful, it stopped seeking converts, and now even a trusted outsider may take years (if ever) to finally gain membership at the Kingston group's center. For some, this may come only through polygamous marriage into one of the families at the core. "Those that go to church together are the Kingstons and their families, and a few people of the Fundamentalist point of view." Even here, economic and business matters dominate Sunday meetings for a people who continue to live in austerity despite the cooperative wealth of their organization. This inner circle is really the only level of the Kingston group where participants can be considered Mormon fundamentalists, because "the Davis County Cooperative isn't really a religious organization." Dominated by descendants of the original core of Kingstons, kin, and early converts, the Kingston group's inner circle is made up of about one thousand persons who can be considered fundamentalist members.[55] This is the last fundamentalist group of significant size.

Outside the Groups: The Independents

Ogden Kraut observes that there is a wide assortment of tiny groups—"splinters of splinters"—some with half a dozen followers.[56] A generous estimate is that no more than one thousand men, women, and children belong to this collection of small organizations of Mormon fundamentalists.

The larger groups duplicate many functions of the LDS church. They have sacrament (Communion) meetings, Sunday school classes, and separate meetings for children, youth, women, and ordained men. In addition, fundamentalist groups accept tithing and have incorporated and obtained tax-exempt status. Nevertheless, in such groups as the Allreds' Apostolic United Brethren, the Priesthood leadership receives no salary, stipend, or living allowance.[57]

This duplication of church functions alienates independent fundamentalists who believe that Lorin C. Woolley's commission of authority was limited to keeping plural marriage alive and nothing more. They affirm that before his death in 1934, Woolley said fundamentalists should not collect tithing, congregate, colonize, or proselytize. Louis A. Kelsch, Jr., was the youngest member of Woolley's Council and became the first independent as early as 1941. Independents share a pessimism that Mormon fundamentalism has also gone "out of order."

The only meetings conducted by independents are private discussions in a family's home, where the sacrament is administered by those with priesthood. If unrelated families gather on Sundays, meeting places rotate so that a different head of household conducts each week, avoiding the appearance of leadership.

Independent fundamentalists estimate their own diverse numbers as 2,000 or 3,000. This is supported by the fact that fundamentalists in the Kelsch family alone currently amount to 300 people.[58] Therefore, it is safe to estimate the total number of independent fundamentalists as approximately 2,500 men, women, and children who live in urban centers like Salt Lake City, Boise, Las Vegas, Denver, Phoenix, and Los Angeles, as well as rural areas throughout the far West.[59] Although they might not define themselves this way, independent fundamentalists are anti-institutional, frequently anti-authoritarian, and very pluralistic.[60]

The polygamist mayor of Big Water, Utah, Alex Joseph, is a well-publicized example. He says, "I'm not an LDS fundamentalist, but I personally subscribe to too many Mormon doctrines to deny I'm a Mormon fundamentalist." His polygamist wives include two Catholics, a Methodist, and a Presbyterian, and neither he nor his wives (unlike other Mormon fundamentalists) observe the LDS Word of Wisdom's prohibition of alcohol and tobacco. At the vernal equinox in 1977, Alex Joseph helped found the Confederate Nations of Israel, which the *Encyclopedia of American Religions* classifies as one of the "Polygamy-Practicing Groups" of Mormonism. Actually, by fundamentalist definitions, this is a nongroup confederation of independent "patriarchs" (including Ogden Kraut, at first). One-fourth of its four hundred members are living in polygamous families throughout the United States, yet few of them have ever been part of any Mormon tradition. Catholics, Protestants, Eastern religionists, atheists, and active homosexuals join independent Mormon fundamentalists as patriarchs in the Confederate Nations of Israel.[61]

Growth by Birth and Conversion

How then have approximately twenty-one thousand men, women, and children become part of Mormon fundamentalism? First, primarily through birth into fundamentalist families. Second, since fundamentalists do not actively proselytize, the relatively few converts actually seek out fundamentalism.

As much as three-fourths of current members in the organized groups were born into fundamentalism. Many fundamentalists today are members of families that have an unbroken pattern of polygamy extending well before the 1890 Manifesto.[62] Since the groups account for 90 percent of the movement, few current Mormon fundamentalists have ever been baptized members of the LDS church.[63]

What of the converts to Mormon fundamentalism? In the early years of the movement, virtually everyone was a convert directly from the LDS church, for which the church excommunicated most of them sooner or later. A plural wife, who has known many converts to independent fundamentalism in the last decade, notes that most of the converts from the church are in their thirties and forties.[64] My fieldwork indicates that recent converts to Mormon fundamentalism come from two directions: previous converts to the LDS church from other faiths, and LDS church members with polygamous ancestry. There seem to be few conversions by those with strictly monogamous Mormon ancestry.

No fundamentalist group now actively proselytizes, so potential converts seek out fundamentalist writers, leaders, or friends. Owen Allred says he is aware of only fifteen or twenty couples annually who convert from the LDS church to fundamentalism.[65] Ogden Kraut's fundamentalist publications cause many investigators to seek him out, and he observes that fundamentalist conversions rise sharply after every change the modern church makes in LDS doctrine and policy. Those changes in the LDS church occur frequently enough that fundamentalism does not suffer by refusing to send out missionaries. Kraut also says that "actually there's a lot of people who are not Mormons who become interested in fundamentalism."[66] Therefore, growth in the groups is primarily through the birthrate, but conversions add significantly to the smaller numbers of independents.

The Appeal of Mormon Fundamentalism

Contrary to popular assumptions, polygamy is not what attracts most converts to Mormon fundamentalism. For example, as a convert to the LDS church, Roy Potter had sought out fundamentalists in 1979 after being censured by church authorities for inquiring about Brigham Young's Adam-God teachings. He regarded ecclesiastical denial of the church's past as evidence that the LDS church "is out of order." Plural marriage was a later consideration.[67] A few years ago, about six English families began reading nineteenth-century teachings of the LDS church, sent a representative to Utah, and eventually joined the Allred group. For these men and women in England, polygamy became significant afterward.[68]

Interviews with fundamentalist youth indicate that a major appeal of fundamentalism is the intensity of its doctrinal emphasis compared with the primarily social emphasis of the LDS church. A fifteen-year-old girl in a plural family did not like the LDS services she attended because she found she was the only one in her LDS Sunday school class who could answer questions, "just simple stuff that you'd think all the kids in the class would know, but nobody knew it."[69] A nineteen-year-old fundamentalist joined the LDS church just to go on a full-time mission and reported back to his friend in the Allred group that "there wasn't really any doctrine presented to the people in their [LDS] meetings." To the LDS rebuttal that its church meetings emphasize faith, repentance, and baptism, fundamentalist teenagers reply, "but not deep doctrine."[70] For these fundamentalist teenagers, the LDS church is too shallow in doctrinal emphasis compared with the sermons and class discussions they are accustomed to.

A young man who converted to fundamentalism at eighteen comments from a different perspective. He had been a strict Mormon since childhood, was the leader of his teenage priesthood quorums, and usually did more than was required, but felt something was missing. "In the Mormon church when I would sit through a meeting I would feel depressed and bored as though I had learned nothing." In LDS classes and release-time seminary, he was always asking questions: "How come this? and How come that?—and they were telling me 'Don't worry about it,' and I told them, 'Well, I've gotta worry about it, because it's buggin' me.'" Two years after his conversion to fundamentalism, this young man no longer pesters teachers or speakers with questions, but instead generally sits quietly in fundamentalist meetings, listening to presentations of "deep doctrine" which he ponders long after the meetings.[71]

The observations of these teenage fundamentalists are consistent with statements by adults who leave the LDS church for fundamentalism. Converts to Mormon fundamentalism do not hunger for polygamy: they thirst for a greater doctrinal and spiritual emphasis than they have known in the LDS church. In particular, interest in Brigham Young's Adam-God doctrine leads many church members to feel there is a chasm between the freewheeling Mormon doctrines of the nineteenth century and the orderly, sanitized theology of the twentieth-century LDS church.

In fact, polygamy can sometimes be the most difficult part of a Mormon's conversion to fundamentalism. The teenage convert's first interest in fundamentalism was the Adam-God doctrine. His second question was whether people should follow "a prophet or was it to be Jesus who we were supposed to follow." This young convert finally got around to polygamy, saying, "that was tough for me to accept at first because I'd always been taught that it was wrong and wicked, and things like that." With the church's exponential conversions in recent decades, relatively few Latter-day Saints have a polygamous heritage, and so polygamy is a social and religious obstacle for most church members. "Except for descendants of pioneer polygamists with a sense of history," notes a feminist expert on Mormon fundamentalism, "polygamy is as foreign to the contemporary Mormon as it might be to someone outside the Church. For some it is barely part of their mythic past."[72]

This teenage convert to Mormon fundamentalism explains his slow acceptance of polygamy: "When I heard that people were taking two or three, I felt that wasn't being very faithful to the first wife, and it took a while to accept it. I had to do a lot of praying, a lot of fasting over it. . . . Gradually I just started accepting it."[73] However, there are exceptions to this reluctant acceptance of plural marriage. One plural wife says that in her conversion in Colorado from the United Church of Christ to the LDS church, she read *Doctrine and Covenants,* section 132, and became convinced of the necessity of plural marriage as part of her conversion to the LDS church. Shortly after her LDS baptism, she was stunned to learn that the church now prohibits plural marriage. A year later, as a transfer student at Brigham Young University, she became a fundamentalist and plural wife at age twenty-one.[74]

Fundamentalist Relations with the LDS Church

Many mainline Mormons do not understand the fundamentalist attitude toward the LDS church, which has certainly not tried to endear itself to Mormon fundamentalists. From the 1930s until recently, LDS church leaders established surveillance teams for fundamentalist meeting places and homes, denied baptism to children of fundamentalists, prohibited fundamentalist children from attending primary classes, and excommunicated adults on the basis of guilt by association, for beliefs rather than acts, and for refusing to deny rumors or sign loyalty oaths. LDS surveillance teams copied down license plate numbers in order to identify those visiting the homes of fundamentalists, and a Brigham Young University professor was once discovered using a telephoto lens to photograph license plates of cars at meetings of the Allred group. There were even some fake conversions so that LDS spies could operate within fundamentalist groups. Beyond ecclesiastical harassment and punishment, LDS church leaders have encouraged punitive legislation, turned over surveillance information to law enforcement, pressured public libraries to remove fundamentalist publications, urged the postal service to deny mailing privileges to fundamentalists, and supported the forced adoption of polygamous children into monogamous homes.[75]

From the earliest years of the fundamentalist movement to the present, LDS leaders have also encouraged an informer syndrome that sometimes poisons family relationships. One plural wife was excommunicated in 1970 after her sister reported her to church authorities. "This was not at all vindictive," the plural wife says, "just the involvement of circumstances which we anticipated—to be excommunicated—but even when you expect it, it's still a real heartache." Then she adds, "The whole life you love is the Church."[76] That love drove one LDS mother to initiate criminal proceedings against her own son for polygamy, and his polygamous daughter comments of her grandmother: "I think she did that mostly because she was really angry that my Dad had gone ahead and entered into polygamy, and she wanted him to stay in the Mormon Church. So my Mom was in hiding, and I was raised in hiding until I was five."[77] Church leaders were mistaken if they expected fundamentalists to repudiate the LDS church in the face of these assaults.

Whether excommunicated or never LDS, nearly all fundamentalists (outside the LeBaron churches) regard the LDS church as the only true church—divinely instituted, with God's full authority to receive revelations, perform saving ordinances, proselytize, and teach. Until recently, the leaders of Colorado City's Fundamentalist Church of Jesus Christ of Latter-day Saints insisted that this title did not refer to a separate church, but only distinguished their Priesthood work from the "monogamous church," and that they revered the LDS church as God's only true church. The Fundamentalist Church legally incorporated in 1991 due to an on-going lawsuit by its separatist Hammond-Timson group.[78]

Like many who were hounded by church repression, Rulon C. Allred felt resentment and pain, but taught his children that the LDS church "was our church—the One True on the face of the earth, he said, although it was currently out of order." Meetings of the Apostolic United Brethren are canceled during the semi-annual general conferences so that the Allred fundamentalists can listen to talks by LDS general authorities. In the Allred academies of Salt Lake and Montana, each morning students pray facing the direction of the Salt Lake Temple to which Mormon fundamentalists are denied admission by the LDS church.[79] Most Mormon fundamentalists so thoroughly indoctrinate their children to revere the LDS church that teenagers even express their love for a church whose meetings they have never attended.[80] In fact, before the groups developed their own churchlike functions, fundamentalists participated in the activities of the LDS church until church authorities discovered this duality and excommunicated them. LeGrand Woolley remained active in the LDS church even after he became a member of the fundamentalist Priesthood Council in 1929. Similar examples include fundamentalists B. Harvey Allred, Jr., Owen Allred, and Ogden Kraut.[81]

Living a dual church-fundamentalist life remains an individual choice today, even for teenagers. A fifteen-year-old fundamentalist girl (an independent) says: "I've kind of dropped out from being active in the church, because I think it's kind of compromising for me because my Mom was a member of the church and they excommunicated her."[82] On the other hand, some teenage boys among the independents today receive ordinations within the LDS church if possible, while those in groups rarely do.[83] A teenage boy in the Allred group says, "they do urge us to go on missions [for the LDS church] but it's not a real common practice,"[84] and the youths I interviewed from the Allred and Colorado City groups have no interest in serving a mission for the LDS church. However, one of these boys has a fundamentalist friend who joined the church for no other reason than to preach the basic principles of the LDS gospel to non-Mormons. This nineteen-year-old is currently serving a two-year mission (during which he supports himself with savings or family assistance). LDS church leaders do not realize that he is a believing fundamentalist.[85]

This study's teenage convert to fundamentalism is not as fortunate. He admitted to local LDS leaders that he believed Mormonism's old-time religion, and they refused to allow him to serve a mission. They rejected his solemn promise to preach only the *Book of Mormon* and other basic principles expected of LDS missionaries today. Now at age twenty, he can hardly contain his sorrow at this disappointment. He had planned and saved since early childhood to serve a full-time mission for the church he still regards as God's own.[86]

Monogamy and Polygamy among Mormon Fundamentalists

Even less understood is the relationship between the actual living of polygamy and the affirmation of each Mormon fundamentalist that plural marriage must be lived today. For example, Albert E. Barlow delayed marrying a plural wife for more than twelve years after his conversion to fundamentalism in 1922. He had the distinction later of serving two prison terms for unlawful cohabitation with his wives.[87] Ogden Kraut was a fundamentalist for twenty-one years as an adult before he married a plural wife in 1969. He says he knows many independent fundamentalists who are bachelors "of all ages, for one reason or another."[88]

Some independent fundamentalists are so disillusioned that they discourage their families from entering polygamy. Roy Potter was dismissed from the police department of Murray, Utah, because of his polygamy. Eventually he took his case all the way to the Supreme Court.[89] Due to the strain on his wives of his legal battle to regain a policeman's badge, Roy Potter is now a monogamist. He is not planning to marry again and has turned down proposals from several women. He also reports that independents who entered polygamy decades ago are now encouraging their children and grandchildren "not to enter into polygamy" because Mormon fundamentalism is "so out of order that you can't possibly do it properly."[90] Nevertheless, such disillusioned independents do not reject Mormon fundamentalist essentials or suggest acceptance of the current LDS church position on those essentials.

Owen Allred reports that only a small minority of his group's adults have married polygamously. Only 10–15 percent of the adults are living polygamously in the Allred group at Salt Lake Valley, Cedar City, Utah, and Pinesdale, Montana. Only 5 percent of the Mexican fundamentalists at Ozumba are polygamous. The Allred fundamentalists in Germany and the Netherlands are monogamous, but several English fundamentalists are polygamous. As presiding elder of the Apostolic United Brethren, Allred says, "actually I discourage it . . . if you're not ready for Celestial Marriage, if you're not qualified to live it, if you do not have a testimony that it is a law of God and not something to satisfy your own personal whims." When a man or woman comes to him seeking permission to court polygamously, Owen Allred usually responds, "Now wait a minute, dear brother or sister, let's be careful."[91]

On the other hand, leaders of the Johnson-Jeffs group actively promote plural marriage among their followers in Colorado City, Arizona, and Hildale, Utah, the Salt Lake Valley, and elsewhere. Bachelorhood among independents is virtually unknown among males who have reached their mid-twenties in the Colorado City group, since unmarried young men can expect intense, personal persuasion from family and the Priesthood of the Johnson-Jeffs group. On-site fieldwork indicates that a majority of the adults in Colorado City and Hildale have entered polygamous marriages and that nearly everyone in these communities is either living in polygamous households and/or was born to polygamous fathers.[92] Nevertheless, married men of great devotion (and real interest in plural marriage) may not be allowed to marry a plural wife in the Colorado City group.[93] The extensive plural marriage in the Johnson-Jeffs group contrasts with near-reticence among independents and the Allred group.

Dating and Courtship

Preparation for marriage, both monogamous and polygamous, is approached in various ways. For the independents and the Allred group, youth activities and dating come before a marriage proposal. A sixteen-year-old boy in the Allred group says, "they have dances for the youth, kind of ballroom dances, but like Virginia reel and stuff like that."[94] A young woman adds that the Allred group's Youth of Zion organizes firesides with speakers, snow-tubing parties at Park City, kite-flying parties, treasure hunts, volleyball, basketball and baseball games, and rents rinks for ice-skating and roller-skating parties.[95] Teenagers in independent fundamentalist families do not usually join these organized activities of the Apostolic United Brethren, even if they have friends in the group.

Independent youth and the Allred youth also have activities on their own for group dates or couple dates. These teenage fundamentalists play Nintendo at home, play tennis, go water skiing and bowling, and see popular movies. In the Salt Lake Valley, teenagers from independent families and from the Allred group also go to the Lagoon amusement park in Davis County, to the 49th Street Galleria to play arcade games, to the Raging Waters water park, and to dance clubs in Salt Lake City such as the Bay and Palladium where they can dance to rock and other modern music unavailable at Allred group dances.[96] A sixteen-year-old boy in the Allred group says, "My Dad was never very strict so I really could go and do anything I wanted, really, unlike most of the kids in the Group." He has played electric guitar in a rock band, but adds, "I'm trying to get off it, because I shouldn't be."[97]

Dating in the Allred group is a serious matter, though. A twenty-two-year-old young woman says that in monogamous dating, young men can ask the girl directly, but usually ask her father first. Her own polygamist father tells the shy young men, "Well, don't ask me; you're not taking me out!" She and a teenage boy from the group both express disapproval of kissing before marital courtship. He also observes that there is no rule for a young man to follow if he learns (as this seventeen-year-old did) that a married man wants to court the teenager's girlfriend: "there's not really any certain way to go about it other than to follow your priesthood head, and by that I don't mean blindly do whatever he says. . . . You need to find out by yourself by prayer and fasting what the proper channel is to take." Monogamous courtship can last a year or more for young fundamentalists among the Apostolic United Brethren and the independents.[98]

In the Allred group and among independents, polygamous courtship can begin early but is usually of short duration. A fifteen-year-old girl in an independent family comments: "In the fundamentalist environment—this isn't true all the time—but a lot of men just think that when a girl turns fifteen, sixteen, seventeen, that she's going to get married." She adds that a married man thinks a girl will marry him if she goes out with him more than once.[99] Unlike monogamous young men, a married man is expected to ask the father's permission to court his daughter, who has the right to turn down the request without ever talking to the prospective suitor. "If the girl feels like she wants to go out with them, she can. If she doesn't want to, she doesn't have to," and this twenty-two-year-old young woman adds that she has told her father to turn down "quite a few married men" who asked him.[100] When one girl joined the Allred group at age seventeen, she had seven polygamous proposals in two weeks, and the first "date" was always a discussion of what the man and his wife (wives) hoped for in a new wife.[101] Some fundamentalists have their other wife (wives) join the first "date" with a prospective new wife.[102] Neither independents nor Allred group members seem to notice the irony that their patterns of courtship give enhanced status to monogamy through prolonged courtship as compared to brief, business-like polygamous courtship.

Arranged Marriage

The Colorado City group eliminates the disparity between long monogamous courtship and brief polygamous courtship. As tersely put by one of its young men: "In our group we don't date."[103] Aside from attendance at classes and youth firesides, the Johnson group authorizes only one kind of close interaction between unmarried boys and girls: ballroom dances which occur several times a month in Colorado City.[104] A plural wife raised in the Johnson group's Salt Lake Valley community observes that dating is absolutely prohibited because "we were raised believing that the Priesthood [Council] would choose our mate and that we were not to allow ourselves to fall in love with anybody." Predictably, some youths at Colorado City try to "get what they called 'sneaky dates.' I mean they'd sneak off and go places and talk." When a seventeen-year-old friend of hers got caught on a "sneaky date" with an eighteen-year-old boy, "they were called into the Priesthood. They were told they were not allowed to see each other again."[105]

Therefore, in the Johnson group, boys alone or girls alone participate in a variety of unsponsored activities such as hiking, camping, horseback riding, and sometimes trips across the border to movie theaters in St. George, Utah. If they live in the Salt Lake Valley, the group's same-sex youth go out together and enjoy fast-food restaurants, bowling, miniature golf, the Lagoon amusement park, movies like *Indiana Jones* and *Batman*, and "whatever's fun."[106]

Although they enjoy the recreational fun of most teenagers, youth in the Johnson-Jeffs group anticipate with faith and solemnity the decision of the Priesthood regarding the most important event of their young lives: the selection of a marriage companion. Arranged marriage in the Colorado City group has three main perspectives: that of the Priesthood leaders, of the prospective husbands, and of the prospective wives.

The president of the Priesthood (or a fellow member of his Council) in the Johnson group seeks divine inspiration to know God's will as the Priesthood selects worthy spouses.[107] After the 1953 raid, Louis J. Barlow (now director of the teenage release-time seminary program in Colorado City) gave a radio address that included a denial of hostile assumptions about arranged marriages at Short Creek: "There have been no forced marriages. Everyone is free to leave or stay as he chooses."[108] His brother further explains that the Priesthood of the Colorado City group arranges marriages to give greater assurance of their stability and permanence, and also to be sure that the couples are not closely related in the tightly knit community. He affirms: "The first consideration, as I've known it, is to make sure the individuals feel free and at liberty to make their own choices."[109]

A young man in the Colorado City group indicates that males also defer to the marital decisions of the Priesthood. At age nineteen, he has never dated a girl, and when asked how he expects to know a girl, he replies, "Basically through the Priesthood. . . . They basically decide who you're gonna marry. You can have a little a bit of your say. It's not just totally that they tell you. You have your say. . . . You go to them. They won't come to you." This nineteen-year-old adds that it is most common for men to be twenty to twenty-one years old when "[you tell the Priesthood] you want to get married. Basically, they'll set it up." These are the marital expectations of young men in the Colorado City group.[110] In first marriages, the husband and wife are usually close in age.[111]

There are some differences in arranged plural marriages of the Colorado City group. The young man says that, unlike the decision for a first marriage, a man does not announce his interest in marrying polygamously: "The Priesthood decides. Basically, they ask you if you would like to do it. You say yes or no." And the man is free to indicate he is not interested in plural marriage "at the time." A faithful male may delay polygamous marriage, but cannot be considered faithful if he refuses the decision of the Priesthood for him to marry polygamously.[112] However, other sources indicate that men who wish to enter plural marriage can also state that interest to the Priesthood, which then advises them who to marry as a plural wife. In this case, even middle-aged men defer to the choices made by the Priesthood.[113]

Females in the Colorado City group are no more deferential to the Priesthood Council's choice of a mate for them than males are, although a female's deference is mediated by her father. "Like if I was sixteen and I wanted to get married," a plural wife observes, "I would go to the Priesthood and I would say, with my father [there], that I'm ready to get married. Please tell me who I should get married to." However, this particular woman's authoritarian father went to the Priesthood without her and obtained the name of a man for her to marry. After her father admitted to her that the intended husband was an "old man," his teenage daughter said she was not even interested in knowing what the Priesthood told him. She eventually left the Johnson group and became a plural wife in the Allred group, where she married a man of her own choosing whom she eventually left. Her five sisters continue in stable plural marriages that were arranged by the decision of Colorado City's Priesthood Council.[114]

Members of the Colorado City group have assured outsiders that "romantic love [is] a frequent element in the courtship,"[115] but that is supposed to happen *after* the Priesthood selects the partners, not before. This is the purpose of prohibiting dating. The discomfort with romantic attachments before the Priesthood's decision is indicated by a comment from one leader of the Colorado City community that if young people "make commitments to each other, then those are respected sometimes."[116] The young woman who lived there in the early 1970s agrees that females could indicate their choice for a husband, but the Priesthood did not welcome such preference: "There was quite a bit of disgrace if you actually did fall in love with somebody who you really did want to get married to." Only a couple of her friends expressed the desire to marry young men prior to the Priesthood's choice, in which case the marriage occurred only after much contrary counseling and a long waiting period.[117]

Ages of Wives and Husbands

The above plural wife's family history raises the question of the age difference between husbands and plural wives in fundamentalist marriages. Her mother became a plural wife at age fourteen, when her father was about thirty-seven. This plural wife herself married in the Allred group at age seventeen to a man who was twenty years her senior; shortly afterward she introduced her seventeen-year-old friend as a new plural wife to her husband. The 1953 raid and investigation showed that "the average age at first marriage for fundamentalist women in Short Creek was sixteen, though fourteen and fifteen were not uncommon."[118] Based on her observations twenty years later, this woman (who left the Johnson group and has now abandoned polygamy) says that for the females there, "it's personal preference," with most choosing to accept an arranged marriage between the ages of sixteen and nineteen: "By the time you're twenty-one, you're an old maid." Despite her own mother's marriage at fourteen in the Salt Lake community of the Colorado City group, this woman disagrees with the 1953 court findings at Short Creek and says it is "uncommon to be married at fourteen" in that group.[119]

But plural wives are often teenagers and sometimes twenty years younger than their polygamous husbands. On the other hand, when a fundamentalist male marries his first wife, she is usually close to his own age. This pattern holds true in all the groups as well as among independent fundamentalists. Rulon C. Allred himself was middle-aged when he married two fifteen-year-old brides.[120] An independent plural wife in this study is twenty-seven years younger than her husband, who is twenty-five to twenty-two years older than his other plural wives.[121] Independents like Ogden Kraut express discomfort at such age differences, and some fundamentalist men marry only wives their age or older.[122] On the other hand, the plural wives I interviewed do not regret their youthful decisions after fifteen to twenty years of marriage.

There are LDS church and Utah state perspectives on fundamentalist teen brides. In his mid-thirties, the founding prophet, Joseph Smith, himself married a seventeen-year-old and a fifteen-year-old as plural wives, and their marriages were not platonic.[123] In Utah, 23.5 percent of females who married monogamously in 1986 were teenagers, compared with 13.1 percent of females nationally who married that year.[124] "Well, in Utah the age of consent for marriage is fourteen, if the parents agree," observes the director of the Utah chapter of the American Civil Liberties Union, "But if they do it for religious reasons, then people get upset."[125]

Utah Children, a child advocacy group, filed amicus curiae briefs in the Fischer adoption case against the right of polygamist families to adopt children, including orphaned polygamous children. The director said, "We also note that young women are frequently given very early in marriage. And we do not think to give girls in marriage is in their best interest." Such opponents regard teenage monogamous marriage as regrettable, but see teenage polygamous marriage as evil. Although Utah Children and others deny that religion is the issue, they actually regard religious belief in polygamy as inherently coercive for teenage girls.[126]

Marriage Dynamics

Fundamentalists also disagree on whether it is necessary to have a minimum number of wives. One author implies that a righteous family "quorum" has a minimum of two plural wives.[127] Ogden Kraut observes that the organized groups regard an increase in the number of wives as requirement or reward for each level of presiding office. Even though Kraut himself now has five wives, he waited two decades to marry polygamously, and says, "Personally, I just don't think that they ought to be running around looking for a bunch of wives. Some of the groups kind of have the idea that the more wives you have the more power, authority, whatever."[128] Rulon Allred's daughter says that is often true among the Apostolic United Brethren.[129] In the groups and among independents, some regard the number of wives as a status symbol for men, whereas other husbands are appalled at such a concept.

Husband-wife dynamics in polygamous families vary as much as those in monogamous families outside Mormonism, but polygamy obviously adds to the complexity. Psychologist Marvin Rytting notes, "What you have in polygamy is basically an intensification of what you see in all sorts of families."[130] Fundamentalist men say they fall in love with each wife in sequence, and argue that this is no more difficult to understand than a father in any family loving each new child as much as he loves his older children.[131] Unless the marriage is arranged (as at Colorado City), a female can propose polygamous marriage, but usually the male does so. Technically, he requires the permission of his first wife to enter polygamy, but that is not necessary if she is opposed.[132] A plural wife in the Allred group observes that a prospective plural wife meets with the first wife and polygamous wives, if any, to "relate with them and take whatever time is necessary. Everybody is very free about their feelings and expressions."[133] Although optional, the first wife's cooperation is essential for a congenial polygamous family, which the first wife traditionally begins by placing the hand of the new plural wife in her husband's hand at the marriage ceremony.[134]

Even the first wife's approval does not eliminate problems with jealousy, which is clearest from the plural wife's point of view. A plural wife in the Allred group says that with her husband's other wives she had a congenial relationship that "was a very easy, wonderful amalgamation," but quickly adds, "That's not necessarily standard."[135] Some plural wives, like one of Rulon Allred's widows, do not acknowledge jealousy: "It was no different for me, really, sharing my sister-wives with my husband than it had been sharing my sisters with my father"; one of his daughters says, "The mothers would sooner die than admit to jealousy or any form of rivalry."[136] On the other hand, plural wives I interviewed volunteered comments on jealousy. Louis Kelsch's widow acknowledged that among his six plural wives, "I have to admit that there are feelings like that, but since we believe that this is a higher principle that we are supposed to live, we believe that we are to control those feelings. And we find out that if we do learn to control those feelings, we become closer than sisters, and we have peace in the family."[137] Girls raised in a fundamentalist family anticipate this necessity, as a fifteen-year-old acknowledges, "I'll probably feel jealousy. I'll have to overcome that." And she adds, "It doesn't really matter if you're the first, second, third, fourth, fifth, whatever."[138] Still, jealousy can be corrosive even for the most devoted fundamentalist families.[139]

Although divorce is a painful topic, fundamentalists do not avoid discussing it. "You have to have a society, if you're going to be civilized, that accommodates for the human error that may occur, and allows for a remedy that is progressive and civilized, and allows for productive things," says Sam S. Barlow of Colorado City. Of the arranged marriages there, he adds, "I don't think anybody's expected to be married to somebody they don't want to be married to."[140] A woman raised in the Colorado City group observes that often there is no formal divorce: "If you were a problem wife you had your own home somewhere else—across the town, preferably. And your husband did not come to see you unless it was a necessity. I mean she was basically just to raise her own family almost like a divorced person, but not quite."[141] Morris Jessop of the Allred group's Priesthood Council says that many polygamists "have lost their families—divorces, breakups, heartaches, you name it—because they fooled themselves to think they could live this way of life and not put an effort to it," but Owen Allred estimates that within his group there is only one divorce for every thirty-seven plural marriages.[142] Ogden Kraut estimates a slightly higher divorce rate for plural marriages among independents: one in thirty.[143]

The estimates by Allred and Kraut translate to 2.7–3.3 percent of polygamous marriages ending in divorce, which fundamentalists define simply as the permanent dissolution of a plural marriage, since there is no civil divorce for polygamy. Standardized divorce rates (crude and refined) based on per thousand of population are not a workable basis of comparison for the small numbers of Mormon fundamentalists. Fundamentalist estimates show that current polygamous marriages are far less likely to end in divorce than civil marriages within the LDS church, Utah, and the United States. In 1981 a representative of the LDS bureaucracy and a sociologist conducted a random survey of 7,446 members of the LDS church and found that 5.4 percent of men and 6.5 percent of women divorced after LDS temple marriage, but that for total marriages (nontemple and temple), 14 percent of married men and 19 percent of married women in the LDS church divorced. In Utah, there is one new divorce annually for every 2.2 new marriages performed, and the percentage of divorce for ever-married men is 21.1 percent, and for women 22.0 percent. Nationally, the percentage of divorce reported for ever-married men is 22.3 percent, and for women 23.3 percent.[144]

However, Mormon fundamentalists contribute to the civil divorce rates through the breakup of their first marriages, particularly those of couples who convert to fundamentalism. First wives obtained civil divorces from some of fundamentalism's earliest leaders: Joseph W. Musser, Louis A. Kelsch, Jr., Charles F. Zitting, Rulon C. Allred, and Rulon Jeffs. In some cases the divorce came after the mere suggestion of polygamy, in other cases after the first wife had tried for years to share her husband with sister-wives and with the fundamentalists over whom he presided.[145] A girl in an independent family reports that the divorce of a first wife is "kind of common" among independents.[146] This is true because first wives in the groups are now likely to be socialized to polygamy through growing up in fundamentalist homes,[147] whereas independents have a higher proportion of converts confronting polygamy for the first time in their lives. Nevertheless, a first wife's divorce does not always mean she has rejected polygamy—in two of the families in this study, the first wives were converts from the LDS church who obtained civil divorces from polygamists, and then became plural wives to other men.[148]

Unhappiness and divorce are part of fundamentalist polygamy, just as dysfunctional families are widespread among LDS and non-LDS monogamists. Of greater interest are the dynamics of polygamous living among Mormon fundamentalists. Polygamous families today manifest several adaptations in the relations of husband and wife, wife with wife, children with parents, children with children, and children with outsiders. Mormon fundamentalist adaptations are sometimes as individual as the persons involved, but the fundamentalist group can also shape family life in prescribed ways. These dynamics can only be sketched briefly here.[149]

Status of Females

Subservience of females to a polygamous patriarchy is one reason the Utah Children advocacy group has legally battled the right of Mormon fundamentalists to adopt children. This organization's director says that fundamentalist teachings that "women were considered property, that women were expected to be submissive . . . are outside of the norms of general society, and we do not believe are in the interest of healthy children growing up to be healthy and normal adults." Thus, one argument against the right of polygamists to adopt is that they teach their sons to be patriarchal and their daughters to be subservient.[150] "But," counters the feminist director of the ACLU's Utah chapter, "the truth of the matter is that not very many religions in this country support the full equality of women. So, if we were going to outlaw every religion that didn't promote equality for women, I think that there would be a lot fewer religions in this country."[151]

Among fundamentalists, that debate may be more relevant to the Colorado City group. One plural wife raised in the group believes that the husband typically "controls the family, controls the wives, controls the income, controls the discipline," and that wives in the Colorado City group are "expected to submit themselves to their husband in all things." However, she admits that her father was stricter than others.[152] On the other hand, the third of five wives in one Colorado City family argues for their domestic power: "Anyone who thinks a plural wife is weak and submissive can't imagine the strength it takes to manage a large home filled with children."[153] But even that seems to be praise for the endurance of wives, not an argument for female autonomy in the Colorado City group, which practices closed communion for priesthood holders only, thereby administering the sacrament only to males above the age of twelve. Females do not receive the sacrament in meetings of the Johnson-Jeffs group in Colorado City, the Salt Lake Valley, or elsewhere, whereas females and males have equal access to the sacrament in the Allred group and among independent fundamentalists.[154]

Deference, not subservience, seems to be the rule for women elsewhere in Mormon fundamentalism. "Pregnant and chained to the kitchen sink is pretty much the image, but that isn't so at all," explains a plural wife in the Allred group. "Our counsel is sought for in the decisions, but we are encouraged to be ourselves. It is not restrictive." "However," she adds, "when you have a head of a family who has four wives, there has to be some system or you have chaotic daily activities constantly. So we do believe in order." Her view of family order is that the husband makes final decisions after consultation with the wives.[155] This is echoed by a plural wife among the independents: "I feel like the husband and the father of the family is definitely the patriarch in that family and should be honored as such."[156] An Allred Council member's plural wife describes her relationship to him as nonsubservient: "And he will say, 'Maybe this would be the better way to do it, but that's up to you, you know.' He usually leaves the final choice up to me."[157]

In fact, plural wives often have a practical autonomy that counters stereotypes of fundamentalist patriarchy. This is especially true when the wives have separate residences and the husband is absent for days or weeks at a time. One plural wife of more than fifty years comments, "Well, when you are in different homes, like we were—we had three different establishments—he is only there a third of the time. So, you have two-thirds of the time when you do have to run your own affairs and you are independent in a small way. . . . We would always consult him about things, but still we had to handle the problems that would come up with the children and with our cars and so on." She admits that her autonomy has sometimes bruised her husband's ego, and so plural wives "have to play dependence one time and independence another."[158] Some fundamentalist wives do not play dependence very well. One plural wife in the Allred group vetoed every choice for a new house her husband proposed, which exasperated her sixteen-year-old son who helped his father pick out one house after another.[159]

In fact, the residential pattern for fundamentalist families tends to be decided by wives among the independents and Allred group and by husbands or the leadership in the Johnson group and Kingston group.[160] Coresidence is common for financial reasons and sometimes is preferred by the wives.[161] Coresidence can involve each wife having a separate section of the building for herself and her children, or it can involve the more complex arrangement apparently standard in the Colorado City group: "All the bedrooms for the children would be on the top floor, and then all the wives' areas, their bedrooms would be on the middle floor. And then maybe on the main floor just one or two wives that basically didn't have children, and the husband's office and bedroom would be on the main floor."[162] Wives can also be in separate cities, or across town, or a few blocks from each other, or in a specially constructed polygamous "compound" of adjacent buildings.[163]

Even though coresidence of wives in a large house eliminates the de facto independence of wives in separate residences, a fundamentalist husband may actually encourage autonomy for his plural wives living under one roof. When the wives in one household expected their husband to make decisions, he usually replied, "You can handle this, dear, I know you can," and one of his plural wives comments: "So he was always encouraging us to be our best selves, to always push forward. And I appreciated that in him." He also handled finances for all the wives, until they decided to control their own income and budgets.[164] At the far end from female subservience is one of Alex Joseph's wives, who explains: "Polygamy is a feminist lifestyle. I can go off 400 miles to law school, and the family keeps running," to which this plural wife adds: "I am a monogamist. My husband is a polygamist."[165]

This discussion risks creating another fundamentalist stereotype—plural wives as feminists. In current polygamist marriages, husbands vary from patriarchal controllers to partners in decision making, and wives from subservient to feminist. No marriage exists in a social vacuum, and all the plural wives in this study volunteered comments about feminism, women's liberation, and society's expectations of the male role in marriage. "But I'm not a feminist or women's libber," was almost a cliché among these plural wives as they described their occupational independence and family autonomy. In fact, American society intensifies the female autonomy that is latent in modern polygamy. Many polygamous couples feel a desire to disprove the stereotype of a polygamous wife's subservience, and they unconsciously turn to feminist-influenced models of partnership marriage rather than to biblical models of patriarchal marriage. That process is common among the independents and in the Allred group, less so in the Colorado City group, but always influenced by the personal preferences of polygamous husbands and wives. Husband-wife dynamics can be as diverse in Mormon fundamentalist marriages as in the monogamous marriages of outsiders.

Female Employment and Financial Stress

Whether by necessity or personal preference, most polygamous wives are employed outside the home. Traditionally, plural wives in the Kingston group work outside the home, often as accountants for the extensive financial transactions of the Davis County Cooperative.[166] The majority of Colorado City's plural wives work in its public schools, its community college, or its Danco clothing factory which manufactures uniforms for medical facilities and for such national chains as Thrifty Drugs and Sizzler restaurants.[167] Many plural wives work in teaching, in clerical positions, or in Utah's service-industry economy. "In the early years it was necessity," one woman says. "We cried when we left our babies, and the sister-wife would hold the baby up at the window and wave good-bye as we left." As a marked advantage over secular society, this sister-wife babysitting leaves children with a trusted adult family member, while allowing the mother to pursue educational or occupational goals. This plural wife is now preparing for a career as a physician.[168] Although Owen Allred prefers that the wives in his group remain with their families, most wives work outside the home, including two of his daughters who are registered nurses.[169] Alex Joseph's wives include a newspaper editor, attorney, fire fighter, and real estate agent.[170]

Separate incomes can give plural wives economic autonomy if they manage their own occupational income. However, very often (especially in coresidence households) each wife's income becomes part of a family budget administered by the husband, and each wife manages only her allotted portion. On the other hand, wives in separate residences (particularly if long distances from each other) tend to manage their own occupational income, in addition to what their husband provides them from his income.

In fact, outside work for plural wives is common because polygamous families in an urban-suburban setting almost always struggle financially. Polygamous husbands frequently have more than one job, and children grow up with a constant awareness of the family's limited resources.[171] Louis Kelsch's widow comments about the general inability of most polygamous families to buy their children a lot of fashionable clothes and to pay for college education. Most of the children in her extended family begin working full time as teenagers.[172] So polygamous families are working families for young and old, male and female.

Child Interaction with Sister-Wives, Father, and Siblings

Sister-wife babysitting also increases the interaction of plural children with the women they call "aunts" and the "other mothers." Teenagers in this study come from large polygamous families representing Colorado City, the Allred group, and the independents. For example, one has twenty-one siblings (ten by one mother), another is from a family of five wives and twenty-six children, and another from a family of three wives and thirty-seven children. Two plural wives point out difficulties in disciplining the other children—resentment between wives if a wife is too severe with a sister-wife's child, and confusion for the children who confront different rules when they enter another wife's "area" in the large house.[173] By an interesting contrast, all the teenagers in this study reported that the other wives disciplined them the same as their own mothers, and their experiences are typical of this boy's: "My other mothers have always just shown all the love that they could give to me, and I'm always welcome at any of their houses at any time. You don't have to knock to go into their houses, because it's pretty much your house, too. And I'm always sleeping over there . . . and I can eat there or whatever." A teenage girl adds, "Sometimes we even call the other moms our Mom."[174]

In practical terms, it is difficult for a polygamist's children to have the kind of closeness with the father that they have with his other wives. This is a result of his heavy work schedule, numerous children, and (for separately housed families) his visitation to his other families. A wife in Colorado City notes, "A father may only spend a few minutes each week with each child."[175] One plural wife in the Allred group admits "he was too busy helping his wives and not doing the fatherly things—not hugging them, and not helping them, and not going to the PTA meetings, and the kids got to where they didn't like their dad. They just didn't because he was too busy. He wasn't a dad to them." Likewise, Rulon C. Allred's daughter published a family memoir that expresses her adoration for him as well as her resentment against his emotional distance.[176]

Despite the logistical problems of parenting a polygamous family, some fundamentalist men are superdads to their children. A teenage daughter reports: "I have a really good relationship with my dad, as far as relationships go. . . . It's incredible having so many children, but he can get around and make us all feel special, and he's helped so much in our upbringing. I think it's really neat that he's been able to make us each feel important. . . . I mean, he's busy. He has a lot of things to do, but he always has time to sit down and talk with us separately, and then if we have any questions for him, he's always there for us . . . just boppin' from house to house."[177] Some polygamists' children have unavailable fathers, but others have fathers as emotionally connected as the best monogamist is to his children.

Another side of polygamous family dynamics is the relationship between children of different wives. All the teenagers from polygamous families in this study report that they regard their siblings as full brothers and sisters, just with different mothers, and the children generally have been in close association all their lives. Similar-aged children by different mothers often report being "best friends," sometimes their only close friends. One plural wife comments that in large polygamous families, "they don't have the need for a lot of outside friends because they've got somebody their own age. They've probably got three or four their own age."[178] However, the elder children of the first wife are less likely to feel this same closeness, since they are often ten to twenty years older than the oldest children of the first plural wife. Estrangement between half siblings is common when the first wife obtains a divorce, but there are always exceptions. A plural wife reports that after polygamy caused her husband's first marriage to end in divorce, the first wife's children drew names each year to send Christmas gifts to their growing number of polygamous brothers and sisters.[179] The "best friend" relationship of siblings in polygamous families raises the question of their interaction with outsiders.

Education

Public school is traditionally the primary agent in the socialization of outsiders, but that is only partly true for the children of Mormon fundamentalists. There is no consistent pattern for the education of these children (even within the same families); they can be found in public schools, private academies, and home schools. Also, distinctions blur between public education and fundamentalist schools.

The educational mode of lowest socialization is home schooling favored by some fundamentalists. Out of dozens of independent fundamentalists participating in home schooling, the John Singer family alone refused school board supervision of the instruction and engaged in an increasingly bitter conflict with authorities in Utah. This resulted in an armed standoff and John Singer's death in 1979.[180] Neither Utah state authorities, local school boards, nor fundamentalist families have repeated the errors of that unfortunate confrontation over fundamentalist education.

Still, some independent fundamentalists are critical of the quality of education that can result from home schools. Ogden Kraut says home schools are fine where wives have good training, but in some fundamentalist home schools "the poor kids never get any training. It had been better for them to go to public schools, than to stay home and to do nothing."[181] A fifteen-year-old girl in a home school agrees that "most fundamentalists do an awful job educating their children. I mean a lot of their children can't even write their names," but in her case her mother and the sister-wives were college graduates with teaching certificates. To get course work beyond the abilities of their home schools, students take correspondence courses or enroll in selected courses at the high schools. This teenage girl is planning on a pre-med program when she enters college.[182]

After decades of operation, the private academy at Colorado City (formerly Short Creek Academy) closed in the 1980s. It had offered instruction through the twelfth grade. A transfer student found the curricula more difficult than those of public schools she had attended in Salt Lake Valley, up until her move to Colorado City in her mid-teens.[183]

Today all the children in the Colorado City–Hildale polygamous commune attend tax-supported public schools, but these "public schools" (two elementary schools larger than many in Salt Lake City, a middle school, and a high school) are operated and staffed completely by fundamentalists for the fundamentalist children of the community. These schools also are rigorously secular and, aside from a moment of meditative silence each morning, have no religious content. Daytime religious instruction comes through the release-time seminary program of the Fundamentalist Church of Jesus Christ of Latter-day Saints in Colorado City, which is almost indistinguishable from the instruction in LDS church release-time seminaries in Utah on the Mormon "Standard Works" of Scripture: the Bible, *Book of Mormon, Doctrine and Covenants,* and *Pearl of Great Price.*[184] Likewise, at Colonia LeBaron and Los Molinos, Mexico, fundamentalist children first attended private schools and then government-supported schools within their own communities.[185]

About 85 percent of the Johnson group's young men and women attend college. Most graduate from Mohave County Community College (also staffed by fundamentalists) right in Colorado City. Many go on to the nearby University of Northern Arizona at Flagstaff or Southern Utah State College at Cedar City, Utah. Some attend the University of Utah at Salt Lake City, and a few even go to the LDS church's Brigham Young University in Provo. In consultation with the Priesthood, the Colorado City's graduates enter occupations that reflect traditional gender roles.[186]

The Allred group and the Kelsch family of independents currently have private academies. The Apostolic United Brethren operates its certified Mountain Valley

School in Bluffdale, Salt Lake Valley, but the school board restricts enrollment to about two hundred students because of the facility's size. Most children in the Allred group attend regular public schools, and only a fourth of the presiding elder's own grandchildren attend his group's school. The Allred commune of Pinesdale, Montana, also has an academy. Aside from opening prayer, the general instruction is secular in the Allred academies, which are also attended by nonfundamentalist and non-LDS children. The academies use the Montessori method, and students graduate on a mastery level at about seventeen or eighteen years of age.[187] The Kelsch family of independent fundamentalists owns and operates the Silver Creek Academy for the benefit of the children who live in a compound of Kelsch brothers and a brother-in-law near Park City, Utah. It also is licensed, but its graduates rarely attend college.[188]

Independent fundamentalists, the Kingston group, many Allred families, and Johnson group families in Salt Lake Valley send their children to public schools. Statistics of higher education are not available for these fundamentalists, but high proportions of males and females attend college in the Allred group and among some independents. Although the independent Kelsch children near Park City have their own academy, most of the children of Kelsch fundamentalists attend public schools, but end their schooling at or before high school graduation in order to work. In fact, if they do not attend a university, fundamentalist boys usually work in the building trades, which Mormon fundamentalists dominate in Salt Lake Valley and elsewhere in Utah, just as the Kelsch family's cabinet factory is one of the largest in the Mountain West. The Kingston group's children also attend public schools, and the Davis County Cooperative may encourage some of its children to attend college and even professional schools in order to provide expert service to the Kingston group as trusted insider-professionals.[189] Despite reservations about the social environment, the majority of urban fundamentalists send their children to public schools, where they interact with outsiders, usually with some discomfort.

Many polygamous children have been taunted as "polygies" by neighborhood children or in elementary school.[190] For some, the situation gets uglier during adolescence. All the teenagers in this study are very reluctant to talk about the religion of those who engage in harassment of polygamists. They finally acknowledge that this harassment comes from LDS church members, but then quickly add that such behavior is not true of all LDS people. Fundamentalist youth find that most non-LDS children and adults shrug when they learn of polygamists in their midst. However, one teenage fundamentalist explains that even in the heavily LDS high schools there has been almost no harassment in recent years, "because there are so many weird people in the school, a polygamist is just another weird group of person."

Converts and their children suffer the most because they have suddenly entered a category feared by their LDS friends and neighbors. The teenage convert to fundamentalism found his LDS friends suddenly stopped talking to him. Their parents were "my second parents," but after his conversion, "they didn't want their kids to have anything to do with me." He had been a youth leader in his LDS ward, but finally stopped attending church meetings because, "I'll go and [offer to] shake someone's hand, and they won't even shake my hand, and they'll just walk away." Aside from a fundamentalist girl he has dated for a year, this teenage convert has not developed any fundamentalist friends his own age, and now at age twenty, his friendships are with the middle-aged men and women of the independent meetings he attends.[191]

"Passing" as Monogamists

Outside the communes, teenagers from polygamous families lead dual social lives. They have many LDS acquaintances who are unaware of their status, but for most their only close friends are other fundamentalist children. Polygamists' children (particularly independents and those in the Allred group) are proud of blending in. One boy says of his high school friends: "None of them even know that I am. They just think I'm just another kid." All the teenagers in this study say they would not deny their status if LDS friends asked, but the dual life goes deeper. To avoid questions concerning their families' polygamous status, most fundamentalist teenagers avoid associating at school with each other.[192] This is not a pattern they will grow out of because their parents are rarely known as fundamentalists to outsiders. Aside from their religious meetings, most urban and suburban fundamentalists do their best to be unrecognizable to outsiders.[193]

In its early decades, the Colorado City group "wore fundamentalist Mormonism like a badge: severe buns, long skirts, black suits, faces scrubbed and plain, persisting in old-fashioned dress even for the children."[194] In Colorado City, this posed no problem, but elsewhere the Johnson group attracted stares, and such pioneer-type dress invited taunts against their children in school. "I resented the fact that I had to be punished for what my parents did," says one woman born and raised as a polygamous child in the Johnson group's Salt Lake Valley community.[195] This has relaxed a bit in Colorado City, but the door of the community's only restaurant (the Early Bird Cafe) displays a sign: "Cover your elbows, knees, shoulders, and toes, or out this door you goes."[196] In Salt Lake City some fundamentalist children of all ages still wear such distinctive dress, including obviously homemade shirts and trousers for the boys. However, that is a rarity which embarrasses children and teenagers in the Allred group and among independents, and is even uncomfortable for those youth in the Johnson group who wear modern clothes.

These teenage fundamentalists have their own dress code. A leader in the Allred's Youth of Zion prefers Reebok high tops, gray acid-wash Levis, and designer-label shirts. A young woman in the Allred group wears high-tops, 900-series Levis, and a sweatshirt. A teenage girl from a family of independent fundamentalists sports black pants, black blouse, high black soft-leather boots, and a white patent-leather jacket. These fundamentalist girls also use makeup consistent with that of their secular peers. Owen Allred's grandchildren at his family compound wear the blouses, shirts, shorts, jeans, and surfer jams typical of any teenagers. "I am opposed to it," their grandfather says, "but it's awful hard because of peer pressure from everywhere."[197] It is not so much peer pressure as it is a determination on the part of most urban fundamentalist youth to be inconspicuous: "We act like normal kids and everything," one boy grins. "We don't dress like polygies, or anything."

Hair is another matter. Raised in the Johnson group, a woman says, "I was always trained that it [the hair] was my crowning glory, that according to the Bible, that one of these days I would get to wash the Savior's feet with it, at least if I lived righteous enough. So to cut it to me was a huge disgrace." Rulon Allred would not allow his wives to cut their hair.[198] Most females in both groups still have long hair, but in the Allred group (and to some extent in the Colorado City group), those with long hair style it in contemporary fashion and avoid the long braid and hair bun. By contrast, women in independent families often have stylishly cut short hair. Most fundamentalist men now avoid beards, and the Colorado City group expects army-style haircuts for all males. The young man interviewed from this group apologized because his hair was just over his ears.[199] On the other hand, teenage boys in the Allred group tend to have collar-length hair, However, if short hair is the style for outsider friends of an Allred group or independent boy, then his hair will be short.

Disaffection of Youth

The desire for outsider approval by youth within the relatively easy going Allred group and among independents often leads to disaffection. One father observes: "There is no middle ground for fundamentalist youth. Either they're very dedicated or they choose to be completely out of the movement. We respect their choice in the Allred group. We don't try to force them one way or the other. On the other hand, the LDS church provides a middle ground for youth because the church is primarily social."[200] Owen Allred volunteers that alcohol, drugs, delinquency, and sexual experimentation are problems among the Allred group's youths, and that twice as many young males leave the group as females.[201] One teenage boy says, "I've had a lot of influences in the world, and sometimes I wonder why I'm even still here [in the Allred group]." Many of Rulon Allred's children and sons of his group's current leadership have abandoned fundamentalism for the LDS church or no religion.[202]

Defection of independent children from fundamentalism is especially understandable since independents feel estranged from the groups, the church, and the secular society. Ogden Kraut observes that "the percentage is not very high" for keeping their children in the movement that many independent parents also regard as "out of order." He adds, "I know of some men who have large families and almost none of them get back into fundamentalism."[203] A twenty-three-year-old son in an independent family says, "I don't think that you should believe in just one thing, in one way like Christian or Mormonism or anything."[204]

At the other end of the fundamentalist scale, the strict demands of the Colorado City group and the Kingstons are too much for many of their youth, again primarily young men. In 1953 the present head of Colorado City's youth seminary program claimed that, as a result of rigid social control, there was no juvenile delinquency or profanity in the town.[205] Colorado City's mayor comments that "If somebody's kids get out of order, you know a man gets some hot breath down his back. It isn't necessarily the police hammering on them. But they get some pressure from the other families and from the people [i.e., the Priesthood] to do something and to take care of them."[206] Many young men leave this control behind as soon as they can.

Raised in the Johnson group until she left it in the mid-1970s, one plural wife says, "There was a very high turnover of young men who left the group." This perception is also supported by recent fieldwork.[207] The disaffection is usually total. One man raised in the commune and now in his twenties recently told me, "I've done my best to put it all behind me and live a different life." One of Colorado City's leaders observes, "Percentage wise there's not a whole lot of them who come back and affiliate religiously. There's quite a high percentage that don't."[208] A plural wife in the Davis County Cooperative says that 50 percent of its young people (especially males) abandon the ascetic Order.[209]

The Guarantee of New Plural Marriages

Since fundamentalists report that twice as many young men abandon fundamentalism as young women, polygamy can continue among fundamentalists with few conversions from the outside. In other words, the rigorous conformity required in the Colorado City group, for example, winnows away the majority of the group's young men. This radically alters the gender ratio of faithful fundamentalists and leaves a disproportionate number of young women free to become plural wives. This pattern of higher religious persistence for fundamentalist females also allows demographic opportunity for polygamy among independents and the Allred group which promote it less.

Even though polygamy is less common among the Allred group and the independents, there is no evidence that it is dying among the minority who remain faithful. In Owen Allred's family, all of his daughters and more than half of his sons have entered polygamy. One independent, Albert E. Barlow, reports that all but two of his first plural wife's eight children married polygamously, as did all but one of the twelve children by his second plural wife. A third of Louis Kelsch's family are living in the Principle.[210]

Among the believing fundamentalist teenagers in this study, attitudes vary from cautious to enthusiastic about entering plural marriage in the future. One boy remarks, "I believe it's a true principle, but I don't know if it's for me to live, either. I just have to wait and see." This is echoed by another who says he does not expect to look for a plural wife because "I don't want to have all that responsibility," even though he believes in it. On the other hand, all the married sisters of another teenage boy have married polygamously, and he says, "I definitely do want to live plural marriage because I have a testimony of it." One young woman responds, "It's a big part of my plans. I mean, I don't know, I can't imagine life without it," and the other teenage girls in this study agree. Even in this small group of faithful teenage Mormon fundamentalists, the commitment to marry polygamously is four times higher for females than for males. Such a gender-skewed trend guarantees that Mormon fundamentalism will continue to thrive as a polygamous subculture in America.

Living with Altered Social and Legal Realities

These young fundamentalists will enter plural marriage in a more hospitable world than when their parents married polygamously. The 1953 Short Creek raid was a climax of government prosecutions of polygamists, and it backfired in a storm of public criticism for its perpetrators and in enormous financial costs to the government. Prosecutorial interest has sharply declined since then. There was a conviction in 1974 for polygamy, but it was due to a formal complaint by the father of one of the man's plural wives.[211] A polygamous husband expresses the view of Mormon fundamentalists today: "We're taking the position that plural marriage is not prosecutable because of so many deviant practices that the Supreme Court has said are justifiable. . . . Because we take that position and because we've had far less persecution over the years, we've become more open." Then he adds, "Some say we'll pay someday. We shouldn't be so open."[212]

Several law enforcement officials explain the lack of prosecutions under antipolygamy statutes. The assistant chief investigator of the Salt Lake County Attorney's Office says, "I really doubt that we'll ever see prosecution of those people for the multiple marriage." Because Mormon fundamentalists marry only one wife civilly, the bigamy statutes do not apply, and prosecutors are reluctant to charge fundamentalists with adultery or unlawful cohabitation because of society's acceptance of sexual cohabitation by unmarried persons.[213] Utah's attorney general agrees, and adds that there is not enough prison space to hold all the polygamists, so there is "an uneasy truce" between law enforcement and polygamists.[214] The Salt Lake County attorney says the polygamy laws should be taken off the statute books because Mormon fundamentalists in all other respects "are not violating the law." His assistant chief investigator adds, "The vast majority of those people are peace loving. They want no problems with outsiders. They want to be left alone to practice their religion as they best see fit, and we respect that."[215] An FBI agent adds: "At least 99 percent of all polygamists are peaceful, law-abiding people."[216]

These remarkable expressions by senior law enforcement officers are symptomatic of dramatic changes that have occurred in the last fifteen years. The murder of Rulon C. Allred in 1977 brought law officers in close contact and cooperation with his successor, Owen Allred, as well as representatives of most other fundamentalist groups anxious to distance themselves from the small band of murderous schismatics connected with Ervil LeBaron. The urgency and intensity of this communication and cooperation broke down walls of suspicion that had previously seemed unbreachable. Owen Allred says, "But as far as the state and the officials of the state—the police departments, head people—they just treat us wonderfully. I am so thankful for that. Right from the governor's office down, they have been very respectful to us."[217]

In 1988 renewal of armed stand offs and bloodshed involving the Singer family and their polygamous son-in-law Addam Swapp again placed local, state, and federal law enforcement agencies in the position of seeking cooperation with fundamentalists, this time with the independents.[218] After the Singer-Swapp family bombed an LDS chapel and barricaded themselves at their family compound, Ogden Kraut's efforts at defusing the situation endeared him to law enforcement agencies. When the resulting publicity of Kraut's polygamous status endangered his position as a civilian employee of the U.S. Army, the local FBI chief and the Utah attorney general intervened with the post commander to protect Kraut's job.[219] It is a long way from the Short Creek raid.

Nevertheless, such developments infuriate powerful elements of Utah and western American society. The *Salt Lake Tribune* printed an editorial in 1988 stating: "Utah officials presumably have tolerated polygamy to keep the peace and to avoid making the dependents of polygamists wards of the state. However, when the state makes special allowances for polygamy, it tacitly approves the practice and scorns its own constitution. Such double-dealing cannot continue indefinitely without generating greater contempt for Utah laws and standards."[220] Although LDS church leaders may wish Utah to be as repressive de facto as it is de jure toward Mormon fundamentalists, the society is in transition not dictated by church headquarters or its allies.

Mormonism has passed the century mark of its public abandonment of polygamy. The Manifesto saved the church from destruction in 1890 and allowed Utah to become a state in 1896. Now government agencies have entered into a de facto gentlemen's agreement with Mormon fundamentalists about their continued polygamy. Some law enforcement officials are even looking forward to a de jure resolution: a case before the U.S. Supreme Court that could reverse the 1879 *Reynolds v. the United States* decision allowing criminal prosecution of religiously based polygamy.[221]

In this instance, disenchanted law officials are joined by legal historians who regard the *Reynolds* decision as an anachronism that could not be upheld if the U.S. Supreme Court agreed to rule on a challenge to the century-old precedent.[222] In 1988 an Arizona superior court judge fired the first shot of what may be a siege to overturn *Reynolds:* "The court holds, in essence, that the [Arizona] constitutional proscription of polygamy may be applied except where it would interfere with genuine religious practices."[223] Those words have begun a judicial battle to fulfill Justice William Douglas's dissent against the 1972 *Wisconsin v. Yoder:* "in time Reynolds will be overturned." Still, the Reagan-Bush Supreme Court may nullify that effort since its neo-conservative majority used the *Reynolds* decision in 1990 to deny the use of peyote in Native American religion.[224] The Supreme Court will never relinquish the essential principle of *Reynolds v. the United States* that there are limits to protected religious practice.

However, the *Reynolds* decision is ripe for circumvention in that it atavistically defines a non-normative family relationship as deprived of legal protections, even though this family relationship is at least as stable as normative monogamy. If religiously motivated polygamists ever have success with the U.S. Supreme Court, they will do so in an appeal that does not use the First Amendment to challenge *Reynolds,* but instead uses the equal protection provision of the Fourteenth Amendment to challenge laws and policies that discriminate against nonmonogamous family life.

That is the constitutional potential of the *Fischer* adoption case. In an unappealed decision in 1991, the Utah Supreme Court ruled: "The fact that our [Utah] constitution requires the state to prohibit polygamy does not necessarily mean that the state must deny any or all civil rights and privileges to polygamists." The court then ruled that a polygamous family has the legal right to adopt children.[225] This 1991 decision established a precedent for future petitions to obtain judicial recognition of all family rights for polygamous marriages.

Triangular Impact: Fundamentalists, the LDS Church, and the Third World

For its part the LDS church strenuously resists reversing any policy, and enforcement of the 1890 Manifesto is a big one. In fact the LDS church applies the Manifesto to countries and cultures where polygamy is legal. For example, Nigerian law allows polygamy, but the LDS church refuses to baptize polygamous husbands or wives in Nigeria unless the husband divorces the plural wives by taking them back to their villages. When the LDS church first sent a representative there, "A Nigerian priest, to become a member of the church, was told that he could not be baptized unless he sent away one of his wives. He slept on it over night and came the next morning and told Brother Williams that he had decided to let one of his wives go back to her father." LDS president David O. McKay lamented: "That is a cruel thing to do." Yet thirty years later that is still the LDS church's policy toward legal polygamists. Nor will the LDS church baptize children of polygamists in Africa, until the children are old enough to convincingly renounce polygamy.[226] Yet polygamous children in Africa are as legitimate as monogamous children.

African polygamy (the normative practice in 78 percent of sub-Saharan tribes) is a challenge for Catholic and Protestant churches as well. Although they lack the LDS church's polygamous scripture and heritage, several Christian churches baptize polygamists. A survey shows that polygamists in Nigeria's capital account for 17.3 percent of Catholics and 23.3 percent of Protestants.[227] Moreover, since polygamy is legal in Nigeria (where there are about twenty thousand Mormons), its polygamists are in compliance with the 1890 Manifesto's wording to "refrain from contracting any marriage forbidden by the law of the land."[228] What African polygamists are not in compliance with are U.S. and Utah laws. Thus, people who marry legally within African culture are now defined as sinful by a church that once advocated polygamy in defiance of U.S. laws. This contradicts the LDS Church's Twelfth Article of Faith as it applies to sub-Saharan Africa: "We believe in being subject to kings, presidents, rulers, and magistrates in the obeying, honoring, and sustaining the law." Moreover, a church that defines family life as eternal has a policy that requires the breakup of Third World families as a precondition for Mormon conversion.

These ironies will become demographically unbearable once black Africa's Mormon population increases significantly beyond its current fifty thousand. Black African Mormons are scattered throughout Botswana, Ghana, Ivory Coast, Kenya, Lesotho, Nigeria, Sierra Leone, South Africa, Somalia, Swaziland, Zaire, and Zimbabwe. In the last two years, the Mormon population increased 50 percent in Nigeria, 62 percent in Ghana, and 250 percent in Zaire.[229]

As early as 1962, church president David O. McKay was inclined to allow wholesale baptisms of Nigerian polygamists on humanitarian grounds and LDS temple marriages for these legal polygamists. He was supported by his lawyer-counselor Henry D. Moyle, who argued that the Manifesto was inapplicable to Third World polygamy. However, they were dissuaded by Counselor Hugh B. Brown's concern that this would confuse the church's policy toward illegal polygamy in North America. Brown, also a lawyer and a lifelong opponent of the fundamentalists, had drafted the 1935 law that made unlawful cohabitation a felony in Utah.[230]

Again, about 1979, Apostle LeGrand Richards reported that a meeting of the First Presidency and Quorum of Twelve Apostles had just debated whether to sanction legal polygamy in Nigeria and elsewhere. However, this temple meeting tabled the discussion, thereby continuing by default the policy of requiring legal polygamists to become monogamists. Apostle Richards explained, "The problem is that if we allow it in other places [such as Africa], the people could argue that it should be allowed here [in Utah], too."[231]

African polygamists who seek admittance into the LDS church are not fundamentalists, but are tarred with the same brush by current application of the 1890 Manifesto. For the past three decades, members of the First Presidency and Quorum of Twelve Apostles have considered changing the scope of the Manifesto without discarding the document itself, which is now regarded as virtual revelation by LDS church members. Although this will be a wrenching administrative change, the LDS church will eventually open the doors of Mormonism to millions of legal polygamists in Africa, the Near East, and Asia by defining the Manifesto to prohibit only marriages that are illegal in the country of their origin.

The change in LDS church policy toward Third World polygamists will also transform the situation of Christianity in Africa. There, Catholic polygamists realize they live in violation of the church's canon law and theology. African polygamists are also second-class Christians even in the few Protestant churches which baptize polygamists, because these churches have simply made a grudging exception to their marital theology in order to accommodate African realities. When the LDS church redefines the scope of the Manifesto, African polygamists for the first time will be able to experience a Christian fellowship whose theology, scripture, and heritage glorify honorable polygamous marriage. The LDS church is the only Christian fellowship that can offer African polygamists more than second class status as Christians, and the Mormon population in Africa will experience explosive growth if the LDS church combines vigorous proselytizing with a redefined Manifesto.[232]

Mormon fundamentalism is the only obstacle preventing the LDS church from making that humanitarianly necessary, theologically consistent, and administratively logical acknowledgment of the sanctity and legitimacy of Third World polygamous family life. The LDS hierarchy is understandably reluctant to do anything that would strengthen the position of its polygamous schismatics, who would demand to receive the same dispensation as African, Near Eastern, and Asian polygamists. But the North American situation is completely different because polygamy is illegal (even if the laws are unenforced) in Canada, Mexico, and most of the United States. The LDS church will never repeal the 1890 Manifesto and accept illegal polygamy in North America, just to allow about twenty-one thousand Mormon fundamentalists to become Latter-day Saints.

Nevertheless, because the 1890 Manifesto's prohibitions were defined in terms of the "law of the land" in the United States, changes in U.S. jurisprudence are undermining the document's relevance to American fundamentalists just as Third World polygamous realities demand the Manifesto's redefinition. The Manifesto's "law of the land" prohibition ceased to apply to federal law as soon as Utah became a state in 1896, because federal antipolygamy laws are legally void within all states of the union. That is why Congress required Utah's state constitution to prohibit polygamy. On the other hand, even if the U.S. Supreme Court continues to uphold *Reynolds,* that 1879 decision's application to polygamists is ironically null in every state that has "consenting adult" statutes which have decriminalized polygamous cohabitation by default. Therefore, the 1890 Manifesto is based on criminal laws that no longer apply in "consenting adult" states where fundamentalist polygamy exists in ironic compliance with the legalistic definitions of the Manifesto.

In addition, even in Utah and other western states with antipolygamy statutes and polygamous families, there is judicial change. The grim hostility of law enforcement officials against continued polygamy has now all but vanished into a live-and-let-live attitude. The numbers of polygamists already make enforcement of these antipolygamy statutes virtually impossible. Mormon fundamentalists have achieved a remarkably successful modus vivendi with the United States, its curiosity, and its laws. If the U.S. Supreme Court eventually rules that nonmonogamous families have legal rights and deserve recognition, then the legalistic basis for the Manifesto will crumble like a house of cards. If there had been judicial recognition of polygamous family rights in 1890, there would have been no Manifesto.

The Mormon fundamentalist population of about twenty-one thousand is a deceptively small percentage of the total population of the LDS church and the United States. Relatively few people who read the *Book of Mormon* and *Doctrine and Covenants* will live polygamy, but the number of Mormon fundamentalists is growing exponentially. Short Creek's polygamous population was four hundred at the time of the 1953 raid, but less than forty years later it has grown to forty-six hundred. Those now living in Mormon-oriented polygamous families rival the number living in plural marriages sanctioned by the LDS church at the time of the 1890 Manifesto. There are ten times more polygamists in the United States now than in 1862, the year of the first federal law against polygamy, or in 1953, the year of the last federal raid against polygamists. Western America is already crowded with Mormons, and will be increasingly so in coming decades, but polygamous family life will also be a growing factor in the West's social fabric. In other words polygamy will be an ever larger demographic reality for

Americans, no matter what the LDS church does regarding its definition of the Manifesto.

But there is an equal irony in the position of Mormon fundamentalists. When the situation in the Third World requires (as it should) the LDS church to sanction current polygamous living, Mormon fundamentalism will face a challenge it will not survive using its present definitions. Mormon fundamentalists have a separate line of priesthood, and they will find it difficult to join a newly polygamous LDS church and be deferential to LDS general authorities rather than to fundamentalist Priesthood Councils. Colorado City's United Effort Plan, the Allred's Apostolic United Brethren, and the Kingston's Davis County Cooperative will be reluctant to turn over their extensive economic assets upon conversion to a polygamous LDS church's Corporation of the President. However, that will be necessary if these groups continue to define the continuation of plural marriage as the fundamental reason for their estrangement from what they define as God's true church.

At a personal level, it will be hard to give up the sense of community within Mormon fundamentalism for a somewhat alien LDS community. Despite all the professed (and sincere) reverence for the LDS church, the Mormon fundamentalist has a religious tradition different from that of the LDS church member, and it will not be easy to walk away from that identity. In other words, one day each Mormon fundamentalist will have to decide whether his or her fundamentalist identity is more important than joining a newly polygamous LDS church.

In fact, LDS church acceptance of Third World polygamists will underscore the fact that (unlike LDS Mormons) fundamentalist Mormons have retained the nineteenth-century sense of being a gathered people. The dual processes of accommodation to American society since 1890 and massive conversion rates since 1960 have undermined the traditional Mormon sense of ethnicity ("peopleness") within the LDS church. "Mormon ethnicity" is dying in the LDS church (and in some respects has died already through a "Correlation Program" too involved to discuss here).[233] By contrast, Mormon ethnicity lives on actively in Mormon fundamentalism.

Not simply caretakers of plural marriage, Mormon fundamentalists have lost their church but retained and even re-created the crucial sense of Mormons as a people, a *Volk,* an ethnicity. The current LDS church is so alien to its nineteenth-century counterpart that even accepting Third World polygamists in full fellowship will not return the current LDS church to its nineteenth-century character. Fundamentalism may therefore have increasing appeal to LDS church members who feel the loss of that identity as their church hurtles toward its projected population of 265 million before the second-century anniversary of the Manifesto. That is one reason there will continue to be fundamentalist Mormons after the LDS church becomes polygamous again.

Many Mormon fundamentalists may realize that their fundamentalist identity is more important to them than even a polygamous LDS church. Undoubtedly most members of Colorado City's Fundamentalist Church, the Davis County Cooperative, and the LeBaron churches will remain fundamentalists even if the LDS church sanctions plural marriage again. On the other hand, significant numbers of Mormon fundamentalists may join the LDS church if it accepts polygamous living. Because of the traditional fundamentalist reverence for the LDS church, some members of the above three groups and at least a large minority of independents and the Allred's Apostolic United Brethren may seek out the LDS church once it sanctions even limited polygamous living. Sanctioning Third World polygamy may be a difficult administrative decision for the LDS church, but it will split and redefine the Mormon fundamentalist movement as nothing else has.

Despite their clannishness and inwardness, Mormon fundamentalists are participating in a transformation of the world around and beyond themselves. Over the objections of the American West's governing elites, Mormon fundamentalists have given the region an enduring polygamous character. The Kelsch family's cabinet business, the Kingston's Davis County Cooperative, Colorado City's United Effort Plan, and the fundamentalist domination of Utah's building trades have a multimillion dollar combined economic impact that is both regional and national. Mormon fundamentalists feel no affinity with practitioners of other non-normative family relationships in the United States, but are participating with all other nonmonogamous households in a domino effect that has altered judicial and social realities of the nation as a whole. Internationally, Mormon fundamentalism is both the deterrent and the key toward a transformation of the Christian status quo in polygamous cultures such as sub-Saharan Africa. Mormon fundamentalism has significant impact far beyond its small numbers which are growing rapidly.

Notes

1. Whitney R. Cross coined the phrase in *The Burned-over District: The Social and Intellectual History of Enthusiastic Religion in Western New York, 1800–1850* (Ithaca, N.Y.: Cornell University Press, 1950). For a penetrating analysis of Mormonism as a new world religion, see Jan Shipps, *Mormonism: The Story of a New Religious Tradition* (Urbana: University of Illinois Press, 1985). For general understanding of Mormon history and beliefs, see also Leonard J. Arrington and Davis Bitton, *The Mormon Experience* (New York: Alfred A. Knopf, 1979).

2. Rodney Stark, "The Rise of a New World Faith," *Review of Religious Research* 26 (September 1984): 22. Five years later he found LDS membership growth actually ahead of his projection. Remarks of Stark at annual meeting of the Society for the Scientific Study of Religion, Salt Lake City, Utah, 27 October 1989.

3. D. W. Meinig, "The Mormon Cultural Region: Strategies and Patterns in the Geography of the American West, 1847–1964," *American Geographers Association Annals* 55 (1965): 191–200; *Deseret News 1991–1992 Church Almanac* (Salt Lake City: Deseret News, 1990), p. 6; LDS church statistical report for 31 December 1991; D. Michael Quinn, "Religion in the American West," in William J. Cronon, George Miles, and Jay Gitlin, eds., *Under An Open Sky: Rethinking America's Western Past* (New York: Norton, 1992); also idem, "From Sacred Grove to Sacral Power Structure," *Dialogue: A Journal of Mormon Thought* 17 (Summer 1984): 9–34; and idem, *The Mormon Hierarchy* (forthcoming).

4. Mormon fundamentalists usually capitalize "fundamentalism" and "fundamentalist" when referring to themselves, although I do not do so in this essay. "They are rightly called Mormon Fundamentalists, for they have not turned with [LDS] Church policy as the main body has, but have reverenced

and upheld the founders." Louis J. Barlow's remarks on KSUB Radio, shortly after the Short Creek raid of 26 July 1953, copy in author's possession; also Leroy S. Johnson's statement in 1977, "I was grateful when I heard that [LDS apostle] Mark E. Petersen branded us as FUNDAMENTALISTS." See Ken Driggs, "Fundamentalist Attitudes toward the Church: The Sermons of Leroy S. Johnson," *Dialogue: A Journal of Mormon Thought* 23 (Summer 1990): 51; and *The L. S. Johnson Sermons*, 6 vols. (Hildale, Utah: Twin Cities Courier Press, 1983–84), 4:1491.

5. Pierre LaForet, "Ce Mormon. Heureux. 'Regne' Sur Ses Quatre Femmes," *Le Figaro*, 16 April 1988; Bella Stumbo, "No Tidy Stereotype. Polygamists: Tale of Two Families," *Los Angeles Times*, 13 May 1988, pt. 1, p. 1; *Reason: Free Minds and Free Markets* 18 (January 1987), photographs on the front page and table of contents page, as well as four illustrations in the same issue for Gerald M. King's article, "The Mormon Underground Fights Back," pp. 23, 24, 26, 28, 29.

6. Example in *Salt Lake Tribune*, 19 March 1986, section NV, p. 1.

7. *Sunstone Review* 2 (January–February 1982): 9. The author watched this film on late-night television in 1991, a decade after its original screening.

8. For the isolated, sensational murders that created this stereotype, see Ben Bradlee, Jr., and Dale Van Atta, *Prophet of Blood: The Untold Story of Ervil LeBaron and the Lambs of God* (New York: G. P. Putnam's Sons, 1981), and Richard S. Van Wagoner, *Mormon Polygamy: A History* (Salt Lake City: Signature Books, 1986), pp. 215–19. The film *Messenger of Death* was also televised more than once in 1990–91.

9. Ken Driggs, "After the Manifesto: Modern Polygamy and Fundamentalist Mormons," *Journal of Church and State* 32 (Spring 1990): 386; Jessie L. Embry, *Mormon Polygamous Families: Life in the Principle* (Salt Lake City: University of Utah Press, 1987), pp. xiii–xiv. Although there was also some nonfatal violence during 1990 involving the polygamous mayor of Big Water, Utah, the conflict involved a political and financial dispute within the community, not a dispute about polygamy or about fundamentalist claims. See Jerry Spangler, "Tidal Wave of Fury in Tiny Big Water," *Deseret News*, 5 September 1990.

10. Stanley S. Ivins, "Notes on Mormon Polygamy," *Western Humanities Review* 10 (Summer 1956): 229–39, reprinted in *Utah Historical Quarterly* 35 (Fall 1967); James E. Smith and Phillip R. Kunz, "Polygyny and Fertility in Nineteenth-Century America," *Population Studies* 30 (September 1976): 465–80; Phillip R. Kunz, "One Wife or Several? A Comparative Study of Late Nineteenth Century Marriage in Utah," in Thomas G. Alexander, ed., *The Mormon People: Their Character and Traditions* (Provo, Utah: Brigham Young University Press, 1980), pp. 53–73; Dean May, "A Demographic Portrait of the Mormons, 1830–1980," in D. Michael Quinn, ed., *The New Mormon History: Revisionist Essays on the Past* (Salt Lake City: Signature Books, 1991); Larry Logue, "A Time of Marriage: Monogamy and Polygamy in a Utah Town," *Journal of Mormon History* 11 (1984): 3–26; Lowell "Ben" Bennion, "The Incidence of Mormon Polygamy in 1880: 'Dixie' versus Davis Stake," *Journal of Mormon History* 11 (1984): 27–42; Larry Logue, *Sermon in the Desert: Belief and Behavior in Early St. George, Utah* (Urbana: University of Illinois Press, 1988), pp. 44–71.

11. U.S. Senate, *Proceedings Before the Committee on Privileges and Elections of the United States Senate in the Matter of the Protests Against the Right of Hon. Reed Smoot, a Senator from the State of Utah, to Hold His Seat*, 4 vols. (Washington: Government Printing Office, 1904–7); H. Grant Ivins, *Polygamy in Mexico as Practiced by the Mormon Church, 1895–1905* (1970; Salt Lake City: Collier's Press, 1981); Kenneth L. Cannon II, "Beyond the Manifesto: Polygamous Cohabitation Among LDS General Authorities after 1890," *Utah Historical Quarterly* 46 (Winter 1978): 24–36; Victor W. Jorgensen and B. Carmon Hardy, "The Taylor-Cowley Affair and the Watershed of Mormon History," *Utah Historical Quarterly* 48 (Winter 1980): 4–36; Kenneth L. Cannon II, "After the Manifesto: Mormon

Polygamy, 1890–1906," *Sunstone* 8 (January–April 1983): 27–35; D. Michael Quinn, "LDS Church Authority and New Plural Marriages, 1890–1904," *Dialogue: A Journal of Mormon Thought* 18 (Spring 1985): 9–105; Jessie L. Embry, "Exiles for the Principle: LDS Polygamy in Canada," *Dialogue* 18 (Fall 1985): 108–16; Fred C. Collier and Knut Knutson, eds., *The Trials of Apostle John W. Taylor and Matthias F. Cowley* (Salt Lake City: Collier's Publishing Co., 1987); Jessie L. Embry, "Two Legal Wives: Mormon Polygamy in Canada, the United States and Mexico"; and B. Carmon Hardy, "Mormon Polygamy in Mexico and Canada: A Legal and Historiographical Review," in Brigham Y. Card, Herbert C. Northcott, John E. Foster, Howard Palmer, and George K. Jarvis, eds., *The Mormon Presence in Canada* (Edmonton: University of Alberta Press, 1990).

12. Van Wagoner, *Mormon Polygamy,* pp. 195–98; D. Michael Quinn, *J. Reuben Clark: The Church Years* (Provo, Utah: Brigham Young University Press, 1983), pp. 183–85.

13. For example, *Salt Lake Tribune,* 24 August 1909, p. 4.

14. *Truth* 15 (October 1949): 133–34. Mormon fundamentalists, like LDS members, capitalize "Church" when referring to the LDS church. In another example of this exaggeration, the fundamentalist periodical claimed that Anthony W. Ivins performed more than four hundred polygamous marriages in Mexico from 1895 to 1904, when in fact he performed forty-three verified plural marriages. *Truth* 5 (April 1940): 246; compare Quinn, "LDS Church Authority and New Plural Marriages, 1890–1904," p. 80, n.281, and Quinn's work in progress.

15. Dennis R. Short, *Questions On Plural Marriage* (Salt Lake City: self-published, 1974), p. 94. *Newsweek,* 19 May 1975, also estimated a total of thirty-five thousand people living in polygamy, which this study regards as too high an estimate even now, and certainly an inflated figure then.

16. Paul Van Dam, Utah state attorney general, interview by Ken Verdoia, 6 December 1989; David Yocum, Salt Lake County attorney who prosecuted Ervil LeBaron in 1980, interview by Ken Verdoia, 7 December 1989. Copies in author's possession.

17. For example, a 1986 study of three suburban polygamous families began by claiming "30,000 people living in polygamous families in Utah today," and the *Salt Lake Tribune* in 1988 reported the estimate of a geographer at Utah State University that "30,000 to 40,000 people could be practicing polygamy in the West from southern Canada to northern Mexico. He estimated that 20,000 to 30,000 of those live in Utah alone." During that same year the *Los Angeles Times* cited an estimate of 60,000 polygamists. Carolyn Campbell, "The Private Place of Plural Marriage," *Utah Holiday,* May 1986, p. 36; *Salt Lake Tribune,* 10 April 1988, section B, p. 2. See also King, "Mormon Underground Fights Back," p. 22; *Los Angeles Times,* 13 May 1988, pt. 1, p. 24. In 1989 the *Encyclopedia of American Religions* article on polygamous Mormon groups estimated "approximately 30,000 polygamists," and the *New York Times* claimed 50,000 people were living in polygamous households as of 1991. J. Gordon Melton, *The Encyclopedia of American Religions,* 3d ed. (Detroit: Gale Research Inc., 1989), p. 579; Dirk Johnson, "Polygamists Emerge from Secrecy, Seeking Not Just Justice but Respect," *New York Times,* 9 August 1991, p. A-22. Fundamentalist publisher Ogden Kraut recently stated that "there are probably at least 30,000 people who consider themselves as Fundamentalist Mormons, espousing at least the belief in the doctrine of plural marriage." Ogden Kraut, "The Fundamentalist Mormon: A History and Doctrinal Review" (Paper presented to the Sunstone Theological Symposium, Salt Lake City, Utah, August 1989), published by Kraut as *The Fundamentalist Mormon,* p. 23. In 1986, Van Wagoner also estimated "30,000 Fundamentalists" (*Mormon Polygamy,* pp. iii–iv).

18. Ogden Kraut, interview by the author, 26 July 1989; Ogden Kraut interview by Ken Verdoia, 17 December 1989, copy in author's possession. After I arrived at

this twenty-one thousand figure, I read the estimate of "twenty thousand or more adherents," in Driggs, "After the Manifesto," p. 388.

19. For that reason, this definition does not include a Mormon schism called the Order of Aaron, the Aaronic Order, or Levites. Its founder, Maurice Glendenning, officially condemned plural marriage shortly after the group's organization in 1942, even though (or perhaps because) about 20 percent of his early followers believed in continued polygamy. This group defines itself as separate from Mormon fundamentalism. Hans A. Baer, *Recreating Utopia in the Desert: A Sectarian Challenge to Modern Mormonism* (Albany: State University of New York Press, 1988), pp. x, 61–63.

20. For a discussion of these issues from different perspectives, see Mario S. DePillis, "The Quest for Religious Authority and the Rise of Mormonism," *Dialogue: A Journal of Mormon Thought* 1 (Spring 1966): 68–88; Shipps, *Mormonism,* and Klaus J. Hansen, *Mormonism and the American Experience* (Chicago: University of Chicago Press, 1981).

21. Van Wagoner, *Mormon Polygamy,* pp. 3–69; Lawrence Foster, *Religion and Sexuality: Three American Communal Experiments of the Nineteenth Century* (New York: Oxford University Press, 1981); Klaus J. Hansen, "The Political Kingdom of God as a Cause for Mormon-Gentile Conflict," *Brigham Young University Studies* 2 (Spring–Summer 1960): 241–60; D. Michael Quinn, "The Council of Fifty and Its Members, 1844 to 1945," *Brigham Young University Studies* 20 (Winter 1980): 163–97; Leonard J. Arrington, Feramorz Y. Fox, and Dean L. May, *Building the City of God: Community and Cooperation Among the Mormons* (Salt Lake City: Deseret Books, 1976); Marvin S. Hill, *Quest for Refuge: The Mormon Flight from American Pluralism* (Salt Lake City: Signature Books, 1988); Kenneth H. Winn, *Exiles in a Land of Liberty: Mormons in America, 1830–1846* (Chapel Hill: University of North Carolina Press, 1989), pp. 4–5, 53–54, 64–73, 218–26; David John Buerger, "The Adam-God Doctrine," *Dialogue: A Journal of Mormon Thought* 15 (Spring 1982): 14–58; *Journal of Discourses,* 26 vols. (Liverpool, England: Latter Day Saints' Book Depot, 1854–86), 1:345–46, 2:82, 210, 3:365, 4:259, 11:328. An excellent one-volume compendium of Mormon fundamentalist doctrine is Robert R. Openshaw, *The Notes* (Pinesdale, Montana: Bitterroot Publishing Co., 1980).

22. Orma Linford, "The Mormons and the Law: The Polygamy Cases," *Utah Law Review* 9 (Winter 1964–Summer 1965): 308–70, 543–91; Gustive O. Larson, *The "Americanization" of Utah for Statehood* (San Marino, Calif.: Huntington Library, 1970); Joseph H. Groberg, "The Mormon Disfranchisements, 1882–1892," *Brigham Young University Studies* 16 (Spring 1976): 399–408; Richard L. Jensen and John W. Bair, "Prosecution of the Mormons in Arizona Territory in the 1880s," *Arizona and the West* 19 (Spring 1977): 25–46; Kimberly Jensen James, "'Between Two Fires': Women on the 'Underground' of Mormon Polygamy," *Journal of Mormon History* 8 (1981): 49–61; Martha Sonntag Bradley, "Hide and Seek: Children on the Underground," *Utah Historical Quarterly* 51 (Spring 1983): 133–53; Hansen, *Mormonism and the American Experience,* p. 145; Edward Leo Lyman, *Political Deliverance: The Mormon Quest for Utah Statehood* (Urbana: University of Illinois Press, 1986), pp. 2, 23; Ken Driggs, "The Mormon Church-State Confrontation in Nineteenth Century America," *Journal of Church and State* 30 (Spring 1988): 273–89; idem, "The Prosecutions Begin: Defining Cohabitation in 1885," *Dialogue* 21 (Spring 1988): 109–21; Edwin Brown Firmage and Richard Collin Mangrum, *Zion in the Courts: A Legal History of the Church of Jesus Christ of Latter-day Saints* (Urbana: University of Illinois Press, 1988); Carol Cornwall Madsen, "At Their Peril: Utah Law and the Case of Plural Wives, 1850–1900," *Western Historical Quarterly* 21 (November 1990): 425–43.

23. Jan Shipps, "The Principle Revoked: A Closer Look at the Demise of Plural

Marriage," *Journal of Mormon History* 11 (1984): 67.

24. *Journal of Discourses,* 13:166, 22: 147–48. A massive collection of doctrinal statements and historical events concerning Mormon polygamy appears in Gilbert A. Fulton, Jr. [pseud.], *The Most Holy Principle,* 4 vols. (Murray, Utah: Gems Publishing Co., 1970–75).

25. Lyman, *Political Deliverance;* Thomas G. Alexander, *Mormonism in Transition: A History of the Latter-day Saints, 1890–1930* (Urbana: University of Illinois Press, 1985), esp. pp. 60–73; Quinn, "LDS Church Authority and New Plural Marriages, 1890–1904," pp. 9–50; Kenneth W. Godfrey, "The Coming of the Manifesto," *Dialogue: A Journal of Mormon Thought* 5 (Autumn 1975): 11–25; Thomas G. Alexander, "The Odyssey of a Latter-day Prophet: Wilford Woodruff and the Manifesto of 1890," *Journal of Mormon History* 17 (1991): 169–206.

26. Thomas G. Alexander, "The Manifesto: Mormonism's Watershed," *This People* 11 (Fall 1990): 23. Jan Shipps had earlier referred to the Manifesto as "a disconfirming event that profoundly altered the character of Mormonism," in "In the Presence of the Past: Continuity and Change in Twentieth-Century Mormonism," in Thomas G. Alexander and Jessie L. Embry, *After 150 Years: The Latter-day Saints in Sesquicentennial Perspective* (Provo, Utah: Charles Redd Center for Western Studies, Brigham Young University, 1983), p. 24.

27. This transition is briefly discussed in Alexander's *Mormonism in Transition* and in Van Wagoner's *Mormon Polygamy,* but deserves more detailed study of how Mormon fundamentalism really developed and why it was shunned by most who secretly entered new plural marriages from 1890 to 1906 with church authority. See also "After the Manifesto"; "Twentieth-century Polygamy and Fundamentalist Mormons in Southern Utah," *Dialogue: Journal of Mormon Thought* 24 (Winter 1991): 44–58; Martha Sonntag Bradley, "Joseph W. Musser: Dissenter or Fearless Crusader of Truth?" in Roger D. Launius and Linda Thatcher, eds., *Differing*

Visions: Biographical Essays on Mormon Dissenters (Urbana, Ill.: University of Illinois Press, forthcoming).

28. Kraut's *Fundamentalist Mormon,* pp. 9–20 discusses the following "Doctrinal Differences": (1) plural marriage, (2) missionary work, (3) office and calling of the Seventy, (4) Priesthood confirmation and ordinations, (5) gathering of Israel, (6) United Order, (7) Adam/God, (8) persecution and world friendship, (9) "One Mighty and Strong," (10) Zion, (11) blacks and the priesthood, (12) Kingdom of God. In his original talk, (11) was Gifts of the Spirit.

29. Van Wagoner, *Mormon Polygamy,* pp. 190–98; Joseph W. Musser autobiography, "Patriarchal," Utah State Historical Society, p. 4; Musser diary, 22 April, 14 June, 7 August 1922, 14 May 1929; *Truth* 1 (January 1937): 117–20; Jerold A. Hilton, "Polygamy In Utah and Surrounding Area Since the Manifesto of 1890" (M.A. thesis, Brigham Young University, 1965), p. 31; Lynn L. Bishop and Steven L. Bishop, *The Keys of the Priesthood Illustrated* (Draper, Utah: Review and Preview Publishers, 1971); Kraut, *Fundamentalist Mormon,* pp. 1–4. Dean C. Jessee, "A Comparative Study and Evaluation of the Latter-day Saint and 'Fundamentalist' Views Pertaining to the Practice of Plural Marriage" (M.A. thesis, Brigham Young University, 1959), was restricted by BYU for several years due to Jessee's relatively even-handed presentation. Paul E. Reimann, *Plural Marriage, Limited* (Salt Lake City: Utah Printing Co., 1974), seeks to refute Lorin Woolley's claims in a legalistic analysis that is flawed by Reimann's historically inaccurate understanding of post-Manifesto polygamy. J. Max Anderson's relentlessly historical analysis of Lorin Woolley's claims is *Polygamy Story: Fiction and Fact* (Salt Lake City: Publisher's Press, 1979), which was reviewed by fundamentalist Fred C. Collier, "Tannering Fundamentalism," *Dialogue: A Journal of Mormon Thought* 13 (Summer 1980): 130–32, and expanded in his *Re-Examining the Lorin Woolley Story.*

30. As an outsider, I find some fundamentalists express suspicion and unwilling-

ness to talk, but many have been patient with my ignorance and curiosity, and have been candid about their experiences. The current mayor of the polygamous commune of Colorado City, Arizona, has provided interviews to more than a hundred reporters. In addition, fundamentalists of various factions have recently invited into their polygamous households such diverse outsiders as a Jewish psychologist and anthropologist, a feminist historian, an LDS legal historian, newspaper reporters from the *Los Angeles Times, Le Figaro, Ladies' Home Journal,* and television crews from local news stations, the University of Utah's public station, the nationally syndicated *Current Affair,* and Italian television. Mormon polygamists have also appeared on the nationally televised talk shows of Phil Donahue, Oprah Winfrey, and Sally Jessy Raphael. For example, *Le Figaro,* 16 April 1988; *Los Angeles Times,* 13 May 1988, pp. 24–25; Dan Njegomir, "Border Towns Embrace Polygamy," *Las Vegas Review-Journal,* 11 December 1988, p. 1; Kathryn Casey, "An American Harem," *Ladies' Home Journal* (February 1990): 117ff.

31. Michael Paul Rogin, *Fathers and Children: Andrew Jackson and the Subjugation of the American Indian* (New York: Alfred A. Knopf, 1975), pp. 241, 247, 248; Jack Norton, *When Our Worlds Cried: Genocide in Northwestern California* (San Francisco: Indian Historian Press, 1979); Arrell Morgan Gibson, *The American Indian: Prehistory to the Present* (Lexington, Mass.: D. C. Heath and Co., 1980), p. 229.

32. Elizabeth M. Lauritzen, comp., *Hidden Flowers: The Life, Letters and Poetry of Jacob Marinus Lauritzen and His Wife Annie Pratt Lauritzen* (Brigham City, Utah: Bradbury Print, 1982), pp. 101–5; Driggs, "After the Manifesto," pp. 367–69, 378–84; idem, "Twentieth-Century Polygamy and Fundamentalist Mormons in Southern Utah," pp. 44–58. Also, Van Wagoner, *Mormon Polygamy,* pp. 195–205; and Sam S. Barlow, interview by the author, 30 January 1990. For the church's quiet encouragement of legal prosecution of fundamentalists, see Quinn, *J. Reuben Clark,* pp. 184–86.

33. Dan Barlow, present mayor of Colorado City, interview by Ken Verdoia, 27 November 1989, copy in author's possession.

34. Sam S. Barlow, interview by the author, 30 January 1990.

35. An "outsider" historian of the Short Creek raid describes a young plural wife who delivered while in detention. At the moment of birth, Arizona authorities "took the baby away from her and wouldn't let her see it for a week." Martha Sonntag Bradley, interview by Ken Verdoia, 5 December 1989, copy in author's possession. Also, Bradley's "The Women of Fundamentalism: Short Creek, 1953," *Dialogue: A Journal of Mormon Thought* 23 (Summer 1990): 23–31; idem, "'We Remembered Zion': The 1953 Raid on the Polygamous Community of Short Creek" (Paper presented at Western History Association, 20 October 1990); and her forthcoming book *Raid: The Fundamentalists of Short Creek, Arizona.*

36. See previous note; Driggs, "After the Manifesto," pp. 384–85; Sam S. Barlow interview; Van Wagoner, *Mormon Polygamy,* pp. 201–5. Utah's test case was Vera Black and her children. See their interview by Ken Verdoia, 28 November 1989, copy in author's possession; Maureen Barlow, interview by Ken Verdoia, 5 December 1989, copy in author's possession; Mabel Allred, interview by Katherine Lundell, 6 January 1990, copy in author's possession; Barbara Owen Kelsch, interview by the author, 20 January 1990; Dorothy Allred Solomon, *In My Father's House* (New York: Franklin Watts, 1984), pp. 82, 125–26; Ken Driggs, "Who Shall Raise the Children? Vera Black and the Rights of Polygamous Utah Parents," *Utah Historical Quarterly 60* (Winter 1992): 27–46.

37. Leroy S. Johnson, sermon at Colorado City, Arizona, 6 March 1977, in *L. S. Johnson Sermons,* vol. 4, p. 1352; Dan Barlow interview.

38. In common Utah pronunciation, it is Short "Crick" and Short "Crickers." Driggs, "Fundamentalist Attitudes toward the Church," p. 51, quotes a sermon by Leroy Johnson that their group was "the

Fundamentalist group of the Church of Jesus Christ of Latter-day Saints." However, after President Johnson's death in 1986, the leaders of the group adopted the unincorporated title of "Fundamentalist Church," as indicated in Sam S. Barlow interview, and in Louis J. Barlow, director of Colorado City Seminary Program of the Fundamentalist Church, interview by Ken Verdoia, 27 November 1989, copy in author's possession. The Colorado City group legally incorporated on 6 February 1991 as a religious corporate sole, The Corporation of the President of The Fundamentalist Church of Jesus Christ of Latter-day Saints, in Utah (#149, 512).

39. Caroline Dewegeli Daley, interview by the author, 28 January 1990.

40. "United Effort Plan's Supplemented Response [as of 27 November 1989] to Order of Court dated July 28, 1989," in Case 87–C-1022J, Roger E. Williams et al. vs. United Effort Plan et al., United States Court for the District of Utah; Jeff Swinton, telephone interview by the author , 14 April 1990; Martha Sonntag Bradley, telephone interview by the author, 27 October 1989; Caroline Dewegeli Daley interview; Sam S. Barlow interview; Lister's population was 586 in the 1986 Canadian census according to author's telephone interview, 17 April 1990, with Mr. McRae, manager of population and social statistics, Ministry of Finance and Corporate Relations, Province of British Columbia, Vancouver, Canada.

41. In a telephone interview on 28 January 1990, Jeff Swinton, the attorney for the Hammond-Timpson group, said that about 20 percent of the former Johnson group members—from Arizona to Canada—have joined the Second Ward, which has 150–200 male heads of household, most of whom live in Colorado City–Hildale. In 1986, during the centennial of the 1886 revelation on polygamy, the Hammand-Timpson group also founded a small residential division of Centennial Park, less than a mile from Colorado City.

42. Van Wagoner, *Mormon Polygamy*, pp. 196–98, 207, 210, 215–16; Lyle O. Wright, "Origins and Development of the Church of the Firstborn of the Fullness of Times" (M.S. thesis, Brigham Young University, 1963), pp. 61–62; Lynn L. Bishop and Steven L. Bishop, *The Truth About John W. Woolley, Lorin C. Woolley and The Council of Friends* (Draper, Utah: self-published, 1972), pp. 33–37; Solomon, *In My Father's House*, pp. 12, 27–29, 47–48, 70–100, 310.

43. Owen Allred, interview by the author, 29 July 1989; Roy Potter, interview by the author, 26 July 1989.

44. Johnson was a polygamous brother-in-law by virtue of being a brother of Joseph Smith's plural wife.

45. The above perspective on the LeBarons comes from Verlan M. LeBaron, *The Lebaron Story* (Lubbock, Texas: Keels and Co., 1981), esp. pp. 122, 134, 170, and 179; also pp. 4–5, 20, 29, 42, 60–61, 64, 71, 99, 105, 112, 115, 117–35. His book states the preference for calling the church over which Joel (and later Verlan) presided by the shortened title Church of the Firstborn. This essay follows that preference, even though there is possible confusion with an alternative Church of the Firstborn organized by their brother Ross Wesley LeBaron. Also see discussion of the claims of various sons of Alma Dayer LeBaron in these outsider studies: Wright, "Origins and Development of the Church of the Firstborn of the Fullness of Times," esp. pp. 89–98, 254–56; Reimann, *Plural Marriage, Limited,* esp. pp. 232–34; Bradlee and Van Atta, *Prophet of Blood*, pp. 45–48, 52, 56, 63–123; Melton, *Encyclopedia of American Religions*, p. 575.

46. See previous note; and *Los Angeles Times,* 18 June 1867, section A, p. 11; Kahile Mehr, "The Trial of the French Mission," *Dialogue: A Journal of Mormon Thought* 21 (Autumn 1988): 27–45; Bruce R. McConkie [an LDS general authority], *How to Start a Cult or Cultism As Practiced By The So-Called Church of the Firstborn of the Fullness of Times Analyzed, Explained, And Interpreted* (Salt Lake City: self-published, ca. 1961); Hector J. Spencer, *Why I Returned to The LDS Church* (Colonia Dublan, Mexico: self-published, ca. 1963); Henry

W. Richards [member of the LDS church's "Special Affairs Committee," then chaired by Apostle Mark E. Petersen], *A Reply to the "Church of the Firstborn of the Fullness of Times"* (Salt Lake City: Deseret Book Co., 1965). For arguments against the LeBarons by mainstream fundamentalists, see Harold Allred, *The Scepter, The Church of the Firstborn, John The Baptist: A Defense of Truth, Peter's Authority* (Fruitland, Idaho: self-published, 1958); Francis M. Darter, *Francis M. Darter versus Joel F. LeBaron* (Salem, Utah: self-published, 1964).

47. LeBaron, *LeBaron Story,* pp. 137–307; Van Wagoner, *Mormon Polygamy,* pp. 214–317; Bradlee and Van Atta, *Prophet of Blood,* pp. 135–350; Richard W. Forbes, assistant chief investigator of the Salt Lake County attorney's office, interview by the author, 26 July 1989; Richard W. Forbes, interview by Ken Verdoia, 7 December 1989, copy in author's possession; Solomon, *In My Father's House,* pp. 88, 92–93, 150, 250; Rena Chynoweth [acquitted of Rulon Allred's murder, but now publicly admits it], *Blood Covenant* (Austin, Texas: Eakin Press, 1990).

48. Richard W. Forbes interview by the author; Forbes interview by Ken Verdoia.

49. Probably the LeBaron colony of Los Molinos in Baja, California. Telephone interview by the author, 29 March 1990, with Leslie Fagen, reporter for television's "Current Affair"; LeBaron, *LeBaron Story,* pp. 228, 250–54, 293–94, 297, 299. Also Fred C. Collier telephone interview by the author, 7 April 1990; *Los Angeles Times,* 13 May 1988, pt. 1, pp. 1, 24.

50. Harold Woolley Blackmore, *Patriarchal Order of Family Government* (Hurricane, Utah: self-published, 1974), p. 94. Owen Allred, presiding elder of the Apostolic United Brethren, expressed similar praise in his interview with the author, 29 July 1989.

51. The above information on the Kingstons comes from Blackmore, *Patriarchal Order,* pp. 94–95; Hilton, "Polygamy in Utah," pp. 38–41; Wright, "Origins and Development of the Church of the Firstborn," pp. 58–59; Bradlee and Van Atta, *Prophet of Blood,* p. 167; Van Wagoner, *Mormon Polygamy,* p. 212; *Wall Street Journal,* 12 February 1985, p. 1; Richard W. Forbes interview by the author. In the years since this publicity, the Kingstons have disposed of some of these businesses and acquired others.

52. Ogden Kraut interview by the author; Owen Allred interview by the author; Ann ____, interview by the author, 28 July 1989.

53. The following comes from "Jane Doe Kingston," information submitted in writing on 25 April 1989, and "George Mason," interview by the author, 26 January 1990.

54. Hilton, "Plural Marriage," p. 38; Owen Allred interview by the author.

55. As indicated earlier, all the above data on the Kingston group come from "Jane Doe Kingston," information submitted in writing and "George Mason" interview.

56. Ogden Kraut interview by the author. For brief discussion of fundamentalist groups of even small size, see Steven L. Shields, *Divergent Paths of the Restoration,* 4th ed. (1990); and Melton, *Encyclopedia of American Religions,* pp. 573–79.

57. Owen Allred interview by the author; Owen Allred, interview by Ken Verdoia, 18 December 1989, copy in author's possession; Sam S. Barlow interview; LeBaron, *The LeBaron Story,* pp. 123–28, 137–82, 297–300. By contrast, in the LDS church there is an ample monthly living allowance provided to its lifetime general authorities and also to church officers in full-time service temporarily. This amounts to fewer than five hundred salaried ecclesiastical officers at one time in a church of eight million, compared with literally hundreds of thousands of unsalaried LDS church officers.

58. The above information on independents comes from Bishop and Bishop, *The Truth about John W. Woolley, Lorin C. Woolley and The Council of Friends,* pp. 11, 85; Ogden Kraut interview by the author; Roy Potter interview; Albert E. Barlow, interview by the author, 27 July 1989; Ann ____ interview; Barbara Owen Kelsch interview.

59. *Los Angeles Times,* 13 May 1988,

pt. 1, p. 24, estimated that in the Los Angeles area alone there are twelve hundred polygamists. This is a wildly inflated estimate, even though my interviews indicate that southern California is home to some independent fundamentalists and some members of various groups.

60. Ernest Strack, letter to the author, 17 June 1989. Strack maintained his Sufi Muslim beliefs as a Mormon fundamentalist.

61. Alex Joseph, interview by the author, 29 March 1990; *Deseret News,* 5 September 1990. Melton, *Encyclopedia of American Religions,* p. 576, gives the organization date as 1978, but this essay follows the 1977 date given in Joseph's interview. For his earlier view of himself and his activities, see Alex Joseph, *A Nickel's Worth: Channel 4 Television Interview with Polygamist Alex Joseph, aired May 22, 1977* (Salt Lake City: Dennis R. Short, 1977). See also Solomon, *In My Father's House,* p. 236, where she discusses Alex Joseph under the name of Ronald Ellison.

62. For example, Louis J. Barlow of Colorado City was the fourth generation to be born in plural marriage, and Morris Jessop in the Allred group was the third generation of his family to be born in the Principle. Both these men were born to fundamentalist parents and now have grandchildren themselves. This pattern of three to four generations of affiliation with fundamentalism is true of the Colorado City, Allred, LeBaron, and Kingston groups and is even true of independents like the Louis A. Kelsch, Jr., family.

63. Morris Jessop, interview by Ken Verdoia, 20 January 1990 and Louis J. Barlow interview; Barbara Owen Kelsch interview; also Ann ___ interview; and "Jane Doe Allred" interview.

64. Ann ___, telephone interview by the author, 27 March 1990.

65. Owen Allred interview by the author.

66. Ogden Kraut interview by the author.

67. Roy Potter interview by the author on 26 July 1989; also King, "The Mormon Underground Fights Back," pp. 24–25; Van Wagoner, *Mormon Polygamy,* pp. 219–322; Royston Potter, *An Offender for a Word: The Polygamy Case of Royston Potter vs. Murray City et al.* (Salt Lake City: Pioneer Press, 1986).

68. Ann ___ interview; Owen Allred interview by the author.

69. Sarah ___, interview by the author, 16 January 1990.

70. Jeremy Thompson, interview by the author, 17 January 1990.

71. Damon Cook, interview by the author, 26 January 1990.

72. Martha Sonntag Bradley, "Changed Faces: The Official LDS Position on Polygamy, 1890–1990," *Sunstone* 14 (February 1990): 32.

73. Damon Cook interview.

74. Carla Foster, interview by the author, 16 January 1990.

75. Quinn, *J. Reuben Clark,* pp. 183–85; Van Wagoner, *Mormon Polygamy,* pp. 195–98; Driggs, "After the Manifesto," p. 381; Albert E. Barlow interview; Ogden Kraut interview; Barbara Owen Kelsch interview; Larry McCurdy, interview by the author, 21 January 1990; Solomon, *In My Father's House,* pp. 12, 97, 244; Rhea Allred Kunz, *Voices of Women Approbating Celestial or Plural Marriage,* vol. 2 (Draper, Utah: Review and Preview Publishers, 1985), pp. 482–87; Bradley, "Changed Faces: The Official LDS Position on Polygamy, 1890–1990," pp. 29, 30, 31.

76. "Jane Doe Allred," interview by the author, 29 July 1989.

77. Caroline Dewegeli Daley interview.

78. Sam S. Barlow interview; Ken Verdoia, telephone interview by the author, 28 March 1990; also Louis J. Barlow, Director of Colorado City Seminary program of the Fundamentalist Church, interview; Driggs, "Fundamentalist Attitudes toward the Church," pp. 51–52. Information on the incorporation of the Fundamentalist Church was obtained in the author's telephone interview, 16 July 1991, with Ken Driggs, who has been requested by leaders of the Fundamentalist Church to emphasize

the fact of its incorporation in his own publications.

79. Solomon, *In My Father's House*, p. 95; Owen Allred interview by the author; Dorothy Allred Solomon, interview by Ken Verdoia, 6 January 1990, copy in author's possession; Carla Foster interview; Mabel Allred, plural widow of Rulon C. Allred, interview; Ken Verdoia telephone interview. Rulon Allred's ambivalence of reverence and resentment is clear in the contrasting obituaries he wrote for church president Heber J. Grant, in *Truth* 11 (June 1945): 17, and (July 1945): 41.

80. For example, Jeremy Thompson interview.

81. Jesse B. Stone, "Jewish Influence on Mormon Church" (Salt Lake City, ca. 1940), by a former Mormon fundamentalist turned pro-Nazi; Owen Allred interview by the author; Ogden Kraut interview by the author.

82. Ruth Foster, age 15, interview by the author.

83. Ann ____ interview; Owen Allred interview by the author; Jonathan D. Robinson, age 16, interview by the author, 26 January 1990; James ____, interview by the author, 30 January 1990.

84. Jeremy Thompson interview.

85. Ibid.; Jonathan D. Robinson interview; James ____ interview.

86. Damon Cook interview.

87. Albert E. Barlow interview.

88. Ogden Kraut interview by the author.

89. See King, "Mormon Underground Fights Back," pp. 24–25; Van Wagoner, *Mormon Polygamy*, pp. 219–22; Royston Potter, *An Offender for a Word: The Polygamy Case of Royston Potter vs. Murray City, et al.* (Salt Lake City: Pioneer Press, 1986).

90. Roy Potter interview.

91. Owen Allred interview by the author; also his interview in *Los Angeles Times*, 13 May 1988, pt. 1, p. 25.

92. Martha Sonntag Bradley, telephone interview by the author, 17 October 1989, concerning her fieldwork in Colorado City;

also estimate that "70 percent of the adults in Colorado City and Hildale engage in the practice of plural marriage," according to dissident Carl Fischer's deposition, p. 90, on 23 August 1988, Fifth Judicial District Court for Washington County, Utah, in re Probate No. 3023, copy in author's possession.

93. Caroline Dewegeli Daley interview. Contrary to his own desires, her father has been a monogamist in the Colorado City group since his plural wife left him nineteen years ago.

94. Jonathan D. Robinson interview.

95. Heather ____, age 22, interview by the author, 17 January 1990.

96. Ruth Foster interview; Heather ____ interview.

97. Jonathan D. Robinson interview.

98. Heather ____ interview; Jeremy Thompson interview; Sarah ____ interview.

99. Sarah ____ interview.

100. Heather ____ interview.

101. Caroline Dewegeli Daley interview.

102. Campbell, "Private Place of Plural Marriage," p. 57.

103. James ____ interview.

104. Ibid.; Sam S. Barlow interview.

105. Caroline Dewegeli Daley interview. She left the Johnson group at age seventeen to become a plural wife in the Allred group.

106. James ____ interview.

107. Martha Sonntag Bradley telephone interview, concerning her fieldwork in Colorado City, Arizona; also Bradley, "Women of Fundamentalism," pp. 14–15.

108. Louis J. Barlow, KSUB talk shortly after 26 July 1953, copy in author's possession; for the negative assessments see Bradley, "Women of Fundamentalism," pp. 12–13; U.S. Senate, Committee of Judiciary to Study Juvenile Delinquency, Plural Marriage, 84th Cong., 2d sess., 28 April–2 May 1955.

109. Sam S. Barlow interview.

110. James ____ interview.

111. Bradley, "Women of Fundamentalism," p. 15.

112. James _____ interview.

113. Bradley, "Women of Fundamentalism," p. 14; Caroline Dewegeli Daley interview.

114. Caroline Dewegli Daley interview. About a year after she formally separated from him, Daley's husband legally divorced his first wife and asked Caroline to remarry him as his legal wife. She did.

115. Bradley, "Women of Fundamentalism," p. 15.

116. Sam S. Barlow interview.

117. Caroline Dewegeli Daley interview.

118. Bradley, "Women of Fundamentalism," p. 14.

119. Caroline Dewegeli Daley interview. Campbell, "Private Place of Plural Marriage," p. 56, also comments, without source citation, that "In Colorado City many girls marry at fourteen," and that unmarried females there are "old maids" at age twenty.

120. Solomon, *In My Father's House*, pp. 47, 79. Of the three polygamist families featured in Campbell "Private Place of Plural Marriage," only one man had married teenagers.

121. Carla Foster interview.

122. Ogden Kraut interview by the author. Campbell, "Private Place of Plural Marriage," pp. 38, 39, gives examples of this alternate pattern of same-or-older-age plural wives.

123. Donna Hill, *Joseph Smith: The First Mormon* (Garden City, N.Y.: Doubleday, 1977), pp. 313, 355; Linda King Newell and Valeen Tippets Avery, *Mormon Enigma: Emma Hale Smith* (Garden City, N.Y.: Doubleday, 1984), pp. 146–47.

124. *Marriage and Divorce: 1987* (Salt Lake City: Bureau of Vital Records and Health Statistics, 1987), p. 10.

125. Michelle Parrish-Pixler, interview by Ken Verdoia, 6 December 1989, copy in author's possession.

126. Rosalind McGee, interview by Katherine Lundell and Ken Verdoia, 15 January 1990, copy in author's possession; also "Utah Children Files Amicus Brief Op-

posing Adoption of Six Children by Polygamist Couple" (Press release by Utah Children, Salt Lake City, 31 May 1989). The specific instance is the Fischer family adoption case, *In the Matter of Wayne Allen Thornton et al.*, No. 890053, Priority No. 7 (Utah Supreme Court). This family is featured in *New York Times*, 12 June 1989, p. 10, and in *Ladies' Home Journal*, February 1990, pp. 116ff.

127. Short, *Questions On Plural Marriage*, p. 77. Cf. D. Gene Pace, "Wives of Nineteenth Century Mormon Bishops: A Qualitative Analysis," *Journal of the West* 21 (April 1982): 49–57.

128. Ogden Kraut interview by the author.

129. Solomon, *In My Father's House*, p. 249.

130. Quoted in Campbell, "Private Place of Plural Marriage," p. 58, but mistakenly identified there as a psychiatrist. Rytting presented his intensive study of the polygamous husband and wives and their children in a single household in "Between Three Cultures: A Polygamous Marriage" (Paper presented at the meeting of the Mormon History Association, Omaha, Nebraska, May 1983), and in "Persecuting and Prosecuting Polygamists: Perplexing Public Policies" (Paper presented at the meeting of the Society for the Scientific Study of Sex at Madison, Wisconsin, June 1986).

131. For example, Owen Allred interviews by the author and by Ken Verdoia.

132. Short, *Questions On Plural Marriage*, pp. 10, 39.

133. "Jane Doe Allred" interview; also Bradley, "Women of Fundamentalism," p. 22.

134. Roy Potter interview; "Jane Doe Allred" interview. Although traditional, the presence of the legal wife has often been eliminated at the ceremony, especially when fear of arrests has made it necessary to reduce witnesses to polygamy, which is defined in the law as the ceremony, not the living arrangement.

135. "Jane Doe Allred" interview.

136. Mabel Allred interview; Solomon, *In My Father's House,* p. 185.

137. Barbara Owen Kelsch interview. One plural wife tells another researcher how she controls jealousy: "But when I felt most hateful I went into my room and closed the door." See Bradley, "Women of Fundamentalism," p. 20.

138. Ruth Foster interview.

139. Caroline Dewegeli Daley interview.

140. Sam S. Barlow interview. For nineteenth century, see Eugene E. Campbell and Bruce L. Campbell, "Divorce Among Mormon Polygamists: Extent and Explanations," *Utah Historical Quarterly* 46 (Winter 1978): 14–23.

141. Caroline Dewegeli Daley interview.

142. Morris Jessop interview; Owen Allred interview by Ken Verdoia.

143. Ogden Kraut interviews by Ken Verdoia and by the author.

144. "LDS Rank High in Marriage, Low in Divorce, Study Says," *Ensign* (July 1984): 79; Bureau of Economic and Business Research, Graduate School of Business, *Statistical Abstract of Utah: 1990* (Salt Lake City: University of Utah Press, 1990), p. 46; Thomas K. Martin, Tim B. Heaton, and Stephen J. Bahr, *Utah In Demographic Perspective: Regional and National Contrasts* (Salt Lake City: Signature Books, 1986), p. 126.

145. Joseph W. Musser and Hugh B. Brown family group sheets, Family History Library of the LDS church, Salt Lake City; Hugh B. Brown interview, 12–13 November 1969, transcription, pp. 24–25, in Edwin B. Firmage Papers, Western Americana, Marriott Library, University of Utah; Laura Tree Zitting, *The Life of Charles Frederick Zitting: One of God's Noble Men* (self-published, 1988), p. 27; Barbara Owen Kelsch interview; Solomon, *In My Father's House,* p. 39. An autobiography of a first wife's gradual disillusionment with fundamentalist polygamy and return to the LDS church is Melissa Merrill [pseud.], *Polygamist Wife* (Salt Lake City: Olympus Press, 1975), which was published by this devotional press as a warning to its LDS clientele. The narrative is true, however, and her husband was a prominent publisher in the Allred group.

146. Ruth Foster interview.

147. Bradley's "Women of Fundamentalism," pp. 22–23, comments on this socialization of daughters in fundamentalist families.

148. Jonathan D. Robinson interview; Caroline Dewegeli Daley interview.

149. Compare following discussion to Vicky Burgess-Olson, "Family Structure and Dynamics in Early Utah Mormon Families, 1847–1885" (Ph.D. diss., Northwestern University, 1975); Lawrence Foster, "Polygamy and the Frontier: Mormon Women in Early Utah," *Utah Historical Quarterly* 50 (Summer 1982): 268–89; Kahile Mehr, "Women's Response to Plural Marriage," *Dialogue: A Journal of Mormon Thought* 18 (Fall 1985): 84–98; Embry, *Mormon Polygamous Families;* and Douglas R. White, "Rethinking Polygyny: Co-Wives, Codes, and Cultural Systems," *Current Anthropology* 29 (August–October 1988): 529–72.

150. Rosalind McGee interview; also "Utah Children Files Amicus Brief Opposing Adoption of Six Children By Polygamist Couple" (Press release by Utah Children, 31 May 1989).

151. Michelle Parrish-Pixler interview.

152. Caroline Dewegeli Daley interview. Bradley's "Women of Fundamentalism," p. 15, does not specifically address this question of actual living dynamics, but does show that subservience was the normative value presented in Mormon fundamentalist literature such as *Truth* 14 (October 1948): 134.

153. Anonymous wife, quoted in Ken Verdoia, "A Matter of Principle," *Utah Holiday,* May 1990, p. 21.

154. Caroline Dewegeli Daley telephone interview; Ann _____ interview; Heather _____ interview; James _____ interview; Jonathan D. Robinson interview; observations by the author of a sacrament meeting of the Apostolic United Brethren, 21 January 1990.

155. "Jane Doe Allred" interview. This is

echoed in Campbell, "Private Place of Plural Marriage," p. 58.

156. Ann ____ interview.

157. June Jessop, interview by Ken Verdoia, 20 January 1990, copy in author's possession.

158. Maureen Barlow interview.

159. Jonathan D. Robinson interview.

160. Ann ____ interview; Caroline Dewegeli Daley interview; "George Mason" interview.

161. Carla Foster interview.

162. Caroline Dewegeli Daley interview.

163. Ann ____ interview; Carla Foster interview; Heather ____ interview; Jonathan D. Robinson interview; Jeremy Thompson interview; Owen Allred interview by author; Barbara Owen Kelsch interview; Solomon, *In My Father's House,* p. 67.

164. Caroline Dewegeli Daley interview.

165. King, "Mormon Underground Fights Back," p. 30.

166. "George Mason" interview.

167. Martha Sonntag Bradley telephone interview; Ken Verdoia telephone interview.

168. Carla Foster interview.

169. Owen Allred interview by the author.

170. King, "Mormon Underground Fights Back," p. 26. For the diversity of employment by nineteenth-century Mormon wives, see Michael Vinson, "From Housework to Office Clerk: Utah's Working Women, 1870–1900," *Utah Historical Quarterly* 53 (Fall 1985): 326–35.

171. Caroline Dewegeli Daley interview; Solomon, *In My Father's House,* pp. 109, 135, 155; Verdoia, "Matter of Principle," p. 21.

172. Barbara Owen Kelsch interview.

173. Ibid.; Caroline Dewegeli Daley interview.

174. Interviews by the author with Jeremy Thompson, Ruth Foster, Sarah ____, Heather ____, Jonathan D. Robinson, and James ____. Compare with Solomon, *In My Father's House.*

175. Anonymous plural wife, quoted in Verdoia, "Matter of Principle," p. 21.

176. Caroline Dewegeli Daley interview; Solomon, *In My Father's House,* pp. 62, 98, 190, 237, 252.

177. Ruth Foster interview.

178. Ann ____ interview.

179. Carla Foster interview.

180. David Fleischer and David M. Freedman, *Death of an American: The Killing of John Singer* (New York: Continuum, 1983).

181. Ogden Kraut interview by the author.

182. Ruth Foster interview; Sarah ____ interview.

183. Caroline Dewegeli Daley interview; also Sam S. Barlow interview.

184. Telephone interviews by the author with Martha Sonntag Bradley and with Ken Verdoia; Sam S. Barlow interview.

185. LeBaron, *LeBaron Story,* pp. 169–70, 254.

186. Telephone interviews by the author with Martha Sonntag Bradley and with Ken Verdoia; Sam S. Barlow interview.

187. *Salt Lake Tribune,* 19 March 1986, section NV, p. 1; Campbell, "Private Place of Plural Marriage," p. 44; Owen Allred interview by the author; Owen Allred interview by Ken Verdoia; Heather ____ interview.

188. Barbara Owen Kelsch interview.

189. Roy Potter interview; Albert E. Barlow interview; Ann ____interview; Owen Allred interview by the author; Barbara Owen Kelsch interview; "Jane Doe Kingston" information submitted in writing.

190. Jeremy Thompson interview; Utah children used a doggerel taunt that was both racially and religiously insulting in Solomon, *In My Father's House,* p. 15.

191. Damon Cook interview.

192. Even if teenagers wanted to be known by their real names in these interviews, I have not identified them here and in other sections of this essay where I felt their disclosures were too personal.

193. Verdoia, "Matter of Principle," p. 22; also specific examples in Campbell, "Private Place of Plural Marriage," pp. 38–39.

194. Solomon, *In My Father's House,* p. 27.

195. Caroline Dewegeli Daley interview.

196. Ken Verdoia telephone interview.

197. Owen Allred interview by the author.

198. Caroline Dewegeli Daley interview; Solomon, *In My Father's House,* p. 32.

199. Caroline Dewegeli Daley interview.

200. Larry McCurdy interview.

201. Owen Allred interview; also Solomon, *In My Father's House,* p. 236.

202. Solomon, *In My Father's House;* "Jane Doe Allred" interview; Owen Allred interview by Ken Verdoia; Morris Jessop interview.

203. Ogden Kraut interview by the author.

204. Brad _____, interview by the author, 30 January 1990.

205. Louis J. Barlow talk on KSUB radio.

206. Dan Barlow interview; also similar observation in Sam S. Barlow interview.

207. Caroline Dewegeli Daley interview; Martha Sonntag Bradley telephone interview.

208. "John Doe Johnson," telephone interview by the author, 28 January 1990; Sam S. Barlow interview. Also, dissident Carl Fischer's deposition, Fifth Judicial District Court for Washington County, Utah, in re Probate No. 3023, pp. 59–60, 105.

209. "Jane Doe Kingston" information submitted in writing.

210. Owen Allred interview by the author; Albert E. Barlow interview; Barbara Owen Kelsch interview.

211. Kraut, *Fundamentalist Mormon,* p. 22; Van Wagoner, *Mormon Polygamy,* 201–7.

212. "George Mason" interview. Fundamentalists, however, have an exaggerated perception of the judicial acceptance of "deviant practices," which have been decriminalized by several states but not by the U.S. Supreme Court.

213. Richard W. Forbes interview by the author.

214. Paul Van Dam interview, quoted in Verdoia, "Matter of Principle," p. 23.

215. David Yocum interview; Richard W. Forbes interview by the author.

216. *Los Angeles Times,* 13 May 1988, pt. 1, p. 24.

217. Owen Allred interview by the author; also Robert G. Dyer, "The Evolution of Social and Judicial Attitudes Toward Polygamy," *Utah State Bar Journal* 5 (Spring 1977): 35–45.

218. "The Return of the Patriarch," *Time,* 1 February 1988, p. 21; Jean Bucher, "Inside Addam Swapp," *Utah Holiday,* October 1988, pp. 31–40, 47; Ogden Kraut, "The Singer/Swapp Siege: Revelation or Retaliation?" *Sunstone* 12 (November 1988):10–17; an account of the Singer-Swapp standoff will appear in the forthcoming second edition of Fleischer and Freedman's *Death of an American.*

219. Ogden Kraut interview by the author.

220. *Salt Lake Tribune,* 9 December 1988, section A, p. 22. See also *Salt Lake Tribune,* 11 June 1989, section A, p. 26.

221. Richard W. Forbes interview by the author; James L. Clayton, "The Supreme Court, Polygamy, and the Enforcement of Morals in Nineteenth Century America: An Analysis of Reynolds v. United States," *Dialogue: A Journal of Mormon Thought* 12 (Winter 1979): 46–61.

222. Laurence H. Tribe, *American Constitutional Law* (Mineola, N.Y.: Foundation Press, 1978), pp. 853–54; G. Keith Nedrow, "Polygamy and the Right to Marry: New Life for an Old Lifestyle," *Memphis State University Law Review* 2 (Spring 1981): 203–49; Penelope W. Salzman, "Potter v. Murray City: Another Interpretation of Polygamy and the First Amendment," *Utah Law Review* (1986): 345–71; Ken Driggs, "Lorenzo Snow's Appellate

Court Victory," *Utah Historical Quarterly* 58 (Winter 1990): 93.

223. Decision of Judge J. D. Howe in *Samuel S. Barlow v. John A. Blackburn et al.,* on 6 June 1988, Superior Court of Arizona, Maricopa County. Copy in author's possession.

224. *Wisconsin v. Yoder,* 406 U.S. 205, 92 S. Ct. 1526, 32 L. Ed. 2d 15 (1972); Van Wagoner, *Mormon Polygamy,* pp. 221–22; Bradlee and Van Atta, *Prophet of Blood,* p. 34; *New York Times,* 18 April 1990, section A, p. 10.

225. *In the Matter of the Adoption of W.A.T., V.E.T., J.T.T., J.S.T., J.L.T., and B.D.T., Minors,* 808 F2d 1083, 1085 (Utah, 1991); also *New York Times,* 29 March 1991; Ken Driggs, "Utah Supreme Court Decides Polygamist Adoption Case," *Sunstone* 15 (September 1991): 67–68; T. R. Reid, "The Adoption Case That Shook Utah," *Washington Post,* 15 March 1989, section B, p. 1; Chris Jorgensen, "Could Adoption Case Affect Polygamy's Future?" *Salt Lake Tribune,* 16 April 1989, section B, p. 1; "Custody Battle in Utah's Top Court Shines Rare Spotlight on Polygamy," *New York Times,* 12 June 1989, p. 10; "Polygamy Battle: Man Fights Utah over 3rd Wife's Children," *Milwaukee Journal,* 12 June 1989, section A, p. 5; *Ladies Home Journal,* February 1990, pp. 116ff.

226. Discussion by members of LDS First Presidency on 19 September 1962, transcript in author's possession; author's telephone interview on 4 April 1990 with Mark and Elma Bradshaw, a married couple who were LDS missionaries in Nigeria in 1980–81 and again from 1988 to April 1989. Mrs. Bradshaw knew of two Nigerian polygamists who received LDS baptism from another missionary shortly after they divorced their wives in this traditional manner, but her husband Mark said he would never baptize a man in such circumstances unless the divorce had occurred long before the baptism request. He could not countenance a man divorcing wives for the purpose of becoming a Mormon, but that ethical scruple is not shared by all LDS leaders or their representatives in Africa. On the other hand, in the mid-1970s a Protestant missionary in Africa wrote that "very few people today advocate a break up of a polygamous household and even conservative pastors in Africa prefer to postpone baptism rather than do such a thing." See Aylward Shorter, "Review," *Journal of Religion in Africa* 8 (1976):150.

227. Eugene Hillman, *Polygamy Reconsidered: African Plural Marriage and the Christian Churches* (Mary Knoll, N.Y.: Orbis, 1975), pp. 34, 94, 96; also G. E. Currens, "A Policy of Baptizing Polygamists Evaluated," *Africa Theological Journal* 2 (February 1969): 71–83; Alan Tippett, "Polygamy as a Missionary Problem: The Anthropological Issues," *Church Growth Bulletin* 5 (March 1969): 60–63; Edward G. Neding, "The Baptism of Polygamous Families: Theory and Practice in an East African Church," *Journal of Religion in Africa* 2 (1970): 130–41; E. Dale LeBaron, "Africa: The Church In," in Daniel H. Ludlow, ed., *Encyclopedia of Mormonism: The History, Scripture, Doctrine, and Procedure of the Church of Jesus Christ of Latter-day Saints,* 4 vols. (New York: Macmillan Publishing Co., 1992), 1:23.

228. *Deseret News 1991–1992 Church Almanac,* p. 153. In the *Doctrine and Covenants* published by the LDS church, the Manifesto has been included at the back of the volume since 1914. It is Document 1 in recent editions.

229. *Deseret News 1991–1992 Church Almanac,* pp. 119, 145, 328–29. Compare to LDS population for Ghana, Nigeria, and Zaire in *Deseret News 1989–1990 Church Almanac* (Salt Lake City: Deseret News, 1988), p. 86. Excluding South Africa, where the vast majority of Mormons are white, there were 31,900 black Mormons in Sub-Saharan Africa as of January 1991. I've allowed for the conversions since then. See LeBaron, "Africa," p. 23.

230. Transcript of First Presidency meeting, 19 September 1962; Joseph W. Musser diary, 28 March 1935; *Truth* 10 (November 1944): 144.

231. Richards described the meeting and made that statement to Paul and Margaret

Toscano, according to their letter to the author, 16 September 1990.

232. Since 1860, the Reorganized Church of Jesus Christ of Latter-day Saints headquartered in Independence, Missouri, officially denied that Joseph Smith had anything to do with polygamy, and the RLDS church defined polygamy as a disgusting aberration from Christian values. However, because of proselytizing among polygamous Africans, in the 1972 RLDS *Book of Doctrine and Covenants,* section 150:10, stated that "Monogamy is the basic principle on which Christian married life is built. Yet, as I have said before, there are also those who are not of this fold to whom the saving grace of the gospel must go. When this is done, *the church must be willing to bear the burden of their sin,* nurturing them in the faith, accepting that degree of repentance which it is possible for them to achieve." (emphasis added). Non–RLDS readers, including the present author, understood the emphasized words to mean that this revelation allowed the RLDS church to baptize African polygamists without requiring an end to their existing plural marriages. However, the RLDS church's official historian writes that monogamy was ultimately required of these polygamous converts: "The RLDS church baptized polygamists in India and Africa during the 1960s, and then took measures to help these families to make the necessary social and economic adjustments to extricate themselves from polygamous arrangements. This was achieved during the 1970s and the RLDS church has not baptized polygamists since that time." Richard P. Howard to the author, 19 December 1990.

233. James B. Allen and Glen M. Leonard, *The Story of the Latter-day Saints* (Salt Lake City: Deseret Book Co., 1976), pp. 595–622; Robert Gottlieb and Peter Wiley, *America's Saints: The Rise of Mormon Power* (New York: G. P. Putnam's Sons, 1984), pp. 15, 59–62, 81–82; Jan Shipps, "Making Saints in the Early Days and the Later Days" (Paper given in a plenary session of the Society for the Scientific Study of Religion, Salt Lake City, 27 October 1989), to be published in Shipps, *Being Mormon: The Latter-day Saint Experience, 1941–1991* (Bloomington: Indiana University Press, forthcoming).

The New Religions, Family, and Society in Japan

Helen Hardacre

The chapters in part 2 present clear examples of the fundamentalist message about the family, women, and interpersonal relations. The Islamic varieties of fundamentalism present in Iran, Egypt, and Pakistan span a broad spectrum of positions and praxis, in combination with varying stages of modernization and Westernization, that impacts very differently on the family. Similarly, Mormon polygamy is clearly related to an economic marginality which fundamentalism is powerless to change. But what of other culture areas or religious movements that are less readily recognizable as fundamentalism in the forms it takes within Western religions?

East Asia is not generally noted for fundamentalist movements. They are not unknown there, but the concept of fundamentalism is less salient in analyzing East Asian religious movements. For example, sacred texts in the Buddhist or Taoist canons rarely are regarded in the way the Bible or Qur'an is in the West: they do not set a standard of orthodox behavior that facilitates approbation for those in conformity with it or stigmatization of nonconformists. History is seen as having a cyclical character rather than as representing a one-time-only cosmic drama.[1]

If we take antimodernism to be an indispensable defining element of fundamentalism, then the phenomenon is not found widely in East Asia, a region which is perhaps more aggressively modernist in its overall character than any other. Perhaps no society better represents the broad social consensus committed to modernism than Japan. There are, of course, parts of East Asia where modernizing processes are proceeding slowly, but the commitment to the associated political and social transformations is very strong. Nevertheless, there are religious movements in East Asia that bear some resemblance to fundamentalisms elsewhere. The New Religions of Japan are one such example, and it is useful to describe their message on women, the family, and interpersonal relations as perhaps a less extreme manifestation of some of the same elements portrayed by other chapters in this section, but with important variations.

Fundamentalism and the New Religions of Japan

In a Yokohama branch church of a Japanese Buddhist New Religion, a small, elderly man stands in his stocking feet at the head of a large meeting room. Tensely resting his right hand upon the doilied lectern before him, he taps with his thumb on the larger beads of his tasseled wooden rosary. He is not pleased; he is not sure his message is getting through. He pauses to survey his audience. About 150 in all, everyone is a member of his church, and virtually all are women. They are sitting formally on their knees upon the straw-matted floor listening to this monthly sermon by the head of their church, the *kyōkaichō*. The leaders among them are dressed in black, as befits a Buddhist gathering in Japan. Some are taking notes. The kyōkaichō tries again:

> You women know that in the animal world, it is the males who are the most powerful. Take the gorilla for example—did you ever hear of a female gorilla leading the pack? No, of course not! And it is the males who are the prettiest. Who ever paid any attention to a drab female duck? Or a female peacock? Ridiculous! Being the strongest and most powerful, naturally the males are the most attractive as well. What I'm trying to tell you today is that it's the same way with human beings. It's the men who are superior, and the women who are behind all the trouble in the world.

This vignette comes from my fieldwork on the Buddhist religion Risshōkōseikai, founded in 1938 and currently the second largest new religious organization in Japan, with some five million members. The message from the Yokohama kyōkaichō was unambiguous: male superiority and authority, a sociobiological argument for female submission and deference. He later connected the assertion of female inferiority with a need to reinstate the *ie,* a patriarchal family form discussed in detail below, in which the authority of elders and the dominance of males were rigidly institutionalized and given legal force under prewar law.

Clear as this man's message was, however, it was not at all obvious how to draw a correct interpretation of the whole situation. The women in the audience, it later emerged, had come to pay tribute to the female founder of the religion, Naganuma Myōkō (1889–1957), whose death anniversary was the occasion for the monthly sermon, and to socialize with each other. Naganuma was a visionary charismatic who kept her younger male cofounder Niwano Nikkyō (1906–) firmly in check during her lifetime, which may account for the present male leadership's desire to write her out of Risshōkōseikai's history. The kyōkaichō himself seemed to recognize that the women sitting so deferentially before him might in fact be ignoring what he had to say, patiently waiting for the end of his tiresome harangue so that they could get on with the business that had really brought them to the church that day: interacting with other women.

Men such as the Yokohama kyōkaichō have no impact on Japan's social policy, because the government steers far clear of any association with religion in that context, no matter how many politicians might personally agree with what was said in the church that day. On the other hand, in terms of the members' thought and religiosity, years of exposure to so vigorous a denigration of women have certainly had a cumulative effect. How many of the women present that day ignored this proclamation of male superiority? To how many does its presentation in religious guise lend a sacrality to the content? For those women, what is the character of religious experience based on a doctrine of their own inferiority? How many will raise their daughters to believe in their own inferiority and to defer to men who proclaim it from the pulpit? When will even one woman have the courage to denounce such a leader in public? Assessing the significance of radical patriarchalism in the New Religions is by no means an easy task.

Most scholars who have studied the New Religions of Japan would probably agree that there is a certain kinship between these religious associations and fundamentalism. Yet this is at best a similarity of ambience, a hewing to social and political conservatism, the perception of an enemy in left-of-center thought and communism in particular, and a pervasive sense that "traditional values," closely associated with the patriarchal family, are both sacred and under attack. These tendencies are more pronounced in newer groups, however, while in the older ones with histories of more than a century they are absent or negligible. Creationism, opposition to abortion, and insistence on textual inerrancy are weak or entirely lacking among the Japanese New Religions. Since the perception of similarity is so amorphous, and since some of the hallmarks of fundamentalism are so conspicuously absent, the appropriate starting point for a comparative investigation is by no means obvious.

Overall it is inappropriate to think of the Japanese New Religions as fundamentalist, because they lack the characteristic antimodernism of the fundamentalist phenomenon as a whole. They affirm the rationalism, bureaucratism, scientism, and nationalism of the modernist hegemony, and in this sense their resemblances to fundamentalist movements, for example, in the field of family, gender, and interpersonal relations, are epiphenomenal.

The New Religions: Background Information

The New Religions of Japan currently number over three thousand organizations, large and small, and include between one-fourth and one-third of the Japanese people, that is, between thirty million and forty million people. A single organization, Sōka Gakkai, accounts for some twelve million persons. While perhaps fifteen of these organizations are truly massive and powerful, with memberships of three million or more, the majority are much smaller in size.[2]

The term "New Religions" refers to those religious associations founded since roughly the beginning of the nineteenth century down to the present which exist outside the ecclesiastical structures of temple Buddhism and shrine Shintō. In terms of their doctrine, the New Religions include Buddhist, Shintō, Christian, and completely novel organizations. The New Religions typically feature a number of elements found also in more traditional forms of religious association, such as ancestor worship, healing, and shamanic practices. The novelty of the New Religions thus lies not in the list of their various practices and beliefs, but in the way they are assembled into a shared perspective on human problems, a common orientation that can be described as a shared worldview. In their incorporation of more traditional practices we can see a continuity with past religious history, at the same time the New Religions, whatever their doctrine, have developed a distinctive approach to the religious life and have adapted traditional beliefs and practices to modern circumstances.

The New Religions were founded in three distinct waves, each in the context of particular social and historical conditions. The first wave occurred during the period 1800 to the Meiji Restoration (1868). Of the organizations founded during that time, three are most significant: Kurozumikyō (f. 1814), Tenrikyō (f. 1838), and Konkōkyō (f. 1858). All were founded in the relatively prosperous area of western Japan: Tenrikyō in what is now Nara Prefecture, while both Kurozumikyō and Konkōkyō were founded in Okayama Prefecture. Contrary to the notion of New Religions being founded by the poor and oppressed, the founders of these three organizations came from stable, even prosperous economic circumstances. Each experienced revelations or religious insight after a severe illness or a series of disastrous yet inexplicable misfortunes.

While none of the founders of these organizations intended to establish a Shintō sect, by the early twentieth century all of them had assumed Shintōized doctrines and practices. During this period the state sponsored the Shintō religion and pressured other religions to conform to Shintō's mythology and emphasis on such state-centered values as loyalty and national service.

The second period of founding New Religions came in the early twentieth century with the establishment of Sōka Gakkai (1930), Seichō no Ie (1929), and Reiyūkai Kyōdan (1919–25). Both Sōka Gakkai and Reiyūkai were Buddhist, while Seichō no Ie expounded the unity of all religious creeds. Sōka Gakkai remained relatively small until 1945, but its growth thereafter was stimulated by the martyrdom of its founder, Makiguchi Tsunesaburō (1871–1944), who was arrested and died in prison. Seichō no Ie's founder, Taniguchi Masaharu, was an eclectic thinker and prolific writer who incorporated such diverse elements as psychoanalysis, spiritualism, and meditation in the thought and practice of his religion. Reiyūkai collected its earliest following from among a very poor stratum, recent migrants to Tokyo from rural areas, largely through the evangelism of its female founder, Kotani Kimi (1900–1971), while the male founder, Kubo Kakutarō (1892–1944), concentrated on developing doctrine. Until 1945 it preached a doctrine of laypersons' ancestor worship combined with frank anticlericalism; it also was a strong supporter of the prewar regime, as was Seichō no Ie. Reiyūkai spawned a number of schisms, which nevertheless have retained much of the parent organization's doctrines and practices—especially the emphasis on ancestor worship—suggesting that it has captured a religious impulse which a broad spectrum of adherents of the New Religions regards as central to the religious life.

The third wave of foundings of New Religions came in the postwar era, when hundreds of organizations were founded. Many of the founders of this wave would doubtless have established religions earlier had they not been prevented from doing so by the repressive prewar state, and many of the organizations formed at this time in fact represented the reconstitution of religions suppressed before 1945. Thus, the appearance of so many New Religions immediately after the war, "like bamboo shoots after the rain," as the Japanese media has often said, is somewhat misleading. It is not that these organizations simply emerged in response to the crisis precipitated by defeat in war, although no one would deny that the defeat was a "crisis" by any definition, but that with the lifting of restrictions on the establishment of religious groups, many persons became able to do so for the first time and sought earnestly to adapt their vision of the truth to the urgent circumstances Japan faced after 1945.

Of the many New Religions founded since 1945, the following stand out. Perfect Liberty Kyōdan (f. 1946) represented the reconstitution of an organization severely persecuted before the war, as did Sekai Kyūsei Kyō. P. L. Kyōdan took as its slogan the expression "Religion is art" and fostered the practice of the arts in daily life. Sekai Kyūsei Kyō practiced faith healing and natural farming without fertilizer. Tenshōkōtai Jingūkyō, informally known as the "dancing religion" because of its "dance of no ego," was founded in 1945 by the highly charismatic Kitamura Sayo (1900–1967), who had begun even before the war's end to castigate the emperor as a puppet, and civil servants as his "maggot beggars."

Women in the Japanese New Religions

The New Religions of Japan present impressive examples of religious change.[3] Of these, none is more significant than the appearance of large numbers of women in active and powerful positions in virtually all lay societies founded since 1800. This represents a major change from the way women participate in more traditional religious associations such as the parishes of temples and shrines. Women's participation in the New Religions has been facilitated by such attitudes as anticlericalism after the Meiji Restoration of 1868 and social changes such as compulsory education for all and urbanization, which have loosened the hold of older religious associations. These changes alone do not, however, account for women's phenomenal participation in new religious movements. That phenomenon rests not only on parallel religious and social change, but also on innovation in religious thought about women.[4] The New Religions offer women a relation to soteriology different from that of other religious groups.

Women's roles in the Buddhist or Shintō parish have largely been restricted to serving male clerics or assisting male lay leaders by performing domestic services (cooking, laundering, cleaning), and these services have not been linked to the salvation of the women concerned. Furthermore, an ideology of pollution has been used to bar women from clerical roles and to insist that it is more difficult for them to achieve salvation than men, if not impossible. For women or men in temple Buddhism or shrine Shintō, salvation is likely to be viewed as a distant goal over which laypersons have limited control, and which depends heavily upon clerical mediation.

By contrast, in the New Religions salvation is typically believed near at hand and within the believer's power to effect. Pollution notions, while present, are used in a different way and do not typically constitute a barrier either to women's full ritual participation or to their enjoyment of the rewards of dedicated practice. Women expect to experience such this-worldly miracles as physical healing and repair of fragmented human relations, and they anticipate that improved health and relationships will result in greater economic stability and good fortune. They exert themselves vigorously to bring about these results and understand their achievement to constitute proof of salvation's imminence.

Women's sustained participation in this mode of religious activity in such large numbers and over nearly two centuries would be inconceivable without basic changes in religious consciousness, leading them to believe that such achievements are indeed possible. One of the most basic changes relevant to women's participation in the New Religions is the shared worldview of these associations.

The Common Worldview of the New Religions

From the foregoing discussion it will readily be appreciated that there is great variety in the doctrines of the New Religions.[5] While some, such as Reiyūkai, derive from Buddhism and contribute significant innovations to traditional Buddhist doctrine and rites, others are purely eclectic; still others have at one time or another in their histories assumed a Shintō identity to escape persecution but without necessarily originating in Shintō doctrine or having institutional connections to Shintō establishments. That being the case, where, then, lies the unity of the New Religions, and in what sense can we speak of them as having something in common?

The New Religions adopt a common perspective on human problems. Typically they present themselves to potential converts as specializing in solving problems of sickness, economic instability, and interpersonal relations. The New Religions, whatever their doctrine, regard human beings as able to gain control over their circumstances through self-cultivation of certain core values embraced by Japanese culture, especially sincerity, harmony, loyalty, filial piety, modesty, and diligence. In contrast to such Western religions as Christianity, they reject the idea that human affairs are determined by the unknowable will of a single creator deity. When a problem arises, they believe, it is because the self has not been sufficiently cultivated in the values they espouse, and the problem's solution is renewed effort in the practice of these virtues. The self exists in a matrix of relations with the body, other persons, society, nature, and the supernatural world. When it is perfected in virtue, the self will naturally be in harmony with each level of the matrix.

This formulation is inverted in the following way in order to diagnose and solve a problem; let us take sickness as an example. An adherent who consults a leader of the New Religions regarding illness will typically be questioned about the quality of personal relations in the household and advised to look there for the origin of the sickness, perhaps recommending repentance for a lapse of personal self-cultivation. It is assumed that illness arises because the self is not in harmony with the body or with other persons, and hence the solution is to restore harmony and a return to health will follow as a matter of course. Sometimes the diagnosis indicates that the sickness arose because the patient has not been sufficiently attentive to ancestral spirits. This idea represents the adaptation of the ancient practice of ancestor worship to the contemporary world; the New Religions typically advise members how to worship their ancestors in such a way that they will maintain harmony with these most proximate representatives of the supernatural world.

It goes without saying that the worldview of the New Religions has limited applicability in treating such diseases of modern life as cancer, but it is undeniable that thousands of adherents of these groups believe that they personally have experienced a healing of a major or minor ailment through the ministrations of their religion. Whatever the status of their therapies in purely medical terms (and it is by no means self-evident that medical institutions in all cases preserve a more "objective" viewpoint about illness than the religions themselves), the psychological reality of healing through a restoration of harmony, however conceived in terms of the doctrine of a particular group, is widespread and remarkably persistent, quite independent of the progress of medical science. Investigation of cases of faith healing often reveals a profound dissatisfaction with Japanese medical practice and the social conventions observed in dealing with doctors.

Ideologies of Gender and the Family

The Japanese New Religions' ideologies of gender present a difficult paradox. Their female founders typically defy social convention and achieve a public voice only by throwing off restrictions of marriage and motherhood—the very restrictions they spend their careers telling other women represent the one true path to salvation. In the postwar period, many New Religions have adopted an agenda of social issues on which reestablishing a patriarchal ideology of the family (which received state sponsorship in the prewar era) heads the list. This prewar family system they seek to reinstate institutionalizes male dominance and the authority of elders and keeps women's status low by restricting the sphere of choice in matters of marriage, reproduction, and divorce. This older family form is imbued with religious significance so that to be a good wife and mother is not only proper—it is essential to women's salvation.

Female gender characterizations among the New Religions idealize the qualities of gentleness, modesty, deference, humility, and self-sacrifice in relation to men, in whom the qualities of forthrightness, assertion, and pride are prized. These idealizations of femininity and masculinity are shared with the rest of Japanese society in broad outline; a distinguishing characteristic of their formulation among the New Religions is a premium placed on exaggerated expressions of humility and deference by women to men, apparently as a demonstration of complete acceptance of the principle of male dominance. Women's rightful arena is the domestic sphere, while men represent the domestic sphere to the outside world. Women should not attempt to take a place alongside men in the public world, or the domestic sphere will be thrown into chaos.

In order to understand the situation in Japan, it is necessary to review major trends in postwar social change and the ideals held in Japan of a "traditional family," an entity we find as mythicized as its American cousin. The composition of that coresident group sharing the tasks of socialization of children and economic sustenance has changed greatly through the course of Japanese history, and at any given time there have been significant regional and class variations and differences of linguistic usage as well as wide variation in patterns of descent, inheritance, and succession.[6] The range of variation that is presently known is probably an index of recent scholarly interest in the history of families and households in Japan, just as contemporary Western scholarship has shown great interest in the topic in the postwar period.[7] As our knowledge of the historical variation in family forms increases, we can assert with confidence that there never existed a single and invariant organization of the domestic group.

Much former regional and class variation in custom was papered over by the Meiji Civil Code, enacted in 1898, by which the new nation adopted the mores of the former samurai class as a standard.[8] It is the ideal of the family embodied in this code, which remained in effect until 1947, which lives on as an ideal in the minds of older Japanese, who hold what we may identify as a semi-fundamentalist mentality. The Meiji Civil Code upheld the ie, or household, as the single form of the family given legal status.

The ie has been characterized as a "joint-stem family," composed primarily of a core of consanguines but sometimes also including unrelated persons who were employees or retainers, existing over generations and including both presently living members as well as ancestors and as-yet-unborn generations. The ie is a corporate group which is an economic unit, the agent of primary childhood socialization, and a ritual group focused on the worship of ancestral spirits. It rests on the twin principles of the authority of elders and male dominance. The ie is inseparable from a code of social ethics built around its role structure, which upholds the values of filial piety, obedience to elders, repayment of benefice, and loyalty to the group. Ancestor worship is carried out by ie units and constitutes a ritual practice sacralizing the ie, its roles and values.

In most cases an elder male served as its head, a position given legal status under the Meiji Civil Code, and he would, except in unusual cases, be succeeded by his eldest son. Daughters and all sons but the eldest normally moved out upon maturity, to marry into other ie and take the new ie's name, or to set up branch households. Both the main branch of the ie, called the *honke,* and branch or collateral households, *bunke,* of which there might be several, were ideally perpetuated by the succession of first sons and their wives.

At any given time in the evolution of a particular ie, it might assume one of several different forms. Starting with a three-generation form, there would be an elder couple residing with their first son, his wife, and the children of the second generation. If the elder generation died before the second generation produced children or before the children of the successor married, the household would have only one or two generations until the first son (the first grandson of the original couple) had married and produced a child, at which time there would again be three coresident generations as the core members of the ie. At any point in the cycle, employees and retainers employed in the business of the ie might or might not reside with core members.

The position of the househead *(koshu, kachō)* carried considerable authority in the Meiji Civil Code. In particular, the househead held authority over all ie property, which made it nearly impossible for women to hold property in their own right. He legally held the ancestral tablets and related ritual equipment that marked the ie's existence as a ritual unit, and he normatively presided over corporate rites of ancestor worship. He also had considerable authority over the marriages of his children, and none of them could marry or establish a separate residence without his consent. If a son's bride did not please him, the househead could divorce her without his son's (her husband's) consent and send her back to her natal family. If she bore no children, or no *male* children, that was sufficient reason to divorce her, even if it was her husband who was infertile.[9]

In the case of infertility or lack of sons, adoption was frequently used to procure a successor. In general, distant kin were preferred over unrelated persons. Adoption had many forms, including adoption of a man to marry a couple's daughter, who then took the wife's surname; this type is known as *mukoiri kekkon.* Alternatively, a childless couple might adopt a boy or a girl and later a spouse for the child, or they might adopt an already married couple. The possibilities were and are wide ranging.

Women's legal capacity was severely limited under the Meiji Civil Code. Women could own real property only in very exceptional circumstances; for the most part, any property a woman brought to a marriage belonged to the husband to dispose of without the wife's consent. It was conventionally believed that women's main duty to the ie into which they married was to bear and raise children. Prewar government policy prohibited use of and education about contraceptive devices. Men could divorce women for adultery, but women could not do the same; women could only initiate divorce proceedings in very limited situations. If a woman were divorced, she was not automatically entitled to financial support from her former husband, and children of their marriage typically were assigned to the man's custody, as members of his ie. Besides these legal strictures, a woman newly married into her husband's ie was normatively under the authority of the househead's wife as well as the authority of her husband and his father. Tensions between these two women were extremely common.[10]

The reality of prewar society, of course, was far from an embodiment of the Meiji

Civil Code. It has been estimated that many household units did not conform to the ie ideal, not because of a temporary cyclic change in the evolution of that household, but because many were in fact living in a variety of other arrangements, from the nuclear family, to single-person households, to coresident groups of assorted, unrelated persons who lived together for any number of different purposes. Nevertheless, the ie remains an ideal family form for many today. Its role structure of househead, wife-of-househead, successor, successor's wife, and the unmarried children of the successor generation remains a powerful grid shaping thought about family life for many people who have never actually lived in the ideal form.

Meanwhile, however, postwar social changes have largely succeeded in relegating the ie to the status of a minority form in contemporary society. The Allied Occupation introduced sweeping reforms in the 1947 revision of the civil code. The ie was deprived of all legal significance, as was the position of househead. Marriage became an arrangement contracted between the principals, requiring the consent of no one else. Primogeniture was replaced by equal inheritance among all children. Women were empowered to own property in their own right and to initiate divorce on terms equal with men. The ritual status of the ie no longer has a determinate form, because the ownership of ancestral tablets, genealogies, graves, and ritual equipment can now be bequeathed and inherited like any other property. In place of the ie, the nuclear family became the legally recognized form of the family.[11]

Just as the Meiji Civil Code was not a blueprint of social reality, neither was the 1947 Civil Code. Occupation authorities recognized that equal inheritance of agricultural land would result in ruinous subdivision of already tiny plots, so no one objected when it became more or less customary for a single child, usually a son, to inherit agricultural land, with other children ceding their right to inherit. Similarly, inheritance of the equipment for ancestor worship continues to devolve disproportionately upon first sons, as does the major responsibility for caring for aged parents, though the latter burden is so heavy that daughters are likely to be called upon as well. Many people continue to think of main and branch households even where the links are quite attenuated, and frequently the authority of the main house is undermined by branch houses whose wealth far exceeds that of the main house.

The percentage of households of the nuclear family type has increased during the postwar decades to around 65 percent of the total, and those households of the ie type, that is, a married couple, with or without children, plus one or both parents of one spouse, have decreased from about 23 percent in 1960 to about 15 percent in 1980.[12] As discussed above, some residential patterns conforming to the nuclear family represent a developmental stage in the ie, but this sustained decrease in the number of ie-type households is definitive evidence of the ie's decline. As Robert J. Smith has said, "The household [ie] ideal has been abandoned in favor of the ideal of the conjugal family, which is no longer a stage along the way to the establishment of a stem family."[13] That the ie is abandoned by many, is undoubtedly true, but today a distinguishing characteristic of that sector of Japanese religious life resembling fundamentalism is a determination to reinstate the ie by limiting women's sphere of choice over marriage, reproduction, and divorce.

During the postwar decades the population of Japan has undergone increasing urbanization. As of 1955 the balance between rural and urban areas has shifted so that a majority of the population now lives in urban areas; since that time agricultural areas have undergone increasing depopulation. In addition, the number of persons per household has decreased dramatically over the postwar decades, from 6.0 in 1955 to 4.5 in 1985. The birth rate has continued to decline as well, from 25.47 per thousand in 1950 to 12.26 in 1986; in other words it has been cut in half in the postwar era. While well over 90 percent of the population marries, the rate of divorce, miniscule by the standards of Western societies, has climbed from around 1 percent in the early postwar period to about 1.39 percent in the late 1980s, a factor that alarms many traditionalists.[14]

Perhaps the most dramatic change of postwar society has been that affecting the female life cycle. Since Japanese women now have the longest life expectancy in the world, at 80.1 years, the changes in the life cycle relative to the prewar period, when the life expectancy of a woman born in 1920 was less than sixty years, have been radical. Women born in the prewar era could expect to live only about fifteen years beyond the birth of their last child, while now they live more than fifty years beyond that time, about eighteen years after the marriage of their last child. Whereas women in 1950 typically gave birth to 3.65 children, the average per couple in 1986 was 1.72. In other words, the birth rate has declined by more than 50 percent in thirty-five years. Comparable changes have occurred in other developed nations only over a much longer span of time.[15]

Women have become increasingly conspicuous in the labor force during the postwar era. There is now a well-established tradition of women working before marriage and until the birth of a first child. Furthermore, from 1965 to 1982 the number of employed married women rose from 38.7 percent to 50.2 percent; if one includes those women who were seeking employment, the increase is from 54.4 percent to 73.0 percent.[16]

The reality that the majority of married women are employed coexists uneasily with the persisting ideal that married women should remain at home. Many married women are employed in a family business or at part-time jobs, so that, in fact, they spend most of their time at home. The issue as religious traditionalists see it is connected to the ie ideal in that the wife's role in that system is a highly professionalized one. Wife and mother is recognized as a full-time occupation which is not less important than men's work and which cannot be combined with employment outside the home without compromising performance in the wife-mother role, which is universally granted greater priority than any other.[17] Hidden within this ideology of full-time motherhood is a fear of married women having independent access to a cash income. This prospect is fearful because it would allow women to become economically less dependent upon, if not independent from, their husbands.

The postwar years have seen a marked increase in women's social participation. They are entitled to equal education, and they may work and marry without anyone's consent. This is not to deny that they are subject to massive and systematic discrimination. The male-female wage differentials in Japan are among the largest of the developed world, with women earning only 57 percent on average of men's wages,[18] and in spite of new legislation promoting women's employment in managerial posts, most are barred from advancing in a career on equal terms with men. Many parents fear giving women "too much" education, and thus the majority of college women are enrolled in two-year junior colleges. Furthermore, while women are free to marry whom they wish and not to marry at all, the pressure brought to bear on women of marriageable age is typically quite intense, both to marry someone—anyone—rather than remain single, and to marry someone regarded by parents as "suitable."[19]

The dramatic decline in the birth rate during the postwar era, cited above, was due to a reversal of the prewar government's pronatalist policy and its encouragement to limit fertility through widespread use of condoms and induced abortion. The drop in the birth rate and the availability of condoms and abortions cannot, however, be taken as indicating that women can now, as they could not under the Meiji Civil Code, exercise full control over their reproductive capacity. Indeed, Japanese family planners cite husbands' lack of cooperation as a major reason for contraceptive failures, leading to decisions to abort in the case of married women. Furthermore, the government's refusal to sanction the prescription of oral contraceptives and physicians' failure to prescribe and fit diaphragms and other female barrier methods of birth control, as well as their general indifference to the state of women's knowledge of their own bodies, act to perpetuate ignorance of basic reproductive functions. A major study, *Family Planning in Urban Japan,* attributes Japanese couples' low "family planning performance," that is, "taking the initiative to find an appropriate contraceptive method and then cooperating with one's partner for effective use," in significant measure to women's low status in marriage.[20]

The changes in women's social position since the prewar period and the changes in their legal status under the revised Civil Code of 1947 relative to the Meiji Civil Code are highly complex and impossible to summarize briefly. Failing that, however, it may still be possible to relate those changes to the issues posed in part 1 regarding compulsion versus choice in American fundamentalism.

In actual situations both choice and compulsion are seldom absolute, and real decisions incorporate varying degrees of initiative and constraint. The mixture is probably more complex and aspects of choice and compulsion more inextricable the more weighty the decision. Choices regarding marriage, divorce, and reproduction are by any standard among the most significant in human life, and hence the most difficult to analyze. Especially for women, pressure to choose in these areas among a limited number of unpleasant alternatives makes choice an illusory freedom. Nevertheless, we can say that relative to the prewar period the sphere in which women can exercise some choice without fear of violating the law has widened. At the very least, women may marry without their parents' consent, they may take steps to control their fertility, and they may initiate divorce. In that they could not do these things without violating civil law in prewar Japan, the principles of male dominance and the authority of elders have weakened since that time.

In asserting that the sphere of matters over which women may exert choice has widened relative to the prewar period, I do not wish to suggest either that choice was absent from prewar women's lives or that compulsion in marriage, reproduction, and divorce is absent in postwar Japan. The change is relative, and there is no doubt that many postwar marriages have been contracted largely to satisfy convention, pregnancies carried to term for the same reason, and divorces heartily wished for by women who, while supposedly "free" to do so, refrain because to do so is economic suicide, given the discrimination they face in the labor market. Similarly, there may have been humane househeads before 1945 who neither abused their authority nor used it to railroad their children into unwanted marriages and divorces. Nevertheless, the idea of an increased sphere of choice for women in postwar society may facilitate this essay's effort to articulate a comparison between Japanese and American fundamentalists.

Identifying Fundamentalism within the New Religions

Recent changes in the leadership of such organizations as Reiyūkai and Risshōkōsei-kai have resulted in efforts to raise the level of women's political awareness and participation, and these may act to broaden women's sphere of choice. Nevertheless, the high priority on ancestor worship, which is an index of patriarchalism, and which seems to be linked to a sacralization of the ie, a desire to reinstate it and to restrict women's sphere of choice as a means to reinstate the ie, may provide an important key for further research that could delimit the field of the New Religions and determine more clearly which may be usefully compared with fundamentalism.

The New Religions showed some slight activity in the 1980s aimed at increasing women's social awareness, and it may be that in the future these will be linked to changes in the general conservatism found there regarding the family, gender, and interpersonal relations. The activity was initiated by male leaders and completely directed by them, so it would be surprising if basic change in this area resulted from these activities. The situation in Reiyūkai Kyōdan and Risshōkōsaikai is informative.

Reiyūkai has been a long-time supporter of a number of conservative politicians, mostly from the Liberal Democratic party, the party that has been in power nearly continuously since 1945. Among them, Ishihara Shintarō, whose dialogue with the founder Kotani Kimi is discussed below, has maintained a sustained relation with the religion. In the 1980s, especially after 1985, significant energy was devoted to considering how the religion can most appropriately contribute to Japan's social and political development, and a body within the organization, called in English the Inner Trip Ideologue Research Center, was formed to coordinate these efforts. One of its activities has been to provide educational programs for women to raise their level of political understanding.

In interviewing Reiyūkai women associated with the research center, I learned that the program consists of occasional lectures to interested women by the wives of politicians, such as Ishihara, who are financially supported by Reiyūkai. At these lectures, wives describe to Reiyūkai women the role of the politician's wife: she is expected to await her husband's return each evening, prepared to offer hospitality to distinguished guests no matter how late the hour, and in other ways be prepared to offer a congenial atmosphere for political guests who require a place where they can discuss political machinations in confidence. Reiyūkai women in the audience reported that they were gratified by the chance to hear about the inner workings of the political world and that they were personally impressed with the women who spoke before them. They said also that these programs had raised their level of interest in politics in a general way, and that they now read the newspapers more and seek to be better informed on current events. They do not themselves, however, anticipate initiating any political activities of their own.

A second manifestation of this new type of activity for women in the New Religions can be seen in Risshōkōseikai's "No Poi" campaign. *Poi to* is an onomatopoetic adverbial expression attached to verbs for "to throw away," as in to toss a bottle or other piece of trash away. This expression provides the origins for the No Poi campaign, which aims to combat littering. This campaign surfaced in the course of interviewing at Risshōkōsaikai's Kosei Institute of Peace and Justice, when I asked whether women were involved in any political activities sponsored by the religion. The No Poi campaign is centered at the Saitama prefectural headquarters of the religion, and its activities consist of women cleaning parks and streets on a voluntary basis. The institute's theory on the matter holds that the questions of peace and justice must ultimately be addressed at an individual level, in terms of the problems that directly affect a community. Of these, trash and the need to assume an attitude of responsibility for the cleanliness and sanitation of one's immediate surroundings are apposite examples. In interviewing in Saitama, however, I did not find any clear reflection of this political theory among women participants.

The two examples just presented of activities among the New Religions in the 1980s aiming to increase women's level of political awareness do not seem to presage any dramatic change in the stance of the organizations concerned on the family, gender, and interpersonal relations. They remain male-initiated and male-controlled. It may be that they constitute rather lukewarm responses to more broad-based efforts in Japanese society during the 1980s to raise women's level of social and political awareness and participation.

Abortion and Pronatalism

Opposition to abortion is conventionally expressed by Japanese Buddhism and Shintō; in addition it is a minor theme in some of the New Religions. Nevertheless, neither temple Buddhism nor Shintō has played a significant role in public debate on abortion or other issues of medical ethics. When called upon to express their views, they are remarkably self-contained and insular, apparently unaware of the history of the discussion.[21] Furthermore, like doctors, Buddhist priests have an economic stake in preserving induced abortion as a means of contraception, regardless of the physical and emotional costs to the women involved. Buddhist temples of virtually every sect reap huge profits from the performance of rites to pacify the souls of aborted, miscarried, and stillborn children (*mizuko kuyō*). Thus they do not wish to displace one of their most reliable sources of income by preaching against the practice of abortion.

Among the New Religions, Seichō no Ie has taken the most vehement stance against abortion. Seichō no Ie was founded in 1929 and presently has about three million members. While its influence outside its own adherents is limited, the voluminous writings of the founder, Taniguchi Masaharu, are widely available and have probably spread somewhat beyond the group's membership. The group's opposition to abortion is based on the twin ideas that abortion prevents the birth of a spirit who should have received human life, and an "anatomy equals destiny" argument holding that women have a duty or "mission" to bear children. "When a woman obeys this 'command of heaven' [i.e., to give birth] she is satisfied and can attain a feeling of 'carrying out the mission.' . . . When it is abandoned through abortion, she is tortured by a sense of guilt which says 'I've killed our child.' "[22]

Implicit in Seichō no Ie's opposition to abortion is the idea that women have a duty to procreate, and that this duty is sacred because it originates in heaven. The sacralization of motherhood thus is invoked to support opposition to abortion, or it might be more correct to say that abortion is opposed because it gives women the option to shirk their duty to reproduce and is tantamount to homicide.

The idea that women have a duty or mission to bear children is shared with the ie ideal. There it derives its rationale from the goal of perpetuating the ie over time. Old timers in the New Religions typically invoke the desirability of perpetuating the ie to support the notion that women are obligated to bear children. In the past, they opine, women "endured" more, were more self-sacrificing, and seldom considered their own interest. In that way, they were more closely conforming to the shared gender ideology which so strongly insists on male dominance.

Seichō no Ie is an eclectic religion that does not derive directly from either Buddhism or Shintō, but the fundamentalist agenda of restricting women's sphere of choice regarding marriage, reproduction, and divorce as a way of reviving the ie is very strong in Buddhist groups as well, particularly Reiyūkai Kyōdan and the thirty-odd organizations that originated by schism from it.

Reiyūkai has not, for the most part, attempted to exert political influence to realize its social agenda, but it patronizes a number of sympathetic politicians on the right of the Liberal Democratic party. One such politician, Ishihara Shintarō, a longtime protégé of Reiyūkai, conducted a series of conversations with the former president of Reiyūkai, Kotani Kimi. The following excerpt is representative of the group's pronatalism in religious guise.

Kotani: Women these days seem to have stopped having many children. Usually they have about two. What do you think about that, Mr. Ishihara?
Ishihara: I think they ought to have five or six, myself.
Kotani: I think so, too [Kotani had no children of her own]. Why is it that women these days won't bear children?
Ishihara: Well, to make a long story short, they're thinking of nobody but themselves. They aren't thinking of mankind as a whole. They have no desire to produce descendants, and in a nutshell, they think only of their own comfort. They think children are a bother, so they put off having them for as long as possible. A concern for humanity is lacking in modern man.

Kotani: If we go on like this, the Japanese people will decrease drastically, as in ancient France.

Ishihara: Well, people talk about a population problem, but when the number of children decreases, I think it's a problem of selfishness on the part of people who ought to become parents. I'm afraid that our great possibilities as Japanese are slipping away. As for me, when my first child was born, for the first time, there were ancestors and descendants, like the links of a chain that had been connected. I felt that I'd become a link in the chain for the first time.

Kotani: That's so true. It's exactly as you say. That's because it is also through children that karma is transmitted. When people do good, good karma is created.[23]

In Reiyūkai the declining birth rate is seen as a social evil attributable to women's selfishly shirking the duty to reproduce. That men might share the responsibility is not considered. In the organization's view the solution to the problem is to encourage women to marry early and to have numerous children. Although childless herself, Kotani saw no irony in her own position as essentially a female religious professional deriving a livelihood from preaching the gospel of "a woman's place is in the delivery room."

Reiyūkai also sees a great evil in divorce, and it charges the foreign (to them, unambiguously American) officials of the Allied Occupation with having confused centuries of stable Japanese social life by granting women the legal power to initiate divorce. Women are more vehement than men in expressing this idea, and during Kotani's presidency it was very strong indeed. The ie can only be protected when women lack this postwar legal right.

In that they seek to reimpose an older model of the family, the New Religions bear a strong resemblance to fundamentalisms elsewhere. They are staunch advocates of strengthened patriarchalism. The ie model of family life which appeals to the New Religions imposes restrictions on women and limits their exercise of choice. Passionate sexuality does not occupy center stage in the hagiographies of female founders of the New Religions, but there is much passion in their singleminded pursuit of religious goals, and men are not expected to fear that passion. While pollution notions applied to women and associated with menstruation and childbirth are not absent in the New Religions, they are frequently used to claim new kinds of power for women, for example, the power to enter trance and to discover the cause of illness or misfortune. In that sense and to that extent, their sexuality receives a positive valuation.

Notes

1. See Martin E. Marty and R. Scott Appleby, eds., *Fundamentalisms Observed* (Chicago: University of Chicago Press, 1991).

2. Material in this and the following sections is largely based on Helen Hard-

acre, *Kurozumikyō and the New Religions of Japan* (Princeton: Princeton University Press, 1986), chap. 1.

3. Material in this section is drawn from Helen Hardacre, forthcoming.

4. This paper adopts the distinction be-

tween religious change and religious innovation delineated by Michael A. Williams in "Religious Innovation: Toward an Introductory Essay" (Working paper, University of Washington, January 1988), in which "religious change" refers to changes of an institutional nature or large-scale change in the climate of thought (such as a shift from pro- to anticlerical attitudes), while "religious innovation" indicates the creation of new myths, ideas, and symbols which may stimulate religious change.

5. Material in this section is based on Hardacre, *Kurozumikyō and the New Religions of Japan,* pp. 7–36.

6. Fukuo Takechiro, *Nihon kazoku seidoshi gaisetsu* (Tokyo: Yoshikawa Kōbunkan, 1959).

7. Robert Netting et al., *Households: Comparative and Historical Studies of the Domestic Group* (Berkeley: University of California, 1984).

8. Harumi Befu, *Japan: An Anthropological Introduction* (San Francisco: Chandler Publishing Company, 1971), pp. 50–52.

9. Igeta Ryoji, "Meiji minpō to josei no kenri," in Joseishi sōgō kenkyūkai, ed., *Nihon joseishi,* vol. 4: *Kindai* (Tokyo: Tokyo Daigaku Shuppankai, 1982), pp. 58–72.

10. Igeta, "Meiji minpō."

11. See Kurt Steiner, "Postwar Changes in the Japanese Civil Code," in John Huston, ed., *Legal Reforms in Japan during the Allied Occupation* (Special edition of *Washington Law Review,* 1977), pp. 97–123; also, Sakae Wagatsuma, "Democratization of the Family Relation in Japan," in Huston, *Legal Reforms in Japan during the Allied Occupation,* pp. 125–45.

12. Shigeru Yamate, "Seikatsu no hendo to kazoku no hendo," in Hamasumi Otohiko et al., eds., *Nihon no shakai,* vol. 1: *Katsudō suru nihon shakai* (Tokyo: Tokyo Daigaku Shuppankai, 1987), p. 91.

13. Robert J. Smith, *Kurusu: The Price of Progress in a Japanese Village, 1951–1975* (Stanford: Stanford University Press, 1978), p. 46.

14. Statistics Bureau, Management and Coordination Agency, *Japan Statistical Yearbook* (Tokyo: Japan Statistical Association, 1988), pp. 51, 53.

15. Ibid., pp. 53, 55; also, Yoriko Meguro, "Josei mondai to josei seisaku," in Hamasumi Otohiko et al., eds., *Nihon no shakai,* vol. 2: *Shakai mondai to kyōiku seisaku* (Tokyo: Tokyo Daigaku Shuppankai, 1987), p. 193.

16. Yamate, "Seikatsu no hendo," p. 95.

17. Suzanne H. Vogel, "Professional Housewife: The Career of Urban Middle Class Japanese Women," *Japan Interpreter* 12, no. 1 (1978):16–43.

18. Statistics Bureau, *Japan Statistical Yearbook,* pp. 100–101.

19. Takie Lebra, *Japanese Women: Constraint and Fulfillment* (Honolulu: University of Hawaii Press, 1984), pp. 50–100.

20. Samuel Coleman, *Family Planning in Japanese Society* (Princeton: Princeton University Press, 1983), pp. 126, 149–54.

21. See the selections by religious leaders in Nakayama Tarō, *Nōshi to zōki ishoku* (Tokyo: Simul Press, 1989).

22. Quoted in Coleman, *Family Planning,* p. 63.

23. Quoted in Helen Hardacre, *Lay Buddhism in Contemporary Japan: Reiyūkai Kyōdan* (Princeton: Princeton University Press, 1984), p. 50.

3

Education and Media

Fundamentalist Impact on Education and the Media: An Overview

Majid Tehranian

The purpose of this essay is threefold: to briefly review the different interpretations of the rise of fundamentalist movements, to provide a perspective that focuses on the impact of fundamentalist movements on education and the media, and to bring that perspective to a comparative analysis of the six case studies that follow this essay.

Seven Models in Search of Fundamentalism

The essays to follow and other case studies prepared for the Fundamentalism Project seem to present at least seven different although overlapping explanatory models of fundamentalism. Common to most of the movements studied under the rubric "fundamentalism" is an *antisecularist* stance. The corresponding explanatory model predicates a reaction against the worldwide penetration of the European Enlightenment and, from the fundamentalists' perspectives, its most insidious consequence, namely, the displacement of the sacred from the center to the periphery of society. This marginalizing or trivializing of the sacred often corresponds to the marginalization of the masses under the pressures of rapid urbanization and modernization in periphery countries (e.g., Iran and Guatemala) and periphery regions (e.g., the Bible Belt in the United States). Thus an *anti-elitist* interpretation of the fundamentalist movements points to the fact that in some movements, especially in the Third World, fundamentalism seems to appeal primarily to the marginal classes, including the lower-middle-class urban populations (as in Guatemala) as well as the intelligentsia from the same social backgrounds (as in most of the Islamic world), suppressed ethnic or religious minorities (as the Shi'ites in Lebanon and Palestinians in Israel), and marginalized majorities such as the Hindu revivalists in India. In the closely related *anti-imperialist* model, fundamentalism is mainly interpreted as a reaction against Western colonial and postcolonial forms of domination. Islamic fundamentalism in both its Shi'ite and Sunni variants is frequently cited as providing strong evidence for this particular interpretation. The *anticommunist* model is presented as at least partially explanatory of aspects of North and South American Protestant fundamentalisms.

Antimodernism seems also to be a shared "family resemblance" of many fundamentalisms. In this model, fundamentalism is explained as a critical reaction against the consequences of modernity and its orientation to secular rationality. These consequences include the erosion of the religious tradition from within and the perverse applications of science and technology by a modern secular intelligentsia. One product of modernity unsavory to most fundamentalisms is the liberation of women from traditional gender roles. Thus an *antifeminist* interpretation of fundamentalism is useful in referring to a variety of fundamentalist movements. A reassertion of patriarchal values against modern feminist values is reflected in the fundamentalist discourses against abortion, coeducation, unveiling, and more generally, women's full and equal participation in social, economic, and political life. In the perceptions of fundamentalists across religious traditions, the combinations of these insidious trends have led to a pervasive deterioration of the moral order and the traditional social nexus that once governed societies. Accordingly, an *antidecadence* interpretation sees fundamentalism as a cultural revolution against these deteriorations and an attempt to restore the spiritual and moral values of religious traditions.

These seven models converge in different configurations in specific interpretations. Fundamentalism appears as a "reactive" phenomenon in all of these interpretations. But it does not appear to be "reactionary" in all cases.[1]

As this schematic presentation suggests, there is no one single explanation of fundamentalism equally applicable to all cases. Each case must be understood in terms of its own unique features. The following case studies provide, therefore, a necessary antidote to the generalizations of this overview essay. Nevertheless, the case studies at hand present a sufficient number of recurrent themes in fundamentalist discourses and practices in education and the media to warrant some generalizations. Given the diversity of causes and consequences of fundamentalism, we may need a hierarchy of explanations.

As indicated above, fundamentalist movements are characterized most consistently as antisecularist, that is, as an expression of a revolt against the so-called secular humanist projects of the European Enlightenment. The failure of the secular ideologies of progress to address (let alone resolve) the human conditions of finitude, fragility, and evil has in our time reinforced the perennial longings for religion and religious ideologies. This is particularly the case in periods of rapid historical change of recent decades in such places as the Bible Belt of the United States, Eastern Europe, and many parts of Asia, Africa, and Latin America. The human conditions of ontological insecurity[2]—insecurity about being and existence itself—have been deepened by the manifest insufficiency of social and political solutions to the persistent problems of transition from an agrarian to an urban, industrial society. In this context, religious sensibilities and solutions return to a level of credibility they had lost in the rationalist, secularist age of European modernization in the eighteenth and nineteenth centuries. However, the reaction to secularizing processes seems to be a necessary and not sufficient condition for the rise of fundamentalism.

Wherever the secularist discourse corresponds with foreign domination tied to the hegemony of an indigenous secular elite, anti-imperialism has found its greatest ally in a revival of primordial identities, including nativistic religions, languages, and ethnicities. In the Third World, secular nationalism, communism, and national liberation movements represented the earlier responses to the challenges of foreign domination. But in the eyes of the natives, the moral and political decline of the West has depreciated the secular ideologies and valorized the nativist religions as an alternative ideological vehicle for resistance against both foreign powers and indigenous secular rulers. This interpretation seems particularly valid wherever the native religion (such as Hinduism and Islam) could also historically be identified with past periods of independence and glory. In such cases, anti-imperialism, populism, and fundamentalism have combined in providing a potent ideological potion. Cultural survival, national independence, and social transformation are the dominant themes of such fundamentalist movements and discourses.

The anticommunism of most fundamentalist movements presents some paradoxes for the previous interpretation. In the United States, the combination of populism and fundamentalism found a convenient ideological ally in American nationalism and Cold War anticommunism. In much of the Third World, anticommunism may be considered as part of the more general antisecularist and antiforeign sentiments. However, in some Latin American countries such as Guatemala, where growth of Protestant evangelism and fundamentalism has been largely assisted by the financial and political support of U.S. fundamentalists, anti-imperialism and anticommunism seem to be sometimes at odds. This paradox appears less so, however, if we consider the fact that Roman Catholicism in much of Latin America is the religion of the ruling elite. The populist revolt against this elite has consequently expressed itself in two competing religious forms—the theology of liberation movement in the Catholic church and the fundamentalist and evangelical movements in the Protestant churches. But as the Guatemala case study demonstrates, Protestant evangelicalism is also caught in the class struggle between rich and poor, deeply divided between the older populist and the more recent counter-revolutionary churches.

The antimarginalist interpretations of fundamentalism explain this paradox in greater detail. The resurgence of religious consciousness in general and political religions in particular may also be viewed as efforts to redefine the world in terms more comprehensible to the peripheries of power while empowering them to act on behalf of their own perceived interests. Politically and economically, modernization processes have privileged the new secular, technocratic, and managerial elites at the expense of the traditionalist segments of the population. In the Third World, the secular elites also tend to be locked into and allied with the world capitalist system and are, therefore, perceived as a fifth column. The religious opposition, by contrast, often constitutes a second stratum of elite ready to challenge the authority and prerogatives of the dominant elites. Furthermore, the resort to religious ideologies and movements to launch counterhegemonic projects is historically rooted in the anti-imperialist and populist movements. In other words, culture has provided a last-ditch defense mechanism for the peripheries against the centers of power. Language, religion, ethnicity, and cultural preferences as reflected in educational and media programs have been thus politicized in a variety of contexts to an unprecedented degree.

The antifeminist aspects of fundamentalist discourse and practice vary greatly from movement to movement, subject to specific cultural and historical contexts. However, a return to the traditional definition of sex roles as found in the holy scriptures or hallowed traditions seems to inspire them all. The division of labor between women as homemakers and men as field, factory, and office workers stands at the root of such traditional sex roles. However, the specific issues on which fundamentalist causes have focused vary from society to society. Freedom of sexual relations is viewed as promiscuity in most fundamentalist discourse. Exclusion of women from certain professions traditionally reserved for men provides another controversial issue among the fundamentalists. Subordination of women to men at home or in society, however, constitutes an implicit if not explicit maxim in most fundamentalist worldviews.

As the previous volume in this series amply demonstrated, the antimodernist sentiments of the fundamentalist movements do not result in a rejection of modernity. The following case studies add further documentation to this point by demonstrating that fundamentalists in Iran, in the United States, and in Guatemala—and to a lesser extent, in northern India and Israel—have shown ingenuity in adopting the modern media of communication for their own purposes. And while the battle against some modern scientific theories such as evolution theory seems to be universally shared, some fundamentalist educators would go to extraordinary lengths to "prove" the scientific validity of the biblical or Qur'anic prophecies. It appears that the power and prestige of modern science and technology are so overwhelming that fundamentalist movements and discourses have generally found their own unique ways of coping with some modern views while rejecting others. The variation in fundamentalist receptivity to modern science, technology, and lifestyles seems to be a function of the different cultural strategies adopted.

Last but not least, the antidecadence interpretation is often put forward by the fundamentalists themselves. To restore spirituality and decency, fundamentalist movements all seem to turn to education and the media for a new socialization, recruitment, and organization of their members. In fact, both traditional and modern networks of communication in the religious institutions, schools, and media have served as the indispensable tools in the formation and dissemination of fundamentalist messages. However, in those historical contexts in which the schools and the macromedia of communication (the national press and broadcasting) have been largely in control of secular authorities, fundamentalist movements have relied heavily on alternative schools and media. In the United States, for instance, the history of recent fundamentalist movements is closely tied with the development of new fundamentalist television stations and higher educational institutions. In the Islamic world, the fundamentalist movements have availed themselves of the traditional educational, cultural, and communication forms and channels in conjunction with the modern micromedia (telephones, cassette recorders, copying machines, and mimeographing) to launch effective campaigns for the dissemination of their ideologies and programs.

Control of educational and media channels appears to be a function of government policy, cost, access, as well as degrees of social engagement and political activism of the fundamentalist groups. In India, the use of micromedia seems to have been somewhat constrained by the low levels of income and access. Hindu fundamentalism concentrates therefore primarily on education and electoral campaigns for the propagation of its message. By sharp contrast, fundamentalism in the United States has extensive access to its own broadcasting facilities and extended some of it to Central America. In many less developed countries, such facilities are directly or indirectly in control of the government and access is therefore limited. In Israel, Egypt, and pre-revolutionary Iran, audio and sometimes video cassettes have found extensive uses in fundamentalist education and propaganda. The Iranian case is the best known.[3] The ayatollah's messages were transmitted from exile via long-distance telephone calls while cheap transistor audio-cassettes recorded them for transcription and then mass production by copying machines at government agencies! They were widely disseminated within a few hours of transmission through the mosque and school networks. The same methods have been used by others such as the Intifada among the West Bank Palestinians,[4] the Jewish fundamentalists in Israel, and the Sunni Muslim fundamentalist groups in Egypt.

Seeking access to the media, however, seems to be a function of the strategy of social and political engagement. The more engaged groups need and employ the media in their cause; the less engaged rely more on religious networks and schooling. Separatist groups such as Farawiya and Hijra wa Takfir in Egypt and the Amish and Hutterites in North America often reject science, technology, and sometimes even literacy as manifestations of an evil modern world. But the socially engaged groups have no hesitation in employing modern means of communication, education, and weaponry in their campaigns.

In Islamic radicalism, as Sivan suggests, modernity is diagnosed as a threefold problem: "the diagnosis—modernity as Jahiliyya [the epoch of 'ignorance' before the dawn of Islam]; the cure—rebellion (first internal, then external); the means for administering that cure—the tali'a (vanguard) of the True Believers organized as counter-society."[5] The counter-society considers secular education and media as the root of all evil while calling for their total control in a religiously reconstituted society. While the strategic goal remains constant, the tactics are a function of time and circumstances. Whenever and wherever the fundamentalist groups have some measure of political power and access, they use the regular commercial or government media and school systems. In the United States and Guatemala, they now are a permanent part of the media and educational tapestry. The Gush Emunim in Israel has its own radio station and recently acquired its own television station. From time to time, for example, after the assassination of Sadat in 1980, the Egyptian government allowed some fundamentalist views to be aired in the mass media so they could be refuted.[6] However, as Sivan notes:

the ubiquitous modern challenge—especially the global village of the media and pervasive state control—made the withdrawal response less and less tenable, at least for all but tiny groups. Long-term educational efforts, designed to convert society segment by segment to "true Islam," has [*sic*] today even less prospect of success than when Sayyid Qutb began to doubt its efficacy as sole means thirty years ago, before the age of transistor radios, television, and the gigantic growth of the higher educational system. Seizure of power from the hands of "Mongol rulers" like Anwar Sadat and Hafez Assad thus came to be perceived as the only answer to the threat.[7]

In summary, fundamentalism appears primarily as a reactive phenomenon—to the unsettling effects of rapid social change (overmodernization in developing countries, postmodernization in the developed), to marginalization (of the ethnic majorities as in the cases of the Malay in Malaysia and the Hindus in India), to relative material or psychological deprivation (among the urban ghetto or yuppie fundamentalists), and to commodity fetishism as an antithesis to its own identity fetishism. It may be a passing social phenomenon as it seizes power (as in Iran), or is frustrated by the superior power of the state (as in Egypt, Syria, Iraq, or Algeria), is gradually integrated into the mainstream of cultural life (as in the case of Moral Majority in the United States), or is allied to the ruling elites in preserving the status quo (as in Guatemala and Saudi Arabia). Its alternative strategies thus consist of revolutionary *militancy* (for total power), *withdrawal* (from mainstream society), *accommodation* (with the rest of society), or a relentless *conservation* of traditional religious values and norms. One of its unintended consequences might be to pave the way for greater epistemological tolerance between religious and secular worldviews as each one softens its monopolistic truth claims. Alternatively, it may take over and rule with an iron fist until it too is chastened by the human facts of diversity and need for tolerance.

Modernity and Its Discontents

To understand the historical roots of fundamentalism, it is useful to consider it in the context of the problematic of modernization. I have argued elsewhere[8] that the transition from agrarian to industrial societies, that is, the complex package of revolutionary changes generally labeled "modernization," seems to have historically entailed a Rousseau effect in most places. Religious fundamentalism might be considered another manifestation of this effect in our own times. As a major theorist of the Enlightenment project, J. J. Rousseau provided one of the first and most intellectually sustained critiques of the Age of Reason by celebrating a return to the original innocence and goodness of the natural man, the so-called noble savage. He also advocated recapturing the lost natural community by a social contract based more on a fusionist "general will" *(volonté générale)* than a divisive "will of all" *(volonté de tous)* or electoral head-counting.[9] This romantic and communitarian theme recurs in a variety of subsequent social movements in modern history. Despite their great variation in context and program, the Romantic movement in Europe, the American transcendentalists, the Russian Narodniks, the Gandhian movement in India, and the Islamic revolutionary movement in Iran have one feature in common: a reaction against the social and psychological dislocations of the transition of millions of peasants from rural into urban areas, and a call for a return to nature and the simple virtues of traditional life. As William McNeill also points out:

> even in affluent communities, most persons do face hardship and disappointment of one sort or another in the course of their lives and then need comfort and support of a kind that cold reason and individualistic pursuit of happiness cannot provide, while among the hundreds of millions of peasants and ex-peasants, whose inherited rural ways of life have become impractical or unacceptable, hardship and disappointment are and will remain the norm, at least for the immediate future. Their need for comfort and support is correspondingly acute and ever present.[10]

The metadiscourse of modernization has thus generated two sets of competing discourses in the modern world. On the one hand, the hegemonic projects of liberalism, communism, and fascism have offered a secular, scientific, and technological path to modernization. On the other hand, a variety of counterhegemonic, communitarian discourses such as those of the European romanticists, American transcendentalists, utopian socialists, religious communalists, and contemporary Green movements have proposed a more decentralized and less rapacious route. Fundamentalism seems to combine elements of these two discourses in a fashion reminiscent of the earlier discourses of secular nationalism; it offers worldly success without sacrificing the affective ties of meaning and community to the cash nexus. For this reason, the label "religious nationalism" for fundamentalism seems apt.

The material challenge facing modernization is how to build the necessary social and economic infrastructure of a modern industrial system. Historically, this task has been achieved by less than liberal means. Generating the economic surplus necessary to get the industrial sector going requires exploitation of the peasantry and working class by keeping food prices and wages low over a few generations. That in turn requires the kind of discipline, order, and effort that only a political dictatorship and an authoritarian ideology have historically been able to produce. The transition from agrarian feudalism to modern industrial societies has been often accomplished by statist (etatist) regimes under the banners of European enlightened despotism, totalitarian communism and fascism (as in the Soviet Union, China, and Japan), or authoritarian leaderships (as in the newly industrializing countries of South Korea, Taiwan, Hong Kong, Singapore, Thailand, Indonesia, and Malaysia).[11] These regimes have employed a variety of ideologies of work ethics and postponed gratification to legitimate the sacrifices necessary for the period of primitive accumulation. In this respect, secular nationalist, communist, and fascist ethics have performed essentially the same function as the Protestant, Confucian, or Islamic ethics.

In the less developed countries, therefore, religious fundamentalism might be considered in light of the ideological role of Calvinism and Puritanism in the earlier periods of capitalist accumulation in Europe and the United States. Contemporary fundamentalism, however, owes much of its potency to a threefold revolutionary process in population, education, and communication. The postwar spread of public health facilities in developing countries has led to a population explosion unprecedented in human history. This in turn has created population structures heavily skewed in favor of the young. Simultaneously, the expansion of educational opportunities to large masses by development-conscious governments has expanded the horizons and expectations of the young. However, the revolution of rising expectations is not matched by rising opportunities. Unemployment rates of 30–40 percent are not uncommon in some developing countries. In the meantime, the mass media of communication are exposing the young to a global pop culture that flaunts sex, violence, and the opulent lifestyles of the more developed countries.

Young persons from a rural or newly urban family background are thus typically exposed to at least three sets of conflicting values at home, school, and society at large. The traditional, often religious, values of the family demand modesty, frugality, and obedience to authority. The secular schools, on the other hand, impart a mix of religious and secular nationalist values primarily calling for loyalty to the national symbols of authority and the application of the scientific method to personal and social problem solving. Finally, urban society exposes the young to a complex range of values reflected in the exhilarating license of the modern lifestyles portrayed on "Dallas" and "Dynasty" as well as in the repression and fear of living under authoritarian regimes. The response to these conflicting messages is initially one of confusion, but subsequently a search for meaning and certainty prone to ideological extremism and syncretism occurs. Combining traditional religious doctrines with selected elements of Marxism, nationalism, liberalism, or even fascism is well known among certain groups such as the Islamic Marxists and the Christian theology of liberation.

The processes of primary, secondary, and tertiary socialization often carried out, respectively, by the family, school, and public discourse (through mediated and unmediated channels) thus tend to be at odds with each other. Most fundamentalist movements clearly understand the pivotal importance of these socializing institutions and the value conflicts among them. Their strategies are therefore focused on a recapture of the family, school, and media institutions as gateways to political and cultural power and influence. Generally speaking, in the premobilized phases of a fundamentalist movement, the family and alternative schooling serve as the main channels for restoring the life of the sacred to an inner core of believers. Islamic, Hindu, and Jewish fundamentalist groups in Iran, India, and Israel seem to have chosen this strategy in their earlier stages. However, as political mobilization assumes momentum, greater resort to the mass media in order to reach out to a broader spectrum of society becomes increasingly possible.

Fundamentalist Education and Media

Despite these general commonalties among fundamentalist movements, there are also vast differences. In order to compare the impact of fundamentalist education and media in a number of different religious traditions and historical situations represented by the following case studies, a typology of fundamentalist movements is necessary. Since "impact" is our primary focus, a typology that highlights the strategic objectives and consequences of fundamentalist movements is preferable to one that might tell us more about their theological tendencies or organizational tactics. As a challenge to secular authority, the simplest and perhaps most appropriate typology of fundamentalism in this context seems to be a political one.

The five countries covered by the following six case studies in part 3 of this volume have all come directly or indirectly under the political impact of fundamentalist movements. Iran became an Islamic republic in 1979. Guatemala gained a Pentecostalist leader when General Efraín Ríos Montt assumed the presidency in 1982; it also elected Jorge Serrano, a Protestant evangelical businessman, president in 1990. India's prime minister V. P. Singh resigned in 1990 in the face of pressures from fundamentalist Hindus and higher castes opposed to his policies of protection for the Muslim minority and compensatory hiring of the lower castes. In the national elections of June 1991, following the assassination of Rajiv Gandhi by a Hindu fanatic, the Bharatiya Jana Party (BJP) won over 25 percent of the ballots cast, took over India's biggest state, Uttar Pradesh, and achieved the status of a national party. It might have emerged as the biggest single party had Rajiv Gandhi not been assassinated.[12] In 1990, Israel's conservative Likud party, in alliance with the Jewish religious parties, once again won a parliamentary majority against the challenge of the liberal, secularist Labor party. American presidents Reagan and Bush have played to fundamentalist constituencies in stressing their opposition to abortion, support for prayer in schools, and approval of the conservative backlash against the sexual and cultural "decadence" of the 1960s and 1970s.

These and similar examples demonstrate only that fundamentalist or fundamentalist-like groups have been recently involved in political life. But the levels, purposes, and outcomes of that involvement vary significantly. One way of establishing a basis for comparison is to stress the commonly held perceptions that inspire fundamentalists' interaction with nonfundamentalists. The movements studied in this chapter have reacted to what they perceive to be the unsettling effects of rapid social change and the uneven and imperfectly integrated process of modernization, to perceptions of their marginalization (in urban ghettoes and among ethnic minorities), and to an awareness of their own material or psychic deprivation. To all of these uncertainties, fundamentalist movements bring the certainties of renewed faith, identity, and community.

However, different fundamentalist movements interact in different ways with nonfundamentalists and enjoy varying degrees of influence upon them. Different movements are also affected in different ways by their interaction with outsiders. The inner tensions of particular fundamentalist ideologies and movements in large part shape the political strategy they adopt toward outsiders (including the apolitical strategy). Struggles exist within fundamentalist movements between populist and elitist tendencies, between dogmatism and pragmatism, and between scriptural literalism and liberalism. While most fundamentalist movements are based on authoritarian leadership, for example, they also thrive by virtue of an equally strong attachment to the common people, their interests, and their salvation. While most fundamentalist movements draw strength from religious dogmas, as movements they have had to formulate and adapt their ideologies to changing circumstances to achieve their political and religious objectives. The relationship between the revealed dogmas and the movement's ideology of the moment is a constant source of tension. And while most fundamentalist movements consider their holy scriptures or traditions as the source of literal truth, they also provide novel interpretations of the revelation significantly at odds with those of the religious orthodoxies.

Having established a general basis of comparison (the phenomenon of religious reaction to a commonly perceived set of enemies in the external order), we may now focus on the diversity within fundamentalisms by examining the four alternative strategies taken in interaction with nonfundamentalists: revolutionary militancy (for total power), withdrawal (from mainstream society), accommodation (with the rest of society), or conservation of traditional values in the face of encroachments of modernity. Each of these responses has in turn called for its corresponding conservative, reformist, revolutionary, and separatist strategies in building educational and communication systems.

Lacking comprehensive political programs, the *separatist strategy* considers the integrity and solidarity of the community as the highest value; groups such as the haredim in Israel consequently emphasize authoritarianism, dogmatism, and literalism almost to the exclusion of populism, dogmatism, and liberalism. Bob Jones University, as portrayed in Quentin Schultze's essay, combines a separatist with a *conservative strategy* that emphasizes authoritarianism at the expense of populism, dogmatism at the expense of pragmatism, and inerrancy at the expense of the more liberal interpretations of the Holy Scriptures. The *reformist strategy* appeals equally to authoritarianism and populism, dogmatism and pragmatism, and literalism and liberalism. Jerry Falwell's approach to Liberty University seems to have settled into this mode, as have the efforts of evangelicals in Guatemala and Hindu revivalists in India. The *revolutionary strategy* tends to favor populism to authoritarianism, pragmatism to dogmatism, and liberalism to literalism. This strategy has been in evidence in Iran in the last decade.

Table 12.1 presents a schematic view of these alternative strategies in terms of their overall aims, political tactics, educational methods, and communication channels. The table clearly presents the "ideal types." In reality, fundamentalist movements may combine two or more strategies in the course of their evolution. The Muslim Brotherhood in Egypt, for instance, was militant before the coup d'etat of 1952, collaborated with the Nasserist regime for a while, then went underground and, under Sadat and Mubarak, has split into radical and moderate factions, with the latter engaged in reformist and electoral politics.

Separatist Strategies

Among the fundamentalist-like movements in our case studies, the haredi "learning community" seems best to fit the features of a separatist strategy of social and educational action. The hallmark of the haredi movement is its opposition to Zionism as a

TABLE 12.1
FUNDAMENTALIST EDUCATIONAL AND MEDIA STRATEGIES

Strategies	Conservative	Separatist	Reformist	Revolutionary
Aims	Conserve tradition	Avoid contamination	Reform society	Overhaul society
Tactics	Reactionary: Alliance with state	Withdrawal: Underground activities	Accommodationist: Electoral politics	Militant: Propaganda, agitation, terror, violence
Typical movements	Wahhabi (Saudi Arabia)	Takfir wa-Hijra (Egypt) Haredi Jews (Israel)	Moral Majority (USA)	Hizbullah (Iran, Lebanon)
Educational methods	State schools	Alternative schooling	Alternative curricula	Educational overhaul
Communication	State media	Underground micromedia	Electronic church	Micro- and macromedia
Channels	Religious networks	Religious networks	Religious networks	Religious networks

profane and secular enterprise. The haredi Jews consider the State of Israel to be a continuation of the *Galut* (Exile), albeit in the Holy Land. They are obligated to refrain from joining this enterprise and to focus their entire being on learning in the holy community for the purpose of transcending this world. The institutions of this learning begin at an Orthodox Jewish home and continue into the synagogue, the elementary school *(heder),* and the high school *(yeshiva).* Torah study creates a total world by which haredi Jews insulate the Torah and the life it prescribes from outside influences. The haredim, Michael Rosenak tells us in chapter 14, disdain cultural interactions that would put them at risk. "They wish to protect themselves against 'false knowledge,'" he writes, "that is, against methodologies or data that allegedly militate against the truth of Torah and undermine the Jewish life of covenant." Haredi learning therefore is not comparable with what connotes learning in the profane world; it does not satisfy curiosity, broaden horizons, gather "useful" information, conduct inquiry for the purposes of problem solving, or theorize in order to understand and control. Instead, the haredi curriculum is to instruct Jews in separatism and the preservation of purity; it must reflect and draw upon the constant struggle against the outside world, with its profane views of teaching, of the child, and of achievement. Traditionalism in methods of rote learning, withdrawal from society, distinctive hair styles, long dark robes, refusal to serve in the army, and a general disdain for the secular world distinguish the haredim.

The attempt to sustain the religious enclave has nonetheless placed the haredim in a paradoxical situation that forces them away from mere traditionalism and into the orbit of modernity as a fundamentalist-like adaptive movement. Rosenak explains that even haredi self-definition is drawn in relation to the outside world: "The Community of Transcendence and Torah, living in a fragile relationship with the 'Zionists' on whom it is so greatly dependent, not only withdraws from the modernists and their false standards and conceptions of knowledge and worth but (except in its most radical sectors) explains this withdrawal as serving the 'real' needs of society and state." This philosophical and cultural dispute with secular Zionism has moved segments of the haredim to modify their tradition-based orientation to more effectively compete with the enemy. Rosenak finds significance in the fact that the extremists among the haredim, aware that educational theories and methods cannot be divorced from philosophies and goals, have nervously castigated "moderate" haredi educators who have introduced modern methods into education, believing them to be "neutral." Another departure from strict separatism and traditionalism noted by Rosenak is the intense "missionizing" of the maverick haredi movement of Habad Hasidism. Open to non-haredi Jews, Habad's outreach work is highly successful and specializes in "soft sell"—in the army, at street corners and bus stations. The general view, even among secular Jews, has been that "Habad is all right," though its recent active role in haredi politics has created suspicion in some circles.

Bob Jones University (BJU) is in some ways the Christian fundamentalist analogue to the cultural separatism practiced by the haredi Jews in Israel. In other ways, BJU also adopts a conservative strategy in its intent to train missionaries and pastors to sustain and expand the fundamentalist subculture in the United States. By the purity of their own lives, Quentin Schultze notes in chapter 17, these Christian fundamentalists are to be witnesses to the truths of conservative doctrine and behavior. From their separatist citadels, they are to militantly defend "biblical authority and infallibility" by attacking "the enemies of the faith." BJU's brand of fundamentalism, Schultze maintains, does indeed imply both defensive and offensive strategies. Faith comes before reason, religion before academics, and personal conversion before formal education. Believers must know where they stand religiously before they are trained academically. "BJU requires students to take at least one Bible course every semester, demands chapel attendance, and generally controls the personal lifestyle of its students, including dating practices, which are strictly regulated," Schultze notes. "Challenges to stated beliefs and practices are nothing short of disloyalty, which Bob Jones, Sr., called an 'unpardonable sin.'"

On the other hand, BJU seeks to prepare its students not just to live and know fundamentalism but also to militantly defend and thus conserve it and the values for which it stands. These fundamentalists openly contend for the faith even when their own separatist communities are not directly under outside attack by critics. The Creed of the College calls upon BJU graduates to combat "all atheistic, agnostic, pagan, and so-called scientific adulterations of the Gospel." This broader mandate, Schultze points out, requires far more than doctrinal knowledge and behavioral purity; it demands a fairly broad, liberal education that examines and evaluates secular ideas and social trends. The fact remains, however, that the university has not fully met these demands; its emphasis on communication skills has not been balanced with serious academic inquiry and open intellectual discussion and dialogue. Such openness would be a challenge to the strict separatism of Bob Jones–style fundamentalism. The cost of failing to relax the separatist stance is counted in BJU's corresponding diminished effectiveness as a genuinely conservative institution.

Nonetheless BJU has trained thousands of fundamentalist elementary and secondary school teachers—graduates who often use textbooks published by BJU Press. And it has supported a flourishing fundamentalist subculture in the United States on its own terms, as evidenced by its refusal to adjust its racial policies in order to reclaim tax-exempt status after losing a Supreme Court case to the IRS in 1982. As Schultze puts it, "racial separation was a matter of religious principle, so there was no way to compromise."

In these separatist circles, mass media play a limited role. The religious networks, schools, and small media serve as the main channels. In this respect, the separatist strategy has something in common with the underground revolutionary movements such as that in Iran, which, under police surveillance, had to resort to low-cost, accessible, and easily concealed micromedia. By contrast, among the ultra-Orthodox Jewish community in Israel, cassette tapes are used to fight secularism from a defensive position, but not for evangelical or revolutionary purposes.[13] In Mea Shearim there are two stores and forty-two lending libraries which distribute religious cassettes. One store has twenty-five hundred subscribers. It may be generalized that (1) a major tactic of fighting secularism, especially among rabbis of Sephardic origin, is to constantly refer to current events, especially to explain disaster as the result of sin, of failure to pray and observe commandments, and to explain miracles as the result of many prayers; (2) sermons are not given to be recorded; they are recorded as an additional activity while being delivered; (3) there is a handful of sermons by rabbis' wives; (4) a rhetorical strategy of some of the rabbis is to play brilliantly with language—using word play and alliteration—and to incorporate slang and army jargon in their sermons; and (5) preoccupation with causal explanations of miracles and disasters was especially prominent during the Gulf War in terms of rewards and punishments.

Conservative Strategies

Elements within fundamentalist Protestant movements in the United States and within the religious Zionist groups in Israel qualify as "conservative." Some may argue that the excesses of some of these movements qualify them as "reactionary" or "fanatical." Yet the movements clearly share a bias for conservative social, educational, and media policies. They have pushed their respective polities toward conservative and nationalistic policies.

The two case studies of fundamentalism in the United States, chapters 16 and 17, focus on its impact on American primary, secondary, and tertiary education. The battle is, in all cases, for the recruitment, socialization, and organization of the young into fundamentalist ranks in pursuit of larger national and global missionary goals. These conservative evangelicals and fundamentalists have departed from a position of strict separatism; the impact of fundamentalist discourse and practice has extended well beyond their own classrooms into the American public school system and national political arena. As Susan Rose reports, the Christian school movement has been the fastest growing sector of private education in the United States. Approximately one million students (K through 12) are now enrolled in some eighteen thousand schools, representing about 20 percent of the total private school population. Since 1965, Catholic school enrollments (still the largest group among religious schools) have declined 54 percent, while enrollments in non-Catholic schools (mostly evangelical) have increased some 149 percent. As evangelicals and fundamentalists have asserted their presence and influence during the past two decades, they have moved away from an earlier separatist to a more conservative and activist strategy. This has drawn them into court battles to protect their schools and to make an impact well beyond. An index of this impact is the production and distribution of textbooks by Accelerated Christian Education (ACE) to some six thousand schools in the United States and eighty-six foreign countries, reaching over 275,000 students. ACE also provides curricula to sixteen hundred families in the United States and three hundred families in foreign countries for home education.

The evangelical curricular contents, methods, and consequences are significantly different from the secular public schools. Fundamentalist education in the United States is a response to a set of perceived threats emanating from the general secularization of life and the legislatively mandated secularization of public schools. It aims at restoring religious and parental authority, providing quality education, and protecting children from the evils of drugs, sex, violence, and lack of discipline. Aside from the fundamentalist emphasis on the Bible, creationism, patriarchal values, and a denigration of secular humanism in general, the curriculum teaches the same subjects as the secular schools. The methods, however, include corporal punishment and standardized pedagogy. "ACE, for instance, provides all the information, materials, and equipment necessary to set up a school quickly and inexpensively. No one teaches in ACE schools; rather, students teach themselves. Little is open to question; all answers lie within the text," Rose writes. The consequences of this pedagogy are remarkable. ACE graduates scored higher than 65 percent in a nationally representative sample of other students, and their Stanford Achievement Test scores appear to be one year and seven months ahead of the national norm. The graduates are considered by the military to be superior workers—disciplined, obedient, with respect for authority.

Evangelical schools draw their students from most socioeconomic groups, particularly from white, middle-class families with an average income of $25,000 and more education than the national mean. Given their relatively homogeneous social background and strong sense of community, the fundamentalists have had an impact on society beyond their numbers. They have managed during the past two decades to put the issues of school prayer, creationism, patriotism, flag burning, and textbook censorship on the national agenda. The Reagan administration, under the leadership of Secretary of Education William Bennett, attempted first to eliminate and then to reduce the Department of Education. Although the fundamentalists have not succeeded in basically altering secular education, they have brought sufficient pressure to bear on secular schools to move them to the right of center, with an emphasis on the neutrality of the basic subjects and control through standardized programs. Rose argues that having partially achieved its educational aims, the movement may have reached a plateau, with the possibility of a convergence of Christian and public schools.

Although frequently identified with the "electronic church" and televangelists such as Pat Robertson, Jimmy Swaggart, and Oral Roberts, fundamentalist higher education that has moved beyond strict separatism is actually represented most clearly by Jerry Falwell's Liberty University. The failure of Pat Robertson in 1988 to win the Republican presidential nomination and the sexual and financial scandals of Jim Bakker and Jimmy Swaggart during the 1980s have somewhat diminished the momentum of the Pentecostalist movement in higher education. However, during the 1980s the movement achieved impressive success in reaching vast audiences through several television stations and programs, raising millions of dollars for its activities, including several institutions of higher learning. And in the 1990s Robertson's Regent University is consolidating the gains made by the television ministry in the 1980s. The marriage of television and higher education indeed proved a potent force in this movement.[14]

Schultze, in chapter 17, demonstrates that the "new evangelical" higher education represented by Liberty University (1) is not totally anti-intellectual, (2) has had an impact on society at large, and (3) will not disappear but may be absorbed into the larger academic world. Although conservative in educational goals and methods, this approach to higher education does not reject modernization or interaction with the secular environment. In fact, it may be viewed as an attempt to reconcile conservative religious traditions with modern science, technology, and education.

As Schultze points out, Liberty and Regent have been willing to compromise in order to gain national legitimacy and accreditation. Even their unconventional academic units such as the Center for Creation Studies and the Museum of Earth and Life History at Liberty University have served the dual purpose of attracting conservative backers and gaining academic respectability. Although each of these universities is identified with a particular charismatic or authoritarian leader, both gained some measure of institutional independence from their founders. Regent University has also gone abroad to establish a branch in Poland.

The evidence shows, therefore, that evangelical higher education might have a dual impact. On the one hand, these institutions may traverse the same evolutionary path as other formerly religious colleges across the country have in the past, from strict separatist (fundamentalist) education into conservative engagement with mainstream culture (new evangelical), until the process leads increasingly to a secular-pluralist model for higher education. On the other hand, both Liberty and Regent have already challenged the more secular institutions on such enduring issues as the "nature of the human condition, the place of norms in scholarship and society, the quest for universal meaning and significance, and even the search for standards of right conduct." Schultze argues that requirements of accreditation, the problems of accepting public funds, and the secularizing effects of higher education will likely temper fundamentalist education toward an accommodation with the rest of higher education in the United States.

As for media strategies, Fore discerns five "generations" of the electronic church, spanning the history of American television.[15] The first, represented by Billy Graham, was typified by the use of television to cover revival meetings, much as it would be used to cover a sport or political event. The second generation marked a change to the style and technique of Oral Roberts, a tent evangelist and faith healer. In the 1960s, a third generation represented by Rex Humbard built a church especially designed for television. A fourth generation was inaugurated by Pat Robertson's "700 Club," adopting a "host show" format in which he brought the viewing audience into intimate contact with the studio through phone-ins and membership in the "700 Club." Robertson also blazed the trail for a fifth generation by establishing his own network, Christian Broadcasting Network (CBN). The CBN format for cable-satellite network has since been copied by many such as the "PTL Club" of Jim and Tammy Bakker. Typically, the audience for the electronic church is more female than male, older rather than younger, of lower income and education, from more southern and midwestern states, and more generally active churchgoers.[16] The size of the audience for the electronic church is a matter of considerable dispute. Estimates range from Gallup's 22.8 million to Annenberg School of Communication's estimate of 13.3 million.[17]

In the Islamic world, the Wahhabi movement in Saudi Arabia represents perhaps the best known and most successful example of a conservative fundamentalist strategy.

As an eighteenth-century movement, the Wahhabis antedated the impact of the modern world in Arabia, but they provided the ideological vehicle for the final triumph of the house of Saud in the twentieth century. The movement has also provided a highly puritanical and fundamentalist Islamic doctrine to legitimate continuing Saudi rule, to seal off Saudi society from the more severe erosions of modernity, and to fend off internal and external challenges.[18]

Reformist Strategies

By contrast, reformist fundamentalist movements provide an example of an interventionist strategy. However, they seem to be characterized by an equilibrium between the forces of populism and elitism, dogmatism and pragmatism, and literalism and liberalism. This may be due to the fact that the status quo under such circumstances is perceived as indefensible—it has to be changed—and yet the fundamentalist discourse presents an appropriate hegemonic project for an alliance of the old and new elites riding on the wave of a populist movement.

The case studies of Guatemala and India present historical evidence that exemplifies this strategy. In both countries, fundamentalist-like movements represent a new hegemonic project combining nationalism and religion to challenge the authority of established secular elites. In Guatemala, in an alliance with North American evangelism and indigenous populism, Protestant evangelicalism is dislodging a corrupt, semi-feudal, Catholic elite. In India, Hindu fundamentalism is undermining the hegemony of the secular Congress party by whipping up religious nationalism and Hindu cultural politics.

In Guatemala the situation has been dramatized by the left-wing guerrillas of the Guatemalan National Revolutionary Union, against whom the government has been fighting for the past three decades, resulting in some one hundred thousand deaths. As Biernatzki reports,

> When General Efraím Ríos Montt, a convert to Pentecostalist church, became president of Guatemala in 1982, he was hailed by the more politically-oriented North American televangelists, particularly the "700 Club" of Pat Robertson. Guatemala was by no means unacquainted with militarism and repression prior to Ríos Montt's presidency, but a new element of zeal was added by his Pentecostalist identity which may have contributed to the slaughter of thousands of Indians during his campaign to repress a leftist rebellion allegedly inspired by Catholic liberation theology but labeled "communist" by the army. By the time Ríos Montt was overthrown, evangelical leaders in Guatemala had come to recognize that they were being blamed for his policies, since he had created the impression that he wanted to set up a Protestant theocracy. They consequently tried to disassociate themselves from him. He had done little for Guatemalan Protestantism, and in fact many evangelical Indians had been caught up in the indiscriminate slaughter.[19]

Despite the predominance of the military in defining the boundaries of civilian power, Guatemala elected its second civilian president in November 1990. The new president, Jorge Serrano, is an evangelical businessman who replaced Vicio Cerezo, leader of the Christian Democrats. Religious identification is as integral a part of the Guatemalan political tapestry as is the military. The failure of the predominantly Catholic elite to make any serious attempt to change the country's semi-feudal power structure has in part led to the rival Protestant evangelicals and neo-Pentecostals gaining ground. Serrano, the only evangelical Protestant ever elected to rule a Latin American nation, won 68 percent of the vote in a run-off ballot in 1990.[20] His campaign promise was to bring Guatemala "total peace." In April 1991 he opened peace negotiations with the left-wing guerrillas of the Guatemalan Revolutionary National Unity movement, but to achieve real peace and democracy he would have to tackle his generals. In the thirty-year war against the guerrillas, the army killed thousands of the highland Indians among whom the insurgents lived and burned hundreds of their villages. The generals are watching over Serrano's shoulders. General Hector Gramajo put down two coups before going last year to the Kennedy School of Government at Harvard, where he explained his doctrinal innovations to the *Harvard International Review*: "We have created a more humanitarian, less costly strategy, to be more compatible with the democratic system. We instituted civil affairs which provides development for 70% of the population, while we kill 30%. Before, the strategy was to kill 100%."[21]

Susan Rose and Quentin Schultze, in chapter 15, provide a case study of how Protestant evangelicalism and neo-Pentecostalism have advanced to serve certain interests in Guatemala. Their analysis challenges some prevailing interpretations such as Peter Berger's contention that we are witnessing the "Second Protestant Internationale" in Central America. That historical analogy suggests "revolutionary" potential for Protestantism while ignoring the essentially reformist and repressive nature of the alliance of fundamentalistic Protestantism with the military, transnational corporate interests, and the United States. However, the case study also points out how the Protestant churches, like the Catholic Church, are torn in the class struggle between rich and poor, government and guerrillas. The authors argue persuasively that (1) we may be overemphasizing the importance of Protestant evangelicalism and neo-Pentecostalism in the same way that we overemphasized the role of liberation theology; (2) that we must recognize the class interests framing the ideological positions of both liberation theology and neo-Pentecostalism (which "represents" Guatemala's professional and business classes); and (3) if evangelical education and media join the chorus of the political right, old and new Pentecostals may find a common voice in opposition to the left. In other words, a politicized fundamentalist Protestant movement may be considered as part of a new reformist, hegemonic discourse aligning the old feudal and new business elites against revolutionary change.

The case study by Rose and Schultze focuses on a careful analysis of the role of education and the media in the remarkable rise of the evangelical awakening in Guatemala. Several factors seem to have contributed to this rise. First, the North American "electronic church" has played an important role in a media blitz of El Salvador, Nicaragua, and Guatemala. Second, there are also indigenous religious and political forces in Guatemala which have paved the way. While it is "not difficult to show how the religious right has tried to turn missionary work into an instrument for U.S. militarism," it is also true that "evangelism has widespread, popular support among the poor." In contrast to Catholic priests, 86.7 percent of whom are foreigners, almost all evangelical priests are Guatemalan. Third, evangelicals have grown in number from 3.5 percent thirty years ago to between 30–35 percent of the population. This remarkable growth has taken place primarily in the last two decades by a shift from written to oral traditions, and from old to neo-Pentecostalism. Neo-Pentecostalism has legitimized indigenous languages and preserved cultures even at the very point when they are undermined by an intrusive and corrosive world. Generally speaking, the neo-Pentecostals have supported the political right, consisting of the government, military, and middle- and upper-class business and professional interests. By contrast, the Catholic theology of liberation has sided with the left in championing the cause of the peasantry.

Turning to the roles of education and the media, Rose and Schultze argue that in Guatemala, where illiteracy rates are high, schooling scarce, and a traditional oral culture prevalent, the media, together with the family and schools, play a central part in the socialization of children. Further, the mass media become more prominent as we move from the fundamentalist strategies of disengagement to one of engagement with the world outside, that is, from separatist to reformist and revolutionary. In the case of separatist groups such as the Farawiya, and Takfir and Hijra in Egypt, science, technology, and even literacy are sometimes rejected.[22] But to the degree that a fundamentalist movement gets involved with reformist or revolutionary projects, the need for the use of modern means of education, communication, and warfare becomes apparent. The Guatemalan situation illustrates the point further. The difference between old and neo-Pentecostalism becomes particularly clear in their respectively conservative and reformist political and curricular projects. Guatemala has one of the lowest per capita expenditures on public education (1.8 percent) in Latin America and one of the highest dropout rates (90 percent never make it to secondary school and 99 percent never to university); in response, the neo-Pentecostals have embarked on an educational venture that the Catholic elite failed to launch. While the old-style Pentecostal churches (the Assemblies of God, the Church of God, and the Jehovah's Witnesses) work extensively among the poor, the new Pentecostals are providing education for the Protestant middle and upper class by establishing relatively expensive private schools. They also import North American fundamentalist values into the curriculum "that strongly support the free enterprise system and condemn communism as the work of Satan. The curriculum communicates that Catholics are non-Christians and Jews are not accepted by God; that secular humanism and relativism are diabolical dangers in the public schools; and that it is essential to restore the United States to the status of a truly Christian nation while simultaneously Christianizing the rest of the world." Modernity is thus accepted as an instrument but not as a value system.

The impact of evangelical fundamentalism on Guatemalan public education, mass media, and national ideology has been far-reaching. Despite their opposition to scientific research, the evangelicals in Guatemala have become the new professional and social engineers. They are interested in social reform in ways that parallel the Social Gospel in the United States at the turn of the century. They are not, however, interested in directly transforming the basic social structures of inequality. They hope to improve society through combinations of personal religious conversion, individual self-discipline, and professional social work. The growth of fundamentalist radio broadcasting has been astounding even compared to that in the United States. By 1988 there were 145 radio stations, 53 of which in the capital. Eighty-seven percent of evangelical radio—preaching, sermonizing, and persuading—is aired live. As a more expensive and less prevalent medium, television programming is dominated by U.S. fundamentalist and Pentecostal imports. Jimmy Swaggart and Pat Robertson are the most represented. Swaggert's organization has established regional centers which answer letters and sell books. His program is oriented toward the lower middle class.[23] Robertson's directly theocratic appeals do not fit Guatemala's need for ecumenical cooperation between the Catholics and Protestants. Anticommunism unites the right, but exclusionary evangelism tends to divide it.

On the longer-range prospects of the impact of evangelism in Guatemala, Rose and Schultze are ambivalent. It remains to be seen, they argue, whether the rise of Protestant ethics will lead to the development of democratic capitalism (as the neo-Weberians such as Peter Berger hope) or end up in another cycle of elite exploitation of the majority in collaboration with foreign capital. However, they offer some reasons to suggest that the results will probably be different from those we have known historically in the West. Religious polarization will continue to persist not only between Catholics and Protestants, but also between conservative Catholics and radical Catholics as well as between old-style, nonpolitical Pentecostals and new-style, political Pentecostals. In any case, religion, education, and the media will continue to play their contradictory, Janus-like role in the formation and dissemination of the dominant hegemonic and counterhegemonic projects.

Religious Zionism in Israel is a second example of a reformist fundamentalist movement. The United States and Israel present two radically different national traditions on issues of religion and state. Whereas the separation of church and state is a constitutional requirement in the United States, Israel was founded on Zionism, a nationalism based on the presumed religious and cultural unity of the Jewish people. As an official Israeli ideology, therefore, Zionism provides a useful litmus test for distinguishing some of the subtle differences between a rich variety of Jewish fundamentalist movements. Religious Zionism, Zionist fundamentalism, non-Zionist Judaism, and anti-Zionist Judaism present different responses vis-à-vis the liberal, socialist, and secular Zionism of the founding fathers of Israel. Not all of these tendencies can be considered fundamentalist. In chapter 14, Michael Rosenak's case study of Jewish fundamentalist education presents a rich tapestry of theologies and movements that pursue both separatist-conservative and reformist strategies, corresponding more or less to what Rosenak calls anti-Zionist and Zionist fundamentalisms. While the haredi Jews are anti-Zionists pursuing a separatist strategy, radical Zionist fundamentalists, messianic fundamentalists (Gush Emunim), and the late Rabbi Meir Kahane's Kach movement (including its offshoot in the United States, the Jewish Defense League) follow a reformist fundamentalist line. They seek neither to overthrow the Zionist state (revolutionary fundamentalism) nor to accommodate it for the sake of conserving their religious traditions (conservative fundamentalism); rather, they intend to transform secular Zionism from within by revealing and bringing to prominence its latent religiosity.

As Rosenak argues, the notion of *Galut* (Exile) is central to an understanding of Jewish fundamentalism. "Exile, Galut, is a heavy-laden concept with political, religious, and existential layers of meaning. It signifies precarious existence among the nations; it bespeaks alienation and remoteness from God, for the Torah cannot be fully carried out in Galut where Israel lacks a society, and it describes the malaise of the world before the coming of the Messiah [redemption]." In the religious Zionist community there were, however, moments of confrontation with Zionism that served as a challenge to religious renewal. Those who were inquisitive and innovative in theological matters became "religious expansionists." Expansionism reinterprets modernity through the prism of the Jewish tradition; "it aspires, in theory, to bring all aspects of life under the rubric of its interpretation of Judaism."[24] When "religious expansionism" was combined with adaptationism, which "affirms that the basic values of modernity are not only compatible with Judaism but partake of its essence," Rosenak points out, there emerged a vibrant and ambitious type of religious Zionism.

Thinkers and educators in this circle perceived no conflict between Zionism and Judaism. Rather, Zionism was the opportunity to fully apply the Torah to the reborn social reality of Judaism in the modern world. The Torah was meant to inform every aspect of life, but this was impossible in Galut. Thus Torah scholars had to engage in dialogue with all knowledge and culture, to be thereby liberated from the shackles of Galut ghettoization and, in turn, to transform the social message of universal ideals. In the religious kibbutz it could be shown that the Torah was the constitution of an ideal society and the foundation of a socially progressive and humanistic religiosity. Conversely, the "expansionistic-adaptationist" religious Zionists held that Galut was ending and that the long-awaited challenge to the truth and viability of Judaism as a social vision was at hand. The Torah would be the "spiritual infrastructure of a new moral and religious-humanistic society."

Each social and existential ideal creates its own educational institutions, and so did the religious Zionists. Their initial innovative yet Orthodox approach was open to outside influences and even rhetoric, yet wished to impose the Torah upon them. This was a difficult educational challenge. The expounders and teachers of this "expansionist" approach had to teach that the Torah was capable of addressing every issue, but it was not clear to them how this worked in practice. As modern Orthodox nonfundamentalist Jews, they lived in a hyphenated valuative world of "Torah" and "general culture," of "Torah" and "labor" (i.e., socialism). Though their ideology was both "expansionist" and "adaptationist," the lives they led and the concrete educational programs they felt qualified to construct and implement were mostly compartmentalized. Some things were Jewish and some were not.

They could not possibly fit into a traditional yeshiva worldview conferring status inferiority on women, disdaining physical work, and deferring the transformation of the world to the coming of the Messiah. Equally committed to Judaism, Zionism, and modernity, religious Zionists have had to create their own educational institutions. Under the leadership of the charismatic first chief rabbi of modern Eretz Israel, Abraham Isaac Kook, radical Zionist fundamentalists established their first Zionist yeshivot for high school youth. The theological justification for such a bold action was to assign messianic meaning to the State of Israel as the concrete Kingdom of God on earth. It followed that the new yeshiva must socialize the youth into the stringently Jewish legal community as embodied in the Israeli society. But this religiously radical approach is profoundly ambivalent about the secular Zionist reality that Rabbi Kook declared to be holy. On the one hand, the Zionist radicals have established their own broadly haredic-yet-Zionist institutions of learning in order to forestall the threats of the decadent secular Israeli culture to religion. On the other hand, as Zionists, the "radicals" serve in the military within a yeshivot framework arranged with the army.

Gush Emunim, the "Bloc of the Faithful," is the most well-known group of the radical religious Zionists who have tied territorial Israeli expansion with messianism and right-wing education. Established after the Yom Kippur War of 1973, Gush Emunim has provided an ideological bridge between religious and secular Zionists and, for that reason, it has had great impact. While pursuing fundamentalist religious education, the movement allows its members to join the army in defense of Eretz Israel and against territorial concessions. Although racially tolerant, the movement has given rise to racist factions such as the late Rabbi Kahane's Kach movement which argues for the expulsion of the Palestinian Arabs. Educationally, Gush Emunim is critical of yeshiva learning and its withdrawal from reality, a withdrawal that in their view is no longer justified.

Hindu fundamentalism in India presents a third example of a movement that challenges the prevailing status quo in favor of social, educational, and cultural reform programs with a complex blending of populism and elitism, dogmatism and pragmatism, literalism and liberalism. In India, as Krishna Kumar argues in chapter 18, "the term 'revivalism' is . . . preferable to 'fundamentalism' mainly because the latter term seems inappropriate in the context of Hinduism. Unlike Semitic religions, Hinduism is characterized by the multiplicity of basic beliefs, texts, and practices. But if we consider a pluralist, secular India as envisaged by the founding fathers of the Indian independence movement (notably Gandhi and Nehru) as progressive, the rise of a Hindu nationalist movement calling for Hindu religious and linguistic hegemony could be considered retrogressive. From another point of view, Hindu revivalism may be considered the Indianization of India. Eighty-five percent of India's 840 million people are Hindus. Lal Krishna Advani, president of the BJP, told a group of foreign correspondents in June 1990 that Hindus were asking only for a recognition of majority rights, and an end to special privileges for religious minorities. Both internal and external forces seem to have combined to bring about this change of heart among the Hindus from secular to religious politics. The rise of Islamic fundamentalism and militancy in Pakistan may have contributed to the growth of Hindu nationalism, but urbanization, the growth of a new middle and lower-middle class, and a redefining of caste and regional identities are perhaps the more basic causes of Hindu religious militancy.[25]

The students who demonstrated and immolated themselves in 1990 were of lower-middle-class origins. They were protesting against the government's plan to set aside 27 percent of federal government jobs for "backward" castes. These students were acting out of a deep despair. The situation in the "Hindi Belt"—India's most densely populated, least literate region, from Rajasthan through Madhya Pradesh, Uttar Pradesh, and Himachal Pradesh to Bihar—is very grim. There pressure is building to find jobs and land for sons and daughters. No job is more secure than one in the civil service, and no political campaign is more powerful than religious militancy.

Religious militancy is, of course, nothing new in India. In 1948 Mahatma Gandhi fell victim to its fanaticism. What is new is its recent political muscle as evidenced by the fact that secular politicians are playing up to its prejudices. The most recent dramatic incident has centered on a mosque at Ayodhya in Uttar Pradesh built on a site that is the birthplace, say Hindus, of their god of war Rama. Militant Hindus have long sought to build a Hindu temple in place of the mosque. In 1950 the mosque was closed down by the government. In 1986 the government ordered the building reopened as a Hindu temple. This move could be interpreted as an attempt by Rajiv Gandhi to purse Hindu votes. Before Rajiv, Indira Gandhi had already appealed to Hindu militancy by taking on Sikh militancy in Punjab. The fall of Prime Minister Singh in 1990 may be also interpreted as his failure to heed Hindu nationalism by increasing appeals to lower castes and the Muslims. The result may be increasing communal violence and appeals to religious politics undermining a secular India.[26]

Kumar's case study focuses on the historical and cultural background of the rise of Hindu revivalism. He argues that the development of Hindi as a medium of modern education has served as a symbol of anticolonialism as well as the consolidation of revivalist ideology. "Unlike some other societies where fundamentalism or revivalism has surfaced as a discrete element in politics, revivalism in northern India must be seen as a phenomenon organically related to the cultural development of a specific stratum of society. But Kumar hastens to add that "opposition to modernity" is not a feature of the revivalist movement, which proposes only "a different political route to modernization from the one proposed and pursued by organizations usually seen as nonrevivalist or secular in the Indian context." Hindu revivalism can be thus interpreted as a movement for both cultural survival and cultural hegemony, including linguistic, religious, and mythological revivals through education and the media. A reconstruction of cultural and political identity in this case as in most other cases of fundamentalism appears to be a recurrent feature. Kumar argues that Hindu revivalism owes much to the Christian and Islamic variants, but we can equally argue that all fundamentalist movements are responding to the specifically modern conditions in which the state has overtaken civil society in its claims for total authority and power over resources and lives of the citizens. To lay equal claims to that power, religious fundamentalism has had to reconstruct history and identity in order to claim state power. In the case of Hindu revivalism, however, Kumar argues that "Hindu society could not find adequate resources for their purposes within religion alone. They had to assemble bits and pieces of relevant material from literature and mythology, history and geography."

Kumar demonstrates how the revival of Hindi as an Indian national language in preference to English, Hindustani, and Urdu has played a central role in this process. He also shows how the development of modern Hindu schools and universities must be understood as part of both the anticolonialist and cultural revivalist movements. He further describes how the development of a Hindu Indian press "provided to the educated, mostly urban parents of the Hindi region, a rich resource for acculturation of their children." He also provides an analysis of the rise of political revivalism as an outgrowth of religious revivalism, in the emergence first of the Arya Samaj movement and its championship of Hindi-language schools (Dayanand Anglo-Vedic or DAV) and then of the Rashtriya Swayamsevak Sangh (RSS) movement upholding the ideal of a militarily strong nation in which the terms "Indian" and "Hindu" would be synonymous. DAV schools have shown remarkable growth in the 1980s, attracting students whose families are from the ranks of urban and small-town shopkeepers as well as professionals and civil servants. Kumar argues that since the beginning of the 1980s, under the impact of Islamic fundamentalism in Pakistan and the Middle East, Hindu cultural revivalism has become politically revivalist as well in order to compete openly for power.

Revolutionary Strategies

In chapter 13, my case study of Islamic fundamentalism in Iran supports Kumar's thesis that in certain contexts, fundamentalism may be reactive but not reactionary. In the Indian and Iranian cases, fundamentalism has also expressed anticolonial aspirations for reform and revolution. Although Iran presents the most spectacular "success story" of a fundamentalist revolutionary movement, it also demonstrates the problems of a theocracy in the position of state power. The tensions between populism and elitism, dogmatism and pragmatism, scriptural literalism and liberalism erupt more violently into the open under revolutionary conditions. As a populist movement, the Islamic revolutionary movement in Iran brought about a broad coalition of secular liberals and Marxists joining hands with Islamic liberals, Islamic Marxists, Islamic traditionalists, and Islamic fundamentalists in opposition to the shah. Following the overthrow of the shah in February 1979, however, this coalition broke down.

One of the central issues that deeply divided the revolutionary ranks revolved around the tensions between populism and elitism. It focused on the question of sovereignty. Whereas the liberals and Marxists argued for popular sovereignty as the basis for the new constitution, Ayatollah Khomeini and his militant followers proposed *wilayat al-faqih* (Trusteeship of the Jurist) as the only valid Qur'anic principle of sovereignty. In his treatise with the same title, Khomeini had argued that sovereignty rightly belongs to God, his Prophet, and the Shi'ite Imams.[27] In the absence of the Hidden Imam (the twelfth Shi'ite Imam who disappeared in the fourteenth century), Khomeini further argued, the duty of governance is passed on to the Muslim *ulama* and their chosen leader, the Supreme Faqih. This theocratic principle was hotly debated before it was written into the new Islamic constitution. Those who disagreed with it were soon either expelled or went underground.

The tension between pragmatism and dogmatism became most evident in the subsequent legislative battles over the issues of land reform, and cultural, media and educational policies. The conflict between pragmatists and dogmatists, also known in constantly shifting alliances as moderates and radicals, was reflected in all debates on matters of domestic and foreign policy. In agricultural policy, land reform legislation became an issue of intense conflict between a radical parliament (the Majlis) and a conservative Council of Experts *(majlis-i-khebregan)*. While the Majlis passed a sweeping land reform law, the Council, ruling on the law's constitutionality, considered it contrary to the Qur'anic injunctions against violations of the rights of private property. At the end, Ayatollah Khomeini intervened by an extraordinary edict declaring all Qur'anic injunctions subject to the current interests and policies of the Islamic state.

Similarly, the conflicts between dogmatists and pragmatists, scriptural literalists and liberalists, have been a source of continuing tension in cultural policy. Before the revolution, Islamic traditionalists were critical of the Pahlavi regime's language purification policies that attempted to purge Farsi of all foreign (including Arabic) words. These efforts were considered part of the regime's anti-Islamic secularization policies. Although Arabic and Islamic studies have been revitalized after the revolution, the modernization of Farsi has also continued its normal course. The process has entailed a twofold effort: to coin new Farsi words for modern scientific and technical terms and to purge the language of foreign (including Arabic) words. A new-style Farsi has consequently emerged, often used in the media, scientific, and government documents, that is less flowery and more precise. The prose of several of the "modernizers" among the clerical leaders, notably the late Ayatollah Beheshti and President Rafsanjani, reflects this shift to purist Farsi. Despite Islamic ideological protestations, language modernization thus reflects the continuity of nationalist traditions.

Women's rights and place in society, however, became an early issue in the life of the revolution. Young women had played a critical role in the revolutionary movement, particularly in urban guerrilla activities. They expected, therefore, recognition of their rights. However, as the clerical factions drove the Islamic liberals and Marxists out of power, new constraints were gradually imposed on women's public place and conduct. Women were declared to have equal but *separate* rights from men. It was required of women to observe *hijab* (covering), to attend primarily to family affairs, and generally to play a supportive role to men in society. Although women are granted the rights of suffrage, education, and pursuit of modern professions, their numbers in public life have been reduced. The new position of women is also reflected in the Islamic regime's media and educational policies. "Indecent" exposures of women, including showing women's hair and bare arms, are banned from film and television programs. Any print and audio-visual media content with sexual overtones is also censored. Following the revolution, boys and girls were completely separated at the primary and secondary school levels. While the universities continue to admit women, male students outnumber female. A few universities have also been designated exclusively for women. The government documents on educational reform emphasize sex role differentiation and the need for educational programs specially suited for women.

Another consequence of the cultural revolution in Iranian media and educational programs has been the shift from "decadent" to wholesome Islamic art forms and cultural programming. The instruction of Qur'an at schools and its regular recitation on radio and television have set a new cultural tone. "Decadent" Western music has been excluded from school curricula and broadcasting in favor of folk and classical Persian and foreign music. Although the making of images is prohibited under the more strict fundamentalist Sunni laws, Shi'a Islam has encouraged both the traditional abstract Islamic calligraphy and mosaics as well as "realistic" paintings of religious subjects such as portraits of the Imams and scenes from religious history and mythology. In view of their mass popularity, feature films, television serials, and historical documentaries have also experienced a rebirth.

As the case study of Iran demonstrates in some detail, the impact of the Islamic revolution on Iranian culture, society, media, and education has been profound. The study shows, however, that the revolution is also characterized by a continuity of problems and processes of modernization. The Iranian revolution may be said to be primarily a political and cultural revolution rather than a social and economic restructuring. Although Islamic ideology and leadership have replaced secular ideology and leadership, the revolution does not appear to have succeeded in creating uniquely Islamic social and economic institutions. The processes of state building and nation building which began with the Pahlavi regime, the centralization of power and authority in the hands of the state, and the efforts to build a social, cultural, and educational infrastructure conducive to economic growth have continued. The Islamic revolution may thus be considered yet another chapter in the relentless struggle of a proud but dependent nation to achieve autonomy in a turbulent world.

Conclusion

Despite their enormous diversity, the six studies in part 3 of this volume have demonstrated that fundamentalist and fundamentalist-like ideologies and movements present a common challenge to the dominant secular ideologies of progress. Return to the certitudes of religious traditions, indigenous cultural roots, sacred languages, and primordial identities is a promise that fundamentalisms hold before the believers. While fundamentalist movements appear to be responses to the increasing penetration of a transnational culture of the secular, scientific, and technological world, their sources of social support and consequent impact vary from case to case. This essay has identified at least four types of movements and strategies, including the conservative, separatist, reformist, and revolutionary. While the conservative and separatist movements may be considered quixotic and limited to special cases, the reformist and revolutionary movements have proved strong enough to seize power in Iran, elect a president in Guatemala, unseat a prime minister in India, provide considerable political support to the conservative social policies of three successive presidents of the United States, and tip the political balance in Israel in favor of the conservative Likud party.

The impact of fundamentalist movements on media and education has been more far reaching. In Iran, the Islamic revolution has revamped the entire educational and media systems. In the United States, the "electronic church" and its educational establishments were the leading growth sectors in media and education during the 1980s. In Guatemala, the Protestant evangelical schools have broken through the elitism of the Catholic hierarchy and education to bring education to greater numbers and layers of society. In India, the Hindu educational and cultural movement has revived Hindi as the leading national language while attempting to desecularize Indian politics. In Israel, however, the fundamentalist Jewish movement has led to a greater schism between the secular and religious Zionists, and secular and religious schools. All fundamentalist movements and ideologies in our case studies have succeeded in redefining the terms of national discourse on culture, education, media, and politics.

Notes

1. Martin Marty, "The Phenomenon of Fundamentalism," *Bulletin of the American Academy of Arts and Sciences* (1988).

2. R. D. Laing, *The Divided Self* (New York: Pantheon, 1969).

3. Majid Tehranian, "Iran: Communication, Alienation, Revolution," *InterMedia 7*, no. 2 (March 1979): 6–12.

4. See Dov Shinar, *Palestinian Voices* (Boulder, Colo.: Lynne Reinner, 1987).

5. Emmanuel Sivan, *Radical Islam: Medieval Theology and Modern Politics* (New Haven: Yale University Press, 1985), p. 186.

6. Ibid., chap. 2.

7. Ibid., p. 129.

8. Majid Tehranian, "The Curse of Modernity: The Dialectics of Communication and Modernization," *International Social Science Journal* (1980).

9. J. J. Rouseau, *The Social Contract* (Hammondsworth, England: Penguin Books, 1968).

10. William H. McNeill, "Fundamentalism and the World of the 1990s," in this volume.

11. For a provocative analysis of the Asian experiences with economic growth and political democracy, see *The Economist*, 29 June 1991, pp. 15–18.

12. *The Economist*, 22 June 1991, pp. 37–38.

13. I am grateful to my friend Brenda Dannet and her student Kimi Kaplan at Hebrew University for the following pieces of information. It is ironic that while revising this chapter, the information came to me through an invisible divine force via electronic mail across the oceans and continents lying between Israel and Hawaii! For further details, see Kimi Kaplan, "The God in the Cassette: Sermons and Cassettes in the Ultra-Orthodox Community" (Paper, Hebrew University, July 1991).

14. For a brief review of the "electronic church," see Majid Tehranian, *Technologies of Power: Information Machines and Democratic Prospects* (Norwood, N.J.: Ablex, 1990), pp. 141–46.

15. William F. Fore, *Television and Religion: The Shaping of Faith, Values, and Culture* (Minneapolis: Augsburg, 1987), as reviewed by W. E. Biernatzki, "Televangelism and the Religious Uses of Television,"

Communication Research Trends 11, no. 1 (1991): 9.

16. Biernatzki, "Televangelism and the Religious Uses of Television," p. 13.

17. Ibid., p. 14.

18. For an official story, see Fouad al-Farsy, *Saudi Arabia: A Case Study in Development*, 2nd ed. (London and New York: Routedge, Chapman and Hall, 1986).

19. Biernatzki, "Televangelism and the Religious Uses of Television," p. 18.

20. "Guatemala: Let the Trials Begin," *The Economist*, 20 July 1991, p. 44.

21. Ibid., pp. 44–46.

22. Sivan, *Radical Islam*, p. 120.

23. Biernatzki, "Televangelism and the Religious Uses of Television," p. 17.

24. Charles Liebman and Eliezer Don-Yehiya, *Religion and Politics in Israel* (Bloomington: Indiana University Press, 1984), p. 122. Liebman, who developed these concepts in "The Rise of Neo-Traditionalism among Orthodox Jews in Israel" (in Hebrew), *Megamot* 27 (May 1982): 231–50, writes of the dichotomies between expansionism and adaptationism and associates expansionism with the radical approaches he finds prevalent in the Zionist yeshivot and in Gush Emunim. I am proposing that in the religious kibbutz movement, both may have been uniquely linked.

25. See the series of articles on India by Barbara Crossette in the *New York Times*, 4 November 1990.

26. For analysis and report of recent events, see *The Economist*, 17 November 1990, pp. 15, 42.

27. R. Khomeini, *Islam and Revolution*, trans. H. Algar (Berkeley: Mizan Press, 1981); Majid Tehranian, "Khomeini's Doctrine of Legitimacy," in A. J. Parel, ed., *Under the Upas Tree* (Newbury Park, Calif.: Sage, forthcoming).

Islamic Fundamentalism in Iran and the Discourse of Development

Majid Tehranian

This chapter analyzes the impact of the Islamic fundamentalist discourse and practice in Iran on the educational and media systems. Education and the media have been perceived as important agents of social change in revolutionary Iran, and the efforts to reform them revealed a good deal about the direction of the Islamic regime in the 1980s. Within a broader historical context, this chapter also focuses on the role of education and the media in the formation and dissemination of the Islamic revolutionary movement and its discourse in the decade before the Islamic Revolution of 1979.

Islamic Fundamentalism and Modernization

Use of the term "fundamentalist" in an Islamic context calls for a few caveats. In the Islamic world, fundamentalism may be considered a reactive but not necessarily a reactionary phenomenon. Characterizations of the Islamic resurgence as a revolt against modernization and as a vain attempt to turn back history do not withstand a careful examination of the empirical evidence. Insofar as fundamentalism may be considered a reactive phenomenon, however, this characterization is not totally devoid of merit. The trouble is that we are dealing with a set of extremely complex and contradictory movements that cannot be pigeonholed under general terms such as "fundamentalist," "revivalist," or "militant." Some scholars argue that application of the term "fundamentalism" to the Islamic movements may contribute to cultural misunderstanding.[1] Muslims consider the Qur'an as the Word of God, the Revelation itself, a veritable miracle, a book of unsurpassed eloquence in classical Arabic, revealed by God to an unlettered Prophet. Furthermore, this revelation is comprehensive of all areas of life and is fully binding on all believers. In this sense, therefore, it has been said that all orthodox Muslims (Sunni and Shi'ite alike) are "fundamentalists."

Interpretations of the Revelation, however, vary greatly in accordance with the different schools of law *(fiqh)* to which individual Muslims belong; at least four schools are generally acknowledged by the Sunnis and one by the Shi'ites. In Shi'ite Iran, however, the term "fundamentalist" could mean something more. In the theological controversies of the seventeenth and eighteenth centuries surrounding the question of *ijtihad* (literally "exertion" to interpret the Revelation), a group of theologians known as the Akhbaris rejected it, arguing that the Qur'an and the record *(akhbar)* of the acts and the deeds of the Prophet and the Imams should be treated as the sole and sufficient source of law and that no new consensus or reasoning was required.[2] By contrast, another group of theologians, the Usulis (literally "the principled faction"), insisted that *mujtahids* were needed to interpret the principles or fundamentals *(usul)* of the faith. By the nineteenth century, this school of thought had become dominant in Iran, and a number of living Shi'ite mujtahids who were authorized to issue *fatwa* (binding religious edicts) on matters of religious interpretation had emerged. In an informal hierarchy that developed in the early twentieth century, the community of the mujtahids in turn generally selected a senior *marja' al-taqlid,* or "source of imitation," by whose interpretation all would be directly or indirectly guided. By comparison with the Sunni ulama who were not as open to ijtihad and largely subordinated to the state, this system of religious authority and legislation has given the Shi'ite ulama considerable power and authority vis-à-vis the state. The Islamic revolutionary movement in Iran and the centrality of Ayatollah Khomeini within it reflected the triumph of the Usuli (fundamentalist) over Akhbari (literalist) principles. The meaning of "fundamentalism" in the Iranian context is therefore significantly different from its meaning in some other contexts.

The focus on "discourse" and "development" also calls for an explanation. Secular and religious ideologies and leaderships have presented competing hegemonic and counterhegemonic projects to deal with the threefold challenges of dependency, development, and democratization in the modern history of the Muslim world.[3] Since most of the Iranian discourse on public issues, including educational and media reform, has been implicitly or explicitly conducted in terms of the global metadiscourse of modernization and "development," this concept is a useful framework for analysis. Therefore, in this chapter the fundamentalist discourse on education and the media in Iran is analyzed in terms of the developmental processes of economic accumulation, political legitimation, social mobilization, and cultural integration. The role of education and communication within each of these developmental processes is particularly emphasized.

This essay argues, then, that the resurgence of Islam should be understood primarily not as a reaction against modernity but as a part of the struggles of the Islamic peoples against dependency and dictatorship and for development and democracy. A limited historical analogy to modern Christianity may make the point in another way. In its fifteenth century A.H. (Anno Hegirae), the Muslim world is undergoing transformations similar in some regards to those that occurred during the Protestant Reformation of the sixteenth century C.E. Islam has faced the secular, Western challenge for about two centuries. This challenge initially came from outside in the form of Western colonialism and domination. The initial appeal of Western secular humanism has worn off, yet the challenge of incorporating the modern democratic values and the scientific, technological worldview within Islam's corpus of knowledge and norms still remains. Just as the Protestant Reformation was in part a response to the secular humanism of the Renaissance, the thrust of the new Islamic resurgence may be also considered fundamentally progressive. A critical difference in the two historical situations is that the Reformation occurred in response to largely indigenous European developments, while the Islamic resurgence is a reaction against threats from both within and without Islamic boundaries.

In recent decades, three recurring patterns have contributed to the resurgence of Islamic ideologies and movements and to their relative political successes. The first pattern is a response to an ontological concern, that is, to the foundational questions of being and existence itself. The failure of secular ideologies of progress such as nationalism, liberalism, and communism to address the human conditions of finitude, fragility, and evil in a particularly turbulent period of historical transition has rekindled the perennial longings for religion and religious ideologies. A second pattern of response takes political and economic forms. Modernization has privileged the new secular, technocratic, and managerial elites at the expense of the traditionalist segments of the population (the ulama, the merchants, the rural population) as well as the new urban middle and lower classes. This elite tends also to be locked into and allied with the world capitalist system and is, therefore, perceived as a fifth column in the Muslim community.[4] The Muslim opposition, by contrast, often constitutes a second stratum of an elite ready to challenge the authority and prerogatives of the dominant elites. In this regard the resort to Islamic ideologies and movements to launch counterhegemonic projects stands in historical continuity with the anti-imperialist movements of the colonial period.

The third pattern of response is the specific subject of this essay. In the absence of ready access to the formal educational system and the major media of communication (the national press and broadcasting), the Islamic movements have used the traditional educational, cultural, and communication forms and channels in conjunction with the small media to launch an effective campaign for the dissemination of their ideologies and programs.

Here the broad similarities in the Islamic world stop and differences begin. Given the enormous diversities of the Islamic world, the same fundamental challenges of modernization have presented themselves under very different historical, economic, social, and political circumstances: in colonial as well as semi-colonial conditions; in resource-rich and resource-poor economies; in tribal, rural, and rural-urban societies; in homogeneous and heterogeneous populations and cultures; in predominantly Shi'ite and predominantly Sunni religious sects and organizations; and in authoritarian as well as relatively democratic polities. Four different Islamic modes of social and political action have developed in response, namely, the *conservative* (traditionalist strategies), the *reformist* (strategies of reform), the *revolutionary* (strategies of transformation), and the *separatist* (strategies of withdrawal from the secular world).

Iran in the late 1970s and 1980s presents a classic case of a revolutionary strategy aimed at total transformation of the economy, polity, culture, and society, including the media and educational systems.

Accumulation and the Development Discourse: The Fall of the Pahlavi Regime

Revolutions in history are often lost rather than won.[5] In other words, the ancien régime often collapses because of its own incapacity rather than as a result of the superior ideology and organization of the revolutionary opposition. The apparatus of an established state is generally too entrenched to be easily dislodged. The Iranian case was no exception to this rule. The Islamic Revolution of 1979 was not well rehearsed either ideologically or organizationally. It came about mainly as a consequence of the moral and political exhaustion of the Pahlavi monarchy, heir to a twenty-five-hundred-year patrimonial political system that had lost much of its legitimacy and efficacy by the second half of the twentieth century.

Despite its economic successes of the 1960s and 1970s under the White Revolution, the strategy of accumulation the regime pursued ultimately proved its undoing. This strategy consisted of a policy of rapid modernization and secularization without political participation. The regime was basically following a policy of "no taxation, no participation."[6] Mounting oil revenues and Western support were, of course, the keys to the partial successes of this strategy. But the successes themselves created a euphoria among the ruling elite during the 1970s that completely blinded it to the gathering storm beneath its feet. In the absence of structures of political feedback and accountability, therefore, the massive degree of popular discontent with the regime came as a surprise to most domestic and international observers.

For fifty years the Pahlavi regime had successfully used modernization ideology as a hegemonic project by which it united the army and the traditional Iranian ruling classes with the Western powers behind a centralized state and the dictatorial prerogatives of the monarchy. The White Revolution, however, further destroyed the relatively autonomous social bases of the traditional elites (notably the tribes and large landholdings) without replacing them with autonomous modern institutions of voluntary association. In the meantime, the regime also created a new urban, industrial, and bureaucratic elite that was almost totally dependent on oil revenues and the monarchy for its own survival. Despite the formal presence of a constitution and the trappings of parliamentary democracy, however, genuine political parties and trade unions were largely banned. Except for the official political parties that were finally reduced to one in 1975, the traditional second stratum of the elite in Iran (the ulama, the bazaar merchants, and the intelligentsia) had been politically disenfranchised by bans on their opposition activities. The regime thus had few programs of its own for political participation and did not allow opposition parties to organize. A few experiments with opposition parties, such as the officially sponsored Mardom party, were too meek and short-lived to be of much consequence. In the meantime, of course, the real opposition parties—the banned Tudeh party, the National Front, and a variety of militant Islamic groups and organizations—were operating underground or in sporadic demonstrations and guerrilla warfare.

All of this occurred under the pressures of social dislocation as mounting oil revenues, industrialization, and urbanization were drawing millions of people from rural to urban areas. The mosque and the religious networks were thus left as one of the few legitimate and available channels for the expression of discontent. The financial and political autonomy of the Shi'a clergy in Iran as compared with their Sunni counterparts in much of the Muslim world also gave the ulama a legitimacy for leadership that other sectors of the Iranian elite did not enjoy. Following the religious riots of 1963, the regime attempted to suppress the Islamic revolutionary movement gathering momentum under the militant leadership of Ayatollah Khomeini. But in the absence of a will to ban, and indeed the impossibility to close down, all mosques and religious gatherings, the opposition coalesced around the Islamic revolutionary movement. The decline in oil prices in the late 1970s, the ensuing rise in unemployment, mounting discontent over government corruption, disgust over the elite's lavish Western lifestyle, and lukewarm support of the shah by the Carter administration were important factors in a virtual collapse of the regime in the autumn of 1978.

The ideology of the monarchical regime rested on three pillars: monarchism, nationalism, and developmentalism. In a country characterized by the heterogeneity of its population and the vastness of its territory, the Iranian monarchy found a powerful source of legitimacy and unity in the model of the Persian Empire of 559 B.C.E. Under the impact of Western domination, however, the Qajar monarchs had come to be identified with weakness, dictatorship, and Western infiltration. Nationalism provided a second powerful source of legitimacy and unity. Reza Shah used this ideology to launch his own Pahlavi dynasty in 1925, and his son, Muhammad Reza Shah, continued in the same tradition by calling his own authoritarian brand "Positive Nationalism," as opposed to the presumably "negative" nationalism of his liberal political opposition in the National Front.[7] With the increasing presence and influence of the United States in Iran, however, his nationalism remained suspect. Developmentalism thus provided the third powerful source of monarchical legitimacy. This ideology was, however, largely imported from the West, notably from the World Bank and International Monetary Fund circles. With rising oil revenues, visible signs of economic progress, and the emergence of new upper and upper-middle classes, this ideology was gaining ground during the 1960s and 1970s. However, as the costs of lopsided development became more apparent in urban congestion and pollution, income maldistribution, and cultural disintegration, the ideology lost much of its appeal, particularly for the youth and the urban lower and lower-middle classes.

Legitimation and Revolutionary Discourse

In response to the development discourse of the shah's regime, the counterhegemonic project of the Shi'a ulama under the leadership of Khomeini employed a militant Islamic, anti-imperialist discourse that called for endogenous development as it severely critiqued the regime's developmentalist ideology. The discourse of revolutionary Islam combined the traditional Shi'a symbols of martyrdom with the modern Iranian nationalist causes as its rallying cries.

In developing the revolutionary discourse of the 1970s and 1980s, militant Islam drew upon its own privileged past, a century of history in Iran beginning with Seyyed Jamal al-Din al-Afghani's pan-Islamic movement, merging into the Tobacco Revolt of 1891 against a British concession, and subsequently into the Constitutional Revolution of 1905–11. In each of these movements, the ulama had forged an alliance with the bazaar merchants and liberal intellectuals to struggle for national independence, constitutionalism, and a reassertion of religious authority over against what was perceived to be foreign-inspired, secular encroachments. Following the Constitutional Revolution, however, the ulama felt betrayed by their liberal, secular, intellectual allies. Although the Constitution called for a committee of five mujtahids to pass judgment on the Islamic validity of the laws passed by the Majlis, this article remained a dead letter. Under Reza Shah, the traditional domains of ulama's authority (the courts, schools, personal affairs, and cultural life) were also taken out of their control and drastically secularized. Following Reza Shah's departure in the popular nationalist resurgence of 1940s and 1950s, the ulama once again forged an alliance with the liberal intellectuals of the National Front parties to struggle for the nationalization of the British-controlled oil industry and the curtailment of monarchical authority. But the CIA-sponsored coup d'etat of 1953, which returned the shah to power, once again reduced their role and influence.

Anti-imperialism was therefore a second important source of the ulama's ideological appeal. Until 1953 Britain and Russia were the chief targets, but with its increasing presence and power, the United States largely replaced the two traditional Great Powers as the main object of nationalist and anti-imperialist hatred. Under the impact of social and cultural dislocations of economic change accelerated by the shah's modernization program, a counterdevelopmentalist discourse assumed a central position in the opposition's ideological arsenal alongside the anti-imperialist rhetoric. Borrowing heavily from the literature of the Third World national liberation movements, this discourse emphasized endogenous and self-reliant development with a focus on the need for the preservation of cultural identity vis-à-vis Western cultural imports and encroachments. These popular sentiments were so powerful that they infiltrated even the court, through Queen Farah and her intellectual entourage.[8]

Given the terms of government and opposition discourses, it was natural for culture, communication, and education to become the central foci of concern.[9] To the Pahlavi government, it appeared that its ambitious goals of economic growth could not be fully achieved unless Iranian culture and society were totally revamped through a new secular, scientific, and technological value system inculcated by the mass media and educational systems. To the Iranian secular elite in general and the shah in particular, the rapid expansion of the educational and broadcasting systems in the 1960s and 1970s was meant to ensure that the regime's programs of economic accumulation, political legitimation, social mobilization, and cultural integration would be supported by a new generation of scientifically and technologically trained, secular, nationalist, and (wishfully) monarchist Iranians. The importance of educational reform and media expansion was underlined by the shah through his own personal involvement in a series of university reform conferences held in Ramsar as well as through a generous funding of the expansion of the broadcasting network.[10]

To the opposition generally and to the ulama in particular in the 1960s and 1970s, the secularist projects of the government were a direct threat against the position of the ulama and the political and cultural autonomy of the country. The projects were thus to be resisted politically through the religious network, alternative media, and educational systems. However, as we shall see, the recourse to alternative media and educational systems had unintended as well as intended consequences for the revolutionaries and the path of their own cultural programs.

Modern educational and media systems create their own sociocultural spaces in society primarily through the institutional linkages they establish domestically and internationally. But in Iran, where dependency has been a preponderant fact of economic, political, and cultural life, these systems became heavily dependent on hardware and software imports.[11] That in turn brought about a high degree of Westernization, cultural alienation, and sociopolitical dualism between the traditional and modernized (read "Westernized") sectors of the population. The introduction of modern schools and media into a largely traditional, oral, and dependent society during the nineteenth and twentieth centuries initially strengthened the ideological and cultural penetration of the traditional, rural peripheries by the modern, urban centers. However, due to the repression of participatory political and communication institutions under the Pahlavi regime, this penetration ultimately resulted in an Islamic revolutionary movement that radically challenged the secularist policies of the earlier era. A movement for the establishment of Islamic schools and Islamic banking began in the 1960s to provide an institutional framework to which the Islamic revolutionaries could later point with pride. In the absence of access to the major media of communication, the movement combined the religious channels of communication (the mosque and minbar, i.e., the pulpit) with the new small media of communication (pamphlets, cassette recorders, and copying machines) to launch an extremely effective campaign of dissemination of its messages.[12] The most well known of these efforts during the late 1960s was a new lecture hall located in central Tehran, Hosseinieh Ershad, at which the religious critics of the regime such as Dr. 'Ali Shari'ati regularly spoke.[13] The lectures were later published in pamphlet form or recorded onto audio cassettes for wider dissemination. The center was soon closed down by the government, but its message spread rapidly through the mosques and universities.

As it became articulated through the new alternative media, the Islamic revolutionary discourse assumed three distinctly different tendencies. Although it was difficult to distinguish between them during the 1970s, following the revolution the three ideological tendencies shaped the three different political groupings of Islamic neotraditionalists, Islamic liberals, and Islamic Marxists.

The neotraditionalist position of wilayat-i-faqih was first and foremost articulated by Ayatollah Khomeini in his Najaf exile lecture notes.[14] From the Qur'anic injunction "to obey God, his Prophet, and those among you who are first in authority," he argued that in the absence of the Twelfth Shi'a Imam, whose ultimate return will bring justice to the world, it is incumbent upon the ulama to assume the mantle of spiritual and political leadership of the Muslim community. He thus advocated an Islamic republic in which a Supreme Faqih, chosen by the consensus of the ulama, should lead the country. This position represented a radical departure from the quietist Shi'a position as represented by Ayatollah Shariatmadari, relegating political authority to a secular government but requiring the observance of the Shari'a.

The Islamic liberals, represented by Dr. Mehdi Bazargan and Dr. Abul Hasan Bani-Sadr, the first prime minister and president of the Islamic Republic, opposed the principle of wilayat-i-faqih and argued for popular sovereignty as well as for less clerical and greater secular control over the reins of government. They suffered a defeat both in the Constitutional Assembly of 1979, which incorporated the new principle into the Islamic Constitution, and subsequently in the political arena.

The third school, that of Islamic Marxism, was largely represented by Mujahidin Khalq led by Massoud Rajavi. This guerrilla action group had been deeply influenced by 'Ali Shari'ati, claimed a large following among the university students, and had played a critical role in the overthrow of the shah's regime. Following a short period of uneasy collaboration with the clerical leadership, however, it fell out of favor and waged a determined and violent campaign to overthrow the clerical hegemony. Following the fall of Bani-Sadr in 1980, the Mujahidin were also forced out of the country and made common cause with Saddam Hussein in the Iran-Iraq War of 1980–88. Their ideological position was a mix of Islamic rhetoric and Marxist ideology that emphasized class conflict, lay Islamic leadership, and revolutionary violence.

Media and Educational Dualism: Competing Strategies of Mobilization

The structure of modern educational and media systems in every society tends to follow the dominant economic and political patterns. In Iran, where the modern educational and media systems were first grafted onto the narrow modern sectors of society, the structure initially followed dualistic patterns of development largely disconnected and alienated from traditional society. In keeping with this pattern, two dominant ideologies began to split Iranian society alongside two increasingly antagonist factions—the secular nationalists celebrating the glories of the pre-Islamic past, and the Islamic revolutionaries commemorating the struggles and martyrdoms of the Shi'ite saints against the tyranny of secular powers. These two ideologies found their fullest expression in the competing claims for sovereignty in the doctrines of Monarchy as the Shadow of God *(Shah saye-ye Khoda)* and the Trusteeship of the Jurist *(wilayat-i-faqih)*. In this ideological struggle, the modern schools and the macromedia (notably the national press and broadcasting) legitimated the monarchical doctrine, while the traditional schools (the Islamic *maktab*, *madresseh*, and *majalis-i-tafsir-i-Qur'an*, i.e., Qur'anic interpretation groups) in conjunction with the micromedia continued to propagate the Shi'a revolutionary ideology.

Modern schools and media had been introduced in Iran primarily through the initiative of the governments in power to advance their modernization ideology and program. Since the rise of mass political movements in the late nineteenth century, however, the traditional communication system has also increasingly utilized some of the modern micromedia to wage a struggle against those in power. The resulting dualism between traditional and modern sectors in education and communication therefore closely reflected the existing economic, political, and cultural dualisms in the country.[15] Given a predominantly government-controlled school and media system, the religious opposition groups had to resort to alternative schools and underground or exile media.

In this tug of war between the two competing modes of discourse and political allegiances in the twentieth century, a distinct pattern emerged: periods of strict media censorship were followed by liberalization, then followed by a new round of censorship. The pattern was repeated several times. The series of cyclical swings moved from centralization to fragmentation of power. The cycles reflected alternating shifts between high accumulation and high mobilization strategies of development. From 1905 to 1921, for example, when a quasi-parliamentary system operated, the press enjoyed some measure of freedom. As political power became centralized under Reza Shah during 1921–41, the press lost its autonomy. Political fragmentation during World War II up to the coup d'etat of August 1953 was reflected in the press by the emergence of ideological diversity and relative political autonomy. Following the coup of 1953, however, to the Islamic Revolution of 1979, the media operated once again under heavy censorship.

The patterns of communication and cultural dualism were exacerbated by the introduction of broadcasting. Radio and television were brought to Iran, in 1940 and 1958 respectively, by a monarchical regime pursuing a relentless policy of Westernization and secularization. Both media were initially prohibited by the ulama, not so much because of their inherent qualities as for the secular content of their messages. Although television was initially introduced as a commercial enterprise by a private entrepreneur, Habib Sabet, it was soon taken over in 1969 by a government monopoly—National Iranian Television. In 1971, radio also was incorporated into a larger organization renamed National Iranian Radio and Television (NIRT). Under NIRT's managing director, Reza Ghotbi, broadcasting achieved important objectives in several domains. Physical facilities were expanded to include a national microwave system, a satellite earth station, three television channels, four radio networks, fourteen regional production centers, and many auxiliary facilities for theater, film, and musical production as well as printing and publishing. Coverage increased to 70 percent of the population for television and 100 percent for radio. The 1976 National

Census indicated a growth in the ownership of radio and television sets to the level of 4.3 million households for radios and 1.6 million households for television sets. At the same time, a worldwide network of short-wave radio was established. Educational broadcasting grew to 2,480 hours of programs for primary and secondary schools and the beginnings of a multimedia system at the tertiary level known as the Free University. Color television production and transmission began in 1975. Iranian news agency offices were established in the major capitals of the world. The School of Cinema and Television, offering undergraduate and graduate programs, opened in Tehran, as did an electronics production plant. Several annual film, musical, theater, and traditional media festivals were held. Research institutes opened, including Iran Communications and Development Institute and a public opinion survey unit. A publishing house, Soroush, was established. To manage these burgeoning enterprises, NIRT's personnel had increased to some nine thousand by 1979.[16]

Similarly, the modern educational system, primarily shaped under Reza Shah's regime,[17] was significantly reformed during the 1960s and 1970s under Muhammad Reza Shah's White Revolution. The educational system was initially patterned after the French scholastic system, but as U.S. power and prestige increased in Iran, the reforms of the 1960s and 1970s introduced some features of the American educational system. The shift was generally away from the French emphasis on a highly theoretical curriculum toward the more practical and vocational orientation of the American system. However, the primary and secondary school curricula continued to emphasize Iranian language, literature, and history—focusing on Iranian monarchy as a unifying theme. The reforms at the secondary level also introduced a new guidance cycle *(dowreh rahnamaii)* at the junior high school level to identify and direct the students' talents toward academic or vocational pursuits. At the university level, the reforms were more dramatic. A Ministry of Science and Higher Education was founded in the mid-1960s that included two auxiliary institutes—the Iran Documentation Center and the Center for Educational Research and Planning. The University of Tehran, a bastion of French-educated academics and political opposition, lost its autonomy after the coup of 1953 and was increasingly staffed by American-educated Ph.D.s who steered it toward a more flexible academic system. In the meantime, a number of competing universities were established with a diversity of missions and academic programs. Under a contract with the University of Pennsylvania, Pahlavi University was established in Shiraz with English as its main language of instruction. Modeled after MIT, Aryamehr Industrial University was established in Tehran to train Iranian scientists and engineers. Bu-Ali Sina University was formed in Hamadan to pursue applied socioeconomic development subjects and programs. Modeled after Harvard Business School, the Iran Center for Management Studies was established in Tehran to train modern managers. Under the supervision of a Harvard team, Reza Shah University was inaugurated in Mazandaran just before the revolution to train scientists and scholars for the higher educational system. A number of provincial universities also were established to pursue academic programs with a variety of regional emphases.[18]

As the size and diversity of Iran's educational system increased, a growing number of students from more traditional, rural, and lower-class backgrounds entered the schools and the universities. The clashes between their Islamic cultural orientations and the secular orientation of the educational system provided the breeding ground for the Islamic revival that became increasingly evident during the 1970s. The outward signs of this revival were the sporting of a beard for young men and the wearing of the *chador* (long veil) or *rusari* (short head-cover) for young women. Another extraordinary sign was the appearance of women with rusari behind the wheels of some of the latest model European or American cars. The Islamic revival was clearly taking place among the lower and lower-middle classes as well as among some in the newly affluent upper classes of north Tehran. At a deeper cultural and educational level, the sale of religious media and underground political opposition tracts was soaring well ahead of the secular, scientific, and literary publications.

Despite its economic and technological achievements, the monarchical regime and its modern communication system largely failed in their major tasks of political legitimation and social mobilization. The repression of modern voluntary associations such as political parties, labor unions, professional organizations, and their autonomous media of communication was at the root of this failure. In a society largely religious in its belief system, heterogeneous in its ethnic and linguistic composition, and traditional in its interpersonal communication networks, the big media came to represent the political and cultural domination of a Westernized, secularized, and privileged elite.

The competing traditional and religious mass communication networks of some 5,000 mosques (the number doubled after the revolution), 1,200 shrines, 90,000 clerics, and 12,000 religious associations in Tehran alone proved more credible and effective with audiences than government broadcasts.[19] As the revolutionary discourse gained momentum in the 1970s, the Qur'an sold some 700,000 copies annually, religious books sold some 500,000 copies (comprising a third of all titles published in 1974–75), and an increasing variety of religious cassettes were sold in the thousands by vendors. While *Maktab-i-Islam* (the leading Shi'a journal) had a circulation of 50,000, *Sokhan*'s (its equivalent as a leading secular, literary journal) circulation was about 3,000. The increasingly dualistic social, economic, political, and cultural structures of Iran under the monarchical regime paved the way for a revolution that shrewdly employed both the traditional and modern channels of communication.

These media, however, should be considered part of a larger network of traditional networks of communication, which may be divided into those used primarily for religious or secular purposes. Religious communication occurs through such institutions as the mosque, shrines such as the ones in Qum and Mashhad, the *madrasa* (theological school), *khaneqah* (the Sufi house of worship), *rowzeh khani* (gatherings for religious mourning), *tafsir Qur'an* (gatherings for the interpretation of the Holy Book), *Hosseinieh* and *Fatemieh* (meeting halls for religious sermons and activities), and *takyeh* (annual tents put up for large religious mournings).

There were few, if any, accurate statistics on the size, management, control, and activities of these institutions in Iran before the revolution. The secularist policies of the Pahlavi regime discouraged any kind of systematic study of the religious institutions. It is significant that the *State Statistical Yearbook* listed mosques and shrines as ancient and historical monuments, neglecting their living social and cultural functions. Furthermore, before the revolution, few Western scholars paid much attention to the importance of these institutions as media of public communication in Islam.[20] For example, Lerner's influential 1958 study of mass communication and modernization, *The Passing of Traditional Society: Modernizing of the Middle East,* had focused almost exclusively on the mass media. By contrast, however, Asghar Fathi persuasively argued that "the pulpit, or *minbar,* in the mosque in the traditional and transitional Muslim society is an organized system of communication operated by a class of professional communicators. It is assumed that prior to the introduction of the press, radio and motion picture in Muslim societies, a system of public communication existed which performed some of the functions of mass media in modern societies."[21]

Traditional secular institutions of public communication in Iran have been often tied to the religious institutions in a variety of ways. The *zur-khaneh* (the house of strength), for example, is a sports house for the practice of traditional sports, particularly those of gymnastics and wrestling, and it has served historically as a channel for the continuation of the pre-Islamic, Iranian traditions of chivalry. As the revolutionary discourse developed in the 1970s, however, the zur-khaneh became intimately tied to the quasi-religious traditions of *futtuwat* and *javanmardi* (chivalry) associated with the name of 'Ali, the Shi'ites' first Imam and considered the legitimate successor to the Prophet Muhammad. It also served as a communication network for a class of *lutis,* men of chivalry in the urban areas, who were closely allied to the ulama and the bazaar merchants.[22]

By contrast, the *ghahveh-khaneh* (the Persian coffeehouse), the *dowreh* (the Persian custom of rotary gatherings of intimate circles of family or friends), and such secret societies as the Freemasons have provided communication networks less visible but no less powerful. In a society characterized by a sense of insecurity generated by extremes of political centralization and fragmentation, these networks have maintained a sense of continuity and connection made possible amid change and turmoil. They have also kept the exchange of news and rumor alive despite considerable control and censorship.

This complex of traditional religious and secular communication networks was pitted against the modern communication network imposed from above. In particular, the relations between the broadcasting organization and the religious institutions were adversarial. There were some religious programs on the air and some clerics on the payroll, but neither enjoyed much credibility. One religious drama, "The Two Children of Muslim," well done by dramatic standards, included a Baha'i in one of its title roles. Another serial, "Dear Uncle Napoleon," which created a political uproar in the late 1970s, mercilessly satirized religious symbols and nationalist megalomania. The Festival of Shiraz, another of NIRT's activities which involved some of the most avant garde of world musical and theatrical groups, created a riot by presenting a group that publicly displayed the sex act. On television, after the French model, women broadcasters were all too seductively dressed and mannered. All this was taken by the ulama as signs of increasing arrogance by a secular and secularizing state that held religious values and institutions in thorough contempt.

Among other things, then, the Islamic Revolution of 1979 signaled the triumph of the "alternative media" and the beginning of a new era in cultural and communication policies. The revolution was achieved through the mobilization of mass protests that employed both the traditional and modern media of communication. Ayatollah Khomeini's messages were transmitted via long-distance telephone calls from Najaf and Paris to his supporters throughout the country, courtesy of sympathetic telephone operators and at His Majesty's expense. The messages were recorded on cheap transistor tape recorders; they were then transcribed, photocopied (often at government offices), and distributed through the oppositionist, religious networks within hours of their reception. The cassette and photocopy revolution thus multiplied the power of the traditional channels by using modern, accessible, inexpensive, and elusive (to the government censors) media.[23]

The revolution, however, became heir to a much more highly sophisticated telecommunication system. Faced with the necessity of governing the newly established Islamic Republic and consolidating and disseminating the Islamic discourse that had brought them to power, the revolutionaries were confronted with the challenge of integrating the traditional and modern cultural and communication systems in a much more sophisticated and systematic way than had been attempted in the years leading up to the revolution.

In meeting this challenge in the 1980s, the revolutionary ideology itself passed through three distinct phases, each of which featured a distinctive role for the media. In the first phase, lasting for about a year during Dr. Mehdi Bazargan's tenure as prime minister (February–November 1979), a *liberal Islamic* ideology allowed a multiparty and competitive media system. The taking of American hostages on 4 November and the resulting resignation of Dr. Bazargan's government signaled a shift of power from the liberal, secular politicians to the clerics led by Ayatollah Khomeini. The hostage crisis thus represented a coup by the clerical leadership to seize power and initiative from the secular liberals. It used to clerical advantage the historical memories of the coup d'etat of 1953 and the powerful anti-American sentiments it had created.

In the second phase, lasting until Ayatollah Khomeini's death in June 1989, a neotraditionalist Islamic ideology expelled its liberal, communist, and Marxist Islamic rivals from the political arena. During this period, Dr. Bazargan came under fire, President Hasan Bani-Sadr was ousted and fled the country, the communist Tudeh party leaders were arrested on charges of espionage for the Soviet Union, and a bloody battle was waged against the Marxist Fadaiiyan Khalq and the Islamic Marxist Mujahidin Khalq. The latter managed to put up strong military resistance through urban guerrilla warfare before their leader, Massoud Rajavi, had to flee the country. Rajavi established his headquarters first in Paris, where he made common cause with

Bani-Sadr, then moved to Baghdad where he came under the protection of Saddam Hussein. In the Iran-Iraq War, the Mujahidin made a few unsuccessful skirmishes over the border into Iran but in the meantime lost much of their political credibility as an autonomous political force.[24]

A third phase in the Islamic Republic, which might be labeled as pragmatic Islamic, began in 1989 with the dual leadership of Ayatollah Sayyid Ali Khamanei as Supreme Faqih and Hojjatolislam Ali Akbar Hashemi Rafsanjani as President of the Islamic Republic. This phase has thus far featured less ideological and more pragmatic policies in order to consolidate the revolution's political gains during its first decade, to pursue the country's economic reconstruction after the devastating war with Iraq, and to reform the social and educational foundations of the country. The new pragmatic policies include an opening to the West, even to the United States, a focus on economic reconstruction, and a softening of the social and cultural strictures.[25]

Media programming has shifted from strictly Islamic to more diversified, entertainment-oriented content. Given the flight of some two million Iranians after the revolution, an active campaign to lure some back started in 1990, including a significant rise in the salaries of the faculty of the universities and invitations to the Iranian investors and managers to consider returning to their homeland.

Following the ascendancy of the clerical factions to power, the Islamic regime followed a dual mobilization policy. The repression or expulsion of the liberal Islamic, Marxist Islamic, Tudeh Communist, and ethnic and religious minority parties and media required some measure of demobilization, but the war with Iraq (1980–88) necessitated a high level of social and economic mobilization. In 1981 the number of officially licensed newspapers in the country was reduced to eight. The two major dailies, *Kayhan* and *Ettela'at,* were taken over by the government, as was Amir Kabir, the country's major publishing house. Liberal and Marxist literature which enjoyed freedom of publication during the first brief phase of the revolution was curtailed. Former Prime Minister Mosaddeq's memoirs, for example, which had reached the status of best-seller, were banned again. And in order to ensure a high degree of self-censorship by the publishers before encumbering the expenses of printing, the old procedure of submitting printed copies of books to the government censors was reinstated: the pre-revolutionary Ministry of Information became the Ministry of Islamic Guidance after the revolution. Except for a period of revolutionary enthusiasm when daily newspaper circulation reached one million and beyond, print runs gradually declined in the 1980s to the vicinity of 150,000. Aside from books of poetry and religious devotion, the highest selling volumes reached 100,000 copies for well-publicized, subsidized, religious titles, 10,000 for popular titles, and 2,000 for scholarly titles. Overall annual title production was back to 2,500.[26] Censorship, price increases, paper scarcity, subject repetition, and declining interest by readers were given as the main reasons for the decline. The print media were still largely an elitist affair, while broadcasting assumed the status of true mass media with a far more sensitive political role.

To mobilize internal and external support under Khomeini's reign, the Islamic

Republic developed a powerful broadcasting network both inside and outside the country. To reflect its new image, the name of the broadcasting agency was changed from NIRT to the Voice and Vision of the Islamic Republic of Iran (VVIRI). While the operation of the national news agency (the Islamic News Agency or IRNA), the press, publishing, and film are under the Ministry of Islamic Culture and Guidance, the operation of broadcasting has been put under the direct supervision of the Republic's leadership.

The (unintended) similarities with the overthrown regime and its discourse survived Khomeini. In a country in which family ties represent the most politically reliable bond of loyalty, the head of NIRT under the shah's regime had been a cousin to Queen Farah. Under President Rafsanjani, the head of VVIRI is the president's brother. However, to ensure some degree of collective leadership in media control, a revised and supplementary constitution adopted in 1990 placed VVIRI under a council composed of two members from each of the three branches of government, while reserving to the leader of the revolution or members of the Leadership Council the right to appoint the managing director.[27]

In 1990 there were two national television channels, one predominantly devoted to light, popular programming and the other to educational programming, corresponding to the division of labor between TV1 and TV2 under NIRT's management. Television broadcast hours ran from 5:00 P.M. to about midnight. Children's programming had an extra two hours on Friday, the Islamic Sabbath. In 1990 there was also a daily two-hour program of news, features, and commentaries in Arabic, directed at the Arab population of Khuzistan Province and the Persian Gulf region as well as Iraqi refugees and prisoners of the Iran-Iraq War. With an estimated audience of twenty million (out of a total population of over fifty million), Iranian television had established itself as a mass medium. Its two channels covered 628,000 square miles, more than three times the area of Spain, larger than the whole of Western Europe, and equal to more than one-fifth of the United States. Its signals could spill over the 1,200-mile border with the Soviet Union to the north and along almost the entire coastline of the Persian Gulf. A mammoth new television house under construction in northern Tehran promised to be the largest broadcasting center of its kind in the Middle East.[28]

To mobilize its foreign communication networks, the regime committed considerable resources to IRNA and foreign radio broadcasting. IRNA established bureaus in some twenty capitals of the world, producing 54,150 words of news daily by 1988. In the print media, the official cultural periodicals (*Soroush, Adineh, Nashr-i-Danesh, Andisheh,* and *Kayhan Farhangi*) showed a new balance between Islamic, Iranian, and foreign themes. The regime also developed an active publication program in other Muslim languages (notably Arabic), including a quarterly journal *Al-Tawhid*, which competes with those of Egypt and Saudi Arabia. Foreign radio broadcasting expanded significantly to 323 hours per week by 1990, making Iran one of the top twenty major world broadcasters.[29]

With the voluntary or forced exile of the opposition as well as the immigration of two million Iranians to the United States and Western Europe since the revolution, an expanding exile media also came into existence in the 1980s.[30] Some of this opposition media may be viewed as countermobilization against the Islamic regime, but some are clearly media serving a high-status immigrant community with its own networks of radio, television, and publishing. In such major concentrations of Iranians as those in Los Angeles and Washington, D.C., Farsi radio and television programs as well as special Yellow Pages and bookshops serve fairly prosperous Iranian communities. In distant Honolulu, which has no more than a few hundred Iranian immigrants, there is now a Farsi radio program with two hours of broadcasting per week. Due to a constantly fluctuating situation, the number of Farsi periodicals published outside the country cannot be accurately ascertained, but it seems that the emergence of new ones has generally outstripped the demise of the old. The highest circulation (about twenty thousand) probably belongs to *International Iran Times* (in English and Farsi), which in 1970 started to publish out of Washington, D.C. This newspaper, published privately, has grown considerably in size, coverage, and circulation since the revolution. By borrowing from all sources, including the government and opposition inside and outside the country, the newspaper has maintained a relatively neutral and professional standard. By comparison, the opposition newspapers in exile cannot claim high circulations. Their fate has often been tied to the political group to which they belong.[31] A number of literary and political journals have also appeared in exile.[32] There is considerable richness and diversity in the Iranian exile media, which may be setting a new tradition in exile discourse.

Following the dislocating effects of the revolution, Iran appears once again to be returning to its historic path of a distinctly Islamic-Iranian cultural and political development. The excessive entanglement with inter-Islamic and Arab politics, caused in part by a reaction against the shah's anti-Islamic policies, is gradually coming to an end. The failures of the Islamic regime in its war with Iraq and involvement in the Lebanese civil war seem to have taught it a lesson. Iranian nationalism is once again on the rise. Appeals to Iranian nationals abroad to return home, a rapprochement with the West, a greater focus on internal rather than external affairs, a revival of Iranian cultural traditions, and a softening of the Islamic image are the most apparent signs of this change of direction. A new phase of involvement with the former Soviet Muslim republics began in 1991–92 with the formation of the Economic Cooperation Organization, which includes Iran, Pakistan, Turkey, and five former Soviet Muslim republics; and the Caspian Council, consisting of Iran, Turkmanestan, Kazakhstan, Azerbaijan, and Russia. As the regime's agents of legitimation and socialization, the media and educational systems are also reflecting this change.

Integration and the Discourse of Identity

As mentioned earlier, cultural integration in Iran, with its heterogeneous population and high rate of illiteracy, has faced serious obstacles.[33] Before the Islamic revolution the Iranian population was increasingly divided between the modern, urban, and secular populations and the traditional, rural, semi-urban, and religious sectors. Against this background, the religious unity of Iran with its 98 percent Muslim population (with a majority of Shi'a) has proved to be an integrating factor.

The modern media before and after the revolution played an important role in increasing cultural and linguistic integration. Iran, like most other developing countries, moved from the oral to the visual stage of communication history without experiencing the literacy revolution. Illiteracy is believed to have increased or stagnated at some 50 percent in the late 1970s. Women's illiteracy rate is probably as high as 80 percent. Rapid population growth in the 1980s (an increase from 2.7 percent to one of the highest rates in the world, 3.3 percent), the abolition of the shah's Literacy Corps, the ideological purge of the school system, and a decline in the quality of instruction contributed to the stagnation in literacy.[34]

Whereas the monarchical regime had followed largely elitist cultural policies, propagating Western-style cultural forms, the Islamic regime in the 1980s pursued an active program of Islamization of culture, media, education, and social conduct. Accordingly, the content of the media changed radically. Television broadcasting hours were considerably reduced, and the new program policy excluded all Western imports and domestic productions that indulged in sex, violence, and "indecent" moral behavior such as holding hands with members of the opposite sex. The new programs included war and revolutionary movies, civil defense instructions (particularly during the war with Iraq), news, public events, audiences with religious leaders, talk shows, and more talk shows. Because of its rural setting and propagation of simple virtues, "Little House on the Prairie" was one of the few American television serials to survive. All the other pre-revolutionary serials, including all westerns, "Kojak," "Charlie's Angels," "Loves of Napoleon," "Days of Our Lives," and domestic and foreign variety shows and musicals (all representing the "decadent" lifestyle of an urban elite) were eliminated. The American popular television series of the 1980s, "Dallas" and "Dynasty," never reached Iran but seem to have overwhelmed some other parts of the world. Imported movies from the Soviet Union, Eastern Europe, and the Third World, dealing with revolutionary struggles, took their place. The attire of television announcers also dramatically changed from coat and tie to revolutionary fatigues or open-neck shirts for men, and from the latest Parisian fashions to Islamic head-cover for women. Female announcers are increasingly conspicuous by their absence.

Like the monarchical regime, however, the Islamic regime of the 1980s faced tenacious problems in their cultural policies of homogenization. Modern communication programs in every society entail some intended consequences such as information, persuasion, education, entertainment, but also many unintended consequences such as the dominance of either visual or print literacy, the reinforcement of either loyalty or opposition to the government, and the promotion of either modern or neotraditional values. Where audience feedback has been weak or conspicuous by its absence, the mass media have often created illusions of power at the centers, while cultural resistance has developed in a variety of ingenious forms at the peripheries. For example, broadcasting before the revolution fostered Iran's emerging consumer industries through commercials that earned as much as 20 percent of NIRT's revenues. Television programs and commercials were particularly seductive in their demonstration of the new standards of living of an emerging, acquisitive society. Items such as new consumer durables, banking services including travelers' checks, and cosmetics were particularly conspicuous in advertising. They demonstrated the chasm between elite consumer behavior and the deprivation of the masses. The flaunting of this affluence brought to the remotest regions of Iran a sense of alienation and outrage that undermined the monarchical regime. Rising expectations and frustration thus seemed destined to lead to a revolution characterized by regression and aggression.[35]

The media policies of the Islamic Republic carried their own unintended consequences. During the 1980s the regime placed a high value on the role of broadcasting in propagating Islamic values. The Islamic Constitution of Iran is perhaps the first of its kind to have a special article devoted to the duties of the mass media. The duty of propagation *(tabligh)* of the faith is a well-recognized Islamic principle; encouraging virtue and discouraging vice *(amr-i-be-m'aruf wa nahy-i-az-munkar)* is also the duty of every Muslim. Accordingly, article 175 of the Constitution maintains that "freedom of publicity and propaganda in the mass media, radio and television, shall be ensured on the basis of Islamic principles." And, although the first director of broadcasting, Sadeq Qotbzadeh, argued that television is bad for the family, President Rafsanjani has gone so far as to suggest that entertainment programs are as important as mosques in the proper education of the people. In his last testament made public immediately after his death, Ayatollah Khomeini made at least fifteen references to the role of the mass media, including the following:

> Television films depicting Eastern or Western products made young men and women stray from the normal course of their work, throwing life and industry into oblivion in respect of themselves and their personalities. It also produced pessimism vis-à-vis their own being, their country, and culture and about highly valuable works of arts and literature, many of which found their way into art galleries and libraries of the East and West through the treachery of the collectors.

> My advice to the Islamic Consultative Assembly [Parliament], to the Guardianship Council, to the Supreme Judicial Council, and to the government now and in the future is to maintain the news agencies, the press, and the magazines in the service of Islam and in the interest of the country. We must all know that the Western-style freedom degenerates the youth, [and] is condemned in Islam's view and by reason and intellect.[36]

Unintended consequences arose from the emphasis on media, however; facing limited technical and financial capacity for production, the Islamic regime has had to import almost as many programs as the monarchical regime, albeit from non-Western sources. Japanese television has provided one such important source for program imports.[37] In November 1987, Iranian television started to dub into Farsi and broadcast the most popular of these programs—a Japanese television serial called "Oshin." "It was believed, from a policy standpoint, that Oshin's spirit of self-sacrifice was what the Iranian people needed at the moment."[38] In addition to the television broadcast, 168 episodes of the serial were also shown on Saturday evenings to packed houses at local movie theaters. The "Oshin" fad was further manifested through clothing, personal effects, and toys displaying Oshin's picture. As in other Asian countries, Oshin soon achieved such popularity that Tehran traffic fell to a minimum during its show time. According to the audience research department of Iranian television, during the three quarters of 1988, "Oshin" enjoyed the highest rating among a number of other television programs.[39]

The effect of "Oshin" is, however, worthy of note. The hero of this serial, Oshin, is a poverty-stricken peasant woman who, through sheer stamina and perseverance, achieves human dignity and worldly success. The cultural impact of this show was so powerful that many parents gave their newborn daughters her name rather than a traditional Islamic one. The issue came to a boil when a young woman on a call-in radio program admitted that she took Oshin as a role model more readily than Fatimah Zahra, the Prophet Muhammad's daughter. Ayatollah Khomeini was so incensed by the broadcast that he ordered the head of radio imprisoned and the director of the broadcasting agency's ideology group sentenced to fifty lashes. Only on the intercession of the chief justice did the ayatollah pardon the participants.

Such instances document the cultural resistance the audiences might show toward officially sanctioned ideologies and norms. However, Mowlana and Rad posed another equally plausible interpretation of the popularity of Oshin in Iran: "The available data . . . provide the first glimpse of evidence on the thesis that television viewers, at least in the case of Iran, are less interested in what they cannot get [i.e., "Dallas"-style wealth, eternal youth, greed, power] and more concerned with what they might perceive as their own cultural setting. This is very well-illustrated in the viewers' absorption of Oshin's life as a tragedy and drama so well depicted within the Iranian cultural and religious setting."[40]

By contrast to foreign imports, the domestic production of films and television serials focused on new historical series in the 1980s. Notable among these television series were "Bu-Ali Sina" (the biography of the tenth century Iranian philosopher and physician known in the West as Avecina), "Mirza Taqi Khan Amir Kabir" (the biography of Nasser ed-Din Shah's reformist prime minister who was put to death by him), and "Hezar Dastan" (about life under Reza Shah in the 1930s). All these programs have commanded respectable audiences.

Iranian cinema seems to have made progress during the first decade of the revolution. Filmmaking techniques greatly improved in all areas, although screenwriting and dialogue were still weak. Dubbing, prevalent despite the technical possibility of live recording, detracts from the credibility of the films. From 31 March to 10 April 1990, a festival of Iranian cinema covering the first decade of the revolution was held at the University of California at Los Angeles.[41] In the presence of such well-known

Iranian film directors as Dariush Mehrjou'i and Abbas Kia-Rostami and a large audience, twenty feature films were screened at this festival. Mahasti Afshar commented:

All the [Iranian] Directors exercised caution in dealing with religious and political issues, a sensibility that the films themselves reflected. With one or two exceptions, the films could have been products of pre-revolution days in that they concentrated on abiding social and personal problems, staying clear of political issues. Even Makhmalbaf's *Marriage of the Blessed,* a film highly critical of the general public's abandonment of the "ideals" of the Islamic Revolution, never pointed to the ruling powers.

Despite this measure of caution, the degree of realism, sincerity, and auto-criticism in these films underscored a new strength in Iranian cinema. The films showed a greater interest in portraying urban society, and to a lesser extent, the impact of international politics on Iran. The roots of this movement go back to the television productions of Nasser Taqvaii and Ali Hatami [among others] in the mid-seventies. Mehrjuii's *Dayere-ye Mina,* a popular film of those years that supplanted stereotypical portrayals with real problems and personalities, was a turning point in Iranian film history. Mehrjuii's latest film *Hamoun,* which Nafici managed to screen virtually the minute it came off the editing machine, continues this probing look by being the first film to focus on the dilemmas of the educated and intellectual classes in contemporary Tehran.

The role of women in society and in film production was only minimally explored. To be sure, restrictions applied to the showing of women with bare heads, sometimes leading to comical results: Female characters in Ebrahimifar's *Nar-o Ney,* a film based on the poetry of Sohrab Sepehri and set in the 60s or 70s, appeared (anachronistically) clad in veils that have become widespread only after 1979! Nonetheless, female directors were surprisingly independent and aggressive in handling their subject matter.[42]

The Islamic regime has embarked on a challenging road to the cultural restoration of Islamic values in a predominantly secular world. Despite the regime's efforts to insulate Iran from the Western world, an oil economy, permeable borders, and a deeply urbanized and internationalized population have undermined such efforts. Sale of audio and video cassettes of Western cultural imports have soared. The sale of VCRs, however, were soon curtailed by government confiscation and a ban on imports. Literature is increasingly popular but also censored if lacking in Islamic values. Several classical poets such as Omar Khayyam (extolling wine, women, song, and skepticism) have been removed from bookshops. However, others such as Ferdowsi (glorifying the pre-Islamic past) and Hafez (castigating clerical hypocrisy) enjoy a new popularity. Fiction, both Persian and foreign, are also enjoying good sales. And sales of foreign translations such as *Ghorresh-i-tufan (Wuthering Heights)* and *Bina-vayan (Les Miserables)* are also on the rise.[43] Following the end of the war with Iraq,

Khomeini's death, and the beginning of the presidency of Rafsanjani in 1989, a more relaxed cultural policy seems to be forming.

Education in the Islamic Republic

To achieve cultural integration in the field of education, the regime has attempted to revamp the entire educational system into an Islamic mold. These reforms have taken two major routes, including textbook and structural reforms. A revolution in the educational system was considered so urgent that only nine days after the victory of the revolution, on 20 February 1979, Ayatollah Khomeini demanded fundamental change in the primary, secondary, and tertiary textbooks to purify them of all past secular and foreign influences. The task of rewriting textbooks was practically complete by 1981. After that time, except for some minor additions or omissions, no major rewriting has taken place. By 1986, seven hundred topics from 636 textbooks had been changed at the elementary and secondary school levels, especially in the social sciences, humanities, and religious studies. By 1989, 10 percent of the textbooks had been written in the post-revolutionary period, while the remaining 90 percent were new editions of pre-1979 ones.[44]

Analyzing the new textbooks from the perspective of socialization of schoolchildren, Golnar Mehran has divided the values they attempt to inculcate into four major categories: (1) the attributes of a New Islamic Person; (2) political beliefs; (3) cultural values; and (4) role models. Martyrdom seems to be the central unifying theme in the socialization of Islamic children into a New Islamic Person. Aside from the traditional Islamic attributes of belief in God, love of nature, piety and chastity, honesty, trustworthiness, thrift and frugality, knowledge, sense of responsibility and dependability, loyalty and devotion, modesty, simplicity, and passion for equality and justice, it is argued that the New Islamic Person must be ready to martyr herself or himself for the cause of the revolution. Schoolchildren are inculcated with the belief that a society based on martyrdom can never be conquered, since surrender and defeat come about only as a result of fear of death. "A nation that believes in martyrdom," declares a chapter on martyrdom in the social science textbook of secondary schools, "will never be enslaved." The idea of martyrdom is then extended to relations between the individual and the state. According to the new textbooks, these relations must be based on unity, support, trust, and mutual assistance. The individual must assist the state in every conceivable way by obeying the laws and acting as "the eyes and ears of the state." Since government is based on the laws laid down by God and the Prophet and government belongs to the people, this is entirely natural. By contrast to dictatorial regimes in which elaborate security organizations are required, in the Islamic Republic people must be the intelligence service of the state.[45]

With respect to political beliefs, the new textbooks teach children that in Islam, religion and politics are not separate. The mosque is presented as a community center in which religious and political matters are jointly discussed. However, before the revolution, the textbooks point out, this cardinal principle of Islamic polity had been undermined by the secular tendencies from two sources of external as well as internal threat: Westoxication *(gharbzadegi)* [46] and Eastoxication *(sharqzadegi)*. Westoxication is a concept borrowed from the modern Iranian novelist and social critic Jalal al-Ahmad, whose book under the same title became a major source of ideological inspiration for the revolution.[47] As a critic of the developmentalist policies of the shah's regime, al-Ahmad argued that Western neocolonialism often penetrated the minds and souls of the nations of the Third World through a pathology called "Westoxication," a total and irrational fascination with everything Western at the expense of the indigenous cultural heritage. His remedy for this disease was a return to the national self. Similarly, the Islamic textbooks argue, Eastoxication is a pathological obsession among intellectuals with Marxist and communist ideologies. Negating religion as "the opiate of the masses," these intellectuals wittingly or unwittingly have detached themselves from the masses and served the interests of the colonial powers in the Soviet camp. "Neither East nor West, Islam is best" is therefore the proud slogan of the Islamic Republic.

With respect to cultural values, cultural imperialism has been the chief target of the new textbooks. This has been defined primarily as neocolonialism, a new form of dependency that operates mainly through cultural dependence by "brainwashing" and humiliating Third World nations, leading them to blind imitation of the West and complete denial of their own values, beliefs, and traditions. Cultural autonomy is not possible, however, unless one rejects alien ideologies and returns to an indigenous cultural self. Franz Fanon is one of the few non-Iranian and non-Islamic sources used to substantiate these views.[48] Both the diagnosis and proposed therapy have been largely inspired by Fanon's psychoanalytical view of the problem. Fanon had argued that to exorcise their colonial oppressors from their psyche, the oppressed need to reject their "white" Western masks and return to their own "black" faces. In the case of Iran, the new textbooks teach, cultural independence can be attained by totally rejecting Western models and returning to an Iranian-Islamic identity.

With respect to role models, the new textbooks provide a hierarchy of the Shi'a Islamic saints and heroes ranging from Imam Hussain and Imam 'Ali [49] to the oppositionist ulama as exemplary lives to be emulated. In this pantheon of heroes, however, a dark corner is reserved for the countermodels to be abhorred, that is, the Westoxicated intellectuals. They are introduced as the "fifth column of imperialism and neocolonialism," the main agents of economic, political, and cultural dependence. The new textbooks have thus undertaken a major rewriting of Iranian history, in which kings and their underlings are castigated while Islamic Imams and ulama are portrayed as true heroes. The focus is particularly on the role of the ulama in the anti-imperialist struggles of Iran in modern history. As Mehran reports:

> Many passages are devoted to Ayatollah Shirazi's role in the Tobacco Protest of 1891–92; the oppositional role of the ulama during the Constitutional Revolution of 1905–11; the "martyrdom" of Ayatollah Modarres during the reign of Reza Pahlavi; the activities of religious leaders during the oil nationalization movement of the early 1950s; and, finally, the role and leadership of

the ulama in the 1979 revolution. Yet the life and struggle of no single religious leader has been discussed as extensively as that of Ayatollah Khomeini. His personal characteristics, social viewpoints, political beliefs and action, speeches, and writings constitute a significant portion of social studies textbooks.[50]

The revolutionary regime also reinforced textbook reform with a structural reform of the educational system. In 1986 the High Council for Cultural Revolution established a Council for Fundamental Change in the Educational System, consisting of two members of the ulama, three deputies of the Ministry of Education, three members of the Planning Commission of the High Council for Cultural Revolution, one member from the High Council for Education, two "conscientious and committed" teachers, a member from the Ministry of Budget and Planning, and the director of the Education Research Planning Institute.[51] The council was given about six months to prepare its report; it consists of five chapters and four appendixes as follows:

1. The Foundations of Islamic Education
2. The Objectives of Islamic Education
3. The Principles Governing the Educational System
4. The Structure of the Educational System
   General Educational Cycle
   Comprehensive Educational Cycle—Scientific and Applied
5. The Implementation Plan of the Educational System

A1. Resolution of the High Council for Cultural Revolution
A2. Survey of the Problems and Bottlenecks of Education
A3. Survey of the Activities Relating to the Reform of the Educational System
A4. Report of the Commission for Fundamental Change in the Educational System.[52]

The structure of the new educational system is summarized in table 13.1. As the figure shows, the pre-university educational system is divided into two main parts. The first part, the General Educational Cycle, lasts nine years and includes three different stages: *(a)* Foundation *(assas)*, lasting two years; *(b)* Core *(arkan)*, lasting four years; and *(c)* Guidance *(ershad)*, lasting three years. The cycle is compulsory, covering the minimum education considered necessary for all Iranian citizens. Compared to the previous admission age of six, the optimum admission age for children is considered to be five and a half years. The aims of education during this cycle are basically the same for everyone with some variations according to gender, age, and geographic location. A Certificate of General Education is granted to all those who successfully complete the cycle.

The second part is the Comprehensive, Applied, and Scientific Educational Cycle. Its duration varies according to which of its two main branches a student pursues. The Comprehensive Secondary Branch lasts three years, including nine proposed

TABLE 13.1
THE OLD AND NEW EDUCATIONAL SYSTEMS IN IRAN

	Old System	New System
Elementary education	5 yrs	6 yrs = 2 yrs Foundation; 4 yrs Core
Secondary education	7 yrs = 3 yrs Guidance + 4 yrs Secondary	6 yrs = 3 yrs Guidance + 3 yrs Comprehensive Secondary
General education (universal and compulsory)	8 yrs = 5 yrs Primary + 3 yrs Guidance	9 yrs = 2 yrs Foundation + 4 yrs Core + 3 yrs Guidance
Pre-university education	12 yrs = 8 yrs General + 4 yrs Secondary	12 yrs = 9 yrs General + 3 yrs Comprehensive Secondary

Source: Islamic Republic of Iran, *Tarh-i-kulliat-i-nezam-i-amuzesh va parvaresh jumhuriy-i-islami-ye iran* (Outline of the educational system of the Islamic Republic of Iran) (Tehran: Headquarters of Fundamental Change in the Educational System, 1988), p. 85.

areas of subject orientation, and leads to a certificate in the student's chosen area. The branch allows students to pursue their special talents and career interests leading to further studies or the job market. The Vocational Branch lasts more or less one year, offering four different fields of training and leading to its own appropriate certificate. Those holding this certificate can receive a secondary school diploma by passing the General Education courses of the Comprehensive Branch and any of its chosen areas of subject orientation.

In both these branches, the government provides the necessary facilities for adult and remedial education. In the design of the curriculum, gender, age, and regional differences are fully considered. Gender differentiation is particularly emphasized by segregation of the sexes until university education and the assignment of different sex roles to boys and girls in their respective educational careers. To implement these reforms, the educational capabilities of the service and manufacturing sectors of the economy are also employed. As compared to the old system, the new primary and secondary educational cycles last about twelve years, as shown in table 13.1.

In contrast to the primary and secondary levels, the universities proved more difficult to change. Due to the political turmoils of the early 1980s in which the liberal Islamic, Marxist, and Marxist Islamic elements among the students posed strong opposition to clerical hegemony, the universities were closed down for a few years before reopening under new management. The new admission rules are based more on ideological commitment than academic achievement. The system has become more selective after the revolution. In a number of disciplines, fewer than one in ten applicants is offered admission to Tehran University. The government reserves more than a third of the available places for handicapped veterans of the Iran-Iraq War, family members of the war dead—"the families of the martyrs"—and others who have somehow sacrificed for the revolution. Some argue that the quota is closer to 40 percent. In the debate between *ta'ahhod* (ideological commitment) and *takhassos* (technical knowledge), the former principle won out in the late 1980s in the selection of both students and faculty. The restructured schools and universities also made rigorous courses on the history and teachings of Islam compulsory. A news report on the state of Iranian universities in 1990 suggests, however, continued student discontent over the lowering of standards and lack of freedom.[53]

To integrate traditional Islamic sciences with modern perspectives, the university curricula in humanities and social sciences were particularly targeted. One notable endeavor in this direction was the creation of an elite Islamic center, Imam Sadeq University, that combines traditional Shi'a curriculum with modern studies of politics, economics, and communications. ISU is located in northern Tehran on the site of the former Iran Center for Management Studies built under the shah in cooperation with Harvard Business School in the style of the medieval Islamic madrasas. The university prides itself on academic freedom and excellence. The students study modern ideologies and Western social science theories in light of Islamic principles.

If the scholarly and literary journals as well as government-sponsored studies are any indication of an emerging Islamic culture, continuities seem to outweigh discontinuities. Islamic concepts and Western intellectual borrowings are used side by side without any apparent concern for possible contradictions. The document on reorganization of the educational system,[54] for example, quotes Islamic sources (the Prophet and Imam Ja'afar Sadeq) as well as Western thinkers (Jean Piaget, Stanley Hill, H. Field) to support its particular curricular proposals for the students' stages of development. In literary journals (e.g., *Keyhan Farhangi*), poststructuralist views are freely presented without much concern that their radical relativism might be contradictory to Islamic views.

On another cultural front also—the language front—continuities seem to outweigh discontinuities. Before the revolution, the issue of language had been greatly politicized. Under the two Pahlavi monarchs, an Imperial Academy of Languages *(Farhangestan)* was engaged in the modernization of Farsi to purge it of foreign (including Arabic) words and to develop a scientific vocabulary. Most of these efforts, particularly the purging of Arabic, were severely criticized by the clerical opposition as another sign of the regime's arrogant tampering with Iran's Islamic heritage. In the post-revolutionary period, however, most of the Academy's coinage are being constantly used in the press, broadcasting, and government publications. In fact, the word *rasaneh,* which had been proposed for the word "medium," found its way into article 175 of the Islamic Constitution on the mass media.[55] Cultural integration thus seems to be taking its natural course, rather independent of passing ideological fads.

At the more grass-roots level, the rise of mosque libraries for young people has placed Iran fourth in the world in the number of active popular or religious libraries.[56] In addition, a revival of the home *maktabs* (Qur'anic schools) in several provincial cities such as Yazd and Tabriz has been identified by government authorities as a positive development in Islamic education of preschoolers. This revival, however, is counterbalanced by the view that government must watch over such maktabs, largely managed by housewives and local mullahs, in order to avoid the health and educational hazards of the traditional ones.[57] The same document argues that in accordance with the 1986 census, some 37 percent of the population have a mother tongue other than Farsi. Although some 82 percent of Iran's fifty million population can understand and speak Farsi, this figure drops to 67 percent for children up to the age of nine. The document argues that the special needs of this population must be carefully taken into account.

Since 1989, private schools at the primary and secondary levels have been allowed and are rapidly growing in number and stature.

Conclusion

This essay has argued that the Islamic revolution in Iran represents a political and cultural backlash against nearly two centuries of Western, secular domination; that the discourse of Islamic fundamentalism reflects the cultural, political, and economic dualism between a secular, compradore, Iranian elite and a second stratum of elite consisting of the ulama, the bazaar merchants, and the liberal intellectuals challenging the dominant discourses of monarchy, nationalism, and developmentalism; and finally, that the impact of the fundamentalist discourse and practice on the educational and media systems, though profound, also reveals some strong continuities in the course of Iranian modernization.

In a larger context, the Islamic revolution in Iran reflects a more extensive revolt in the Islamic world. Under the spell of Western domination, the Islamic world has employed several competing secular and religious ideologies and the technologies of traditional and modern media and schools for economic accumulation, political legitimation, social mobilization, and cultural integration. The cultural schism of the Muslim world between the Western-oriented, secular elites, armed with their scientific and technological discourse, and the religious masses and leaderships, engaged in an Islamic counterdiscourse, has erupted into the open. While the secular ideologies of progress (nationalism, liberalism, and Marxism) have lost much of their appeal, the Islamic ideologies of reform and revolution have gained momentum. The Islamic revolution in Iran has presented the first model for those who have argued for a wholesale Islamization of polity, economy, and society. However, given the intractable domestic and international problems of modernization, Iran has also demonstrated that the road to a purely Islamic society is not an easy one. Although the repressive forces that led to the Iranian revolution continue in most other Islamic countries, the lessons of Iran seem to have already alerted the ruling elites and somewhat tempered public enthusiasm for the radical projects of revolutionary Islam.

To achieve modern, industrial, democratic, and integrated societies, Iran and the rest of the Islamic world face the central problems of defining their national identity, legitimacy, and community in renewed terms. The resolution of these problems in ethnically heterogeneous and multilingual societies such as Iran's is not an easy task. The fundamental challenge before Islamic societies, as elsewhere in the world, is how to build progressive and prosperous societies without losing those delicate ties of identity, legitimacy, and community which bind modernity with traditions of civility. These national needs also correspond to the cultural and communication needs of the individual, consisting of the needs for identity, legitimacy, and community in an increasingly atomized, individualistic, and callous world. These provide the cement that links the individual needs to those of an increasingly centralized and bureaucratized social system. How adequately these needs are fulfilled in a modern society seems to depend on the extent to which society has provided for individual autonomy, social justice, and political solidarity.

Notes

1. A typical objection by a Muslim reads as follows: "As a Concerned reader interested in accuracy I encourage you to discontinue the Western media practice of referring to Muslim or Islamic fundamentalists. According to my Oxford, Webster's and Thorndike dictionaries, the word 'fundamentalist' relates to orthodox Christian beliefs based on a literal interpretation of the Bible and particularly relates to an American Protestant movement. Obviously this term does not apply to Muslims or Islamic belief.

The very basis of Islamic belief and practice precludes concepts such as orthodox or fundamentalist." The editor of the *Washington Report on Middle Eastern Affairs* 9, no. 6 (November 1990): 82, replies, "We concede entirely that use of the term Islamic fundamentalist seems redundant, since Muslims accept the Holy Qur'an as the word of God, period." Although "fundamentalist" seems redundant, this article uses the term in the specific sense referred to above.

2. Juan Cole, "Shi'i Clerics in Iraq and Iran, 1722–1780: The Akhbari-Usuli Conflict Reconsidered," *Iranian Studies* 18, no. 1 (Winter 1985): 3–34; Edward Mortimer, *Faith and Power: The Politics of Islam* (New York: Random House, 1982), p. 302.

3. The concept of hegemony is borrowed from Antonio Gramsci to suggest the ideological formulations employed by the ruling classes or groups to gain the consent and to enlist the active cooperation of other groups in society, particularly the mobilized sectors. See Antonio Gramsci, *Prison Notebooks* (New York: International Publishers, 1971).

4. Afghanistan and the central Asian Soviet Muslim republics are clear exceptions to this generalization, but since communists are perceived as "godless," that is even more cause for religious revolt.

5. The voluminous studies of the Islamic revolution in Iran available in English mostly bear out this contention. See Ervand Abrahamian, *Iran between Two Revolutions* (Princeton: Princeton University Press, 1982); Shahrough Akhavi, *Religion and Politics in Contemporary Iran: Clergy-State Relations in the Pahlavi Period* (Albany: State University of New York Press, 1980); Shaul Bakhash, *The Reign of the Ayatollahs: Iran and the Islamic Revolution* (New York: Basic Books, 1984); Farideh Farhi, "Class Struggles, the State, and Revolution in Iran," in Berch Berberoglu, ed., *Power and Stability in the Middle East* (London: Zed Books, 1989); Nikkie Keddie, *Roots of Revolution: An Interpretive History of Modern Iran* (New Haven: Yale University Press, 1981); Jerrold D. Green, *Revolution in Iran: The Politics of Countermobilization* (New York: Praeger, 1982); Farhad Kazemi, ed., "Iranian Revo-

lution in Perspective," special issue of *Iranian Studies* 13, no's 1–4 (1980); idem, *Poverty and Revolution in Iran: The Migrant Poor, Urban Marginality and Politics* (New York: New York University Press, 1980); Farhang Rajaee, *Islamic Values and Worldview: Khomeini on Man, the State and International Politics* (Lanham, Md.: University Press of America, 1983); Homa Katouzian, *The Political Economy of Modern Iran, 1926–1979* (New York: New York University Press, 1981); Haleh Afshar, ed., *Iran: Revolution in Turmoil* (Albany: State University of New York Press, 1985); Assef Bayat, *Workers and Revolution in Iran* (London: Zed Press, 1987); Robert E. Huyser, *Mission to Tehran* (New York: Harper and Row, 1986).

6. Marvin Zonis, "The Political and Social Systems of Iran in the Year 1990" (Paper, December 1977).

7. Richard Cottam, *Nationalism in Iran; Updated through 1978*, 2d ed. (Pittsburgh: University of Pittsburgh Press, 1979).

8. Queen Farah headed a number of social and cultural organizations but exerted considerable influence on cultural policy through her able cousin Reza Qotbi, who headed National Iranian Radio and Television, a nine thousand–member organization with its own theater, symphony orchestra, and publishing, public opinion survey, and social research affiliates; for greater detail, see Majid Tehranian et al., eds., *Communication Policy for National Development: A Comparative Perspective* (London: Routledge and Kegan Paul, 1977), chap. 12.

9. In 1975, I interviewed some one hundred members of the Iranian communication elite, including major government officials responsible for cultural, educational, media and religious affairs, education and media professionals, and members of the Iranian Shi'a ulama. A few of the ulama interviewed, such as Ayatollah Mottahari and Ayatollah Nuri, played leading roles in the subsequent revolutionary developments. For a fuller account of these interviews and survey findings, see Tehranian et al., *Communication Policy for National Development;* and Majid Tehranian, *Socio-Economic and Communication Indicators in Development*

Planning: A Case Study of Iran (Paris: UNESCO, 1981).

10. An anecdote reported to me by Dr. Mehdi Zarghami, chancellor of Aryamehr University at the time, reveals the extent of the shah's naive belief in the power of the media. In a personal audience, Dr. Zarghami reported to the shah that his students were more affected by Islamic than Marxist ideologies. The shah, who believed otherwise, admonished him that if so, television and its seductive programming (e.g., Gugush's songs and dances!) would soon take care of that problem.

11. Tehranian et al., *Communication Policy for National Development;* Tehranian, *Socio-Economic and Communication Indicators;* Elihu Katz and George Wedell, *Broadcasting in the Third World: Promise and Performance* (Cambridge: Harvard University Press, 1978).

12. Majid Tehranian, "Iran: Communication, Alienation, Revolution," InterMedia 7 (March 1979).

13. In his monograph *Che bayad kard?* (What is to be done?) (Tehran, 1352/1973), Ali Shari'ati provides a manifesto for this center and its Islamic educational mission.

14. Literally, "Trusteeship of the Jurist," published also under the title "Hokumat-i-Islami" (Islamic government); see R. Khomeini, *Islam and Revolution,* trans. and ann. by Hamid Algar (Berkeley, Calif.: Mizan Press, 1981). For a more detailed analysis of the doctrine, see Majid Tehranian, "Khomeini's Doctrine of Legitimacy," in A. J. Parel, ed., *Under the Upas Tree* (Newbury Park, Calif.: Sage, forthcoming).

15. The first printing press in Iran was introduced by the Armenian scholar and priest Katchadur in 1639, just 190 years after its introduction in Germany. It was, however, mainly devoted to printing books in Armenian. Printing in Persian was brought to Iran by the two leading nineteenth-century reformers, Crown Prince Abbas Mirza and Prime Minister Amir Kabir. During the last two decades of the nineteenth century, two types of publications were emerging in Iran which corresponded to the cultural and political dualism that erupted forcefully into the open in the Islamic revolution. The rise of a pan-Islamic movement led by Seyyed Jamal ed-Din Assadabadi (known as al-Afghani) gave rise to the publication of a number of newspapers, including the famous *Al-Urwatul Wuthqa,* published in Paris and circulated in many Islamic countries. A second type of publication consisted of the newspapers of a secular, liberal, and nationalist orientation edited by a Western-educated elite promoting Western ideas. These included *Qanun* (London), *Akhtar* (Istanbul), and *Hab al-Matin* (Calcutta). In addition to the daily press, a very lively tradition of *shabnameh* (nightly press) was also initiated by the underground, secret societies of the Constitutionalist movement. Their function was similar to the function of *zamizdat* (the Soviet underground press) in the Russian revolutionary and dissident movements. The emergence of a popular, anti-imperialist, and Constitutionalist movement at the turn of the century brought these two trends together for a while. Some twenty-two newspapers were published in exile before the Constitutional Revolution of 1905–11, returning home in the ensuing years. This gave rise to a virtual renaissance of modern Persian poetry and prose experimenting with new genres and topics dealing with a new sense of national and social consciousness. However, the political alliance between the liberal intellectuals, the bazaar merchants, and the ulama in the Constitutionalist movement proved itself ultimately ineffective in challenging the authority of the Great Powers and the domination of the traditional ruling elites. The secret Anglo-Russian Treaty of 1907 dividing the country into spheres of influence, the wartime occupation of the country by the Allied forces, withdrawal of the Russians subsequent to the October Revolution of 1917, the abortive Anglo-Persian Treaty of 1919 reducing Iran to the position of a virtual British protectorate, and the rise of Reza Khan as a new strongman in the coup of 1921—all these events brought the new, liberal press to a sudden halt. New rules of strict censorship were soon imposed. Opposition newspapers had to flee once again into exile, while domestic papers remained largely

under censorship. For the history of the press in Iran, see E. G. Browne, *The Press and Poetry of Modern Persia* (Cambridge: Cambridge University Press, 1914); Hamid Mowlana, *Seiri-i-irtibatat-i-ijtima'i dar Iran* (Evolution of social communication in Iran) (Tehran: College of Mass Communication Publications, 1979); and Hamid Mowlana, "Mass Media Systems and Communication," in Michael Adams, ed., *The Middle East* (New York: Facts on File Publications, 1988).

16. Tehranian et al., *Communications Policy for National Development*, chap. 2.

17. Amin Banani, *The Modernization of Iran* (Stanford: Stanford University Press, 1961).

18. Majid Tehranian, *Andishe daneshgah* (The idea of the university) (Tehran: Bu-Ali Sina University, 1976).

19. Unless otherwise indicated, all the statistics in this article are drawn from Majid Tehranian, *Socio-Economic and Communication Indicators*, where their exact sources in Iranian government publications and census reports are indicated. Despite their government source, or rather because of it, statistics in developing countries such as Iran are often subject to irregularities and sometimes to conscious doctoring. The figures should be considered therefore only as estimates based on the best information available.

20. Notable exceptions to this rule were Algar and Keddie; see Hamed Algar, *Religion and State in Iran, 1785–1906* (Berkeley: University of California Press, 1969); and idem, *Mirza Malkam Khan: A Study in the History of Iranian Modernism* (Berkeley: University of California Press, 1973); as well as Nikki Keddie, *Religion and Rebellion in Iran: The Tobacco Protest of 1891–1892* (London: Frank Cass, 1966); idem, *An Islamic Response to Imperialism: Political and Religious Writings of Sayyid Jamal al-Din "al-Afghani"* (Berkeley: University of California Press, 1968); and *Sayyid Jamal al-Din "al-Afghani": A Political Biography* (Berkeley: University of California Press, 1972). In the post-revolutionary period, however, a number of excellent studies have somewhat rec-

tified the situation; see Peter J. Chelkowski, ed., *Ta'ziyeh: Ritual and Drama in Iran* (New York: New York University Press and Soroush Press, 1979); Roy Mottahedeh, *The Mantle of the Prophet* (New York: Pantheon Books, 1985); Said Arjomand, ed., *From Nationalism to Revolutionary Islam* (Albany: State University of New York Press, 1984); and idem, *Authority and Political Culture in Shi'ism* (Albany: State University of New York Press, 1988); Michael Fischer, *Iran: From Religious Dispute to Revolution* (Cambridge: Harvard University Press, 1980); Shahrough Akhavi, *Religion and Politics in Contemporary in Iran: Clergy-State Relations in the Pahlavi Period* (Albany: State University of New York Press, 1980); Nikki Keddie, ed., *Religion and Politics in Iran: Shi'ism from Quietism to Revolution* (New Haven: Yale University Press, 1983); and Nikki Keddie and Eric Hoogland, eds., *The Iranian Revolution and the Islamic Republic* (Syracuse: Syracuse University Press, 1986).

21. Asghar Fathi, "The Role of Minbar in Islam," *Journal of Communication* (1979).

22. Mehrdad Bahar, "Lecture Notes," Iran Communication and Development Institute, 1978.

23. Tehranian, "Iran: Communication, Alienation, Revolution"; idem, "The Curse of Modernity: The Dialectics of Communication and Modernization," *International Social Science Journal* 32, no. 2 (June 1980); idem, "Communication and Revolution in Iran: The Passing of a Paradigm," *Iranian Studies* 13, nos. 1–4, (1980).

24. Ervand Abrahamian, *Radical Islam: The Iranian Mujahedin* (London: Tauris, 1989).

25. See, for instance, "Iran's Nice New Face," *The Economist*, 1 June 1991, p. 37.

26. John Harvey, "Information Service in the Islamic Republic of Iran," *International Library Review* 20 (1988): 273–306.

27. Hamid Mowlana and Mehdi Mohsenian Rad, *Japanese Programs on Iranian Television: A Study in International Flow of Information* (Washington, D.C.: International Communication Program, School of

International Service, American University, 1990), p. 32.

28. Ibid., pp. 22, 34.

29. As Mowlana and Rad, in *Japanese Programs on Iranian Television,* p. 22, report, "Broadcasting has increased from some 170 hours a week in 1978 to 323 in 1986, in thirteen different languages and ranking eighteenth among the world's top twenty major broadcasters. These include such countries as the United States (2,368 hours), the Soviet Union (2,259), China (1,411), Taiwan (1,098), West Germany (821), and Egypt (including Middle East Radio) (820). Iran's external Arabic-language programming exceeds any other initiated in the Arab world. In terms of the weekly program hours to the Middle East, Iran ranks fourth among major international broadcasters with 233 hours/eight languages, following Egypt (495 hours/three languages), the Soviet Union (371 hours/eleven languages), and the British BBC (250 hours/four languages). The United States Voice of America (VOA ranked fifth with 168 hours weekly/three languages)." Mowlana and Rad note that these statistics are compiled from a number of sources, including the BBC, Voice of America, and UNESCO.

30. For an analysis of Iranian immigration to the United States since the revolution, see Mehdi Bozorgmehr and Georges Sabbagh, "High Status Immigrants: A Statistical Profile of Iranians in the United States," *Iranian Studies* 11, nos. 3–4 (1988): 5–35.

31. Published by a monarchist group in Paris, for example, *Iran va Jahan* (Iran and the world) ceased publication after internal schisms occurred within that camp. The Tudeh, the Mujahideen, and the National Front groups have all had their own organs as well, but no single publication out of the opposition groups has achieved much regularity and continuity. Another newspaper, *Kayhan,* published by Mustafa Mesbahzadeh out of London with promonarchy sentiments, may be the closest rival to *International Iran Times.*

32. The oldest of these scholarly journals is *Iranian Studies* (in English), founded by a group of seven Iranian scholars (including the author) who formed the Society for Iranian Studies in 1967. Published by the Foundation of Iranian Studies (financed out of an endowment fund from Princess Ashraf), *Iran Nameh* (in Farsi) was initially edited by Jalal Matini in Washington, D.C., and covered historical and literary themes; it is now edited by Dariush Shayegan and Dariush Ashuri and covers social science topics focusing on problems of modernization. A number of other literary and political journals, such as *Par* (Feather), *Cheshmanadaz* (Perspective), and *Azadi* (Freedom), have a more polemical style to suit their oppositionist readerships.

33. Tehranian, *Socio-Economic and Communication Indicators.* According to the preliminary census report of 1986, the population of the various ethnic and linguistic regions is as follows: Farsi-speaking regions, 31.2 million; Azari-Turkish-speaking regions, 8 million; Mazandarani- and Guilani-speaking regions (excluding Turkish), 5 million; Kurdish-speaking regions, 3 million; Arab-speaking regions, 1.8 million; Baluchi-speaking regions, 1 million. Islamic Republic of Iran (IRI), 1990, p. 107. This account leaves out some other minority ethnic and linguistic groups such as the Lurs, the Qashqais, the Bakhtiaris, and the Semnanis. Nevertheless, the total of non-Farsi-speaking regions comprises 37 percent of the country's population.

34. Harvey, "Information Service in the Islamic Republic of Iran."

35. Tehranian et. al., *Communication Policy for National Development;* and Tehranian, *Socio-Economic and Communication Indicators.*

36. As quoted by Mowlana and Rad, *Japanese Programs on Iranian Television,* p. 35, from "Imam Khomeini's Last Will and Testament," in *Kayhan International* (Tehran) 10, no. 2446 (24 June 1989): 6.

37. For an overall analysis of Japanese television programs in Iran, see Mowlana

and Rad, *Japanese Programs on Iranian Television*.

38. Ibid., p. 16; Youichi Ito, "The Changing Trade Winds," in *Communication Yearbook,* ed. J. Anderson, vol. 13 (Newbury Park, Calif.: Sage Publications, 1989).

39. The ratings were as follows: "Oshin," 76 percent; two Iranian series, 64 percent and 63 percent each; a British series, 52 percent; another Japanese film, 45 percent; and a third foreign-made program, 37 percent. See Mowlana and Rad, *Japanese Programs on Iranian Television,* p. 40.

40. Ibid., p. 60.

41. Taqvaii's *Nakhoda Khorshid,* Kia-Rostami's sensitive *Khan-ye Dust Kojast,* and Beyzai's *Bashu* are the notable exceptions. The industry has grown considerably in the last decade. According to Hamid Nafici, organizer of the festival, film is very much in demand as one of the few sources of mass entertainment. Box office sales of some, notably *Tenants* by Mehrjou'i, have exceeded all expectations. According to Mehrjou'i, "While there is every opportunity to keep up to date with foreign cinema through local theaters and festivals, the public is increasingly interested in Iranian films." See Mahasti Afshar, "Notes on a Decade of Iranian Cinema at UCLA," *Newsletter of Association of Harvard and MIT Iranian Alumni* 1, no. 2 (July 1990): 4–5.

42. Afshar, "Notes on a Decade of Iranian Cinema," pp. 4–5.

43. Harvey, "Information Service in the Islamic Republic of Iran," p. 277.

44. Golnar Mehran, "Socialization of Schoolchildren in the Islamic Republic of Iran," *Iranian Studies* 12, no. 1 (1989): 37.

45. Ibid.

46. This term has been also translated as "Westomania," but "Westoxication" connotes a richer meaning in English in that the individual so addicted, just like any intoxicated individual, enjoys the conditions of his own addiction.

47. Jalal Al-Ahmad, *Gharbzadegi* [Westoxication] (Tehran, n. d.). For an anthol-ogy of Al-Ahmad's writings in translation, see Jalal Al-Ahmad, *Iranian Society: An Anthology of writings by Jalal Al-e Ahmad,* comp. and ed. Michael C. Hillmann (Lexington, Ky.: Mazda Publishers, 1982).

48. Franz Fanon, *The Wretched of the Earth* (New York: Grove Press, 1965); idem, *A Dying Colonialism* (New York: Grove Press, 1967); *Black Skin, White Masks* (New York: Grove Press, 1967).

49. Imam Hussain, the son-in-law of the Prophet, is the third Shi'a Imam, considered to be the Shah of Martyrs *(shah-i-shahidan)*. Imam Ali was Imam Hussain's father, the Prophet's cousin, son-in-law and, according to Shi'ites, the rightful successor.

50. Mehran, "Socialization of Schoolchildren," p. 48.

51. For a list of the membership, see Islamic Republic of Iran (IRI), *Tarh-i-kulliat-i-nezam-i-amuzesh va parvaresh jumhuriy-i-islami-ye iran* (Outline of the educational system of the Islamic Republic of Iran) (Tehran: Administrative Headquarters of Fundamental Change in the Education?ʾ. System, 1988).

52. Ibid.

53. "Yes, the revolution has done some good things, but maybe we will need a second revolution, especially in the way we are educated," said Leila, a twenty-one year-old science student at Tehran University, perhaps the most important and prestigious university in Iran. As she hurried between classes, her black head scarf fluttering in a steamy breeze, Leila asked an American visitor whether college students in his country were forced to wear special restrictive clothing, or were plagued by a shortage of professors, or were barred from even the most innocuous classroom conversation with a student of the opposite sex. Her questions were clearly rhetorical. "Universities must have freedom," said Leila's friend, who gave her name as Maryam. "This university and this nation must have more freedom." A twenty-four-year-old theater student compared the university to a gardener who "has picked out the best flowers—us, the stu-

dents—but who will not water them." She added, "there are so few teachers that it seems we must teach ourselves." *New York Times,* 23 July 1990, pp. 1–2.

54. Islamic Republic of Iran (IRI), p. 99–100.

55. Through membership in the Social Science Committee of the Farhangestan, I had a role in the introduction and dissemination of some of these neologisms.

56. Harvey, "Information Service in the Islamic Republic of Iran," p. 306.

57. Islamic Republic of Iran (IRI), pp. 106–7.

Jewish Fundamentalism in Israeli Education

Michael Rosenak

We may approach fundamentalism and fundamentalistic education in one of two ways. The first is to limit the study to its culture of origin, Christian Protestantism, and to insist that kindred phenomena in other religious traditions and communities be termed and treated differently. Thus we may speak of Islamic zealotry or Jewish fanaticism, but not of Jewish or Islamic fundamentalism. The other option is to use the term "fundamentalism" whenever we are confronted with specific traits among extremists of various faith-communities who articulate their discontents with modern liberal societies, feel threatened by them, and devise strategies of self-defense, or even aggression, against them. In our discussion of "extreme" Jewish education in Israel, we assume that the term "fundamentalism" is indeed useful for understanding discrete religious cultures and educational concepts and systems, and that it helps shed light on data that might otherwise remain obscure or even exotic.

At the same time, in assuming certain commonalities between fundamentalist-like groups, we may not lose sight of differences in culture, theology, and social context among them. Therefore, two essential prerequisites for honest and accurate investigation of our subject must be kept in mind: First, a particular fundamentalism should not be defined, described, and subsequently evaluated from within a cultural framework and tradition that is alien to it, so that the term does not become a pretext for polemics and cultural self-aggrandizement. For example, whether a particular Jewish movement is indeed fundamentalistic cannot be established on the basis of its spiritual distance from particular doctrines or assumptions of, say, Western liberalism or American Protestantism.[1] Such an approach would imply that to be religious or a member of the "wrong" religion makes one a fundamentalist. To escape such biases, one must carefully examine each movement within the context of its own religious tradition, the one it claims to represent "most authentically." Thus, the historical-spiritual tradition within which the fundamentalist movement arises must be considered alongside the historical, political, and social forces that provoked the "zealots" to make their specific emphases and perhaps unintended innovations in the heritage they are intent on protecting.

Second, since various fundamentalist movements within the same religion have access to the same traditions and appropriate them, it makes sense to anticipate that all of them, and their educational conceptions, will have something in common. Yet, if they stress diverse aspects of the tradition and interpret sacred texts and present historical circumstances differently, they are indeed disparate movements and we may expect them to champion different social ideals and to have different priorities. Thus, we wish to see how diverse movements understand and adapt the theological and educational traditions of Judaism and which alternatives for conceiving the "educated person" proceed from each of them.

Accordingly, a brief statement of the biblical story as it sets foundations for Jewish theology and its cultural language, and the place of education or the "study of Torah" within that universe of discourse, is a necessary first step in understanding what fundamentalist groups claim to be continuing and, under present circumstances, defending.

Elements of Jewish Theology and Educational Philosophy

The theological foundations of Judaism laid out in its sources and elaborated in its ongoing life and literature may be summarized along the lines suggested by such thinkers as Kaufmann, Fackenheim, and Buber, as follows.[2]

God created the world in accordance with a design, that it be "good." Yet the moral purpose of the creation dictated that the pinnacle of God's handiwork be a free agent "created in His image" who would choose to live in a loving (thus free) and moral (thus obedient) relationship to God, expressed largely, perhaps mainly, in his relationship to other people. Humankind constitutes both the ultimate promise of God's creation—that it be good—and the only impediment to its successful consummation. For human beings, having free will, can obey or disobey, can live in covenant and love, or rebel ("sin") and suffer alienation.

The biblical "story" is elaborated in a medley of descriptions and digressions in the talmudic and midrashic literature. God gave commandments to humans as evidence of His loving relationship and of His moral purpose and sovereignty. But twice (in Eden and in the generation of Noah) He was spurned and the world became violent and corrupt. God then made His covenant with a particular "family" which promised to "do righteousness and justice," the family of Abraham. The terms of this covenant—and testimony to God's "presence" and partnership in it—is the Torah. The Torah makes it possible and obligatory for its recipients, Israel, to live a holy life even in a world of idols. The Torah, the blueprint for God's all-inclusive kingdom, holds the promise that ultimately all will accept "the yoke of Heaven." The choosing of Israel constitutes, therefore, a strategic retreat by God, who requires witnesses that He is the Lord, until the latter days when all nations "will ascend to the mount of the

Lord." This will mark the advent of Redemption, the achievement of God's purpose in creating the world. And the Torah is also a testimony of God's love for His witnesses, who have chosen Him and His way.

The Torah and the covenant are eternal, yet they are a heavy burden, both historically—for the world is not yet God's—and normatively. For while pious Gentiles need observe only the seven Noachide commandments[3] to be accounted righteous individuals, Israel has undertaken to be a holy people and to observe a comprehensive social and political regimen in addition to the laws of individual morality.

As a holy people, covenanted to carry the "yoke of God's kingdom," Israel has received a land from the "Maker of Heaven and earth." This is the Lord's inheritance; Israel must carry out the edicts of the divine king. This kingdom is to be a microcosm of the anticipated universal domain of God. When Israel sins by not discharging its mandate, God exiles the people from their land, as He exiled Adam and Eve from Eden. Having been disloyal to God's purpose, Israel is "vomited out of the land,"[4] sent into exile.

Exile, *Galut,* is a concept laden with political, religious, and existential layers of meaning. It signifies a precarious existence among the nations; it also bespeaks alienation and remoteness from God, for the Torah cannot be fully carried out in Galut, where Israel lacks a society. Moreover, Galut describes the malaise of the world before the coming of the Messiah (redemption). On this existential level, Galut connotes that the Torah, meant to be the teaching for humanity, is not at home in the unredeemed world. Thus, those who remain faithful to it, carrying it with them through the centuries and lands of exile, are really somehow living outside the world. The (unredeemed) world is transient, while the Torah and its adherents are eternal, waiting for Galut to end, for history again to become invested with meaning.

The notion of Galut introduces a startling paradox. The choosing of a historical people, the assignation of a land, and the demand that every concrete aspect of life be lived "according to the commandments" testify to the earthly and concrete disposition of the biblical-talmudic tradition. Holiness, in its ideal state, is not achieved through the escape of the soul from the world but in the "descent" of Transcendence into the concrete realities and experiences of people—who are themselves required to bring down the Divine Presence, to be worthy of having it dwell among them.

The symbolic—yet characteristically concrete—depiction of this ideal reality, of God in the midst of His people, as an ongoing reality, had been first represented in the Bible by the Sanctuary in the wilderness. Later, the Presence "dwells," according to the biblical narrative, in the Temple in Jerusalem and in the kingdom established by Israel in His land. It requires radical reinterpretation for this major theme of Judaism, God dwelling in the midst of His people, to remain meaningful in Galut; this is achieved by investing the concept of Torah with all possible attributes of glory, significance, and Providence. For the talmudic sages, who sought constantly to "increase Torah and to magnify it," it is the pinnacle of worth: the "crown of Torah" is greater than the crowns of priesthood and royalty.[5] For Torah is everything: law, sanctuary, devotion, and hope. In Galut, and even in postcommonwealth *Eretz Yisrael*

(Land of Israel), God and Israel have no "ground" for covenantal meeting but the Torah.

Accordingly, the rabbinic sages elevate to the status of a primary *mitzvah* (commandment) the biblical requirement to "rehearse these words" of religious creed and action to one's children; the obligation to study the Torah is declared equivalent to all others. [6] Everyone, not only children, must study Torah. Education is an obligation imposed on parents and the community to enable the young person to become an adult capable of studying Torah and carrying out its commandments. In the talmudic conception, the world "exists only by virtue of the Torah." Hence its acquisition by the young is of cosmic significance in that it enables them to continue the world-preserving activity of adult "learners." Therefore, one who studies Torah for extrinsic goals unrelated to the very meaning of life has not understood what "learning Torah" is. For while education in Torah, like any educational enterprise, is a community act of cultural socialization, it is also a religious quest. The "world" that must be "maintained" by Torah study is not only the community but also the individual soul.[7]

Maimonides, the renowned medieval philosopher and codifier of Jewish law, set down the *halakha* (law) of Torah study as follows: "Every man in Israel is obliged to study the Torah, whether he is firm of body or suffers from ill health, whether a young man or of advanced age with his strength abated. Even a poor man who is supported by charity and who is obliged to beg at doors and even one with wife and children is obliged to set aside a period for Torah study by day and by night, as it is said, 'Thou shall meditate therein day and night.'"[8]

The Torah which must be studied is not synonymous with, or limited to, the Bible. While the term "the Torah" often refers to the Pentateuch, "Torah" refers to the entire corpus of sacred literature, from the Bible through the Talmud, which is often called the "Oral Torah," and its commentaries. The latter encompasses legal responsa, homiletical and exegetical works, mystical and philosophical treatises, codes of law, and moral as well as pietistic writings.

The basic method and thrust of Torah learning is termed *Midrash,* which denotes *halakhic* (legal) and *haggadic* (nonlegal, homiletic, "philosophical") ways of exploring its "innumerable" meanings. For in the midrashic tradition, the Bible's seeming literal sense is only one of its myriad "true understandings." Therefore, study of the "Oral Torah," most specifically the Talmud, has often been considered the most refined form of "Torah learning." By the first centuries of the Christian era, the Bet Midrash (House of Study) or yeshiva, in which the Talmud was studied almost exclusively, had developed into Jewry's most prestigious educational institution.[9]

Though the entire literature of Torah has traditionally been considered as, in some sense, God's revealed teaching, the Oral Torah is largely a record of deliberation, opinion, decision making—that is, of controversy. The Talmud states that controversy "for the sake of Heaven" contains, on both sides of the argument, "the words of the living God," for the Bible says (Exod. 20:1), "And God spoke all these words."[10]

The scope of the Torah to be studied is itself a subject of controversy. The Talmud rules that "a five-year-old is introduced to the study of Scripture, a ten-year-old to

Mishnah, a thirteen-year-old (to observe) the commandments and a fifteen-year-old to Talmud.[11] Yet it is not exactly agreed what Talmud entails. Maimonides, for example, considers Talmud to consist of philosophical reflections upon the truth of the Torah and a study of its principles.[12] Furthermore, it is clear that Torah, in any canonized sense, does not exhaust the subject matter of education. The Talmud stipulates that parents are also required to teach their children a means of livelihood (a trade) and the arts of self-preservation in the physical environment. From talmudic times to the present, Jews have argued about what real and worthy education should entail. Some associated "real" education almost exclusively with talmudic halakhah and commentaries, even at the expense of Scripture; others insisted that the mystical lore of the *kabbala* was the essence of Torah. As for "external wisdom," some scholars condemned it as leading to heresy; others considered the knowledge of universal wisdom to be a religious duty. In any case, throughout medieval Jewry the primacy of learning and the ideal of being a *talmid chacaham* (Torah scholar) were universally acknowledged.[13]

Modernity, Contemporary Jewish Life, and Fundamentalism

Since the advent of modernity, the ethos of learning described above has been largely abandoned by the mainstream Jewish community. Contemporary educational fundamentalism is, in the main, a response to this state of affairs. Thus it is comprehensible only against the background of circumstances and ideologies which called learning and the theological understanding of Jewish existence into question. These developments include the *Haskalah* (Enlightenment), during which the absolute and adequate truth and value of Torah were qualified or even denied on rationalistic, scientific, or Western-cultural grounds. Typical, yet quite moderate, was the celebrated distinction of Naftali Herz Wessely (late eighteenth century) between *Torat HaShem* (the divine Torah) and *Torat Ha-adam* (the culture of humanity)[14]—whereby he introduced a dichotomy between religion and culture and valued each equally. Such prescriptive distinctions were previously unknown or viewed as sacrilegious. Rabbinic leadership in Eastern and central Europe reacted militantly and uncompromisingly, in part by placing increasing emphasis on learning as a beacon of faithfulness to tradition, which stood opposed to all profane intrusions into Jewish life. A social and spiritual elite was thereby oriented toward ultra-conservatism.[15]

As the Enlightenment spread throughout Europe, there was a steady drift away from traditional belief and practice, exacerbated by the political process of "Emancipation." Emancipation offered Jews full membership in liberal societies (i.e., citizenship) and implicitly encouraged assimilation by way of immersion in the culture of "the nation." Emancipated Jews were required to accept the legal system of the state as exclusively binding (at the expense, ultimately, of the halakha). The privatization of religious life followed as a consequence of the displacement of halakha; religion no longer conferred a clear collective identity.

Two important responses to the threatened demise of Jewish faith and identity which have had an effect on Israeli education were cultural Zionism and neo-Orthodoxy. Cultural Zionism was intended as a solution to the dilemmas posed by Emancipation and as a positive response to the challenge of the Enlightenment. It embraced modernity and secularization, but sought to reconstitute an indigenous national Jewish culture in a modern nation-state that would itself be Jewish, in which Jews would emancipate themselves.[16] The neo-Orthodox, on the other hand, wished to harmoniously blend modern sensibilities, loyalties, and bodies of knowledge with traditional religious attachments, norms, and even a modicum of traditional study. Their slogan was *Torah im Derech Eretz* (Torah and general culture). A far-reaching attempt at such a synthesis was later made by the religious Zionists who wished to be both Orthodox Jews and part of the national renaissance. The most thorough program for blending Orthodox Judaism with socialist Zionism was that of leaders of the religious kibbutz movement, who adopted as their educational ideal the person who would be "a *talmid chacham* (Torah scholar), a *chalutz* (pioneer) and a citizen."[17]

The various modern movements in Jewish education were institutionally established in mandatory Palestine. By the late 1920s, the new Yishuv (the Zionist community) had created three distinct school systems or trends representing the varieties of Zionist ideology. There were the General Zionist schools, with a civic and humanistic-cultural orientation; the Mizrachi (religious Zionist) schools, which combined modern Zionistic civic ideals with adherence to Orthodox Judaism; and the Labor trend, which emphasized pioneering and socialist ideals and reinterpreted the Jewish religious tradition most radically. In addition, there were the educational institutions associated with the ultra-conservative old Yishuv (non-Zionist community). These were later to become a fourth trend, the Independent system, under the auspices of the ultra-orthodox Agudat Yisrael movement. To the right of this system were the ultra-traditionalist institutions that looked askance at the Independent system's willingness to receive authorization—and monies—from the Zionists.

The growth of fundamentalism, originally identified with the fourth trend, was dramatically furthered by a number of contemporary developments. First was the much-celebrated "crisis of modernity" experienced by many Jews with particular intensity because of the trauma of the Holocaust—and what it was perceived to mean about the worth and stability of modern culture, as well as the feasibility and desirability of Jewish participation in it. Second, secular socialist Zionism, the dominant ideal of Israeli society in its formative years, experienced difficulties in transmitting its pioneering ethos and its antimaterialistic ideology to an increasingly consumer-oriented society. Many post-1948 children resented the burden of such seemingly outmoded social idealism, especially since it appeared to represent no more than their parents' rebellion against their parents. Moreover, it often appeared that these ideals were given lip service in the classroom but were not carried out in the increasingly permissive society. A third and ironic development was the large-scale financial support given to ultra-Orthodox education by the secular Israeli government, and the decision to "defer," usually indefinitely, the army service of yeshiva students. This encouraged the development of a haredi "learning community" subculture, in the very midst of the modern Israeli metropolis.[18] Fourth, the Mizrachi schools, surviving in the Israeli government school system under the National-Religious party label, were not notably successful in cultivating loyalty to Orthodox Judaism. This failure led to the establishment of more traditional forms of Zionist religious education, especially of yeshiva high schools, which became the educational "home ground" of a young elite within religious Zionism. Fifth, the dramatic victory of Israel in the Six Day War of 1967 created a sense of deliverance and elation among most of the religious public, especially the youth. Many were convinced that these contemporary events corresponded to prophetic promises of redemption and that the long-awaited messianic era had begun.[19]

In this situation, in which the fabric of modernity seemed to be unraveling, ultra-Orthodox fundamentalism thrived and religious Zionism gradually developed its own fundamentalist-type branches. This essay examines the educational philosophies, ideals, and institutions of these anti-Zionist and Zionist fundamentalists, with particular emphasis on their respective orientations to the outside world. That is, I am concerned with their outreach and influence on outsiders as well as on their own discrete communities. Each of these groups draws upon the common tradition described above; in its affirmations and rejections, each also expresses an educational worldview that is translated into ways of teaching and patterns of influence.

Jewish fundamentalism is here understood as a tradition-based orientation that considers Torah, as interpreted by traditional or charismatic leaders, to be totally comprehensive and exclusive. Torah is the locus of all values; it is religiously adequate and culturally self-contained. Fundamentalists wish to insulate the Torah and the life it prescribes from outside influences; they disdain cultural interactions that would put them at risk. They wish to protect themselves against "false knowledge," that is, against methodologies or data that allegedly militate against the truth of Torah and undermine the Jewish life of covenant.

By fundamentalistic lights, Torah is never enhanced nor will it reveal more of its divine truth by synthesis or even contact with worldly wisdom. Therefore the tension between Torah and anything else, such as socialism, democracy, modern science or general scholarship, is unnecessary at best and usually injurious. It is not productive of greater understanding and should not be seen, as the "modernists" do, as a continuation of the perennial dynamic of Midrash. To engage in significant interaction with anything other-than-Torah as delineated by "Torah authorities" is inconsistent, confused, and heretical.

In all cases, adherents of fundamentalist groups and their educational spokesmen see themselves as steadfastly loyal to the tradition and pointing the way to "return" from culturally foreign adventures. Fundamentalists aim for the unchallenged centrality of religion, as defined by the fundamentalist community and its rabbinical authority, in the behavior, experience, and personality of the "faithful" person. This unqualified religion-centeredness as defined by the fundamentalist authority is seen not only as an existential requirement of individual life but also as the sine qua non of Jewish existence and identity.

It should be clear that fundamentalists, despite their zealous and rigid traditionalism, often propose idiosyncratic interpretations of tradition that are, in some senses, departures from it. Fundamentalists deny or ignore the richness or ambiguity of tradition which, as noted, invites ongoing midrashic-interpretive creativity. Fundamentalists see sacred texts, whether of the Written or the Oral Torah, as monolithic, ahistorical, and straightforward directives to be inculcated by the educator. In fundamentalistic education, there is almost no teaching for deliberation and Midrash-making. Likewise, there are no inconsistencies or genuine valuative dilemmas in the tradition itself nor any positive historical influences upon it.[20] The curricular ramifications of this, as we shall see, are far-reaching.

In examining the educational philosophies and activities of Jewish fundamentalists, we must keep in mind that education, in the learning tradition of Judaism, is addressed to adults as well as children and, as in most religious traditions, cannot be exclusively identified with schooling but actively engages the home and the community. The home has traditionally educated through the inculcation of its assumptions and standards of behavior. In modern society, education in the home is enhanced by appropriate literature, newspapers, retreats, communal outings, and other occasions for learning or inspiration. The *community,* in turn, educates through its norms of Torah study and religious practice. For example, every observant Jew will hear a reading of Scripture, "the portion of the week," at least every Sabbath in the synagogue. He will also hear short sermons or discourses on the chapters of the Pentateuch and Prophets assigned for that week; he may also read printed materials distributed in synagogues and schools on the portion, providing inspirational or exegetical discussion, often with comments on the portion's relevance to contemporary events.[21] The community educates another way as well, namely, through the social controls engendered by the largely public character of the halakha and the need of the community's members for legal decision-making by its authorities in various situations. Thus, each fundamentalistic community, to a greater extent than nonfundamentalistic ones, is headed by authorities who interpret the norms of the Torah. Their authority derives from their reputations as learned and their charisma. Finally, schools reinforce the lessons of the home and prepare young people for active participation in community life, for normative behavior (including reverence for Torah authorities), and, at least with regard to males, for life-long learning.

Foundations of Haredi Educational Philosophy

Haredi Jewry is diversified in its subgroups, which set themselves apart one from another and often quarrel. Haredim differ in dress, read different (haredi) newspapers, and entertain diverse accommodations with the Zionists and their Hebrew-speaking culture. Most haredim speak Hebrew in daily life and participate in Israeli politics. Some, however, ban even haredi politicians and condemn those who speak anything but Yiddish. But all haredim consider the State of Israel and its epoch to be a continuation of Galut, albeit in the Holy Land.[22]

Most haredim also admit that though the State of Israel is a commonwealth of heresy and profanity, it is also the locus of an unprecedented haredi renaissance.[23] A group, 90 percent of which was destroyed in the Holocaust, has been vouchsafed a wondrous rehabilitation. More yeshivot and students exist in Israel than there were in Eastern Europe. The Torah, as haredim understand and study it, is more at home in Zionist Jerusalem than it was in the pre-State Diaspora. Yet, paradoxically, the curricular philosophy of these yeshivot holds that haredim are not at home in this world—be they in Jerusalem or New York. Indeed, Jerusalem is, in some respects, worse than New York, for exile in Eretz Yisrael, under the Zionists, is more bitter and painful than elsewhere.

Haredi educational philosophy is based on the stark reality of Galut, an existential category of sin and alienation from God, even and especially among Jews. Amid the glitter of modernity, its latest and most pernicious manifestation, Galut has won the hearts of most Jews. They feel at home in the world as it is; they think that the exile is ended. In Israel, they have created a Jewish culture, a bogus redemption, which expresses their modernity. A haredi Jew must, first and foremost, not be at home in this situation; children must be taught the courage of solitude. In the words of a haredi educational leader: "Our fathers and grandfathers set the educational paths for us. We strive to reach a situation in which their worldview will be ours and that of our children. We stand alone in this. We are different from all around us. . . . Reform historians . . . poets (are seen as great men by all the others). . . . Streets are named for historical figures whom we see in an utterly negative light. . . . We stand all alone."[24]

The educational philosophies of haredim are variations on the theme of aloneness and alienation, on maintaining a community of transcendence in a world of exile. The haredi child must become a member of a holy community absolutely different from the profane world. He must learn the Torah and accept the authority of *gedolim,* the "great ones," who alone have the wisdom and authority to interpret it. Then he may become a *ben Torah,* a Torah personality who is really at home in the holy community.

Paradox abounds in haredi philosophy and education. The subject matter of Torah, such as the halakhic laws of damages, agriculture, and sacrifices, becomes, in the false world of Galut, at least partly ethereal and abstract. This is not because the Torah is abstract; quite the opposite, it is very concrete. But it is being learned in Galut, where the Torah is not at home. As a result, the haredi learner has a style of study that sets him apart. The studied disregard for the surrounding reality makes learning seem like a kind of disembodied spiritual exercise, even when it deals with the laws of damages. Haredi learning may be applied to some particulars of a holy life in the holy community, but it is not comparable with what connotes learning in the profane world. There, among "the others," it refers to satisfying curiosity, broadening horizons, gathering "useful" information, conducting inquiry for the purposes of problem-solving, theorizing in order to understand and control. But when one learns Torah, in the haredi view, it is quite different: one enters the sphere of the divine. Learning shapes character in line with God's blueprint for goodness and knowledge. The average person cannot fathom exactly how learning does this, but the great ones of Torah understand and guide. Only they can be trusted to set the principles of curriculum and to direct the community in every detail of its life.

R. Friedman writes adventure stories for children that exemplify the haredi ideal.[25] In one of them, the young hero, Motti, has survived the Holocaust in hiding. After the war, he was kept from his people and faith by deceitful and missionizing Christians. Ultimately, Providence intervenes: a pious Jew rescues him, takes him into his home, and soon enrolls him in the yeshiva in which his own son is learning. There

> the melody [chanted in reciting the Talmud] echoes between the walls of the yeshiva. Some hundred boys sit in fellowships of two and the sound of their learning wells forth in song. Fresh air flows in through the windows. . . . The boys wear bright white shirts, their faces are refined and endearing—they are sitting and arguing about the halakhah. The hand supports the chin, furrows form on the forehead . . . they are perturbed, trying to understand the [halakhic] issue. Suddenly, the faces clear up, pleasant smiles spread over them: the matter is clear, there is no difficulty. . . . The purity which sweeps all faces shows that they are indeed completely absorbed in profoundly understanding the Holy Torah which refines and purifies the inner heart and leaves its trace also on the outer features.[26]

An outsider might demur that youngsters who learn only this, and whose ideal is in almost direct contradiction to the dominant youth culture of Israel, from the "bright white shirts" to the hands "supporting chins," will hardly find their place in the world as it is. The principled reply is that this failure indeed constitutes success; the children, through learning of Torah, are being socialized into the holy community.

Yet an education for transcendence in the profane world raises some problems. One must make a living, and relationships with society must be maintained. Also, while science may be based on mistaken premises regarding value and even reality, technology makes life easier and actually creates better conditions for learning. Moreover, the profane world, with its innumerable temptations, is always there. Education may insulate and protect, but it must also create the capacity for limited access and use of the outside world. While the rank and file of boys and young men are learning, who shall negotiate this relationship so that it is effective yet not harmful? The gedolim, the great scholars, of course do this: one must assume that in addition to Torah, they know the sociology of knowledge well. But in daily and mundane affairs, the role of bridging is largely assigned to women, which has far-reaching and paradoxical educational ramifications.

Traditionally, women were not required to study Torah and were often discouraged from doing so. In part, this was because study, like all formal education, was an institutional, hence public, activity, and prevailing concepts of modesty dictated that women be "within the tent"—a phrase suggesting a romanticized yet somewhat manipulative view of charm and chastity.[27] There was also the notion that women were intellectually and temperamentally unsuited for study of the details and dialectics of halakhah.[28]

In bridging between the holy and profane communities, women leave their sons, brothers, and husbands free to learn; they do this by keeping house, running stores, and today, again paradoxically, teaching school (for girls) and even operating computers. Thereby women are placed in an ambivalent position. Being enjoined to enter the profane world to facilitate the initiation of males into the world of transcendence and separation, women have an inferior status. Tainted by the profane, they are different from men and, in many social contexts, are actually separated from them. At the same time, they are honored for their selfless (modest) service to the sanctity of the community. By virtue of this service, they are members of the community, even without learning. But an interesting question arises: what kind of education is suitable for making young women capable of, and content with, such a role? We return to this problem in due course.

The theological ground of the haredi worldview and the rhetoric of their educational philosophy are well represented by Rabbi David Zvi Hoffman,[29] a contemporary haredi-oriented educator. Like many writers trained in Talmud, Hoffman begins with a puzzle: Why has God "commanded us to work six days and rest on the Sabbath alone?" (Rest connotes spiritual activity, especially learning.) How could we have been commanded to spend six days a week on (profane) labor, and only one day in the pursuit of holiness? Further, should one study Torah continually or devote most of one's time to making a living? In answering, Hoffman follows the talmudist's practice of citing seemingly opposing opinions. "Our sages, of blessed memory, taught us that ours is a world of activity, a world of cause and effect, a world of precise and set laws of nature," he writes. "The task of man is to fit into this framework and to take care of his livelihood according to the laws which are all around him."[30] God, the relevant texts instruct, wants people to work so that they will not rob for bread, nor spend their time in vanities—in useless leisure that activates the evil impulse. It is therefore a positive value to work, to withstand the temptation to do the wrong thing or to still the evil impulse that is aroused when we have nothing to do.

Yet the fabric of reality and the temptations within it are much more complex. What the Sages tell the ordinary man about causality is pedagogically but not ontologically true. The created world, with its natural and determined laws, does not expose the real truth but hides it: for everything that happens is the direct will of God. When people see the operation of the laws of nature, they are likely to conclude that understanding the natural world through science and philosophy will lead them to wisdom. But he who views the world as a causal system that requires no Providence has fallen into a trap. He has succumbed to the lure of determinism and has failed to exercise his free will—which allows him to see God's handiwork behind the mask of causality. If the sages say that work is precious, this is because it is God's way to bring man into the system of nature, where it appears that work is the cause of livelihood. But God does this to present us with a test of faith. If a person passes the test, work will have become a means of serving God; he will work not because nature requires it but because God commands it.

The conclusion is clear: work builds faith in the spiritually maturing person, who learns to look to God through the disguise of causality. It is, of course, also the downfall of the wicked, who choose to consider nature as governed by causality. Ultimately, therefore, "the whole purpose of life is to constantly diminish natural endeavor and to reach the heights of spirit, represented by the Sabbath, and to be completely sanctified." Torah study should always be the permanent and cardinal activity of a person, for it alone brings one directly in touch with the revealing God, that is, with the authentic truth. Work should be transitory: it is basically an exercise in faith and a religious requirement. "Yeshiva education that is nothing but Torah" teaches the youngster "total dedication to Torah"; he learns to "distance himself from the experiences of this world."[31]

By this view the Zionist enterprise, which valued work and responsibility for this world as a spiritual enterprise, was a demonic snare. Likewise, to one who has real knowledge, the dedicated scientist is a victim of illusion and the world of the university is a Platonic cave populated by immobile fools. However, given a world in which causality does "seem" to apply at least in a superficial sense, the haredi understanding of divine Providence assumes a hierarchy of knowledge and value. Women and others remote from Torah learning, but especially women, should do the work of the world; those who study Torah, the learners, bring transcendence down into the world. The learners' task is by far the more valuable.

This notion is used to justify exempting yeshiva students from army service. For it is actually God who directly protects society, and those who learn call down God's grace upon it. As for those who have the spiritual talent to learn and yet go into the army instead, they are shirkers.[32]

The Practice of Education: Unbending Traditionalism

If the educational philosophy of haredi fundamentalism is centered on holy community and transcendence, the hallmark of educational practice is unbending traditionalism. Especially among Ashkenazic haredim,[33] any new idea is seen as a clear and present danger to everything Judaism stands for, a blatant attempt to introduce reform, atheism, or Christianity surreptitiously. The only way to educate is the way it was (presumably) always done.

This extreme conservatism has been particularly pronounced in the Land of Israel, where the Zionists were seen as trampling underfoot everything sacred. Thus, the dangers are everywhere. Even when German Orthodox and non-Zionist Jews who were associated with the neo-Orthodoxy of "Torah and general culture" established their own comprehensive school in Jerusalem in 1934, haredi leaders demanded its closing: "They . . . write on blackboards, ring bells like in a church and study from maps."[34] The haredi ideal is to continue the tradition without change, indeed, to accentuate it, in order to counteract the dangers of modernity.

Traditional Jewish education begins in the home and is bound up with the norms of the family.[35] In the traditional home, existing of course within the framework of the traditional community, the child learns immediately who has status and authority—and why. Even as the child begins to speak, he or she is taught several verses of the Bible and begins to pray. The child sits at the table with the family and observes that blessings are recited before and after the meal. At an early age, the child takes part in preparing for the Sabbath and festivals, some of which, like Passover, require elaborate preparation indeed. If a Bible or other holy book falls to the ground, the child sees it being kissed. Charity is given every supplicant who comes to the door, and every Sabbath and holiday brings guests and the needy to the table. Everything in the traditionalist home is done for a reason that can be traced back to some religious obligation or sanction. While modern people have no compunction about inviting others to their homes socially simply because they feel like it, persons in the traditional community generally invite guests because it is commanded or the occasion (like a wedding) requires guests.[36] The home is thus the primary educator; for women, it was, until recent generations, almost the only educator.

A second educational institution is the synagogue. The child joins the parent at prayer. For boys, this is a considerable segment of the daily schedule, for father goes to the synagogue every morning and evening. At the synagogue the child observes the workings of community life: who is honored and why; who is held in contempt and why. The "language" of community life learned in the synagogue and in social encounters is intricate. He who has learned it is, in the traditional universe of discourse, substantially educated. The child discovers who is called to the reading of the Torah and on which occasions; he hears the Torah lessons given by the rabbi at specific times during the service; he participates in the change of garb on Friday afternoons, and joins the family in singing at festive meals; he observes the drama of mourning. All these rituals, performed according to the elaborate rules of pious conduct, comprise the child's education. Today, in order to maintain this tradition as it is remembered by authorities, the fundamentalist family conducts itself as though every custom were an iron-clad rule. For parents, and eventually for children, every law is a precious and indispensable aspect of one's innermost being.

The elementary school, the *heder,* is in a sense a mere cognitive supplement to all this. The curriculum of the heder is one of basic texts, practices, and attitudes appropriated "alongside" the home and the community. For example, one learns to read by reading the prayerbook. One studies the Torah (Pentateuch) parallel to the portion of the week. (Consequently, children often know the first part of every section, but never learn the last parts. But this is "the way it was always done," so it is unobjectionable—and holy.)

As the children in the heder progress, the commentary of Rabbi Shlomo Yitzchaki (Rashi), doyen of medieval biblical exegetes, is added to Bible study. Children also learn the laws that pertain to their daily lives and the rhythms of community life, particularly the laws and stories of the various holidays. At a more advanced stage, boys begin to study the Oral Torah: Mishnah and Gemara (together, Talmud). After the age of thirteen, some will advance to a yeshiva for youth and then a high (or holy) yeshiva. Here, with the exception of some study of the portion of the week and of halakhic codes, learning deals exclusively with the Talmud and its commentaries.

The yeshiva is not merely an educating and socializing institution, alongside the home and community, but is truly an embodiment of the haredi ideal for life, a microcosm of the real world in which the divine Presence dwells. Outsiders to the yeshiva world, even if they are nominally haredim, cannot understand this.

How peculiar are the claims made . . . even by the pious . . . that the yeshiva does not train haredi physicians . . . or pious academicians . . . that it doesn't provide teachers for schools. . . . What these reproaches have in common is that the essence of "a place of Torah" is alien to them and they do not give the yeshiva intrinsic worth. . . . The yeshiva is the place of vital spirit. . . . Today there are thousands throughout the world who study Torah and labor in it without the addition of "enlightened" study, and they must be the bearers of the Divine Presence in this generation.[37]

Naturally, those to whom the significance of "a place of Torah" is alien make the "ludicrous" demand that yeshiva students serve in the army. Rabbi Shlomo Volve of the Be'er Yaakov Yeshiva, the author of the previous ideological statement, explains: "If only the State of Israel understood how the yeshivot protect its existence—it [Israel] would station soldiers around the yeshiva to guard its learners, lest they waste one minute, for the life of society depends on them."[38]

Here, then, is an additional paradox. The community of Transcendence and Torah, living in a fragile relationship with the Zionists on whom it is so greatly dependent, not only withdraws from the modernists and their false standards and conceptions of knowledge and worth, but (except in its most radical sectors) explains this withdrawal as serving the "real" needs of society and state.

School for Girls: Innovation for the Sake of Traditionalism

Perhaps the height of paradox in haredi educational thought and practice is in the realm of women's education. On the basis of halakhic rulings in the talmudic and medieval sources, women need not learn Torah; the haredi community, on the basis of one talmudic opinion and pietistic traditions, has posited that they shall not. Ironically, well-to-do pious parents who would not have dreamt of sending their sons to good "general" schools, did send their daughters.[39] Consequently, girls from haredi families, in Eastern Europe and in Israel, often received a broad humanistic education, usually in "secular" or Christian schools. This education, of course, tended to alienate them from their traditional communities; even worse, the girls had a "bad influence" on their brothers who were dutifully "learning," but who blatantly lacked the general knowledge and sophistication of their allegedly "ignorant" sisters. In these circumstances, haredi rabbinical leadership was faced with a serious dilemma.

When the issue of girls' education arose in this acute form in the first decades of the twentieth century, it was handled in a manner that testified to sociological analysis and deliberation. Rabbi Yisrael Meir of Radin, known as the Hafetz Chaim, ruled, in a responsum of 1933, that girls in our generation may indeed be taught Torah, though not the halakhic disputes of the Talmud: "Now, because of our great sins, the tradition of the fathers has been greatly weakened. . . . It is surely a great mitzvah [meritorious act] to teach girls the Pentateuch and also other books of Scripture and the ethics of the sages . . . and so on, so that our holy faith will be verified for them. Because if not, the girls are likely to stray completely from the path of the Lord and transgress the foundations of our religion, God forbid."[40]

Through the energetic efforts of a devout woman, Sarah Schnirer, a network of haredi schools for girls, called *Bet Yaakov* (the House of Jacob), was established, first in Eastern Europe and then in Israel. While the educational goal was to produce the "modest" and God-fearing young woman who "knew her place" in the haredi community, the curriculum was actually much broader than that of the boys. The syllabus included literature and history, albeit with a heavy dose of "moral lessons" to be learned from events. The schools developed a general presentation of "Judaism," centering on its philosophy and spiritual "message" in addition to teaching handicrafts, business, child care, and education and related fields through which women could be expected to contribute to their families and communities.

However, the Bet Yaakov network could not break the fundamental haredi norm: it could not make girls equal to boys in the "learning" deemed most important—Talmud. Dr. Yehudah Leib Orlean, onetime director of the Bet Yaakov movement, explained that even the outstanding Sarah Schnirer could not study in a yeshiva. "Such is the demand of Judaism," which a "modern European woman couldn't possibly understand . . . but this in no way detracts from the importance of the woman." There is a division of labor within the Jewish people, and if one accepts the notion of the essential unity of Israel, then one accepts this division as natural and positive.[41] Once again, the needs of the holy community take preference over the individual; education serves transcendental religious norms. The young woman is to see herself as part of an organic community, in which everyone has his or her "place." In a world of seeming anarchy, this conception of community can bestow order and spiritual comfort; if it is seen as God's will, it also promises significance and salvation.

Protection against the Outside World in the Haredi Curriculum

If curriculum may be defined as "everything that goes on in school for the purposes of education," then the haredi curriculum must reflect the constant struggle against the outside world, with its profane views of teaching, of the child, and of achievement. In Israeli society, where Torah is studied in all Jewish school systems, including nonreligious ones, one of the greatest dangers is a wrong or tainted conception of Torah itself.

In the more extreme haredi circles, like the Eda Haredit, rabbinical leaders have well understood that educational theories and methods cannot be divorced from philosophies and goals. Moderate haredi educators have introduced modern methods into education, believing them to be "neutral." In response the Eda Haredit leadership has attacked such adaptation.

For example, the Eda Haredit abhors recourse to psychologists: "Research into the thoughts and feelings of people, called psychology, is based on contaminated Gentile investigations . . . without faith and without Torah and holiness . . . psycho-

logical and psychiatric wisdom is built on the words of one degenerate who constructed the entire edifice on degeneracy. And their entire way and theory is to lead
man in the ways of abandon and lawlessness like the beasts of the field." Psychology
is "the inquiry of mortals, and thus full of mistakes. . . . And every year and in every
generation they themselves change their theories and ways." Children's problems
should be dealt with as they have always been, by teachers imbued with Torah wisdom. The answers are found "in the books of the righteous and great Torah scholars
who are the true physicians of the soul, for the Holy Spirit rests on them and their
words." Teachers are urged to return to the true and tested ways, and not to shirk
their responsibilities by sending their charges to psychologists, with their contaminated theories.[42]

A telling illustration of fundamentalist self-protection against the profane environment and its highest scholarly institution, the university, is a response of Rabbi Eli-
yahu Dessler, a foremost theological-educational thinker and an acknowledged leader
in the midcentury haredi yeshiva world.[43] Rabbi Dessler was approached by several
yeshiva men who wished to establish a (haredi) teachers' seminary attached to the
yeshiva. He, in effect, forbade them to proceed with their plan. The existence of
such an institution may weaken many a young man who, "were there no devout
seminary . . . would study only in the yeshiva and remain a real ben Torah and it
would not even occur to him to prepare for the university and he would make no
plans to take a B.A. or something like that."[44] Even if some weak souls leave the fold,
that is a price worth paying for the purity of the yeshiva ideal.

The university world's interest in Bible and other Jewish studies is particularly
threatening to fundamentalistic educators, and they must not to be influenced by
research or literary approaches in any way. All secular scholarship with regard to
Torah is false; only Torah sages can begin to fathom the transcendental reality it reflects, and which is reflected in the community into which children must be initiated: "[God's] Torah is broader than the earth and deeper than the ocean. If man
approaches Torah with his limited mind and evaluates it with his miniscule compre-
hension, he reduces Torah to his own level—and there is no greater profanation of
Torah than that . . . you cannot evaluate Torah with your own faculties, but must
accept Chazal's [the talmudic sages'] explanations of every word, every letter of the
Torah."[45]

In 1989 the haredi world was shaken by the "exposure" of Rabbi Adin Steinsaltz,
one of Israel's greatest talmudists. Steinsaltz had been working for many years on the
translation of the Talmud (from Aramaic) into Hebrew and had been composing a
running commentary on the text. His work was meant to facilitate Talmud study for
nonscholarly learners. A man of phenomenal scholarship, Steinsaltz illuminated talmudic concepts and modes of discourse for wide circles; in addition, he lectured,
broadcast, and wrote widely on the Bible, Jewish mysticism, and other domains of
Judaica.

In July 1989, Rabbi Eliezer Menachem Schach, the acknowledged leader of
"Lithuanian" (anti-Hasidic) haredi Jewry, denounced Steinsaltz's work. In *Yated
Ne'eman,* the haredi newspaper published under Schach's tutelage, readers were

warned that Steinsaltz had made the lives of the patriarchs and matriarchs into "romantic tales, God save us"; also, his literary and psychological explanations of sacred events marked his books as heretical. The *Yated Ne'eman* reporter apologized to his readers for quoting from Steinsaltz's writings and explained that rabbinic authorities permitted citation from these terrible books so that the public will realize the enormity of the danger to faith they contain. There was a time when "no permission was given to print books of . . . commentary like these except if the writers . . . had been carefully examined, [to determine] that his heart was pure and his faith perfect."[46] The argument that Steinsaltz, himself a Jew who "returned" from secularism to Orthodoxy, had brought many people back to religious Judaism was beside the point, for he had not brought people back to fundamentalist Judaism. To Rabbi Schach, Steinsaltz's "way of learning takes [away] every bit of holiness and faith, for it presents the Talmud as though it were like a book and like the wisdom of the Gentiles, God save us, and clearly this way will cause the forgetting of the Torah, God forbid." Regarding his ban on Steinsaltz, Schach said: "And let no one claim that [the ban will] reduce [the number of] learners, for it is our duty to preserve the pure vessel of oil in its purity and not to make an increase which is not pure. A little bit of light drives away much darkness."[47]

Haredi Outreach and the Crisis of Religious Zionist Education

Rabbi Schach's declaration that he prefers the preservation of one vessel of pure oil to "an increase which is not pure" notwithstanding, haredi leaders and educators are keenly interested in "outreach." They have had a significant and dialectical influence, for example, upon the "vessel of oil" they consider impure, the world of religious Zionism.

This influence can be traced to the theological and ideological ambiguity that characterized the religious Zionist position vis-à-vis the "yeshiva world," on the one hand, and secular Zionism and the *chalutzim* (pioneers) on the other. The haredi "yeshiva world" never allowed itself to be drawn into ideological confrontation with religious Zionism, but simply scoffed at it. Moreover, religious Zionism put itself at an ideological disadvantage by grudgingly admitting that the haredim were religiously more consistent than they and that the "learning" that prevailed in the "yeshiva world" was unmistakably authentic and, after the Holocaust, even dramatically heroic.

The Mizrachi (later, National-Religious) schools were meant to foster the social, religious, and personal ideals of religious Zionism, but were ridden with ambivalence and doubts. The norm was supposed to be both modern Zionist and religious Jew, but the connection between the two identities was unclear, and sometimes embarrassing. The secular Zionists were envied and esteemed for being *more* Zionistic than the religious Zionists, with greater pioneering accomplishments and a firmer "at-homeness" in the new society, while the haredim were perceived as *more* religious than the religious Zionists. The National-Religious Jew observed the mores of Orthodox Judaism and held a respectable if generally low profile place in society, but he was compartmentalized. He was both national and religious, and he was not taken very seriously in either dimension.

This unheroic image and self-perception were reflected in the religious-Zionist school from its inception in the 1920s.[48] The curriculum was like that of the "general" schools, with the addition of religious subjects and the goal of molding a man or woman who would be at home in the observant community as well as in modern science and culture. But the young people who went through that school often were not really at home in either world, nor did they feel they had mastered the bodies of knowledge that distinguished each world. Having never fully and consciously rejected the haredi ideal of what constitutes Torah and Torah study, the thoughtful National-Religious pupils knew that they didn't "know Torah" or really study it; in their school it was one of a series of subjects, not the focus of existence.[49] Torah study was thus experienced as boring, arbitrarily restrictive, and confining—dictating what a religious Jew "couldn't do" that everyone else could and did. Meanwhile, "general" studies were taught conscientiously by well-trained Western and central European pedagogues, but were actually treated less seriously than in secular schools. There was usually less time for such studies and religious doctrine and social dogma set limits on the exploration of certain areas such as biblical research, comparative religion, the cultural conflicts between Judaism and the "Western" (Greek, Christian, or liberal/ secular) heritage, and the modern trend by which faith is viewed as a personal choice rather than as the fate of a particular sector of the population.

In the religious Zionist community there were, however, moments of confrontation with Zionism that served as a challenge to religious renewal. Those who were inquisitive and innovative in theological matters identified with what Charles Liebman has called "religious expansionism." "Expansionism affirms modernity by reinterpreting it through the prism of the Jewish tradition. . . . It aspires, in theory, to bring all aspects of life under the rubric of its interpretation of Judaism."[50] When "religious expansionism" was combined with adaptationism, which "affirms that the basic values of modernity are not only compatible with Judaism but partake of its essence," there emerged an ideationally vibrant and ambitious type of religious Zionism, most fully embodied in the religious kibbutz movement and members of its spiritual circle, many of them academicians of Western and central European background.[51]

Thinkers and educators in this circle perceived no conflict between Zionism and Judaism. Rather, Zionism was the opportunity to fully apply the Torah to the reborn social reality of Judaism in the modern world. The Torah was meant to inform every aspect of life, but this was impossible in Galut. Thus Torah scholars had to engage in dialogue with all knowledge and culture to be thereby liberated from the shackles of Galut ghettoization and, in turn, to transform the social message of universal ideals. In the religious kibbutz it could be shown that the Torah was the constitution of an ideal society and the foundation of a socially progressive and humanistic religiosity.

In a sense, the approach of these theologically oriented and socially conscious religious Zionists was diametrically opposed to that of the haredim. The latter also considered Torah comprehensive, but for them the world was still in Galut, and they did not believe that the Torah could shape any society beyond the confines of the faithful sectarian community. Conversely, the "expansionistic-adaptationist" religious Zionists held that Galut was ending and that the long-awaited challenge to the truth and viability of Judaism as a social vision was at hand. Thus, the ultra-Orthodox could be perceived by the modern Orthodox Zionists as "not religious enough." In the words of Pinchas Rosenbluth, one of the leaders of this religious-Zionist movement: "We accept upon ourselves the entire Torah, its commandments and ideas. The [old] Orthodoxy made do in fact with a small part of the Torah . . . observed in synagogue or the family . . . or certain areas of life. We want to carry out the Torah all the time and in every area, to grant [Torah] and its laws sovereignty in the life of the individual and of the public."[52]

Rosenbluth and his friends wished to educate a religious Jew who would not seek through the Torah a narrow individual or even a sectarian-communal salvation: that was the diminutive Torah of Galut. Rather, the Torah would be the spiritual infrastructure of a new moral and religious-humanistic society in which the inner idea of the Torah would come to light. Obviously, in this conception, neither traditional rabbinic authorities nor the yeshiva were educationally appropriate. As Moshe Unna, a leading educational personality of the religious kibbutz movement wrote, each social and existential ideal creates its own educational institutions; the yeshiva served an elite of learners in a restrictive and restricted environment.[53] The yeshiva world and its rabbinic leaders wished to cultivate, through learning, spiritual individuals, but there was no intention on their part to change society. Built into the yeshiva worldview were features that Zionism categorically rejected: status inferiority for women, disdain for physical work, disinterest in transforming the world (a task assigned to the Messiah!). As for the rabbis of that yeshiva community, they understood nothing of emerging social ideals, the very ideals the religious Zionists felt were required (by the Torah!) in the contemporary situation; the haredim spoke a spiritual language of passiveness and quietism. Religious Zionism wished to build a new society in the image of the Torah, and thus needed a new school system in which general and Jewish knowledge lived not merely in compartmentalized mutual tolerance, but in harmony and mutual enrichment.

In the general spirit of this ideal, the religious Zionist youth movement, Bnai Akiva, was begun in 1929. One of its founding members declared that Bnai Akiva

> shares the general worldview of the [Zionist] youth of all streams that youth must be imbued with the spirit of rebellion against social convention but Bnai Akiva [also accepts] . . . the view of their great teacher, Rabbi Akiva, about [the nature of] the rebellion. Rabbi Akiva called for rebellion in Israel not against the God of Israel but against the pagan gods that had a hold then in Eretz Yisrael. And we, his disciples, Bnai (sons of) Akiva, must call for a rebellion against the rebellion, against the view of the [secular] youth which is opposed to Judaism and Jewish tradition.[54]

The innovative yet normative approach of Bnai Akiva's founders, who were open to outside influences and rhetoric upon which they wished to impose the norms of tradition, made for a difficult educational challenge. The expounders and teachers of this expansionist approach had to teach that the Torah was capable of addressing every issue, but it was unclear to them how this worked in practice. As modern Orthodox nonfundamentalistic Jews, they lived in a hyphenated valuative world: of Torah and general culture; of Torah and "labor" (i.e., socialism). Though their ideology was both expansionist and adaptationist, the lives they led and the concrete educational programs they felt qualified to construct and implement were mostly compartmentalized. Some things were Jewish and some were not.

What caused this discrepancy between the expansive ideal of Torah and the compartmentalized reality? In the early years of Israeli statehood, it became abundantly clear that this circle had found no rabbinic authorities who had the clout, courage, or even the inclination to interpret the Torah as they perceived it. And, as devout traditional Jews, they dared not do it themselves, because they felt unqualified and did not want to alienate themselves from the wider religious Zionist community, which in turn had not fully liberated itself from the authority of the haredi world.

This point is central in explaining the religious-Zionist turn to fundamentalism. Recall that Torah is never just written canon; it is always, in addition, Oral Torah. The corpus is wide, varied, and deliberative: it states its demands and meanings only through the prism of cumulative learning in diverse historical circumstances, through the tradition of valuative debate and struggle. The revelation of God is "in all these words."[55] It is the ground of the discussion itself. One cannot know what the Torah says and what to do by simply reading a chapter of the Bible. The text comes with layers of commentary, mountains of Midrash. The text is Presence, inviting encounter with God, who wishes to dwell in the midst of the community of Israel. This is its religious significance and thus has it been experienced. But that requires learning in the sense of undergoing the experience of understanding, deciding, and doing. This is what learners do, and the scholars who teach them provide the normative context to their life of Torah.

Having no scholars who were genuinely theirs, who understood what Unna and Rosenbluth were saying, the kibbutz theologians and educators, together with their entire circle, had no real social context for learning Torah in their own spirit.[56] Therefore, when they spoke of Torah as "everything," this was a slogan. It was not a program for learning under the guidance of Torah scholars. And so they slowly retreated, becoming more polemical and frustrated in their writings, becoming more cautious and conservative in their lives.[57] And the general mood within wider religious-Zionist circles was religious apathy and, for the religiously sensitive, discontent.

Yeshiva High Schools and Radical-Zionist Fundamentalism

The discontent within religious-Zionist circles aroused certain Bnai Akiva teachers and youth to create frameworks wherein the Torah could be studied seriously, which would indeed spark a veritable counter-reformation within Bnai Akiva. This was the origin of the Zionist yeshivot for (high school age) youth. The development came from below as well as from above: in the early 1950s, a religious elite of Bnai Akiva members in their early teens organized themselves into an almost secret society for seriously studying Torah and revolutionizing Bnai Akiva and religious youth culture along more pious lines.[58] Within fifteen years of the founding of the Zionist Kfar Haroeh Yeshiva, there were five such institutions, and later more were added. All but one of these yeshivot were formally connected to Bnai Akiva; they were all meant for Zionist pioneering youth. However, conflicts between the desire to learn and teach only Torah and the ideal of kibbutz settlement and service to the wider community, including army service, soon emerged. There were also conflicts with the academic demands and cultural expectations of middle-class parents. Thus, eventually, the Bnai Akiva yeshivot began, usually against the explicit wishes of their rabbinical leaders, to introduce general studies (in the afternoon) and to prepare pupils for government matriculation examinations. In the course of these developments, girls' schools *(ul-panot)* were created, parallel to the yeshivot, now called yeshiva high schools. It rapidly became the norm for the best youth of the Bnai Akiva movement to attend either a yeshiva or an ulpana.

Originally part and parcel of the Bnai Akiva world, marked by informal relations between rabbi-teachers and pupils, and casual Israeli dress (sports shirts, khaki trousers, sandals), the yeshivot began to move away from this ambience and return to the roots of the yeshiva world—with its East European conception of learning. The rabbi-leaders of the Bnai Akiva-oriented yeshivot were adamant that the real purpose of their institutions was to "bring their boys into the world of Torah"; they refused to adapt the subjects and themes studied to the "new realities and challenges facing us in our own society," as demanded by religious kibbutz educators.[59] And so, quite naturally, they brought into the yeshivot teacher-educators who were graduates of haredi yeshivot, men who "really know how to learn," and who could inspire youth with a love of Torah. These haredi teachers often saw their employment in these Zionist yeshivot as an opportunity to win back for real Judaism the confused young souls of the Bnai Akiva world. So, even if, when they were not overtly missionizing, these teachers hardly shared a spiritual world with the youth of Bnai Akiva, they considered movement work by pupils on evenings and Sabbaths a waste of time, and they thought the study of secular studies was, at best, useful for making a living. When all was said and done, this viewpoint was shared by the heads of the Bnai Akiva yeshivot, who, as men living in the world of Torah, were more anchored in the haredi yeshiva than in the religious kibbutz or in Bnai Akiva.

Ultimately, Bnai Akiva realized that its greatest educational achievement, the Zionist yeshiva, was weaning its best youth away from its professed ideology and cut its organizational ties to the yeshivot. But before it did so the leadership of the movement, many of whom were graduates of these very yeshivot, agreed to the principle that learning Torah was an acceptable alternative to kibbutz and pioneering for young men. (Obviously this also implied a new and once again inferior role for women. The boys who came to kibbutz instead of going on to Higher yeshivot were of secondary quality—like the girls!) Midrashiat Noam was the first yeshiva high school in Israel to introduce secular studies in principle, and its founder decided that it should not be called Yeshiva but rather Midrashia (an academy). It was designed to create a "religious intelligentsia."[60] Yet the credo of Rabbi Yehoshua Yogel, educational head (*Rosh Yeshiva*) of Midrashiat Noam, was indicative of the direction in which all the yeshiva high schools were moving. Rabbi Yogel cited his own (haredi) mentors, who maintain that Torah must be learned "for its own sake, not as 'a spade with which to dig' [i.e., for instrumental and extrinsic purposes] but *because this is the purpose of man*. . . . This concept [of general studies] should not be understood in the narrow sense of livelihood *but in the broadest sense* as a means for economic, military and political existence—but this is not Torah for its own sake" (emphasis added).[61]

The ideal presented here is, in essence, the haredi one, with the addition of a strictly circumscribed political-civic-national supplement. Not even lip service is given to building a more ideal society on the basis of a new interpretation of Torah. Moreover, general studies are narrowly practical; science is understood in an instrumental and technological sense, and these studies have no intrinsic cultural value. It was, in fact, seen in the same way as was the new situation of Zionism: as economic, military, and political. The State of Israel is almost a technological phenomenon, requiring no theological innovation, but merely patriotic application. (The only religious innovation often found in such statements is a historical belief that the state has messianic meaning, but this does not require creativity in the realm of the normative Torah, but only a new historical orientation which makes no social-moral demands.) It is not surprising that Rabbi Yogel declared the yeshiva high school to be a bridge to the Higher yeshivot, whether to the "old [haredi] ones or the yeshivot which sprung out of the yeshiva high schools, the Hesder Yeshivot."[62] For they serve the same purpose, to create Torah personalities.

The yeshiva high school was hardly the bastion of "Torah and general culture" that some hoped it would become; rather, it emerged as a primary center of haredi outreach.[63] This was less the result of haredi deviousness than of religious-Zionist hesitation to break away from traditional modes of Torah learning. However, the religious-Zionist youth in the high school were committed to Israel and had a Zionist identity, and Bnai Akiva, together with the dramatic circumstances of Israeli life, did shape their worldview and character. So these young people were genuinely ambivalent about their haredi teachers. They respected them but felt uncomfortable with them; they honored them for their learning yet subtly looked down on them. Their black suits and white shirts; the empty spaces in their personal biographies where army service should have been; their gestures and experiential detachment from national crises and challenges—all of this placed them in the world of Galut.

For the religious-Zionist youth, Galut was over; they had learned that unmistakably in Bnai Akiva, the bastion of the "Torah and labor" ideology. The end of Galut meant taking Torah seriously, applying it to everything, making it a truly comprehensive worldview. But their mentors in the yeshivot had not given them a dialectical concept of religious Zionism with which to meet the challenge of cultural and philosophical Enlightenment, but instead the narrow political view that saw Israel only as a response to the challenge of Emancipation. This was much easier to handle theologically and could be accepted even by moderate haredim. The end of Galut meant the end of foreign domination and cultural subversion. There was thus no longer any need to modify the all-inclusive cultural demands of the Torah; the halakha could now be fully carried out, in its own environment, in its own land. But this view, that the halakha could again, comprehensively, come into its own, was only semantically and superficially similar to the religious kibbutz ideal of the decades before. For the religious-Zionist youth in religious high school circles assumed that the halakha's religious-cultural demands were to be applied to society as it was, and with the tradition basically as it was. It was not a program for reverent reexamination of the tradition so as to make it a unique religious platform for changing and redeeming society. The only changes were national: political, civic, military, and matters of style (i.e., casual dress) rather than substance (e.g., "a Torah view of social justice").

During the 1950s and 1960s, this orientation was developed by graduates of the yeshivot who went on to Higher yeshivot, especially by those who studied in the one yeshiva which had a national-Zionist worldview, the Mercaz Harav Yeshiva, founded by the charismatic Chief Rabbi Abraham Isaac Kook and then headed by his son, Rabbi Zvi Yehuda Kook. This worldview was a synthesis of the haredi convictions about real Torah study and the civic nationalism that had become stronger in secular (and religious) Israeli society after the weakening of the socialist-pioneering ethos. As graduates and leaders of Bnai Akiva, these young men identified with this type of nationalism and felt that their view of Torah was destined to replace the empty and now defunct ideologies of secular-socialist idealism.

In this context Zionist fundamentalism became fully developed. The young men in the Mercaz Harav Yeshiva wished to defend the Torah against the onslaughts of alien cultures, and they believed that, in the State of Israel, it was now possible to apply the Torah to everything—unlike the haredim, who saw no special significance in the state or society of Israel. For the Mercaz Harav group, the Torah addressed itself not only or even primarily to the individual soul, but to the nation. The Torah should not be, as the haredim taught, seen merely as the sanctuary carrying God's presence in the (Galut) wilderness; rather, the wilderness had been traversed and the present epoch and the State of Israel were the harbingers of redemption. The State of Israel was intrinsically holy, for it was destined to become the concrete Kingdom of God as the ancient kingdom had been. As for the haredim, Rabbi Zvi Yehuda Kook could describe them as righteous unbelievers, for while they were pious, they did not understand the significance of Israel. This explained the haredi hatred for nonreligious Jews; they did not know that, as subjects of the emerging kingdom, the secular Jews were "holy in spite of themselves."[64]

The educational ramifications of this development were clear. Education was a socialization into the stringently (yeshiva-oriented) halakhic community, which saw itself as an integral part of Israel, and as an elite within Israeli society as a whole. The pinnacle of education was yeshiva education. Girls, too, were to learn Torah, though certain restrictions on the study of Talmud remained in force.[65] Children would learn that the Torah, both as practice and as worldview (as interpreted by national-religious rabbis, associated mainly with the Mercaz Harav Yeshiva), had something to say on every issue, and a solution to every problem. Though this was similar in rhetorical style to the position of the religious kibbutz movement, the emphasis had shifted from social to national issues, with a strong "holy community" orientation. In turn this orientation led to an emphasis on devoting time to Torah (i.e., Talmud) study and promoted a holistic halakhic pattern of behavior conforming to the strict standards of the community. Most significantly, it also stood behind the settlement of "liberated" territories.

This approach is "fundamentalist" in the unmediated, authoritarian, and narrow character of its "comprehensiveness." It is *unmediated* in the sense that the tradition is presented as monolithic, holy, and binding in accordance with premodern theological formulations that do not *engage* modern sensibilities or funds of knowledge but are merely *applied* to modern attitudes and situations. The approach is *authoritarian* in that its proponents do not see the tradition as vast, variegated, and requiring valuative deliberation; instead, proper explication of and fidelity to the tradition require total reliance on the proper authorities who can say "exactly what it all means." And the approach is *narrow* in that the focus of interest is on particular external-ritual matters and on political-national ones that are simplistically resolved by way of mythic structures and associations. (For example, one educational sermonette, the story of Hagar, who was exiled with her son Ishmael by Abraham, shows that "transfer" of Palestinian Arabs is the best and most "humane" solution to the Intifada.)[66]

Yet this "religiously radical" approach, as it is sometimes called in Israel, is profoundly ambivalent about the secular Zionist reality that Rabbi Kook declared to be holy.[67] The blatant secularism and libertine behavior that these religious people observe in their society distresses them; they cannot but feel alienated from Tel Avivian culture. They know that materialism and individualism are the norm of the day and that the gap between them and the nation they are commanded to love for its (all-too-hidden) holiness is wide. They are therefore impelled to be greater Zionists and patriots than the secularists—indeed, they sometimes claim to be not only the best but the last Zionists—and, at the same time, to withdraw into communities of like-minded Zionist fundamentalists.

Like the haredim, they want to recognize one another: men wear a particularly large knitted skull-cap, and a kerchief or hat modestly covers the hair of married women. Many wear their ritual fringes, worn by most Orthodox males under their shirts, hanging out, framing their trousers, for "here, in our own country, there is no need to tuck them in." They diligently study Torah together in small groups, perhaps several evenings a week; husbands and wives also study together, though rarely Talmud. The more extreme send their children to the radical-religious youth movement Ariel, founded a decade ago, where boys and girls conduct separate activities. But most continue to see themselves within the Bnai Akiva "family," where their children, hopefully, will work at making the movement more religious, more "consistent"— that is, less influenced by Western culture.[68] Of course they expect their children to conform to strict standards of sexual modesty, standards that are indistinguishable from moderate haredi ones, and far removed not only from those prevailing in Israeli society, but also from those of Bnai Akiva in its earlier days.

Formal Zionist "radical" education also has a platform and even a group of schools called *Noam*.[69] The ideological position of Zionist-fundamentalist education was first presented by Rabbi Yaakov Filber, a member of the original group of Bnai Akiva youngsters who demanded a Torah-centered revolution (1951) and in 1990 head of the yeshiva for high school-age boys attached to the Mercaz Harav Yeshiva. In an essay entitled "From Religious Education to Torah Education,"[70] Filber decries the ignorance and lack of faith prevalent, in his opinion, within the National-Religious school system. This school system, he claims, is run by political functionaries who kowtow to secular bureaucrats in the Ministry of Education. National-Religious education did not establish curriculum teams which included "wise men of Torah, educators, subject-matter experts, fearers of God and lovers of Torah." Instead the curriculum teams were led by Western European pedagogues and educational officials who "in blind enthusiasm, strove to squeeze into the framework of the religious school everything studied in the general [secular] school and [only] the remaining time was devoted to sacred subjects." This flies in the face of the "revolution" in the hearts of religious Israeli youth, who "hold compromising education in contempt, as well as the impotence of Western European religiosity, devoid of the warmth of faith. Rather [this youth] asked for something authentic and rich [rooted in] . . . Torah and commandments. This revolution was not taken into account by the functionaries of religious education, and they continued their old ways, ignoring the spiritual aspirations of the young believing person."

Noam, the radically religious school, meets the needs of this youth. "Men of Torah" (that is, graduates of Higher yeshivot, who usually have no general or academic training) set the educational goals and syllabi. Filber, among others, calls for a syllabus of Bible, Mishnah and Talmud, but also ethics and "faith." Curricular materials must be prepared, but not by "secular" educators who are the present leaders of religious education in Israel: "Neither the School of Education at the Hebrew University nor the Department of Curriculum of the Orthodox Bar-Ilan University can save us in this."[71]

In 1990 there are six Noam institutions that operate according to Rabbi Filber's guidelines, in addition to several Zionist heder schools that limit secular learning even more stringently. The purpose of these is to cultivate "Torah personalities," so that the Zionist radical community may free itself from all dependence on haredi teachers.

The irony is blatant: the Zionist radicals, intent on establishing their independence from "righteous nonbelievers," have established institutions of learning that are broadly haredi yet Zionist. Unlike the haredim, they have an expansionist conception of how society at large may be influenced by Torah because they (the Zionists) believe that Galut is over. Yet their view of general culture and the dangers it poses to faith and religious identity is substantially the same as that of the haredi.

Ideologically, the Zionist radicals' contempt for modern culture cannot extend to the defense of Israel. For the most part, therefore, the radicals serve in the army—within the framework of Hesder yeshivot. These are yeshivot established through an "arrangement" (Hebrew: *Hesder*) with the Ministry of Defense. These yeshivot are structured to release young men for given periods of military training and service; and the young men commit themselves to almost five years of study and army duty. During this time, the student-soldier spends a year and a half on active duty. (In wartime, of course, Hesder students immediately leave the yeshiva to join their units.) Hesder soldiers usually serve in clusters, so that they can carry out the requirements of communal religious life. Thus one finds them in army bases together, yet among others.

Here is a powerful locus of influence and outreach. While many soldiers resent these Orthodox Hesder men for their superior airs, and hold them in contempt for their ritual "fixations," for their (frequent) political extremism and their gratuitous "love" of the people they hardly talk to, others are quite impressed by them. On the basis of many conversations it is my conviction that many newly religious young people who have found their way to places like Machon Meir, a yeshiva for Zionist-radical returnees, first became interested in religion through observing Hesder soldiers while in the army. They saw Hesder men eating their Sabbath meals together, worshiping and singing together, learning together—in short, having and being a community—while others often seemed bored and lonely (especially on the Sabbath). As one testified on an Israeli television show: "These guys know why they're alive. They're together. They're on to something. I saw them and realized I had to find out what they knew that I didn't."[72]

The question may be asked: When approached by religious seekers, what do radical-Zionists have to say? Have they been educated to deal profoundly, or even adequately, with the problems of religion, modernity, and Israeli society?

Yochanan Ben-Yaakov, former secretary-general of Bnai Akiva and a member of Kibbutz Kfar Etzion in Judaea, believes that their yeshiva high school education has taught these young people to flee from problems and from "the complexity of reality." Their education has convinced them that "human reasoning, differences of opinion, argument and confrontation all . . . have their place only in mundane matters. In the realm of Judaism, in thought and practice, there is no room for human thought, independent judgment. The authority of the rabbi-teacher is absolute."[73] Again, the parallel with the haredi community is striking.

Ben-Yaakov describes the consequences of the religious-Zionist educational method: "when young people who think in one-dimensional, black-and-white terms find themselves in a complex reality [because they] . . . have been shaped by an education that blocks thought and criticism and encourages surrender to authority, the result will be, given the complicated circumstances of Israel, extremism in attitudes and actions."[74] In the nonfundamentalistic religious education favored by ben Yaakov there are always dilemmas and the ability to tolerate dichotomies and ambiguities.

In explaining why Israeli religious education has moved in a fundamentalistic direction, away from the universalistic and humanistic emphases of the early educational leaders of the movement, Lawrence Kaplan cites the impact of the haredi worldview on the curriculum of the Zionist yeshiva: "The Jewish component of education in religious Zionist yeshivot still follows in all essentials the educational model and approach of the Eastern European yeshivot and their latter-day imitators [i.e., the present-day haredi yeshivot], except that this education is overlaid with a coating of messianic, nationalist Zionism. . . . The Israeli religious Zionist schools never effected a successful reform of their classical yeshiva curriculum, and approach."[75]

Gush Emunim: Messianism, Right-Wing Education, Expansionism

The group of radical religious Zionists who have attracted most public attention is Gush Emunim, the "bloc of the faithful," founded after the Yom Kippur War (1973) by members of the inner circle of young Mercaz Harav learners, disciples of Rabbi Zvi Yehuda Kook.[76] While it is generally assumed that Gush Emunim ideology is synonymous in principle with that of "radicals" like Filber, there are several reasons for doubt.

First, a distinction should be made between the normative position that the Torah must now be applied in a certain way because the exile is over (the radical position) and the belief that "the redemption has begun and we are now living in messianic times." The latter belief, from within the context of historic Judaism, is either a correct or incorrect theological reading of events. One can, in principle, be a halakhic moderate or even reformer and believe that these are messianic times; indeed, in terms of the messianic tradition of Judaism, it even makes sense to associate messianism with religious innovation and a rejection of former orthodoxies.[77] Since messianism is ultimately of universal significance, one would expect messianists (unlike radicals) to be open to the world and critical of the yeshiva culture, which was a merely protective framework designed for more prosaic, pre-redemptive days than these.

Second, since the messianic convictions of Gush Emunim are theological-historical rather than halakhic, we may expect them to make their primary demand a correct view of events rather than an Orthodox mode of religious behavior. Specifically, we may expect them to aim for a political consensus about Eretz Yisrael. This is, in fact, what we find. While the inner circle of Gush Emunim are Orthodox Jews and, for the most part, are personally of the "radical-fundamentalist" persuasion, they are, as Gush Emunim leaders, remarkably tolerant of religious and irreligious diversity—even while they are extremely intolerant of Orthodox Jews who do not believe in the "integrity" of Eretz Yisrael at all costs. In the religious Gush Emunim settlement of Kadumim, for example, about 10 percent of the families are nonreligious, and they send their children to a "general" school in a neighboring settlement.[78] This tolerance is explained by Gush Emunim leaders as flowing from Rabbi Kook's doctrine of "love of Israel," but it is at least partially related to the Gush political conviction and calculation that all elements of the public must be wooed if Israel is to withstand international pressure for the relinquishing of territories. Indeed, Gush educational seminars on Zionism usually include secular lecturers, especially hawkish labor and pioneering types, who are Eretz Yisrael believers.

Third, while radicals are spiritually utterly dependent on their (rabbinical) authorities, this is not the case of Gush Emunim. The culture of debate and semi-public introspection, so characteristic of the early secular pioneers, has been largely adopted by the inner group of Gush Emunim; they devotedly and regularly debate what they should do now and how they strayed or failed. Moreover, they readily disagree with one another and have no compunctions about discussing these disagreements.[79]

Finally, though Gush Emunim, like the radicals, grew out of Bnai Akiva and its yeshiva "world" of Mercaz Harav and is enormously influential within the religious-Zionist public, it should not be identified with that public's educational elites. Bnai Akiva has never fully endorsed it, though Gush members (probably in greater numbers than its opponents) are well represented in Bnai Akiva ranks. In fact, Bnai Akiva leaders, including secretaries-general who are sympathetic to it, have accused Gush Emunim of bad faith or disloyalty for, among other things, organizing public excursions in Judea and Samaria on days when Bnai Akiva had scheduled nationwide educational activities.[80] Furthermore, Mercaz Harav has given only qualified support, and there is at times tension between the yeshiva and the Gush. Rabbi Kook considered learning more important than political activity and urged Gush activists to devote more time to study. Prestigious yeshiva high schools, bastions of radical ideology, forbade pupils to take part in Gush demonstrations, including those that preceded the evacuation of Yamit in Sinai (1982). Such demonstrations were declared to be *bitul Torah*—a wasteful expenditure of time that should have been devoted to Torah study. Indeed, the well-publicized mass excursions in Judea and Samaria that Gush Emunim regularly conducted in its early years actually ceased when the word went out from Mercaz Harav that these were immodest, because of the free and easy mingling of the sexes.[81] Gush Emunim is caught between the radical fundamentalists they cannot cast off and with whom their leaders, for the most part, personally identify—and their messianic convictions which bid them build a politically right-wing consensus on Eretz Yisrael and "the continuation of the redemption."

Educational programs of Gush Emunim, such as the multimedia sound and light show screened to Israeli and foreign groups at Kadumim's Educational Center for Judea and Samaria, include elements that are particular to Gush Emunim and that are at loggerheads with the style and sensibilities of the radicals.[82] The musical background features European light classics as well as classic Zionist songs and religious (neo-Hasidic) melodies; the message is designed to make sense to religious and secular Zionists as well as to devout Christians.[83] Indeed, the thrust of the presentation, usually followed by discussions, links the return of the Jewish people to the Land, to faith and to the Bible, and to the religious, prophetically foretold drama of Jewish history.

The program is, of course, designed for outside consumption; the lessons children are taught in schools and the sermons Gush settlers hear from their rabbis in synagogues are often much more dogmatic and shrill.[84] Yet the sound-and-light show reflects what its educational leadership wishes to project as the Gush educational message. An analysis of the program yields *(a)* a strong belief in classical Zionism which many classical Zionists might nonetheless repudiate, for *(b)* it is given a biblical covenant-oriented basis providing *(c)* theological rationales for right-wing politics.

Gush Emunim educators evidently believe that faith can be translated for the secular public into national, historical, and cultural terminology without losing its (religious) essence.

The faith of Gush Emunim may best be termed Zionist-messianic. It is doubtful whether this is fundamentalistic in the context of the tradition of Judaism (the very emphasis on the Bible rather than on the Talmud makes the Gush suspect of hetero-doxy!)—though most Gush leaders are personally close to the fundamentalist-radicals of Mercaz Harav. The opponents of Gush Emunim ideology, in their polemical writings against it, have expressed the fear that it represents what, in Jewish history and theology, has been termed "false messianism."[85] But that too is a subject of controversy. In any case, to identify Gush Emunim as Jewish fundamentalism in Israel, as was recently done,[86] is questionable.

Nevertheless, Gush Emunim has a great impact, and there is no doubt that its influence strengthens fundamentalistic forces within the religious community and that it has fundamentalist repercussions in even wider circles. It represents what appears to be the best hope of religious Zionism to seize center stage in the drama of Zionism and to effectively get its message across. If we bear in mind that the radical-fundamentalists have come increasingly, in their own eyes as well as in the perception of outsiders, to represent the entire religious-Zionist public, we can readily see how Gush Emunim fits into the picture. The radical group, which has included top educational leaders, believes that territorial compromise is forbidden by halakha, and they find their fundamentalistic rabbinical leadership willing to issue rulings that support them.[87] In educational forums such as Gesher (Bridge), an institute for religious-secular dialogue between pupils, it was reported that "radical youth no longer agreed to even discuss 'the integrity of Eretz Yisrael'; the rabbis had 'already decided.'"[88] Gush Emunim thus are placed in the role of "idealistic practitioners" of what all religious Zionists ostensibly know and believe.

This "radical" ambience is reenforced from a surprising source: the maverick haredi movement of Habad Hasidism. Habad is intensely missionizing and open to non-haredi Jews. Its outreach work is highly successful and specializes in soft sell—in the army, at street corners and bus stations. The general view, even among secular Jews, has been that Habad is "all right," though its recent active role in haredi politics may have cost it some sympathy. While Habad is anti-Zionist in a rather idiosyncratic theological manner, it is extremely national: "the nations" want to take Eretz Yisrael away from us, but it is forbidden to relinquish any part of it. Habad thus joins the Zionist Gush Emunim in creating an ostensible "consensus" in religious Jewry about Eretz Yisrael.

To this we may add the influence of the late Rabbi Kahane's radically nationalistic and racist movement.[89] Kahane supplied the "simple solutions" that many seem to desire to the complex problems of Israel. His viewpoint was genuinely fundamentalistic insofar as he adopted the sectarian approaches of the haredim (and their hatred of irreligious Jews) together with the messianic politics of Gush Emunim. Unlike Gush Emunim, he did not tolerate the very tensions and paradoxes that the Gush (paradoxically) heightens. If Gush Emunim wants "the whole Land of Israel" and rights for the Arab inhabitants, religious piety and tolerant love for the nonreligious, and so forth, Kahane utilized the psychic stress created by these dichotomies and offered a solution: expulsion of Arabs and, ultimately, war against irreligious and "leftist" Jews. Kahane's fundamentalist solutions to the problems that Gush Emunim has helped bring to the fore have influenced Gush members and convinced many that "Kahane has the answers."[90]

Some of the particular and perhaps idiosyncratic qualities of Gush Emunim education can be observed in the curricular and ideological writings of Dan Be'eri, a central educational personality of the Gush. Be'eri was one of the key figures of the Jewish underground in the early 1980s. His activities occasioned much soul-searching in the Gush, though he and his friends won the warm support of the Hebron firebrand and Gush leader Rabbi Moshe Levinger. Be'eri is now head of the Kiryat Arba Talmud Torah or heder, a school in which "Torah and piety" are the main educational objectives. (The irony of an extremist-Zionist institution of learning being called heder, the trademark of passive Galut-oriented haredi Jewry, beggars description.)

Be'eri, like his Gush Emunim colleague Rabbi Yoel Bin-Nun, head of the Girls' High School in Ofra,[91] believes in integration of Torah and wisdom, of Jewish and "general" subject matter. In the Kiryat Arba Talmud Torah, all general studies except mathematics are integrated with Jewish studies, including language, nature, geography, history, "society," and "culture." Teachers are required to be men who have studied for many years at yeshivot, but who also have a wide knowledge of science and humanities, pedagogic skills, and a talent for warm relationships with pupils and colleagues.[92]

Be'eri is extremely critical of the "yeshiva learning," which he considers a withdrawal from reality, a withdrawal that is no longer justified. Like Unna a generation before, he finds fault with the purely "personal ideal" of the yeshiva. His critique, in fact, is very reminiscent of the "expansionism" and "adaptationism" of the religious kibbutz movement, though it grows out of a radically different political and social soil and draws on different theological sources:

> From now on, we must direct all our human powers to a new pioneering effort . . . not to educate our children to some undefined "occupying oneself with Torah" but the acquisition of the entire Torah. Systematic and harmonious . . . together with wide knowledge of the world we live in, with all its scientific and human dimensions; the very world we are called upon to perfect . . . as God's kingdom. Not the scarecrow of a "halakhic state" which is dry, clerical and totalitarian, but rather, we must set on its feet the nation of Israel in its rebirth, in the fullness of its creative powers in all fields.[93]

The educational conception is romantic, perhaps utopian, and draws upon the mystic harmonizations of Rabbi Abraham Isaac Kook. If implemented by fundamentalists, it is also likely to be dry, clerical, and totalitarian. But it need not be. Though there is a close family relationship between the radical-fundamentalists and Gush Emunim, they are not identical, and they are in disagreement over several issues.

The General Impact of Fundamentalism on the Educational Scene

We have discussed at length how haredi fundamentalism has radically affected National-Religious education. We have also noted how Gush Emunim reenforces fundamentalistic tendencies among the larger religious public. We must now make some more general remarks about the ramifications of educational fundamentalism on Israeli society, both religious and secular.

Ahad Ha'am, the father of cultural Zionism, was convinced that the era of religiously authorized norms was ending, that the explicitly religious understanding of Jewish culture was, in the modern era, a fixation to be overcome. Judaism was overdue to liberate itself from cultural childhood (i.e., religion) and to move into a mature stage of rational and scientific self-understanding. In this stage, Torah would be understood as Jewish (moral and national) culture; Jewish learning in the yeshiva manner would be supplanted by the learning of scholars at the Hebrew University and kindred institutions. And the emerging Jewish commonwealth would be the locale for a new and modern Judaism which translated the moral character of the Jewish people and culture into contemporary categories, facing contemporary challenges.[94]

For various reasons, this program, though it had many adherents, including most of the cultural and political leadership of Israel, has not been easy to transmit to younger generations. Ahad Ha'am's thesis—historical continuity should be maintained through national forms and moral fervor that would not require religious belief or halakhic norms—often seemed sentimental and artificial; he appeared to be demanding traditionalism without the specific contents of tradition.[95] Educators, for several generations, have been attempting to work out in philosophical and curricular terms what that meant.

The task has been made more difficult still by the unexpected survival and vibrancy of Orthodox Judaism, in the very midst of physical destruction in Europe and cultural assimilation worldwide. When Ben-Gurion gave army exemptions to yeshiva students in 1948, he thought he was dealing with an archaic yet cherished remnant of a world destroyed; he did not know that he was setting the foundations for a subculture that considered itself Zionism's spiritual successor and not only its historical predecessor. Ahad Ha'am and his disciples thought in terms of inevitable historical processes; the haredi world, on the other hand, worked with Providence, catastrophes, and miracles. At first, no one took them seriously, and they themselves disdained all cultural and cognitive negotiation with the "heretics." But then, as the cultural and educational crises of the secularists became more apparent, they began to look more and more sane, plausible—and threatening.

This may be stated as follows: The obstinate insistence of religious fundamentalists that they are the only true representatives of the national tradition and future, coupled with the cultural dilemmas of secular Zionism, has given some intellectual respectability to the notion, among religious and nonreligious Jewish Israelis alike, that secular Zionism is bankrupt or played out. This thesis is, of course, systematically nourished by fundamentalists.[96] They declare, and few offer energetic repudiations, that secular culture is not Jewish. And this, it appears, is a double-edged sword. On the one hand, it leads a small minority to seek Judaism from authentic spokesmen and sources; conversely, it convinces the great majority that historical Jewish culture is incorrigibly religious and therefore not for them. The first reaction has led some prominent Israelis, especially from the entertainment world and the army, to return to (haredi) Judaism; the second weakens the cultural roots and search of almost everyone else.

A prominent example of the latter is the decreasing interest in Jewish studies on the university scene. Most areas of Jewish learning are seen more and more as somehow the province of the religious. For example, the kibbutz movement, which in the early 1970s initiated important Jewish learning programs, especially in its Teachers' Seminary at Oranim, has since 1987 "temporarily suspended" its curricular work on teaching Jewish sources. There is, quite simply, less interest. The appearance of religious teachers of Judaica on the Oranim campus also created suspicion. The teaching of Judaism seemed, in the spiritual and political situation of contemporary Israel, less like a bridge between religious and secular Jews and more like a threatening beachhead of fundamentalists.[97] Secular Jews are more wary, thus more insistent that they must go their own way, without help or cooperation with the religious. Yet they are unclear what that way is, and how it will be linked to the traditions of the Jewish people.

For both the non-Orthodox and the Orthodox, the radical groups are increasingly seen as the religious wave of the future, as more authentic and legitimate. They have more children, and so they require more schools. (It is also widely held that the demographic vitality of the haredi and radical-Zionist communities is a healthy response to the danger of physical extinction that, since the Holocaust, hangs over the Jewish people.) Because of their disproportionate political power under the current Israeli electoral system, the haredi parties have made every coalition agreement dependent on more "aid" for their schools and more benefits for those who learn. Though this creates great resentment, it also puts formerly marginal mores and assumptions into the center of the cultural and social stage. Among these mores and assumptions that are, in fact, antithetical to the ethos of classical Zionism we note the following: that rabbis are better off and more profoundly learned without secular knowledge and that, consequently, the university is spiritually useless or even pernicious for religious leaders; that it is better to learn than to go to the army; that Zionism is not a serious revolution in Jewish life but an episode, or it is serious but not understood properly by its (secular) historical representatives.

It is obvious that this development seriously weakens the status and educational power of traditional religious Zionism. The radicals consider themselves the future of religious Zionism; to a large extent, they are also its present. The result is that the moderate educational ideology of, say, the religious kibbutz movement as envisioned by its shapers has no social hinterland. Most religious youth accept more haredi-type standards as normative as schools move to the right in their curricula and expectations. In National-Religious educational circles, especially for social elites, there is increasing radicalization, which means a stronger emphasis on external manifestations of halahkic loyalty, and increasing isolation from nonreligious youth throughout the educational process, extending in many cases through army service. Likewise, there is an increasing disposition to take rabbinical pronouncements as definitive judgments on all issues, including political ones. Schools which try to keep their distance from this radicalization, prominently those of the religious kibbutz movement, find to their dismay that large percentages of their graduates "leave religion" (and thus, too, the religious kibbutz framework) in the early stages of their army service. The religious Orthodoxy which characterized the Western European leadership, which blended a humanistic orientation and strict halakhic observance, appears in retreat. Even where it is respected, it, and not the haredi approach, is considered a relic. This relic is sometimes venerated for its nobility and sometimes despised for its naiveté. A veteran religious kibbutz educator described (religious) educational deliberations in which he found himself in a perennial minority position: "They count our votes, but our votes don't count."

In 1954, several years before immigrating to Israel, I spent a few months as a student in Jerusalem. One Sabbath afternoon an Israeli friend took me for a tour of the haredi neighborhoods of Jerusalem. She was, like myself, a religious Zionist, of the Mizrachi persuasion. But she approached the haredi section of the city with something approaching reverence. I was surprised at this, and my own background made me skeptical and derogatory; after all, these people were not building kibbutzim, defending the country, speaking Hebrew. They were part of the past, exotic, not "with it." My companion was patient with me, but pedagogical. "But Mike," she said, "these Jews are really religious." Thinking back, I now realize how that conversation has helped me understand some of the processes described above.

Fundamentalism and Education: A Postscript

As I noted at the beginning, all fundamentalist groups claim to be authentically and exclusively continuing the tradition, and protecting it against the challenges of a degenerate and destructive modernity. Many of Lazarus-Yafe's categories[98] apply to both the haredim and the Zionist radicals: they are countercultures; they reject Western ideologies and see no need to harmonize their religious convictions with democracy; they are antagonistic to scientific method, despite their general comfort with technology; their understanding of religion is monolithic and ahistorical, and their theology is crude insofar as they refuse to engage in serious discourse with modern thought and culture.

From a specifically Jewish point of view, fundamentalist thought and education may be severely criticized for refusing to take the midrashic method and "language" (of interpretation) with real seriousness. It is the midrashic method and language that made it possible for Torah to remain, in the words of the psalmist, "perfect, restoring the soul." An education that lacks a true midrashic-interpretative dimension is not only dogmatic and ahistorical, but it cannot teach children to recognize the challenges of their own time through the prism of their religious traditions.

Richard S. Peters, the renowned English philosopher of education, once wrote that all education consists of teaching a language, that is, a basic method and a broad culture—with all its civilizational assumptions, cultural idioms, modes of communication. But, he added, the purpose is not only to learn the language, but to be enabled to do "literature" in it; to make it possible for children to express themselves in and through the culture, say new things, in short, creatively continue the language.[99]

Where education is in the hands of fundamentalists, it seems to be all language and no literature: children learn to speak but they are incapable of saying anything new. Our religious traditions, in this age more than ever, need an education for both conviction and intelligence, for spontaneity and creativity as well as loyalty. Fundamentalism, by indoctrinating instead of educating,[100] is liable to protect religion to death and thus, once again paradoxically, to deny children (and all who learn) that which education and, some would say, religion too is meant to bestow upon them—spiritual life.

Notes

1. Ian S. Lustick, *For the Land and the Lord: Jewish Fundamentalism in Israel* (New York: Council on Foreign Affairs, 1988). See, for example, p. 153.

2. Some useful readings on these theological foundations are Emil L. Fackenheim, *Quest for Past and Future: Essays in Jewish Theology* (Bloomington: Indiana University Press, 1968); Martin Buber, *Israel and the World* (New York: Schocken Books, 1963); Leo W. Schwartz, ed., *Great Ages and Ideas of the Jewish People* (New York: Random House, 1956), especially part 1, "The Biblical Age," by Yehezkel Kaufmann.

3. For a brief discussion that enumerates and explicates this talmudic formulation of the laws of universal morality, see S. S. Schwartzschild, *Encyclopedia Judaica*, vol. 12 (Jerusalem: Keter Publishing House, Ltd., 1971), col. 1189–1190. The Noachide laws are the prohibitions against idolatry, blasphemy, bloodshed, sexual immorality, theft, the eating of limbs from living animals, and the positive injunction to establish courts of law.

4. Lev. 18:28; see also Deut. 29.

5. Avot (Ethics of the Fathers) VI-6. A large part of this tractate of the Mishnah deals with the virtues of Torah and of its study.

6. (Mishnah) Peah I-1. A central biblical source for teaching is Deut. 6:7, though there are many others.

7. In the words of the talmudic sages: "Suppose you say, I shall learn Torah in order to be called learned, to have a seat in the academy, to have endless life in the world-to-come, the teaching is: (Study in order to fulfill the commandment) 'to love the Lord thy God.'" *Sifrei*, Deut. 48.

8. Moses Maimonides, *Mishneh Torah, Hilchot Talmud Torah* (Laws of Torah Study), I-8.

9. For a detailed discussion, see Moshe Aberbach, "Educational Institutions and Problems during the Talmudic Age," *Hebrew Union College Annual* 36 (1966): 107–20.

10. B.T. (Babylonian Talmud) *Hagigah* 3b.

11. Avot V-24.

12. Maimonides, *Mishneh Torah, Hilchot Talmud Torah*, I-11. On the argument regarding the primacy of distinct fields of Torah study, see Isadore Twersky, "Talmudists, Philosophers, Kabbalists: The Quest for Spirituality in the Sixteenth Century," in Bernard Dov Cooperman, ed., *Jewish Thought in the Sixteenth Century* (Cambridge: Harvard University Press, 1983), pp. 431–57.

13. See Dov Rappel, "The Central Status of Torah Study in Jewish Consciousness in the Middle Ages" (in Hebrew), *Niv Hamidrashia* (Tel Aviv, 1972), pp. 155–63, in which he describes social and educational legislation and halakhic decisions in various communities. See also idem, "Be Diligent to Study . . . What to Answer the Heretic" (in Hebrew), in which he surveys diverse views about the study of "external wisdom" vis-à-vis Torah study as reflected in different commentaries on one Mishnaic passage, in *Avot. Techumin: Halakhic Compendium*, vol. 3 (Alon Shvut, Tzomet, 1982), pp. 477–84.

14. Naphtali Herz Wessely, "Words of Truth and Peace," in Paul R. Mendes-Flohr and Jehuda Reinharz, eds., *The Jew in the Modern World: A Documentary History* (New York: Oxford University Press, 1980), p. 63.

15. See Shaul Stampfer, "*Heder* Study, Knowledge of Torah and the Maintenance of Social Stratification in Traditional East European Jewish Society," in Janet Aviad, ed., *Studies in Jewish Education*, vol. 3 (Jerusalem: Magnes Press, 1988), pp. 271–89.

16. For a full discussion, see, for example, the introduction to Arthur Hertzberg, *The Zionist Idea: A Historical Analysis and Reader* (Garden City, N.Y.: Doubleday and Co. and Herzl Press, 1959), pp. 15–100.

17. See Marc Silverman, "The Educational Ideal of the Founders of the Religious Kibbutz: Talmudic Scholar, Pioneer and Citizen" (in Hebrew with English abstract), in Aviad, *Studies in Jewish Education*, vol. 3, pp. 102–24 (Hebrew), pp. 304–6 (English).

18. Samuel C. Heilman and Menachem Friedman, "Religious Fundamentalism and Religious Jews: The Case of the Haredim," in Martin E. Marty and R. Scott Appleby, eds., *Fundamentalisms Observed* (Chicago: University of Chicago Press, 1991).

19. I have dealt with this issue in "Religious Reactions: Testimony and Theology," in Stephen J. Roth, ed., *The Impact of the Six Day War: A Twenty Year Assessment* (London: Macmillan Press and Institute of Jewish Affairs, 1988), pp. 209–31.

20. For an illuminating example, see Rabbi S. Wagschal, *Successful Chinuch (Education): Guide for Parents and Educators* (Jerusalem and New York: Feldheim, 1988). The guide is replete with talmudic and other rabbinic sources which authorize the unambiguous (but not unsophisticated) instructions conveyed to the reader.

21. The ambience of the Orthodox synagogue is such that the worshiper will feel quite comfortable reading such study sheets between chapters of prayer and Scriptural reading. There are a number of agencies, ranging from the national-religious movement to Habad Hasidim that compete for the synagogue reader's attention in this regard. We may note, too, that the ultra-Orthodox community has had no difficulty in applying communications technology to its own educational needs. Thus, taped Torah lessons, talk and sing cassettes, and even taped daily Talmud lessons are popular. On my own daily walks around Jerusalem I usually listen to taped music. More than once I have been asked: "Mozart or Mishnah?"

22. See Aviezer Ravitzky, "Exile in the Holy Land: The Dilemma of Haredi Jewry," in *Israel: State and Society, 1948–88: Studies in Contemporary Jewry*, vol. 5 (Jerusalem: Institute of Contemporary Jewry, Hebrew University, 1989), pp. 89–125.

23. Menachem Friedman, "Religious and Haredi Society in Israel after the Elections to the Twelfth Knesset: Tendencies and Processes" (in Hebrew), *Skira Chodsheet* (Monthly Review) (Publication for army officers, Chief Education Officer, I.D.F.), vol. 36, no. 5 (30 June 1989).

24. Avraham Yosef Wolff, *Education in the Face of the Generation* (in Hebrew) (Tel Aviv: Netzach Publishers, 5714/1954), p. 12.

25. R. Friedman, *The Boys across the Bridge* (in Hebrew) (no publisher or date listed).

26. Ibid., p. 81.

27. An ideal based on an interpretation of Gen. 18:9.

28. For example, on the basis of Exod. 19:3, which states that Moses shall speak the words of revelation to "the children of Israel" and say them to "the House of Jacob," the talmudic sages in the midrashic

work *Mechilta* deduce that the "House of Jacob" are the women who must be told the laws of the Torah more gently and in less detail. (The word "say" is interpreted as less demanding than "speak.")

29. David Zvi Hoffman, "Make Your Torah Study Fixed and Your Work Transient" (in Hebrew) *Niv Hamidrashia* (journal of Midrashiat Noam Yeshiva High School, Tel Aviv), Spring 1969, pp. 184–92.

30. Ibid., p. 186.

31. Ibid., p. 191.

32. Thus, for example, a group of haredi youth leaders were reported to have "explained" at a seminar run for high school seniors of National-Religious schools, in *Torah V'avodah* (Torah and labor), publication of *Ne'emanai Torah V'avodah* (Adherents of Torah and labor) (Jerusalem), January 1986, p. 5. The pupils were reportedly told that "a shirker is one who is capable of going to a yeshiva and goes to the army instead." *Ne'emanai Torah V'avodah* is an antifundamentalist Orthodox-Zionist group which regularly conducts seminars and documents instances of educational and social influences of haredi Jewry on the religious-Zionist public.

33. The situation of Sephardic haredim is somewhat different. Though many Sephardic pietists have been "assimilated" to the Ashkenazic "yeshiva world," much of Sephardic haredi life is much in the nature of religious-cultural traditionalism, which does not share the Ashkenazic antagonism to the State of Israel or to traditionally minded Jews who are lax in religious observance. The Sephardic-haredi party, Shas, reflects this ambivalence between haredi and neotraditional orientations. See Heilman and Friedman, "Religious Fundamentalism and Religious Jews," pp. 321–26.

34. Menachem Friedman, *State and Society: The Non-Zionist Orthodox in Eretz Yisrael, 1918–1936* (in Hebrew) (Jerusalem: Yad Ben-Zvi Publications, 1977), p. 362.

35. Jacob Katz, *Tradition and Crisis: Jewish Society at the End of the Middle Ages* (New York: Schocken Books, 1971), chap. 18.

36. Jacob Katz, "Traditional Society and Modern Society" (in Hebrew), in Jacob Katz, *Jewish Nationalism: Essays and Studies* (Jerusalem: Zionist Library, 1979), p. 162.

37. Rabbi Shlomo Volve, "The Yeshiva in Our Age" (in Hebrew), Mordecai Bar-Lev, ed., *Religious Education in Israeli Society: Anthology* (Jerusalem: Hebrew University, 1986), p. 128.

38. Ibid.

39. Deborah Weissman, "Bais Ya'acov" (Paper presented at the International Conference on Jewish Education, Hebrew University of Jerusalem, Samuel Mendel Melton Center for Jewish Education in the Diaspora, 24–29 June 1984).

40. Ibid.

41. Quoted in Deborah Weissman, "Bais Ya'akov as an Innovation in Jewish Women's Education: A Contribution to the Study of Education and Social Change" (Paper).

42. These declarations and those that follow are found in a *kuntress* or declarative brochure issued by the council of the Eda Haredit and signed by the one time acknowledged leader of Jerusalem haredi Jewry, Rabbi Yoseph Haim Sonnenfeld, in 1919. The kuntress is entitled "Do No Injury to My Anointed" (in Hebrew) (n.d.). It deals with "pernicious" attempts to make innovations in traditional education.

43. Rabbi Eliyalu Dessler, *A Letter from Elijah*, vol. 3 (in Hebrew), ed. A. Carmel and A. Halperin (Bnai Brak, Israel, 1974), pp. 355–58.

44. It is noteworthy that the editors of Dessler's writings see fit to print "B.A." in Latin (and not Hebrew) letters and to explain to their readers, in a marginal note, that B.A. means "an academic title granted by the university," a fact of which, it is hoped, they are not aware (Ibid., p. 355).

45. Rabbi Aaron Kotler, "How to Teach Torah" (Lakewood, N.J.: Rabbi Aaron Kotler Institute for Advanced Learning, 1972), p. 3. Rabbi Kotler was not part of the Israeli haredi leadership, but with regard to haredi leadership and ideology, this is not a relevant factor.

46. The writer is "sorry and our hearts are stricken that we have to deal with such

garbage and bring it . . . into the homes of pious people." *Yated Neeman*, Friday, 10 Av 5749 (11 August 1989).

47. Ibid., p. 10. The vessel of pure oil is an allusion to the undefiled vessel of oil found in the Temple after its desecration by the Greeks, which made possible its rededication in 165 B.C.E., according to the Talmud (B.T., Shabbat 21b).

48. On the problems of the "trends" and the place of the Mizrachi trend within them, see Zvi Lamm, "Ideological Tensions in Education," *Jerusalem Quarterly*, no. 6 (Winter 1978): 34–110, and especially 96–97.

49. On the basis of conversations with graduates of such schools. Written critiques are legion, for example, Yisrael Sadan, "The Application of 'Torah and General Culture' in Our Time: The Yeshiva High School (in Hebrew), in *Niv Hamidrashia*, vols. 16–17 (Tel Aviv: Midrashiat Noam, 1984), esp. p. 257. However, these critiques, often written by advocates of yeshiva high schools, may be suspected of considerable bias. In *Amudim*, the magazine of the religious kibbutz movement, there have been frequent discussions as to whether this kibbutz movement needs yeshiva high schools of its own or should send its sons to existing ones, in order to "strengthen the religiosity" of its children. See, for example, A. Shaffir and Yedidya Cohen in *Amudim*, no. 353, (Nissan 5735/April 1975), pp. 282–85. The most pithy example in my own experience: when my oldest son transferred from a yeshiva high school to a standard religious high school, he returned from his first day of studies with the remark: "In this [new] school, they teach Talmud as though it were a subject." That remark catches the essence of the controversy.

50. Charles Liebman and Eliezer Don-Yehiya, *Religion and Politics in Israel* (Bloomington: Indiana University Press, 1984), p. 122. Liebman, who developed these concepts in "The Rise of Neo-Traditionalism among Orthodox Jews in Israel" (in Hebrew), *Megamot* 27 (May 1982): 231–50, writes of the dichotomies between expansionism and adaptationism and associates expansionism with the radical ap-

proaches he finds prevalent in the Zionist yeshivot and in Gush Emunim. I am proposing that in the religious kibbutz movement, both may have been uniquely linked.

51. This "circle" is difficult to delineate precisely, but it includes, in addition to the leadership of the religious kibbutz movement, most of the religious academicians of the time, religious intellectuals in education departments of the Jewish Agency, and other scholarly and educational personalities. In Israel they are often identified by their subscriptions to *Deot*, a journal of religious university students and academicians, and *Amudim*, the journal of the religious kibbutz movement. The editor of *Deot*, Dr. Gabriel Cohen of Bar-Ilan University, informs me that the index lists hundreds of contributors to *Deot* throughout the years; there are significantly fewer regular contributors to *Amudim*.

52. Pinchas Rosenbluth, cited from the Archives of the Religious Kibbutz, in Silverman, "Educational Ideal," p. 103. Among the ideological leaders active in this discussion are Moshe Unna, Yeshayahu (Isaiah) Leibowitz, Zuriel Admonit, Eliezer Goldman, and Simcha Friedman. Unna has written extensively on these problems. For a comprehensive religious kibbutz perspective, see Zuriel Admonit, *Within the Current—And against It* (in Hebrew) (Tel Aviv: Kibbutz Hadati, 5737/1977).

53. Silverman, "Educational Ideal," p. 103.

54. Mordecai Bar-Lev, Yedidyah Cohen, and Shlomo Rosner, eds., *Fifty Years of Bnai Akiva in Israel, 1929–1979* (in Hebrew) (Tel Aviv: Bnai Akiva Movement, 5747/1987), p. 14.

55. For a learned discussion of the cultural processes being described, see Judah Goldin, "Of Change and Adaptation in Judaism," in Barry L. Eichler and Jeffry H. Tigay, eds., *Studies in Midrash and Related Literature* (Philadelphia: Jewish Publication Society, 1988), pp. 215–37.

56. This is not, of course, to imply that they do not engage in much Torah study but that this has remained an academic and

spiritual exercise and a normative-halakhic practice, which has not become applicable to "changing the total reality in the light of the Torah."

57. An outstanding example is that of the radical yet Orthodox thinker Prof. Isaiah Leibowitz, who, as late as the 1950s, spoke of the challenge posed by the creation of the State of Israel to halakhic authorities for innovation and rethinking. In his later writings his emphasis has been on the innate tension between political and religious leadership, between the power of the state and the conscience of the religiously observant (therefore "free") individual and his or her religious community. See Isaiah Leibowitz, *Judaism, the Jewish People and the State of Israel* (in Hebrew) (Tel Aviv: Schocken Publishing, 1975). On the other hand, there have been periodic attempts to "revive" this circle, for example, in the Ne'emanai Torah V'avodah (Adherents of Torah and labor) group and in the Yahadut Shel Torah (Judaism of Torah) movement of the sixties and seventies, the latter led by the one-time head of the Israel Academy of Sciences, Prof. Ephraim Urbach.

58. Gideon Aran, "The Origins and Culture of Gush Emunim: A Messianic Movement in Modern Israel" (in Hebrew) (Ph.D. diss., Hebrew University of Jerusalem, February 1987), pp. 80–99. See also idem, "From Religious Zionism to Zionist Religion: The Roots of Gush Emunim," in Peter Y. Medding, ed., *Studies in Contemporary Jewry*, vol. 2 (Bloomington: Indiana University Press, 1986).

59. On these developments and tensions, see Mordecai Bar-Lev, "The Educational Institutions of the Bnai Akiva Movement" (in Hebrew) in Bar-Lev, Cohen, and Rosner, *Fifty Years of Bnai Akiva in Israel,* pp. 289–349. On the orientation of the yeshiva leadership to the "Higher yeshivot" and its consequences, see also Mordecai Bar-Lev, "The Yeshiva High School and the 'Torah and General Culture' Approach" (in Hebrew) in Mordecai Breuer, ed., *Torah and General Culture: The Movement, Personalities, Ideals* (Ramat Gan, Israel: Bar-Ian University, 1987), pp. 237–53.

60. Israel Sadan, in conversation with the writer, 8 September 1989.

61. Rabbi Yehoshua Yogel, "The Way of the Midrashia" (in Hebrew) in Bar-Lev, *Religious Education in Israeli Society,* pp. 147–56. The citation is on p. 114.

62. On this quasi-deterministic viewpoint, see Michael Rosenak, "State of Israel," in Arthur A. Cohen and Paul Mendes-Flohr, eds., *Contemporary Jewish Religious Thought* (New York: Charles Scribner's Sons, 1987), pp. 909–16.

63. Bar-Lev, "The Yeshiva High School and the 'Torah and General Culture' Approach."

64. Conversation with Rabbi Jochanan Fried, founding member of Gush Emunim and longtime disciple of Rabbi Zvi Yehuda Kook, 5 September 1989.

65. Aran well describes the learning and lifestyles of radical-Zionist couples who are attached to the Mercaz Harav "family." Husbands and wives are likely to study together, and women, most of them graduates of the ulpanot, are well versed in Jewish learning, though not in Talmud. Aran, "The Origins and Culture of Gush Emunim," pp. 294–322. In terms of my thesis that the haredi woman does not "learn" because she is a major "bridge" between the holy and the profane communities, one may expect that the antilearning ideology (for women) will dissipate among the radical-Zionist fundamentalists since they consider the entire society holy. At the same time, haredi-type separation of the sexes at public occasions remains in force, as a kind of formal halakhic requirement and as a conspicuous indicator of the community's high standards of sexual morality.

66. This is a sermonette published in the "portion of the week" bulletin, *Oneg Shabbat,* distributed by a right-wing Society for the Implementation of Jewish Values, published "in cooperation with the Likud," for 28 July 1989. On various approaches in Israeli education to the Abraham stories, see J. Schoneveld, *The Bible in Israeli Education* (Assen/Amsterdam: Van Gorcum, 1976), pp. 150–66.

67. The term is used by one of its fore-

most spokesmen, Rabbi Shlomo Aviner. See Aviner, "Radicalism and Liberalism in the National-Religious Camp" (in Hebrew), *Amudim* (Journal of the religious kibbutz movement) 404, (Av 5739/August 1979): 375–82, in which he chides those who seek a synthesis between Judaism and Western culture. Among the responses, see Amnon Shapiro, "On Fundamentalism and Radicalism" (in Hebrew), *Amudim* 407, (Elul 5739/September 1979), in which he insists that Aviner's "radicalism" is quite simply fundamentalism. It is noteworthy that Shapiro can express this opinion despite his sympathy for Gush Emunim. See discussion on the relationship between Gush Emunim and the radicals, below.

68. Yochanan ben Yaakov, in conversation with the writer, described discussions with leaders of Ariel, in which he, as secretary-general of Bnai Akiva, attempted to dissuade them from breaking away from that movement. The response he received from one of them was: "The difference between us is that you belong to Western culture, while we belong only to Jewish culture." Ben Yaakov, a strictly Orthodox Jew and an outspoken opponent of what he considers "cosmopolitan" tendencies among "left-wingers," related this with a smile.

69. For descriptions and critiques of Noam, see *Haid Hachinch* (The educational echo): *Journal of the Teachers Association of Israel,* for 4 and 25 November 1976 (in Hebrew).

70. Rabbi Yaakov Filber, "From Religious Education to Torah Education" (in Hebrew), in Bar-Lev, *Religious Education in Israeli Society,* pp. 198–203.

71. Ibid. p. 200.

72. For discussion of this search for roots and meaning among potential "returners to Judaism," see Janet Aviad, *Return to Judaism: Religious Renewal in Israel* (Chicago: University of Chicago Press, 1983), chap. 4. This attraction to religious Hesder groups in the army by others who remark enviously that "they have a group" was also discussed by Rabbi Yochanan Fried, formerly head of Jewish studies in the Education Corps of the Israeli army in conversation with the writer.

73. Yochanan Ben-Yaakov, "Religious Youth and the Manner of Its Education" (in Hebrew), *Amudim* 467 (Heshvan 5745/November 1985): 80–83.

74. Conversation with Yochanan Ben-Yaakov, 14 September 1989.

75. Lawrence Kaplan, "Education and Ideology in Religious Zionism Today," *Forum* (Jerusalem, World Zionist Organization) no. 36 (Fall/Winter 1979): 30.

76. On the history and ideology of the movement, see Gideon Aran, "Jewish Zionist Fundamentalism: the Bloc of the Faithful in Israel (Gush Emunim)," in Marty and Appleby, *Fundamentalisms Observed.*

77. See Gershom Scholem, "Towards an Understanding of the Messianic Idea in Judaism," in his *The Messianic Idea in Judaism* (New York: Schocken Books, 1971), pp. 1–36. For an example of the religiously innovative tendency in Gush Emunim thinking, see Moshe Ben-Yosef (Hagar), "The Revolution at an Intermission" (in Hebrew), *Nekudah* 139 (March–April 1990), which argues that the halakhah must undergo a Zionist revision.

78. Zvi Slonin, the director of Kadumim's educational center, remarked to me that one of the nonreligious members is "so non-observant" that he doesn't enter the synagogue even on Yom Kippur. "He always takes over guard duty for the rest of us on Yom Kippur so we won't be kept from our prayers. What a great fellow. Everybody loves him." Conversation with Zvi Slonin, director of the educational center at Kadumim in Samaria, 10 September 1989.

79. Conversations with Gush Emunim activists give this impression, though it may not be true of the inner circle that Aran deals with in his monograph "Jewish Zionist Fundamentalism." To give a recent and well-publicized example: In September 1989, Menachem Fruman, a leading Gush personality and rabbi of Tekoah, a settlement in the Judaean Hills, conducted conversations with Faisal Hussaini, a leading Palestinian spokesman, in Jerusalem,. on a variety of religious and political subjects including "how our two peoples can live together in this land." Fruman explained to the press that he had

stated his position "as a right-winger"; this, he said, had in no way disturbed the two in creating a cordial relationship. While Fruman was promptly condemned by his colleagues in Gush Emunim and declared to have "read himself out" of the Gush, it was only a matter of days before a televised discussion was held between him and other West Bank settlers, at Kfar Etzion, a kibbutz closely associated with Gush leaders. See Aran, "Jewish Zionist Fundamentalism: the Bloc of the Faithful in Israel (Gush Emunim)," in Marty and Appleby, *Fundamentalisms Observed.*

80. Bar-Lev, Cohen, and Rosner, *Fifty Years of Bnai Akiva in Israel,* pp. 195–96.

81. These points were repeated by Yochanan Ben-Yaakov in conversation with the writer.

82. Presently to be found in the library of the Fundamentalism Project.

83. According to Zvi Slonin, in conversation with the writer. In his words: "Often they [Christian audiences] understand better than the secular Jews; they have a feeling for the Bible and a faith in it that our secular youth has lost."

84. Rabbis in Gush Emunim settlements are, of course, usually of the radical "school." But such rabbis are found in many synagogues elsewhere; Gush Emunim is not a separate sect. Likewise, though schools in Gush Emunim settlements are invariably of the national-religious type or are yeshiva-type institutions inspired by the Mercaz Harav model (since the settlers are religious Jews), they are not inherently different from such schools in the cities. However, almost all national-religious schools have moved to the right in the past two decades. See Aviezer Ravitzky, *The Phenomenon of Kahanism: Consciousness and Political Reality* (in Hebrew) (Jerusalem Institute for Contemporary Jewry of the Hebrew University, 1985). What may strike the observer is the importance attributed to educational touring in settlement schools, with emphatic use of the Bible to show the close link between Land and Book. One must also note the influence of the community on the ethos of the school, especially in such monolithic and radical communities as Kiryat Arba (He-

bron). An extreme example: When Rabbi Moshe Levinger, Gush firebrand of Hebron, was taken to prison for "negligence leading to the death" of an Arab (May 1990), community leaders demanded that school classes be released for the day to accompany the rabbi. The deputy-principal (in the absence of the principal) allowed school to be dismissed for an hour. When I inquired at the Ministry of Education whether the school authorities of Kiryat Arba had been reprimanded for this decision, I was told that the deputy-head's decision was not deserving rebuke. He had turned down the local council's request and had come up with a plausible compromise solution. "Educational institutions belong to communities and, within limits, must be sensitive to them," a high official at the ministry explained to me.

85. Most outspoken in this direction has been Isaiah Leibowitz. See Liebowitz, *Faith, History, and Values* (in Hebrew) (Jerusalem: Acadamon, 1982), especially pp. 218–19.

86. Lustick, *For the Land and the Lord.*

87. A perusal of *B'Sede Chemed* (In the field of national religious education), issued by the Department of National-Religious Education in the Ministry of Education (in Hebrew), shows a steady increase in nationalistic emphases, touched with theological intimations and rhetoric, in educational proposals since 1967. These also affect, and in some cases reflect, changing curricular aims and objectives. For an early discussion of this, see Schoneveld, *The Bible in Israeli Education,* pp. 131–32.

88. In conversation with Dr. Daniel Tropper, director of Gesher.

89. Ravitzky, *Phenomenon of Kahanism.*

90. Ibid., pp. 26–27.

91. Rabbi Bin-Nun has, in recent years, been the leader of the most moderate group within Gush Emunim, strongly opposed to Rabbi Moshe Levinger. It is noteworthy that Bin-Nun has recently consulted with Hebrew University educators with regard to his integrative program. One cannot, of course, imagine "radicals" like Filber doing this.

92. From *The Hebron Torah Academy* (a

curriculum outline in Hebrew), n.d., p. 1.

93. Dan Be'eri, "To Uproot the Galut Which Is Being Rehabilitated among Us" (in Hebrew) *Nekudah* (Journal of settlers in Judaea, Samaria and Gaza) 103 (New Year 5747/October 1986): 20.

94. For Ahad Ha'am's ideas on this, see *Selected Essays of Ahad Ha'am,* trans. and ed. Leon Simon (New York: Meridian Books, 1962).

95. See Eliezer Schweid, "A Secondary Relationship to Tradition: A Study of One Particular Aspect of Ahad Ha'am's Doctrine," in *Israel at the Crossroads,* trans. Alton Meyer Winters (Philadelphia: Jewish Publication Society of America, 1973), pp. 69–83.

96. Aviad, *Return to Judaism,* cites representative statements. See, for example, pp. 9, 114. Articles on this sense of crisis are legion, prominently in the secular kibbutz movements.

97. I am indebted to my student, Eric Caplan, who has studied this issue in his Master's thesis: "Faces of Jewish Thought at the Center for Jewish Studies at Oranim and Their Reflection in Education" (Hebrew University, 1990).

98. Hava Lazarus–Yafe, "Contemporary Fundamentalism in Judaism, Christianity and Islam," *Jewish Quarterly* 47 (Summer 1988): 27–39.

99. On R. S. Peters' concepts of "language" and "literature," see "Reason and Habit: The Paradox of Moral Education," in Peters, *Moral Development and Moral Education* (London: George Allen and Unwin), pp. 51–54.

100. On this distinction with regard to religious education, see Michael Rosenak, "Jewish Religious Education and Indoctrination," in Barry Chazan, ed., *Studies in Jewish Education,* vol. 1 (Jerusalem: Magnes Press, 1983), pp. 117–38.

The Evangelical Awakening in Guatemala: Fundamentalist Impact on Education and Media

Susan Rose and Quentin Schultze

Let There Be Light: Proyecto Luz, a media extravaganza engineered by M. G. "Pat" Robertson's Virginia-based CBN Network, Inc., swept through three Central American countries in the spring of 1990. Robertson cast his mass-media net wide, hoping to convert two million new souls to evangelicalism in El Salvador, Nicaragua, and Guatemala. His organization, along with assistance from Bill Bright's North America-based Campus Crusade for Christ, used television, film, radio, newspapers, leaflets, and revival meetings to spread the Word. The long-term impact of the campaign is unclear. For one thing, the outgoing Sandinista government of Daniel Ortega decided at the last minute not to air CBN's prime-time television programs. Also, many Central Americans may accept "Jesus Christ as their Savior and Lord" simply as a matter of courtesy, preferring not to offend people, even North American televangelists. Finally, the TV blitz included various segments which were poorly adapted to local cultures.[1]

In the short run, however, Robertson's campaign reached vast audiences. In Guatemala alone over 60 percent of homes with television watched the first of CBN's three hourly prime-time specials—20 percent more than had ever watched any Guatemalan program, including the previously top-ranked World Cup soccer.[2] Of course Guatemalans had little choice; CBN had purchased simultaneous time on all television stations in the country.

Ambivalent about the millions of dollars being spent on a short-lived gringo media blitz, many Guatemalan evangelicals nonetheless saw the campaign as a way of celebrating the growing presence of evangelicalism in the region and creating a spirit of solidarity among a myriad of evangelical groups, which often compete with one another intensely. The campaign was also meant to impress Robertson's North American viewers and supporters with the apparent evangelization of so many "unsaved" souls. For the first time, via Robertson's domestic version of his daily "The 700 Club" show, many North American evangelicals and even Catholic charismatics were exposed to the rising tide of dynamic Protestantism in Latin America. Excited about the region's evangelical awakening, Robertson asked his North American viewers to contribute to the cause. On one show he preached from the back of a flatbed truck to abjectly poor Guatemalans living in shacks near the city garbage dump where they scavenged for food. CBN's staff then distributed bags of beans to the converts. Wishing to promote an anticommunist message of evangelicalism in Central America, Robertson was willing to pay as well as pray. The media blitz cost about $1.5 million, which went much further in economically depressed Central America than it would have in North America. (In comparison, one thirty-second spot during the Super Bowl sold for more than half that amount in the United States in 1992.)

Critics wondered if Proyecto Luz was politically motivated. Robertson's commitment to the Nicaraguan Contras and the Salvadoran army is well documented, as is his support of Efraín Ríos Montt, the former Guatemalan "president" by coup from 1982 to 1983, and a candidate for president in 1990 (before a constitutional law disqualified him from the election).[3] Indeed, in a "700 Club" program broadcast live from Guatemala in March of 1990, Robertson interviewed and enthusiastically endorsed Ríos Montt as the candidate who could return the nation to God.

Do Robertson's evangelistic and political motives represent those of the evangelicalism in Guatemala? How much of the growth and character of evangelicalism in Central America today is attributable to the religious, political, and economic interests and influence of the United States? To what degree is it or has it become an indigenous movement? These questions are addressed in this essay. To anticipate one answer: Robertson's religiopolitical style of evangelism is only one influence and one version of the North American gospel in Central America. The nature and scope of Central American evangelicalism are both more complex and more interesting—as well as potentially more powerful in shaping the region's political and economic direction.

The political and economic conspiracy thesis, which links the rise of Latin American evangelicalism to right-wing interests in North America, has many supporters; political, academic, and religious observers have repeatedly attributed the growth of Latin American Protestantism to particular North American policies and movements, from the Central Intelligence Agency to New Right evangelical broadcasters. Archbishop Penados, in a widely quoted pastoral letter in January 1990, denounced the "invasion of the sects" as an imperialist maneuver by North Americans interested in furthering their own business and political interests. According to Penados, "The diffusion of Protestantism in Guatemala is more part of an economic and political strategy than a genuine religious interest."[4] Other accusations, some well documented, point to the politicization of evangelicalism and its alignment with right-wing, military dictatorships.[5] Whether or not particular evangelicals identify themselves as apolitical, the perception that they are serving as "foot soldiers in the advancement of U.S. foreign policy" is not uncommon, either in Latin America or in the United States.[6] As anthropologist David Stoll states in the conclusion to his book

Is Latin America Turning Protestant?: "It is not hard to show how the religious right has tried to turn missionary work into an instrument for U.S. militarism."[7]

On the other hand, as Stoll and others acknowledge, evidence also indicates that evangelicalism has widespread popular support among the poor, who are more interested in survival than ideology. To explain the growth of evangelicalism in Central America purely in terms of North American influences, whether they be implicitly or explicitly political, would be both patronizing and inaccurate. For one thing, the Roman Catholic church is not as vibrant in the region as it once was. As Dennis Smith, a Presbyterian lay missionary associated with the Latin American Center for Pastoral Studies (CELEP), comments: "The whole conspiracy theory that there's a spook behind every evangelical doesn't take into account the pastoral crisis in the Catholic church. It's much easier and more convenient to attribute growth of Protestant churches to the CIA or North American imperialism."[8] In fact, most evangelical churches, schools, and broadcasts are now firmly rooted in Guatemalan culture, with little or no direction from North America. Almost all evangelical pastors are Guatemalan. By contrast, 86.7 percent (603) of Catholic priests are foreigners and only 13.3 percent (93) are Guatemaltecos.[9] In this sense the evangelical movement is far more populist and indigenous than is the ecclesiastical structure of the region's Roman Catholicism.

However, evangelicalism is hardly a unified movement, theologically or ideologically. In some areas, particularly among urban upper-middle-class neo-Pentecostals, ideology is a significant factor. Ríos Montt and Jorge Serrano Elías, who became president of Guatemala in January of 1991, are from this group.[10] Central American evangelicalism is deeply fragmented and predominantly anti-ecumenical. Some upscale, urban, evangelical churches refer to themselves as "Christian" rather than "evangelical" in order to appeal to elite Catholics in the cities, but even they do not collaborate much; they share a Catholic enemy more than a common commitment to a movement characterized by a shared leadership, similar doctrines and styles of worship, and collectively articulated goals.

In spite of these divisions, however, it is safe to say that in Central America one is either a fundamentalistic evangelical or a Catholic; the culture offers few other options. The past and present have conspired, without the pressure of any single indigenous or imported individual or group, to breed a wildly dynamic and richly competitive interplay between the Catholic and evangelical "movements."

In this cultural context, so different from that of North America, fundamentalism becomes a pervasive style of, and approach to, religion, rather than a circumscribed subculture within one larger religious body. Because religious change is quite rapid and cultural conditions exceedingly fluid, fundamentalism as a religious style may be discernible on the religious "left" as well as the "right," and among Catholics as well as Protestants. Fundamentalism in this sense is in Latin America a distinctive strategy for survival, a way of identifying and asserting one's collective existence amid the escalating cacophony of religiously defined voices, whether they have a political language or not. Only those who do not want a voice in the hum of religious competition can easily avoid fundamentalism. For them, however, other versions of a "fundamentalist" rhetoric are found in politics, which itself often breeds militancy, anti-intellectualism, and even separatism, qualities also characteristic of fundamentalist religion.

In this religiocultural climate, contemporary evangelicalism in Guatemala is a popular, fragmented, and adaptable movement that is flourishing both among the rural and urban poor, and the urban middle and upper-middle classes. Whether in the countryside or the city, evangelical churches in Guatemala are essentially fundamentalistic: they tend to be dispensationalist, anti-intellectual, anti-ecumenical, and culturally separatist. This is true even of Pentecostals, who are not directly identified with fundamentalism in the North American context. While all Protestants are referred to as evangelicals in Central America, the majority of Protestants in Guatemala would be considered fundamentalist by North American standards, including the Pentecostal groups. Guatemalan evangelicals tend to be either apolitical or politically conservative. In either case, evangelicals generally support the civil authorities and the political and economic status quo,[11] with a few notable exceptions. There are some evangelicals, neither Pentecostal nor neo-Pentecostal, who uphold their own version of liberation theology and tend to work with Catholics. These evangelicals—a few Mennonites, Episcopalians, and Presbyterians, along with a few Central American Mission, Church of God, and Prince of Peace pastors and lay leaders—are much more ecumenical than traditional Pentecostals and even than the neo-Pentecostals.[12] They are the closest to North American mainline Protestants, but they hold a more clearly evangelical faith than their North American counterparts.

Consistent with patterns of Protestantism in other cultural contexts, Protestant churches in Guatemala proliferate when splinter groups break away from the "mother" church, as a result of either conflict or deliberate church "planting." These churches emphasize evangelism, so "rarely does a church not have [extension] congregations, missions or preaching points *(campos blancos)*."[13] Lay leaders from a "parent" church or newly trained pastors are likely to establish a new congregation in a neighboring locale. Moreover, the country is dotted with small, loosely organized, and often poorly funded Bible institutes and seminaries that train pastors of varying educational backgrounds to evangelize and instruct. In many cases, newly trained pastors return to their home communities, but often they meet with resistance. While Indian congregations expect their pastors to wear a suit while preaching and to have a working knowledge of Spanish as a symbol of their authority and status, a congregation will cease to recognize a pastor's authority if he becomes too "Latinoized" as a result of study at a Bible institute. In such cases, the rejected pastor is likely to move away to start a church in one of the barrios of Guatemala City, and the congregation elevates one of its own to the pastorate.[14]

For many of the large urban churches that cater to the small but influential middle and upper-middle classes, the evangelical message tends to legitimate wealth and prosperity. Many of these neo-Pentecostal churches have embraced some facet of "prosperity theology," the "name it and claim it" school of thought or the "health and wealth" gospel that has filtered down from the North. Prosperity theology (as espoused by proponents such as North American televangelist Kenneth Copeland, or

Kenneth Hagin, who runs the Rhema Bible School in Tulsa, Oklahoma) teaches that by invoking the name of Christ, one can have power over evil spirits and disease as well as over money, material goods, and property.[15] Within this framework, poverty is typically considered the result of sin and laziness, not of social conditions or any form of injustice within society.[16]

These large neo-Pentecostal churches also thrive on practical ministries designed to help the middle class cope with widespread personal and family problems. Like North American "megachurches," they offer educational and worship experiences for the entire family. Sermons and courses address topics such as raising children, building strong marriages, managing households, avoiding work-related stress, and establishing relationships with God through prayer, fellowship, and especially Bible study. Most of their members are lapsed or unhappy Catholics or, increasingly, members of other Protestant churches. For example, one upper-class woman left the Presbyterian church for one of Guatemala City's large neo-Pentecostal churches because the latter "gives power" *(da poder)* in a way that the old denominations do not. Neo-Pentecostal churches of this type also stress the importance of self-discipline as measured by various cultural prohibitions, such as abstention from alcohol and smoking. Here, too, they reflect patterns of North American fundamentalism.

While these urban churches are very visible and influential, largely due to their professional and business-class constituencies and their access to the media, it is still the older Pentecostal fundamentalist churches (such as the Guatemalan versions of the Assemblies of God, Central American Mission, Church of God, Nazarenes, Baptists, and Presbyterians) that remain the backbone of the evangelical church in Guatemala.[17] Three-quarters of Protestant churches are located in the provincial towns and countryside, where one-half of the population lives. And from one-fourth to one-third of all Guatemalan evangelicals are indigenous, representing an adult population of 125,000 out of a total of 400,000.[18]

The majority of evangelicals, like the rural and urban population overall, is poor. Older Pentecostal churches with large memberships, like the Church of God and the Assemblies of God, are scattered throughout every region of the country. Their church members, in the words of one Church of God minister and educator, "do not serve the poor, they are the poor."[19] Marginal in status but not in numbers, for 85 percent of the Guatemalan population lives in poverty, many Guatemalans turn to such Pentecostalism hoping to find solace in small communities that may allow them greater opportunities for involvement and eventually leadership.

The rapid growth of Elim and the Principe de Paz Church, organizations without any foreign affiliations, and the Iglesia de Dios Evangelio Completo, a group officially affiliated with the Church of God (Cleveland), attests to the popular character of the evangelical churches in Guatemala. These groups are self-sustaining, self-directed, and appeal to peasant and indigenous populations. In addition, approximately one-third of the members of the Assembly of God churches are Indian.[20] The vast majority of indigenous congregations are tiny, local sects. If they have any affiliation with a denomination, it is rather loose and informal. Often numbering no more than a dozen people, many of these little sects meet in peoples' homes or in storefronts. Most are led by pastors whose only training is divine revelation. They are highly schismatic by nature; virtually all splinter periodically into new congregations.[21]

Although the spread of evangelicalism in Guatemala can sometimes be linked to the influence of North American money and interests,[22] evangelical faith in Guatemala is not monolithic, shallow, or predominantly under the control of North American preachers or denominations. Today, virtually all Protestant pastors are Guatemaltecos, and in many cases there is considerable resistance to North American culture, which is typically viewed as worldly and secular. The large, local churches which have recently emerged, including the Prince of Peace, Elim, Fraternidad Cristiana, and El Shaddai, are controlled by Guatemalans.

In order to gain a better understanding of the dynamic character and role of evangelicalism in Guatemala, we now examine the impact of fundamentalist Protestantism on education and the media, as well as these social institutions' impact on fundamentalism. In the context of many developing nations like Guatemala—where illiteracy rates are high, schooling is not universal, and a tradition of oral culture is still strong—the media are more likely to serve as secondary forms of socialization, along with the schools. We believe that Latin American fundamentalism today is transmitted by classroom and media "teachers" as well as by grass-roots church evangelization. Schools and the media increasingly establish the cultural context for the growth of evangelicalism. The media primarily legitimize evangelicalism by giving it a public presence, while the schools usher evangelicalism into daily local life.

The Impact of Evangelical Education

The evangelical impact on education in Guatemala is profound. From Christian day schools to a whole range of Bible institutes and seminaries that train people for the ministry, extension schools, Sunday schools, and orphanages, evangelicals are teaching basic literacy skills and evangelical values and beliefs to hundreds of thousands of Guatemalans. Moreover, social services run by evangelicals are provided within the boundaries of secular state schools and institutions, such as youth shelters. Like Catholicism, evangelicalism has reached educationally beyond the walls of the church.

With an evangelical population of over two million, representing 31–35 percent of the total national population of almost nine million, Guatemala has some 10,500 churches and congregations, if one includes "house" churches. This translates into a ratio of one church for every 808 inhabitants.[23] Most of these churches have active Sunday schools, Bible studies, and prayer meetings in addition to regular church services. As in the United States in the nineteenth and early twentieth centuries, Sunday schools play a major role in the evangelical education of both children and adults. Over 90 percent of Protestant churches have Sunday schools,[24] and most of the ones we visited strongly emphasized their Sunday school programs. For example, Fraternidad Cristiana boasts about the six hundred school-age children it teaches every Sunday morning. Moreover, materials designed for Sunday schools in the United States or Mexico are often used in the curricula of the Christian day schools.

In addition, some fifty or more Bible institutes are training people for Christian service. According to a survey that Martha de Berberian conducted in 1982, twenty-eight Bible institutes in the capital and eighteen in the departments were providing Christian education at four different levels: a certificate for those who had not finished elementary education; a diploma for those who had finished primary but not secondary school or the equivalent; a *bachillerato* for those who had finished secondary school or the equivalent (that is, primary school plus three years of study); and the *licenciatura* for those who had finished secondary school plus (that is, primary school plus six or seven years of schooling).[25]

The extension schools, developed originally by Presbyterian missionary Ross Kinsler, provide similar kinds of training for the ministry without disrupting regular employment, family, or congregational obligations. While the seminaries, Bible institutes, and extension courses tend to be denominationally based, correspondence courses tend to be interdenominational.[26] These programs generally depend heavily on funding from abroad, especially from the United States and Europe. Teaching basic literacy skills as a central part of these programs is a necessity in a country where official sources place the illiteracy rate at 45 percent of the population, the highest rate in Latin America. Most independent specialists argue that at least 70 percent of the population is functionally illiterate, ranging from about 25 percent for young people in the urban areas to 95 percent for Mayan women in rural areas.

One of the appealing aspects of Protestantism is the opportunity for people to become religious leaders within their own communities, whether or not they have a formal education, and the possibility to receive more training that is adapted to their individual needs. For example, Samuel de Berberian, owner and principal of Frederico Crowe, established this evangelical school in 1989 to prepare students who had not finished their secondary schooling for university studies in theology. Like a number of Christian schools, Frederico Crowe offers a variety of programs during the school week, evenings, and on Saturdays to meet the needs of students of varying ages, educational levels, and religious involvements. Most of his students are post-adolescents, and some of them are already ordained and practicing ministers who have no secondary schooling. In contrast to Protestant pastors, who need little formal education to start a church or even to be ordained within most denominations in Guatemala, Catholic priests must go through extensive postsecondary training before being allowed to enter the priesthood. Therefore, it is not surprising that there is a much greater variety of evangelical education offerings than Catholic ones.

Like the more typical Catholic private schools, Christian day schools also help fill an educational as well as a religious vacuum. Catering primarily to the children of the middle and upper-middle classes, they take the pressure off the government to provide universal schooling within a public school system that currently is grossly overcrowded and inaccessible to many school-age children. According to a 1987 survey by the Guatemalan National Institute of Statistics, 2,652,000 people (representing 42.5 percent of the population over seven years of age) have never received any formal education, and approximately 500,000 school-age children do not have the opportunity to attend school. A study conducted by the Ministry of Education found that of every 100 Guatemalan school-age children, 30 never enter the school system, 76 never make it to third grade, 86 never make it to sixth grade, 90 never make it to secondary school, and 99 never make it to university.

Why is so little being done in the area of education when the government argues that providing universal education is one of its priorities? Why does Guatemala have the second lowest GNP per capita expenditure on public education (1.8 percent) in Latin America?[27] The answer, in part, can be found in the tax structure, which has been instituted by a succession of repressive governments over the last thirty years. The wealthy classes in Guatemala have been very successful in keeping the vast majority of people in dire poverty, while maintaining an extremely low level of taxation. The overall rate of government taxation in Guatemala, reported to be the lowest in Latin America and the second lowest in the world, is only 5.3 percent, and most of that is raised through indirect, regressive levies.[28]

The majority of students who attend school enroll in public schools, but a significant proportion of students attend private religious schools. According to a study published by the Guatemalan news service, ACEN-SIAG, in December 1989, 800 private educational institutions served 41 percent of the 300,000 students in Guatemala City, and 611 public institutions served the rest. At the primary level in Guatemala City, there are 397 private institutions, of which 80 are Roman Catholic and 60 are Protestant. At the secondary level, most high school students attend private institutions. Of the 459 high schools in Guatemala City, 83 percent are private and attended by 53 percent of the teenagers in school.[29]

Although there are only some one hundred Christian day schools, educating approximately twenty thousand students throughout the country, they are highly visible in a country where 42 percent of the population has had no schooling at all and only 5.2 percent graduate from high school.[30] The inequality and lack of opportunity created by the Guatemalan class structure provide fertile ground for evangelical schools to offer basic education, especially if the cost of private education is borne by evangelizing churches. When Christian schools for the poor are supported with the help of Jimmy Swaggart scholarships, donations from a myriad of evangelical sources in the United States and Western Europe, and small tuition payments scraped together by working-class parents or, in the case of the more affluent Christian schools, from parent tuitions, there is less pressure put on the government to raise taxes for public education. Thus, evangelical and other private schools relieve the burden and responsibility of the public schools and the government.

Catering primarily to the middle and upper-middle classes, the vast majority of Christian schools reinforce the predominant evangelical message that legitimates the authority of the status quo. This message blames poverty (and by default, illiteracy and high infant mortality rates)[31] on sin and laziness. Rather than challenging the structures that make schooling inaccessible and working toward better health care, nutrition, and education for Guatemalans, the "new" (neo-Pentecostal and affluent) evangelicals in Guatemala tend to protect their own well-being at the expense of those less fortunate. This is where they part company from the more historic Protestant churches in Guatemala, even when those churches may represent conservative branches of Protestantism, and from the old-style Pentecostal churches, such as the Assemblies of God and the Church of God, which tend to work extensively among the poor.

While there is some connection between the dramatic growth of the Christian school movement in the United States and the (more modest) growth of evangelical schools in Guatemala, the context and nature of "Christian schooling" in the two countries are quite different. While in neither the United States nor Guatemala do evangelical schools primarily or even significantly educate the poor, neither are they servicing the same populations. The Christian school movement in the United States involves primarily a middle- and working-class constituency. In Guatemala, evangelical schools cater to the upper-middle and middle classes, but compared with the vast majority of the population which lives in poverty, the Guatemalan middle class enjoys a much higher standard of living relative to the working and poor classes than does the middle class in the United States. As one would expect, the radically different cultural, social, political, and economic contexts affect the accessibility and quality of both public and Protestant education in each country.

Christian education in both the United States and Guatemala provides an alternative form of education. But while North American evangelicals turn away from the secular, public schools that once represented Protestant thought and leadership, Guatemalan evangelicals turn away from public schools that were and are imbued with Catholic thought and tradition. And while some North American evangelicals decry the poor quality of public education (quite aside from their not offering a "Christian perspective and ethos"), the difference in quality between public and private schools in Guatemala is typically far greater than what one finds in the United States. Moreover, while there has been great tension in the United States between public and evangelical schooling, and controversy over church rights and responsibilities vis-à-vis the state, in Guatemala the government is generally supportive of Christian schooling. In order to be accredited a school must follow the curricular guidelines set by the Ministry of Education. Most schools easily meet the guidelines and are accredited, with little interference from the government. Even some schools which do not appear to follow the guidelines closely are accredited.[32] Perhaps for political reasons, but most certainly for economic reasons, the Guatemalan government makes it easy for evangelicals to maintain their own school systems.

Christian Curricula

Guatemalan evangelical schools import some North American curricula, but by and large these curricular packages are simply too expensive to use in Guatemala, even in the more affluent schools. One bilingual school, organized by El Shaddai and catering to an upper-middle-class constituency, uses some North American Christian school materials (A BEKA, published in Pensacola, Florida, and Bob Jones's materials, which represent a militantly fundamentalist perspective), but only as supplements to their general curriculum. Other schools have experimented with Accelerated Christian

Education (ACE), a prepackaged, individualized system of instruction produced by a for-profit corporation in Lewisville, Texas. ACE presents pro-U.S., fundamentalist values and beliefs that strongly support the free enterprise system and condemn communism as the work of Satan. The curriculum communicates that Catholics are non-Christians and that Jews are not accepted by God, that secular humanism and relativism are diabolical dangers in the public schools, and that it is essential to restore the United States to the status of a truly Christian nation while simultaneously Christianizing the rest of the world.

In order to sell Accelerated Christian Education in Guatemala and other Spanish-speaking nations, ACE president Donald Howard focused on the threat of communism. In a promotional pamphlet, Howard states that Joseph Stalin advised his followers to corrupt the young in order to plant and spread the seed of communism. Howard then "quotes" Joseph Stalin: "Undermine the loyalty of citizens in general, and young people in particular, by making it easy for them to obtain drugs of all kinds, giving them alcohol, extolling their savagery, and strangling them with sexual literature" (translation from the Spanish).

Advertised as efficient and inexpensive, the ACE curriculum package explicitly states that experienced teachers are unnecessary because students are capable of teaching themselves. Supervisors, as the ACE teachers are called, simply monitor students, who are told to find all the answers within the instruction packets, which emphasize rote learning and memorization. Group discussion is avoided, which eliminates the need to contend with different points of view. Well-trained ACE pupils may be well equipped to read certain kinds of "how-to" manuals, but not to formulate questions or explore alternative answers.[33]

Church of God minister Rick Waldrop chose to use ACE at Casa Shalom, a small orphanage and school that he runs outside of Guatemala City. While he takes issue with some of ACE's pedagogical methods, he found the ready-made packets which match the pace of individual students to be very helpful in teaching children in a situation where there is not much money to hire experienced teachers, and he can use both the English and Spanish versions. In addition, the Agua Viva school that educates only North American missionary children uses the English version in its school and plans to use it in a new school for Guatemalan orphans. Typical of the pattern of use in the United States, Guatemala City's Christian Academy, which caters to a mixed group of North American missionary and Guatemalan children, used it for a few years and then began developing its own curriculum, as did Escuela Christiana Verbo, an elite Christian School in Guatemala City that predominantly educates middle- and upper-middle-class Guatemalan children.

Instituto Evangelica America Latina, Guatemala's largest Christian academy with approximately three thousand students, was involved in early attempts to translate ACE into Spanish. Headmaster Virgilio Zapata, past president of CONELA (Latin American Evangelical Confraternity), was very impressed by the "latest technology in American education" and ACE's focus on "individualized instruction."[34] Some of his staff, including his wife, began translation of ACE materials in the mid-1980s, but then abandoned the project, presumably in favor of the evangelical system of education that Zapata himself tried to market to other church and school groups throughout Central America.

Generally speaking, ACE has met with limited success in Central America, partly for ideological and methodological reasons, but primarily because of its cost.[35] While it is very inexpensive by North American standards and one of the simplest ways for a U.S. congregation to set up a Christian school, by Guatemalan standards ACE is costly. Even with the 50 percent discount that ACE initially offers schools in developing countries, it is unaffordable for lower- and working-class schools, and even for many middle-class schools. In 1987, children in Guatemalan public primary schools were paying fifteen to twenty dollars a year for their books, which was the cost of just one course of study in an ACE school.

More significantly, however, a number of the teachers in middle- and upper-middle-class Christian schools believe that while ACE may be useful in initially establishing a school, in the long run it does not teach students how to reason. One such instructor, a North American, taught at the Escuela Christiana Verbo. He defined his primary mission as preparing students to do intellectual battle against the evil ideas of secular humanism: "In order to prepare students, we have to go beyond rote learning to analytical thinking. . . . ACE does not give students enough opportunity to reason, and they have to be able to reason in order to oppose the evils which the humanists have instigated."[36]

This instructor helped select the curriculum for the Verbo school, which is set up to serve the children of Iglesia del Verbo, the Church of the Word. This very large church of over two thousand members caters to some of the city's most prominent residents and is located in the hotel district of Guatemala City across the street from the U.S. embassy. Founded by North American missionaries who arrived in Guatemala City immediately after the earthquake of 1976, the church helped rebuild neighborhoods that had been destroyed. Relief workers so impressed some upper-class Guatemalans with their faith and energy that they began a small church the following year.

El Verbo has chosen a Christian curriculum from the United States, the "Principle Approach," for use in the Verbo school (which has over six hundred students) and the ten satellite schools (with over thirteen hundred students) which it has propagated. Modeled after Paul Jehle's school program in Plymouth, Massachusetts, "Principle Education" is based on the following seven principles: individuality, stewardship, unity and union, Christian character, self-control, sovereignty of God, and planting and harvesting. Jehle writes that Principle Education emphasizes "basic Biblical principles first, and . . . America's history and patriotism as one outgrowth of this." In his book *Go Ye Therefore and Teach,* Jehle argues that

> America is the *only* nation that has embraced some fundamentalist Bible principles and *extended* them into the civil sphere to affect their civil government *since* Christ's coming to earth. Therefore, the example of America, though not perfect, can stand as a beacon light in history for our children who live in the fruit of civil liberty. . . . We do not want to "Americanize" Christianity, for to

confine Christianity to one nation or national race of people would be to deny the power of the Cross (Ephesians 2:11–22; Galatians 3:26–29). The restoration of America's Heritage, though a necessary goal so that people are not led astray, is not the "ultimate" goal of all of our teaching. Our goal is to teach our children so that they can fulfill our Lord's commission to disciple the nations and to spread the Gospel of the Kingdom to all nations for a witness, and therefore the vision is much higher than America or any one nation's restoration.[37]

Jehle, principal of the New Testament Christian School in Plymouth, Massachusetts, and author of a number of books on how to establish a Christian school, is a reconstructionist. He and other reconstructionists would like to see a theocracy established in the United States and abroad.[38] In his introduction to *The Principle Approach to Political Involvement,* Jehle writes that

Without an apology, this is written from the standpoint of an American and a proud one. I am sick and tired of the way Christians have let our nation slide into evil under the guise of "spirituality," when in reality it is simply a lack of stewardship over what God has given us. . . . After years of silence when we have surrendered away our liberties in America, the giant of humanism is coming out and defying the church and all it stands for. It looms large, threatening, and mouths out blasphemous threats that haven't been dared to be uttered in this land ever before, so openly, and defiantly. . . . There is a small band of believers . . . preparing to do battle . . . , armed in the name of the Lord. They will sling the Lord Jesus (that godly stone) into the ideologies of humanism (the forehead), and at once cause the armies to flee, and cut the head (false leadership) off of the nation. Is this the army you wish to join, and fight in? If so, read on.[39]

The military imagery is not new to fundamentalism, but it takes on particular meaning in Guatemala, where evangelical activity has been and continues to be aligned with military regimes and the suppression of popular unrest. Many of the North American evangelicals we talked with spoke proudly of having been in the U.S. armed forces and continuing the fight against communism now in God's Army.

The two primary texts on which the Principle Approach has been built are Verna Hall's *The Christian History of the Constitution of the United States of America* (1966), and Rosalie Slater's *Teaching and Learning America's Christian History* (1965), both published by the Foundation for American Christian Education in San Francisco. Hall and Slater left service in the U.S. Department of Education in 1947 when they "experienced the beginnings of socialism; I saw the thoroughness of socialistic organization descend like a pall upon every facet of our economy and culture."[40] Hall left in order to start a Constitution study group for people interested in economic and constitutional principles. "Communism and socialism are anti-God and anti-Christian; the battle against communism and socialism was not, and is not now, just economic and political; it is religious," she writes. "Shall Christianity be taken captive?"[41]

Her series of texts on American history and the history of the Constitution is now used in the New Testament School in Plymouth, Massachusetts, and as "guide" books in the eleven schools sponsored by El Verbo in Guatemala. While the emphasis is definitely on the United States, Hall explains why her texts and discussion are relevant to any and every country:

> To the kindly influence of Christianity we owe that degree of civil freedom, and political and social happiness which mankind can now enjoy. In proportion as the genuine effects of Christianity are diminished in any nation, either through unbelief, or the corruption of its doctrines, or the neglect of its institutions; in the same proportion will the people of that nation recede from the blessings of genuine freedom, and approximate the miseries of complete despotism. I hold this to be a truth confirmed by experience. . . . Whenever the pillars of Christianity shall be overthrown, our present republican forms of government, and all the blessings which flow from them, must fall with them.[42]

Other than these books which serve as teachers' guides, no specific texts are used at Escuela Christiana Verbo. Instead, teachers xerox materials from a variety of sources and attempt to integrate the seven principles into everything they teach. For example, one teacher in an upper-level social studies course was lecturing about the culture of the Mayans. While praising the Mayans for some of their accomplishments, he argued that they lost their lands because they were not good stewards. He then proceeded to talk about the principle of stewardship, which denotes both self-discipline and private property: "If God has chosen to allow you to accumulate certain amounts of property, then it is your sacred duty as His steward to guard that property and develop its full productive, and profitable, potential."[43]

According to the teachers at the Verbo school, they must arm their children against the corrupting ideas of secular humanism and communism. One source of inspiration is a newspaper, *The Forerunner,* published by the Maranatha Church headquarters in Gainesville, Florida; its byline, "Taking the Lead in the Battle of Ideas," expresses the mission of the school. In order to prepare their students, teachers involve them in rigorous class discussions, asking them to critique the information they are reading. This emphasis on discussion and the flexibility of the curriculum may, in part, reflect the class interests of those involved at El Verbo. They expect their children to have the opportunity to lead the future Christian government of Guatemala.[44]

The Guatemalan woman in charge of teacher education for Verbo's satellite schools repeatedly mentioned the one quality of North American character and education which Guatemalan society as a whole needed: *disciplina.* The twin themes of obedience and discipline are constantly interwoven by Verbo's preachers and teachers to reflect the primary demands of God and the state. On three successive Sundays in June 1987, Ramirez's sermons related to the concerns of the ruling class: the national politics of Guatemala and its reactions to international pressure. The words repeated over and over again as part of God's message for Guatemala were "discipline, obedience, and authority." Everyone should submit to the authority of Christ, the wife should submit to her husband, members should submit to the elders of the church, and citizens to the nation and the army. Ramirez reminded his congregation that God chooses who should rule in various countries and that it is the duty of believers to always obey the authority of the given ruler: "At times God chooses to unite the religious world and the political world under one leader, as He did when he chose King David to lead the nation of Israel. Similarly He picked General Ríos Montt to temporarily lead Guatemala as prophet and king in 1982–83 and he may choose to do so again."[45] The message of local sermons is reinforced by North American publications. In the newspaper *Radiance,* produced by the Church of the Word in California, Jim DeGolyer, another elder at the Verbo Church, wrote that true obedience requires discipline and that "the laziness and lack of discipline that rules us is the real tyrant that causes poverty."[46]

Blaming poverty on laziness and sin is characteristic of evangelicals in Guatemala, be they poor or wealthy. The need for discipline, self-control, and obedience was emphasized in all the congregations and schools we visited in 1987 and 1990. These schools include the following ones in Guatemala City: America Latina, Bethesda, Colegio del Verbo, Christian Academy, El Shaddai, Fraternidad Cristiana, Frederico Crowe, Wycliff Center, Cristo del Mundo, Maranatha, and Elim. It also includes various schools in Quetzaltenango and Antigua, the old capital. The lower- and working-class churches (e.g., Elim) and schools tended to focus on the need to resist the temptations of the flesh and evil spirits more than on international and national politics. They also emphasized the need to work hard in order to become upwardly mobile. Rather than having a clearly articulated educational philosophy or their own curriculum, they tended to follow the Ministry of Education's curriculum, integrating it with fundamentalist readings and interpretations. In short, they were proud to be offering a basic Christian education to students who might otherwise not have been educated at all.

The only Christian schools reaching out to the poorer classes and offering an education to Guatemalan children who may not otherwise receive an education are the Assembly of God schools.[47] While some scholarships are given to working-class children at America Latina in Guatemala City and its sister school in Chimaltenango, El Calvario, a small Central American Mission school in Antigua, and Bethania in Quezaltenango, the vast majority of evangelical schools are clearly catering to the middle and upper classes. According to a number of alumnae with whom we spoke, the schools are money-making enterprises; some evangelical educators disagreed, however, citing high operating costs. Regardless of profitability, it is clear that evangelical education is primarily a recruiting tool aimed at the middle and upper-middle classes rather than an outreach program designed to serve and convert the less fortunate.[48]

Within the last few years both El Shaddai and Fraternidad Cristiana opened bilingual (Spanish and English) elementary schools, which are considered highly desirable by the upper-middle and middle classes and, therefore, effective in recruiting members. Their tuitions represent the high end of the scale for Christian schools in

Guatemala, averaging Q60 a month (or roughly $16, plus additional costs for bus service, swimming, etc.) for elementary school, in contrast to the Assembly of God schools, which on average charge Q15 a month (roughly $3.75). Considering that the average monthly working-class family income in Guatemala City is about Q250–300, such schooling is hardly affordable for everyone. In addition to the tuition (which is four times as high at the more affluent schools), there are registration, uniform, and book fees that place Christian education out of the reach of the majority of Guatemalan children. For those children who do attend Christian schools that serve the poorer and working classes, there is a dramatic difference in the quality of education they receive.

Students of the upper-middle-class school sponsored by El Shaddai not only have ample space within their classrooms, where each desk is bedecked with pencils, crayons, books, art materials, and a Charlie Brown thermos that matches the Charlie Brown posters on the walls, but they also have weekly swimming lessons in an Olympic pool and gym privileges. In the case of Bethesda School, which is located in one of the poor colonies of Guatemala City, students do not always have their own desks or writing materials; not only do they not have the opportunity to swim or have a thermos, they do not have access to potable water.

Servants of the Poor: Assembly of God Schools

The Assembly of God churches in Guatemala are predominantly churches of the poor. The people who organize and teach in their Christian schools are happy to have any kind of job in a society characterized by very high unemployment and poverty rates. They generally settle for salaries at less than half the minimal rate paid to public school teachers, who in turn receive less than the cashiers at McDonalds restaurants in Guatemala City. The teachers in these evangelical schools are dedicated people who will teach without textbooks and other materials when, as is often the case, they cannot afford them. They are proud that their students have escaped the *humanismo* that pervades the public schools. The teachers, who generally are required to be evangelical Christians,[49] do not receive training in any specific North American curriculum like the Principle Approach. Their educational philosophy is supplied mainly through the consistent messages coming from their pastors and the evangelical radio and television programs of Jimmy Swaggart, the "700 Club," and others.

These evangelical schools offer a basic education to students who might not otherwise receive one. They also help relieve the overcrowding of the public schools, which are often severely limited in terms of space, desks, teachers, and basic resources. The differences in the quality of education among evangelical schools are readily acknowledged by evangelicals and non-evangelicals alike. People are quick to identify which evangelical schools compete with the elite Catholic private schools and which are at the lower end of the spectrum. A principal in a working-class school in Quetzaltenango compared her church and students with another in the area: "Because we are lower class we have to move more slowly; because they are ministering to a higher class of people they can grasp more complicated ideas and make faster spiritual progress."[50]

Established in 1973, Liceo Bethesda is located in Zone 19, one of the poor colonies on the outskirts of Guatemala City. Bethesda was the first Assembly of God school in Guatemala; its enrollment grew from eighty students in 1973 to nine hundred students in 1987 to thirteen hundred students in 1990. From 1983, when North American televangelist Swaggart first visited Guatemala and regular weekly broadcasts of his television show began appearing on Guatemalan stations, Swaggart's ministries helped support Bethesda and fifteen other Assembly of God schools in Guatemala, sending down some $9,000 to $10,000 a month.[51] With his fall in 1988, Swaggart's money flow to Central America dried up and a number of schools and programs he was helping to support were forced to close.

According to Ministerio Piedad,[52] a local Guatemalan organization created in 1989 through the Assemblies of God to coordinate the schools' programs, Guatemala appears to be the only country in Central America in which no school had to close for lack of funding after Swaggart's fall. Some money continued to be channeled through the Assemblies of God, and U.S. missionary Gregory Austin helped reorganize the school ministries through the control of Ministerio Piedad. In the reorganization, only those schools whose director was pastor of an Assembly of God church were eligible for funding, and one superintendent was appointed to coordinate all of the Assembly of God schools. Therefore, as of March 1990, thirteen Assembly of God schools were operating throughout the country, with a total enrollment of some seven thousand to eight thousand students. A number of health clinics and lunch programs the schools were sponsoring, however, had to be discontinued. While five of the schools had lunch programs in 1987, only two schools had them in 1990; health clinics that were run by the schools had to close, some of them indefinitely, others for a few months.

When we first visited Bethesda School in July of 1987, we found a crowded school of nine hundred students with a student-teacher ratio of 48:1, a health clinic that helped serve the needs of students and their families, and a food lunch program. Bethesda had few curricular materials but a desk for every student. In March of 1990 the school was still operating with four hundred more students but fewer teachers, none of whom had received a salary increase since 1987. The food lunch program was no longer available, and the clinic, which had been closed for a number of months, had just reopened on a part-time basis. It occupied three rooms: a waiting room, a room with a couple of beds for those who needed to rest, and a little room that stored drugs that had been shipped from a German mission, even though a number of major international drug companies flanked the Pan American Highway only a few miles away. Although they had begun to dig a well in 1987, little progress had been made by 1990 so that neither the Bethesda clinic nor school had potable water, particularly ironic given the name of the school.

Regardless of the differences in resources and pedagogical methods, all the evangelical schools teach some form of creationism as well as anticommunism. Moreover, the North American materials that are used reflect a kind of fundamentalist Americanism that has become one of the United States's primary cultural exports to many developing countries. Given the repression of more liberal religious forces since the late 1970s (especially Catholic priests and lay workers in the countryside, but also a number of Protestant ministers preaching to poor congregations), there is little opposition to these evangelizing efforts.

While the support that U.S. evangelical groups have given Guatemalan evangelical churches and schools in terms of money, personnel, and even curriculum has been substantial, Guatemalan evangelical schools are not simply by-products of North American evangelicalism nor primarily dependent on it for support. According to Stuart Salazar, former faculty member of America Latina and currently the head of the Central American branch of the American Association of Christian Schools International (ACSI), private evangelical schools are receiving little outside funding; most rely on parent tuitions. ACSI is experimenting with different ways to provide scholarships for students in developing countries.[53]

Christian schools in Guatemala tend to operate as islands unto themselves. In general, there is a great deal of competition and very little cooperation or even contact among Christian schools. Principals were aware of the existence and general orientation of a number of other Christian schools, but they expressed little interest in exploring issues that might be of common interest. The one exception is the association of the Assembly of God schools which, since the downfall of Swaggart and the transfer of power to the local level, has begun to coordinate efforts and plan a common curriculum for their thirteen schools throughout Guatemala. Interested in coordinating efforts among Christian schools throughout the world, ACSI, whose headquarters is located in Whittier, California, appointed a regional coordinator for Latin America in 1990. Stuart Salazar's first step in trying to establish a national Christian school association in Guatemala, that would in turn be an associate member of ACSI, was to survey the landscape of Christian schooling throughout the region.

The Impact of Fundamentalism on Public-Sector Education

Christian education in Guatemala has an impact not only on evangelical institutions but on secular institutions as well. According to a report published by AVANCSO,[54] a social science research center in Guatemala City, and various evangelical informants, evangelicals are welcomed into the public schools to offer programs and provide counseling. Youth for Christ (Juventud para Cristo), a newcomer to Guatemala and perhaps the most successful postwar parachurch organization, is an international ministry oriented to young people. Radio and television are central to its evangelical mission,[55] and Youth for Christ members volunteer in public schools. "Offering antidrug programs, conferences and individual counseling, . . . [many of the volunteers] function as school guidance counselors."[56] Moreover, many of the curricular materials used in the antidrug campaigns are published by evangelicals. Evangelical educator Salazar has offered such programs in public schools in Guatemala; he believes this is a wonderful avenue for evangelizing not possible in the United States, but which should be exploited in Guatemala.[57]

The AVANCSO report also refers to the influence of a well-known evangelical and clinical psychologist who "does not believe in psychology as a solution to delinquency and does not employ it at [a] shelter" he runs for young women. Instead, "he offers a traditional family environment (the young women call him 'Papa') and the Bible, teaching that accepting Christ resolves problems." In addition to lecturing about drug abuse and delinquency on television, he writes a column for *El Gráfico,* one of Guatemala's major newspapers. *El Gráfico* calls him "one of the most outstanding professionals of Guatemala psychiatry," and he has been invited by the Ministry of Education to lecture to public school administrators about how to handle young people and by the minister of the interior to speak to cadets at the National Police Academy.[58]

Beyond the public schools, then, evangelicals are active in running orphanages and youth shelters. In many cases, the National Police have chosen to take children to an evangelical shelter rather than to juvenile court. In the case of at least one evangelical shelter, a structured arrangement has been agreed upon; the shelter sends monthly reports to the court on consigned minors. The judge "thinks that there is little choice; given the scarcity of state programs, the evangelicals are useful."[59]

In spite of the fact that fundamentalists often tend to resist or oppose scientific research and discovery, they have become the new service professionals, the new social engineers in Guatemala.[60] According to the AVANCSO report, "Since the early 1980s, evangelicals have emerged as the new technicians in the field of social work and education."[61] In this sense, evangelicals (mostly neo-Pentecostals with members of Elim quite prominent) *are* interested in social reform, in ways that parallel the Social Gospel popular in the United States at the turn of the century. But as critiques of the products of the North American middle-class social reformers suggest, the new system of professional service did not so much break cycles of dependency and delinquency as reconstruct them.[62] In other words, like the early Child Savers or the contemporary neo-evangelicals in the United States, even in the cases where Guatemalan evangelicals are actively involved in trying to reform society, they are not interested in directly transforming the basic structures of inequality—an emphasis which characterizes the liberation theology movement. Instead, they hope to improve society through a combination of personal religious conversion, individual self-discipline, and in some cases, personal professional care.

While social pain, of which there is no scarcity in contemporary Guatemala, is the proof of evangelicals' message that humanity has lost faith in God, for members of the street gangs *(maras)* which are growing rapidly in Guatemala City, it is an indication of a corrupt system that is stacked against them. While evangelicals tend to teach youth to obey the authorities, the maras encourage their members to express their anger and frustration. Interestingly, the AVANCSO report argues that probably the two most important organizations for urban youth are the maras that roam the streets and the evangelical churches.[63] Indeed, both are growing, and they share certain characteristics: "Like the *Maras,* Evangelicalism orders life, explains society and offers an intense [personal] experience."[64] But unlike the evangelical youth groups which are run largely by adults, the maras are led by young people who resist authority and challenge conventional social institutions, including the traditional family and religion.

Whether in providing education or trying to control the maras, the Guatemalan government is quite willing to have evangelical organizations actively involved: "The state legitimizes Evangelicalism by allowing Evangelicals to administer to the problems of civilian life in the public schools, the streets and the reform centers. The state has, intentionally or not, taken up with Evangelicals. . . . By allowing the Evangelicals to handle what it does not have the tools to deal with as a civilian power, the state opens its door to transforming state institutions into religious, rather than secular, ones."[65]

Given the current structures and politics, the Guatemalan government has little choice but to rely on private, nongovernmental organizations to provide services it cannot. It makes sense that the easiest alliances are made with those who are willing to put their own time, energy, and money into working on social problems while asking few questions, making few demands, and leaving the status quo unchallenged. The government is at least implicitly supportive of evangelicalism when it comes to media outreach as well.

History of Fundamentalist Broadcasting in Guatemala

The rapid growth of evangelicalism in Guatemala would not have occurred without the incredibly creative and dynamic infusion of fundamentalist radio and television programming. Fundamentalist broadcasting did not cause the rapid proliferation of Pentecostal and neo-Pentecostal churches in the country. As we suggested earlier, there were numerous other factors in the rise and spread of Latin American evangelicalism. Nevertheless, radio and television were important conduits for the transmission of fundamentalist values, beliefs, and practices throughout the country, especially in the Spanish-speaking cities and regions. More than everything else, the electronic media legitimized Protestant fundamentalism and helped make it socially acceptable for Roman Catholics to jump over to evangelicalism.

In other words, fundamentalist broadcasting, like fundamentalist education, amplified and shaped Guatemalan evangelicalism, giving it particular form and content. Guatemalan society and culture produced the seeds of fundamentalism, while the broadcast media scattered the seeds, fed them, and increasingly became part of the soil in which they took root and prospered. At first it appeared that North American evangelical broadcasting, led by enormously popular televangelist Swaggart, might determine the direction of Guatemalan evangelicalism, especially among neo-Pentecostals and old-style Pentecostals. However, by the early 1990s it was abundantly clear that evangelical radio in Guatemala was largely setting its own course, and television might soon follow.

The story of evangelical radio and television in Guatemala begins in the years after

World War II when North American missionaries brought their technical skills and financial resources to the country. In 1945 the Mision Evangelica Centroamericana (Central American Mission, or CAM) first investigated the possibility of establishing Protestant broadcasting in the country. Five years later CAM started 2 of 4 eventual stations, TGN (AM medium wave) and TGNA (shortwave), both called Radio Cultural.[66] Other mission groups soon began broadcasting as well, establishing the competitiveness that increasingly characterized evangelical broadcasting throughout Central America, particularly when Ladino evangelicals took to the airways. By 1961 there were 23 Protestant programs on commercial (nonreligious) stations in Guatemala.[67] CAM had 5, followed by the Church of God's Foreign Mission Board (4), the Primitive Methodist Foreign Mission Board (4), the Seventh Day Adventists (4), the Southern Baptist Convention Foreign Mission Board (4), and especially the nonfundamentalist United Presbyterian Church in the U.S.A., which had started 8 of its own programs.[68]

Between 1961 and 1988 the growth of evangelical broadcasting in Guatemala was astounding even compared with its development in the United States. By 1988 there were 145 operational radio stations in all of Guatemala, 53 of which were located in the capital of Guatemala City.[69] Thirteen of the stations were nonprofit evangelical broadcasters, 10 were dedicated to Roman Catholic programming, and another 6 were commercial religious stations.[70] More striking was the fact that 63 percent of all AM stations and 43 percent of all FM stations in Guatemala aired religious programs. Some stations did not air religious broadcasts because of internal politics or because of direct orders from station management.[71] Probably because of both the nation's political turmoil and its religious competition, such stations simply refused to air potentially controversial or at least divisive programming that might alienate part of its audience or bring on the wrath of the government. Nevertheless, every week in 1988, Guatemalan radio stations aired a total of 28,205 minutes of religious programming. Seventy percent of that radio time was controlled by evangelicals, compared with 20 percent by Catholics, 7 percent by Seventh Day Adventists, and 3 percent by other groups, including spiritualists, naturalists, Jehovah's Witnesses, and even parapsychologists.[72]

Clearly the most important aspect of evangelical radio in Guatemala is the live, local character of so many of the broadcasts. Ladino evangelicals have naturally moved beyond the rather dull, pedantic, and literary styles of North American religious radio stations to entertaining and dramatic programs that are typically broadcast live. Eighty-seven percent of evangelical radio is aired live in the studio, compared with only 66 percent of Catholic programming.[73] Moreover, nearly all evangelical broadcasts are produced in Guatemala, even those made by North American mission organizations.[74] On the air evangelicals preach, sermonize, persuade, cajole, interpret, and encourage. In short, fundamentalists enthusiastically and commitedly witness to their faith via the spoken word to a culture that loves conversation and discussion, with the apparent authority of the voice of a real person presenting the word of God. Catholic radio broadcasters, by contrast, have tried relatively unsuccessfully to be far more of a cultural presence through music, information, and to some extent, instruction.

North American Television in Guatemala

As in other developing countries, television has played an increasingly important role in Guatemalan life. Even in the barrios many Guatemalans own television sets principally for evening entertainment. Communal viewing, particularly among neighbors and extended families, is common, building the potential national television audience to over 70 percent of the population and approximately 80 percent of churchgoers.[75] Children are especially fond of the medium both as an escape from some of the hardships that surround them and as a source of visual and aural pleasure.

Largely because television is far more expensive to produce than radio programming, North American broadcasters have been significantly more influential with both secular and religious fare. By and large Guatemalans cannot afford to produce programming that competes with North America's slick and technically superior programs. Most religious television in Central America is evangelical programming produced in the United States.[76] If Guatemalan radio is largely a reflection of the richness and breadth of the region's evangelicalism, television reflects primarily North American Pentecostalism and neo-Pentecostalism. Eventually native fundamentalists may rule the television roost, but for now the same economic factors that make Central America heavily dependent on North American television make Guatemalan evangelicals dependent on the productions of their media-rich neighbors to the North.

Louisiana's Swaggart used satellites and syndicated tapes to become the closest thing to a Protestant pope in Central America. His popularity in Guatemala in the mid-to-late 1980s far exceeded his television appeal in the United States, even though he was the highest-rated televangelist. During his heyday, before the sex-and-money scandals among top-rated televangelists in the late 1980s, Swaggart's weekly program reached an estimated two million to three million adult viewers in the entire United States—roughly 2-3 percent of the population. By contrast, in Guatemala Swaggart's show was seen regularly by at least one-half of the nation.[77] Roughly three-quarters of the country's active churchgoers had seen his program—more than had seen or heard any other media evangelist, including the popular radio broadcasters Hermano Pablo (65 percent) and Luis Palau (59 percent), and the Spanish version of Jim Bakker's PTL television program, funded by PTL but hosted by Elmer Bueno (52 percent).[78] Moreover, Swaggart's appeal largely transcended the divisions and animosities among Guatemala's religious groups, including the Catholic-Protestant split. About one-quarter of churchgoers regularly watched one of the four major radio or TV evangelists.[79]

Swaggart's popularity can be attributed to a number of things. First, his program was simply one of the most engaging religious broadcasts on Guatemalan television. Pentecostalist Swaggart communicated in a powerful aural and visual style that conveyed great spiritual anticipation and showed enormous dramatic flair. In spite of the great technical effort behind every one of his broadcasts, especially the taped crusades, the programs nearly always created the illusion of being live, unrehearsed, unplanned events. Compared with the ritual of the Catholic mass or even the academic style of a mainline evangelical preacher, Swaggart's emotional appeals established considerable trustworthiness among Guatemalans—more than other television preachers in the region.[80]

Second, Swaggart's Pentecostalism matched the growing style of evangelicalism already present in Guatemalan culture. The televangelist seemed to resonate with the rising impulse of spirit-led Protestantism breaking out across the country, especially in the Spanish-speaking regions. Even Swaggart's Spanish translator, used extensively at revivals taped in Latin America, effectively duplicated the televangelist's kinesics and vocal style and habits. Swaggart's popularity in the region reflected far more than clever marketing, choice air time, or dramatic flair. It mirrored a natural communicative affinity between the oral cultures of Pentecostal Guatemala and the Pentecostal southern United States. This helped Swaggart overcome his gringo roots and speak to Guatemalans in their own Pentecostal tongue.

Third, Swaggart's outspoken attacks on liberal social and personal mores resonated with Latin American cultural prohibitions and taboos. Compared with much television and especially popular films, Swaggart's broadcasts were seemingly pointed and unequivocal attacks on many of the very things that plagued the region's families and neighborhoods: alcohol abuse, drug use, infidelity, and so forth. Unlike many North American television preachers who appealed in the United States to the middle and upper-middle class with their more liberal attitudes toward culture, Swaggart was a clear and forceful voice for fundamentalism. Many Guatemalans liked that. In fact, the evangelical churches of Guatemala had largely thrived on such cultural fundamentalism—much more than did mainline evangelicalism in the United States.

Aside from Pat Robertson's Proyecto Luz in 1990, the former U.S. presidential candidate has not been particularly well received in Guatemala. His outspoken support for former Guatemalan president Ríos Montt and the Nicaraguan Contras elicited considerable news media attention in both Latin America and the United States.[81] In terms of religious respect and influence, however, Robertson was not nearly as significant as Swaggart and numerous other radio and television broadcasters from both Central and North America. If anything, Robertson's public support of various political figures and causes scared away most Guatemalan evangelicals, who generally believe that religion and politics should be kept separate. We can only speculate that Robertson was misinformed about the actual impact of his programming or he was using the Latin American broadcasts as a means of eliciting donations from sympathetic North American supporters.

The openly political style of the media-orchestrated New Christian Right in the United States, represented in the 1980s by people such as Falwell and Robertson, and by organizations such as the Moral Majority and the Religious Roundtable, has not made major inroads in Latin America. For one thing, fundamentalists in Guatemala still generally believe that political work can easily get in the way of the believer's first task—evangelization. For another, they know that politics can be injurious to one's health—even deadly. Finally, evangelical leaders in Guatemala realize that an openly politicized gospel would make little difference in Guatemala unless it were at least somewhat ecumenical. Few people will listen seriously to fringe religious groups' political rhetoric, which invariably gets squelched by media or government. At the same time, there is little room in the public square for almost any kind of ecumenical appeal.

In the United States a Robertson or Falwell can bring Protestants and Catholics together in a symbolic display of their common political interests. Such is not the case in Guatemala. At least for the 1990s, it appears that the general kind of moralistic rhetoric of Swaggart is much more acceptable to Guatemalans than the apparently theocratic message of someone such as Robertson. While North American evangelical pietism and dispensationalism took firm root in Latin America, New Christian Right politics did not. As a result, Guatemalan evangelicalism tends to be implicitly rather than explicitly ideological, and evangelical leaders, whether broadcasters or pastors, nearly always preach salvation and moral living before social transformation or political and economic reform. In other words, Guatemala's New Right is not yet militantly religious in public life, even though past president Ríos Montt and recently elected president Serrano Elías were open about their evangelical beliefs.

The most successful television, then, like the most successful radio, tends to be Pentecostal or neo-Pentecostal and explicitly apolitical. It is also dramatic, entertaining, and seemingly spontaneous. It is usually directed toward the personal crises experienced by many people in a society convulsed by political oppression, economic problems, and cultural flux. The most effective messages are delivered by apparently authentic individuals who speak from the heart rather than from the mind. This is not the rationalistic fundamentalism of North American Presbyterianism between the world wars, but much more the romantic fundamentalism of Southern Pentecostals such as Swaggart, who preach triumphantly against the sins of the flesh in front of the cultural backdrop of modernization.

Robertson learned this the hard way in his Proyecto Luz media campaign during March of 1990. In spite of the enormous television ratings for his three prime-time television specials, viewed in over 60 percent of Guatemalan homes, two problems dogged the mass media campaign. First, not all evangelical churches were willing to support the campaign by helping with viewer follow-up. Many Guatemalans, including many evangelicals, were skeptical of Robertson's intentions, given his political activities in the past and his gringo style of evangelism. It was not that they disagreed with Robertson's politics; rather, they did not think it appropriate to mix ideology and religion.[82] Second, Robertson committed what some Guatemalan evangelicals considered a nearly unforgiveable sin: he included a positive segment on a Roman Catholic, Mother Teresa. Such a positive portrayal of Catholicism was perceived by some as a significant media blunder reflecting either cultural misunderstanding or insensitivity to the culture of Latin American evangelicals. Indigenous broadcasters know better.

Guatemala's Nascent Religious Right

Most Guatemalan fundamentalists, influenced by North American dispensational theology and cultural moralism, define religion in terms of saving souls and living a moral life. Evangelical broadcasting in Guatemala proudly proclaims this view of fundamentalism on radio and television as well as in churches, Bible studies, and Protestant schools. However, in the middle- and upper-middle-class neo-Pentecostal churches, personal piety and morality are expressed in increasingly social and political terms. This approach to Guatemalan fundamentalism sounds much like the inchoate New Christian Right in the United States of the late 1970s, when the Religious Roundtable and the Moral Majority were formed. However, it is far more tentative and less boldly assertive than its North American counterparts.

In Guatemala City, home of the nation's most influential media and its political and economic center, the new politicized fundamentalism is emerging in a number of the largest neo-Pentecostal churches which typically use the broadcast media. Unlike the old-style Pentecostal churches of the barrios, these megachurches are made up largely of professionals who have found personal and family comfort in the practical advice and emotional worship found in such gatherings. At the Fraternidad Cristiana, Pastor Jorge Lopez preaches to as many as thirty-one hundred on Sunday mornings in three successive services—up from the thirty-five people he started with in 1979. As indicated earlier, his sermons stress topics relevant to the family, for example, financial stewardship, raising children, and building strong marriages. The group's slogan, *Una iglesia para la toda familia* (One church for the whole family), is used as a recruiting tool to gather the whole family into the fold. At present, many Guatemalan families are split not only between Catholicism and Protestantism but also among various Prostestant churches. In trying to draw in new families or new members from families who already belong, Fraternidad Cristiana organizes bimonthly breakfast meetings, for which tickets are sold, at the elegant Camino Real or Sheraton Conquistador. The cost of an average breakfast for a family of four (approximately Q75 or about $19, the monthly income of many Guatemalan families) indicates the middle- and upper-middle-class constituency.

Most of the members are former Catholics who visited the church for the first time at the invitation of friends, through their own curiosity, or sometimes because they saw or heard Lopez's television or radio programs. Lopez is a former radio and TV personality who joined one Protestant denomination and then split off to form his own church.[83] His services are often rebroadcast on television and radio, and he writes editorial columns regularly in *Prensa Libre,* a conservative daily that is the nation's largest newspaper.

Lopez is not afraid to preach on the necessity of personal political involvement as he offers the congregation biblical principles for selecting the right candidates for political office. Privately he even advises congregants as to whom they should support in upcoming elections. Church members have been associated with the MLN,[84] the ultra right-wing National Liberation Movement, which in turn has been linked to the military death squads that have kidnapped and murdered thousands of moderate and progressive leaders over the past twenty years. The MLN would like to keep labor unions at bay or ban them entirely, and would like to keep Guatemalan taxes as low as possible.

In one of his sermons concerning management,[85] Lopez referred to a study from an eminent North American university explaining that 80 percent of the population cannot work adequately without constant supervision and direction, that 16 percent can work on their own with just a little direct supervision, and that only 4 percent have what it takes to be self-sufficient, give orders and effectively manage enterprises and the work of others. Lopez went on to explain that God wants those who are in authority, the managers, to be good stewards of various kinds of property and make them productive and bountiful. Their responsibilities are great, so therefore it is altogether fitting that their compensation be great, for they have earned it.

Lopez explained that the attitude of good management will be passed down through the ranks so that the lower echelons will appreciate their duty in keeping things orderly. In the same way, he noted, the wife will learn from the husband how to communicate appropriate orders on cleanliness to her maid, for it would be silly for her to attempt to do everything herself just because she has not learned to manage effectively the work of her servants.

Fraternidad is a native-born church, independent of either a North American denomination or direct missionary influence. The church is not dependent on direct theological wisdom from the North, like that which El Verbo receives from the California church, and seems not to welcome the charitable instincts which the North Americans are trying to inculcate in Verbo's more "Americanized" membership. Still, Lopez acknowledges intellectual sources from the United States and supports the health-and-wealth gospel while cautioning that it is important to preach about the evil side of life as well.[86]

Churches such as Fraternidad Cristiana, influenced by education and relative prosperity, are openly addressing the personal problems faced by tens of thousands, or perhaps even several hundred thousand, of former Roman Catholics in urban areas. These converts are not so much interested in a purely emotional escape from the world or a transcendent experience, but instead want a practical faith that will serve as a map for living a meaningful and stable life in a changing society. Such churches look out to the world, not just inward to personal religious experience. Along the way they typically embrace conservative political values, which in Guatemala usually translate into support for the government and military. Not surprisingly, then, Pastor Lopez has aired his religious broadcasts free on the government channel operated by the Guatemalan army.

In spite of the success of the new Guatemalan megachurches, the old-style Pentecostalism, strongly pietistic and moralistic, continues to dominate the airways and the churches throughout the country. So far, evangelical broadcasting has been one of its most important allies in filling old-style Pentecostal churches and especially creating a publicly legitimate voice in a society formerly defined religiously by the Catholic church. Radio VEA (Evangelical Voice of America), for example, pumps the airways with the Pentecostal "full gospel" all day long, and at night even into southern Mexico. With only about four hours weekly of North American–produced programming, Radio VEA tries to protect its viewers from non-Pentecostal or other questionable fare from theologically or morally unknown places. Suspicious of all non-Pentecostals, and competing directly even with CAM's Radio Cultural, the station hopes to continually energize the Pentecostal movement while fighting against moral decay and personal sinfulness. It receives from one thousand to fifteen hundred letters per month from listeners.[87]

Catholic Media

Evangelical broadcasting has both legitimized evangelicalism as a viable religious alternative and elicited Roman Catholic combatants in the media. There has long been Catholic radio in Central America, but the stations never broadcast particularly religious programs. Partly to gain listeners in an increasingly competitive and expensive radio market, Catholic broadcasters turned to musical programming. A few stations boldly offered editorials and commentaries on the region's political situations, sometimes even criticizing right-wing governments, but for the most part the major Catholic stations remained apolitical.

While approximately 20 percent of all religious programming in Guatemala is Roman Catholic (compared with 70 percent evangelical), evangelicals dominate the larger cities where most of the population resides. For example, in the Guatemala City area evangelicals broadcast about 5,900 minutes weekly compared with less than 300 minutes by Catholic stations.[88] Catholic stations are generally funded and operated principally by rural Catholic groups likely rooted in the Catholic Action movement. They are highly localized operations, offering entertainment and information. Unlike Honduras, where some of the unlicensed stations have been shut down by politicized battles among the military, left-wing groups, and unidentified terrorists and hit squads, Guatemala's Catholic stations largely avoid politics in favor of Catholic cultural programming. Nevertheless, it is probably true that the Guatemalan stations, like their other Latin American counterparts, increasingly represent a Roman Catholic church which is changing "from the vertical, centrally controlled structure of communication of a hierarchical society to a system which permits wider popular participation and many alternative channels."[89]

Popularization often breeds a different message, however, especially when the medium is market-driven. In the midst of the Catholic church's decline come even louder calls for more creative and certainly more North American uses of the mass media. Consider the case of radio and television evangelist Salvador Gomez, who left Catholic seminary to start a broadcast ministry. The equivalent of what in the United States would be called a charismatic, Gomez took to the airways with the style and even some of the substance of Swaggart, launching the independent Ministerio Trigo (Wheat Ministry). Some Catholics understandably disowned him, including Catholic prelates, who are typically opposed to anything that even looks like Pentecostalism. Initially, Gomez was viewed by the Catholic church as a turncoat or traitor.

But as Gomez became more successful at attracting audiences and raising his own funds, he looked better and better to some Catholics. He was both a thorn in the flesh of the Latin church and a rising star in the competitive world of media ministry. The result was predictably practical and necessarily unsatisfactory to many Catholics.

Without official ecclesiastical support, Gomez continued to preach his charismatic version of the Catholic faith, even receiving some funds from dioceses and parishes. He and twenty-one other full-time employees worked vigorously against four "problems" with the Catholic church in Latin America: (1) a clergy mentality, (2) excessive humanism, (3) the loss of true spirituality, and (4) the disappearance of personal faith in Jesus Christ. Along the way, they presented some traditional Catholic doctrines in new wineskins, while avoiding any ecumenical efforts, which might cause new Catholic charismatics to jump over to the evangelical camp—a much shorter jump thanks to Trigo.[90]

In 1990 some Latin American bishops still refused to let Gomez preach in their dioceses. He and his successful ministry were caught between two powerful forces in the region's history—the traditionalism of Rome and the dynamism of Pentecostal evangelicalism. How ironic that Rome might look to North American media techniques to save the Catholic church in a region that it once so thoroughly dominated! Nevertheless, with the support of North American producers, and apparently the Vatican, the Catholic church launched its own *electrónico* evangelization campaign in Latin America in the early 1990s.[91]

The Battle for the Airways

Evangelical radio in Guatemala has already become a major voice for Protestant fundamentalism. If television follows suit, eclipsing North American televangelists in favor of Ladino broadcasters, both Protestant and Catholic fundamentalism might grow even more rapidly than they have in the past decade. Protestant radio broadcasters (evangelical *locutores*) have proven their ability to adapt creatively Pentecostal and neo-Pentecostal messages to the medium. Meanwhile, the popularity of Salvador Gomez suggests that Catholic television is poised for its own creative responses to Protestant competition.

Guatemala City's channel 21, the nation's first full-time religious television station, is a revealing test of the winds of revivalism on the Ladino airways. Started in the early 1980s with local support from the Sandovals, a wealthy newspaper-publishing family, modest financial support from Arkansas-based Youth with a Mission, and equipment from California's Trinity Broadcasting Network (an independent, charismatic satellite network), the station has struggled with low power and a very small audience. In fact, both Youth with a Mission and Trinity apparently raised considerable funds for the project from their North American constituencies but passed little of the money to the North American station manager, lay preacher, and television producer Steve Smith. The station survived largely by using Smith's personal equipment to produce profitable commercials and videotapes for Guatemalan businesses. Desperate for programming, the station continued broadcasting reruns of Trinity productions from Los Angeles as well as a few local preachers and church services, but it was increasingly operated by Catholic charismatics. Overall, the station was a dismal failure, both technically and programmatically. Unable to secure continued North

American funding or to rally the divisive Guatemalan evangelical community around the station, Smith left the transmitters and studios in a defunct nightclub to a largely inexperienced group of frustrated young broadcasters.[92]

Television, it seems, is generally too expensive for relatively small Guatemalan evangelical subgroups to finance on their own. As a result, it is either used by Catholics, who have trouble raising adequate funding as well, or by the already established North American fundamentalists. Given the suspicion that Ladinos and Indians generally harbor about North American political intentions in the region, only the most apolitical and culturally sensitive evangelical televangelists will make it in Guatemala. Swaggart was able to accomplish what no natives could, but his success suggests that a home-grown Pentecostal television star with adequate funding might make the big time. In 1990 it appeared that both Catholics and Protestants in the country were split over whether such a Guatemalan ministry would be good for their respective movements. Evangelicals debated Protestant ecumenism, while Catholics were divided over whether or not high-profile television would warp the historic mission and message of the Roman church by reverting to Protestant methods fashioned by North American evangelicals.

On the Protestant side, an optimistic cheerleader for fundamentalist broadcasting is A. Edmundo Madrid, pastor and president of the Alianza Evangelica de Guatemala (Evangelical Alliance of Guatemala). One of the few evangelicals to call himself a fundamentalist, Madrid has the difficult task of trying to bring together the disparate factions of Guatemalan evangelicalism. The Alliance, which is the equivalent of the National Association of Evangelicals in the United States, includes the Association of Christian Communicators of Guatemala (something like the National Religious Broadcasters). Only six of the ten evangelical radio stations are members. Moreover, most of the 1,020 evangelical programs on commercial stations are produced by evangelical organizations that so far have refused to join the Alliance, including the Assemblies of God.[93] The extent and variety of home-grown evangelical radio in Guatemala have made it exceedingly difficult for people such as Madrid to harmonize fundamentalist broadcasting. Home-grown television, where the stakes are even higher and the funding more competitive, could produce even greater splits in the country's religious landscape. Or it might force greater Protestant ecumenism than now exists.

In the past, much North American evangelical television has survived because of the infusion of North American finances and the establishment of a relatively small neo-Pentecostal audience carved out of the Guatemalan middle class. This was not as true of Swaggart's old-style Pentecostalism, but it was certainly the case with programs such as "The 700 Club" and "PTL Club." These shows, like their Guatemalan audiences, were less apt to criticize Catholics and were far more open to ostentatious North American lifestyles frequently depicted on the air. However, nearly all indications in the early 1990s suggest that even these types of programs could not easily survive on the contributions of middle-class Ladino evangelicals financially strapped by the nation's economic plight in the 1980s.

For the time being, then, fundamentalist broadcasting in Guatemala continues to reflect the many disparate directions of religious life in the country. Along with extensive North American–produced television and an incredible array of local evangelical radio broadcasting are Catholic radio and Catholic-charismatic television. Not all of it is fundamentalist, but in a region of great cultural flux and social strain, religious broadcasting from all traditions tends to take on fundamentalist styles and messages. The CAM's four radio stations are generally the Protestant exceptions, with the help of U.S. funding, while the older Catholic radio stations provide the Catholic connections to a more placid and less competitive religious past. Whether these types of broadcasters will be able to survive successfully without external funding, however, is greatly open to debate. Evangelical radio, on the other hand, both thrives on and fuels the fundamentalist explosion in the area.

Conclusion

To evangelize is to spread God's Word so that others may hear and come to believe. Through their churches, schools, and media, Guatemalan evangelicals rely on preaching, teaching, and singing as effective channels of communication to win others over to Christ. From speaking in tongues to divine laughter, they express their fear and frustration, their hopes and joys.[94] Enthusiastic religion has been especially appealing to those who find their daily lives a grind, and this is no less true in the case of Guatemala.

While evangelicalism was initially imported from the North, it has grown fundamentally as a grass-roots movement. Guatemalans of many persuasions, socioeconomic backgrounds, and regions have embraced evangelical religion. They, in turn, express their faith in a variety of ways: from old-style revival meetings to high-class prayer breakfasts; from tents pitched on Catholic-owned plantations to storefront Pentecostal churches in the cities; and from loudspeakers attached to the outside of small churches in rural villages to remote-control televisions directed to overflow crowds in the large city churches.

Some Guatemalan evangelicals, mainly the lower and working classes, take, in Niebuhr's terms, a "Christ-above-culture" or "Christ-against-culture" position, while others, primarily from the middle to upper classes, tend very cautiously toward a "Christ-as-transformer-of-culture" position.[95] But whatever the particular orientation, more and more Guatemalans are becoming engaged not only in listening to God's Word but also in telling it. As evangelicals, they give testimony to their own religious experience, rehearsing and dramatizing the story of their faith as they attempt to influence others. In this way, as well as metaphorically through speaking in tongues, many Guatemalans may be turning to evangelicalism in order to find a new "voice." That voice is now almost universally fundamentalistic, whether it comes from the United States or local media, schools, and churches.

While evangelicalism is not yet the majority religion in Guatemala, its presence is felt by all. Thousands of evangelical institutions dot the landscape of Guatemala, the "land of eternal spring." Certainly for some, evangelicalism brings a message of hope, a new start to building communities and lives that have been torn apart by violence and economic depresssion. For others, it brings a message of compliance to inequitable conditions that make life miserable for the majority of Guatemalans.[96] Some scholars writing in the neo-Weberian tradition see evangelicalism as enabling people to take greater control of their personal lives, helping them to improve the daily conditions of their lives by developing good work habits and "clean" lifestyles; others see evangelicalism as enabling the political, military, and economic elite to carry on the capitalist exploitation of the majority by preaching obedience to the powers that be. Whether evangelicalism will serve as the handmaiden to capitalist development that entraps the majority in oppressive conditions, or whether it will usher in more democratic forms of capitalist development that better serve the majority, remains to be seen.

While the Protestant faith was introduced into Latin America between 1870 and 1890, bringing attitudes favoring democracy, science, and liberal progressivism, it has not been such a modernizing force in areas dominated by the developed world.[97] Miguez Bonino describes the process of modernization in Latin America over the past century:

> The leaders of emancipation and modernization had their faces turned toward Europe and the U.S.A. and their backs to the interiors of their countries. There, Indians and peasants were simply incorporated as cheap labor for production. . . . A free press, free trade, education, politics—all the "achievements" of liberalism—were the privilege of the elite. For the growing Latin American masses, undernourishment, slavery, illiteracy, and later on forced migration, exploitation, crowding and finally repression when they claim their rights—these are the harvest of one century of "liberal democracy."[98]

Indeed, evangelicalism has grown most rapidly in the last few decades in countries like South Korea, the Philippines, and Guatemala, where repressive right-wing, military governments have been the rule.

The rapid growth of evangelicalism in Guatemala comes at a time when the advanced capitalist countries have already established a hierarchy of dependency relations, with Guatemala in a subordinate and dependent position. It is clear that Guatemalan evangelicalism often legitimizes capitalism. However, so far evangelicalism alone has not created conditions under which successful entrepreneurship can develop into major industrial change. In fact, small-scale entrepreneurship has existed for a long time; just observe the number of rural and urban markets, and the number of people who hawk their goods on the streets or scrape together a living as best they can from a myriad of sources. If anything, it may be the existing "entrepreneurial spirit" of Guatemalans (whether voluntary or involuntary) that makes fundamentalistic evangelicalism attractive to them. The incredible growth in the number of little congregations in Guatemala in recent decades may, in part, be aided by this spirit. The Protestant pastor, who embodies the persona of the entrepreneur, must compete with others for funding and loyalty within a market of religious options. He resembles the "mumi" big-men who offer handouts to attract followers and impress others; one can choose to follow him, to follow another, or to establish oneself as leader of a newly founded group.

Ironically, the forms of capitalist development that many Guatemalan fundamentalists currently tend to support could possibly hinder the "spirit of entrepreneur-ship." As large-scale agriculture and industrial development continue without opening up other forms of employment for the majority of people, various kinds of entrepreneurial activity could be pushed out. That is, given the configuration of the global economy, the kinds of economic development (e.g., *maquiladora* factories established by South Koreans an hour outside of Guatemala City, or large-scale agro-exports where the farmers take the risks and the middle men the profits on new ventures) occurring in Guatemala today may reduce the likelihood and viability of small-scale entrepreneurial activity. In this context, the entrepreneurial growth of evangelical churches is not eliciting a parallel development in the economy. This puts enormous pressure on fundamentalist leaders and institutions to provide for peoples' material as well as spiritual needs.

There are those who see hopeful signs of the Protestant ethic at work; people are being trained in good work habits, entrepreneurialism, and even democratic partici-pation in society. David Martin in *Tongues of Fire,* his valuable survey of Protestantism in Latin America, seems tentatively hopeful, even though he has reservations about the undemocratic, inegalitarian societies in which these movements prosper. Peter Berger, whose Boston University Institute for the Study of Economic Culture funded Martin's research, seems intent on finding ways to celebrate entrepreneurialism world-wide. He is enthusiastic to the point of saying that we are witnessing the "Second Protestant Internationale,"[99] a label that suggests the "revolutionary" potential of Protestantism while ignoring the context of political repression within which it prospers.

The explosion of evangelicalism in Guatemala parallels new patterns of interaction between religious developments and political and economic transformations. While a number of scholars have noted the similarities between industrializing England (1750–1850) and late twentieth-century Guatemala, the differences in the political economies of each country and their respective relationships to the political econo-mies of other countries in the global system must be seriously considered.[100] We do not believe that in Guatemala, Protestantism will have precisely the same effects as it has had in other historical periods and regions. However, we do believe that trends in Guatemala probably foreshadow similar developments in many other Latin Ameri-can countries. Certainly the Guatemalan religious experience is being spread directly and indirectly to other nations in Central America. Just as Guatemala historically has been the cultural soul of the region, today it is the religious parent of spiritual move-ments—including educational and mass communication movements—that are spreading across the land. The impact of fundamentalistic Protestantism will un-doubtedly vary across the region, but its dynamic, expansionary soul will continue to radiate from Guatemala, which will probably soon be more Protestant than Roman Catholic. With these developments in mind, we offer the following future scenarios for Guatemala.

First, religious polarization will likely continue. Liberation theology and funda-mentalist dispensationalism will continue to grow side by side in a land where many of the struggles of daily life are the result of a long history of nationwide social, economic and political problems. We do not believe that any "Reformation" of either Catholicism or Protestantism will alone dominate the area's religious and hence its cultural landscape. Instead we see ongoing adoption, assimilation, and rejection of religious ideas and practices from within and without Guatemala. In short, we see ongoing religious competition. Although anchored in different theologies, liberation theology and dispensational fundamentalism are essentially grass-roots phenomena based on rebuilding community life as well as on religious faith. In their own ways, each captures powerful visions of the kingdom of God on earth as well as in heaven. In the past, scholars have tended to overemphasize the significance of liberation theology; now they may be overemphasizing the recent gains of Protestantism. After all, government oppression historically has elicited countermovements, including left-wing organizations tied to liberation theology and support from right-wing movements. As we indicated earlier, Guatemalan religion tends toward a fundamentalistic style of belief and expression, including militancy. This feeds the religious competition as well as the parallel political instabilities.

Second, neo-Pentecostalism and liberation theology may increasingly exacerbate as well as reflect existing ideological battles in the region. In the past, the old-style Pentecostalism was largely an implicitly apolitical phenomenon that led believers inward to the life of personal piety far more than outward to the word of politics and social action. Neo-Pentecostalism, by contrast, shows significant signs of entering the public arena as an increasingly political force that would support various candidates while openly grappling with the implications of the evangelical faith for a wide range of social and economic issues. While liberation theology has significantly shaped the religiously inspired political left, neo-Pentecostalism, as a middle- to upper-middle-class phenomenon, has mirrored and advanced the political positions of the nation's professional and business people.

Third, the old-style Pentecostalism of the rural and urban poor may eventually become openly politicized. Presently there are few signs of this happening, but as Ríos Montt and Serrano Elías took their faith to the public square, they also legitimized evangelicalism as a religion that has something to say about how the country should be run. At this writing it is unclear what form of expression the newly elected President Jorge Serrano's evangelical convictions will take. Most old-style Pentecostals remain skeptical or even strongly opposed to openly politicized religion. If evangelical education and media join the chorus of political voices, however, old-style and neo-Pentecostals may find a common voice in opposition to the left. Such a scenario could potentially make the country's political landscape even more polarized and militarized.

Notes

1. "U.S. Evangelist's Expensive Nicaraguan Campaign Encounters Rocky Ground," *CEPAD Report*, March–April 1990, pp. 5–7.

2. Stan Jeter, Project Light coordinator, interview, Guatemala City, 3 April 1990.

3. See Sara Diamond, *Spiritual Warfare: The Politics of the Christian Right* (Boston:

South End Press, 1989); David Stoll, *Is Latin America Turning Protestant? The Politics of Evangelical Growth* (Berkeley: University of California Press, 1990).

4. Archbishop Penados quoted in Colum Lynch, "Catholics, Evangelicals Tangle amid Latin Turmoil," *San Francisco Chronicle,* 10 May 1989, p. 4.

5. See Stoll, *Is Latin America Turning Protestant?;* Diamond, *Spiritual Warfare;* Tom Barry and Deb Preusch, *The Central American Fact Book* (New York: Grove Press, 1986); Deborah Huntington, *The Salvation Brokers: Conservative Evangelicals in Central America,* NACLA Report on the Americas 18, no. 1 (1984); Bruce Larmer, "Guatemala: Evangelical Spurt Meets Spiritual Needs and Political Goals," *Christian Science Monitor,* 9–15 March 1989, p. 1; Bill Moyers, "God and Politics," part 1, Public Broadcasting System, 8 December 1989.

6. Lynch, "Catholics, Evangelicals Tangle amid Latin Turmoil," p. 4.

7. Stoll, *Is Latin America Turning Protestant?* p. 308.

8. Lynch, "Catholics, Evangelicals Tangle amid Latin Turmoil," p. 4; Dennis Smith, interview, March 1990.

9. Dennis Smith, "Guatemala in Numbers" (Manuscript), p. 1.

10. Lindsey Gruson, "Right-Wing Protestant Elected President of Guatemala," *New York Times,* 8 January 1991, p. A3.

11. David Martin, *Tongues of Fire: The Explosion of Protestantism in Latin America* (Oxford: Basil Blackwell, 1990).

12. In the case of some of the neo-Pentecostal megachurches, there may be quite a bit of ecumenicism that tends to operate covertly within an international circle where political and economic concerns may transcend religious concerns. For instance, there is some indication that the elders of Verbo have made alliances with Opus Dei and the Knights of Malta.

13. Quoted in Everett Wilson, "The Central American Evangelicals," *International Review of Missions,* p. 99.

14. Virginia Garrard Burnett, "Jerusalem under Siege: Protestantism in Rural Guatemala, 1960–1987" (Paper presented at the Latin American Studies Association, September 1989), p. 15, and Rick Waldrop, interview, Guatemala City, July 1987.

15. In his booklet "How to Write Your Own Ticket with God," Kenneth Hagin shares a vision he had of Jesus: "He [Jesus] said, 'If anybody, anywhere, will take these four steps or put these four principles into operation he will always receive whatever he wants from Me or from God the Father.'" According to Hagin, the four steps are (1) Say it (whatever you say you will get—put words to your faith); (2) Do it (put actions with your faith); (3) Receive it (plug it into the powerhouse of heaven); (4) Tell it (tell others so that they may believe). Kenneth Hagin, "How to Write Your Ticket with God" (Tulsa, Okla.: Faith Library Publications, 1980), p. 5; see also Kenneth Copeland, "The Laws of Prosperity" (Fort Worth, Tex.: Kenneth Copeland Publications, 1974); Elda Susan Morran and Lawrence Sclemmer, in *Faith for the Fearful* (Durbin, South Africa: Center for Applied Social Science, University of Natal, 1984), provide a good discussion of prosperity theology, especially in relation to evangelical churches in South Africa.

16. See Susan Rose and Steve Brouwer, "The Reproduction of Secular Worlds in Sacred Institutions: A Critique of Christian Schools," Issues in Education 4, no. 2 (1987): 136–50.

17. Barry and Preusch, *The Central American Fact Book,* p. 1.

18. *Directorio de Iglesias, Organizaciones y Ministerios del Morimiento Protestante Guatemala* (Guatemala City: Instituto Internacional de Evangelizacion a Fondo [IINDEF] y Servicio Evangelizador para America Latina [SEPAL]).

19. Rick Waldrop, interview, July 1987.

20. Wilson, "Central American Evangelicals."

21. Burnett, "Jerusalem under Siege," p. 15.

22. See ibid.; Diamond, *Spiritual Warfare.*

23. "Retrato de Guatemala" (Guatemala City: Equipo Sepal con Alianza Evangelica, Vision Mundial, Cruzada Estudiantil y

Profesional para Cristo, December 1988), p. 2.

24. For a numerical description of types of Christian education in Guatemala, see Martha de Berberian, "Analisis de la educacion cristiana en Guatemala" (Tesis: Escuela de Teologia, Universidad Mariano Galvez de Guatemala, 1983).

25. Ibid.

26. There are certainly exceptions here. For example, Christ for the Nations is an interdenominational Bible study institute located in Guatemala City. Part of the pretribulationist charismatic movement, it draws students from various city churches, and members of the "teaching team" attend different area churches.

27. "Assessment of Guatemalan Education" (Guatemala City: Academy for Educational Development Report, 1985), p. 6; "Diagnostico de la Educacion Guatemalteca" (Guatemala City: Ministerio de Educacion, Oficina de Planeamiento Integral de Educacion, 1985).

28. *Guatemala 1986: The Year of Promises* (Guatemala City: Inforpress, 1987).

29. "On Their Own: A Preliminary Study of Youth Gangs in Guatemala City," *Cuadernos de Investigacion* 4 (Guatemala City: AVANSCO, 1988), p. 40.

30. Ibid. A 1985 AED (Academy for Educational Development) report on the state of education in Guatemala indicates that the current educational system reaches only 60 percent of the seven to fourteen age-group: 75 percent in the urban areas and only 34 percent in the rural areas. Of the children who did attend first grade in 1978, only 26.2 percent were enrolled in the sixth grade in 1983.

31. Infant mortality rates are 84.5 per 1,000 in rural areas and 65.3 per 1,000 in urban areas.

32. Interviews with the minister of education and principals of fourteen Christian schools indicate that the government knows which schools are operating and in fact has more complete records than the U.S. or various state Departments of Education, July 1987.

33. See Susan Rose, "Christian Fundamentalism and Education in the United States," chap. 16, this volume; and idem, *Keeping Them Out of the Hands of Satan* (London: Routledge and Kegan Paul, 1988), for greater detail on ACE.

34. Virgilio Zapata, interview, June 1987.

35. Where the school is small and loosely structured, it is possible to reuse ACE packets and xerox only the test pages, a practice that is, of course, not encouraged by ACE. See also "'Escuela del futuro' y el proyecto neoconservador," in *Infopress Centro Americana*, 21 de Marzo 1991, pp. 3–5, for a discussion of the conflicts between ACE and the state of Honduras.

36. Paul W. Jehle, *Go Ye Therefore and Teach: Operation Manual for Christian Day School* (Plymouth, Mass.: Plymouth Rock Foundation, 1982), pp. 13, 35 (emphasis in original).

37. Ibid.

38. Bill Moyers has produced an excellent documentary on the reconstructionists in the United States and Central America, in his "God and Politics" series.

39. Paul W. Jehle, *The Principle Approach to Political Involvement* (Buzzards Bay, Mass.: Heritage Institute Ministries, 1985), p. 5:1.

40. Verna Hall, *The Christian History of the Constitution of the United States* (San Francisco: Foundation for American Christian Education, 1966), pp. iii–iv.

41. Ibid., p. ii.

42. Ibid.

43. Visit by one of the authors to Escuela Christiana Verbo, Guatemala City, July 1987.

44. See Rose and Brouwer, "Reproduction of Secular Worlds," for a more detailed discussion of socioeconomic status and classroom styles.

45. Verbo unsuccessfully prepared the path for Ríos Montt's election, despite the fact that the Constitution prohibited anyone who took power by virtue of a coup to run for the presidency. Ríos Montt claimed, however, that he was a servant of God and

would do what God called him to do. His campaign message appeared on billboards that flanked the Pan American Highway ("Montt es Honesto"), in newspaper reports, and on Pat Robertson's "The 700 Club."

46. James DeGolyer, "Unlearning the Ways of the World," *Radiance,* May 1985, p. 13.

47. We tested the evidence of our fieldwork by asking every school principal and evangelical educator we interviewed in March 1990 whether they thought this was an accurate assessment. All concurred that it was and offered no contradictory evidence.

48. Most evangelical schools admit children who are from non-evangelical backgrounds quite readily, being less selective about their evangelical pedigree than are most North American Christian schools. Moreover, most schools do not have a totally evangelical teaching staff—a consequence of necessity, not philosophy. Most of the directors with whom we spoke would prefer to enroll solely or predominantly children of evangelicals, and their explicit goal is to convert the families of the students who come to their schools as well as the students themselves. Approximately 70 percent of the schools in Guatemala are church-run, and the churches are quite explicit about using them to attract potential new members and retain old ones.

49. Though according to Stuart Salazar, 80 percent of evangelical schools do not have a full evangelical staff. Interview, Guatemala City, 22 March 1990.

50. Interview with Christian school principal, March 1990.

51. According to Penny Lernoux, *People of God: The Struggle for World Catholicism* (New York: Viking Penguin, 1989), p. 16, Swaggart alone spent $15 million a year on overseas missions, including a private school system in El Salvador that educated over thirteen thousand children, and a similarly large one in Honduras.

52. An acronym for Program Integral Educativo de las Asambleas de Dios.

53. The Inasmuch program, which encourages North American schools, teachers, and families to sponsor a child in developing countries, was begun in 1988 and as of 1990 was sponsoring 400 students in South East Asia and 250 in Latin America, including a couple of students at America Latina, the only Guatemalan school involved to date. In addition, ACSI has initiated Partners for Nationals, which helps support a Christian school teacher's salary (approximately $150 a month in Guatemala) and the SOS (Students Organized to Serve) program, which sends small groups of North American high school students to work on development and missions projects in developing countries.

54. "On Their Own."

55. See Stoll, *Is Latin America Turning Protestant?* for further details on Youth for Christ.

56. "On Their Own," p. 42.

57. Stuart Salazar, interview, 22 March 1990.

58. "On Their Own," pp. 43–44.

59. Ibid., p. 44.

60. This is often the case in the United States as well, where many born-again Christians (especially charismatic evangelicals) have become employed in the social services, taking, in Niebuhr's terms, a "Christ as transformer of culture" approach. In Guatemala, such social reformers tend to come from the neo-Pentecostal churches such as Elim.

61. "On Their Own," p. 42.

62. See Anthony Platt, *The Child Savers* (Chicago: University of Chicago Press, 1977); David Nasaw, *Schooled to Order: A Social History of Public Schooling in the United States* (Oxford: Oxford University Press, 1979); Linda Gordon, *Heroes of Their Own Lives: The Politics and History of Family Violence* (New York: Viking, 1988).

63. "On Their Own," p. 49.

64. Ibid.

65. Ibid., p. 50.

66. Dennis Smith, "The Gospel According to the United States: Evangelical Broadcasting in Central America," in Quentin J.

Schultze, ed., *American Evangelicals and the Mass Media* (Grand Rapids, Mich.: Zondervan/Academie, 1990), p. 279; Anibal F. Duarte, "Radiofonia religiosa en Guatemala" (Licenciado en Ciencias de la Communicacion thesis, Universidad de San Carlos de Guatemala, 1989), pp. 3–4.

67. Clyde W. Taylor and Wade T. Coggins, *Protestant Missions in Latin America: A Statistical Survey* (Washington, D.C.: Evangelical Foreign Missions Association, 1961), p. vii.

68. Ibid., p. 152.

69. Duarte, "Radiofonia religiosa," pp. 27–28.

70. Taylor and Coggins, *Protestant Missions*, p. 83.

71. Ibid., p. 32.

72. Ibid., pp. 50–51.

73. Ibid., p. 56.

74. Ibid., p. 57.

75. Dennis Smith, "The Impact of Religious Programming in the Electronic Media on the Active Christian Population in Central America," *Latin American Pastoral Issues* 15 (July 1988): 76.

76. Maria C. Wert and Robert L. Stevenson, "Global Television Flow to Latin America," *Journalism Quarterly* 65 (Spring 1988): 182–85.

77. Gustav Niebuhr, "Poor, Rich Alike Stay Tuned to TV Preachers," *Atlanta Constitution,* 2 March 1987, p. 6A; Smith, "Impact of Religious Programming," p. 77. Smith measured church-going in three countries.

78. Smith, "Impact of Religious Programming," p. 77.

79. Ibid., p. 78.

80. Ibid., p. 79.

81. Penny Lernoux, "The Fundamentalist Surge in Latin America," *Christian Century* 20 (January 1988): 52–53; Stoll, *Is Latin America Turning Protestant?* p. 192.

82. Interviews with numerous evangelical leaders by one of the authors, Guatemala City, 2 and 3 April 1990.

83. Fraternidad Cristiana, whose large church edifice resembles a fancy auto dealership, sits just outside Guatemala City on the Pan American Highway near the glass and steel headquaters of several North American drug companies. As you enter the auditorium, which holds eight hundred people, equal numbers of men and women, well dressed in understated light blue uniforms that resemble those worn by pilots and stewardesses, usher you to your seat. Services at Fraternidad are lively and entertaining. Lopez is preceded by an imposing gentleman in a white jacket who is the lead singer; he is backed by a band and a well-dressed chorus of attractive young women. He alternates between leading the congregation in song and singing solos which have the sound and trappings of tasteful nightclub music. After about an hour, Lopez takes the stage and begins delivering a fast-paced sermon laced with humorous one-liners which evoke laughter from his audience. Clearly the church is attracting many new members who more than pack the three successive services held there every Sunday morning. In fact, extensive church and school construction is currently under way.

84. Interviews with one of the authors, June 1987.

85. Attended by one of the authors, June 1987.

86. Service attended by one of the authors and conversations with church members, June 1987; interviews with members of the church and school director, 24 March 1990, and with Jorge H. Lopez, 3 April 1990.

87. José Adonias Corado, station manager, interview with one of the authors, Guatemala City, 3 April 1990.

88. Duarte, "Radiofonia religiosa," p. 53.

89. Robert White, "The Church and Communication in Latin America: Thirty Years to Search for Patterns," in *Communicatio Socialis Yearbook* (Indore, India: Sat Prachar Press, 1982), p. 98.

90. Ricardo Echevaria, Ministerio Trigo, interview with one of the authors, 2 April 1990.

91. See Mike Tangeman, "'Evangelización 2000' and 'Lumen 2000': Their Im-

pacts on the Catholic Faith in the Developing World" (Manuscript); See Fernando Torres, "La fe vía satélite," *Solidaridad,* June 1989, no pages; "Luman 2000," *L'Actualité Religieuse,* March 1988, pp. 17–28.

92. Niebuhr, "Poor, Rich Alike Stay Tuned"; Steve Smith, interview with one of the authors, Guatemala City, 3 April 1990.

93. A. Edmundo Madrid, interview with one of the authors, Guatemala City, 3 April 1990.

94. See Pablo A. Deiros, "Protestant Fundamentalism in Latin America," in Martin E. Marty and R. Scott Appleby, eds., *Fundamentalisms Observed* (Chicago: University of Chicago Press, 1991).

95. H. Richard Neibuhr, *Christ and Culture* (New York: Harper and Row, 1951).

96. According to a 1982 UNICEF study, Guatemala has the lowest "physical quality of life" index in Central America, and the third lowest in Latin America, after Haiti and Bolivia (Barry and Preusch, *The Central American Fact Book,* p. 79).

97. Michael Kearney, "Religion, Ideology, and Revolution in Latin America," *Latin American Perspectives* 13, no. 3 (Summer 1986): 3–12; Jose Miguez Bonino, *Doing Theology in a Revolutionary Situation* (Philadelphia: Fortress, 1975).

98. Miguez Bonino, *Doing Theology,* p. 15.

99. Peter Berger, in "Foreword" in Martin, *Tongues of Fire.*

100. See Martin, *Tongues of Fire;* Michael Dodson and Laura O'Shaughnessy, *Nicaragua's Other Revolution* (Albany: State University of New York Press, 1990).

Christian Fundamentalism and Education in the United States

Susan Rose

"Baptist church padlocked. Minister arrested along with seven other parishioners." In September 1982 Faith Baptist Church was padlocked to prevent its operation of a Christian school that had not been authorized by the state. On 31 January 1983, the pastor of the church, Reverend Everett Sileven, was released from Cass County Jail after having served four months for operating the unaccredited school in violation of a court order to close it. Upon release, he made the following statement to reporters who had gathered in front of the jail: "I do ask in the authoritative name of Jesus, the supreme law of the universe that God Almighty bind the officials of the state of Nebraska and Cass County from further interference with the ministry of God at Faith Baptist Church . . . by either converting them or restraining them or removing them or killing them."[1]

What led government officials to lock up a church, challenging the right to free exercise of religion, and the right of a pastor to pray that his enemies be exterminated?

For supporters of Faith Baptist Church, the issue is religious freedom. They argue that their First Amendment rights are violated if the state is allowed to regulate how parents should educate their children. For supporters of the state, the issue is the state's responsibility to ensure a quality education for all children, and minimum standards for all schools. The central question is basic: whose right and responsibility is it to teach what to whom?

Controversy over the resurgence of fundamentalist activity has characterized the latter decades of the twentieth century. In the United States, significant litigation and legislation have accompanied the proliferation of "Christian" (private, evangelical) schools. Centering on the issues of states' rights versus parents' rights, and church-state relations, the legal and philosophical battles have influenced both private and public education. As "battlegrounds for social change,"[2] the public schools have become a contested terrain of political, ideological, and religious struggle. Although the mission of the common school was to rise above politics, public education has not escaped the conflicts that come with the pressures of interest-group politics. Conflict is central to the educational arena as educators and policymakers contend with the meaning and realities of democratic pluralism. Thus it is not the presence of conflict that is surprising but rather the absence of an ideology that explains it, particularly in a society that celebrates competition in the political and economic arenas.[3] "The multifarious events and occurrences that define the history of education in urban America can be understood as attempts by one or another group to preserve, protect, nurture, rebuild, and/or transform community," Barbara Finkelstein writes. "It is a history of conflict between increasingly diverse groups for control over the network of relationships enclosing the young, and for the power to censor, filter, and define significance."[4]

Until the 1970s, fundamentalist perspectives were largely ignored by mainstream educators.[5] But during the past two decades, fundamentalists have mobilized, voicing their grievances and extending the controversy over public education from the class-room to the courtroom. As a consequence, they have had a significant impact on religious and secular schooling in the United States. Across the nation, public schools have been pressured to remove books from classrooms and libraries, to teach scientific creationism as well as evolution, to eliminate sex education, to adopt textbooks that reinforce "traditional" American values, and to avoid "controversial" subjects in the classroom.

While the contemporary proliferation of Christian schools represents the first widespread secession from public schooling since the establishment of the Catholic parochial school system, it is not a new phenomenon.[6] Most denominations experi-mented with religious weekday education throughout the nineteenth century al-though the idea never took off; by the early twentieth century most mainline denominations had abandoned the idea of religious day schools altogether.[7] While fundamentalists continued to establish a number of independent postsecondary edu-cational institutions and bible colleges, it was not until Protestant control of public education gave way to secularization in the mid-twentieth century that fundamental-ists actively began to establish their own primary and secondary schools. They called their schools "Christian," in contrast to other religious schools (those established by Catholics, Lutherans, Episcopalians, Quakers, and Amish, among others). The term "Christian" is used to emphasize a distinction fundamentalists draw between them-selves as "saved" and others who are "unsaved."

Interdenominational and Protestant, "Christian schools" actually represent a range of *evangelical* groups. The term "evangelical" is often used inclusively, as I employ it in this essay, to refer to coalitions or alliances of fundamentalist, charismatic, and neo-evangelical Christians, all of whom share basic evangelical tenets, including belief in Christ as personal savior and the necessity of a conversion experience in order to be saved, the Bible as the inerrant word of God, and the necessity of spreading the gospel and converting others to Christ. While it is difficult to assess how many of the Chris-tian schools are strictly fundamentalist (distinctions among types are not necessarily made by Christian school associations), it appears that Christian schools are most popular among the more separatist, uncompromising, and conservative wing of the evangelical movement—that is, among those to whom the term "fundamentalist" most readily applies and by whom it has been most readily accepted. However, as we shall see, many fundamentalist and nonfundamentalist evangelicals alike have entered, and been drawn into, national, state, and local politics—and thus into the heart of compromise—both to defend their separatist schools and to reform public schools in order to make them acceptable and viable (for Christians) once again. In examining the education-related activism of fundamentalist and nonfundamentalist evangelicals during the past two decades, sharp distinctions between the two groups are difficult to sustain.[8]

At the same time, fundamentalists and evangelicals together do not constitute the full list of participants in the Christian school movement. The Dutch Calvinist schools, representing the longest tradition of Christian elementary and secondary schooling, are among those that consider themselves part of the larger Christian school movement but are not fundamentalist. The Calvinist schools, started in the Netherlands in the nineteenth century, were established in the United States beginning in the mid-nineteenth century. While they are technically part of the Christian school movement, they distinguish themselves from the other fundamentalist and evangelical schools in a number of ways. Established not as a protest against public education, but as a way of educating children according to the customs and beliefs of the Dutch Reformed, they are closely connected to an ethnic group. Believing that educational authority lies within the family, not in the church or state, the Calvinist schools are parent-run rather than church-run or board-run. Neither individual schools nor their association, Christian Schools International (CSI), tends to interact with other Christian schools or associations.[9]

Therefore I focus on the contemporary Christian school movement only as it expresses the ethos of participating fundamentalists and evangelicals (who, together, do constitute the large majority of players in the movement), and as it has played a significant role in the efforts of the New Christian Right to influence the course of North American education. In assessing the influence of Christian schools or students, one must recognize that they remain a small percentage of the total and that Christian school growth appears to have reached a plateau in the early 1990s. The influence of these schools, however, reaches beyond their numbers, as we shall see.

The Christian School Movement

The Christian school movement has been the fastest growing sector of private education and represents one of the most important mobilization efforts of fundamentalists to regain influence in American society. Approximately one million students (K–12) are enrolled in some ten thousand schools. These enrollments represent approximately 20 percent of the total private school population and 2–3 percent of the national school population.[10] The numbers may be larger than this, for the character of the Christian school movement renders a precise record of the number of schools and students impossible. Separatist schools often choose not to register with the state, report data to any state or federal education agency, or belong to a Christian school association.[11] Many Christian schools open and then close within two to three years. Nonetheless, it is clear that there has been dramatic growth. Even during a period of reported high unemployment "when there existed a very real threat of a national economic recession, with reports of declining enrollments in both public and non-public schools, and increased educational budgets being submitted by all levels of government, the Christian School movement grew [dramatically]."[12] Although the Roman Catholic schools still comprise the largest group in private education, with approximately 2.8 million students, a realignment has occurred within the private sector where Christian schools have grown in numbers and relative influence. Since 1965, enrollments in non-Catholic religiously affiliated schools (the majority of which are evangelical) have increased some 149 percent, while Catholic school enrollments have declined 54 percent and the number of Catholic schools has decreased by 28 percent.[13]

A grass-roots movement of the 1950s, Christian schools proliferated in the late 1960s and 1970s. Until the 1970s the schools tended to be scattered and relatively powerless, but throughout the 1970s they began to organize through Christian school associations. In 1972 the American Association of Christian Schools was founded, and in 1990 it numbered 1,360 schools with enrollments of 151,214. In 1978, a merger of several small associations took place, forming the Association of Christian Schools International which now has 1,930 schools with enrollments of 348,912. The third major association, Christian Schools International, was founded in 1920 by Dutch Calvinists with some 459 schools and enrollments of 88,165.[14]

These associations offer a variety of services including monitoring legislation at the state and federal levels; legal assistance; school and teacher accreditation; professional training; teacher placement; insurance packages; and national competitions in athletics, academic debates, music, and Bible. They serve primarily as lobbying organizations which monitor legislation and defend individual cases at the local, state, and federal levels. Politically active evangelicals of the 1970s and 1980s "cut their political teeth defending Christian schools they had helped to organize."[15]

The irony of the situation is not lost on the advocates of the Christian school movement. Once the sponsors and regulators of the mainstream educational system, evangelical Protestants feel compelled to pursue alternative forms of education in the closing decades of the twentieth century. Their actions are motivated by their desire to restore religious authority in American society, to reinforce parental authority, and to provide quality education for their children while protecting them from drugs, sex, violence, and the lack of discipline in the public schools.

Evangelicals and fundamentalists act in response to a series of perceived threats, the most serious of these being the general secularization of life and the legislatively mandated secularization of public schools. Supreme Court decisions prohibiting prayer (*Engel v. Vitale*, 370 U.S. 421 [1962]), and Bible readings and devotions in public schools (*School District of Abington v. Schempp*, 374 U.S. 203 [1963]) offended evangelicals and fundamentalists because these actions excluded God. Just as the Vietnam War and Watergate challenged the notion of America as the "Righteous Empire,"[16] fundamentalists were becoming convinced that their own "civil religion" had also suffered erosion—a righteous patriotism had been excluded from the public schools.

Evangelicals were similarly convinced that "secular hegemony" was undermining the supremacy and legitimacy of the traditional, white Protestant, middle-class, patriarchal family.[17] They pointed to the Supreme Court decision desegregating schools (*Brown v. Board of Education of Topeka*, 374 U.S. 483 [1954]), to the increase in the divorce rate and single parenting, and to the civil rights, women's, and children's rights movements of the 1960s and 1970s.

Seeking to preserve the "traditional" patriarchal family, evangelical parents needed allies rather than adversaries. Some withdrew their support from public schools and established their own schools so they could hire teachers who would reinforce their values and authority as parents. Personal character and religious commitment were more important in hiring Christian school teachers than academic credentials or pedagogical expertise; in many cases, the most valued B.A. degree was the Born-Again degree. However, evangelical and fundamentalist parents were also concerned with the academic quality and social environment of the public schools. The school atmosphere, the way students are taught, and the whole matrix of social relations was and is as important as the specific information that is taught.

The following discussion of the philosophy and structure of "Christian education" draws on a number of Christian school ethnographies in which the large majority of the schools are fundamentalist.[18]

The Educational Philosophy of Christian Schools

"The nation would consider utterly ridiculous the idea of sending its soldiers to Russia to be trained in order to later fight that nation," Marianne Brown wrote in the *Gospel Herald*. "Just so, it is ridiculous to have children trained in the world to combat the forces of evil." Many fundamentalists agree that Christians should maintain their own separate form of schooling; if they are true believers, they could not possibly entertain the idea of sending their children to public schools. These strict separatists are accompanied along the fundamentalist-evangelical spectrum by accommodationists, who see Christian schooling as an alternative to public schooling and leave the choice to parents, and by interventionists, who see the public schools as a type of mission field and suggest that it may be unchristian to withdraw from and abandon them.

But whatever their philosophical and strategical differences, evangelicals and fundamentalists are united in their opposition to secular humanism and values clarification in public education. Antihumanist, anticommunist, and antifeminist, they rally around the teaching of "the basics" that once represented the foundations of Protestant, patriotic, and patriarchal culture. As the alternative to public education, Christian schools offer wholistic, authoritative, disciplined, and God-centered education that emphasizes character development and spiritual training. Affective and moral domains are considered at least as important as cognitive domains.

When people at two Christian schools (one a working-class, fundamentalist Baptist school that I refer to as Lakehaven Academy, and the other a middle-class, independent charismatic school that I refer to as Covenant) were asked what they wanted to teach their children, they responded: "We want to introduce our students to certain disciplines of knowledge that will cause them to develop their God-given intelligence, gifts, and abilities to their potential and cause their true identities as God created them to develop" (Covenant founder). "We want the individual child to find their identity and salvation in Jesus" (Covenant teacher). "To teach them to love the Lord. Academics will pass away" (Academy teacher). "We want to guide and influence character growth. It is more important that they learn not to be selfish and not to lie; they'll eventually learn that $2 + 2 = 4$" (Covenant teacher).

Excerpts from the Covenant handbook articulate the general educational philosophy of the Academy as well and of the Christian school movement in general:

Mathematics: In light of the order God has produced in the material universe and its set relationships in space and time, we cannot overlook Mathematics as being an instrument for teaching our students concepts of order and logic that Creation itself portrays as a very attribute of God. Mathematics is an exact science and in this present age of "relative truth," it affords the Christian school an excellent opportunity to teach each student how to comprehend the orderly world around him, created by God who presents Himself as Absolute Truth (John 14:6).

Science: Students should come to view Science not as a discipline that destroys the traditional values of Christian faith, but as a secondary interpretive aid to the Biblical revelation (i.e., understanding how creation works). Because the Biblical perspective is far deeper and more inclusive than the scientific viewpoint, reaching to the area of ultimate meaning, the Biblical revelation has the final priority.

English: In the Kingdom of God our communications skills are a prerequisite for our walk, for to know God is to understand Him as He is revealed through the Word (John 1:1, 14 and 2 Timothy 3:16). We receive this revelation through listening or reading. Once we come to know Christ, that knowledge of Him must flow through us to others as we speak and write (Matthew 28:19–20).

The Word is manifest in language . . . Kingdom people must become skillful craftsmen in communication, language artists. Ineffective and unclear communicative endeavors hinder unity and one-mindedness (Genesis 11:6–7).

Social Studies: Genesis 1 tells us that God created the heavens and the earth as well as every living and non-living thing in them. In light of his revealed fact, we need to accumulate and transmit to our children what God has created and how it may affect us who are a part of that creation. We need a working knowledge of the world, its geography, and its people that will enable us to better be "in this world but not of it." We learn in our study of Scripture that the Lord God acted upon and in the world's history to shape and mold it according to His plan. He raised up kings and nations and tore them down, always with a purpose in mind that was not at times clear to those participating.

In general, Christian schools stress the Christian history of the United States of America, the fight for religious freedom, the integral relationship between patriotism and Christianity, the religious foundation of the polity and educational system, and the religious character of traditional American leaders such as George Washington and Abraham Lincoln. Free-enterprise economics is emphasized, and government and economics tend to be taught as one subject.[19]

While Christian school advocates want to remedy what they consider ungodly and un-American progressivism in the schools, they acknowledge that they are struggling with how to construct a "Christian curriculum." Much debate among Christian educators concerns the "true" integration of Christian beliefs and values with academic subjects, and the development of a "truly Christian curriculum." Acknowledging that one does not yet exist, evangelical educators James Bidwell and Ronald Chadwick challenge their colleagues to "free themselves of a secular mindset in order to approach all things from a godly perspective."[20]

Some evangelical leaders are trying to create a new, in this case Christian, epistemology that draws on earlier conceptions of a Christian cosmos. The fact that these attempts often fall short of the mark is an indication of how difficult and radical the challenge is. An English teacher at Bethany Baptist Academy may be representative in his unsystematic efforts to integrate Christian principles into the curriculum: "I like to teach all kinds of truths and philosophy and it all pretty much agrees with the Bible. If it doesn't, I just don't teach that part in literature."[21] Most Christian school educators fall back on this strategy, selecting what will be read or blacking out passages from books that are read; a few are more actively searching for ways to integrate more dynamically their religious and educational worldviews.

While there is disagreement about which curricular materials should be used, and whether or not they must be Christian or can be secular, Christian school educators agree that secular humanism, the "man-centered" philosophy that serves as the "established religion" of the public schools, is to be avoided, and countered, at all costs. In 1987, 624 evangelicals filed suit against state and local officials in Mobile, Alabama. They convinced Judge Brevard Hand that secular humanism was a privileged religion in the state school system. In *Smith v. Board of Education,* Judge Hand concludes that "teaching that moral choices are purely personal and can only be based on some autonomous, as yet undiscovered and unfulfilled, inner self is a sweeping fundamental belief that must not be promoted by the public schools. . . . With these books, the State of Alabama has overstepped its mark, and must withdraw to perform its proper nonreligious functions."[22]

Although the plaintiffs won the case, the decision was overturned by the federal appeals court in Cincinnati in August of 1987. The Cincinnati court could find no evidence that the children were required to "affirm or deny a religious belief," and it rebuked Judge Hand for turning the First Amendment requirement that government be neutral about religion into "an affirmative obligation to speak about religion." The Supreme Court refused to review the case in 1988.[23]

Evangelicals and fundamentalists blame secular humanism for all sorts of evils, including "today's wave of crime and violence in our streets, promiscuity, divorce, shattered dreams and broken hearts."[24] The 1988 U.S. presidential candidate and evangelist Pat Robertson and anti-ERA crusader and founder of the conservative Eagle Forum Phyllis Schafly attribute the decline in test scores, increasing promiscuity, and violence in the schools to secular humanism.[25] Televangelist James Robison warns:

> Although it [secular humanism] ostensibly champions the dignity of man, it denies that he has a soul or is capable of salvation, and it leads inexorably to his degradation and a level of existence barely superior to that of animals. Its "creed book," the *Humanist Manifesto,* favors freedom of sexual choice, equality between men and women, abortion on demand, suicide, euthanasia, and one-world government. It is ultimately responsible for crime, disarmament, declining S.A.T. scores, "values clarification," and the new math. And it seeks to limit free enterprise, distribute wealth to achieve greater equality, and place controls on the uses of energy and the environment. What is the origin of such consummate evil? It is spawned by demonism and liberalism, and that's a fact.[26]

Yet it is difficult to find adherents of "humanism." The closest thing to an organized movement is the American Humanist Association (AHA), whose credo was published in the *Humanist Manifesto I* (1933) and *II* (1973). Neither manifesto made a great impact. The AHA has approximately three thousand members, and its *Humanist Magazine* has a small circulation. As Barbara Parker and Christy Macy point out in their editorial memorandum "Secular Humanism, the Hatch Amendment, and Public Education" for People for the American Way, "In terms of influence, these humanists rank with militant vegetarians and agrarian anarchists, and were about as well known—until the Religious Right set out to make them famous."[27]

Indeed fundamentalists have been at their most effective in claiming and naming an enemy. The rationale for the creation of Christian schools rests on the premise that they are necessary to inculcate Christian values to combat the forces of secular humanism. How schools resist it varies, however, depending on the theological and class orientations of the sponsoring body.

While both Covenant and the Lakehaven Academy define the secular world as evil, their ways of dealing with that world differ. Like the Covenant charismatics, the Academy fundamentalists support the free enterprise system and the privacy of the family, and feel threatened by big government, affirmative action, and the women's movement. In response to changing social norms and economic conditions, the Academy fundamentalists tend to withdraw from the world and do the best they can within their own community. The Covenant charismatics, on the other hand, feel they are responsible for counteracting unacceptable trends in the larger society. "In folk religion people were told to close the windows and keep out the devil," a Covenant preacher explained. "We, however, are on the offensive. The blows we receive are from a retreating enemy (Col. 2). This does not mean that the blows are not serious—they are, for the enemy is trying to recapture lost ground."

These theological orientations toward the outside world determine how evangelical groups socialize and educate their children. Contemporary fundamentalists are instructed by a history of separatism and instinctively seek to protect their children from the world. "Some people say we are protecting them from the world, sheltering them," an Academy mother acknowledged. "Well, that's right. I don't want them in the world. I want them to go into Christian service. It's like tomatoes in a greenhouse; you have to protect them and nourish them until they grow strong before you put them in the garden." The Academy fundamentalists pray that their children will be able to preserve their faith in the midst of a contaminating secular world. To be a good Christian and citizen means to work hard and take care of the family; it means taking care of one's own rather than trying to effect social and political change.

But while the Academy fundamentalists emphasize the ability of the individual to withstand opposition, the Covenant charismatics emphasize the power of the collective to change. They are preparing their children to act on the world. "We do not want to keep them from the world but from the evil one (John 17:15–16). We want them to be able to discern right from wrong, good from bad," the Covenant handbook proclaims. "Kingdom education comes to its fullest when the home-church-school community surrounds the student with a consistent environment where Jesus Christ is the center. . . . The children who can weave in and out of these three institutions and find life abundance will be able to form a well-equipped army of mature individuals ready to go out into a deteriorating world and conquer every domain for the King."

The process of socialization reflects the interaction of the theological and class orientations of these two communities.[28] The predominantly middle-class charismatic parents and educators rely on intensive interaction with students in an attempt to instill their values and beliefs. They are communicating their view of the world as a place in which individuals are actors who can change the world. Taking, in Niebuhr's terms, a "Christ as transformer" position, the Covenant educators want their students to be well prepared for higher education and professional careers so that they, as Christians, can transform the society from within. Part of the process involves discussion and joint activities as a form of interactive learning whereby ideologies are explored and explanations are given. Different editions of the Bible are read and discussed; exposure to a range of reading and media materials is encouraged.

In contrast, the Lakehaven fundamentalists want their students to be well trained in order to secure a dependable job and support their family. Recognizing that in today's market that standard increasingly means their children will need some college education, many Lakehaven parents encourage their children to go to Bible college or community college. Most of their children will be the first generation college-bound.[29] Anticipating the service jobs their students will eventually fill, Lakehaven Academy relies heavily on rules to regulate students' behavior. They have chosen a highly standardized and individualized system of instruction, Accelerated Christian Education (ACE), which encourages privacy and reinforces conformity to external demands.[30] Their school is characterized by a high degree of supervision, routinization, and tradition.[31] Bible verses are recited from the King James version only; few supplementary materials are used other than ACE, and the reference books that constitute a very small library date from the 1950s. Neither group discussion nor essay writing is part of the regular curriculum.

Educational Organization and Curricula

In summary, then, the Christian school movement, like the evangelical movement, is not monolithic; rather, the variation among schools reflects the ideological, organizational, and demographic characteristics as well as the talents and personal styles of those who establish and operate them.[32] Curricula range from secular materials to Christian-based instruction. While the majority of schools follow traditional styles of classroom interaction and teaching practices, others use more behaviorist models of prepackaged, individualized instruction or intensive group recitation. Facilities range from poorly equipped church basements to modern, multi-building campuses; some have computerized labs while others have no lab equipment at all. The majority of Christian schools offer only elementary education, but as the children grow older the school often grows with them; increasingly Christian schools are offering secondary education. The enrollment of the average Christian school falls between one hundred and two hundred students, although the schools vary in size from ten to over two thousand. The majority of the Christian schools are church-sponsored, but some (like the Calvinist day schools) are parent-run or board-run.[33]

Whether the schools are using Christian (e.g., ACE, A BEKA, Alpha Omega, or Bob Jones texts and materials) or secular materials, Bible readings, worship and prayer times accompany regular instruction. Moreover, certain policies and practices are typical of the majority of Christian schools. Discipline is a primary concern. In order to prepare the children for the ultimate submission to God, they teach them to obey their parents, teachers, spiritual leaders, and civil authorities, although they warn against nonbelievers. Referring to the Scripture that to "spare the rod is to spoil the child," Christian schools generally use corporal punishment. One visible way of maintaining school discipline and reinforcing standards about appropriate behavior is enforcing a strict dress code. The emphasis is on modesty and propriety.[34]

Many parents who enroll their children in Christian schools are trying to control not only their children's behaviors but also the behaviors of those with whom their children associate. Admissions (and suspension) policies enable this type of control. Based on voluntarism, enrollment in a Christian school is a mutually self-selecting one for both school and family. Whether to accept non-Christian students or students from outside the fellowship is usually an issue for debate. The controversy involves the tension between evangelism as the primary mission of the church and the desire to build a community that protects children from the contamination of the secular world and the "unsaved." Most schools have decided on a policy which accepts a minority (5–15 percent) of "non-Christians" (those who do not come from families of the proper fundamentalist or evangelical persuasion, and the unchurched).[35] The variation in policies among schools reflects the kind of balance they have achieved between these two, often competing, goals. But each of the twenty-two Christian schools I visited explicitly stated their educational philosophy and policy as a Christian school. Before enrolling their children, parents had to agree to the stated policies (e.g., chapel, Bible studies, spanking, dress codes).

Admissions policies also vary with regard to enrolling "problem" students. Nancy Ammerman reports in her study of Southside Academy that students who have had academic or behavioral problems in other schools, or who are emotionally disturbed, physically or mentally handicapped, or learning disabled are not permitted to enroll at the Academy "if their condition were to hold back the progress of the entire class."[36] In contrast, Lakehaven Academy, which uses ACE, finds that one of its strengths is the ability to accept students who have had learning and, at times, behavioral problems in the public schools. Since each student works at his or her own pace in the ACE curriculum, they are not competing with other students nor are they affecting the pace of the class. The principal estimates that about 20 percent of the students at the Academy have learning problems, including one of the oldest students in the school who was reading at a fourth grade level. In fact, a number of students who had been considered "emotionally disturbed" or "delinquent" in the public schools were attending the Academy. According to the upper-level supervisor, a number of these students "would probably have dropped out of high school, but this way they don't have to be embarrassed because no one knows how they are doing. They aren't called on in class, nor are they forced to compete against other students."[37] ACE has recently made its success with problem students a selling point in its expanding market. [38]

The question of admissions policies relative to race and ethnicity is also an important and controversial one. In the 1970s, approximately one hundred schools lost their tax-exempt status because they were avoiding integration.[39] While some began as segregationist academies, it appears that most do not now actively discriminate on the basis of race or ethnicity.[40] Some, like Jerry Falwell's Christian Academy, which initially advertised "for whites only," have changed their admissions policies. Other Christian schools are actively committed to racial and ethnic diversity. Still others are serving black and, to a lesser extent, Hispanic and Native American communities. In fact black Christian academies constitute half of the over two hundred schools, serving more than twelve thousand students, listed in the 1988 *Directory of Independent Schools* published by the Institute of Independent Education.[41]

Nonetheless, most Christian schools are predominantly white, despite their admissions policies. The data on minority enrollments in private schools indicate that in 1988, 54 percent of non-Catholic, religious schools, 42 percent of Catholic schools, and 24 percent of nonsectarian schools enrolled less than 5 percent minority students.[42] Ammerman suggests that there is often an implicit, if not explicit, assumption that many black students are simply unwilling or unable to live by their standards.

Moreover, while many Christian schools may not be ideologically committed to segregation, many are committed to separation.[43]

While there is diversity among Christian schools, the research to date points to a pattern of instruction that tends to minimize critical thinking and to limit students' exposure to diverse materials and perspectives. Similar to the fundamentalist schools that Peshkin, Ammerman, and Gehrman studied, the Lakehaven Academy students are not taught to think critically, to formulate significant questions, or to explore alternative answers. If they have a question about the reading, they are told to find the answers within the prepackaged texts. Additional reference books are carefully screened and often censored. Moreover, students often have little voice within the context of the classroom.

Concern over authority and discipline has an impact on pedagogical styles as well as teacher-student relationships and the climate of the classroom. Educators at Bethany Baptist Academy and the Lakehaven Academy share similar ideas about the role and authority of adults in general, and teachers in particular: "The more you do that is student centered, the more you surrender control to the class. . . . Don't apologize for telling the kids what is right. They should be taught not to question you. Tell them, 'This is my classroom and this what I expect. The classroom is not a democracy. It's a dictatorship. You don't vote on anything!' This is what I tell the kids."[44] This paternalistic relationship is related to both pedagogical styles and curricular content; knowledge is "a fixed body of facts, all of which have their origin with God and can be found in one form or another in the Bible." Students are preoccupied with copying, memorizing, and reciting; they "faithfully reproduce in their notebooks what the teacher has written on the board." Even in high school, "there is no attempt to move toward creative, critical, or integrative thinking."[45]

Many evangelicals have withdrawn their children from the public schools because they expose the children to values and beliefs that conflict with their own. Some parents say explicitly that they do not want to broaden their children's perspectives; they hope to contain them within a Christian context. In fact, some consider the exposure of students to the realities of life to constitute child abuse, and they want to protect them within the confines of a Christian school.[46] Other evangelicals have become actively involved in trying to reform the public school curriculum in order to make it more compatible with their own objectives. The nature and degree of "political" activity will depend in large part on whether, in Niebuhr's terms, the school takes a "Christ-against-culture," a "Christ-above-culture," or a "Christ-as-transformer-of-culture" position. Let us examine, then, the mobilization of evangelicals and fundamentalists and the impact they have had on other sectors of the educational system.

Evangelical and Fundamentalist Impact on Public Policy

The New Christian Right has had an impact not only through the establishment of Christian schools but on education in the society at large. It has been influential in blocking the passage of public school referenda, in pressuring publishers to alter the content of public school textbooks, and in minimizing state-regulated standards for private schools.

Private Education

One evangelical and fundamentalist cause célèbre has been the battle to deregulate the private schools, that is, to exempt private schools from the accreditation standards required of public schools. New Right victories minimizing the standards for operating a private school, as in the Nebraska case eliminating the requirement for teacher certification by the state, have benefited nonevangelical groups as well. Russell Means, leader of the American Indian Movement, indicated that the successful attempts at removing state certification standards for private schools in South Dakota have made it easier to establish a private school in the Black Hills encampment of the Dakota Sioux. Means can now hire uncertified teachers to instruct children in traditional Sioux ways and values.[47] Deregulation has also benefited the home schooling movement, now numbering somewhere between 248,000 and 354,000 students.[48] This represents a fifteen-fold increase from the school year 1980–81 to 1987–88.[49]

The "National Conference of State Legislatures Report on Home Schooling" (1989) suggests that the growing momentum of home schooling and the litigation surrounding it are in large part the result of the resurgence of religious activism, building upon widespread concern about drug use and the lack of discipline in the public schools.[50] John Holt and Ivan Illich, founders of the liberal private school movement and home schooling, have found their efforts aided by the fundamentalist victories that revoked certification standards.[51] Experts on home schooling indicate that religious motivation is a major factor and contend that the large majority of home-schoolers are evangelicals and fundamentalists.[52] Ironically, many Christian school leaders initially opposed home schooling, fearing it would draw students away from the Christian schools. Their position was difficult to sustain, however, since much of their rationale for Christian schooling rested on the biblical premise that parents are the ones primarily responsible for the education of their children. While fighting for greater parental choice and control in the larger policy arena, resistance to home schooling on the part of Christian school educators appears to have waned.[53]

Public Education

Activists of the New Christian Right have also called for a reduction in federal funding of public schools. In 1975 U.S. Congressman John Conlan, Jr., of Arizona introduced a bill that would have eliminated federal funding for any course that purportedly taught secular humanism. The legislation passed the House but was defeated in the Senate.[54] In the absence of such legislation, evangelicals and fundamentalists argue, they cannot in clear conscience send their children to public schools and thus should not be required to support the schools. In testimony before a 1979 congressional hearing on tax exemptions for Christian schools, the Reverend James E. Lowden, Jr., executive director of the Alabama Christian Education Association, espoused this basic philosophy, echoed many times since: "I believe, given the philosophy of public school education today, [that] it is a sin for a true believer in the

Lordship of Jesus Christ to send their children to a public school."[55] In *America Can Be Saved,* Jerry Falwell anticipated the day when it would be unnecessary for Christians to make that choice. "One day, I hope in the next ten years, I can trust that we will have more Christian day schools than public schools. I hope I live to see the day when, as in the early days of our country, we won't have any public schools," he wrote. "The churches will have taken them over again and Christians will be running them. What a happy day that will be."[56] Other fundamentalists have gone even further. An activist in Louisville, Kentucky, pronounced his desire to eliminate public schooling altogether: "We want public schools abolished. We believe public schools are immoral . . . the public schools breed criminals. They teach [children] they're animals, that they evolved from animals. Christianity has been replaced by humanism in the public schools. It's disgusting."[57]

A small but vocal minority group within the larger evangelical movement, the reconstructionists, take a similar position. Paul Lindstrom, pastor and principal of the Christian Liberty Baptist Academy in the Chicago suburbs of Arlington Heights, rejects the authority of the state in all matters related to education. Rejecting public school as an option for concerned Christian parents, he implies that parents commit "blasphemy against Jesus Christ by enrolling their children in the schools of the Philistines."[58] Paul Heidebrecht, reporting on a conference organized by Lindstrom, quotes him as saying that public education is a "multi-billion dollar taxpayer rip-off"; to rectify the situation, Lindstrom calls for "warfare against the humanist elite that controls America's culture and its schools."[59] One tactic is to support home schooling. Lindstrom and his Christian Liberty Academy oversee a satellite school system for home educators with an enrollment of over twenty-two thousand children in thirty-six countries. The largest distributor of home schooling curricula, they offer a year's education at a very modest cost: $210 per child in 1986.[60]

Believing in and working toward a theocracy, in which there would be no separation of church and state and conservative Christians would govern, the reconstructionists take a separatist stand. Their thinking is expressed through the words of Rousas J. Rushdoony, one of the most influential reconstructionist theorists and head of the Chalcedon Institute: "We believe a child needs to learn to be a conqueror in this world," for "a generation of barbarians is busily destroying this civilization."[61] Writer and educator Samuel Blumenfeld praised the reconstructionist movement for its separatist stance and its willingness to oppose the "satanic control of the public schools." According to Heidebrecht, "Blumenfeld alleged that public educators have deliberately downgraded literary skills of Americans to make them more amenable to socialism."[62] In fact, Lindstrom indicated that his school was "founded, in part, to oppose the creeping socialism of the public school curricula."[63] Blumenfeld's solution is to counteract their control: "First we must remove the obstacles, including the restrictions on home schooling, mandatory attendance laws, and teacher certification requirements."[64]

While the reconstructionists represent an extreme position within the evangelical community, they joined other evangelical groups and social forces in putting public education on the defensive in the 1980s. Public school educators became concerned about poor public perceptions and declining support for public education, especially when it came to funding. One National Education Association (NEA) spokesperson declared: "We are fighting like hell to save our public schools."[65] Accordingly public school associations in the early 1990s have become more vocal in advocating universal and compulsory education. The NEA argues that public education is not atheistic but rather "nontheistic"—as required by the Constitution.

Other groups also emerged or organized more effectively to counter the activities of the New Christian Right (NCR) on the educational front. Television producer Norman Lear founded People for the American Way in 1980 in part to counteract fundamentalist influence. Other existing organizations, such as the American Civil Liberties Union's Coalition Against Censorship, sponsored by the National Council of Churches, and the American Library Association's Committee on Intellectual Freedom, became actively engaged in research about the activities of the NCR and informed legislators and the general public.

As vulnerable to political pressures but not as accountable to the public, textbook publishers have also been influenced by the organized efforts of the NCR and have avoided "publishing material that might be construed as unpatriotic, anti-capitalistic, or anti-Christian."[66] Phyllis Schafly, conservative activist and president of the Eagle Forum, argues that the public schools "should use textbooks that do not offend the religious and moral values of the parents. [They should] use textbooks that honor the family, marriage, and man's role as provider and protector. [They should] permit children to attend school in their own neighborhoods and separate the sexes for sex education, gym classes, athletic practice, competition, academic and vocational classes."[67]

One of the most successful attempts to control the content of texts has been Norman and Mel Gabler's textbook review service which they began in 1975 out of their home in Longview, Texas. Since that time, their operation, Educational Research Analysts, has grown into a worldwide organization with a mailing list of over twelve thousand. Reviewing fifty to sixty books a year, they highlight what they consider objectionable passages and send their reviews to the Texas Textbook Selection Committee. In the early 1980s, over two-thirds of the books they objected to were rejected by the committee. Since Texas has one of the largest school-age populations and therefore one of the largest textbook markets, their decisions helped determine the content of school books sold all over the nation.[68]

The Gablers, like many other evangelicals, want textbooks to stress traditional, patriotic values. They disapproved of Magruder's American government text because of the line, "year after year the Defense Department takes a very substantial slice of the federal budget." The Gablers argued that "this showed a subtle bias in favor of disarmament." In his analysis of the Gablers' operation, Hefley writes in *Textbooks on Trial* that "progressive education threatened to undermine church and home teaching of biblical Christianity, and the principles on which America was founded. It was materialistic, humanistic, atheistic, and socialistic; an ideology foreign to a nation whose motto was, 'In God We Trust.'"[69]

The protestors in the Kanawha County controversy expressed similar concerns about the public school curriculum. To combat secular humanism and preserve fundamentalist principles in the public schools, over twelve thousand Kanawha County citizens signed a petition and submitted it to the public school board in 1974. Among the principles they wanted to preserve were the following: the "traditional" patriarchal family; belief in God, the American political system, the free enterprise economic system, and the history of America as "the record of one of the noblest civilizations that has existed"; and the need for study of the traditional rules of grammar.[70] The victories of the Kanawha County protestors fueled the efforts of fundamentalist groups around the country to challenge their local school boards. Joseph Kincheloe reports that the "American Library Association documented a dramatic increase in textbook controversies in the years immediately following the Kanawha County episode."[71]

In attempting to institute curricula that would reinforce "traditional" American values, the NCR has targeted specific texts and curricula. Funded in the late 1960s by the National Science Foundation (NSF), *Man: A Course of Study* (MACOS) was one course that received much negative publicity within evangelical circles. Designed for upper elementary students, MACOS provided an examination of various human cultures. In comparing middle-class American culture to that of the Netsilik Eskimos, "the course," Pat Robertson claimed, "obviously teaches evolution, but even more important it condones the practice of senilicide" (the practice of killing the elderly as a form of population control). Between 1970 and 1974, approximately seventeen hundred schools in forty-seven states were using the MACOS curriculum. By 1975, however, protests were flaring up all over the country; ultimately Congressman John Conlan, Jr., was successful in ending the funding for this NSF-sponsored program.[72]

In the late 1980s and early 1990s, the U.S. Department of Education's National Diffusion Network (NDN), which distributes curricula that have proven successful in experimental programs to schools across the country, was targeted by a number of right wing groups, including the Liberty Lobbyists, the Pro-Family Forum, and Schafly's Eagle Forum. Shirley Curry, former head of the Tennessee chapter of the Eagle Forum, lost her job at the Department of Education when she announced she was out to eliminate the NDN. As an alternative, the Pro-Family Forum and Charlotte Iserbyt, former Reagan appointee in the Department of Education, urged parents to use the Hatch Amendment to lobby against the NDN.[73] The Hatch Amendment of 1978 requires parental consent when a federally funded program calls for "a student to submit to psychiatric evaluation, or treatment, or psychological examination, testing, or treatment, in which the primary purpose is to reveal information concerning: political affiliations; mental and psychological problems potentially embarrassing to the student or his family; sex behavior and attitudes; illegal, antisocial, self-incriminating, and demeaning behavior." In 1984 the Family Educational Rights and Privacy Act Office was established in the Department of Education to provide information about the requirements of the amendment and to investigate, process, and review violations and complaints that may be filed.[74] With the publication of the regulations, the Hatch Amendment "suddenly became a divisive, disruptive force in school districts throughout the U.S."[75]

The Eagle Forum used the Hatch Amendment to urge parents to protect their children from psychological manipulation in the classroom. A version of a letter distributed by the Maryland Coalition of Concerned Parents on Privacy Rights in the Public Schools told parents to question activities that include death education, including discussions about suicide; curricula pertaining to drugs and alcohol; globalism curricula; education on human sexuality; autobiography assignments, logs, diaries, and personal journals; and talk-ins and magic circle techniques.[76] Malcolm Lawrence, president of the Maryland Coalition, said that forty-five Christian-oriented radio stations were promoting the letter.[77]

In response, a coalition of thirty education associations (including the American Education Research Association, the American Psychological Association, the American Association of School Administrators, and the National PTA) organized to demand more precise definition and to protest federal intervention in the affairs of local school districts. The regulations of the Hatch Amendment "spawned such a gargantuan raid on the integrity of a free public education that even its sponsor, Senator Orrin Hatch (R-Utah), has called for the 'rule of common sense.'"[78]

But given political and religious differences, the "rule of common sense" needed to be spelled out. In Hillsborough, Minnesota, for example, several parents charged that the district was violating the Hatch Amendment by offering state-mandated sex education courses, holding mock elections, and requiring students to keep personal journals. They also objected to the Walt Disney movie *Never Cry Wolf*. Parents in Gallipolis, Ohio, used the Hatch Amendment to protest a voluntary high school drug and alcohol abuse project.[79] Finally in February of 1985, Senator Hatch took to the Senate floor to say that "some parent groups have interpreted both the statute and the regulations so broadly that they would have them apply to all curriculum materials, library books. . . . [But] because there are no federal funds in such courses, the Hatch Amendment is not applicable to them."[80] So far, less than a dozen complaints have been filed with the Department of Education. The greatest activity has been at the state and local levels.

That is one reason why the NDN, which does use federal funds, has been singled out. Especially controversial is a course of study on the Holocaust called *Facing History and Ourselves*. Various conservative parent groups have effectively blocked its distribution. Phyllis Schafly argues that teaching children about the atrocities of history constitutes child abuse.[81] In *Child Abuse in the Classroom*, she cites some of the congressional testimony of a student who had been exposed to the *Facing History and Ourselves* materials: "Life used to be so easy. There always seemed to be an answer to everything. Everything fit into place, getting up at 7:00, going to school at 8:00. . . . In my tightly scheduled life, I left no time to reflect. In these past four months, however, I have been forced to think. It hasn't been easy."[82] Protecting children from the "harsh realities of life" was also the reason given for objecting to the use of *Time, Newsweek,* and *US News and World Report* in the classroom.[83] Disturbed by materials that contradicted their view of the world, evangelicals and fundamentalists targeted books because they expose children to the "expectations and orientations of Black Americans" *(The Learning Tree);*[84] and to homosexual authors (Oscar Wilde, Tennessee Williams, Gore Vidal, Walt Whitman).[85]

The treatment of racial and ethnic diversity in the United States is also a major curricular issue, with evangelicals tending to want to limit the discussion of racial pluralism. In the Kanawha County controversy, for example, Alice Moore claimed that the proposed ban on books was not inspired by racism. However, the list of authors accused of corrupting the basic values of Christian parents included Gwendolyn Brooks, Dick Gregory, Eldridge Cleaver, Langston Hughes, James Baldwin, and Malcolm X.[86] Moore, one of the proponents of the ban, argued that these authors were excluded not because they were black but because they espoused moral and philosophical positions contrary to those of the protestors; she suggested that the best solution would be for the schools to ignore the question of ethnicity and racism, and concentrate on the "inculcation of Americanism."[87]

While Christian schools were allowed to ignore questions of cultural pluralism in their curriculum, they were not allowed to avoid integration and still maintain their tax-exempt status. As mentioned earlier, in the 1970s approximately one hundred schools lost their tax-exempt status because they were avoiding integration.[88] The Reverend Robert Billings, former executive director of the Moral Majority but at the time a top official of the Department of Education, led the fight against the IRS proposal to tax religious schools that were discriminating on the basis of race.[89] Then in 1982, President Reagan reversed an eleven-year-old federal policy and ordered the IRS to reinstate the tax-exempt status to certain Christian schools which had been denied it on the basis of their racial segregation policies, thus kicking up a storm of protest from civil rights advocates. In May 1983, the Supreme Court upheld the denial of tax-exempt status to segregationist schools. The decision, based on the case of Bob Jones University, Robert Billings's alma mater, struck a blow to the evangelical right.[90]

Other academic controversies have been taken out of the classroom and local school board and into court. In Tennessee, a group of fundamentalist parents filed suit over a series of reading textbooks.[91] Vicky Frost, primary plaintiff in the case, contended that one of the second-grade stories, which dealt with a magical trip to Mars, advocated mental telepathy which she thought gave a positive portrayal of occultism. In October of 1986, a federal district court judge in Greensville, Tennessee, ruled that the school district had violated the families' civil rights by requiring children to read books they considered "anti-Christian." In December 1986 the same court awarded $50,521.59 to the Frost family and their coplaintiffs as reimbursement for legal expenses incurred.[92] In this case, the plaintiffs were asking for alternative readings for their children.

At the same time, another group of over six hundred evangelical parents sued the Alabama public school system over its use of "objectionable" textbooks. Their approach, however, was broader. The Concerned Women of America's attorney Michael Farris sought to have "secular humanism" declared a religion. If the case was won, all traces of "secular humanism" would have to be removed from curricular materials or given status equivalent to other religions. On 4 March 1987 a federal judge in Mobile, Alabama, banned forty-four textbooks from the local public school system on grounds that they promoted the "religion" of "secular humanism."[93] Several weeks later a federal appeals court overturned the decision, and the Supreme Court declined to review the case in 1988. Given this defeat, evangelicals are likely to concentrate their energies on influencing the policies of local school boards and the process of textbook selection.[94]

And this they continue to do. Often under the pressure of the New Christian Right, many school systems and state legislatures have substituted free enterprise classes for the old survey of economics course. In the petition signed by the twelve thousand Kanawha County protestors, free enterprise economics was one of the eight principles listed.[95] Other efforts are aimed at limiting sex education in the schools. The American Library Association reported in the late 1970s and early 1980s that one-half of the documented parental efforts to remove materials from schools involved sex education literature.[96] In the late 1980s and early 1990s, the most common objections were directed toward books that use "objectionable language" or those that make reference to satanism, witches, or the occult.

Moreover, parents' and pupils' rights acts, often referred to as "baby Hatches," were introduced in at least eight states by the mid-1980s.[97] Many were directed against teaching of sex education or counseling that would ask a student "any question that may be of embarrassment to the parent." Given the history of evangelical lobbying against mandatory child abuse reporting, these bills are particularly problematic. Most of them have been defeated or vetoed by governors; some, like the Pupil-Parent Protection Act (House Bill 2277), introduced in Pennsylvania and sponsored by Rep. Stephen Friend, have been reintroduced and were still before the state legislature at the time of this writing (1990). Policymakers believe the "baby Hatches" have little chance of passing.

Evangelicals and fundamentalists have also had a significant impact on the curriculum of the public schools, if not to the degree they would have liked. While numerous law suits have been introduced, only small victories have been won—usually an alternative readings clause whereby teachers must give students the option of reading another text. Recent California guidelines state that while students may elect not to participate in class discussions of sexual reproduction or experiments with animals, they may not be excused from class attendance "based on disagreements with the curriculum."[98]

Evangelical pressure groups have been most influential deposing rather than proposing, that is, in impeding the introduction of innovative ("progressive") public school programs rather than in establishing their own curricula. One possible exception is the impact evangelicals and fundamentalists have had on the content and pedagogical approach to classic texts. Activists have chipped away at *Romeo and Juliet* to the point where publisher Scott Foresman and Co. deleted nine lines from act 2, scene 3, in which Juliet dreams of a last tryst with her exiled lover, removing the famous words, "if love be blind." In an approved text for ninth graders, 320 lines were cut from *Romeo and Juliet* and approximately 100 lines from *Hamlet*.[99] Notwithstanding these occasional fundamentalist "victories," it appears that *Florey v. Sioux Falls School District 49–5* expressed the general consensus of the courts on this matter: "If we are to eliminate everything that is objectionable to any [of the religious bodies existing in the United States] or inconsistent with any of their doctrines, we will leave public education in shreds."[100]

Nonetheless, attempts at censorship continue into the 1990s. A review of the seven annual reports on censorship published by People for the American Way (PAW) from 1982 to 1989 indicates a continual (and in some years a dramatic) increase in censorship cases. The 1989 report, "Attacks on the Freedom to Learn," cited incidents occurring in forty-two states and in every region of the country. The report found that all aspects of the school curricula, from library books and sex education courses to science instruction and literary classics, came under attack. Censors were successful in banning educational materials or restricting their use in nearly half the legal challenges to instruction. School libraries were the target of significantly more censorship attempts in 1989 than previously; more than half the challenges were leveled against materials that are not required reading for young people but are simply available in the library.[101]

The reports demonstrate that members of groups representing the religious right were responsible for the large majority of the censorship efforts in 1982 (and that many of the earliest protests were against materials that portrayed minority groups in a negatively stereotyped fashion). As the 1980s continued, the "coalition" of would-be censors grew to include a variety of groups and individuals; Donna Hulsizer, director of education for PAW, estimated that by 1989 only one-third of the censorship cases were initiated by evangelicals and fundamentalists.[102] This is an important finding in that it corroborates data from other sources suggesting that one important consequence of fundamentalist and evangelical activism in the late 1970s and early 1980s was the "empowerment" of educationally like-minded groups and individuals (that is, people who shared the searching criticisms of the fundamentalists without necessarily sharing their proposed remedies or the particulars of their worldview or political ideology). These groups learned much from the political strategies and success, however limited, of the New Christian Right.

Indeed, developments in the late 1980s and early 1990s provided testimony to the limits of fundamentalist activity, to the inroads it has made, and to its unintended and sometimes ironic consequences. For example, the textbook review process in Texas was revised in 1989. Hulsizer argues that the fundamentalist-inspired controversy led to a type of liberalization of the review process. "Before there was no way of defending why an idea should be left in; one could only argue that something should be left out. Now there is greater representation from all sides."[103] Ron Fields, director of the Federal Relations Office for the National Conference of State Legislatures, also argues that Texas and California, two of the most targeted and influential states in the textbook adoption process, have recently "turned around." "States like California and Texas that were strongly influenced by fundamentalist activity [in the early 1980s] are starting to reevaluate."[104] The reevaluation comes with growing concern about the need for a literate work force, and the need to be competitive both educationally and economically in the world system. Poor test scores of U.S. students compared with those of students in other industrialized nations (especially West Germany and Japan) have generated a new concern for strong educational content, and a demand for less "watered-down" textbooks. "Facing a skilled worker shortage and international competition, the new reform school movement is motivated, as usual, by economic concerns more than by religious pressures."[105] The implication is that "creationism won't do."[106] Half-realized victories are part of the record of fundamentalist activism in education. Regarding creationism, for example, the Supreme Court in *Edwards v. Aguillard* (482 U.S. 378 [1987]) struck down (in a seven-to-two vote) the 1981 Louisiana balanced treatment law. However, the ruling does not ban the teaching of creationism; it simply stipulates that the state legislature cannot require it. To take another example, in March 1989 the Texas State Board of Education approved guidelines for publishers to include "scientific evidence of evolution and reliable scientific theories, if any" in high school biology textbooks. The guidelines were heralded as a victory by both evolutionists and creationists. The evolutionists were able to lobby against the inclusion of "scientific creationism" and to amend the previous clause from "include scientific evidence of evolution and reliable scientific theories *to the contrary*" to "scientific theories, *if any*." The Gablers, along with other creationists, also claimed it as a victory, arguing that it opened the door for creationist views to be taught.[107]

It is striking that the United States is the only modern, industrialized nation engaged in a serious debate over the status of creationism and whether or not evolution must be taught. The 1988 platform of the Republican party of Texas supported "the teaching of a balanced view of the origin of life in Texas Public Schools."[108] Whether creationism is a religious belief that should be relegated to social studies courses that teach various religious systems or whether it is a legitimate "scientific theory" that could be taught as an alternative to evolution theory is still a controversial issue in many states.[109] Some of the confusion revolves around the use and interpretation of the words "scientific theories of the origins of life." Although the Alabama State Board of Education mandated that evolution be taught, its 1987 "Course of Study" curriculum guide included this qualifier: "Consistent with the expression of the U.S. Supreme Court in *Edwards v. Aguillard,* teachers shall have the freedom and flexibility to supplement the curriculum with the presentation of various scientific theories about the origins of life, if done with the secular intent of enhancing the effectiveness of science instruction." Not only in Alabama, but in other states including Texas, Ohio, and California, Justice Brennan's decision has been used to promote creationism by arguing that "scientific creationism" represents another scientific theory about the origins of life.[110]

Not only has creationism been promoted, but the teaching of evolution has been held to higher standards and in some cases avoided altogether. For example, the California State Board of Education recently rejected all junior high school science textbooks submitted for adoption, in part because members thought their treatment of evolution was inadequate.[111] In an ironic outcome for the fundamentalists, the Texas State Board of Education announced in 1988 that high school geology textbooks must include the topic of evolution and extended that rule to high school biology texts in 1989.[112] In 1985 California State Superintendent William Honig and the Board of Education rejected entire series of seventh and eighth grade science textbooks because they failed to explore topics such as evolution and reproduction; New

York did likewise. People for the American Way's 1985 review of biology textbooks indicated that one-sixth of the books reviewed did not mention evolution; half covered it insufficiently.

Much of the problem has been the dilution of textbooks as publishers have tried to respond to the pressures of various groups. But the tide seemed to be shifting in 1990. California's Science Curriculum Framework and Criteria Committee produced a statement that passed the State Board of Education in the fall of 1989, affirming that matters of religion belong in classes on social science and literature, not science. Superintendent Bill Honig argued that such a "clearing-the-air document" was needed because there was confusion over what teachers could and could not teach. The confusion stemmed from the state's previous policy on science education which singled out evolution as a tentative scientific theory. According to Honig and the committee, although "few science teachers give equal time to creationism, many are so intimidated by the fundamentalists and confused by current policy that they omit evolution instruction."[113]

Evangelicals and fundamentalists have thus had mixed results in the attempt to alter the structure of the American educational system. On the one hand, as Bruce Cooper points out, they "have amassed an impressive array of public policies in their favor: tax-free status for private schools; services under Title I (now Chapter I) of the new Education Consolidation and Improvement Act which allows state governments to fund private schools directly should local school boards refuse to grant them educational services guaranteed under the law; and aid under categorical programs such as special education."[114] One of the most important victories has been the legal precedent set by the Supreme Court decision in Mueller v. Allen (463 U.S. 388 [1983]) affirming as constitutional the tax deduction plan in Minnesota which allows parents who send their children to private schools to claim a deduction on their state income tax. As William Reese argues, "Far from being a persecuted minority, Christian school reformers have enjoyed many legal victories [defeating state regulation of private schools in landmark decisions in Kentucky and Ohio], a testimony to their political savvy and the support the courts have given to First Amendment freedoms."[115] Moreover, their political lobbying efforts helped squash attempts at more restrictive state regulation proposed elsewhere. Due in large part to evangelical efforts, the tendency over the past eight years has been toward deregulation.

On the other hand, evangelicals who wanted to eliminate federal funding for education and decentralize education opposed the Department of Education but were unsuccessful in their attempts to do away with it. Instead, President Reagan stacked it with political conservatives, some of whom were evangelicals and many of whom were responsive to the organized activities of evangelicals. Fundamentalist PACs had the ear of many of those in office, especially Senator Hatch, who chaired the Senate Human Labor and Resource Committee which dealt with educational policy issues.[116] Reagan also appointed William Bennett as secretary of education, who agreed to an "ideological screening by ultrarightist leaders" and was sympathetic to the New Christian Right.[117] Bennett replaced Under Secretary Gary Jones with Gary Bauer, a prominent NCR spokesperson. Bauer attracted some attention because he deleted material from a department report indicating that tax tuition credits would cost more than anticipated. One of his special assistants was Rosemary Thompson, former Illinois leader of the Eagle Forum. Bennett also hired Eileen Gardner from the Heritage Foundation. She briefly headed a specially created Office of Educational Philosophy and Practice before it was revealed that her "educational philosophy" included the conviction that "the proper role of the federal government in education is no role," as she wrote in a 1983 Heritage report. Of her novel view that the handicapped have brought it all upon themselves and deserve no help from society, Bennett initially said it was consistent with "respected traditions of theological thought."[118]

Evangelical groups were also successful in dismantling the National Institute of Education (believing it to be too independent and too liberal), and replacing it in 1985 with the Office of Educational Research and Improvement. Its appointed head, Chester Finn, was hospitable to evangelical concerns and supported research on family issues.[119]

But a number of primary goals on the evangelical agenda were not achieved. Their attempts at instituting tax credits and tuition vouchers that would have promoted greater school choice and school prayer were unsuccessful, despite the support they received from Reagan. Although the Bush administration's support of the evangelical agenda was initially unenthusiastic, it began supporting school choice initiatives as of 1991–92. Nonetheless, if significant progress toward evangelical goals is to be made, it will likely be at the state level.

This assessment of the direct influence that evangelical activity has had on American education does not address a more elusive, although very important, question. Has fundamentalist activity had a chilling effect on public education? The answer is yes, but it is difficult to determine to what extent. Certainly the targeting of certain programs like MACOS and *Facing History and Ourselves;* the amendment added to the magnet school program whereby monies cannot be spent on courses that promote secular humanism (the definition of which is left to the discretion of the local school board), and the use of the Hatch Amendment to challenge local school curricula have had obvious impacts. But more subtle consequences have resulted from the work of the New Christian Right.

A number of public high school teachers and principals acknowledge that they are more careful in bringing up or dealing with controversial issues. Many, afraid of organized pressure, are side-stepping controversy and playing it safe. A history teacher in Texas spoke of avoiding controversial subjects: "I think about what I am doing twice. Is there anything controversial in the lesson plan? If there is, I won't use it. I won't use things where a kid has to make a judgment."[120] In a conversation with Dan Leçlerc, head of social studies in an affluent and fairly progressive school in a Boston suburb, he likewise indicated that the teachers he supervises think twice now about what they are teaching. "You know that there are parent groups there who may challenge you. So you choose carefully. The tendency is to avoid anything controversial." This has influenced not only curricular content but also the introduction of innovative teaching methods. As Kincheloe argues, "Back to the basics involves much more than a renewed emphasis on skills. It's also a politically and economically conservative movement based on moral absolutism."[121]

In this sense evangelicals have been influential in raising questions that are resonant with the culture at large: What are we teaching our children? What moral and ethical content is found, or is absent from, the education of American children? Gene Wilhoit, executive director of National School Boards Association suggests that "fundamentalists have been instrumental in raising questions about 'values education,' questioning what it is we are teaching in the schools. They have made policymakers more aware."[122] As a result the role of values and ethics in education has come to preoccupy the attention of many educational policymakers in the early 1990s. Wilhoit argues that while the fundamentalists have helped raise the issues, curricular reform is not likely to go in the direction they want. Other interest groups, including those concerned with civil rights and equality for women, have as much if not more influence than the "Christian lobbyists." In the early 1990s, issues of equity and accountability have increasingly occupied the thoughts and energies of educators and policymakers. The "threat" or "challenge" of the New Christian Right on the federal level has diminished in the minds of most of the educational policymakers with whom I spoke. The powerful influence evangelicals and fundamentalists exerted in the early 1980s on the national level has abated somewhat, but evangelicals still have a powerful presence at the state and local levels and seem to be concentrating organizational efforts there.[123]

While they see the Christian school movement and its advocates as having played a significant role in raising the issues that they now are addressing, most of the policymakers with whom I spoke indicated that American public education was and is driven more by economic concerns than religious forces. While this concurs with my assessment, it is also important to recognize the potential conservative impact that evangelicals can and have had, not only on educational issues but on economic issues as well.

If the demand for equity is taken seriously and legitimated by the U.S. Supreme Court, which is likely to hear at least one of the many equity cases that are making their way through the court system in 1990 (the Texas Supreme Court voted 9–0 that the state school-financing structure is unconstitutional),[124] then evangelicals who tend to be conservative and politically active are likely to challenge a major increase in funding for education, especially if this is to be achieved through an increase in taxation.

The equity cases are extremely important in challenging the inequalities that exist in the public school system, but the political will must be mustered to fund greater equality while maintaining reasonable quality within the public schools. Although public schools do reproduce the inequalities of the economy and workplace,[125] in some ways they also challenge the legitimacy and practice of such discrimination. By operating within the political arena, they have to contend with the pressures of a variety of interest groups. In fact, the participation in government at the school board level is probably more accessible and democratic than anywhere else in the American system.

Among the possibilities is a policy whereby states might allocate a minimal amount for each public school, with the likely result that more parents may opt to send their children to private schools. We may find greater bifurcation of the public and private school systems, and of the already stratified system of private education, with Christian schools offering private education at a lower cost than many of the more elite schools.

Indeed, the Christian school system itself is becoming more stratified. We already see variation in the quality of education that Christian schools offer. Part of this may be due to ideological factors, but much of it is related to the economic resources available. Economic determinism is perhaps too strong a term, but the link between economic realities and educational philosophy and method is noteworthy, For example, many schools open with the Accelerated Christian Education (ACE) curriculum program precisely because it is inexpensive. A church can cheaply and quickly set up a school in its basement, hiring teachers who do not need to be certified or college educated. While ACE is not representative of the entire Christian school movement, it is the largest distributor of Christian school curricula and claims close to six thousand schools nationwide. ACE estimates that approximately two-thirds of Christian schools established in the last decade initially used ACE, mainly because it is inexpensive, costing less than $1,000 per child per year.

ACE's headquarters are in Lewisville, Texas. It began in 1970 as a nonprofit venture and then became a for-profit corporation in 1972; by 1979 it was grossing one million dollars a month.[126] When it began in 1970 it worked with 45 students; by 1972, there were 4,000; by 1976, 80,000; by 1978, 160,000; by 1980, 275,000 students. As of 1987 ACE reported close to six thousand schools, with an additional six hundred schools in eighty-six foreign countries using its curriculum. The size of the average school it serves is 35 to 70 students. ACE also provides curricula to sixteen hundred families in the United States and three hundred families in foreign countries who are educating their children at home.

A highly standardized system of education, ACE provides all the information, materials, and equipment necessary to set up a school quickly and inexpensively. Christian curricula, furniture, procedural guides, administrator and teacher training, even uniforms (red, white and blue, with American flags on the boys' ties), can be purchased.

A modern, behavioral system of education whose curriculum is based on traditional values of Christian Americanism, ACE dictates educational philosophy and policy. Perhaps the most distinguishing and controversial feature is the belief of founder Donald Howard that "teaching is not important." No one "teaches" in ACE schools, rather, students "teach themselves" through the medium of prepackaged instruction packets called PACEs. Teachers, who are called supervisors, circulate around the room, responding to American flags that students post when they have an "academic" question. Little is open to question, for teachers—and in turn their students—are instructed that "all the answers lie within the text." Monitors respond to Christian flags which are raised when students have a procedural question or need to check their test scores; they also pray with students before they take tests, and help maintain discipline. Students work in "offices" that are designed to promote independent work and to limit student interaction. Although they are in close contact, students are separated by wooden blinders that run alongside the cubicles; they do not have ready access to eye contact with anyone—including the teacher. Instead, they are to direct their attention straight ahead and sit straight in their chairs with feet firmly planted on the floor.

The walls display charts that mark the successes (and by default, failures) of students in memorizing Scriptures, making the One Hundreds Club, and performing certain duties. Everyone is aware of how each student is doing, although they do not necessarily know what the student is doing, for each works at his or her own "PACE." A student may be working on seventh-level math, nineth-level English and eighth-level science. All tests involve multiple choice, true-false, or fill in the blank type of responses; students are not asked to write essays. Both the curriculum and the day are tightly structured, leaving little to no opportunity for group discussion. The ACE program stresses the extreme self-discipline and isolation required of each student at his or her "work station." The prepackaged learning program of ACE creates a monologue of instructions rather than a dialogue; no longer is the teacher needed to communicate knowledge to or engage in joint activities with students.

Both ACE and secular critics have recognized ACE as innovative and potentially influential in providing leadership for educational reform. The education offered at the Baptist Academy appears to anticipate the future of efficient, corporate-oriented instruction. The emphasis on orderliness and discipline at the "office" learning station realistically mirrors the working stations of many present and future jobs. The increasingly automated or computerized clerical or office job requires someone who is willing and able to sit at a word processor or computer terminal for an entire day with little or no interaction with fellow workers. It also corresponds to the standardization of production and procedures now practiced by many large corporations in the service, manufacturing, insurance, and banking fields. Low-level and middle managers all over the county (and all over the world) use extensive operations manuals to instruct and govern the smallest procedures performed by the employees they supervise; the manuals severely limit the kinds of decisions the managers themselves can make.

ACE methods likewise reflect, in a more extreme form, the deskilling and reskilling process which is taking place in curricular reform in the public schools.[127] "The encroachment of technical control procedures is exemplified by the exceptionally rapid growth in the use of prepackaged sets of curricular materials . . . that include statements of objectives, all of the curricular content and material needed, prespecified teacher actions and appropriate student responses, and diagnostic and achievement tests coordinated within the system."[128] ACE takes such prepackaged curricular systems and teaching models to their extreme.

Some American parents, many of them working class, are asserting their right to control their children's education—at a price they can afford. Their sense of empowerment should not be lightly dismissed, even if their real control is limited to the degree that they purchase a franchised corporate product. But in ten or twenty years, it may be evident that these "sacred" schools were the experimental testing grounds that preceded a massive invasion of the education business by corporate America.[129] Even more poignantly, by resisting what parents and educators often think of as the "snobbish intellectuality" of the public schools (where their children are disproportionately tracked into the lower classes), they reproduce patterns of communication and thinking that are likely to limit their children's possibilities in the future.[130] The children may become "good workers," but they may not become full citizens. In fact, because of the process as well as the content of their education, ACE students are unlikely to challenge the kind of education they are receiving, or even to question whether or not they have been "educated."

The parents and educators of the ACE students are making compromises; they realize that their own and their children's opportunities are limited. Therefore, they "create" an educational environment that will better insure that their students learn the basics and become well-disciplined workers. Moreover, their most fundamental values and beliefs are not challenged, nor is their self-esteem put on the line by teachers who may devalue their working-class and fundamentalist culture.

In the case of the ACE program at Lakehaven Academy, the teachers come from the same background as the parents, and the children do not experience any great disjuncture between the language and values of their working-class, fundamentalist homes and the school. In this sense, the Academy and ACE may have something to offer the working-class and problem student; they escape much of the humiliation and devaluation they might experience in the average public school. In fact, Academy students report feeling quite comfortable with the structure of their schooling. Academy parents and educators are pleased that their system is well suited to preparing disciplined, punctual, obedient, conforming, and self-instructed students who will make "good workers." The principal of the Baptist school, in extolling the virtues of his ACE school, remarked that the military is pleased with ACE students because they are disciplined, obedient, and respect authority: "They make good workers. And that's not all that easy to come by these days. Not that I want all of them going into the military—I'd like to see some of them going into Christian ministries."[131]

By and large, the Academy is successful at getting its students to finish high school without dropping out and increasingly successful at preparing them for college. And they are proud of the fact that the majority of Academy students are now going on to college. The vast majority enroll in Christian colleges (including Pensacola, Bob Jones University, Liberty University, Grace, and Practical Bible College); the remaining few tend to enroll in community colleges.

Conclusion: The Compromises of Success

Christian schools represent the mobilization efforts of evangelicals to establish greater control over the socialization and education of the young, and therefore over the future of society. These parents and educational leaders of the Christian school movement want to protect their children from the degradation of modern, secular life—although they attempt this in very different ways. How successful they are depends on the criteria by which one judges success.

In the creation of Christian schools, we see neither total rejection of secular processes (can we even envision what this might mean?) nor total acceptance of traditional, patriarchal, evangelical ways. This act of compromise involves a myriad of contradictions as evangelicals selectively reject, accept, and appropriate modern ideas, conveniences, and lifestyles. While evangelicals react against the commercialization of culture, many develop, sell, buy, and use mass-marketed curriculum packages which dictate virtually every aspect of school life. Although Christian schools stress the values of the traditional patriarchal family and the "natural" submission of women, because of their size and curriculum the schools tend not to segregate boys from girls, nor do they offer them different curricula. The education for boys and girls tends to be quite similar, although traditional gender roles are reinforced in the texts themselves, and adult men clearly have more status and authority than adult women within the community.

Given that Christian schools tend to select a relatively homogeneous student population, most often drawn from the ranks of the sponsoring congregation or neighboring congregations, there is a high degree of consistency among the major socializing institutions of school, church, and family. The majority of parents tend to share similar class backgrounds, interests, lifestyles, and aspirations for their children.

A number of studies of Christian schools suggest that their students are well behaved, obedient, and well mannered, without being overly pious.[132] Students tend to express political and attitudinal beliefs similar to those of their family, and to spend a good deal of their time with "Christian" friends.[133] This is not to say that there are no forms of rebellious activity. While many espouse a deep Christian faith, for others it may be a more superficial conformity to the norms of the school community, against which they may rebel once given a chance.[134]

Moreover, the available data (which come from limited and selective Christian school samples) suggest that Christian school students are doing no worse, and on average better, than the average public school student, given the criteria commonly used to test academic achievement. (How accurate the measures of academic achievement are is another question.) In May 1983 CTB/McGraw-Hill conducted a major testing survey of 7,500 students who had been using ACE for at least four years. The results indicate that the average student using ACE materials scored higher than 65 percent of the students in the control group, a nationally representative sample of students. The American Association of Christian Schools International also coordinated a nationwide testing program of Christian school students. Results from their administration of the Stanford Achievement Tests to 175,000 Christian school students showed that the average achievement level was one year and seven months ahead of the national norm.[135]

In terms of organizational impact, Christian schools have contributed to the momentum of the New Christian Right. Their accomplishments in establishing alternative forms of education (both through the schools and the media), and the increasing legitimacy they have derived from these successes, have influenced not only others' perceptions of them, but their own perceptions of themselves.

Arguing for greater community and lay control of education, the New Christian Right raised the question of who should be teaching what to whom: "Since the Bible demands that children be trained properly, the question is, who should be doing that training? the state? the NEA? the ACLU? the Utopians? the Behaviorists? the parents?"[136] The answer is clear to them: Evangelical parents enroll their children in Christian schools believing that their authority and roles as parents are reinforced, even though they do not necessarily gain greater control over their children's education.[137] Evangelical teachers say they are able to express their beliefs and values more freely and to form more intimate relationships with their students. Many evangelical pastors also serve as school principals, increasing the influence they have on their flock. With mutually reinforcing institutions, based on consensus and dedicated to similar goals, one can expect to find more consistent results in socializing children.

The establishment of Christian schools in the midst of a society that values educational conformity requires energy, confidence, and resourcefulness. It represents both an act of rebellion (against the dominant culture) and of commitment (to "Christian" community). Furthermore, an examination of the curricula used in Christian schools reveals that they represent both resistance and accommodation to standard forms of educational content found in the public schools. While Christian schools resist public school materials because they are too secular and humanistic, and mass, commercialized culture because it is too materialistic and crass, they nonetheless often use those materials or buy mass-produced packages of Christian curricula.

Moreover, as fundamentalists have reasserted their presence and influence in the last two decades, they have become less separatist. While they have established their own, separate schools, they have become engaged in political battles that have drawn them into the secular courts. In order to preserve their rights as evangelical Christians and to protect their schools, fundamentalists have increasingly moved beyond the borders of their own communities.

What might the future hold? It appears as though the growth of the Christian school movement has plateaued but that Christian schools will remain a viable option for educating children in the United States for some time to come. Some suggest that we may be seeing a convergence of public and Christian schooling. If this is the case, and the public schools continue to move right of center, with an emphasis on the "neutrality" of status quo "basics," and increasingly approach "accountability" through standardized programs, then evangelical parents may become less dissatisfied with public education and less willing to bear the costs of Christian schooling.[138] But while this may be true for some, it ignores the religious motivation of many Christian school parents who want their children to go to school in an explicitly Christian environment. We must recognize the complexity of the decision-making process; there are mixed motivations and different priorities assigned to choices involving the education of one's children, be they in public or private schools. Some evangelical parents are totally committed to Christian schooling, but probably the majority make decisions a year or two at a time, choosing among various Christian and public school and, increasingly, home schooling options. As it is, some evangelical parents send one child to Christian school and another to public school, depending on what each might have to offer the particular child in question. Shopping among Christian schools is not uncommon.[139]

The greatest challenge for Christian schools in the next decade may be internal rather than external. Jim Carper, professor of education at the University of South Carolina and a supporter of Christian education, argues that the major concerns facing Christian schools today are no longer government control (that has largely been settled at the state level, with the exception of Iowa and Michigan), but rather financial stability and spiritual vitality. How they are able to balance these two concerns will be a test of their maturity as they come of age in the late twentieth century.

In the process of trying to "revitalize" American education, both fundamentalists and the educational system are being transformed. While evangelicals have been influential in raising relevant questions that have commanded the attention of many both within and beyond their borders, they have not convinced the culture at large that they have the answers. Thus the debate about what kinds of "revitalization" American education needs and how we will go about that process will continue to be part of the contested terrain as the United States enters the twenty-first century as an increasingly heterogeneous and stratified society, and one whose position and power in the world is shifting.

Notes

1. Quoted in David Moshman, "Faith Christian v. Nebraska: Parent, Child, and Community Rights in the Educational Arena," *Teachers College Record* 86, no. 4 (Summer 1985); see this article for a thorough discussion of the case.

2. Diane Ravitch, *The Great School Wars: A History of Schools as the Battlefields of Social Change* (New York: Basic Books, 1974).

3. David Tyack and Elizabeth Hansot, "Conflict in American Educational History," in the special issue "American Schools: Public and Private," *Daedalus*, Summer 1981.

4. Barbara Finkelstein, "Cultural Transmission and the Acquisition of Identity: Learners and Learning in American Educational History" (Paper presented at American Educational Research Association Meetings, New York, 1982).

5. Point made by Joe Kincheloe, personal correspondence.

6. James Carper and Thomas Hunt, *Religious Schooling in America* (Birmingham, Ala.: Religious Education Press, 1984), pp. 111–13.

7. See Carper and Hunt, eds., *Religious Schooling in America*. Others who document earlier experimentation with Protestant day schools include Francis Curran, *The Churches and the Schools: American Protestantism and Popular Elementary Education* (Chicago: Loyola University Press, 1954); Otto Kraushaar, *Nonpublic Schools: Patterns of Diversity* (Baltimore: Johns Hopkins University Press, 1972); Richard Ognibene, "Religious Education in the Late Nineteenth Century," *Religious Education* 77 (January–February 1982): 5–20. See Carper and Hunt, *Religious Schooling in America,* for a more detailed discussion and bibliography.

8. It is important, however, to distinguish between types. See Nancy T. Ammerman's excellent discussion of North American Protestant fundamentalism and her distinction between fundamentalists and evangelicals, in "North American Protestant Fundamentalism," in Martin E. Marty and R. Scott Appleby, eds., *Fundamentalisms Observed* (Chicago: University of Chicago Press, 1991). See also Richard Quebedeaux, *The Worldly Evangelicals* (New York: Harper and Row, 1978); idem, *The Young Evangelicals* (New York: Harper and Row, 1974); Carper and Hunt, *Religious Schooling in America*, p. 123.

9. Carper and Hunt, *Religious Schooling in America,* one chapter is devoted to Christian day schools and another to Calvinist day

schools. While the Calvinist or Reformed schools are considered part of the Christian school movement, they are also considered quite different from the other Christian schools. See Donald Oppewal and Peter DeBoer, "Calvinist Day Schools," in Carper and Hunt; Harro Van Brummelen, *Curriculum: Implementation in Three Christian Schools* (Grand Rapids, Mich.: Calvin College Monograph Series, 1989); idem, *Telling the Next Generation: Educational Development in North American Calvinist Christian Schools* (New York: University Press of America, 1986); Donald Oppewal, *The Roots of the Calvinist Day School Movement* (Grand Rapids, Mich.: Calvin College Monograph Series, 1963); *Christian Schools International Directory, 1989–1990* (Grand Rapids, Mich.: Christian Schools International).

10. James Carper, "Evangelical Christian Schools: Old Values, New Trends," *Private School Monitor* 11, no. 2 (Winter 1990): 2; Bruce Cooper, "The Changing Demography of Private Schools," *Education and Urban Society* 16, no. 4 (1984): 429–32; James Carper, "The Christian Day School," in Carper and Hunt, *Religious Schooling in America;* James D. Hunter, "Evangelical Schools in Growth, Catholic Schools in Decline," *Wall Street Journal*, 8 March 1989, p. 34, estimates that there are two million Christian school students, but this figure is considerably higher than indicated elsewhere. The National Center on Educational Statistics released a report in December of 1989 that gives figures for enrollments in public and private (Catholic, other religious, and nonsectarian) schools but does not specify evangelical schools as a major type among "other religious schools," although they would represent the majority group. Marilyn Miles McMillen, "Key Statistics for Private Elementary and Secondary Education: School Year 1989–90," in *Survey Report* (NCES 90–026) (Washington, D.C.: U.S. Department of Education, National Center for Education Statistics, December 1989).

11. For example, a 1979 study found that 72 percent of Kentucky and 50 percent of Wisconsin Christian day schools did not belong to any national association. Virginia Davis Nordin and William Lloyd Turner, "More Than Segregationist Academies: The Growing Protestant Fundamentalist Schools," *Phi Delta Kappan,* February 1980, p. 392. See also James Carper's detailed discussion of this in his chapter "The Christian Day School," in Carper and Hunt, *Religious Schooling in America.*

12. George Ballweg, "The Growth in the Number and Population of Christian Schools since 1966: A Profile of Parental Views Concerning Factors Which Led Them to Enroll Their Children in a Christian School" (Ph.D. diss., Boston University School of Education, 1980), p. 3.

13. Hunter, "Evangelical Schools in Growth," p. 34. According to "Characteristics of Private Schools: 1987–1988" (NCES 90–080) (Washington, D.C.: National Center for Education Statistics, April 1990), Christian schools represent 22 percent of private, religious schools and 39 percent of non-Catholic religious schools. Because of the proliferation of Christian schools which tend to be small, one consistently finds that the relative percentage of the numbers of Christian schools as part of the whole private school system is higher than their relative percentage of enrollments. For example, while Christian schools represent 22 percent of all private schools, their enrollments represent 13 percent of enrollments in private schools; while Christian schools represent 22 percent of all religious, private schools, their enrollments represent only 16 percent. This stands in contrast to Catholic schools, which represent 44 percent of all private, religious schools but 64 percent of enrollments; and 35 percent of all private schools but 54 percent of their enrollments.

14. Ibid.; *Christian Schools International Directory, 1989–1990.*

15. Robert Liebman and Robert Wuthnow, *The New Christian Right* (New York: Aldine, 1983), p. 2.

16. Martin E. Marty, *Righteous Empire* (New York: Dial Press, 1970).

17. See essays by Helen Hardacre, Andrea B. Rugh, Shahla Haeri, Jorge E. Mal-

donado, and D. Michael Quinn, this volume.

18. Nancy Ammerman, *Bible Believers: Fundamentalists in the Modern World* (New Brunswick, N.J.: Rutgers University Press, 1987), p. 182; Mary Beth Gehrman, "Reading, Writing, and Religion," *Free Inquiry*, Fall 1987, pp. 12–14; Paul Parsons, *Inside America's Christian Schools* (Macon, Ga.: Mercer University Press, 1987); Alan Peshkin, *God's Choice: The Total World of a Fundamentalist Christian School* (Chicago: University of Chicago Press, 1986), p. 79, see also p. 80; Van Brummelen, *Curriculum: Implementation;* Susan Rose, *Keeping Them Out of the Hands of Satan: Evangelical Schooling in America* (New York: Routledge, 1988).

19. Rose, *Keeping Them Out of the Hands of Satan;* Ammerman, *Bible Believers*, p. 182.

20. Conference for Christian school administrators, American Christian Schools International, Grace Theological Seminary, Winona Lake, Ind., 1982.

21. Peshkin, *God's Choice*, p. 79, see also p. 80.

22. *Smith v. Board of Education*, 655 F. Supp. 939, 987–88 (D.C. Ala. 1987), as quoted in Eugene Provenzo, Jr., *Religious Fundamentalism and American Education: The Battle for the Public Schools* (Albany: State University of New York Press, 1990), p. 81.

23. *Smith v. Board of School Commissioners of Mobile County,* 827 F. 2d 684 (11th Cir. 1987).

24. Tim LaHaye, *Battle for the Mind* (Old Tappan, N.J.: Revell, 1980), pp. 9, 26.

25. Joe Kincheloe, *Understanding the New Right and Its Impact on Education* (Bloomington, Ind.: Phi Delta Kappa Educational Foundation, 1983).

26. James Robison, quoted in William Martin, "God's Angry Man," *Texas Monthly*, April 1981, p. 226.

27. Barbara Parker and Christy Macy, "Secular Humanism, the Hatch Amendment, and Public Education" (Editorial memorandum, People for the American Way, Washington, D.C., 1985), p. 8.

28. It is important here to distinguish between fundamentalists and charismatics. The fundamentalists, emerging at the turn of the twentieth century, took on recognizable form after World War I. They became an opposition movement against the modernists, who, in accepting biblical criticism, evolutionary theory, and the Social Gospel, departed from orthodox belief. Believing that the secular world is sinful and corrupting, they took, in Richard Niebuhr's words, a Christ-against-culture position. As fundamentalists, people involved in the Lakehaven Academy are inclined to be separatists, politically and socially conservative, holding anticommunist and premillennial, apocalyptic beliefs. The charismatics, on the other hand, tend to be less separatist, believing in the potential of Christ to transform the culture. The movement itself is a more middle-class expression of the older "classical" Pentecostalism that, like fundamentalism, was also very exclusive and separatist. The major theological differences find expression in the charismatic emphasis on religious experience and testimony rather than on defense of doctrine and the letter of the law that is central to fundamentalist tradition. While the charismatics believe in the "baptism of the Holy Spirit," divine healing, prophecy, and speaking in tongues, the fundamentalists condemn these practices as the work of the devil and divisive to the Christian community.

29. Students in non-Catholic religious schools have lower application rates to college and are less likely to be enrolled in college preparatory classes than students in Catholic or nonsectarian, private schools. It would be important to analyze the data according to those schools which fall into the Christian school movement, including the Assemblies of God, Baptists, Christians (specifying no particular denomination), and Calvinists. See "Characteristics of Private Schools: 1987–1988," p. 6.

30. A recent study by Harro Van Brummelen *(Curriculum: Implementation)* offers more insight into schools that have accepted and rejected the ACE curriculum. A survey of the kinds of schools choosing to use ACE

for extended periods of time would be useful in order to begin to unravel the complex interactions among theological, socioeconomic, organizational, and curricular orientations. At present, as in the past, many schools begin using ACE since it is an inexpensive and quick way to set up a school, and then shift to another curriculum after the first few years.

31. Rose, *Keeping Them Out of the Hands of Satan.*

32. See Van Brummelen's comparison of three neighboring schools in a British Columbia community for a discussion of factors influencing organizational and curricular variations (Van Brummelen, *Curriculum: Implementation*).

33. For greater detail see Rose, *Keeping Them Out of the Hands of Satan;* Carper and Hunt, *Religious Schooling in America;* Carper, "Evangelical Christian Schools."

34. Most Christian schools require that girls wear dresses or skirts, with hems just at or below the knee. For boys, it is hair length that is specified: usually above the collar and ears, and off the brows. Girls are usually not permitted to wear pants, and boys are not allowed to wear blue jeans, T-shirts, or sandals. No low-cut blouses or dresses are allowed; shirts must be buttoned and tucked in. See Peshkin, *God's Choice,* p. 100; Alan Peshkin, "The Truth and Consequences of Fundamentalist Christian Schooling," *Free Inquiry,* Fall 1987, pp. 5–10; Ammerman, *Bible Believers,* pp. 180–81; Rose, *Keeping Them Out of the Hands of Satan.*

35. This figure is taken from my sampling of twenty-two schools (Rose, *Keeping Them Out of the Hands of Satan*) and Ammerman's case study (Ammerman, *Bible Believers*).

36. Ammerman, *Bible Believers,* p. 179.

37. Rose, *Keeping Them Out of the Hands of Satan,* p. 122; see also chaps. 6 and 7.

38. Their recent literature, which turns a perceived weakness into a potential advantage, reflects a shift in thinking from the 1970s: "In the early years conventional Christian educators counseled ACE not to take the slow learners—that the ACE pro-gram would be overrun with problem kids and that it would ruin the reputation of ACE. By the 1980s, ACE became known as 'a school system for problem kids.' Most of the problem kids came from conventional schools. . . . How can you practice Christianity if you reject those who need help most?" Donald Howard, "The Strength and Weaknesses of the A.C.E. Program" (Lewisville, Tex.: A.C.E., Inc., 1985), p. 34. Moreover, ACE has used the same argument to extend its curriculum to those beyond the fundamentalist community, both within and beyond the borders of the United States. The company publishes a new curriculum under the neutral academic label of Basic Education which now provides materials in English, Spanish, and French. Acutely aware that many of their constituency may disapprove or at least question whether they are "selling out," they are careful to explain that Basic Education represents ACE's outreach ministry and as such, is a "fulfillment of the Great Commission." *Facts about A.C.E.* (Lewisville, Tex.: A.C.E., Inc., 1985).

39. Patricia Lines, "Private Education Alternatives and State Regulation," *Journal of Law and Education* 12, no. 2 (Spring 1983): 191.

40. Peter Skerry, "Christian Schools, Racial Quotas, and the IRS," *Public Interest,* no. 61 (Fall 1980).

41. Jack Layman, "The Irony of Black Christian Academies," *Private School Monitor* 11, no. 2 (Winter 1990): 4–6. Directed by Joan Davis Ratteray, the IIE was started in 1984 in Washington, D.C., to encourage and assist independent neighborhood schools, both religious and secular, in Afro-American and other minority communities.

42. "Characteristics of Private Schools: 1987–1988," p. 2.

43. Ammerman, *Bible Believers,* p. 177.

44. Quoted in Peshkin, *God's Choice,* p. 59.

45. Ammerman, *Bible Believers,* p. 183. This is indicated by research on other fundamentalist Christian schools as well, although nonfundamentalist Christian schools may exhibit a very different pattern of instruction. Peshkin and I describe similar patterns of

"nonquestioning"; it may be this that distinguishes the more strictly fundamentalist schools from some of their evangelical counterparts. For example, my research on a middle-class, independent charismatic school revealed much greater interest in using a variety of texts, encouraging more creative thinking, and exploring alternative explanations. Interacting with this is the greater likelihood that the fundamentalist schools will take either a "Christ-against-culture" or "Christ-above-culture" position rather than a "Christ-as-transformer-of-culture" position that typifies the charismatic school I studied. The latter stance would require not only greater interaction with the culture but also greater understanding of it in order to effectively transform it. See Rose, *Keeping Them Out of the Hands of Satan;* Peshkin, *God's Choice;* also, Van Brummelen, *Curriculum: Implementation.*

46. Phyllis Schlafly, ed., *Child Abuse in the Classroom* (Wheaton, Ill.: Crossway Books, 1985).

47. Kincheloe, *Understanding the New Right,* p. 32.

48. Estimates vary from 248,500 to 353,500 according to Patricia Lines who has been systematically studying the movement. Patricia Lines, "Estimating the Home Schooled Population" (Working paper, OR 91–537, Office of Research, Department of Education, October 1991. See also idem, "An Overview of Home Instruction," *Phi Delta Kappan* 68, no. 7 (March 1987): 510–17; Brian Ray, "The Kitchen Classroom," *Christianity Today,* 12 August 1988, p. 23.

49. Ray, "Kitchen Classroom," p. 23.

50. In 1988 alone, Colorado, Hawaii, Maine, New York, North Carolina, and South Carolina either passed laws or set regulations for home schools. "National Conference of State Legislatures (NCSL) Report on Home Schooling" (Washington, D.C., 8 February 1989).

51. Kincheloe, *Understanding the New Right,* p. 23.

52. "NCSL Report, 1989"; Mark Weston, "Home Schooling: A Primer for State Legislatures," *State Legislative Report* (Den-

ver) 14, no. 1 (January 1989); Mary Anne Pitman, "Compulsory Education and Home Schooling: Truancy or Prophecy," *Education and Urban Society* 19, no. 3 (May 1987): 280–89; Ray, "Kitchen Classroom," p. 26; Jane Van Galen, "Explaining Home Education: Parents' Accounts of Their Decisions to Teach Their Own Children," *Urban Review* 19, no. 3 (1987): 161–77; idem, "Becoming Home Schoolers," *Urban Education* 23, no. 1 (April 1988): 89–106; Diane Divoky, "The New Pioneers of the Home-Schooling Movement," *Phi Delta Kappan* 64, no. 6 (February 1983): 395–99. At least three major categories of home-schoolers have been identified: evangelicals, "New Age" types, and those who have chosen to home-school for a variety of reasons (primarily that they believe they can do a better job of teaching their children or because of a child's illness) without espousing a particular religious or political ideology.

53. These preliminary observations come from my research of a charismatic Christian school that was experiencing internal conflict because some parents in the fellowship wanted to home-school their children for a period of time, and from a telephone conversation with James Carper, who shared similar observations in "Evangelical Christian Schools." It appears that most children who are home-schooled move in and out of home schooling and some other kind of educational setting. It would be interesting to study the kinds of schools they enter and exit from in the course of their education, how those choices are made, how the transitions are negotiated by the children, and the timing of the transitions. It may be that those engaged in home schooling and various forms of private schooling, including Christian schooling, are some of the greatest shoppers.

54. Kincheloe, *Understanding the New Right,* p. 30.

55. Quoted in William Reese, "Soldiers for Christ in the Army of God: The Christian School Movement in America," *Educational Theory* 35, no. 2 (1985): 178; House Subcommittee on Oversight of the Committee on Ways and Means, *Tax-Exempt*

Status of Private Schools, pt. 2, 96th Cong., 1st sess., 1979, p. 949.

56. Jerry Falwell, *America Can Be Saved* (Murfreesboro, Tenn.: Sword of the Lord Publishers, 1979), p. 53.

57. Quoted in Reese, "Soldiers for Christ in the Army of God," p. 178. In fact, at least one evangelical has attributed the "streaking craze" of the 1970s to the teaching of evolution, arguing that if children are taught they are descended from animals, they will begin to act like them.

58. Quoted in Paul Heidebrecht, "Reconstructionists: War Is Declared on Public Education," *Christianity Today* 30, no. 7 (18 April 1986): 40, 43.

59. Ibid., p. 40.

60. Ibid.; Lines, "Overview of Home Instruction"; idem, "Home Instruction: Size of the Movement and Public Impact" (Working paper, 1989); Ray, "Kitchen Classroom."

61. Quoted in Heidebrecht, "Reconstructionists," p. 40. Eugene Provenzo argues that Rushdoony's thinking and writing has contributed more to the fundamentalist interpretation of American educational history than any other. See his *Religious Fundamentalism and American Education,* p. 5. See also Sara Diamond, *Spiritual Warfare: The Politics of the Christian Right* (Boston: South End Press, 1989), pp. 135–39, for a discussion of Christian political activism and the role of reconstructionists.

62. Quoted in Heidebrecht, "Reconstructionists," p. 40. This concern with socialism is echoed in the writings of Verma Hall and Rosalie Slater. Verna M. Hall, *The Christian History of the Constitution of the United States* (San Francisco: The Foundation for American Christian Education, 1966); Rosalie Slater, *Teaching and Learning America's Christian History* (San Francisco: Foundation for American Christian Education, 1965). See Susan Rose and Steve Brouwer, "The Export of Fundamentalist Americanism: U.S. Evangelical Education in Guatemala," *Latin American Perspectives* 17, no. 4 (Fall 1990): 42–56, for a more detailed discussion of evangelical reactions to their perceptions of socialism in the public schools.

63. Kincheloe, *Understanding the New Right,* p. 35.

64. Heidebrecht, "Reconstructionists," p. 43.

65. Kincheloe, *Understanding the New Right,* p. 21.

66. Ibid., p. 36. A recent airing of Roger Mudd's "Learning in America" (September 1989) presents the problem of "diluted texts" as pervasive. Watered down to the point of offending no one, most high school textbooks are no longer of interest to anyone.

67. Eagle Forum, "Membership Form," cited in Charles J. Park, "Rise of the New Right: Human and Civil Liberties in Jeopardy," *New Jersey Education Association Review* 53 (March 1980): 14.

68. James Hefley, *Textbooks on Trial* (Wheaton, Ill.: Victor Books, 1976); Kincheloe, *Understanding the New Right,* pp. 34–35.

69. Hefley, *Textbooks on Trial,* p. 32.

70. Kincheloe, *Understanding the New Right,* p. 15.

71. Ibid., p. 8.

72. Ibid., p. 30; Provenzo, *Religious Fundamentalism and American Education;* Dorothy Nelkin, *The Creation Controversy: Science or Scripture in the Schools?* (New York: W. W. Norton, 1982).

73. "How Can the Pupil Rights Amendment Be Used Effectively?" *Pro-Family Forum Newsletter,* March 1985, pp. 7–8; Anthony Podesta, "Ignoring History Is a Misguided Protection Effort," *Houston Post,* 29 May 1985; Donna Hulsizer, education director, People for the American Way, telephone interview, 4 October 1989; Ed Kealy, director, Federal Programs, National School Boards Association, telephone interview, 30 August 1989.

74. *Federal Register* 49, no. 174 (6 September 1984): 35, 318–22.

75. Anne Lewis, "Little-used Amendment Becomes Divisive, Disruptive Issue," *Phi Delta Kappan,* June 1985, pp. 667–68.

76. *Phyllis Schlafly Report,* January 1985; see also, "Asserting Parental Rights in Education: A 'How-To' Complaint Kit" (Washington, D.C.: Contact America, 1986).

77. Anne Bridgman, "Groups Press Parent-Control Campaign, Get High Level Support," *Education Week,* 20 February 1985; James Wall, "A New Right Tool Distorts Regulations," *Christian Century,* 24 April 1985, p. 403.

78. Lewis, "Little-used Amendment," p. 667; Edward Fiske, "The Hatch Act Comes Alive," *New York Times,* 7 July 1985; Dennis Doyle and Terry Hartle, "The White House in the Schoolhouse," *Washington Post,* 20 May 1985; Anne Bridgman, "Bills Patterned after Federal Hatch Act Pressed in States to Spur 'Discussion,'" *Education Week,* 29 May 1985.

79. "The Hatch Amendment Regulations: A Guidelines Document," prepared by the Hatch Amendment Coalition, 1985.

80. "Pupil Protection Rights Regulations," *Congressional Record,* 99th Cong., 1st sess., 19 February 1985, pt. 15: S1389–S1390; Lewis, "Little-used Amendment," p. 668.

81. Schlafly, *Child Abuse in the Classroom.*

82. Ibid., p. 193.

83. Rebecca Coudret, "Policy Governs Local School Decision," *Courier* (Evansville, Ind.), 1985.

84. "Controlling Curriculum Content," *Inquiry and Analysis,* NSBA, May 1985, p. 3; see also *Grove v. Mead School District No. 354,* 753 F. 2d 1528, 1534 (9th Cir. 1985).

85. Coudret, "Policy Governs Local School Decision."

86. Kincheloe, *Understanding the New Right,* p. 31.

87. Ibid.

88. Lines, "Private Education Alternatives and State Regulation," p. 191.

89. Sara Diamond, *Spiritual Warfare,* pp. 63–64.

90. See Ibid., p. 64, especially her footnotes; "Koop for Surgeon General, Billings in at Education," *Christianity Today,* 13 March 1981; Charles Babcock, "Bob Billings: Christian Right's Inside Man," *Washington Post,* 25 March 1982.

91. *Mozert v. Hawkins County Board of Education,* 827 F. 2d 1058 (6th Cir. 1987); see also Charles Glenn, "Religion, Textbooks, and the Common School," *Public Interest* 88 (1987): 28–47.

92. *New York Times,* 16 December 1986, p. 10.

93. *New York Times,* 5 March 1987; Glenn, "Religion, Textbooks, and the Common School."

94. See Diamond, *Spiritual Warfare.*

95. Kincheloe, *Understanding the New Right,* p. 29.

96. Ibid., p. 8.

97. Anne Bridgman, "Bills Patterned after Federal Hatch Act Pressed in States to Spur 'Discussion,'" *Education Week,* 29 May 1985.

98. Robert Rothman, "California Policy Calls for Curb on Science 'Dogma': Board Backs Teaching of 'Observable Facts,'" *Education Week,* 25 January 1989.

99. Jennifer Spevacek, "Awful Truths about Hamlet's Mom and Ardent Romeo Cut from Texts," *Washington Times,* 17 December 1984.

100. *Florey v. Sioux Falls School District 49–5,* 619 F. 2d 1311, 1318 (8th Cir. 1980), cert. denied, 449 U.S. 987 (1980).

101. "Attacks on the Freedom to Learn: 1988–1989 Report" (Washington, D.C.: People for the American Way, 1989), pp. 1–2.

102. Hulsizer interview. A 1986 PAW report indicates that 24.1 percent of the censorship incidents reported were initiated by organized censorship groups aligned with evangelical organizations such as the Moral Majority, the Pro-Family Forum, Educational Research Associates, and the Eagle Forum. Approximately 65 percent of the protests were led by legislators, preachers, and individual parents. Whether initiated by organized groups or individuals, the majority of the cases are resolved at the local level and receive little or no national atten-

tion. See "Attacks on Freedom to Learn: A 1984–1985 Report" (Washington, D.C.: People for the American Way, 1986), p. 32.

103. Hulsizer interview.

104. Ron Fields, director, Federal Relations Office, National Conference of State Legislatures, telephone interview, 29 August 1989.

105. Fields interview. The same sentiment was expressed by Gene Wilhoit, executive director of the National School Boards Association, telephone interview, 31 August 1989; and John Myers, director, Denver Office of State Services, National Conference of State Legislatures, telephone interview, 29 August 1989.

106. Fields interview. This was also expressed either directly or indirectly by several spokespersons for the national educational and legislative associations.

107. Siva Vaidhyanathan, "Ruling on Evolution in Texts Altered," *Dallas Morning News,* 12 March 1989, pp. 33A, 35A; Michael Hudson and Thomas Warren, "Should Schools Have to Teach Evolution?" *Dallas Morning News,* 9 March 1989.

108. This statement was a plank in the education section of the 1988 Republican party platform, entitled, "Balanced View of Origin of Life," reported in *NCSE Reports,* "What Did Justice Brennan Mean?" March–April 1989, p. 16.

109. See essays by Everett Mendelsohn, James Moore, Bassam Tibi, and Farhang Rajaee, this volume.

110. Ibid., pp. 14–16.

111. Rothman, "California Policy Calls for Curb on Science 'Dogma,'" pp. 16–17.

112. Vaidhyanathan, "Ruling on Evolution in Texts Altered." These requirements will affect books purchased for the 1991–92 school year.

113. Diane Curtis, "State Refining Policy on Science Teaching," *San Francisco Chronicle,* 6 January 1989.

114. Cooper, "The Changing Demography of Private Schools," *Education and Urban Society* 16, no. 4 (1984): 437.

115. Reese, "Soldiers for Christ in the Army of God," p. 184.

116. Fred Pincus, "From Equity to Excellence: The Rebirth of Educational Conservatism," *Social Policy* 4, no. 3 (Winter 1984): 50–56; Kealy interview.

117. The Moral Majority report later boasted that "[Reagan's] appointment of William Bennett as [secretary] . . . was a clear indication that the President understands who his friends are." Reported in Christopher Hitchens, "The Minority Report," *The Nation,* 8 June 1985, p. 694. The regional liaison officer in the department's Denver office, Tom Toncredo, sent out a mailing advocating fundamentalist private schools and complaining that "godlessness" was taking over America, once a "Christian" nation. The mailing went on to announce that "humanism and Christianity cannot exist side by side." Its author, Robert Billings, was director of the department's ten regional offices and a former officeholder in the Moral Majority. Bennett evaded questions from Senator Lowell Weicker, Jr., and others about the constitutionality of the mailing. When Congresswoman Patricia Schroeder wrote the department about the matter, she received a reply written by Billings, who maintained that the mailing "was well within the parameters of the statute governing the use of mail for official purposes."

118. Hitchens, "Minority Report."

119. Kealy interview.

120. Quoted in Dena Kleiman, "Parents' Groups Purging Schools of Humanist Books and Classes," *New York Times,* 17 May 1981.

121. Kincheloe, *Understanding the New Right,* p. 32.

122. Wilhoit interview.

123. Wilhoit interview.

124. On 2 October 1989 the Texas Supreme Court ruled 9–0 that the state's school-financing structure was unconstitutional because many tax-poor districts could not raise and spend nearly as many dollars per student as their more affluent neighbors, and the state was not adequately making up the difference. See David Maraniss, "A Texas School District Celebrates Death of Two-

Tiered System," *Washington Post,* 8 October 1989, p. A3.

125. Michael Apple, *Teachers and Texts* (New York: Routledge, 1986), p. 194.

126. Felicity Barringer and Barbara Vobejda, "Franchising the Classroom: Texas Firm Sells Churches on Teacherless Education," *Washington Post,* 3 February 1985.

127. Michael W. Apple and Lois Weis, "Curriculum Form and the Logic of Technical Control," in *Ideology and Practice in Schooling* (Philadelphia: Temple University Press, 1983).

128. Michael Apple, *Cultural and Economic Reproduction* (London: Routledge and Kegan Paul, 1982), p. 149.

129. Indeed, such evidence may be much closer at hand. Note Whittle Communications, creator of Channel One, the controversial news program that some 6.6 million American teenagers in more than nine thousand schools watch every day. The national PTA, among other educational groups, opposed Channel One because of the two minutes of ads during every program. California state superintendent of public instruction Bill Honig accused Whittle of "converting the educational purpose of a school to a commercial one." Chris Whittle (who, according to John Friedman, has "many interlocking ties with Education Secretary Lamar Alexander") has announced plans to open two hundred private schools by 1996. Tuition would likely be just below the per-pupil cost of public education in the community. One way to contain costs, Whittle suggests, is to "harness student power" in order to reduce support staff and use televised instruction. See John S. Friedman, "Big Buisness Goes to School: The Whittle-Alexander Nexus," *The Nation,* 17 February 1992, pp. 188–192. In 1992 Benno Schmidt resigned as Yale University's president to become president and chief executive of Whittle's "Edison Project," which

plans to establish one thousand day care–high school campuses by the year 2010.

130. In *Bible Believers,* pp. 178–79, Nancy Ammerman makes a similar point. Also, see Rose, *Keeping Them Out of the Hands of Satan,* especially chap. 8, for greater detail on class and codes of communication in relation to classroom styles.

131. Rose, *Keeping Them Out of the Hands of Satan,* pp. 204–5.

132. See Rose, *Keeping Them Out of the Hands of Satan;* Peshkin, *God's Choice;* Ammerman, *Bible Believers.*

133. Rose, *Keeping Them Out of the Hands of Satan;* Peshkin, *God's Choice.*

134. See Ammerman, *Bible Believers,* pp. 184–87.

135. Paul Kienel, "A Special Message to Christian Leaders about Christian School Education" (Whittier, Calif.: ASCI, 1979); Andrew McDearmid, "Student Achievement in Accelerated Christian Education Schools in Pennsylvania" (Ph.D. diss., Temple University, 1979).

136. President of the Religious Roundtable testifying before a congressional committee studying tuition tax credits in 1982, quoted in Reese, "Soldiers for Christ in the Army of God," p. 181.

137. This is a point that both Alan Peshkin and I make. See Rose, *Keeping Them Out of the Hands of Satan;* Peshkin, *God's Choice,* pp. 94–96.

138. This is an observation Joe Kincheloe offered in response to reading an earlier draft of this paper.

139. As Jim Carper suggested in a phone interview (April 1990), either through self-selection or experience, those who have resisted the pressure to send their children to public school and have actively sought out other options may be more likely to continually reevaluate their options at every juncture.

CHAPTER
17

The Two Faces of Fundamentalist
Higher Education

Quentin Schultze

What is today a matter of academic speculation begins tomorrow to
move armies and pull down empires.

J. Gresham Machen, *Princeton Theological Review* (1913)

In 1886 the Chicago Evangelization Society
raised $250,000 to prove to urban revivalist Dwight L. Moody that it was serious
about starting a school for training evangelical leaders. Moody stood before the group
and enthusiastically endorsed their plan. "I believe we have got to have 'gap men,'"
Moody exhorted, "men who are trained to fill the gap between the common people
and the ministers."[1] Within three decades Moody Bible Institute, as it was eventually
called, was a regional center for fundamentalism, teaching hundreds of lay workers
about the Bible and training them to be missionaries.

When radio broadcasting began in the 1920s, Moody's school was one of the first
on the air. By 1930 its station, WMBI, was receiving over twenty thousand letters
annually from listeners. In the next decade its programs were syndicated to 187 different stations across the country.[2] Moody Bible Institute eventually launched its own
satellite network, feeding radio programs from its Chicago studios to even more radio
stations throughout the United States. Not only was the "gap" filled, but a national
constituency was linked directly to Institute headquarters in the Windy City. Along
with *Moody Monthly,* one of the highest-circulation religious magazines in the country,
the radio network became the hub of a national, transdenominational network of
fundamentalist pastors, lay leaders, students, and financial supporters.

American fundamentalism from the 1920s to the present has been organized
around media and schools—two of the major agents of socialization in modern society. At first there were relatively simple combinations of Bible institutes, national periodicals and local radio programs. Already in 1922, before radio reception was very
clear, the Bible Institute of Los Angeles started radio station KJS, where Charles E.
Fuller began his broadcasting career. Later Fuller used contributions from his national
"Old-Fashioned Revival Hour" to establish Fuller Theological Seminary in Pasadena.

Fuller even recruited the seminary's first class over the radio. Providence Bible Institute, Columbia College in South Carolina, and Denver Bible Institute all had their own radio programs.[3]

During the 1950s and 1960s, fundamentalists similarly combined mass communication and education to attract sympathetic constituencies and to raise funds. Billy James Hargis gained national publicity in the sixties for his criticism of sex-education curricula in the public schools. Soon he was on both radio and television, broadcasting anticommunist messages and investing in the most sophisticated direct-mail fundraising equipment available in that era. Hargis founded American Christian College in Tulsa in 1971, dedicating the school to "God, government, and Christian action." The college, modeled after Bob Jones University, opened with an auspicious enrollment of two hundred but soon closed when Hargis was accused of sexual misconduct with students.[4] Fundamentalist radio broadcaster Carl McIntire started Shelton College in the mid-1960s at a seaside resort hotel in New Jersey as a training ground for his small Bible Presbyterian Church. He recruited students and generated contributions through a nationally syndicated radio show, "The Twentieth-Century Reformation Hour." Eventually his school's state accreditation was revoked after a bitter and protracted battle over academic standards. McIntire refused to permit the government to dictate curriculum.[5]

Overall, fundamentalist higher education has not greatly influenced American intellectual life or society. Most fundamentalist colleges have catered to rather small and typically separatist constituencies. Bob Jones University and Tennessee Temple University are the two largest and most successful. Even Moody Bible Institute is not widely known outside of fundamentalist and certainly evangelical circles. While higher education flourished in the United States after World War II, opening the floodgates of the academy to middle- and working-class students, fundamentalist schools still served a rather small group of true believers. Moreover, for every dozen or so attempts to establish a fundamentalist college, only two or three were successful.

Partly to survive, and partly because of changing cultural currents in America, most fundamentalist colleges and universities began by softening their fundamentalist rhetoric, academically professionalizing their curricula, and joining the movement toward mainstream evangelicalism. The most significant change was the transformation of Bible colleges and institutes into liberal arts colleges, but the academic professionalization of seminaries was also important. Marsden traced the latter in the case of Fuller Seminary, which maintained the fundamental beliefs of the evangelical faith while largely eliminating the anti-intellectualism, cultural separatism, and rhetorical belligerency that generally characterize militant Protestant fundamentalism in the United States.[6] This neo-evangelical impulse has elevated the academic status of many formerly fundamentalist institutions, from Wheaton College to Taylor University, but in the process it has changed their character both as educational institutions and as symbols of the rising status of evangelicals in American society.

This chapter suggests that it is time to reexamine the significance of fundamentalist higher education in America. A new style of fundamentalist higher education, softened by neo-evangelicalism but still committed to the fundamentals of the faith, is forming out of the seeds of old-fashioned fundamentalist higher education. To some extent Fuller Seminary foreshadowed the new style in the 1950s and 1960s. However, the new university-oriented evangelical higher education is organized around the integration of nonministerial professions with the fundamentals of the faith. Today it is championed by Jerry Falwell's Liberty University and M. G. "Pat" Robertson's CBN (Christian Broadcasting Network) University (CBNU), renamed Regent University in 1990. Although coming out of very different social and theological backgrounds—independent Baptist vs. contemporary charismatic renewal—the schools hold up similar academic ideals. However, some of the same trends can be seen even among the older, more belligerent and separatist schools like Bob Jones University and Tennessee Temple University. The differences between Liberty and Bob Jones are in degree of cultural co-optation and academic professionalization; they are the two faces of fundamentalist higher education. Both want to maintain the *fundamentals* of the faith, but Bob Jones University seeks to maintain *fundamentalism* as an expression of its commitment to cultural separatism and academic autonomy.

In spite of what fundamentalists might think, media technologies are not socially, culturally, or even theologically neutral. Partly for this reason, the new television-related universities, such as Liberty and Regent, are different institutions than separatist schools such as Bob Jones, which are less dependent on television for raising funds and building national constituencies. National, audience-supported television invariably shapes the ways these educational institutions see themselves and the ways they define themselves for the public. Just as most television programming is produced by no one in particular for everyone in general, universities that expand via the medium tend to establish a relatively broad constituency that does not share a clearly identifiable religious tradition. Such schools therefore emphasize the new and popular over the historic and the particular; they are motivated by a vision of the future much more than by the reality of the past. Bob Jones and Tennessee Temple, on the other hand, are beholden to relatively small and clearly defined constituencies that generally want to keep the schools on a militantly separatist track. They use media to maintain communication with constituencies and to "win souls," not to principally raise funds or to grow.

Fundamentalist schools of the 1920s and 1930s, often formed initially by independent-minded leaders and publicized via radio or print media, were able to establish their own "tradition" of nondenominational education. If nothing else, mass media enabled them to form quickly—far more rapidly than in the days of circuit riders, revivals, or even pamphleteering and book publishing. By comparison, the new "fundamental" universities, such as Liberty and Regent, are dynamic, adaptable organizations that may not need links to traditions or denominationally defined constituencies to survive or even to prosper. However, the lack of such links might impoverish their education as well. Some of these schools seem so easily to grab the latest educational fad—or even to start their own—that they can become too excessively market-driven for their own long-term good. Broadcast ministries enable universities such as Regent and Liberty to grow quickly and to fashion novel curricula, whereas scarce resources and long-standing constituencies prohibit most fundamentalist and neo-evangelical colleges from responding rapidly and dynamically to opportunities in the changing educational marketplace.

The rapid proliferation of home schooling and the growth of fundamentalist day schools have been widely examined by numerous scholars, but no one has seriously addressed the scope and impact of conservative Protestant colleges and universities. One reason, perhaps, is that many liberal scholars assume that "fundamentalist higher education" is an oxymoron. Given their own liberal education, they hold particular stereotypes of fundamentalism as separatist, anti-intellectual, dogmatic, authoritarian—characteristics which, they believe, could not possibly characterize genuine higher education. In addition, it seems obvious that fundamentalist higher education has not yet produced any noticeable impact on the broader academic community or on society in general. Finally, scholars might assume that fundamentalist higher education is merely one characteristic of transitory fundamentalist movements which will eventually disappear.

All three assumptions could be wrong. First, much fundamentalist higher education is no longer so anti-intellectual or anti-academic, even at a place like Bob Jones University. At the fundamental schools such as Liberty and especially Regent, academic dialogue and debate are alive, well, and even cherished. The new fundamental schools, strongly influenced by broader movements within evangelicalism, increasingly distinguish between the non-negotiable fundamentals of the faith—a few basic doctrines and beliefs—and academic epistemologies and professional practices. Philosopher Arthur Holmes at Wheaton in Illinois summarized this epistemology: "All truth is God's truth."[7] In short, the new "fundamentalism" disassociates the particular doctrinal or confessional fundamentals of the faith from the old epistemology, which summarily baptized or denounced particular professional practices and intellectual ideas. The strident militancy and intolerance of earlier fundamentalism has given way to a remarkably open-minded attitude toward learning, teaching, and education at the college and university levels.

Second, the new fundamental education will likely have significantly more impact on society because it is directed toward engaging and transforming the outside world rather than merely escaping from it or firing salvos at it. This is partly a result of the emphasis on professional education over ministry and "soul winning." At Liberty and Regent the real institutional struggles have been between old-style fundamentalists who tend to view the organization as a church, and the more academically professionalized staff who see it as a college or university. Although constituencies and founders sometimes cling to the ecclesiastical model, faculties and administrations increasingly look to higher education for their visions of institutional mission and organization. In this respect, fundamentalist schools such as Bob Jones are less progressive; education is much more clearly organized around the need to train "church" workers for administration and evangelism. Nevertheless, the rapid proliferation of nonministerial professional programs at these schools suggests that they, too, are being shaped significantly by academic trends in North America.

Third, the new fundamental higher education will not likely disappear quickly. It is better financed, more widely promoted, and increasingly better organized. With the help of national television, in the case of schools like Liberty and Regent, it has established itself as the hub of new transdenominational movements and organizations. If the schools avoid particular financial and administrative mistakes, they could establish significant endowments that would guarantee the long-term viability of the institutions. Moreover, if they carefully market their academic programs to the broader evangelical community—including evangelical-minded youth from mainstream Protestant and Roman Catholic churches—they will likely continue to grow and prosper, attracting students who would otherwise attend state universities, not fundamentalist colleges. On the other hand, what fundamentalist schools such as Bob Jones lack without the publicity of television, they make up for somewhat with faithful constituencies.

In short, the new fundamental higher education has been transformed by evangelicalism's more moderate style and more tolerant rhetoric. Less militant and belligerent, more open to academic discourse and debate, and suited to the professional goals and aspirations of middle- and upper-middle-class students and their families, this education is forming a new, more wealthy constituency while hanging on to the "fundamentals" of the faith. The new "gap" is not evangelistic workers, as it was in Moody's day, but evangelical professionals who are being trained to transform all corridors of society, from Wall Street to Madison Avenue and skid row. In this new gap lie both the strengths and weaknesses of the new fundamental education. Will these new workers for the Kingdom of God change the world or be co-opted by it? Will the new fundamental schools, some of which are not really so fundamentalist after all, hang on to the fundamentals of the faith in the midst of rapid academic professionalization and worldly success?

This study of the new fundamental higher education shows clearly that not all conservative Protestants completely reject modernization. In fact, they often seek to use modern ideas and technologies to challenge aspects of modernization. The picture here is one of fundamentalist action through curricular changes, funding innovations, and academic professionalization—all for the purpose of making the new education more popular and more explicitly religious. In terms of Majid Tehranian's patterns of response to modernity, we may say that the new fundamental higher education ironically seeks to demodernize aspects of modern society by using the latest educational methods and contemporary media technologies to train a new generation of believers who will restructure society into a more biblically "natural" place for all humankind.

It appears that for some of the most revolutionary and popular fundamental universities, the mass media, especially broadcasting, cable and satellites, are crucial tools for accomplishing their goal of limited demodernization. For one thing, among these educators the mass media symbolize power and authority. In a society where they have been largely disenfranchised from the existing channels of social and cultural influence, from schools to mass media, the latest media technologies represent a means of reclaiming lost authority. The media create the illusion, if not the reality, of power. For another thing, the mass media are indeed a crucial means for North American religious minorities to organize themselves—to become national groups or movements with identifiable leaders, to establish common concerns and desires, and especially to raise funds in the name of the movement. The new fundamental higher education does not have to use cable or satellite communication, but such media have enabled it to organize more quickly and successfully.

Bible Institutes and Bible Colleges

Formed prior to the rise of early twentieth-century Protestant fundamentalism, Bible schools and Bible institutes became the seeds of Bible colleges, evangelical liberal arts colleges, and eventually even universities. Fundamentalist leaders established and transformed their educational institutions to meet the changing needs of the fundamentalist movement, on the one hand, and to take advantage of broader changes in American culture and higher education, on the other. From the beginning, fundamentalist higher education was shaped by both the perceived educational needs of fundamentalists and the wider educational trends in American society.

Brereton suggests that no other set of institutions was more significant in the development of conservative evangelicalism than Bible schools.[8] Started in the 1880s and 1890s, many of them became regional centers of fundamentalism during the religiously turbulent 1920s and 1930s. Bible school leaders were often popular educators who not only taught day and night classes, but frequently instructed students of all ages via periodicals, correspondence, radio, and extension classes.[9] The original impetus behind Bible schools was primarily urban evangelism. They were generally established by theologically conservative ministers and evangelists who believed that evangelism should "reach beyond comfortable congregations to appeal to the urban masses by dispensing with pew rentals, elaborate sermon styles and formal worship." Like their liberal counterparts who espoused the Social Gospel, Moody and the other architects of successful Bible schools hoped to widen the churches' scope of service by "transforming them into virtual city missions."[10] Between 1880 and 1920, 32 Bible schools were started in the United States. In the next two decades an additional 43 were established.[11]

Even into the 1930s and 1940s, fundamentalist parents had few acceptable educational options beyond Bible schools. Some decided to send their children to the more mainstream evangelical schools such as Grove City College in Pennsylvania and Taylor University in Upland, Indiana. There were only a few fundamentalist liberal arts colleges, such as Wheaton and Bob Jones (then located in Cleveland, Tennessee).[12] These colleges prospered, but not nearly as much as the more practical Bible schools. By 1948 there were 120 Bible institutes and colleges in the United States with an estimated enrollment of fifteen thousand students.[13]

In 1947 a group of Bible colleges formed their own accrediting organization, the Association of Bible Colleges, as a way of recognizing their distinctive emphasis on Bible teaching and limited liberal arts instruction. The regular regional associations would not accredit Bible colleges, which were caught between "demanding a sufficient study of the Bible to give [a] thorough grounding in Christian thinking," and "meeting the requirements of the secular accrediting agencies."[14] As one of the supporters of separate Bible college accreditation put it, the schools suffered from the "stigma of being short-cut training schools rather than educational institutions."[15] Accreditation further legitimized Bible colleges academically and boosted the combined institute and college enrollment in 1960 to about twenty-five thousand.

During the 1970s and 1980s, however, the Bible college movement waned under the weight of educationally related social and cultural changes in the United States. Most importantly, growing numbers of students and their parents saw college and university education as a stepping stone to obtaining a high-paying job and building a career. "The materialistic mood of the times has students thinking more of well-paying jobs than of service," lamented the president of one Bible college.[16] Some Bible colleges hoped that the booming fundamentalist Christian day school movement alone would build enrollments in their teacher education programs. Others responded by broadening their own academic missions to attract a wide array of career-minded students interested in programs in nursing, journalism, missionary aviation, linguistics, music, and other applied areas.[17] But by the late 1980s the overall prospects for fundamentalist Bible colleges looked rather bleak. Between 1981 and 1987, 6 Bible colleges listed by the American Association of Bible Colleges closed, while about another 20 of them were in serious financial jeopardy. Only about one-quarter of the 112 accredited Bible colleges were fiscally sound in the late 1980s.[18] Some of the older Bible schools refashioned themselves into separatist colleges and universities, while others clung hopefully to the Bible college model. In both cases, however, the surviving old-style fundamentalist institutions carefully cultivated rather small and generally separatistic constituencies from coalitions of independent churches. Bob Jones and Tennessee Temple, the two major survivors, both changed their names to universities while courting the support of the independent Baptist churches of the South and Midwest.

The overall trend was clear: fundamentalist Bible colleges became liberal arts colleges and then sometimes universities. Along the way they generally became less fundamentalist, which meant less anti-intellectual, less separatist, and more academically respectable in mainstream higher education. One list of fundamentalist colleges in 1983, compiled by a fundamentalist educator, included only 32 "militant" schools such as Bob Jones (then the only one calling itself a "university") and Temple Baptist Bible College (later Tennessee Temple University). Enrollments were usually between two hundred and five hundred students, and most of the schools sought either Bible college accreditation or no accreditation at all. The same list included 65 "moderate" fundamentalist schools, including the Assemblies of God's Evangel College, Hyles Anderson College, Moody Bible Institute, and Liberty Baptist College (later called Liberty University). These had larger enrollments than the militant schools and generally sought accreditation either as Bible colleges or sometimes as liberal arts colleges. Finally, the list added 48 "modified" fundamentalist schools such as Wheaton, Gordon, and Oral Roberts University.[19] According to a different classification, in 1985 there remained only 15 fundamentalist Bible colleges and 19 fundamentalist liberal arts colleges, compared with 54 evangelical Bible colleges and 36 evangelical liberal arts colleges.[20]

The most striking thing about such lists of fundamentalist schools is the inverse relationship between militancy and academic status and success. In the 1980s, militant fundamentalist colleges remained rather small and virtually invisible in the wider academic community. Most of them were Bible colleges, whereas nearly all of the "modified" fundamentalist schools were liberal arts colleges. Militant schools such as Bob Jones University served small constituencies and received little publicity. Their faculty did not normally attend traditional academic meetings or even belong to mainstream professional associations. Moreover, the U.S. Department of Education did not receive information from most of them, and they were not even listed (with seven exceptions) in the Carnegie Foundation's classification of institutions of higher education.[21] The "modified" schools were typically larger, accredited by regional associations, and significantly more visible in professional academic associations and in professional publications.

By the 1980s, then, it was clear that old-style fundamentalist higher education had thrown its lot largely with the Bible college movement and that the movement was in serious trouble. It peaked in the 1940s, when 66 new Bible colleges were started, and began declining precipitously in the 1980s.[22] Students and parents wanted more than a Bible-centric education, even if they still held strongly to fundamentalist beliefs and life styles. They wanted an education for success in life, and in middle-class America that meant more than Bible school or even Bible college. Accreditation was increasingly important, even to many fundamentalists. No amount of publicity or promotion could effectively sell fundamentalist higher education to parents who wanted "the best" for their children. And the best higher education was a more worldly, less separatist, and more academically respectable college or university. Caught in the trends of academic professionalization and the winds of American culture, fundamentalist higher education increasingly found solace, hope, and especially success in more broadly evangelical institutions. The major exception was Bob Jones University, which flaunted its separatism in the face of major obstacles to its continued success. It still represents the old face of fundamentalist higher education.

Bob Jones University and Old-Fashioned Fundamentalism

In 1967 *McCall's* magazine surveyed college newspaper editors across the country about their perceptions of various schools. Among the more humorous categories addressed in the survey was the "most square university." Bob Jones University (BJU) in Greenville, South Carolina easily won that award. In a revealing response to the school's unusual publicity, Bob Jones III, then the university's vice-president, complimented both *McCall's* and the college newspaper editors: "These college newspaper editors have hit Bob Jones University square on the nose. Their 'poking insult' is a very true description of Bob Jones University. This institution is square and would have reason to be ashamed if anyone thought otherwise."[23] The four thousand students at BJU agreed, bursting into thunderous applause when the poll results were announced in chapel.[24] As the school's promotional literature says repeatedly, BJU may indeed be the "world's most unusual university."

If the conservative Bible institute and Bible college movement comprised the educational arm of North American Protestant fundamentalism in the United States, BJU became the most visible fruit of that movement. While never called a Bible college, BJU took much of its fundamentalist spirit from the movement. BJU and a handful of other schools thereby stood like anachronistic archipelagoes in a sea of educational and social change. In the background at BJU were always the four central tenets of American fundamentalism: separatism, biblical inerrancy, premillennialism, and evangelism.

In the foreground, BJU adopted new programs and vigorously promoted tough academic standards among its students, but it refused to compromise with American higher education in any way that would detract from its preeminent goal of promoting a militant style of fundamentalism. It even shunned academic accreditation. BJU would rather fight than change, even when its tax-exempt status was challenged by the Internal Revenue Service in a case that went all the way to the United States Supreme Court. By the 1980s the result was a thriving school of about four thousand students with a small constituency that valued religious truth more than academic dialogue or inquiry, and rigorous instruction more than scholarship or research.

The philosophy and practices of BJU cannot be understood apart from the separatist ideals of the school's three visionaries: evangelist Bob Jones, Sr., founder and for many years president; Bob Jones II, a gifted actor and student of Shakespeare who became chancellor; and Bob Jones III, a practical administrator who eventually took over the school's presidency. In his book *Cornbread and Caviar,* Bob Jones II called the "scriptural teaching on separation . . . the very foundation and basis of a fundamental witness and testimony."[25] In other words, by the holiness of their own lives fundamentalists are to be witnesses to the truths of conservative doctrine and behavior. Moreover, from their separatist citadels, fundamentalists are to militantly defend "biblical authority and infallibility" by attacking "the enemies of the faith."[26] BJU's brand of fundamentalism always implies such defensive and offensive strategies.

Oddly enough, in fundamentalist higher education these strategies naturally move schools in paradoxical directions. On the one hand, BJU and its conservative counterparts such as Pensacola Christian College, Faith Baptist Bible College, and Maranatha Baptist Bible College seek to "teach the faith." As Bob Jones, Sr., used to say, "If you will give God your heart He will 'comb the kinks out of your head.'"[27] This requires the largely uncritical dissemination of literal biblical truths by professors, administrators, chapel speakers, and others. As Bob Jones II put it, no subject is so important in the curriculum that it must be included if the school cannot find a "dedicated, born-again, Bible believing Christian who can teach it."[28] This doesn't leave much room for a discipline like archeology.

Faith comes before reason, religion before academics, and personal conversion before formal education. All of this is meant to ensure that believers know where they stand religiously before they are trained academically. Largely for this reason BJU, even though it is not a Bible college, requires students to take at least one Bible course every semester, demands chapel attendance, and generally controls the personal lifestyle of its students, including dating practices, which are strictly regulated. Challenges to stated beliefs and practices are nothing short of disloyalty, which Bob Jones, Sr., called an "unpardonable sin."[29]

On the other hand, BJU seeks to prepare its students to militantly defend, not just to live and know, fundamentalism. Unlike the historic Anabaptists, these fundamentalists will openly contend for the faith even when their own separatist communities are not directly under outside attack by critics. The Creed of the College, part of an unchangeable charter, specifically says that BJU's mission is to combat "all atheistic, agnostic, pagan, and so-called scientific adulterations of the Gospel."[30] This broader mandate required far more than doctrinal knowledge and behavioral purity; it demanded a fairly broad, liberal education that examined and evaluated secular ideas and social trends.

Instead of emphasizing this type of liberal education, however, BJU focused on communication skills rather than apologetics. The school strongly encouraged students to take speech lessons offered free as personal tutorials. It further established a regional debate team that competed successfully against many schools. In the 1950s the school started one of the most technically advanced film programs in the world. Boasting state-of-the-art equipment, a modern production studio, and significant operating capital, BJU's motion picture instruction was ranked with leading universities such as the University of California at Los Angeles and the University of Southern California by the Society of Motion Picture and Television Engineers. BJU's own radio stations and Bob Jones II's syndicated television program were also important vehicles for publicly defending fundamentalism.[31] The fact remained, however, that the university's emphasis on communication skills was not balanced with serious academic inquiry and open intellectual discussion and dialogue. Such openness would be a challenge to fundamentalism.

Founder Bob Jones, Sr., was an early twentieth-century evangelist known for his wit and wisdom, not his intellectual prowess. Hardly anti-intellectual, but certainly not a scholar, he was no great supporter of ivory tower academicians. Jones valued practical ideas about how to live the fundamentalist life; he left behind after his death dozens of short sayings that followers found helpful for guidance in the complex modern world: "When in doubt, play safe"; "No man is *high born* until he is *born on high*"; "Don't sacrifice the *permanent* on the altar of the *immediate*"; "It is a sin to do *less* than your best."[32]

At the same time, the evangelist saw clearly that battles over religious faith often took place in the world of ideas visited by the modern academy. His venture into university administration was purely pragmatic: to establish a "safe" school to help young people keep their faith while learning how to combat the "atheistic drift in educational institutions," especially evolutionary thought.[33] But for the sake of academic integrity he would not settle for a second-rate school that pandered to anti-intellectualism or cultural unsophistication. He sought to "dispel the idea that is going around that if you have old-time religion, you have to have a greasy nose, dirty fingernails, baggy pants, and that you must shine your own shoes." Jones wanted a school that would have high academic standards and would have "an old-time country mourner's bench where folks can get right with God."[34]

This unusual combination of old-fashioned fundamentalist religion and high cultural and academic standards set the direction for the development of BJU under all three Jones administrations. The emphasis on fundamentalist religion would keep the school "safe," while the high cultural and academic standards would safely make it respectable. First in Panama City, Florida, in 1927, when the school was founded, then in Cleveland, Tennessee, in 1933, and from 1947 at the current Greenville campus, the school charted an interdenominational course designed to appeal principally to the fundamentalist families of first-generation college youth.[35] Commonsense Christianity and liberal arts instruction were innovatively combined to assure the safety of fundamentalist youth while creating a cultured atmosphere.

As one reporter aptly put it, BJU had put a "red carpet over the sawdust trail."[36] From the early years to the present, this combination of old-style religion and new-style liberal arts education created an attractive ethos for many fundamentalists who wanted to transcend the limited academic vision and cultural myopia of Bible institutes and Bible colleges. In fact, Jones, Sr., purposely never called the school a Bible college; it was Bob Jones College beginning in 1927, long before most fundamentalist liberal arts colleges emerged from the bible college movement.[37] Jones was ahead of his time in stressing music and speech training as part of the fabric of the red carpet.

Bob Jones II later became the champion of the arts on campus, criticizing the puritanical view of culture as "dull and gloomy" and vigorously endorsing a classicist view of culture centered on the drama of Shakespeare, which became a focus of public life at the university.[38] BJU eventually established its own opera association and even began a university art museum that by 1990 included thirty galleries of some of the finest European religious (especially baroque) art in the Western world.[39] And there would be no jazz, rock, or hillbilly music on the university's radio stations.[40] As Louis Gasper put it, BJU promoted "Art without Bohemianism."[41]

In spite of the classicist emphasis on the arts at BJU, there is little evidence that the school deserves the title "university." First, about one-quarter of the students still major in religion.[42] The emphasis on Christian and lay ministry is still strong on campus, in spite of the fact that in 1978 about 18 percent of the students majored in business, another 15 percent in arts and sciences, and 10 percent in fine and performing arts.[43] Second, BJU does not foster much advanced research or scholarship on campus, although it has a few faculty who are known in their fields. Teaching loads are very high, and faculty will even volunteer to teach additional courses. There is little incentive for scholarship. BJU promoted itself as a "university" both to enhance its academic status and to reflect accurately its wide array of programs, majors, degrees, and certificates offered by six "schools": Religion, Arts and Science, Fine Arts, Education, Business Administration, and Applied Studies.

At BJU the drive for academic status is always kept in check by the demands of the constituency and administration for a predictable education in tune with old-style fundamentalism. Safety is maintained in three ways: careful recruiting of like-minded faculty, administrative autocracy, and non-accreditation. The result is a truly fundamentalist institution which has little or no impact on the wider academic community in the United States.

In the name of fundamentalist quality control, BJU is one of the most academically incestuous colleges or universities in the country. The best way for BJU to safely recruit like-minded faculty is to hire its own graduates. Bob Jones II learned that the hard way, dismissing a number of faculty in the school's early years.[44] In 1990, 75 percent of the 322 undergraduate faculty at BJU had at least one degree from the university.[45] Moreover, a mere 14 percent of the faculty had doctorates, and about one-third of them had been awarded by BJU. Even only 29 percent of the graduate faculty held doctorates.[46] The school apparently hires faculty on the basis of institutional loyalty and fidelity as much as on academic reputation or status, although it expects all faculty to be competent teachers.

BJU's administrative autocracy is both legendary and generally well liked at the school.[47] Each of the "Dr. Bobs," as the three Bob Joneses are called on campus, has been a benevolent dictator over virtually every aspect of university life. The school is not run by the faculty, and terms such as "academic freedom," "tenure," and "faculty governance" are simply irrelevant. The Dr. Bobs have been patriarchal leaders in the BJU "family," which has no room for rebellion or disloyalty. Students and staff go to BJU knowing that they must obey the family rules and follow the guidance of their campus fathers. BJU represents as close to a religious monarchy as one finds in fundamentalist higher education, and the monarchy is vested with political as well as ceremonial authority.

BJU's refusal to seek institutional accreditation has probably been its toughest decision in the name of fundamentalist integrity and purity. Accreditation would surely enhance the school's academic reputation, make it easier for graduates and transfer students to receive full credit for their work at BJU, provide additional potential sources of student recognition and support (such as the National Merit Scholars program), and convince some parents to send their children to BJU instead of to one of the competing fundamentalist institutions. But BJU has always had a vocal constituency that sincerely believes all types of "worldly" compromises are sinful—including academic association with nonfundamentalist schools, which accreditation would involve. In spite of the potential liabilities, the administration has maintained that accreditation is too great a threat to the school's independence. As Bob Jones II put it, "No academic recognition or approval is essential enough for Bob Jones University to become unequally yoked together with unbelievers or to sacrifice a biblical principle in order to achieve it. To join an academic association is to sacrifice God's blessing through disobedience."[48] By refusing even to seek accreditation, BJU has been able to maintain greater control over its admissions standards, curricula, faculty compensation policies, library resources, and the like.

Nevertheless, the school is adequately self-conscious about its nonaccredited status to publish a promotional booklet titled *Why Bob Jones University Was Founded—Why It Has Never Sought Membership in a Regional Educational Association*. In that publication the school argues against unholy yokes and strongly in favor of its own record of academic accomplishments. "Our opinion," it says, "is that the only way any educational institution should be judged or accredited is by the results the institution produces." The document then cites the following: BJU's graduating education majors score above the national average in national teachers' examinations; the university's accounting majors do the same on the certified public accountants' examination; the school's Unusual Films productions achieved national and international honors; and students at BJU have won top honors in state and regional competition in arts, music, and speech.[49] The fact is that BJU's graduates are indeed highly sought by numerous employers, including the big-six accounting firms and Christian schools across the country. BJU is probably the largest supplier of fundamentalist elementary and secondary school teachers in the country.

It appears that in spite of its separatist style, BJU indeed produces successful students and graduates. These students are unlikely to be as liberally educated as most university undergraduates in the United States. There is an obvious dearth of theoretical and philosophical inquiry in many majors at BJU. For example, in Radio and Television Broadcasting there are twenty-five "applied" courses, but not one which is concerned principally with theory, criticism, history, or ethics.[50] Nor are BJU students as likely to be "educated" about the worldly ways of contemporary university student culture, from drugs to sexual promiscuity. BJU does not permit the establishment of any "outside" organizations on campus, including fraternities, sororities, and honor societies. It does have its own literary societies. Also, the school does not participate in intercollegiate sports, preferring instead to focus on a campus-wide, highly competitive intramural sports program. BJU redirects students' natural rebelliousness and curiosity in more pragmatically productive ways than do other universities .

In short, BJU emphasizes self-discipline and self-motivation, two traits frequently lacking among American undergraduates. Regardless of the particular content of their education, BJU students learn habits and attitudes which will be enormously helpful in becoming an academic and professional success. As Bob Jones III put it, "Our product is superior on the basis of their ability to compete. . . . They're desired because they're honest, they're dedicated, they're disciplined, and they produce."[51]

North American fundamentalists are notorious for their bickering and infighting, but a visitor to BJU would hardly know it. BJU directs its salvos off campus. As Bob Jones III put it in the university catalog, the school opposes "all atheistic, agnostic, and humanistic attacks upon the Scripture." It also combats the "so-called 'Modernists,' 'Liberal,' 'Neo-Orthodox,' positions" and protests "the unscriptural compromise of the 'New Evangelicals' and the unscriptural practices of the 'Charismatics.' "[52] These common enemies, along with the paternalistic and monarchical authority on campus, foster an unusually strong sense of collective identity at BJU.

Hiring and compensation practices further the sense that BJU is really a family, not merely an academic institution. BJU employees, from student workers to faculty, administrators and maintenance people, are motivated more by a sense of divine mission and familial allegiance than by professional status or personal financial gain. In fact, BJU has very unusual compensation practices which might be considered socialistic by some observers. No one works for a wage or salary equivalent to what they might make outside the family; instead they are paid according to their needs.[53] For faculty, this means salaries of about one-third of those paid in other universities.[54] However, the university normally provides meals in an enormous dining hall and campus housing for faculty and their families. Moreover, BJU provides medical care, including the delivery of children, at is own one hundred–bed hospital.[55] Faculty spouses are expected to work for the school as part of this compensation package.[56] After all, they too are part of the family.

Among other things, BJU's unusual compensation system is a remarkably effective way of keeping down tuition and other costs even in the face of the school's loss of is tax-exempt status in 1982. For the 1990–91 school year, the tuition per semester was only $1,650, and room and board another $1,590.[57] This may appear expensive to some parents of BJU students—after all, many students are first-generation college students—but in reality the costs are incredibly low for a private college or university, and even lower than state universities. Most amazing of all, BJU operates almost totally on tuition income. It rejects all forms of government support, both institutional and student support, and has never sought a large endowment to subsidize operating costs. The "family" ethos of BJU faculty, staff, and students drives down educational costs by stressing institutional allegiance and personal loyalty over other values.

BJU's family includes over fifty thousand former students.[58] The Jones families spend considerable time cultivating alumni support and maintaining strong relations with like-minded pastors and secondary school teachers. BJU's *Faith for the Family* magazine, which had a circulation of over seventy thousand in the mid-1980s, kept the school and its on-campus family in the minds and hearts of supporters around the world.[59] However, the BJU family grew primarily because of student recruiting by graduates who pastored fundamentalist churches or taught in Christian schools. Unlike most American colleges and universities, BJU hardly needed a professional admissions staff. As long as it could graduate enthusiastic pastors and Christian school teachers, the family would grow on its own. By 1957 BJU alone graduated more than one-fifth of all teachers who graduated from South Carolina colleges and universities.[60] And BJU graduated in the late 1950s more ministerial candidates than any other school in the country.[61] These graduates shepherded thousands of potential BJU students in later years, such as the early 1980s when enrollment peaked at about five thousand.[62]

In marketing terms, BJU has successfully positioned itself as the major fundamentalist university in the country. It became the mother of thousands of fundamentalist elementary and secondary school teachers—graduates who often use textbooks published by BJU Press.[63] After all, as Bob Jones, Sr., warned, disloyalty was an unpardonable sin. Graduates who wavered from the fundamentalist faith might suddenly receive a letter from BJU informing them they were no longer alumni in good standing. They were effectively excommunicated from the BJU family, as if it were its own ecclesiastical body.

BJU has two governing boards, one that approves major administrative decisions and the other, a nonvoting "Cooperating Board," that merely extends the BJU family by recognizing important fundamentalists with whom BJU shares ideals. The most widely known member of the latter is Irish fundamentalist Ian Paisley, to whom BJU gave an honorary degree while he was in prison. In 1980 Paisley, Bob Jones, Sr., and others organized the Second World Congress of Fundamentalists. According to the two leaders, the purpose of the meeting was to "give united witness to the fact that there are thousands around the world who have not bowed the knee to compromise, who stand strongly in defense of the Scripture, and who are opposed to 'liberalism,' Romanism, false religions and heresies."[64] This extended family knows where it stands.

It frequently seems that fundamentalists are able to generate considerably more publicity than warranted by their relatively meager power in modern society. But because they are often so openly militant, fundamentalists tend to be at newsworthy points of history—at critical times and places where history is being made. Their militant style frequently generates media coverage.

BJU made history in the 1980s when the school became entangled in a series of complex legal suits that eventually led to a case before the United States Supreme Court. Since 1909, because of congressional action, private schools and colleges have been exempt from paying taxes.[65] The seeds of the BJU case were sown in 1970, when the Internal Revenue Service decided it could no longer give tax-exempt status to any private school with racially discriminatory admissions policies. BJU was one of those schools until 1971, when it decided to admit married blacks while instituting on campus a policy banning interracial dating and marriage among students. Four years later, the Supreme Court ruled against racial exclusion from private schools, and BJU began admitting unmarried blacks as well.[66]

In 1982 the IRS revoked BJU's tax-exempt status, but the university fought back on the grounds that its religious freedoms were being compromised.[67] BJU's attorney, William B. Ball, stated the university's position before the Supreme Court: "Bob Jones University, as an exclusively religious organization, qualifies as a tax-exempt organization. It is a pervasively religious ministry whose raison d'etre is the propagation of religious faith. Its rule against interracial dating is a matter of religious belief and practice."[68] Many nonfundamentalist religious groups filed friend-of-the-court briefs on behalf of BJU's right to establish its own policies.[69] Careful to take issue with BJU's racial theology, evangelicals nonetheless spoke forcefully against the way BJU was being treated by the courts.[70] The high court ruled eight to one against BJU, which continues to operate without tax-exempt status.[71]

BJU spent over $800,000 in court costs and legal fees to unsuccessfully protect its preferred tax status.[72] In the strong tradition of fundamentalist militancy, it was simply unwilling to back down before the high court. Racial separation was a matter of religious principle, so there was no way to compromise. Legal experts disagreed over the implications of the case, which was widely applauded by antidiscrimination groups and criticized by religious organizations.[73] But there was no appeal. The Court had spoken, and BJU's only acceptable recourse was to maintain its position that God intends the races to be separate. In the eyes of old-style fundamentalists, universities are religious first and educational second. That is what William Ball argued before the court, and that is what distinguishes the old-style fundamentalist higher education from its more liberal counterparts in what Bob Jones III critically called the "New Evangelicalism."

Liberty University and the Impact of Television
on Fundamentalist Higher Education

The rapid growth of televangelist Jerry Falwell's Liberty University in the 1970s and 1980s is a remarkable story of how quickly fundamentalist higher education can be willingly transformed by the drive for academic prestige and institutional success combined with the financial pressures of big-time televangelism. Built from contributions generated through television and direct-mail solicitations, Liberty relied on ministry funding until 1989, when it first became self-sufficient.[74]

Liberty sought from the beginning to become a fully accredited liberal arts college and even a "world-class university."[75] Falwell envisioned a large university offering dozens of majors for career-oriented students who would help transform the world by becoming influential leaders. The college would provide "high academic standards in an atmosphere of Christian learning with emphasis on practical application and spiritual development."[76] Falwell understood the value of a strong core curriculum, clearly articulated lifestyle codes for staff and students, a major intercollegiate athletics program, and especially a strongly pietistic but nondenominational atmosphere. The school's mission was to raise "up a generation of leaders who are educationally superior and whose strength of character and commitment to absolutes will be felt in key positions in all areas of our society."[77] Falwell wrote that the "Christian school movement is the movement of the future. We need a spiritual army of young people who are pro-life, pro-moral, and pro-American. We need to train a generation of young people who can carry this nation into the twenty-first century with dynamic Christian leadership."[78]

Liberty began as Lynchburg Baptist College in 1971, the same year that Falwell launched his coast-to-coast television ministry, the "Old-Time Gospel Hour."[79] The television program would help build the college, Falwell hoped, into a fifty thousand–student university which would compete athletically and academically with the best universities in America. "I am certain that we will become a world-class university training champions for Christ in every important field of study," wrote Falwell. "What Notre Dame is to Roman Catholic youths and what Brigham Young is to Mormon young people, Liberty University will become to the Bible-believing fundamentalist and evangelical students of America."[80] This was hardly the separatist model of the old-fashioned schools.

In order to get the school established, Falwell needed a smaller, more accessible constituency which would provide financial support and especially students. The school would have to appeal to the constituency Falwell knew best—independent Baptist fundamentalists. He hired Elmer Towns, former president of Winnipeg Bible College and member of the accreditation committee of the American Association of Bible Colleges, to create an "arts" college (the phrase "liberal arts" was unacceptable) which would appeal to this group.[81] "Many of the schools and churches that were once true to God have gone into liberalism," said Falwell. "As a pastor I find it impossible to financially support any program that, in turn, supports liberal professors and instructors. Here at Liberty Baptist College, every professor, instructor, administrator, and staff member must subscribe to the articles of faith before he or she is employed. If, during their employment, they depart from this declaration of faith, they are immediately dismissed."[82] From the beginning, Liberty was to be an alternative to the humanistic educational philosophies and methods that Falwell believed saturated public education. "The educational philosophy of the modern world permeates the lives of our young people," he lamented, "and we see them controlled by a rationalistic approach where there are no absolutes, no right and wrong. . . . It is man-centered. As a result, we live in a century of conflict and revolution. On every hand we see our society crumbling because of national decay and moral deterioration."[83]

The first classes were held at Thomas Road Baptist Church, of which Falwell was senior pastor, and houses nearby were purchased for student residences—a campus plan based on the model of Tennessee Temple.[84] Then the church bought the downtown Virginian Hotel and renovated six floors for four hundred student residences. Later it rented a high school and a block of rooms from a local motel.[85] Finally, the church began construction of the master campus on Candler Mountain (later renamed Liberty Mountain), a beautiful five thousand–acre tract purchased for $1.25 million from U.S. Gypsum in the late 1960s.[86] "It was our dream," wrote Falwell in his autobiography, "that one day God would use our television ministry to create and support that great educational complex on Liberty Mountain with its accredited university, graduate schools, and a seminary."[87]

In spite of the conservative Baptist constituency and the vocationally oriented, Bible college model, Liberty was not conceived of as merely a training ground for church work or missions. In the conservative Baptist tradition, missions meant evangelism or "soul winning." Falwell and Towns were deeply committed to that goal for Thomas Road Baptist Church, but they believed that evangelism was not an adequate purpose for establishing a highly respected university. Moreover, there were plenty of conservative and even fundamentalist Bible colleges in the United States and especially the South, and the enrollments of many of them were declining steadily.[88] Liberty would serve the church and the cause of worldwide evangelization indirectly by training leaders for service in all areas of life, especially the professions. The school would remain under the authority of the church, and all faculty would have to abide by the doctrinal statement of Thomas Road Baptist Church, but the university would be far more than a Bible school. Liberty would "save" society by preparing students for careers in all of the major professions, not just church work. In this manner the professional goals of students and parents could be harmonized with the religious thrust of the university. The fundamental beliefs of the faith could be maintained in the midst of rapid academic professionalization.

As planned, in the mid-1970s, Falwell and Towns quickly transformed Liberty from a Bible college to a liberal arts college, but not without criticism from some fundamentalists. In 1977 it hired thirty-eight new liberal arts faculty to supplement the existing ones in religion and a few other disciplines. Members of Bible Baptist Fellowship, a nondenominational group of fundamentalist Baptists, criticized Falwell for the apparent "liberal" direction of the school and even for Falwell's goal of seeking accreditation. These separatists felt that accreditation would accommodate the school to the winds of academic secularization.[89] More moderate fundamentalists, on the other hand, often quietly supported Liberty's goal of providing an accredited education in the context of a conservative campus life. In the early years the vast majority of Liberty students were first-generation college students from families that highly valued academics as a way to become professionally successful in the world.[90]

The school's strong commitment to conservative campus life and its mandated church involvement convinced many parents and pastors that Liberty was truly fundamentalist. Liberty required all students to complete an approved "Christian Service assignment" for every semester they were registered as full-time students. Freshman normally had to register for Christian Service Orientation classes, while other students fulfilled the requirement by working at Thomas Road or any theologically similar church in Lynchburg.[91] Liberty also required noncommuting students to join Thomas Road Church, to participate in scheduled devotional times in the residence halls, and to attend thrice-weekly chapel services.[92] Students were prohibited from "immoral behaviors" such as drinking and smoking. Campus dress codes required women to wear their "Sunday best" every day in the tradition of the Southern finishing school.[93] In 1989 Liberty even instituted the nation's first mandatory drug-testing program for students.[94] Students were often the biggest defenders of Liberty's lifestyle rules and campus regulations.[95]

Liberty's relatively unique combination of increasingly rigorous academics and Christian atmosphere attracted growing numbers of students from nonfundamentalist backgrounds, especially the more conservative wing of the fourteen million–member Southern Baptist Convention (SBC). Generally speaking, Southern Baptists are Southern Baptists first and Baptists second, and will usually attend a Southern Baptist college or university over an independent institution. The battles between conservative and moderate factions within the SBC in the 1980s coincided with Liberty's rapid growth to about five thousand on-campus students in 1989. Falwell and Liberty cultivated supporters from among the disenchanted conservatives in the SBC. He wrote critically about SBC schools in a special issue of his *Fundamentalist Journal* in 1989: "Schools founded to train pastors and missionaries had become 'high places' of idolatrous intellectual pursuits."[96] Liberty was able to attract Southern Baptist students whose parents were unhappy with some of the liberal trends within SBC colleges but who wanted their children to attend a fully accredited school which would prepare them for a career.[97] To them, a school like BJU was simply unacceptable. Liberty's academic emphasis appealed to these and other nonfundamentalist and moderately fundamentalist students and their parents, who were more likely to have attended colleges themselves compared with independent fundamentalist Baptists. By 1989 about 30 percent of all Liberty students were Southern Baptists, and slightly more were independent Baptists. Moreover, children of some of the SBC leadership attended Liberty.[98]

Academic integrity was essential for Liberty to attract Southern Baptists and moderate independents who might otherwise attend respected Baptist universities such as Baylor or Furman. Although the requirements were later relaxed, in the beginning

Liberty required all students to take two semesters of English, history, literature, mathematics, and speech, as well as biology, psychology, and sociology. It also required students to take courses in theology, although that was later changed to Bible courses.[99] Perhaps more important, Falwell and other university administrators spoke repeatedly to church and community groups of Liberty's academic excellence. They created an upbeat rhetoric of success about the university that appealed to parents and students alike. Liberty's first full-time professor, Elmer Towns, called it an "I'm gonna be a winner" attitude.[100]

Liberty's academic competition eventually shifted from the more fundamentalistic colleges and Bible colleges to community colleges and state universities.[101] In the early years it competed for students against fundamentalist schools such as BJU and Tennessee Temple. Then it began competing with more moderate conservative liberal arts colleges such as Cedarville and Wheaton.[102] By the mid-1980s it was clear that Liberty was no longer competing very directly with the more militant and even most of the more moderate fundamentalist schools.[103] At the same time, about half the university's board of trustees was made up of Southern Baptists while the rest were independent Baptists. The academic quality of applicants for admission increased steadily during the period, also reflecting the university's broadening student base.

Liberty was never denominational or sectarian in admissions. It remained committed to an "open-door" policy that evaluated students more on the basis of their "moral behavior and character" and "personal testimony for the Lord Jesus Christ" than on the basis of religious affiliation or even high school or previous college work. (These are fundamentals shared with evangelicals, but which are insufficient to be considered fundamentalism.) Liberty welcomed any student who could affirm its doctrinal statement. It also established a successful assistance program to help marginal admissions and an honors program for outstanding students. In short, Liberty was becoming all things to all conservatives, who increasingly perceived it as an island of academic integrity and excitement in the middle of an ocean of collegiate liberalism, on the one hand, and second-rate fundamentalist academic separatism, on the other. Few of the more moderate fundamentalist colleges could successfully compete with Liberty as the university defined itself in those terms on television, in periodicals, and from the pulpits that Falwell used across the nation.

Amid such rapid growth and changes in institutional character, faculty governance was perennially an issue at Liberty. Clearly Liberty was Falwell's school, but primarily because he was founder and senior pastor of Thomas Road. Liberty was officially owned and operated by the church, which in 1967 had formed a subsidiary called Old Time Gospel Hour Incorporated, which enabled the church to circumvent Virginia law prohibiting churches from owning more than twenty acres of property.[104] Through such an arrangement the church could control the university. The pastors and deacons of Thomas Road were the highest officials of the university. In the early days of the university the faculty were even officially part of the pastoral staff of Thomas Road, but in the 1980s that designation was reserved for the religion faculty, while other faculty were considered merely part of the "leadership" of the church. Faculty could participate in other churches, although they were expected to tithe to

Thomas Road. That policy protected the cultural sanctity of the Baptist tradition, where tithing was expected. It also maintained the ecclesiastical ties between the church and the university.[105]

As senior pastor of the church and chancellor of the university, Falwell could exert considerable influence over all campus affairs. In 1989 the church formalized the implicit requirement that all faculty tithe to Thomas Road. It similarly "Zeused" (a term used by some staff) the faculty with a requirement that all students had to take a course on creationism offered by the university's own Institute for Creation Studies. Titled "The History of Life," the two-hour course taught by members of Liberty's biology department addressed the issues surrounding the origins of life. Actually, Falwell had to create the course as a compromise with the state of Virginia in order to remove creationism from the biology department. Protests from the American Civil Liberties Union had moved the state to challenge Liberty's accreditation for teaching creationism in biology. Falwell's solution was to shift the academic location of creationism within the curriculum, from science to "creation studies," thereby satisfying the accreditation standards while simultaneously appeasing the college's more conservative constituency, which insisted that creationism be taught at Liberty.[106]

Falwell's decisions in the late 1980s to build a new, twelve thousand–seat (expandable to thirty-five thousand) multi-million-dollar outdoor sports stadium and to hire former National Football League coach Sam Rutigliano were criticized by some faculty and students who felt that athletics was becoming more important than academics.[107] However, the Rutigliano decision was clearly in tune with the overall vision for a "winning university." "Certainly I'm not scripturally where Dr. Falwell is," said Rutigliano, "but we basically believe in the same things about kids and discipline."[108] Moreover, the $10 million cost for the stadium and a 9,000–seat convention center was borne principally by two major donors who offered to finance them.[109] Liberty president A. Pierre Guillermin replied to critics in the school paper, "A university should provide an outstanding sports program that will attract students and supporters who would otherwise not be interested in its philosophy or its programs."[110] Sports, too, would support Falwell's long-range goal of putting Liberty on the academic map in North America and eventually the world.

Except for the occasional strong arm of Falwell and the church, however, Liberty's campus was remarkably open to serious intellectual and political debate. Liberty attracted many faculty from state universities who were disillusioned with the institutional politics and secular self-righteousness among faculty at such schools. They genuinely supported the concept of a Christian university and hoped that Falwell could indeed turn Liberty into a Protestant Notre Dame. The faculty did not unanimously support Falwell's right-wing political stands, his involvement in the Moral Majority, and even all of his biblical exegesis. Nor did the students, who would sometimes openly express their dissent. Although the students and faculty agreed on the fundamentals of the faith, as represented in the church's and university's doctrinal statement, they represented a fairly broad range of academic views.

In essence, the doctrinal statement simply asserted what many moderate-to-conservative American Protestants and certainly the majority of evangelicals believed in : the Trinity, the Creation, the authority of Scripture, the Fall, redemption through Christ's atoning blood, the literal resurrection, and the imminent return of Christ.[111] The only potentially controversial sections of the doctrinal statement for some evangelicals concerned the nature of the Creation (human beings were "not evolved") and the premillennial return of Christ. In the classroom, however, evidence for other views of the Creation, including theistic evolution, was openly presented and discussed.[112] The premillennialist doctrine was not particularly significant since its logical impact on day-to-day life was not especially clear. Falwell's own long-range vision for the university itself seemed to contradict the logical consequences of such premillennialism.

Liberty offered no tenure, but very few faculty were ever dismissed. Academic freedom at Liberty was dictated indirectly by the kinds of faculty hired rather than directly by the doctrinal statement. Faculty necessarily agreed on the fundamentals of the faith and were largely free to disagree about the implications of those fundamentals for their teaching, writing, and research. Scholarship was limited more by the heavy teaching loads (thirty credit-hours per year) than by a lack of academic freedom. As of 1989, only two Liberty faculty had ever received grants from the National Endowment for the Humanities. In an effort to become more of a recognized research university, and under the recommendation of the Southern Accreditation Association, Liberty established in the late 1980s a sabbatical program to encourage faculty scholarship and publication, although it granted sabbaticals only to faculty with proven research records.[113] It also increased academic conference travel budgets and initiated a university lecture program to bring to campus scholars of national stature, including evangelical theologian Carl F. H. Henry and Notre Dame's Alvin Plantinga, one of the foremost philosophers of religion in the world. The university additionally planned to hire a director of grants and fellowship.[114] In 1989 about half the faculty held doctorates, and the university hoped to increase that number to 75 percent by 1995.[115]

In only twenty years Liberty had evolved from a nascent Southern Bible college to a comprehensive university with graduate programs in business, religion, and theological studies. It had about five thousand full-time students, including three hundred graduate students.[116] Although its professional credibility in the national and international academic community was still to be determined, Falwell's own image as a right-wing televangelist clearly affected many peoples' views of the university. Falwell had made himself a very public figure in American political life, and that, more than anything, made it difficult for the university to establish its own academic integrity in American higher education. Both the public and the wider academic community associated Liberty with Falwell and the Moral Majority. In fact, Falwell's politics undoubtedly tarnished the academic reputation of Liberty among American intellectuals and mainstream academe even if it helped sell Liberty to some conservative constituencies. Irving J. Spitzberg, general secretary of the American Association of University Professors, criticized the Moral Majority in 1981 for its "yahooism" and blasted its leaders for trying to "legislate religious belief into public law."[117]

It remained to be seen in the early 1990s whether or not Liberty could step out from under Falwell's public shadow and establish its own status as a bona fide university. And it would certainly be difficult for Liberty to hire top-ranked scholars to boost the academic prestige of the university. For one thing, it was already difficult for Liberty to find highly qualified undergraduate faculty in some fields, especially the social sciences and, ironically, communications. American fundamentalism had not yet produced many scholars or even many doctorates in a host of academic fields.[118] The university's doctrinal statement, which codified the institution's fundamental religious beliefs, significantly limited the potential faculty pool even among evangelicals. Liberty's library was weak for graduate-level and faculty research, as the Southern Accrediting Association pointed out.[119]

In the early 1990s the university still needed to please a vocal conservative constituency, including Falwell and Thomas Road Church. And as long as Liberty continued to court the fundamentalist student market, it had to deal with a sometimes militant and anti-intellectual constituency that devalued scholarship and academic inquiry and sought a safe environment for its children. Falwell was criticized in 1983 by university friends and supporters when he invited liberal Senator Edward Kennedy to speak on campus.[120] Liberty clearly took the safe route in 1989 when it hired as a university scholar Norman Geisler, a militant defender of biblical inerrancy who was known for his attacks on the hermeneutical views of some mainstream evangelicals. However, Geisler wrote, with other Liberty faculty, a book on relating the conservative Christian faith to scholarship in various disciplines.[121] Clearly some Liberty faculty sought greater academic respectability for the school and hoped to contribute to evangelical scholarship.

Without question, by 1990 Liberty was no bastion of fundamentalism. The university under Falwell's direction had figured out its own way of being many different things to many different styles of conservative Protestantism. Although the school officially belonged to the Thomas Road Baptist Church, it served a far broader and more diverse constituency. Its expanding national athletics programs served not only the church and the university, but the city of Lynchburg. As Liberty entered Division 1 NCAA athletics in the early 1990s, its team and the new stadium were a source of revenues and pride for the city. At the same time, the university's plethora of programs and majors (seventy-five undergraduate majors alone), mostly oriented toward particular careers, served an expanding national market of second- and especially first-generation college families that greatly valued the opportunity to get an accredited baccalaureate degree at a respectable but religiously safe university with national visibility. And the faculty remained divided on its support for Falwell's nationalistic religiosity. If Falwell died, the university would undoubtedly be left without clear leadership and some kind of power struggle would likely take place within the university and Thomas Road Baptist Church. Although he held only a Th.G. degree from Baptist Bible College, Falwell had become the visionary leader for one of the largest Protestant colleges or universities in the country.[122]

The impact of television on Liberty, however, was a mixed blessing. The televangelism scandals of the late 1980s lowered Falwell's television ratings and donations to the ministry. Nevertheless, the Liberty University's School of Life-long Learning

(LUSLL), which offered fifteen accredited bachelors degrees and over one hundred courses on videotape, and its Home Bible Institute, which offered diplomas, became the major capital-generating arms of the university. While donations to the "Old Time Gospel Hour" dropped, television-generated admissions to LUSLL skyrocketed. In the fall of 1989 over sixteen thousand people registered for classes in LUSLL, which the state of Virginia was studying as a model for other accredited home-video programs. The vast majority of students in both programs heard about the videotaped courses from the "Old Time Gospel Hour" broadcast. Over thirty thousand students had signed up for the Home Bible Institute courses since the program was launched in 1976.[123] LUSLL and Home Bible Institute tuition greatly helped fund the growth of the university on Liberty Mountain.[124]

For the first time in the history of Falwell's ministry, he was clearly involved more in the business of education than in the ministry of saving souls. And in 1989, for the first time in the history of the university, it was operating in the black. A combination of new revenues, budget cuts, higher tuition, and reorganization made Liberty solvent. Falwell was keeping Liberty on the safe side of the ledger—and Liberty's growth was accomplished without direct government aid. Falwell rode the crest of American televangelism for the sake of Liberty University. By 1990 Liberty was largely free from the unpredictable and frightening swings of the market for televangelism, but the school still had many debts to pay from earlier expansion.

Falwell perceived the growing market for professionally oriented higher education among religiously conservative first- and second-generation college families. He charted a course between cultural separatism and accommodation. He emphasized academic quality in the context of religious lifestyles and personal piety. He figured out how to anchor educational philosophies in the goal of training Christian leaders rather than in the old-style, Bible college concept of missions. Finally, Falwell learned how to sell his vision of education to sometimes divergent groups within conservative Protestantism, not just fundamentalism. In 1981 he wrote that "there is little difference theologically between Fundamentalists and Evangelicals."[125] In 1990 this was particularly evident at Liberty University, where graduates were more likely to refer to themselves as Christians rather than evangelicals or fundamentalists.[126]

Perhaps the story of Liberty's transformation is best summarized by the shifting makeup of the student body and the new demographics of the contributors to the "Old Time Gospel Hour." In 1989 over half of the students were business or education majors, while the number of religion majors, about 10 percent in 1989, continued decreasing proportionately and numerically.[127] Even though it needed a larger library, the university planned to build a new business building after completion of the stadium.[128] Meanwhile, the age of the average contributor to the ministry dropped from about sixty-two to thirty-seven. Partly because of the televangelism scandals of 1987 and 1988, and partly because of the ministry's increasing emphasis on education, baby boomers had become significant supporters.[129] Still, Liberty was extremely dependent on the "Old-Time Gospel Hour" broadcast to generate funds—both contributions and student tuition—to pay off the many loans used to construct the rapidly built campus.

Falwell's lasting legacy to American culture will probably be Liberty University rather than the Moral Majority or even the "Old Time Gospel Hour" broadcast. Falwell brought a new vision of higher education to fundamentalism. Along the way he honed the more militant and separatist edges of American fundamentalism and prepared it for assimilation into the wider society. Falwell's professionally oriented views of university life, although wrapped in personal piety, emphasized secular vocation over distinctly missionary work and religious worldviews. He attractively harmonized the fundamentals of the faith with the commitments of academic professionalization and vocational instruction. It was simply not possible to maintain a distinctly sectarian educational vision under the pressures of academic professionalism, rapid institutional growth, and television support.

To some observers, Falwell went too far in 1990 when Liberty sought to issue bonds to purchase the campus from Old Time Gospel Hour Incorporated. Liberty received approval from the Lynchburg Industrial Authority, the Lynchburg City Council, and a Circuit court, but an appeal to the Virginia Supreme Court by Americans United for Separation of Church and State reversed the decision. According to Virginia law, such bonds could not be used to finance pervasively religious activities, so Falwell specifically excluded the university's School of Religion, religious radio station, and campus church from the refinancing plan. The university's catalog was also changed to downplay aspects of the university's religious practices: "chapel" was changed to "convocation," and "Christian" service requirements became "community service." Most striking, the university's application for admission no longer asked prospective students if they "received Christ" as their "personal savior."[130] Some people read these twists in Liberty's story as shrewd financial moves by an increasingly respected university that had done much over the years to bring revenues to Lynchburg. Instead, it was likely that the changes in catalog copy were primarily a way of positioning Liberty financially and academically as more than a fundamentalist university.

The recession of the late 1980s and early 1990s, coupled with the lingering suspicion brought on by earlier scandals involving televangelists, plunged Falwell's entire organization into financial trouble. A taxable bond issue underwritten by Kemper Securities of Chicago failed to materialize for Falwell, reportedly because of a lack of buyers. Meanwhile, Liberty began selling assets, including a fifty-one-acre north campus and the broadcast ministry's FamilyNet satellite television network. As a result, Falwell was forced to exert greater financial control over his religious empire. The preacher and university chancellor was increasingly becoming a businessman. "Everything General Motors does, we have to do," Falwell said in late 1991.[131] Ironically, Falwell's plight mirrored the financial state of many North American universities—and so did the business-like response.

Regent University and the New Evangelical Graduate School

While Liberty flourished as primarily an undergraduate institution, hoping one day to become a major graduate-level university, CBN University, renamed Regent University in 1990, became the major graduate-level evangelical university in North

America. Once again, public perceptions of CBNU were deceptively formed around the activities of its founder, religious broadcaster M. G. "Pat" Robertson. It was certainly Robertson's vision and energy, as well as his enormously successful work as a television fund-raiser, which gave birth to CBNU. Just as Bob Jones and Liberty belonged to their founders, CBNU has always been Robertson's institution. When Robertson ran unsuccessfully for the Republican presidential nomination in 1987, effectively diverting funds from both the university and the Christian Broadcasting Network, both institutions faced serious financial crises. Like Liberty, Regent had to face the fiscal realities of overdependence on the fund-raising abilities of one person and the unpredictable winds of television ministries. By 1990, however, it was clear that Regent would one day not be Robertson's university. More importantly, it seemed that Regent might become Robertson's well-endowed gift to the cross-denominational church renewal movement and an important legacy in the history of evangelical education.

Throughout his broadcasting career Robertson was sloppily referred to by the popular media as a fundamentalist. While there was little question that Robertson personally held to the fundamentals of the evangelical faith, he was not a traditional Baptist or Presbyterian fundamentalist. He strongly supported evangelism, biblical inerrancy, and premillennialism, but never separatism. Robertson's mission was neither to escape from the world nor to evangelize it from a distance. His "fundamental" faith was both ecumenical and belligerent—ecumenically tied to the cross-denominational charismatic movement of the late twentieth century, and belligerently focused on the immorality and injustices that he believed plague the modern, secular world. In short, Robertson was a fighter who wished to change the world by enlisting the help and support of like-minded people of all denominations. In his mind Christianity was not just a religion, but the truth of eternal life and the dynamic seed of social, cultural, and personal redemption. To put it differently, Robertson was never really an old-fashioned fundamentalist who battled against other fundamentalists over doctrinal issues and the fine points of cultural separatism. He was a new-fashioned fundamentalist born out of neo-Pentecostal evangelicalism who battled against the evils of secularism. Although a member of a Baptist church, Robertson was too committed to charismatic renewal to limit his academic vision to a church, denomination, or some narrowly conceived religious in-group.

In the mid-1970s, after successfully launching his cable television network, Robertson began thinking about establishing an educational institution. His for-profit CBN, Inc. (later called the "Family Channel"), in its own way was educationally directed at spreading "Christian values" throughout society. Like evangelical theologian Carl F. H. Henry in the 1940s, Robertson in the 1980s had an "uneasy conscience" about conservative Christianity's other-worldliness.[132] Even Robertson's more devotional books, such as *The Secret Kingdom,* were usually oriented toward social as well as individual change.[133]

His own daily talk-show, "The 700 Club," one of the highest-rated religious programs on cable and broadcast television in the United States, attracted a broad range of religious and even many nonreligious viewers. On that program Robertson and his guests taught viewers about the implications of the Christian faith for social and cultural life. The program always combined personal evangelism and social change; it assumed that saved individuals would transform the structures of society. Perhaps more than anything else, the "700 Club" encouraged evangelicals to take their own faith seriously outside of the walls of the church and to respect their rich heritage.[134] On the "700 Club," evangelical Christians of all occupations and traditions were taken seriously as first-class citizens. In spite of the fact that Robertson openly used the controversial "gifts of the spirit," including healing and prophecy, many noncharismatics viewed the show and supported the ministry.

When Robertson founded the university in 1978, he carefully decided to emphasize professional instruction over research and scholarship. The new "gap men," to use Moody's phrase, were to be evangelistically inspired social activists. Their vocation was not to be "preacher," "evangelist," or "theologian," but "professional." CBNU was established primarily as a graduate professional school that would train and teach evangelicals from all denominations how to practice their professions "Christianly." The "goal was gradually to infiltrate secular society with committed Christians who were at least as well prepared as their uncommitted colleagues and thereby to permeate the social fabric with biblical values."[135] In effect, CBNU would carry on Robertson's vision of evangelical social transformation long after he died. "The most important thing that anyone can do in life is set up an institution that will live after them," Robertson said of both his own and Moody's work.[136]

As a graduate institution, Robertson assumed, CBNU would more easily accomplish such goals. For one thing, there were already many independent and denominationally affiliated evangelical colleges in the United States. In the Christian College Coalition, a loose coalition of Protestant schools, there were in 1990 nearly eighty member institutions representing about ninety thousand students nationwide.[137] For another, few evangelical colleges offered graduate degrees. Oral Roberts University (ORU), one of the leaders in charismatic-evangelical graduate education, had some financial problems because of its commitment to the City of Faith hospital and the medical school. ORU eventually gave its law school and law library to CBNU. Finally, and probably most importantly, graduate students were simply more serious about academic study and professional instruction. "What I wanted," said Robertson, "was older students who were already pretty much set in their life's pattern and who wanted to get the training needed to focus on a major career goal. I didn't want a bunch of kids who were still trying to have big parties and grope around in life in more than one way."[138]

Robertson decided to establish a freestanding set of graduate programs without an undergraduate institution or baccalaureate degrees—probably the only institution of its kind in the country. The Virginia Beach property of the cable television network, purchased in 1975, eventually became the campus for CBNU. In the meantime, classes started in rented facilities in 1978 with seventy-seven students in the school of communications. By 1984, when CBNU was awarded full accreditation by the Southern Association of Colleges and Universities, there were about seven hundred students in six programs.[139] A $13 million, 152,000–square-foot library was dedicated in 1981, and two enormous classroom and office buildings were added to the campus.[140] The large, Williamsburg-style brick library became the focus of intellectual life for the five graduate colleges that comprised CBNU in 1990.[141]

From the beginning, the university was heavily subsidized by the for-profit television network. Robertson's policy was never to borrow money, and all buildings were erected on a pay-as-you-go basis. But the university needed constant cash flow. In 1989–90, when the university budget was about $10 million, the network still contributed over half of the cash needed to keep the school going. In addition, the university received about $2 million worth of recruitment advertising on the network.[142] Moreover, CBNU refused direct and indirect government support, including grants from the Virginia Tuition Assistance Program. In 1989–90 that meant the university refused about $600,000 in state assistance. Instead, the university gave its own financial aid to students, subsidizing them with money generated by the network. The average student had nearly half of his or her tuition paid by the network. If a student worked on campus or for the network, the student normally graduated debt-free.[143]

The network also was the major recruiting tool for CBNU. In the early years virtually every student heard of the university through the "700 Club" or advertisements on the network. Lacking alumni and without any reputation, the university had the difficult task of attracting students to a school that had neither a history nor an existing campus. Largely for this reason, Communications was the first program; if nothing else, prospective students could relate to the professionally produced programs they saw on the network. A decade later, however, the "700 Club" remained an important recruiting vehicle. In 1988 over half of the new students at CBNU first heard about the university from the show. By comparison, less than one-third of the new students first heard about CBNU from a friend or relative and less than 2 percent first heard about the school from a pastor.[144]

Enrollments at CBNU peaked in 1986, the year before Robertson ran for the Republican presidential nomination. About 950 students took classes at CBNU that fall. The School of Law, acquired the same year from ORU, had the most students, followed by communication, education, and religion. In both student enrollments and campus atmosphere, the university was not merely a divinity or theological school. Its religious perspective was integrated largely into the various professional programs rather than divorced from them in separate classes in Bible or religion—with the exception of the College of Theology and Ministry. After the university was reorganized into the many schools and institutes in 1987, the School of Christian Ministry, which offered M.A. and M.Div. degrees, suffered the largest drop in enrollment.[145] Clearly CBNU's students were more interested in the pursuit of traditionally secular professions and not primarily in missions or other church work. Nevertheless, the administration hoped that the university's growing identification with the charismatic movement would eventually boost enrollments even in theology and ministry. In 1989, after Robertson returned from his unsuccessful presidential bid, enrollments increased dramatically. When CBNU announced it would change its name to Regent University in the fall of that year, Robertson stated publicly that the school was hoping to have three thousand students by the year 2000.[146]

CBNU's professionally oriented graduate instruction attracted students from a wide spectrum of denominational and geographic backgrounds. One-half of the first class at CBNU was Roman Catholic, probably mostly charismatics.[147] ORU was the major "feeder" school, sending forty students to CBNU in 1988, but about 35 percent of the students that year officially listed their religion as nondenominational. Almost 20 percent said they were from the Assemblies of God, 10 percent Baptist, 7 percent Presbyterian, and 3 percent Roman Catholic. Approximately 17 percent of the new students at CBNU in the fall of 1988 were from Virginia. The remaining 83 percent were from all over the country, Canada, and a few other nations, particularly Nigeria and Venezuela.[148] As with Liberty, CBNU's major academic competition was state universities. Few evangelical colleges or universities had significant reputations for their graduate schools.

Students were generally pleased with the quality of instruction at CBNU. The university recruited some excellent professors from state and private schools, even though prospective faculty were not always sure where the university was headed academically and financially. Faculty went to CBNU both to escape some of the politics and academic pretension of state universities and to become part of a rapidly growing evangelical graduate institution. The faculty thought of themselves as Christians first, and evangelicals second, but not fundamentalists. It became an amazingly ecumenical faculty, considering the university's evangelical emphasis. In 1989 there were faculty at CBNU from mainline evangelical, charismatic, Pentecostal and mainline Protestant churches. There was also one Roman Catholic. Yet they shared a strong conviction that the fundamental beliefs of the evangelical faith should shape what professors teach and what students do when they graduate. In this ecumenical—but strongly religious—context, faculty appreciated the quality of their relationships with each other and with students. Most of all, however, they liked the religiously defined academic freedom.

Far from what one might expect, CBNU strongly supported academic freedom. Unlike Liberty, the university established and supported a tenure program for its faculty. There was no sectarian doctrinal requirement, only a statement of faith that required belief in the inspiration of the Bible, the Trinity, the Fall, salvation through the blood of Christ, the Second Coming, and the mission of the church as "worldwide evangelization and the nurture and discipline of Christians."[149] In practice, a professor's personal "experience" of faith was more important than sectarian doctrine.[150] The official statement of academic freedom declared that "true academic freedom comes from each individual's commitment to Jesus Christ, not from each individual's conscience tempered by the collective conscience of his peers."[151] The fundamentals in the statement of faith were perceived as "enabling" beliefs—not restricting ones—that protected the faculty's freedom to explore the relationships among faith, various disciplines, and professional practices. Gross immorality was far more likely to be the reason for dismissal than was any kind of heretical opinion or perspective. As with BJU and Liberty, faculty recruitment automatically limited hiring to individuals who could affirm the statement of faith.

Nor has the CBNU faculty always unanimously agreed on how to relate the Christian faith to teaching, scholarship, and professional practice. The School of Law, for example, adopted its paradigm from earlier work done by faculty at ORU and published annually in that university's *Journal of Christian Jurisprudence.* Not all former ORU faculty transferred to CBNU with the law school in 1986, but the program's emphasis on common-law theory and scholarship, and its publication of the journal, continued at the new institution. In short, the curriculum was based largely on the fundamental assumption that God "impressed upon His creation an objective legal order that man is bound to obey. The study of law, therefore, involves the discovery of the principles of law, the communication of those principles, and the application of them to all of life." [152] The first purpose of a Christian law school, according to ORU's law dean, was "to equip . . . students with the ability to bring God's healing power to reconcile individuals and to restore community wholeness." [153]

The CBNU law program's strongly religious perspective created significant accreditation problems for the new school in the late 1980s. The school's dean, Harvard Law School graduate Herb Titus, believed that the American Bar Association's initial refusal to grant accreditation was primarily a conflict over academic freedom. Like ORU a decade earlier, CBNU had to argue that academic freedom was not reduced by the requirement that students and faculty hold a shared religious faith. [154] From Titus's perspective, all universities and colleges had limits on academic discussion and debate established by the academic disciplines themselves. CBNU chose the "objective" standards of the Bible instead of the contemporary norms of the professional academic community. According to Titus, the ABA exposed its lack of academic freedom by assuming that religion was irrelevant to the study and practice of law. He believed that the CBNU School of Law was actually reclaiming the historic roots of common law in the Judeo-Christian tradition. That academic philosophy attracted to the law school plenty of bright and highly motivated students, most of whom went into local practice across the country rather than into corporate law. [155]

In the same college at CBNU, the School of Public Policy was influenced by "dominion" or "reconstruction" theology, which searched for the "laws of Creation" which should guide human thought and action in the world. Adherents such as CBNU professor Joseph Kickasola, a graduate of Brandeis University, believed that Christians must refashion all social institutions according to biblical commands found largely in the Old Testament. [156] Gary Amos of that school published a book in 1989 defending the Declaration of Independence on the basis that its writers, framers, and adopters were significantly influenced by the Bible. [157] Some critics have argued that Robertson himself has been influenced by dominion theology, but the evidence is not clear. [158]

However, other colleges at CBNU were not significantly influenced by dominion theology. Far more theologically liberal was the College of Communication and the Arts, which challenged many of the evangelical commonplaces about the nature of distinctly "Christian" communication. As Harrell suggested, the faculty of that college understood their mission not merely in terms of evangelism, but in terms of art. [159] Godly communication was to be well conceived, well structured, attractively produced, and technically superior. It was not sufficient, for example, to rely solely on moralistic criticism of television programs. Artistic quality was as important as morality and ethicality. From this perspective, Christians were called to be excellent communicators, not just righteous ones, and the evangelical community was to learn much from the artistic endeavors of pagan film and television producers, directors, and writers. This was a far cry from the separatist stand of BJU. That philosophy attracted some evangelical students who might otherwise have attended some of the major film and television schools. It also enabled CBNU students to take first prize in a national film competition.

In its first decade of existence CBNU was clearly a professional school rather than a research university. In the 1990s, however, CBNU planned to influence American academic life by establishing doctoral programs and supporting faculty scholarship. Some of the faculty raises were dependent upon scholarly publication. Moreover, the College of Communication and the Arts launched the university's first doctoral program in 1991. One dean said that every college at CBNU needed to attract at least one well-known scholar within five years if the university was to gain the kind of academic reputation necessary for doctoral programs. Boosted financially by the sale of the "Family Channel," it was hoping to hire established researchers and scholars.[160] Faculty generally supported these changes, believing that there was a significant market for Christian academicians, especially among the growing evangelical colleges, and that CBNU could adequately staff and fund expensive doctoral work. Already in 1989, CBNU graduates taught at such colleges as Evangel, Southern California, Geneva, Lee, Colorado Baptist, Bethany Bible, Liberty, Oral Roberts, Hampton, and Old Dominion.[161]

Such student successes occurred in the face of recurring faculty discontent with CBNU's administration. Many faculty believed that the university's administration did not completely understand the importance and value of scholarship. They felt that too many of CBNU's administrators were from the business world or church work rather than from academe. As one faculty member put it, too many administrators saw the university "more as a church to be pastored or shepherded rather than a university to be provided academic vision and organization."[162] There was little question that faculty did not have as much power at CBNU as most faculty did at other institutions of higher education, though certainly more than at most old-style fundamentalist colleges. In 1990 the administration began seriously to address these concerns by appointing a highly respected dean, George Selig, as provost and initiating steps toward establishing a faculty governance structure. These steps, too, distinguished the new Regent University from its fundamentalist cohorts.

Nevertheless, CBNU faculty generally agreed in 1989 that the only major obstacle to making the institution the first truly outstanding evangelical university was lack of financial resources. With a meager $5 million endowment and a large television-network subsidy, the university was greatly affected by economic vicissitudes that were completely out of its own control. In the early years the university operated with fairly lavish budgets, while during Robertson's presidential campaign the university dropped faculty retirement benefits, required employees to pay some of their own health and medical insurance, and froze faculty salaries.[163] The financial condition changed radically in 1990. The Southern Accrediting Commission had recommended that CBNU substantially increase its endowment, but the TV network, which subsidized the school all along, was asset rich and cash poor. As the fifth-largest cable network in the country, the "Family Channel" reached over forty-four million homes on over 8,300 cable systems.[164] In 1981 the network revenues from the the "Family Channel" surpassed for the first time the revenues received from contributions.[165] Partly to build the endowment, CBN, Inc., sold the network in 1990. One hundred million dollars were earmarked for the university, which adopted the name "Regent University" at the same time. Regent might eventually "emerge as one of the centers of truly fresh learning in the evangelical world," said David Clark, dean of the College of Communication and the Arts.[166] Certainly the $100 million endowment could go a long way with Regent's faculty of about sixty. The accrediting organization recommended a full ten-year renewal. Having not only survived Robertson's presidential bid but also reveling in the rapidly growing endowment, Regent's administration announced in 1990 that it would start a satellite campus in Poland—the first of any American university.[167]

In many respects Robertson and Falwell represent very different strands of conservative American Protestantism. Falwell's staunchly fundamentalist roots in independent Baptist religion are a far cry from Robertson's more ecumenical roots in the charismatic movement. Each of these university founders comes to higher education with his own religiocultural baggage. Robertson's brand of conservative Protestantism is generally more open to cross-denominational association and to nonbiblical authority, including reason and personal guidance from the Holy Spirit. Educationally speaking, however, Robertson and Falwell are on the same track. Both hope to have their religion *and* their academic status. Both desire to influence society by training biblically informed but professionally competent graduates. Both are being swept along by the same social currents that will make it impossible for their schools to turn back toward the old-fashioned concept of separatist, fundamentalist higher education. Indeed, neither school was ever there; each jumped in the water after the currents had been flowing for decades. Robertson just jumped in the water farther downstream than Falwell in an attempt to beat other schools to the tributaries of big-time higher education.

The Christian College Coalition and the New Evangelical Higher Education

The academic professionalization of fundamentalist higher education is reflected collectively in the Christian College Coalition. Some older fundamentalist colleges and a host of more moderate ones representing nearly all of the major conservative Protestant traditions formed the coalition in 1976. Reshaping the tradition of the bible institutes and bible colleges, which many of them once were, they collectively asserted their commitment to religiously informed education and increasingly to evangelical research and scholarship. Originally the coalition was composed of older, more established colleges, including Wheaton, Seattle Pacific, and Asbury. Two-thirds of the member institutions had been founded before 1924.[168] By 1989 the group of about eighty colleges and universities was seriously challenging the long-standing independence that characterized both evangelical higher education and fundamentalism generally. As a whole, these schools held steadfastly to the fundamental beliefs of evangelicalism while largely rejecting the fundamentalist impulse of separatism.

Probably the most important work of the coalition was upgrading the overall academic quality of member institutions, which varied widely in their commitments to faculty scholarship and overall academic excellence. The coalition sponsored dozens of faculty development conferences and workshops, with funding for an series of ten workshops from the National Endowment for the Humanities. It organized the publication by Harper and Row of a series of supplemental textbooks designed to help faculty and students grapple with the interplay of historic Christian thought with major fields of study, from psychology to economics and biology.

Largely because of the work of the coalition, it was clear in the 1980s that evangelical and some fundamentalist scholars and students were working together across the theological and cultural barriers that had been erected earlier in the century. About half the coalition schools were listed in a directory of "fundamentalist" colleges— Biola and Wheaton, for example. Others were from Reformed and Presbyterian confessional traditions. Yet others were evangelical colleges affiliated with mainline Protestant denominations. Some were associated with Pentecostal traditions, including the Assemblies of God. Many were outgrowths of the Holiness tradition. Together the schools represented nearly ninety thousand students.[169]

Unlike the fundamentalist higher education represented by the old-style Bible school and Bible college traditions, the coalition schools generally favored academic professionalization. In fact, these schools tended to embrace the goals of liberal education and, at least verbally, faculty scholarship. To some extent they saw themselves as reclaiming the heritage of religiously inspired education that spread throughout the United States during the second half of the nineteenth century. Their goals in the 1980s were increasingly to redefine the meaning of the specialized disciplines in the wholistic context of an openly religious academic community. Their response to secular higher education was not simply reactionary and defensive, but proudly self-assertive. Beyond "knowledge and experience" they sought "enduring values and a spiritual rudder, a global vision."[170]

The creation and growth of the coalition in the late 1970s and early 1980s reflected important transformations in fundamentalist higher education. Already in the 1970s some professors at coalition schools were arguing that conservative Christianity had to embrace scholarship and take an active role in the arts and sciences as well as professions. Two Wheaton professors wrote that through "her lack of biblical scholarship," conservative Christianity has "replaced the authority of Scripture over all of life with the authority of personal experience in conversion, service, and holiness. . . . While liberal Christianity is 'this-worldly' conservative Christianity is 'other-worldly.'" Echoing evangelical theologian Carl F. H. Henry's hopes of the 1940s, they concluded that the "demand which rests upon the new evangelical is to return to a Christian world and life view drawn from the authority of scripture. . . .

It is the message of coherence between the divine and human reality that flows from a biblical Christianity."[171]

In effect, many of these new evangelical colleges became hybrids of the old-fashioned, church-related liberal arts college of the nineteenth century, the German-inspired, early twentieth-century research university, and the late twentieth-century professional school. On the one hand, they strongly supported education which built Christian character and moral and ethical discernment. On the other hand, they increasingly valued academic specialization and professional education. Constituencies of these colleges were sometimes still skeptical and even suspicious of the apparent scholarly posturing and intellectualism of the colleges, but the growing necessity among American evangelical youth of attaining a college degree led many parents to favor the rising evangelical academic establishment over its larger, more diffuse, and seemingly more secular counterpart, the state university. Parents were often willing to pay the extra price of a private education if it were presumably Christian rather than pagan. As some of the coalition administrators described member colleges, they were not mere "defenders of the faith," a phrase used by the Danforth Foundation, but "faith-affirming" and even "faith-developing" colleges.[172] The new evangelical college was emerging at a time when the market was ripe, not the least because changes in American society were producing interested parents, eager students, and professionally inspired young faculty.

Largely because of a steady increase in evangelicals with doctorates in the 1970s and 1980s, the coalition colleges were increasingly able to improve the academic quality of their institutions. A few of them, most notably ORU (which discontinued membership in 1989) and Seattle Pacific, moved seriously into graduate education. However, none of them alone had the resources to create a research university. Graduate education generally meant, after teacher-education programs and perhaps religious degrees, professional programs. In other words, the coalition both reasserted religious wholism and followed the higher education market toward professional and preprofessional education. Even the largest coalition school in the early 1980s, ORU, directed its graduate education toward professional schools rather than toward full-fledged university status, which would require endowed chairs, ample research budgets, significantly more faculty travel money, and reduced teaching loads. The fact that so many coalition faculty produced scholarship was a sign of their love of and passion for it rather than a reflection of any professional duty required for promotion and tenure.

It became increasingly clear in the coalition schools in the 1970s and 1980s that it was possible to adhere to an explicitly religious educational mission while also engaging in remarkably free and open intellectual discussion and scientific research. These schools generally held strongly to the theological fundamentals of the evangelical faith while discarding the anti-intellectual and antimodernist impulses characteristic of earlier fundamentalism and schools such as BJU. At the same time, however, it was not obvious that academic freedom was especially important in the new approaches to organizing and marketing evangelical higher education. Struggling sometimes to market themselves in the competitive world of college and university admissions, these schools were occasionally tempted to peddle jobs and middle-class security over their religious purposes and mission. One critic said these colleges were "more and more difficult to distinguish from Revlon or Miller Beer. Increasingly, and particularly in times of economic contraction, [their] goal is that of any modern corporation, namely, financial stability and institutional longevity."[173] Overall, though, coalition colleges found that it was entirely possible to educate students according to the fundamentals of the faith while simultaneously giving them a liberal education. Students graduated with their theological beliefs intact even though they experienced noticeable liberalization of aesthetic, moral, and sociopolitical beliefs.[174] However, it was unclear if such graduates significantly shaped society, or if they were merely integrated comfortably into the consumer society.

In spite of their independent success, the new evangelical universities connected with religious broadcasting operations sought membership in the coalition. ORU became the largest member in the mid-1980s, when its enrollments were above four thousand. Liberty, in spite of Falwell's own independent Baptist background, began discussions with the coalition in the mid-1980s. Lacking an undergraduate program, Regent was not qualified to join, but during the same period it also initiated discussions with the coalition about the possibility of a new category of membership. By contrast, schools such as BJU had no intention of yoking themselves with the coalition.

The success of the coalition in helping to advance the academic quality of evangelical higher education reflected the overall direction of much conservative Protestant education in the United States in the 1980s. Instead of compromising its religious criteria for membership, the coalition held fast to the fundamentals of the faith as the basis for evangelical education. At the same time, the coalition sought academic excellence and established programs to help its member institutions achieve it. The Coalition's goal was not only to upgrade the image of evangelical education, but to advance the quality of education at its colleges and universities. That meant, among other things, more distinctly evangelical scholarship, which had never been a major goal of fundamentalist schools. But scholarship could not be taken as seriously by the schools as teaching and curricular innovation, which were much more likely to attract students. While the coalition helped professionalize its member institutions, those schools simultaneously enhanced their marketability with new, vocationally oriented programs and degrees. Members found in the 1980s, while national college enrollments were declining, that the combination of religious integrity and career-oriented programs was a strong selling suit.

The Impact of Fundamentalist Higher Education

The impact of fundamentalist higher education is wrought with irony. Certainly such higher education is more academically respected, by both parents and educators, than it has been since the 1920s. This is less true for the separatist schools like BJU and Tennessee Temple than it is for the more aggressive and market-driven schools like Liberty and Regent. New schools cling just as tenaciously to the fundamentals of the faith as did earlier schools in previous decades, but both the style and substance of the educational experience have been gradually transformed by pressures from within and outside fundamentalism. Overall, fundamentalist higher education has been assimilated, sometimes even co-opted, by both the desire to achieve greater academic respectability and the need to survive in the shifting sands of student interest and the prevailing winds of American higher education. For every BJU there is a host of colleges that have willingly given up their fundamentalism for the sake of academic success.

One possibility is that American culture and American higher education have had more impact on fundamentalist education than such education has had on America. Accordingly, conservative Protestant higher education is becoming more like nonreligious education. From this perspective, twentieth-century fundamentalist education in the United States is only now undergoing the same kind of secularization that took place at the elite colonial colleges primarily in the early nineteenth century and at the midwestern church-related colleges in the late nineteenth and early twentieth centuries. As those colleges focused less on training what Moody called "gap men" and more on building Christian character and providing "Christian, social leadership," they were transformed from explicitly religious institutions into private holders of the public trust.[175] That process was slow but steady and influential.

Among the vast majority of nonfundamentalist colleges and universities, secularization was nearly complete in the 1940s, except for a few major divinity schools at major institutions. By then there was virtually no evangelical presence in major American educational institutions, from the Ivy League colleges to the land grant universities.[176] During the same decade the number of students in public institutions surpassed those in private ones.[177] Church-related institutions secularized so rapidly that it was difficult in the 1960s to determine what made them distinctive any longer. Many of them were "invisible" colleges in both size and prestige. Their students often received an excellent liberal arts education, but it was not a particularly religious experience in or out of the classroom.[178]

According to this scenario, academic professionalization and vocationally oriented instruction will eventually eclipse the distinctly religious mission of all fundamentalist colleges and universities. As prospective students, from ever more cosmopolitan backgrounds, look beyond the limited educational opportunities of small, regional evangelical colleges, such colleges will have to secularize to survive.[179] In the 1980s, church-related education made up about one-fourth of all postsecondary institutions and enrolled about 10 percent of the United States's university and college students. At the same time, denominationally affiliated religious education represented about 786 out of about 3,300 institutions nationally. Only a handful of those schools and students were evangelical or moderate fundamentalist; most were mainline Protestant and especially Roman Catholic.[180] The more conservative schools, so the scenario goes, will simply join the secular academic parade as small floats in a long procession of previously religious institutions in a yet larger parade of state universities. Fundamentalist colleges are merely at the end of the parade, the last schools to be seriously affected by the "ideals of science, professionalism, standardization, and cosmopolitanism."[181]

A far different scenario suggests that in American culture there will always be a market for religiously inspired and shaped higher education. Although some schools might secularize beyond the bounds of an organization such as the coalition, new ones will form out of the energy of visionary evangelicals and even new fundamentalists. Some of these new schools will be reactionary and militant, while others will adopt the more moderate stance of the typical evangelical liberal arts college. Also in this scenario is the recognition that secularization is not always good marketing. In the 1960s and 1970s, secularization helped Roman Catholic colleges attract additional students, but it had the opposite effect on Protestant ones. The revival of religious interest among young Protestants aided the explicitly religious colleges more than it did those that secularized.[182]

By and large, older colleges which expanded their constituency base without clarifying it jeopardized their product appeal in the crowded educational marketplace.[183] By maintaining a distinctly religious identity, some Protestant colleges served an identifiable need in the educational marketplace and thus were able to raise their tuition without driving all students toward the less-expensive public universities. The fiscal health of church-related colleges has always depended largely on the tenacity with which they held to the religious, spiritual, and moral principles that undergirded their historical institutional mission and purpose.[184] In order to survive, church-related colleges have had to maintain a clear identity, distinct educational goals, a loyal and vocal alumni, powerful religious commitments, an active and involved board of trustees, first-rate administrations, a "good story," and intensive denominational financial support.[185] In that mix, religious commitments often have been exceedingly significant.

The new, broadcast-funded evangelical colleges and universities have succeeded largely because they could raise funds and effectively communicate their "story" to a new constituency. Their story was framed by the drive for academic excellence, religious perspective, and professional education. In the 1980s those were powerful symbols that attracted thousands of students and even hundreds of thousands of supporters to the more independent and cosmopolitan evangelical schools. In part, new institutions such as Regent and Liberty were able to create a market for their services by appealing via television to widely held evangelical sentiments about American higher education's secularization and moral equivocation. Among fundamentalists these trends were part of the "secular humanism" that, as fundamentalist leader Tim LaHaye put it, controlled the "most powerful institutions in our country today," namely, the media, government, education, business, church, and pressure groups.[186] All fundamentalist and evangelical higher education was partly an alternative to the immoral campus life and poor academic quality sometimes publicly associated with secular education.[187] Concerns about "secular humanism" were merely the more militant expressions of widespread public fears about the general direction of American society and culture. This is likely why so many of the students of the new evangelical education would otherwise have gone to state universities.

Neither of the scenarios depicted above is entirely correct. Fundamentalist higher education will continue to be co-opted by sweeping changes in American higher education as a whole. At the same time, because of both institutional commitments and pressures from the marketplace, conservatively religious higher education will regularly redefine and strengthen its distinctive purpose in higher education. Without returning to anti-intellectualism or cultural separatism, most of these schools will probably hang on to their religious commitments. As long as some parents and their children perceive the threats of secularism, even the most militant fundamentalist institutions will survive or be replaced with other, competing institutions. Militant fundamentalist colleges and universities will likely remain small and largely uninfluential in American society, however, because of their separatist attitudes toward both the wider academic community and society in general. The more interesting question is what will happen with the new style of higher education represented by schools such as Regent and Liberty, as well as the more academically prestigious members of the Christian College Coalition.

The most important legacy of fundamentalist higher education will likely be the renewed inclusion of religious questions and perspectives in modern academic dialogue and scholarship. Although militantly American fundamentalist institutions rarely participate significantly in the nation's or the world's intellectual life, escapees from fundamentalism will increasingly influence both evangelical higher education and the larger worlds of scholarship and ideas. The reformation of Fuller Seminary created what Marsden has called "neo-evangelicalism," but at the same time it helped keep alive evangelical issues and perspectives in American theological life. Similarly, each in their own ways, schools such as Liberty and Regent, as well as a number of members of the coalition such as Wheaton, Gordon College and Seattle Pacific, may help keep alive distinctly religious and broadly evangelical questions and ideas.

It appears that the new-style evangelical higher education is prepared to enter into new waters of academic debate and dialogue. Having focused on the "fundamentals of the faith" rather than on a pervasive fundamentalistic style, these colleges and universities are poised to inject their religious agendas and issues into the intellectual life of the academy. Schools like BJU are not there yet, but many others are well on the way. This will likely not be a threat to academic freedom, but yet another agenda for the pluralistic world of research and scholarship. From the religious and academic "right" will continually come the enduring issues that have always intrigued individuals who value the life of the mind: the nature of the human condition, the place of norms in scholarship and society, the quest for universal meaning and significance, and even the search for standards of right conduct.

Nevertheless, three developments could stall this infusion of academic life and thought. First, the mainstream academic community, largely through its professional associations, could force upon colleges and universities accreditation requirements that would snuff out most serious attempts to keep alive religiously inspired scholarship. The United States relies on independent accrediting agencies rather than on the federal government to regulate higher education. The agencies examine such things as admission requirements, general academic standards, and institutional self-improvement.[188] A few of the more militantly fundamentalist institutions like BJU simply refuse even to apply for accreditation, some of the new-style evangelical institutions have had significant problems gaining certain kinds of accreditation, while the new evangelical schools want it, but cannot always get it. Both ORU and CBNU had difficulty achieving accreditation for their law schools. Liberty had to compromise its educational mission somewhat in order to keep its state accreditation. Generally speaking, though, evangelical institutions have had little difficulty gaining regional accreditation.

In recent years, some accrediting agencies have become increasingly skeptical about "church-related" higher education, especially such schools' purported lack of diversity, their consideration of religious belief in admissions and hiring policies, their religion-based codes of student and faculty behavior, and their professed practice of teaching from an explicitly religious perspective. As a result of these practices and purposes, some accrediting agencies have "promulgated standards aimed at restricting, directly and indirectly, the sectarian character of church-related schools."[189] In 1984 the Northwest Association of Schools and Colleges revised its eligibility standards to require that students and facilities in its accredited schools have a "high degree of intellectual independence. . . . An institution owned by or related to an outside agency, such as a church . . . should ensure that it maintains an atmosphere in which intellectual freedom and independence exist."[190] Since virtually all federal funding is contingent upon accreditation by an agency recognized by the U.S. Department of Education, and since most accredited schools will accept transfer credits only from other accredited schools, this is a particularly important issue for a pluralistic society.

The most significant battles so far have taken place between religiously oriented professional schools and professional accrediting bodies. ORU's and CBNU's law schools ran into difficulties largely because of their requirement that students adhere to particular religious beliefs.[191] It appears, however, that the disputes involve definitions of "professionalism" more than religious discrimination or lack of academic freedom. The contemporary liberal faith in pluralism, which values the struggle between conflicting ideas and perspectives, is not applied nearly so broadly in national professional accreditation as it is in regional institutional accreditation. Professions have relatively narrow views of what it means to be a professional. When those are applied as accreditation requirements by the American Bar Association, for example, all kinds of religious institutions look professionally suspect.

In one sense the dean of Brigham Young's law school was right when he wrote that "the tensions in accrediting the new church-related law schools had nothing to do with professional or academic credibility."[192] As the former president of the Association of American Law Schools put it, academic integrity is not adequate for accreditation; schools must be held to the moral weight of nondiscrimination on the grounds of religion.[193] In another sense, however, professionalism today often implies obeisance to some standard of objectivity or professional detachment from the subject under study. As two critics of the law school accrediting process put it, "A pervasive secular orthodoxy which contains religious-like dogmas, a definable value-laden education, an emphasis on individual rather than institutional freedoms, an academic elitism and a hearty mistrust of religious institutions has permeated the accrediting process of American law schools."[194] If anything, the trend toward professional education in evangelical institutions will lead to more battles between accrediting agencies and religious institutions.

Second, evangelical institutions could face difficulties with accepting public funds. The constitutional separation of church and state has raised many issues pertaining to public support of religiously oriented education. Some of the militant fundamentalist colleges and universities simply refuse to accept any federal or state money directly and even indirectly in the form of students loans, grants, or work-study compensation. At least one legal scholar has concluded that a "pervasively sectarian institution would not be eligible for [state] aid."[195] Others have concluded that "if a college were to seek to impose upon its faculty or student body a narrow definition of sectarian orthodoxy or orthopraxy, it may have to forego institutional assistance."[196] And some observers believe that religious schools will face increasing pressure for government regulation in the future.[197] Clearly this is not an important issue for the more separatist institutions, but it directly relates to the mission and purpose behind the newer, more professional and cosmopolitan evangelical colleges and universities.

Finally, fundamentalist higher education may be significantly corrupted by its own nonfundamentalistic success. Higher education generally secularizes both individual students and faculty, and eventually this leads to the secularization of the social institutions which the students enter upon graduation. It is not certain how these trends will affect fundamentalist colleges as they strive for greater academic quality and as they reorient their institutions to the desires of students for career-directed degrees and academic programs. However, James Davison Hunter's study concluded that evangelical higher education has likely eroded the "symbolic boundaries of conservative Protestantism."[198]

One of the harshest critics of the new-style evangelical education believes that such schools are sailing with the winds of the modern consumer culture. He argues that college administrators and parents of students at these institutions practice a politics of deception and self-deception that creates the illusion that their "children will remain respectable evangelicals and will make it in the consumer society. . . . The Christian college . . . joins the biggest game in town, the compulsive but unconscious and unremarked genuflection before the idol of consumerism."[199] Such criticism is probably too harsh, but it certainly is true that conservative Protestant students attend like-minded colleges and universities for essentially the same reasons that most young Americans seek a higher education—to earn a marketable degree. In other words, from the perspectives of students and parents, whether they are fundamentalists or evangelicals, college degrees are increasingly stepping stones to careers. This is as true at a place like BJU as it is at many coalition schools.

From the early 1900s to the present, American fundamentalist higher education has always oriented itself to the need for what Moody called "gap men." Along the way the gap was increasingly filled with women as well. Moreover, the nature of the gap changed along with the general transformations of both American fundamentalism and American higher education. The goal of training lay missionaries was increasingly harmonized with the vocational interests of middle- and eventually working-class families. These changes affected even the most fundamentalistic colleges. By 1990 it was clear that the growth of Liberty and Regent, as well as the overall success of the Christian College Coalition, symbolized major changes in Protestant higher education as well as in American society. The new colleges and universities were far from Bible schools or institutes, and their academic professionalism and vocationally oriented curricula reflected little direct concern with evangelization.

The new "gap men" are in a far better position to transform society precisely because fundamentalist higher education has been transformed by society. Largely shed of its militancy and separatism, the new evangelical higher education seeks to transform the entire culture and society, not just the church. Ironically, that may be closer to Moody's initial vision for urban evangelism than were the goals of Bible schools and institutes, as well as the goals of the few colleges and universities, like BJU, that held tenaciously to their old-style fundamentalism. Much of fundamentalist higher education has been transformed by its own success into something that is neither so fundamentalistic nor a significant threat to the fabric of democratic and academic life. In fact, the new education, transformed by the world it sought to change, may contribute religious and even intellectual vitality to American higher education. Meanwhile, the old-style fundamentalist schools will continue serving their relatively small constituencies. Neither face of fundamentalist education should concern the trustees of the public weal.

Notes

1. S. A. Witmer, *The Bible College Story: Education with Dimension* (Manhasset, N.Y.: Channel Press, 1962), p. 36.

2. Joel A. Carpenter, "Fundamentalist Institutions and the Rise of Evangelical Protestantism, 1929–1942," *Church History* 49 (March 1980): 67.

3. Ibid.

4. Gary K. Clabaugh, *Thunder on the Right: The Protestant Fundamentalists* (Chicago: Nelson-Hall, 1974), p. 30; *Current Biography* (1972), s.v. "Hargis, Billy James"; James Morris, *The Preachers* (New York: St. Martins, 1973), p. 294; "The Sins of Billy," *Time,* 16 February 1976, p. 52.

5. Clabaugh, *Thunder on the Right,* p. 94; Laurence R. Marcus and E. M. Perkins, "New Jersey v. Shelton College: State Regulation v. Religious Freedom?" (Paper delivered at the Annual Meeting of the American Society for Higher Education, Washington, D.C., 2–3 March 1982).

6. George M. Marsden, *Reforming Fundamentalism: Fuller Seminary and New Evangelicalism* (Grand Rapids, Mich.: Wm. B. Eerdmans, 1987).

7. Arthur F. Holmes, *Contours of a World View* (Grand Rapids, Mich.: Wm. B. Eerdmans, 1983), p. 133.

8. Virginia Lieson Brereton, "The Bible Schools and Conservative Evangelical Higher Education, 1880–1940," in Joel A. Carpenter and Kenneth W. Shipps, eds., *Making Higher Education Christian* (Grand Rapids, Mich.: Christian University Press/ Wm. B. Eerdmans), p. 110.

9. Virginia Lieson Brereton, *Training God's Army: The American Bible School, 1880–1940* (Bloomington: Indiana University Press, 1991).

10. Brerton, "Bible Schools," p. 112.

11. Witmer, *Bible College Story,* p. 40.

12. Carpenter, "Fundamentalist Institutions," p. 68.

13. Wallace Emerson, "Christian Educa-

tion Today—The Bible Institute," *Christian Life,* September 1948, p. 47.

14. Ibid.

15. Witmer, *Bible College Story,* p. 18.

16. Ken Sidey, "Bible Colleges Search for Students, Future," *Moody Monthly,* October 1987, p. 97.

17. L. John Eagen, *The Bible College in American Higher Education* (American Association of Bible Colleges, 1981), p. 7.

18. Sidey, "Bible Colleges," p. 94.

19. George W. Dollar, *Facts for Fundamentalists,* rev. ed. (Sarasota, Fla.: self-published, 1983).

20. Edward G. Dobson, "An Analysis of the Environmental Perceptions of Undergraduate Students in Evangelical and Fundamentalist Bible Colleges and Liberal Arts Colleges," (Ed.D. diss., University of Virginia, 1986), pp. 119–21.

21. Carnegie Foundation for the Advancement of Teaching, *A Classification of Institutions of Higher Education,* 1987 ed. (Princeton, N.J.: Carnegie Foundation, 1987).

22. Witmer, *Bible College Story,* p. 40; Eagen, *Bible College,* p. 60.

23. Quoted in Melton Wright, *Fortress of Faith: The Story of Bob Jones University,* 3d ed. (Greenville, S.C.: Bob Jones University Press, 1984), p. 309.

24. Ibid., p. 310.

25. Bob Jones [II], *Cornbread and Caviar* (Greenville, S.C.: Bob Jones University Press, 1985), pp. 203–4.

26. Ibid., pp. 163, 165

27. Bob Jones [Sr.], *Things I Have Learned* (Greenville, S.C.: Bob Jones University Press, 1986), p. 47.

28. Jones, *Cornbread and Caviar,* p. 217.

29. Wright, *Fortress of Faith,* p. 295.

30. Ibid., p. 50.

31. Ibid., p. 185.

32. Dr. Bob Jones, Sr., *Chapel Sayings* (Greenville, S.C.: Bob Jones University, n.d.), pp. 4–6.

33. Wright, *Fortress of Faith,* p. 56. Also see Bob Jones, Sr., *Three College Shipwrecks* (Greenville, S.C.: Bob Jones University, n.d.).

34. Wright, *Fortress of Faith,* p. 45.

35. Ibid., pp. 50, 56, 63–65, 89–97.

36. Quoted in ibid., p. 27.

37. Ibid., p. 180.

38. Ibid., pp. 145–47.

39. *One of America's Finest University Art Collections* (Greenville, S.C.: Bob Jones University, n.d.). For one attempt to explain this combination of classicism and fundamentalism, see Daniel Lynn Turner, "Fundamentalism, the Arts and Personal Refinement: A Study of the Ideas of Bob Jones, Sr., and Bob Jones, Jr." (Ed.D. diss., University of Illinois, 1988).

40. Wright, *Fortress of Faith,* p. 153.

41. Louis Gasper, *The Fundamentalist Movement* (The Hague: Mouton, 1963), p. 105.

42. Apparently this figure has not changed significantly in the last decade. For information on BJU in the early 1980s, see Christopher Connell, "Bob Jones University: Doing Battle in the Name of Religion and Freedom," *Change* 15 (May–June 1983): 38–47. Current enrollment data come from Gail Dental, BJU Office of Public Liaison, interview with author, 30 November 1990. I also discussed the university with numerous people—past students and employees—who did not wish me to use their names.

43. Connell, "Bob Jones University," p. 44. Also see *Why Bob Jones University Was Founded—Why It Has Never Sought Membership in a Regional Educational Association* (Greenville, S.C.: Bob Jones University, n.d.).

44. Jones, *Cornbread and Caviar,* p. 217.

45. These are my own calculations from the listing of faculty in *Bulletin: Undergraduate 1990–91* (Greenville, S.C.: Bob Jones University, 1990), pp. 243–51. This figure compares with the data for 1983 as reported by Connell, "Bob Jones University," p. 44.

46. I calculated these data from *Bulletin: Graduate 1990–91* (Greenville, S.C.: Bob Jones University, 1990).

47. My interviews with people connected with the school suggest considerably more support for the administration and its policies than that found by one scholar in the early 1960s. See Gasper, *Fundamentalist Movement*, pp. 108–9.

48. Jones, *Cornbread and Caviar*, p. 217.

49. *Why Bob Jones University Was Founded*, pp. 11–12. Also see Wright, *Fortress of Faith*, pp. 313, 407. These accomplishments were confirmed in Dental, interview.

50. This is according to the course descriptions provided in the catalog.

51. Connell, "Bob Jones University," p. 43

52. *Bulletin: Undergraduate 1990–91*, pp. 2–3.

53. Wright, *Fortress of Faith*, p. 247.

54. Connell, "Bob Jones University," p. 42.

55. Wright, *Fortress of Faith*, p. 328.

56. Ibid., p. 247.

57. *Bulletin: Undergraduate 1990–91*, p. 25.

58. Ibid., back cover.

59. Wright, *Fortress of Faith*, p. 399.

60. Ibid., p. 198.

61. Ibid., p. 195.

62. BJU says enrollment was about six thousand, but nearly one thousand of those were actually students in the fundamentalist academy located on campus.

63. BJU Press was formed largely to publish texts for fundamentalist elementary and secondary schools. It has titles in physical science, math, heritage studies, earth science, biology, and chemistry.

64. Wright, *Fortress of Faith*, p. 339.

65. "Religion, Race and Taxes," *Newsweek*, 25 October 1982, p. 102.

66. Edward F. Taylor, "Bob Jones University Loses Its Preferred Status," *Change* 15 (July–August 1983): 21.

67. "Religion, Race and Taxes." Also see "The Bob Jones Case," *National Review* 15 (October 1982): 1262, 1264.

68. Wright, *Fortress of Faith*, pp. 382–83.

69. Ibid., p. 386.

70. See Kenneth S. Kantzer, "The Bob Jones Decision: A Dangerous Precedent," *Christianity Today*, 2 October 1983, pp. 14–15; "Bob Jones versus Everybody," *Christianity Today*, 19 February 1982, pp. 26–27.

71. Wright, *Fortress of Faith*, p. 386; Dental, interview.

72. "Talking with Bob Jones III," *Change* 15 (May–June 1983): 47.

73. See Stanley J. Hanna, "Bob Jones University v. United States: Interpretation and Conclusions," *Journal of Education Finance* 9 (Fall 1983): 235–40.

74. W. David Beck, interview with author, Lynchburg, Va., 28 September 1989.

75. Jerry Falwell, *Strength for the Journey* (New York: Simon and Schuster, 1987), p. 306; Elmer Towns, interview with author, Lynchburg, Va., 28 September 1989.

76. Gerald Strober and Ruth Tomczak, *Jerry Falwell: Aflame for God* (Nashville: Thomas Nelson, 1979), p. 94.

77. Ibid.

78. Jerry Falwell, with E. Dobson and E. Hinson, *The Fundamentalist Phenomenon: The Resurgence of Conservative Christianity* (Garden City, N.Y.: Doubleday, 1981), p. 219.

79. Falwell, *Fundamentalist Phenomenon*, p. 313.

80. Ibid., p. 393. Interviews with various colleagues of Falwell suggest some discrepancy as to when the "world-class university" concept was first developed. It may have been in the late 1970s—not in the first few years of the school when the university was considerably more separatist. In any case, by 1985 the concept was clearly part of the established public rhetoric of the institution. See Jerry Falwell, "Training Leaders for the Twenty-first Century," *Fundamentalist Journal*, December 1985, p. 10.

81. Towns interview.

82. Strober and Tomczak, *Jerry Falwell*, pp. 170–71.

83. Ibid., p. 91.

84. Towns interview.

85. Falwell, *Strength for the Journey*, p. 307.

86. Ibid., p. 310.

87. Ibid., p. 311.

88. Towns interview.

89. Beck interview.

90. Towns interview.

91. Beck interview.

92. *1989–90 Undergraduate Studies* (Lynchburg, Va.: Liberty University, 1989), p. 42.

93. Towns interview.

94. Douglas Lederman, "Liberty University Seeks Success in Football to Spread Fundamentalist Message," *Chronicle of Higher Education,* 15 March 1989, p. A32.

95. Towns interview.

96. Jerry Falwell, "The SBC: Revived and Rebuilding," *Fundamentalist Journal,* July–August 1989, p. 10. The journal ceased publication in 1990.

97. Beck interview.

98. Ibid.

99. Towns interview.

100. Ibid.

101. Earl S. Mills, interview with author, Lynchburg, Va., 28 September 1989.

102. Towns interview.

103. Towns interview.

104. Falwell, *Strength for the Journey,* p. 395.

105. Beck and Mills interviews.

106. Ibid. Also see "Liberty Center for Creation Studies Announced," *Fundamentalist Journal,* October 1984, p. 61; A. Pierre Guillermin, "Creationism and Biology at LBC," *Fundamentalist Journal,* October 1984, p. 12; idem, "LBC Biology Accreditation," *Fundamentalist Journal,* October 1982, pp. 63–65.

107. Lederman, "Liberty University Seeks Success in Football," pp. A29, A32; Barry Jacobs, "Building from the Ground Up," *New York Times,* 21 March 1989, pp. B9, B12; "Liberty University Announces New Stadium and Sports Arena," *Fundamentalist Journal,* February 1989, p. 41.

108. Jacobs, "Building from the Ground Up," pp. B9, B12. For additional insight on sports at Liberty, see David J. Miller, "The Last Temptation of Price," *Sport,* July 1989, p. 12; Montville Leigh, "Thou Shalt Not Lose," *Sports Illustrated,* 13 November 1989, pp. 82–86; John Capouya, "Jerry Falwell's Team," *Sport,* September 1986, pp. 72–74.

109. Letter from R. Mark DeMoss to author, 13 January 1992.

110. A. Pierre Guillermin, "Liberty University Balances Academics with Athletics," *Liberty Champion,* 27 September 1989, p. 2.

111. *1989–90 Undergraduate Studies,* p. 10.

112. Beck interview.

113. Mills interview.

114. Beck interview.

115. Lederman, "Liberty University Seeks Success in Football," p. A32.

116. Towns interview.

117. Irving J. Spitzberg, "Speaking Out: Presidents, Faculties, and the Moral Majority," *Academe* 67 (1981): 401–2.

118. Towns interview.

119. Beck interview.

120. Falwell, *Strength for the Journey,* p. 378. The Kennedy-Falwell dialogue was an important symbol for both parties. See Robert J. Branham and W. Barnett Pearce, "A Contract for Civility: Edward Kennedy's Lynchburg Address," *Quarterly Journal of Speech* 73 (1987): 424–43; W. Barnett Pearce, Stephen W. Littlejohn, and Alison Alexander, "The New Christian Right and the Humanist Response: Reciprocated Diatribes," *Communication Quarterly* 35 (1987): 171–92; Deryl Edwards, "Kennedy Speaks At," *Fundamentalist Journal,* November 1983, p. 65.

121. W. David Beck, ed., *Opening the American Mind* (Grand Rapids, Mich.: Baker, 1991).

122. Strober and Tomczak, *Jerry Falwell,* p. 90.

123. "Liberty Home Bible Institute Enrollment Growing," *Fundamentalist Journal,* January 1989, p. 51.

124. Beck interview.

125. Falwell, *Fundamentalist Phenomenon,* p. 222.

126. Edward G. Dobson, interview with author, Grand Rapids, Mich., 19 September 1989.

127. Towns interview.

128. Beck interview.

129. Towns interview.

130. Kim Lawton, "Church-State Questions Vex Falwell's University," *Christianity Today,* 19 February 1990, pp. 36–37. Also see Joseph L. Conn, "Don't Buy Liberty Bonds," *Church and State* 43 (March 1990), pp. 4–6.

131. "Trying Times for the Founder of the Moral Majority," *Parade Magazine,* 19 January 1992, p. 10.

132. Carl F. H. Henry, *The Uneasy Conscience of Modern Fundamentalism* (Grand Rapids, Mich.: Wm. B. Eerdmans, 1947).

133. Pat Robertson, *The Secret Kingdom* (Nashville: Thomas Nelson, 1982).

134. David Clark, interview with author, Virginia Beach, Va., 19 September 1989.

135. John B. Donovan, *Pat Robertson: The Authorized Biography* (New York: Macmillan, 1988), pp. 157–58.

136. Ibid., p. 157.

137. Christian College Coalition, "The Case: Never Has the Need Been Greater," promotional brochure.

138. Donovan, *Pat Robertson,* p. 158.

139. Dwight "Butch" Maltby, interview with author, Virginia Beach, Va., 29 September 1989.

140. "Upfront News," *Wilson Library Bulletin,* November 1984, p. 166.

141. These included Administration and Management, Education and Human Services, Communication and the Arts, Law and Government, Theology and Ministry; also, nine schools (Education; Counseling and Family Services; Radio, Television and Film; Journalism; Communication Studies; Law; Public Policy; Biblical Studies; Christian Ministry) and the Institute of the Performing Arts.

142. Maltby interview.

143. Author interview with a group of CBNU faculty, Virginia Beach, Va., 29 September 1989.

144. Maltby interview.

145. Ibid.

146. Philip Walzer, "CBNU Changing Name to Regent University," *Virginia Pilot,* 9 November 1989, p. D1.

147. Faculty interview.

148. Maltby interview.

149. *Graduate Catalog 1989–90* (Virginia Beach, Va.: CBN University, 1989), p. 3.

150. Faculty interview.

151. *Graduate Catalog, 1989–90,* p. 4.

152. Ibid., p. 69.

153. Charles A. Kothe, "Preface," *Journal of Christian Jurisprudence* (1980): 2.

154. See Bruce Barron, "Bible-Based Law: CBN Law School versus the American Bar Association" (Paper presented at the Annual Meeting of the Society for the Scientific Study of Religion, Virginia Beach, Va., November 1990).

155. Herb Titus, interview with author, Virginia Beach, Va., 29 September 1989; Titus's own conversion is described in Bob Slosser, *Changing the Way America Thinks* (Dallas: Word, 1989), pp. 1–6.

156. For a fairly balanced assessment of the school, see Steven W. Fitschen, "Paradoxes of Christian Public Policy Marketing: Reactionary and Radical Elements of the Vision of Regent University's School of Public Policy" (Paper presented at the Annual Meeting of the Society for the Scientific Study of Religion," Virginia Beach, Va., November 1990).

157. Gary T. Amos, *Defending the Declaration: How the Bible and Christianity Influenced the Writing of the Declaration of Independence* (Brentwood, Tenn.: Wolgemuth and Hyatt, 1989).

158. H. Wayne House and Thomas Ice, *Dominion Theology: Blessing or Curse?* (Portland, Ore.: Multnomah, 1981), pp. 383–84.

159. David Edwin Harrell, *Pat Robertson: A Personal, Religious, and Political Portrait* (San Francisco: Harper and Row, 1987), p. 66.

160. David Clark, Dean of the College of

Communication and the Arts, telephone conversation with author, 15 March 1990.

161. Faculty interview.

162. Ibid.

163. Ibid.

164. "Top 25 Cable Networks," *Electronic Media,* 22 May 1989, p. 52.

165. Pat Robertson, *The Plan* (Nashville: Thomas Nelson, 1989), p. 185.

166. Clark interview.

167. Philip Walzer, "Regent University Plans to Open Facility in Poland," *Virginia Pilot/Ledger Star,* 19 May 1990, pp. C6, C7.

168. Stanley A. Clark, "A Comparative General Study of Member Institutions of the Christian College Coalition" (Report prepared for the Christian College Coalition, Washington, D.C., April 1989).

169. Christian College Coalition, "The Case" (Brochure).

170. Ibid., p. 1.

171. Marvin K. Mayers, Lawrence O. Richards, and Robert Webber, *Reshaping Evangelical Education* (Grand Rapids, Mich.: Zondervan, 1972), p. 44.

172. "Faith-Developing Colleges," *Christian College Coalition News* 15 (January 1990): 2.

173. Douglas Frank, "Consumerism and the Christian College: A Call to Life in the Age of Death," in Carpenter and Shipps, *Making Higher Education Christian,* p. 262.

174. Jack Balswick, Dawn McN. Ward, and David E. Carlson, "Theological and Socio-Political Belief Change among Religiously Conservative Students," *Review of Religious Research* 17 (1975): 61–67.

175. Leslie Karen Patton, *The Purposes of Church-Related Colleges* (New York: Bureau of Publications, Teachers College, Columbia University, 1940), p. 235.

176. George M. Marsden, "Why No Major Evangelical University? The Loss and Recovery of Evangelical Advanced Scholarship," in Carpenter and Shipps, *Making Higher Education Christian,* pp. 294–304; Carpenter, "Fundamentalist Institutions," p. 22.

177. Manning M. Pattillo, Jr., and D. M. MacKenzie, *Church-Sponsored Higher Education in the United States* (Washington, D.C.: American Council on Education, 1966), p. 16.

178. Alexander W. Astin and C. B. T. Lee, *The Invisible College* (New York: McGraw-Hill, 1972), p. 91.

179. Michael D. Wiese, "Strategic Implications of Cultural Analysis: Preserving Purpose through Market Research," *College and University* 65 (Winter 1990): 95–108.

180. Center for Education Statistics, *Digest of Education and Statistics* (Washington, D.C.: Government Printing Office, 1987), pp. 127–28.

181. Dorothy C. Bass, "Ministry on the Margin: Protestants and Education," in William R. Hutchinson, ed., *Between the Times: The Travail of the Protestant Establishment in America, 1900–1960* (Cambridge: Cambridge University Press, 1989), p. 49.

182. Richard E. Anderson, "A Financial and Environmental Analysis of Strategic Policy Changes at Small Private Colleges," *Journal of Higher Education* 49 (1978): 30–46.

183. John D. Moseley and Glenn R. Bucher, "Church-Related Colleges in a Changing Context," *Educational Record* 63 (Winter 1982): 47.

184. Anderson, "Financial and Environmental Analysis."

185. Dean L. Hubbard, "The Seven Commandments," *Currents* 11, no. 10 (November–December 1985): 12–15.

186. Tim LaHaye, *The Hidden Censors* (Old Tapan, N.J.: Revell, 1984), p. 19.

187. Patrick Welsh, "Are You Sure You Want to Send Your Kid to College?" *Washington Post,* 25 September 1988, pp. C1, C4.

188. Matthew B. Durrant, "Accrediting Church-Related Schools: A First Amendment Analysis," *Journal of Law and Education* 14 (1985): 147.

189. Ibid., p. 148.

190. Ibid., p. 154.

191. Ibid., p. 151.

192. Carl S. Hawkins, "Accreditation of

Church-Related Schools," *Journal of Legal Education* 32 (June 1982): 187.

193. Sanford H. Kadish, "Church-Related Law Schools: Academic Values and Deference to Religion," *Journal of Legal Education* 32 (June 1982): 161–71.

194. April Kestell Cassou and Robert F. Curran, "Secular Orthodoxy and Sacred Freedoms: Accreditation of Church-Related Law Schools," *Journal of College and University Law* 11 (Winter 1984): 294.

195. Julie Underwood O'Hara, "State Aid to Sectarian Higher Education," *Journal of Law and Education* 14 (1985): 183.

196. Philip R. Moots and Edward M. Gaffney, Jr., *Church and Campus* (Notre Dame, Ind.: University of Notre Dame Press, 1979), p. 83.

197. Ibid., p. 140.

198. James Davison Hunter, *Evangelicalism: The Coming Generation* (Chicago: University of Chicago Press, 1987), p. 206.

199. Frank, "Consumerism and the Christian College," p. 262.

Hindu Revivalism and Education in North-Central India

Krishna Kumar

I have profound respect for Dayanand Saraswati. I think that he has rendered great service to Hinduism. His bravery was unquestioned. But he made his Hinduism narrow. I have read *Satyarth Prakash,* the Arya Samaj Bible. Friends sent me three copies of it whilst I was residing in the Yarvada Jail. I have not read a more disappointing book from a reformer so great. He has claimed to stand for truth and nothing else. But he has unconsciously misrepresented Jainism, Islam, Christianity, and Hinduism itself. One having even a cursory acquaintance with these faiths could easily discover the errors into which the great reformer was betrayed. He has tried to make narrow one of the most tolerant and liberal of the faiths on the face of the earth. And an iconoclast though he was, he has succeeded in enthroning idolatry in the subtlest form. For he has idolized the letter of the Vedas and tried to prove the existence in the Vedas of everything known to science. The Arya Samaj flourishes, in my humble opinion, not because of the inherent merit of the teachings of *Satyarth Prakash,* but because of the grand and lofty character of the founder.

Mahatma Gandhi (1924), *Collected Works* 24:145

All political discourses that we can distinguish in Indian public life today can be traced back to India's struggle for independence. The revivalist discourse, which gained considerable political ground in the 1980s, can be traced back to the philosophical, religious, and social movements that originated in the latter half of the nineteenth century as part of a quest for India's independence from British rule. Search for self-identity was an important part of the vision of an independent India, and revivalist movements have played a key role in this search.

This role of revivalism proved highly relevant to the development of indigenous educational concepts and practices because education had served as an instrument for the dissemination of a colonial identity. Dissatisfaction with colonial education gave revivalism one of its raison d'êtres. Educational enterprise thus became a favorite sphere of revivalist mobilization. The interplay of political, religious, and pedagogic strategies that characterizes the contribution of revivalist movements to education over the last one hundred years is a highly intricate phenomenon. In this chapter, I focus on one segment of this phenomenon—Hindu revivalism in the Gangetic-

Vindhya belt of northern-central India. Broadly approximating the territories of modern-day Uttar Pradesh (U.P.) and Madhya Pradesh—formerly the United Provinces and Central Provinces—this area is the seat of Hindi. The argument I propose is that the development of Hindi as a medium of modern education was the major function that Hindu revivalist forces assigned to themselves. They appropriated a mass language and, in the name of education and national development, turned it into a class dialect. Furthermore, the political value of Hindi as a symbol of anticolonialism combined with a trend toward Hindi-Urdu differentiation to make Hindi a potent instrument for the consolidation of revivalist ideology.

In this context the term "revivalism" is preferable to "fundamentalism" mainly because the latter seems inappropriate to Hinduism. Unlike Semitic religions, Hinduism is characterized by the multiplicity of basic beliefs, texts, and practices.[1] Fundamentalism of the kind we notice in some societies in a Christian or an Islamic context is incompatible with the Hindu religious philosophy. Indeed, the revivalist movements had to make a conscious attempt to systematize Hinduism by constructing a set of fundamental dictums and texts. It is historically valid to say that such attempts represent the influence of Islam and Christianity on Hindu revivalist leaders. Moreover, the attempts to systematize Hindu society could not find adequate resources for their purposes within religion alone. They had to assemble bits and pieces of relevant material from literature and mythology, history, and geography. The common element in their different approaches was the use of the past, especially the distant past, to evoke a wistful mood. All the necessary ingredients of social action consistent with revivalism—a sense of lost utopia, the territorial outlining of the utopia and its anthropomorphization, the collective naming of a scapegoat, and the determination to rebuild the utopia—were believed to be logical outcomes of the wistful mood.

In the course of my analysis I refer to two specific sources of revivalist influence on education, namely, the Arya Samaj and the Rashtriya Swayamsevak Sangh (RSS). In the development of the revivalist ideology in modern India, these two sources have undoubtedly played prominent roles. Yet revivalism is a wider phenomenon than what may be grasped by studying these or other specific sources of revivalist influence. Unlike some other societies where fundamentalism or revivalism has surfaced as a discrete element in politics, revivalism in northern India is a phenomenon organically related to the cultural development of a specific stratum of society. When we study revivalism as a manifestation of the social personality of a particular stratum, we run the risk of ignoring those aspects of this manifestation which are not consistent with the customary understanding of the connotations of revivalism as a term. "Opposition to modernity" is one such connotation. Neither of the two sources I talk about provide proof of such opposition. On the contrary, as Erdman[2] noticed in a somewhat different context, modernity is subsumed in the philosophy of the political right in India. Neither Arya Samaj nor the RSS was or is antimodern, as one might expect while calling them revivalist or fundamentalist. Rather, they suggest a different political route to modernization from the one proposed and pursued by secular organizations in the Indian context.

The Shaping of Modern Hindi

The Hindu region came under colonial control long after the penetration of coastal India by English administration, language, and education. By the time colonial education policy found an operational structure in the Hindi region, with its avowed goal of spreading literacy, an important change was already taking shape in the social milieu. This change had to do with the arrival of printing technology. Availability of the printing press had altered the uses of reading and writing and thereby the meaning of literacy. Any individual or institution could now create a text and disseminate it. Literacy now meant not just the ability to decode a text with the help of one's familiarity of a script, but also implied the power to project meanings and to share them with a scattered audience. Text creation was no more a function of some few individuals, nor was textual communication any longer confined to local spaces defining a proximate community. The growth of colonial administration brought about substantial expansion of literacy-related employment and the development of a postal system.

Under these circumstances, literary journalism acquired the distinct cultural function of shaping a heterogeneous town-based society into a distinct community consisting of salaried professionals and office hands, merchant groups, property owners in towns, and rural landowners with urban links. Heterogeneous though this educated town-based society was in terms of its economic character, it was mainly upper caste, dominated by Brahmins and Kayasthas. This emerging community included a literati committed to controlling the processes of symbol creation and dissemination in a highly fluid cultural situation. The literati chose to accomplish these goals by first developing a standardized prose diction. Apart from diction, the choice of content for newly recognized prose genres such as the essay and the short story was also important. Leadership in these matters was provided by a literary magazine called *Saraswati,* started by the Indian Press of Allahabad in 1901. Allahabad had become a center of administration, commerce and political activity, and also had a university—the only one in northern India.[3] Its illustrious editor from 1903 to 1921, Mahavir Prasad Dwivedi, is now remembered as the "father of Hindi prose."[4]

The Hindi-Urdu differentiation had considerably deepened, although it was still treated as a matter of controversy. Reaction to the Persianization of Urdu was well established along the lines of religious separatism.[5] Among both the Muslim landed and salaried gentry and the Hindu upper castes, language became the means as well as the symbol of community creation. But while both Hindi and Urdu were being used for this purpose, Hindi was also perceived as the symbolic instrument for fighting colonialism and English, whereas Urdu was perceived essentially as the instrument for preservation of Muslim self-identity. The decision made by the English administration to use Urdu as the court language had tainted it, rendering it unsuitable for the anticolonial struggle. Hindi represented a far more ambitious program, that of crowning the emergent vision of an independent India with a pan-Indian language. This role was assigned to Hindi not just by the Hindu literati, but also by the leaders of two major social reform movements of the late nineteenth century—the Arya Samaj and the Brahmo Samaj. The shaping of modern Hindi and its dissemination throughout northern India were perceived as tasks of immense cultural significance by the leaders of the Arya Samaj.

The Arya Samaj

The Arya Samaj looms so large on the intellectual and social scene of late nineteenth-century northern India that it is unnecessary to establish linkages between the major tenets and concerns of the Arya Samaj and discrete currents of thought and expression available to individuals growing up during this period. Biographies of numerous eminent literateurs and social leaders who came to maturity in the last quarter of the nineteenth century provide testimony that the Arya Samaj acted as a major agency of socialization. And even in cases where the influence of Arya Samaj was absent or rejected, its presence in the wider social milieu seems to have made an impact on symbols available for socialization within the family. The Arya Samaj provided the upper caste, literate elements of Hindu society with norms and symbols to define a sense of self-identity and collective goal. A lengthy discussion of the origins and the ideology of this movement has been provided by Daniel Gold in an earlier volume.[6] My present purpose requires only a brief addition to Gold's extensive discussion. In the program of organizing a reformed Hindu society that the Arya Samaj had proposed an important role was given to the development of a lingua franca of reformed Hindus or the "Aryas." Dayanand Saraswati, the founder of Arya Samaj, was a great scholar of Sanskrit, which he used for his discourse until he met Keshub Chandra Sen, the Brahmo Samaj leader, in Calcutta in 1872. Sen gave Dayanand the idea of using Hindi as the medium for propagation of religious and social reform. Also during his visit to Calcutta, Dayanand was exposed to the early nationalist thought of Bengali intellectuals such as Bhudev Mukhopadhyay and Rajendralal Mitra, who regarded the adoption of Hindi as an important preparation for India's reconstruction.

Dayanand gave his first lecture in Hindi two years later in Benares. In this lecture, writes his biographer, "hundreds of words, and even sentences still came out in Sanskrit."[7] Hindi soon acquired the title "Aryabhasha" (the language of the Aryas) in Arya Samaj parlance, and its Sanskritized form became part and parcel of the movement's vision of a reformed Hindu society. Arya Samaj leaders took an active part in the campaign for the popularization of the Devnagari script and its acceptance for official use. Indeed, the initial impetus for the construction of an institutional base for this campaign—the Nagari Pracharini Sabha (literally, the "Conference for the Propagation of Nagari" script) in Benares—came from the Arya Samaj movement in the final years of the nineteenth century. The biographer of Shyam Sunder Das, the founder-secretary of the Sabha, noted that the idea of starting the Sabha had come from a speech delivered by an Arya Samaj preacher, Shankarlal.[8] The Nagari Pracharini Sabha's leadership proved crucial for the acceptance of Hindi as a court language in the United Provinces.

It is difficult to find a parallel for the attention and symbolic value that the graphology of a language acquired in the course of its battle for introduction in state offices and courts. The adversary against which the Hindi stalwarts fought their battle was Urdu. Apparently the Persian script of Urdu was a concrete reminder to the literate upper castes, particularly the Brahmins and Kayasthas, of the United Provinces of their subservient status vis-à-vis the Muslim aristocracy. In retrospect, it seems ironic that the Arya Samaj, whose early leaders freely used Urdu to propagate their ideas, made a vital contribution to the movement which aimed at distancing Hindi from Urdu.

Dayanand Saraswati had established a few schools, on his own initiative, but after his death an organized effort was made to propagate the ideas of the Arya Samaj with the help of formal educational institutions. The first institutions of this kind were the Dayanand Anglo-Vedic (DAV) school and college at Lahore. The DAV movement, which celebrated its centenary in 1986, was born with this college. The spectacular success of this institution was due to the dedication of Lala Hansraj, who is now remembered in the history of Arya Samaj as Mahatma or "the great spirit." As the name "Anglo-Vedic" indicates, the purpose of this college was to pursue the aims of the Arya Samaj while providing for the study of English and Western knowledge. Promoting the study of Hindi was among the foremost aims of the college, and Urdu was made available in it only as an optional subject, even though several members of the original managing committee wanted to give Urdu a more important place.[9] The role Hindi was expected to play in the educational endeavor of this institution can be understood from the point Lala Hansraj made in one of his writings for young men. He listed three elements as essential for the progress of the Hindu *jati* (in this sense, "community," although usually the term connotes "caste"): that its members are in unity and share a common origin; that religion is held in common; and that members share a common language.[10]

After the celebrated beginning of the DAV school and college at Lahore, a split occurred in the Arya Samaj over the educational philosophy to be pursued by the movement. On one side were the more practical-minded Samajists who wanted English and Western school subjects to be taught in Arya Samaj institutions. On the other side were men who wanted Arya Samaj institutions to make a radical departure from the existing colonial education system by returning to the ancient ideals of *gurukul* or *ashram* style of education. Popularly labeled as the "college" wing and the "gurukul" wing, respectively, these groups cannot be neatly distinguished in terms of progressive versus orthodox views as is sometimes attempted. On the question of higher education for women, the gurukul wing, supposedly the more orthodox, took a more forward-looking stand than the college wing, which thought that the time for higher education for women had not yet come. The famous Arya Kanya Mahavidyalaya of Jalandhar was started by Lala Devraj who belonged to the gurukul wing. The remarkable achievements of this college in terms of providing a new kind of institutional ethos for girls and in the preparation of new curricula and texts have been studied in detail by Kishwar.[11] As she notes, the Jalandhar college could not last in its original character, nor could this experiment be transplanted elsewhere. The gurukul wing had better success with the school they established at Kangri near Haridwar in 1902, which developed into a university famous for Sanskrit scholarship and indigenous Indian sciences. The founder of this institution was Lala Munshiram, who later became known as Swami Shraddhanand. In his own words, the gurukul at Kangri was started with the aims of "reviving the ancient institution of Brachmacharya, of rejuvenating and resuscitating ancient Indian philosophy and literature, conducting researches into the antiquities of India, of building up a Hindu literature, incorporating into itself all that is best and assimilable in Occidental thought, [and] of producing preachers of Vedic Religion and citizens."[12]

Benares Hindu University

These goals were not all that different from the ones Madan Mohan Malviya had in mind in setting up another university on the banks of the Ganges, in Benares. The Benares Hindu University (BHU) was not linked as such to the Arya Samaj movement, but it contributed more than any other institution toward promoting a sense of community among educated Hindus which is what the Arya Samaj was also after.

The creation of the Benares Hindu University in 1915 as a modern institution with a religiocultural agenda gave considerable strength to the self-image of the Hindi literati and its reading public. Efforts to create the BHU had started as early as 1905, and money had been collected over the years with the help of a large network of upper-caste, landed, and feudal interests which was spread over districts all over the United Provinces, the Central Provinces, and Bihar.[13] The location of the only "Hindu" university of the country in the heart of the Hindi region had obvious symbolic significance. It complemented the process whereby significant geographical symbols, such as the Ganga, the Himalayas, and the Vindhyachal, had been appropriated in literary writings to project a hegemonic destiny for the Hindi region. The BHU was a community project, not a gift of the administration as Allahabad was. It quickly became the mint where the modern cultural coinage of the north Indian plains was stamped and approved for circulation. To have been educated at Benares became symbolic of a new status, that of a "modern" Indian with a cultural consciousness which no other university could supposedly give. The name of BHU was supposed to wash away the associations of Macaulay and his legacy from one's education.

Together with Allahabad, Benares produced the overwhelming majority of literary writers and critics of Hindi, and a large number of the trained teachers who worked at schools all over the Hindi region—from Rajasthan to Bihar and southward in the Central Provinces. At BHU the codification of "worthwhile" knowledge of Hindi literature and language in the shape of syllabi, textbooks, and teacher education took place. M. S. Golwalkar, who later became the *sarsanghsachalak*—the "highest director"—of the RSS, was a student at BHU from 1924 to 1928 and was a teacher there from 1930 to 1933.[14]

Hindi Curriculum and Texts

Teaching Hindi at the college level and subsequently establishing Hindi departments in universities during the first quarter of this century were major factors in the success of the Hindi literati's cultural agenda. Syllabi and anthologies were required for the teaching of Hindi in colleges. Preparation of syllabi meant the systematization of available knowledge and its codification in a formal way. Once codified as a syllabus, the knowledge would gain legitimacy from the university's name and from the rigor and reputation of its examination. No one contributed more toward the codification of Hindi-related knowledge than Acharya Ramchandra Shukla, who started teaching Hindi at Benares Hindu University in 1919. A man of extraordinary talent and energy, Shukla shaped not only the format that the syllabi of Hindi in colleges continue to follow to a great extent to this day, he also defined the heritage of Hindi language and literature in a manner with which few have dared quarrel.

This he did in his famous *Hindi sahitya ka itihas* (History of Hindi literature), which was first published in 1929. It was a work of enormous and painstaking research, and it immediately gained a halo of authority in Hindi academic circles because no work of its caliber existed before it. Shukla went well beyond the territory of the literary historian and took a strong ideological position indicating the irrelevance of the Urdu-Persian tradition for the development of modern Hindi. He ignored major Urdu poets of the eighteenth and nineteenth centuries in his otherwise meticulous chronology. This was indeed a rather strange response of a prolific reader of literature to a genuine part of the Hindi tradition. Earlier in an autobiographical essay, Shukla had written that his father had a good knowledge of Persian and used to enjoy mixing lines of Persian poetry with the lines written by Hindi poets.[15] Ramchandra Shukla gave no sign, either in his history or in his other prolific works of literary criticism, of having taste or tolerance for this kind of mixture. By denying the literary works written in the mixed Hindi-Urdu tradition a valid place and status in Hindi's literary history, he performed a decisive, symbolic act that shaped the cultural identity of college-educated men and women for generations.

The identity Shukla gave to the Hindi heritage was a distinct Hindu identity. His appreciation of a Muslim poet like Jaisi, and his acknowledgment of the achievement of Premchand, who symbolized the confluence of Hindi and Urdu at a time when the two had traveled far apart, made little difference to this.

Ramchandra Shukla also edited a school textbook of Hindi for the higher primary grades.[16] Published in 1932, this textbook was the prescribed literary reading in vernacular schools of the United Provinces. At the time, the basic Hindi readers were composed in Hindustani, which was the mixed code of Hindi and Urdu. These readers were available in both Devnagri and Arabic scripts. Premchand mentions how both Hindi and Urdu supporters had started to complain that instruction in a mixed language gave no literary knowledge to the student.[17] Associates of Nagari Pracharini Sabha voiced the perspective of Hindi supporters, and the Anjuman Tarakkiye Urdu represented the supporters of Urdu. Men like Pandit Roopnarayan Tripathi and Pandit Sitaram Chaturvedi stood for the cause of Hindi in this campaign over primary-level textbooks, and Hasrat Mohani led the cause of Urdu.[18] In response to these complaints, the government prescribed a literary reader (in addition to the basic reader) for the higher primary grades.

The literary reader prescribed for Hindi was Ramchandra Shukla's *Hindi sahitya*. It exemplified the manner in which the process of text-creation for the school system contributed to the crystallization of the educated Hindi-speaker's identity. The portion of *Hindi sahitya* for grade three has twenty-four lessons, and the portion for grade four has twenty-three. In both sections, one-third of the lessons consist of literary materials that symbolize a Hindu configuration. The configuration consists of mythology and symbols derived from religious practices and from history, projecting a specific religiocultural identity. This identity is embedded in the manner in which the book recognizes its readership. In the lesson "Twelve Months," for example, the author says: "In the Pitrapaksha as Ashwin, *we* Hindus remember our ancestors." Vijayadahni reminds us, the lesson says, that "our country was also victorious once." The concept of "country" is obviously associated here with pre-Mughal times. This reference to a distant past as part of one's search for a happier, proud period in the life of the "mother country" *(matribhoomi)* is a prominent motif appearing in several different forms throughout the book. In the lesson on the "Kumbh Fair of Prayag," to take another example, the motif takes the form of nostalgia and longing. The lesson says that in older times the Kumbh was an occasion for assemblies of devout men and for the pursuit of physical and spiritual health by common men. That has changed: "Now we neither have true sages, nor do people have that kind of desire to acquire knowledge. All that is now left to do is to bathe at the Triveni for two or four days or a month, to have one's meals, and to go off home. Let us hope that when better days will again return to our country, the real face of the Kumbh fair will come back too."[19] The hope that India's mythologized past will return is elsewhere expressed in the form of a question, asking whether a woman like Sita will be born again in our country.

It is within this wistful mood of the book that we ought to interpret the recurring reference to India as a nation. The idea, or rather the vision, is of a community of people who have won the freedom to return to what they regard as their glorious, unsullied, precolonial past. The process of return involves the dissemination of knowledge about the religion and traditions of the community. It is clearly identified as a Hindu community.

The process of return to its bright past also involves the dissemination of Hindi. Though it is never labeled specifically as a language of the Hindus, the symbolic association in which it is placed in relation to the religion and the traditions of the community functions as such a label. The poem *Matribhoomi* (Motherland) sharply brings out this linkage: "One who has no thought for one's own language, nor has a knowledge of one's community [*jati*] and religion; who feels no pride for his country—such a person is dead even though he lives." In another poem, the "nation" is projected as a cluster of symbols including religion, cultural norms, language, and dress. Here, too, the reader is left in no doubt that the religion the poet is referring to is Hinduism.

Although Ramchandra Shukla was not in any way linked with the Arya Samaj movement, he grew up and worked in a milieu in which the ideas of Arya Samaj were rapidly gaining popularity. To what extent his reading of social messages in literature—which is often seen as his single contribution to literary criticism in Hindi—can be attributed to the milieu in which he lived is a matter of interpretation. But if we look at Shukla's textbook for children as an anthology of didactic writings, one can certainly see in it the tendency to imbue didacticism with a revivalist view of nationhood. The spread of Arya Samaj in Uttar Pradesh and later in the Central Provinces and Bihar made a substantial contribution to this tendency among the Hindi literati. Mahavir Prasad Dwivedi's painstaking efforts to set the norms of Hindi usage were matched by efforts to establish ethical norms, and in this latter effort the contribution of Arya Samaj was clearly visible in the early issues of *Saraswati*. In this period, writing literature with a sense of moral responsibility was also meant to be a departure from the Riti poetry of the post-Bhakti era in which poets had directed their literary repertoire and their feudal patron's attention to the marvels of the female body. The pathos of child marriage, widowhood, and dowry became a frequent motif of poetry in the Dwivedi era under the influence of Arya Samaj.[20] Motifs such as these were evoked within a specific view of history—a view of the Hindu society's moral decline under "foreign" influence over a thousand years.

The literature written during the first decades of the century with this kind of moral inspiration acquired a more specific educational function when Hindi was accepted in 1924 as an optional subject for the intermediate examination in the United Provinces.[21] Textbooks now became a major agency for the dissemination of the moral, revivalist consciousness of the Hindi literati. The form that the Hindi textbook inevitably took, following its counterpart in English, was that of an anthology of poems and essays. In the case of Hindi, textbooks provided an important outlet and motivation for the essay as a genre. The fact that the educational market was so important for writers of both prose and poetry accentuated the overtly didactic character of literary writing. In both prose and poetry, moralizing within a revivalist worldview became so entrenched in school textbooks that the powerful movement of romantic liberationism, Chhayavad, could make little impact on school learning when it swept the literary scene in the late twenties. The lyricism of the greatest Chhayavad names like Prasad and Nirala had failed to melt the reformist hearts of Mahavir Prasad Dwivedi and his influential contemporaries. Poetry and essays preaching a hundred lessons in moral behavior and featuring meticulous attention to grammar and the purity of diction remained the staple of textbook anthologies.

The Indian Press emerged as a near-monopoly house of textbooks in Hindi, matching the monopoly Macmillan enjoyed in English at this time. As the publisher of *Saraswati,* the Indian Press had access to a vast resource of literary writings suitable for textbooks. The dominance which this publishing house had over both the literary and the educational markets undoubtedly strengthened the linkage between the writings appropriate for the two markets. The association between literary and pedagogical writing became even stronger when the Indian Press started a monthly magazine for children called *Balsakha* in 1917. For nearly half a century, but particularly in the first forty years of its life, *Balsakha* provided to the educated, mostly urban parents of the Hindi region a rich resource for acculturation of their children. Brought out with great editorial and graphic care, it came month after month as a symbolic exhortation to view the growing, struggling nation as a child. Nationalist dreams and visions found in the metaphor of the child an expression that conveyed both innocence and design. Inevitably, these dreams were rooted in a Hindu configuration of collective memory. Hindi language and Hindu beliefs and ethics were warmly intertwined in this memory.

Influence of the RSS

From the 1930s onward, the region received further impetus to nurture a distinct Hindu vision of India's future from a source that lay to the south. This source was the Rashtriya Swayamsevak Sangh—a blossom of the vigorous seed of revivalist nationalism that Tilak had sown in western India. Gold has narrated the genesis of the RSS and examined its social ideology in an earlier volume, therefore, I present here only a brief outline of how the RSS was born and with what aims.[22] Its founder, Keshav Hedgewar, was a Maharashtrian Brahmin from Nagpur, the capital of the Central Provinces. Educated at an English-medium school, Hedgewar became a medical doctor but decided to spend his life serving the cause of India's freedom and reform. To pursue this cause he joined the Indian National Congress, but soon enough grew disenchanted with it, particularly with its ideology of nonviolent resistance as developed by Gandhi. The Hindu-Muslim rioting that followed the noncooperation movement waged by the Congress in the early 1920s provided the context for Hedgewar to develop his thesis and strategy, leading to the formation of the RSS in 1925. The RSS was to him an answer to the need for India's national revitalization. The answer lay essentially in the RSS's potential for becoming a force of Hindu unity and cohesion.

The main instrument used by the RSS to spread its ideology was to be the *shakha*—an open-area evening class for socializing male adolescents into a quasi-military brotherhood.[23] Three principles underlying the shakha program have been neatly listed by Golwalkar, the contemporary RSS leader who succeeded Hedgewar: (1) to reflect on the chosen ideal; (2) to keep regular company with those pursuing that ideal; and (3) to participate in activities consistent with the ideal. The ideal the RSS is committed to disseminating by means of the shakha is that of Hindu unity for building a strong Indian nation. Any afternoon or evening, youngsters of the RSS gather to listen to didactic stories and discourses, to play games designed to inculcate a sense of togetherness in a joint enterprise, and to exercise together—a maneuver centered around the skill of wielding a short wooden stick. Although the average shakha in a small town may not impressively represent it to an outsider, these activities—and the very raison d'être of the "school"—are grounded in the RSS philosophy of a militarily strong nation in which the terms "Indian" and "Hindu" are synonymous.[24] Indeed, the shakha has been designed to act as a slow, unobtrusive socializing agency with a long-term agenda that is always described today as cultural rather than political by the RSS leadership.

By the early 1930s, the RSS leadership had started to cast its aspiring glance at the Hindi areas of the Central Provinces and farther northward, at the Gangetic plains. The RSS leader Hedgewar was invited to Karachi by Bhai Parmanand, a prominent leader of the Arya Samaj, to attend the All-India Young Men's Hindu Association. This visit gave the RSS leadership its first opportunity to initiate RSS activities in areas where the Arya Samaj had found its lasting audience, namely, the Punjab and the United Provinces. RSS shakhas multiplied at a rapid rate in the Hindi region during the 1930s. A measure of its increasing influence can be found in the notification issued by the government in the Central Provinces prohibiting its employees, including teachers, from being involved in RSS activities.[25]

The attraction of the RSS ideology and its mode of functioning for teachers and students was considerable. Here was an articulate program that promised to inspire youth with a sense of values and idealism in pursuit of the dramatic objective of sparking Hindu resurgence. The atmosphere in the towns of the Central Provinces was conducive to the deepening of RSS influence. Marathi landowners and professionals committed to Tilak's notion of Swaraj had resisted Gandhi's followers in the twenties, and the English administrators were only too eager to keep nationalist loyalties divided. For Hindi-speaking Indian National Congress politicians to subdue their Marathi-speaking rivals, the practical route was to imitate the latter's aggressive stands in matters relating to religion, education, and language. Broad-mindedness in consideration of religiocultural matters was passé by the early forties, when nationalist consciousness expanded from its original narrow base. In literary and educational matters, the people of the Central Provinces resisted the inroads of Hindu revivalism less strenuously than had the people of Uttar Pradesh. The supremacy of the Congress before and after independence made no difference to this aspect of the political life of the Hindi region in central India. Here Congress leaders like Govindadas could freely propagate Hindi as the means of fulfilling India's cultural destiny and face even less questioning than Sampuranand or Tandon had to face in the United Provinces.

New Hindi, Old Hindi

The great dream of the U.P. literati to provide the future nation with an indigenous lingua franca thus became colored by an association between religious revivalism and language. The association cast its shadow on both the nature of Hindi and the identity consciousness for which it stood. The impact on Hindi was mainly through Sanskritization and sharp disassociation of the written from the spoken form. The process had already begun with the Persianization of Urdu. By the mid-nineteenth century there had emerged two "distinct" languages, and the two had begun to be associated with two "communities," namely, Hindus and Muslims. Nevertheless, until the end of the nineteenth century no eminent writer of Hindi had written in a style entirely devoid of Urdu mannerisms. Bhartendu's prose, both in his essays and plays, had the vibrancy of a spoken language. His syntax as well as his word choice showed a sense of freedom to utilize the Urdu tradition and scholarly acquaintance with its Persian heritage. Even his contemporary, Pratap Narain Mishra, who is accredited with the slogan "Hindi, Hindu, Hindustan," gave evidence of the same sense of freedom vis-à-vis the Urdu tradition.

This freedom, and the absence of prejudice toward Urdu that it implied, became inaccessible to the Hindi writer of the early twentieth century. The differentiation between Hindi and Urdu deepened as the two languages became increasingly associated with Hinduism and Islam, respectively. The attempt made by the Arya Samaj to use Hindi to develop the self-perception of a Hindu community in the urban, educated groups of Punjab and Uttar Pradesh made a signal contribution to the formation of the Hindi-Hindu association. Lajpat Rai noted in his autobiography that the most powerful influence on his character was the Urdu-Hindi movement. "This conflict taught me the first lesson of Hindu communality," he wrote.[26]

When Hindi was approved as a subject for the intermediate examination in the United Provinces in the late 1920s, it had already become a language different from the one Bhartendu had used. It had become the chosen vehicle of an upper-caste literati's self-image in a fast-changing national scene. A new register was developing, that of studied complexity in syntax and circumspect word-choice. This register was proposed as especially suitable for educational purposes, on the strength of the argument that educational or scholarly discourse by its nature requires a more complex register, that the language spoken by ordinary people cannot be used for serious dialogue. This argument was used as an answer to Gandhi's plea for the use of Hindustani—a mixture of Hindi and Urdu or, rather the old Hindi/Urdu. Hindustani was referred to as a language of the bazaar, which could hardly fulfill the requirements of a national language. Sampurnanand wrote, "In any country, the dialect of the village and the bazaar cannot be adequate for the needs of civilized society."[27] Support for Hindustani among the Hindi literati was scarce. Premchand was the only major writer who supported it.[28] The two powerful institutions working for the promotion of Hindi, namely, the Nagri Pracharini Sabha of Benares and Hindi Sahitya Sammelan of Allahabad, vigorously opposed Hindustani. Gandhi's plea for Hindustani proved a straw in the wind. In his autobiography Govindadas wrote that Gandhi's plea was a political one.[29] Of course it was. To challenge it, Hindi supporters used two grounds: (1) that Hindustani, as a spoken idiom of the common man, is inadequate for serious discourse, as in education and Parliament; and (2) that it cannot promote national integration as Sanskritized Hindi can, for traces of Sanskrit are found in all Indian languages.

Neither of the two arguments revealed the core "problem" of Hindustani and Urdu from the perspective of the supporters of Hindi. The problem never fully surfaced in the long debate on the national language question. This was nothing unusual, of course. Many problems remain buried in Indian political dialogue and are consistently denied by the very men who want these premises to become accepted by all. In the case of Hindustani, the hidden premise of Hindi supporters was that it was not purely Indian. They saw its Urdu legacy as a "foreign" element, in line with perceptions that became popular in the later part of the nineteenth century. Govindadas gives us a tiny glimpse of this hidden premise. Referring to the two groups, one representing English imperialism and the other representing Mughal imperialism, he says: "Due to the conspiracy of these two groups it was no easy matter to install a purely Indian language as India's state language."[30]

The struggle for Hindi, in a form from which its Urdu heritage was deodorized, became a means for the upper-caste groups, some of whom had substantial landed interests, to establish political identity. Once established, this identity was used from the late thirties onward to fulfill a hegemonic political agenda. This political use of Hindi accelerated its transformation from a spoken language to a narrow dialect of educational and political communication. This form of Hindi not only denied the Urdu heritage its share, but also closed itself off to the powerful spoken varieties of the region, including Awadhi, Bundeli, Chhatisgarhi, Bhojpuri, and the several tribal languages of central India. The "new" Hindi became the symbolic property of the college educated, and especially of those who had studied Hindi literature. Literary publications had to find their audience within this group. In a society where literacy was very narrowly spread, this meant a very restricted sphere indeed. The confinement of literate Hindi within this sphere meant the exacerbation of syntactical complexity and the Sanskritization of vocabulary. These tendencies, in turn, strengthened the reproductive role of education. Only children of upper-caste background could feel at home in a school culture where the language used was so restrictive.

Another implication of the Hindi taught at school had to do with the perception of Urdu and Muslims. Words of Urdu origin were labeled "foreign" in the classification taught as part of Hindi in secondary school classes. This labeling impelled the student to perceive the Muslim population as a "foreign" and separate group. The average student had, of course, no access to the aesthetic patterns associated with Islam, since the heritage he came to be acquainted with as part of his language education excluded the symbols of Islam and the literary patterns of Arabic-Persian traditions. The Muslim child, on the other hand, was unlikely to find any symbols of his home culture in the curriculum. His language, and the cultural patterns associated with it, were not recognized by the school. As a social institution, the school was unable to provide him with the feeling that he "belonged." To this aspect of the school's failure, the teacher made a vital contribution. Himself drawn from an upper caste, though with a low economic background, he received as part of his own education and training a social perspective consistent with the new Hindi of the urban, educated groups. A manual for Hindi teachers used in training colleges in the United and the Central Provinces since 1940 gives us ample evidence of this tendency. The first chapter of the book sets the tone by taking the position that "only Sanskritic Nagri can become the national language."[31]

After Independence

The shaping of modern Hindi under the influence of Hindu revivalist ideology constituted a major process in the emergence and spread of modern education in the Gangetic-Vindhya belt. The Sanskritization of Hindi described above was one salient feature of this process. After independence, the tendency toward Sanskritization received substantial impetus from the state. Hindu revivalist leaders were able to ensure this impetus by engineering a tactical victory for their cause in the Constituent Assembly which framed the Indian Constitution. The question facing the Assembly was essentially concerned with the task of replacing English with an Indian language. This question, however, assumed a more complex shape when a tussle arose between the supporters of Hindustani and those of Hindi. Influential Congress leaders like Nehru and Azad were advocating Hindustani as India's national language. Hindustani also had the blessing of Gandhi. On the other hand, prominent supporters of the Hindi movement, such as P. D. Tandon, Dr. Raghuvir, and Ravi Shankar Shukla, were also members of the Constituent Assembly.[32] They not only worked hard to mobilize support for Hindi within the Assembly but also waged a propaganda war against Hindustani and Urdu outside the Assembly, in the Congress party and in other cultural and literary organizations.

The partition of India made the task of Hindi stalwarts easier since it enabled them to freely associate Hindustani and Urdu with Muslims and Pakistan. Gandhi anticipated this strategy of the Hindi leaders when he wrote in his paper four days before the parirition: "During the crisis the Congress must stand firm like a rock. It dare not give way on the question of the lingua franca for India. It cannot be Persianized Urdu or Sanskritized Hindi. It must be a beautiful blend of the two simple forms written in either script."[33]

The supporters of Sanskritized Hindi were able to stage a crucial display of their influence in the Congress party while the language debate was on in the Constituent Assembly in 1949. In a vote that took place at a meeting of the Congress party, the supporters of Hindi won by seventy-eight votes against seventy-seven votes cast in favor of Hindustani.[34] In view of this precarious balance, a compromise was attempted and reached in the shape of a formula permitting an escape from the choice of a national language and providing for the term "official language of the Union." This status was given under article 343 of the Constitution, on "Hindi in Devanagari script." An attempt was made to record the importance of Hindustani in article 351, which dealt with the development of Hindi language. It said:

> It shall be the duty of the Union to promote the spread of the Hindi language, to develop it so that it may serve as a medium of expression for all the elements of the composite culture of India and to secure its enrichment by assimilating without interfering with its genius, the forms, style and expressions used in Hindustani and in the other languages of India specified in the Eighth Schedule, and by drawing, wherever necessary or desirable, for its vocabulary, primarily on Sanskrit and secondarily on other languages.

This masterly act of dispute settlement could not save Hindustani from disappearing from the affairs of state in the years following independence. As minister of education, Maulana Abul Kalam Azad was severely attacked by Tandon in the Parliament for attempting to provide state patronage for the development of Hindustani. On the other hand, the Board of Scientific Terminology, established in 1950 and later replaced by the Commission for Scientific and Technical Terminology, went about coining new terms for Hindu usage, overwhelmingly drawing on Sanskrit. Already by the end of the 1960s, some two hundred thousand terms had been prepared in this manner. In 1960 the government established the Central Hindi Directorate to supplement the work of the commission and also to coordinate the many different activities already underway for the development of Hindi. Also in 1960 the government established an institute in Agra to make pedagogical expertise available for training Hindi teachers.

Apart from this kind of institutional support, the Union government also provided funds for preparation and translation of textbooks, and for scholarship, libraries, standardization of Hindi shorthand, and improvement of the Hindi keyboard. Numerous voluntary organizations were able to benefit from state funds made available under the various programs to develop Hindi. The state-controlled radio, and later television, provided another powerful channel for promoting Sanskritized Hindi. The state's Hindi industry became a major agency of employment, including hiring Hindi ideologues in influential positions. But apart from providing a financial cushion for the cause of Hindi, the government's Hindi industry provided a means whereby the religiocultural agenda of the Hindi movement could be absorbed by the state apparatuses of formal education and broadcasting. The state's commitment to secularism was in no position to resist this process because the cause of Hindustani and its symbolic value had been successfully checkmated and because the bureaucratic and intellectual elite continued to be dependent on English. The elite's dependence on English implied that they remained somewhat indifferent to the growth and character of Hindi and were also insufficiently equipped to interfere in the buildup of etatiste Hindi.

Thus, having shaped Hindi in accordance with their ideology, the Hindu revivalists were able to develop a device uniquely suited for working within the secular state's apparatus. However, the specific revivalist organizations we have been studying were not dependent on this subtle instrument alone. The DAV organization suffered considerably due to the partition,[35] but stability and strength did not take more than a decade to achieve. The DAV movement already enjoyed great respect in Punjab and the region close to it. The new challenge lay in expanding from this base. A steady though slow pace of expansion was maintained during the 1960s and 1970s, but in the 1980s a sharp increase occurred in the number of DAV institutions throughout northern India. This recent progress has apparently been due to the organizational enthusiasm shown for the celebration of the centenary of the DAV movement. The DAV Managing Committee reported the opening of sixty-seven new schools in the centenary year, 1986.[36] A rapid pace of expansion has been maintained to this writing (1990). According to the latest available documents, there are over five hundred DAV institutions in the country, including colleges of teacher training, medicine, and engineering. A significant new category is that of "public" schools, the term denoting British public school ideals which have continued to enjoy popularity in India. The DAV Managing Committee's decision to go in for "public" school-type institutions represents an attempt to exploit the popularity of the "English-medium public school" label.

Although the DAV movement continues to be committed to the development of Hindi and preservation of Vedic ideals and knowledge, many DAV schools now flaunt their "English medium" character along with values and ideals of ancient India. The number of students in DAV "public" schools varies; in some of the bigger schools attendance runs as high as five thousand, but in most schools the number is about two thousand.

The clientele of DAV schools remains largely the children of small-scale businessmen and professional and salaried people who are economically below Westernized elites. The DAV schools present to these groups the opportunity to educate children in line with the syllabus and examination pattern of the state system but in an ethos featuring Vedic rituals and a yearning for the revival of India's ancient glory. This latter feature expresses a specific view of history in which the conquests of India by the Mughals and the English are seen as causes of India's cultural and moral decline. Special respect for warriors like Rana Pratap and Shivaji, both of whom fought the Mughals, is symbolic of the ideological themes embedded in this view of history. This ideological preoccupation with history aroused a major controversy over history schoolbooks during the Janata party government (1977–80), which has been investigated in detail by Rudolph and Rudolph, among others.[37]

Large pictures of medieval heroes such as the ones named above, and modern ones who symbolize Hindu revival, are commonly used in DAV schools to decorate assembly halls and corridors. In this regard, at least, it is difficut to distinguish a DAV school from a school affiliated with the RSS. In both DAV- and RSS-affiliated schools, the communication of a Hindu heritage serves an important role in constructing a relevant cultural ethos. The relevance of the ethos lies in the anti-Muslim messages which are consistent with the character of the Hindi language shaped by the forces of Hindu revivalism. Indeed, use of this Hindi in school rituals like the daily morning prayer and in other collective activities makes an important contribution to the ethos I have tried to characterize.

Organizing formal school education has become part of the RSS's activities relatively recently, but RSS members have been running private schools for a long time. Many RSS-affiliated schools in the Hindi states are now commonly known as Saraswati Mandirs (literally "Saraswati temples," Saraswati being the goddess of learning), although variations on this name also exist. The first Saraswati Shishu (meaning "little children") Mandir was started in Gorakhpur, Uttar Pradesh, in 1952, in the presence of Golwalkar, Purushottam Das Tandon (referred to earlier as a leader of the Hindi movement), and Hanuman Prasad Poddar, editor of a massively popular religious monthly.[38] The inaccessibility of accurate records prevents us from tracing the precise source of the growth of RSS-affiliated schools, but evidently the 1980s was a period of rapid growth of these schools too. In all there are about three thousand RSS-affiliated schools in the country at this writing, the highest number being in Uttar Pradesh.[39]

The term "RSS-affiliated" is mine and should not be taken as an indication of acknowledgment by the RSS that it is directly involved in any institutional network. On the contrary, the independence of networks (like the school network we are discussing) from the main body of the RSS is a salient part of RSS policy. The RSS-affiliated schools are run as part of a chain governed by a voluntary body registered under the Societies Act in each state. Some are run as purely private schools affiliated to the appropriate voluntary organization in each state. An All-India amalgamating body called Vidya Bharati was set up by the RSS leadership in 1977 to provide an organizational umbrella to these schools.[40] The need for such an umbrella body was undoubtedly triggered by the State of Emergency imposed by Mrs. Indira Gandhi in 1975 under which the RSS was banned. The end of the Emergency and the defeat of

Mrs. Gandhi in 1977 brought the Janata party into power. The Hindu revivalist party Jana Sangh, which had strong links to the RSS, was part of the Janata coalition. The Jana Sangh's presence in the governing coalition boosted the sphere of RSS's educational (and other) activities, including the establishment of Vidya Bharati to better coordinate these activities. A grand display of the popularity of the Saraswati schools was staged in November 1978, in a rally of children brought to Delhi from several states under the auspices of Vidya Bharati. Since then, the RSS-affiliated schools have flourished in the Hindi states. Their progress was not affected by the end of Janata rule in 1980.

These schools attract not only the children of urban and small-town shopkeepers, which is probably their core clientele, but also those of professional and government-servant families, as is the case of DAV schools. Like the DAV schools, the Saraswati Mandirs also follow the curriculum and textbooks prescribed by the government. Only in areas of study that are peripheral to the core curriculum, such as physical education, music, and cultural heritage, has the Vidya Bharati worked out its own curriculum. The RSS ideology is conveyed to the children studying in Saraswati schools primarily through co-curricular activities and publications, including children's magazines.[41] The morning assembly is used for this purpose. Children are taught to sing prayers and songs steeped in religious devotion and the spirit of patriotism addressed to the concept of the Hindu nation defined in RSS ideology. Assemblies and stage performances organized on Hindu festivals are another example of ideologically relevant activities. The virtual absence of non-Hindu children in these schools adds to the collective sense of a distinct self-identity, which these activities evoke in a Saraswati school.

Arousing a collective sense of Hindu identity may be seen as the underlying philosophy of education in these schools. A commentator from within the Vidya Bharati establishment explains this philosophy by saying: "dedication to the motherland with a deep Bharatiya spirit inculcates in the child the will to change his character [and] adjust his nature and programme so as to fulfill the nation's will and necessity."[42]

The aim of education in both the DAV schools and the Saraswati Shishu Mandirs is customarily explained as "character building." Even though it is a very broad and common term, it nevertheless evokes the philosophies propagated by social reformers and leaders of the nineteenth-century renaissance and the freedom struggle. Prominent among these leaders are Vivekanand, Sri Aurobindo, and Tilak. Along with several other illustrious men, these leaders thought that building "strength of character" was the major responsibility of the patriotic educators. I have argued elsewhere[43] that the diagnosis of India's problems implied in this prescription was itself a reflection of the colonial image of Indians as people with a weak morality. The emphasis that the public schools of England placed on building character was readily assimilated by the nationalist discourse on education that developed in India as part of the freedom struggle. There were only two prominent exceptions to this trend, Gandhi and Tagore, both of whom propagated a modernist vision of education. In Gandhi's case, the vision was centered around the idea of productive activity; in Tagore's, the child's autonomy was the central issue. Understandably revivalist movements had no use for such ideas. Gandhi and Tagore represented a "liberal" course in politics and culture which conflicted with the strategies of revivalist organizations. The revivalists built an agenda of mobilizing people around symbols of a mythologized Hindu past. As we have seen, a major political aim of this process in the Gangetic-Vindhya region was to establish the hegemony of a provincial upper-caste elite on the national scene.

The adversary was the Westernized elite, living mainly in the metropolitan areas and larger towns, and possessing a tight hold over key apparatuses of the state. Despite having its roots in the colonial era, this Westernized elite succeeded in asserting its legitimacy as a ruling class of independent India, but it had neither the means nor perhaps the strong urge to consolidate its legitimacy by nurturing relevant symbols of India's incipient nationhood. Language was a key area in which the elite's weakness as a ruling class was sharply expressed. The elite were content not only to use English as the medium of daily communications, but also to run the affairs of state and educate their children in English. English medium schools guaranteed mastery of written and spoken English. They also socialized their clientele to attach status to poor command of one's mother tongue and almost certain ignorance of its literature. In the world in which members of the elite strata chose to live their professional as well as personal lives, development of Hindi as a national language was only a tactical, and not a real, necessity. Hindi was a deity to which they paid homage as it symbolized India's free status in the community of nations, but for which they had little affection or use.

As this study shows, Hindu revivalist organizations had grasped the political potential of Hindi worship well before independence. After independence, they continued to use Hindi as a major ingredient in their politics of religious and cultural separatism, while resolutely denying that their aim of cultural revival had anything to do with politics. This kind of denial had little value given the existence of Jana Sangh and its dependence on RSS and the Arya Samaj for the supply of activists. Since the beginning of the 1980s, with the increased prominence of the Hindu revivalists on the political scene and the awareness that many Hindu activists had been trained in the RSS and Arya Samaj schools, the denial lost what little relevance or tactical value it might have had earlier. Revivalism came into the visible arena of competition for power at this point.

The rise of fundamentalist forces in other countries certainly helped revivalists in India gain popular sanction in the 1980s. Islamic fundamentalism in Pakistan and the Middle East made a definite impression on Indian Muslim leaders, and this in turn further strengthened the morale of Hindu revivalists. The penetration of revivalist ideology into a political organization like the Indian National Congress, which has always professed secularism, had been deepening gradually all along, as had the penetration of revivalism into professional and salaried urban groups. Eventually, by the 1980s, however, differential points of emphasis and the finer distinctions of dominant themes within the revivalist ideology had either disappeared or become irrelevant. This happened because the Hindu revivalist force was no longer confined to the active followers of the Arya Samaj, the RSS, and the BJP (Bharatiya Janata Party, formerly the Jana Sangh), but had now become disseminated throughout the general population of northern India.

Hindu revivalism has now found a voice that seems remarkably well organized and, in the perception of the Westernized elite, rather frightening. The elite are alarmed and have proved willing to compromise on many fronts. The prolonged serialization during the latter half of the 1980s of the epic Ramayana on government-controlled television was one mark of such compromise. True, the Ramayana (and also the Mahabharata, which was serialized afterward) is an essential part of India's national heritage, but the manner in which it was scripted and visually presented left little doubt about its being used to evoke nostalgia for a mythologized Hindu past.

What gave this telecast a distinct political significance, however, was the parallel buildup of a movement aimed at reclaiming Ram's alleged birth place from a mosque at Ayodhya. This Ramjanmabhoomi movement has been the biggest symbolic drama staged in India since Gandhi's salt *satyagraha*. The contrast between the narrow communal ends of the Ramjanmabhoomi movement and the secular message of the salt satyagraha is a measure of the pressure liberalism in India has had to bear over the last sixty years.

To return to the religiously inspired telecasting of the Ramayana, such signals of the elite's readiness to bend toward the popular world of revivalist ideology raises the question, "How far would the elite be willing to compromise before it barters away its secular identity which is linked to its legitimacy as a ruling group?" The politics of revivalism has recently entered an advanced round of its struggle for power, symbolized by the significant gains made by the BJP in the last parliamentary elections and by the intensifying of the Ramjanmabhoomi movement. Meanwhile, champions of secular values have also gained political ground among the poor and oppressed sections of north Indian society. How much better they will fare than did the Westernized elite in taming the forces of revivalism is one of the crucial questions to be answered in the coming years.

Hindu Revivalist Education in the 1990s

In November of 1990 the Janata Dal government fell when the BJP, unhappy with the treatment of Ramjanmabhoomi activists, withdrew its support. The fall of the Janata Dal government led to a fluid political situation which in turn necessitated a parliamentary election (along with assembly elections in some states) in the summer of 1991. While the 1991 parliamentary election failed to yield a majority government, the Congress (I) party improved its position and formed a minority government which continues, at this writing, to face pressure by its opponents—especially the BJP—to compromise on a variety of issues. The BJP radically improved its own position in the 1991 election and emerged as the ruling party in Uttar Pradesh, the seat of the Ramajanmabhoomi movement.

Increasingly the social climate in India favors Hindu revivalism. In 1991 a ground-swell of communal emotions reached a high point unprecedented in electoral politics. The BJP electoral gains, based in part on its connection with the Ramajanmabhoomi movement, occured in this context. However, many observers of Indian politics believe that this was the apex of BJP influence. Secular political groups have shown strength in at least one significant corner of the Hindi heartland, namely Bihar, the state where the Janata Dal continues to rule with a following largely among "backward" peasant groups.

Nonetheless the BJP continues to pursue its hegemonic agenda in educational and cultural spheres with the help of the RSS, as well as a variety of quasi-cultural organizations and fellowships composed primarily of unemployed or self-employed youth. In October 1991 Vidya Bharati, the umbrella organization for RSS-affiliated schools, held a major conference to discuss future educational strategies. One of these strategies was the proposed expansion of the Vidya Bharati network to the extent of establishing a school in every development block in the country. Programs such as para-military training of RSS activists were also outlined.

In 1992 the Vidya Bharati prepared a new set of history textbooks which are expected to replace the text currently used in the four BJP-governed states in northern India. The controversy over the writing of history texts for school children, a major point of ideological conflict between Hindu revivalists and secular-minded intellectuals, erupted again in the wake of the BJP's involvement in the preparation of the Vidya Bharati textbooks. The Congress (I) Party's Ministry of Human Resource Development established a committee of secular historians to write a history of post-Independence India. Representation of the past has been a major concern, as well as a strategy of mobilization, of the Hindu revivalist camp. One focus of this concern is the treatment of the medieval period, when Mughal monarchs ruled large parts of India. The revivalists depict the Mughals as foreigners and oppressors, and interpret India's achievement of freedom from English rule as but the latest episode in a long, ongoing struggle to free India from foreign influences. Muslims are, by this interpretation, the contemporary incarnation of the Mughal pattern of dominance.

Hindu revivalists do not belittle the Independence struggle in public, but they do suggest that the Hindu genius has not yet been fully liberated in India. The glorification of ancient heroes and intellectuals in the media promotes this kind of rhetoric and gives a sense of direction and purpose to RSS-BJP educational and cultural enterprises. In 1991, for example, the BJP's campaigned vigorously for the extension of a Sunday morning television serial depicting the life of the famous Indian political philosopher, Chanakya (also known as Kautilya). The serial portrays Chanakya's struggle to assist Chandra Gupta Maurya in ancient India in a way to suggest its similarities to the struggle waged by the BJP today. Another television serial, on the life of Lord Krishna (who has already figured extensively in the long "Mahabharata" serial), will undoubtedly raise questions and anxieties similar to those raised by "Chanakya." In all such media controversies, the bureaucrats of the government's professional media establishment inevitably come into conflict with the politicians of the ruling Congress (I) party. In such a conflict the formally educated professional or civil servants have been more amenable to the persuasive pressures of the revivalist ideology than the politician who has his own ideology to defend.

The gains made by the BJP in the 1991 election suggest to some observers that India is headed toward a Hindu revivalist hegemony. Such a prediction overlooks the importance of India's regional diversity and political tensions. Hindu revivalism has remained a northern phenomenon despite the concerted efforts to expand it and the favorable political and social circumstances in some areas. Over recent years, gains made by the RSS-BJP in certain parts of the south have not been particularly impressive.

Whether or not the RSS-BJP gains greater prominence in the years ahead, one must acknowledge that the impact of Hindu revivalism on education in India has been significant. As this study shows, the impressive rise of Hindu revivalism in the Hindi region is the outcome of a specific historical experience—the sustained attempt by a provincial literati to gain a competitive advantage over an entrenched, geographically scattered, Westernized elite. From all signs in this last decade of the century, one may anticipate that the ideology of Hindu revivalism will at the very least compel secular and democratic forces to find credible and legitimate leadership among the Indian masses.

Notes

1. See Romila Thapar, "Syndicated Moksha?" *Seminar* 113 (September 1985).

2. H. L. Erdman, *The Swatantra Party and Indian Conservatism* (Cambridge: Cambridge University Press, 1967).

3. For details of Allahabad's development, see C. A. Bailey, *The Local Roots of Indian Politics: Allahabad, 1880–1920* (Oxford: Clarendon Press, 1975).

4. For a detailed study of *Saraswati*, see Ram Vilas Sharma, *Mahavir Prasad Dwivedi aur Hindi Navjagran* (Delhi: Rajkamal, 1977).

5. Cf. Amrit Rai, *A House Divided* (Delhi: Oxford University Press, 1984).

6. See Daniel Gold, "Organized Hinduisms: From Vedic Truth to Hindu Nation," in Martin E. Marty and R. Scott Appleby, *Fundamentalisms Observed* (Chicago: University of Chicago Press, 1991).

7. Cf. J. T. F. Jordens, *Dayanand Saraswati: His Life and Ideas* (New Delhi: Oxford University Press, 1978).

8. Cf. Sudhakar Pande, *Shyamsunderdas* (New Delhi: Sahitya Academy, 1978).

9. Satyaketu Vidyalankar, "Dayanand Anglo-Vedic School" (in Hindi), in *DAV Centenary Souvenir* (Delhi: 1987), pp.

10. Lala Hansraj, *Mahatma Hansraj Granthavali*, vol. 4 (Delhi: Govindram Hasanand, 1986).

11. Madhu Kishwar, "Arya Samaj and Women's Education," *Economic and Political Weekly* 21, no. 17 (1986): WS 9–24.

12. M. R. Jambunathan, ed., *Swami Shraddhanand* (Bombay: Bharatiya Vidya Bhawan, 1961), p. 138.

13. Cf. S. L. Dar, *History of the Benares Hindu University* (Benares: Benares Hindu University Press, 1968).

14. *Organizer,* 26 February 1978.

15. See the essay "Premdhan ki chhaya-

smriti," in Ramachandra Shukla, *Chinta-mani-3* (New Delhi: Rajkamal, 1983).

16. Ramachandra Shukla, *Hindi sahitya* (Lucknow: Hindustani Book Depot, 1932).

17. Cf. Premchand, *Sahitya ka uddeshya* (Allahabad: Hans Prakashan, 1967).

18. This information is based on a letter, dated 22.May.1988, I received from Pandit Sitaram Chaturvedi.

19. Shukla, *Hindi sahitya,* pp. 65–66.

20. Cf. Kshemchandra Suman, *Hindi sahityaa Ko Arya Samaj Ki Den* (Delhi: Madhur Prakashan, 1970); and idem, Bhaktram Sharma, *Dwivedi Yugin Kavya Par Arya Samaj Ka Prahbav* (Delhi: Vani, 1973).

21. M. L. Bharghava, *History of Education in U.P.* (Lucknow: Supdt. Printing and Stationery, 1958).

22. This discussion is based mainly on Walter Andersen and Sridhar Damle, *The Brotherhood in Saffron* (New Delhi: Sage, 1987).

23. For an insider's view, see Dina Nath Mishra, *RSS: Myth and Reality* (New Delhi: Vikas, 1980).

24. Savarkar, whose influence on the RSS's founder, Hedgewar, has been well recognized, defined "Hindu" as a person who feels united by blood ties with all who trace their ancestry to "Hindu antiquity" and who accept India as their fatherhood and holy land. See Anderson and Damle, *Brotherhood in Saffron,* p. 34.

25. See D. E. U. Baker, *Changing Political Leadership in an Indian Province* (New Delhi: Oxford University Press, 1979).

26. Lala Lajpat Rai, *Punjab Kesari Swarqiya Lala Lajput Rai Ji Ki Atmakatha* (Lahore: Rajpal, 1915), p. 144.

27. Sampurnananda, *Kuchh Smritiyan Aur Kuchh Sfhut Vichar* (Kashi: Gyanmandal, 1962), p. 135.

28. See Premchand's article, "Urdu Hindi aur Hindustani," in *Sahitya ka uddeshya.*

29. Seth Govindadas, *Atma-Nirikshana-III* (Delhi: Bharatiya Sahitya Mandir, 1958).

30. Ibid., p. 147.

31. Acharya Pandit Sitaram Chaturvedi, *Bhasha Ki Shiksha,* 7th ed. (1940; Varanasi: Hindi Sahitya Kutir, 1962), p. 18.

32. For details, see Granville Austin, *The Indian Constitution* (Bombay: Oxford University Press, 1966).

33. *Harijan,* 10 August 1946.

34. See Jyotirindra Das Gupta, *Language Conflict and National Development* (Berkeley: University of California Press, 1970).

35. "March of DAV Movement," *Aryan Heritage,* June 1989.

36. "DAV Movement in the Service of Education since 1886" (Pamphlet issued by the DAV Managing Committee).

37. L. I. Rudolph and S. H. Rudolph, "Rethinking Secularism: Genesis and Implications of the Textbook Controversy, 1977–79," *Pacific Affairs* 56, no. 1, (1983): 15–37.

38. See *Organizer,* 12 November 1978.

39. Based on the pamphlet "Vidya Bharati Akhil Bharatiya Shiksha Sansthan" (n.d.).

40. "Vidya Bharati," *Organizer,* 12 November 1978.

41. See, for example, *Devputra.*

42. S. P. Gulati, "Shishu Mandirs and the Concept of Developed Child," *Organizer,* 12 November 1978.

43. Krishna Kumar, *The Political Agenda of Education* (New Delhi: Sage, 1991).

_____ EPILOGUE _____

Fundamentalism and the World of the 1990s

William H. McNeill

Readers of *Fundamentalisms and Society* and its companion volume, *Fundamentalisms and the State*, may well wonder whether the essays deal with a general phenomenon of the contemporary world that runs across cultural, religious, and ethnic lines or whether each religious group dealt with in the separate chapters is unique unto itself. Our use of a single term "fundamentalism" to describe them all obviously implies some sort of commonality. Yet the meaning of this originally Protestant term alters drastically when applied to Jewish, Muslim, Hindu, or Buddhist movements and groups; even within the Christian community it is often difficult to say who is and who is not a fundamentalist. On the surface of things, surely, different heritages operating in different circumstances reduce the common denominator among all the groups described in these pages to little more than high emotional commitment to a program for reform which draws its inspiration from religious faith rather than from secular this-worldly hopes.

This perhaps only proves that the editors chose carefully what to write about so as to assure a minimal level of commonality. In and of itself this scarcely will convince skeptics that these groups have enough in common to be called by a single name and accorded serious attention. I propose, therefore, to look for other commonalities in hope of showing that the editors and authors of these two volumes are indeed addressing themselves to an important dimension of contemporary affairs.

One obvious common feature that emerges from the essays is not really surprising, for despite the different contexts in which they operate, religiously inspired programs for reform of family life and education are a good deal more precise and practically significant than are programs for political, and especially for economic, change. After all, it is easier for fellow believers to alter personal and private life and to agree upon their own distinctive educational programs than to overcome the evils of society as a whole. Reformation of politics and economics requires the faithful to convert or sup-

558

press unbelievers and halfhearted fellow travelers. Hence, even when religiously inspired reformers come to power, efforts to make over society are sure to dilute or distort their initial vision of a world made new. Recent developments in Iran simply conform to the numerous historic examples of the compromises that successful revolutionaries always have to make, regardless of how emphatically they seek holiness or some other, more secular goal.

Other commonalities are less obvious, reflecting social changes that in and of themselves have no particular religious dimension. But before I come to them, it seems well to ask whether the movements dealt with in these pages are in any sense unusual or simply constitute a normal part of the cacophony that arises from the diversity of civilized societies. Assuredly, religiously inspired reform has been around for a long time. Ever since the dawn of prophecy during the first millennium before the Christian era, urbanized societies have accommodated reformers who cast their reproaches against existing conditions in religious terms. The Hebrew prophets were especially influential, since their utterances and examples had profound impact on the subsequent history of Judaism, Christianity, and Islam. But the Persian Zoroaster, together with Gautama Buddha in India, resembled the Hebrew prophets in the magnitude of their influence on later generations, and in their roles as religious critics and reformers of the society around them. Ultimately, the diverse groups dealt with in these volumes all hark back to one or another of these prototypes. They are thus contemporary exemplars of a tradition of religious protest—voices crying in the (often urban) wilderness—that descends unbroken from these founding figures.

If so, what importance should we accord them? Is the level of discontent in our world on the increase? Do we live in an age when religiously inspired reformation is becoming more likely? Or is the disenchantment with existing conditions, which these movements express, normal and to be expected? Unfortunately, there is no good way to measure the levels of discontent that prevailed in times past. Hence historical comparisons with today's occurrences become merely impressionistic. Let me try nonetheless.

As a prolegomenon it may be useful to remind ourselves of how important religiously inspired reform movements have been in civilized history. The Reformation of the sixteenth century is an obvious instance that springs to mind for those raised in the Christian tradition; in fact many of the characteristics of contemporary Protestant fundamentalism in the United States stem directly from the biblical emphasis and moral energy that characterized the radical fringe of that movement. But Christendom experienced a multiplicity of reformations both before and after Luther, and it is probably correct to claim that reform movements have had a continuous, tumultuous history ever since about 50 C.E., when Peter disagreed with Paul at a conference in Jerusalem over whether Christians should observe Jewish law.

Muhammad's revelation was itself a reformation of Jewish and Christian teaching. And, just like Christians, Muslims have subsequently experienced multiple reformations, including one that was almost contemporary with Luther's and divided the realm of Islam into mutually hostile factions by bringing Shi'a reformers to power in Iran in 1499. Khomeini's revolution of 1979 harked back to that reformation a good deal more consciously than contemporary American fundamentalists do to the Anabaptists of the 1520s and 1530s. The Ottoman Empire experienced another, rather less successful, reformation after 1656, when Kiuprili viziers unleashed dervish-led popular piety in the streets of Istanbul as part of their effort to repel Christian attack. The declining success Muslim rulers had in repelling Christian armies after 1699 provoked many other local reform efforts, some of which attained political power, as the Mahdi did in the Sudan (1885), while others were violently repressed, as happened to the Wahhabis in Arabia (1818).

A long series of reform movements shaped modern Judaism as well, beginning with the Old Testament prophets and continuing to the present. For European Jews, the eighteenth century was more significant than the sixteenth, for it was then that the Enlightenment ideal of assimilation into European society was born (primarily in Germany), only to be countered by a resurgence of Hasidic piety in Poland.

Buddhists have a reformist past too, though efforts to use state power to enforce doctrinal uniformity—taken for granted by Christians and Muslims through most of their history—have been less common in Buddhist lands. But Buddhist reform movements did sometimes collide with political authorities. This happened to the followers of Nichiren Daishonin (d. 1281) in Japan, for example, and in Tibet a monastic reform movement, sometimes referred to as the "Yellow Church" from the color of the hats the monks wore, actually seized power in 1642 and established the Dalai Lamas as rulers of the country until 1949.

With the self-styled Enlightenment of the eighteenth century it became fashionable among many European and American intellectuals to suppose that traditional religions were about to fade away along with all the other errors to which the human mind was susceptible. Optimists expected that practical betterment through the application of reason to the problems of human society would, eventually, erase injustice and suffering, thus bringing Heaven to earth in a fashion analogous to the way Newton's mathematical reasoning, by discovering the laws of motion and universal gravitation, had united earth and the heavenly bodies into a single world system. But even at the time when faith in rational, earthly progress peaked—say, about the time of the Great Exhibition in London (1851)—it is easy to find evidence of the continued vitality of religious commitment in the most prosperous European countries; in less favored places, religiously expressed reform and revolutionary movements flourished just as they do today.

The Taiping Rebellion in China (1850–64) was by far the most massive and violent revolutionary movement, combining, as it did, elements of Christian and Buddhist doctrine with old-fashioned peasant revolt. Among Muslims, Wahhabi reform was advancing by mid-century in spite (or perhaps even because) of its military defeat in 1818, and so were other, sometimes openly heretical movements like the Bahai of Persia. Among Christians, Adventist and Mormon churches were beginning to flourish in the United States, and an enormous variety of other sects, together with missionary orders and social reformers who drew their inspiration from more established churches, deeply affected all parts of the European world as well as Europe's colonial possessions overseas.

I conclude that since about 700 B.C.E., in urban and civilized societies, where inequitable social relations were always present to offend tender consciences, energetic groups of reformers have persistently and perpetually sought to remake the world along juster, religiously sanctioned lines. If so, it is obvious that the movements considered in this book are not unusual and may not signify any notable departure from the normal confusion and controversy of civilized existence.

Yet there are considerations that point in another direction. The basic reason for supposing that religiously inspired reform movements may be gaining momentum in our time is that perceptions of inequity in human affairs—and the tangible realities that provoke those perceptions—are on the increase. Population growth on the one hand and new forms of communication on the other brought disruption to local use and wont on a massive scale, creating personal uncertainty, isolation, and disappointment more often than not. Resulting distress can and often does find expression in fundamentalist movements that counteract uncertainty by emphatic affirmation of eternal truths, and counteract isolation and disappointment by forming supportive communities of fellow believers. All of the groups discussed in the pages of the companion volumes conform to this pattern, although some, like Mormon polygamists and Jewish haredi, have a lengthy sectarian history behind them and recruit members primarily by educating their children to conform to inherited prescriptions for holiness, while others, like the Pentecostalists of Guatemala, have sprung up very recently and continue to recruit their numbers from society at large.

Obviously, a sect of long standing that does not recruit many members from outside its own ranks is not really trying to transform the society around it. Polygamous Mormons, therefore, are not likely to matter much for the rest of the United States, though in Israel the quirks of electoral politics do allow religious sectarians to make and break governments because parliamentary representation of the two main parties is so nearly deadlocked. But this sort of influence is adventitious and irksome rather than indicative of far-ranging social transformation. The movements that matter, as auguries of change that may or may not be enduring, are those that recruit from society at large and spread because they answer, or seem to answer, newly felt human needs. The Pentecostalists of Guatemala fit that pattern; so perhaps do the politicized Buddhist monks of Ceylon, Burma and Thailand, the Shi'a of Iran and neighboring Arab countries, and the Sikhs and Hindu militants of India.[1]

It is no accident that these movements are all based in countries where population pressure on the land is making continuation of old village ways impossible for a majority of the population, and where urban-based mass communications, by penetrating the villages, have begun to erode an age-old framework of peasant life. If that framework actually does dissolve, not merely in Central America, Southeast Asia, the Middle East and India, but throughout the globe, our age will turn out to be truly revolutionary. Peasants who depend mainly on what they can produce themselves and enter the market only marginally still, in the 1990s, probably constitute a majority of the human race. In proportion as they really do begin to participate more fully in urban-based exchanges of ideas, goods, and services—as seems possible and even probable—profound new strains will be felt in the fabric of civilized societies everywhere.

To see the breakup of peasant society in proportion one must understand that civilization was originally based on harsh exploitation of rural cultivators, who paid rents and taxes in return for what was at best an imperfect protection against rival human predators. Across the centuries of recorded history, urban-based artisans and peddlers slowly reached out toward the rural majority, offering iron tools and other useful articles in return for food and raw materials. But since taxes and rents removed almost all available surpluses from the villages, market exchanges remained marginal and peasants continued to depend for most essentials of their everyday life on what they could produce by their own efforts within walking distance of where they lived.

This urban-rural regime failed to establish itself in English-speaking colonies of North America, though a more drastically polarized society, in which black slaves took the place of European peasants, prevailed in some of them. Americans prefer to remember frontier-generated rural equality, and for that reason we are not acutely conscious of the worldwide prevalence of rural-urban inequity. But peasant society broke up in western Europe only within the past two hundred years or so, and peasant life endured in eastern Europe well into the twentieth century. Ironically, under the banner of Marxism, the old regime in Russia mutated into a bureaucratized, statist exploitation of the peasantry after 1917, and the resulting communist system spread to China after 1949 where it still prevails. Elsewhere, as the twentieth century draws to a close, straightforward, old-fashioned urban exploitation of the countryside through unrequited rents and land taxes is breaking down. But even where landlords have been dispossessed (or never existed), more often than not bureaucratic ways of exploiting the rural majority have been substituted, favoring urban dwellers through price controls on food and excise on things the rural folk have to buy.[2]

One class of fundamentalist movements dealt with in these volumes derives its energy and importance from the acute discontents felt by peasants and ex-peasants. Ex-peasants, who have migrated to town seeking a better life than is possible in over-crowded villages, are particularly vulnerable and volatile. Deprived of (or emancipated from) traditional village contexts, they have to construct a new moral and social life for themselves in city slums. Mere survival in their new urban environment requires regular participation in market exchanges and frequent dealings with strangers. Rampant selfishness and ruthless disregard for traditional ties with others may flourish under such circumstances. An alternative response is to strive to invent new social contexts within which mutuality and justice of the old-fashioned sort may still prevail. This is where religious groups come into play, for they affirm truth, morality, and justice amid the corruptions of an urbanized world, bring like-minded people together so they may support one another, and may even aspire to punish unrighteousness and reform society as a whole.

When village ways alter, making room for more persistent immersion in urban-based exchanges, the same need to remodel norms of behavior reaches out into the countryside as well. But economic change is not necessarily decisive. Thanks to the penetrating capability of modern mass communications, ideas and information commonly outstrip economic transformation. Hence, even when village routines of work remain what they were, radio and television can sow discontent in the countryside by making peasants acutely aware of the gap between themselves and privileged urban dwellers. In such circumstances, reaffirmation of eternal truths and religiously inspired programs of reform compete and blend with Marxism among discontented villagers, though the mere fact that they live dispersed in relatively small communities means that established governments are unlikely to pay much attention unless or until discontent becomes armed and insurrectionary.

Urban protest is, by comparison, far more effective since governments operate from cities and an angry crowd surging around official buildings cannot easily be overlooked. In this sense modern communications have not altered the age-old advantage that urban dwellers have against their rural contemporaries. To be noticed by constituted authorities, rural discontent has to reach a higher threshold than is true for urban distress. And whenever the interests of urban crowds and of the rural peasantry diverge, as regularly happens when governments try to set prices for foodstuffs, one may expect governments to favor the urban crowd. That is why bureaucratic exploitation of the peasantry has become so widespread in the twentieth century, often displacing landlords' rents completely.

The elemental fact that a majority of humankind on the face of the earth today is properly described as peasant and ex-peasant means that their responses to the harsh conditions of life they confront are sure to remain of capital importance. Insofar as their distresses find religious expression, fundamentalist movements like that in Guatemala will continue to flourish throughout the foreseeable future. Frustration and suffering will not diminish as long as population continues to grow, for in many parts of the world excessive rural numbers are making established patterns of village life unworkable. Once all available land has been brought into use, wherever families of more than two children prevail, the rising generation finds itself unable to replicate the lives of their parents simply because there is not enough land. The resulting dilemma is only intensified by the fact that radio, television, and other new forms of communication, having exhibited urban wealth and ease before the astonished eyes of remote villagers, make innumerable rural youths loathe to accept their parents' style of life even when they can do so. In this way the pull of urban wealth and comfort and the push of land shortage and rural immigration point in the same direction, impelling vast numbers of young people to migrate into cities, where their overwhelming number and low level of skill guarantee continued hardship and disappointment.

In these circumstances, it is hard to doubt that fundamentalist movements will continue to command heartfelt response among millions and perhaps billions of persons who desperately need to find new forms of community because the customary routines of traditional village life have suffered such drastic disruption.

These pages also describe another, quite different sort of fundamentalism, rooted not in rural poverty and frustration or in the slums of Third World cities, but in the comparative ease and luxury of professional and urban life in the United States. Instead of embarking on the pursuit of happiness by trying to satisfy individual and personal desires, as most Americans are (more or less) content to do, these people yearn after firm rules for leading a good life, and find them in the words of preachers who derive their teaching from the Bible.

Knowing what is right and how to behave is, indeed, critical for all human society. A tissue of expectation and prescription woven by those around them nurtures children from infancy, and when such nurturing succeeds, adults acquire a workable repertory of responses to all expected, ordinary situations. What a person says or does is then understood by others nearly as was intended, and in turn elicits more or less expected responses. But in modern urban environments, the process of nurturing, whereby common understandings pass from generation to generation and spread throughout society, appears to be in serious jeopardy. Existing apart from a firm network of shared expectations means that an isolated, private life is liable to lose its meaning and savor. Individualized pursuit of happiness, restrained only by public laws that prohibit some behavior but do not prescribe what ought to be done, may leave the individual lonely and unsatisfied, even when outward material wants have been abundantly satisfied. This, I think, is what leads comparatively affluent Americans to join fundamentalist churches, where they can enjoy the fellowship of other believers and find fresh meaning for their lives by conforming to clearly defined expectations of those around them.

How widespread the need for more meaningful and prescribed modes of life may be in cities of the United States is hard to tell. And how the affluent (and so far almost entirely American) style of fundamentalism may interact with the fundamentalisms of the peasants and ex-peasants of the Third World is even more obscure. But the future importance of fundamentalism for the world as a whole seems likely to depend on these two factors.

In reflecting on how the two forms of fundamentalism may interact in time to come, it is worth reminding ourselves that all of the world's higher religions took shape and flourished in the context of urban anomie and only subsequently penetrated the countryside and established roots among the peasantries of the earth. Judaism became preponderantly urban after the destruction of the Temple in 70 C.E. and the first Christians were recruited from the urban populations of the Roman Empire. Buddhism likewise flourished initially in Indian cities, and spread with trade and urbanism throughout eastern and southeastern Asia. Islam, the last born of the world's important faiths, was based in the cities of Mecca and Medina from the start; its spread into Africa and central Asia was closely associated with the spread of trade and urbanism, just as earlier Buddhist expansion had been.[3]

Synagogue, church, mosque, and temple all made the anonymity and uncertainty of urban living more nearly bearable by creating a supportive community of like-minded persons within which individual private lives could attain (or maintain) meaning and value. By also promising redress of injustices in a future life, the suffering and inequities of everyday became more bearable as well. The effect was to make urban, civilized forms of society far more stable than could otherwise have been the case. The alliance of throne and altar that became traditional in all civilized societies reflected this elemental fact.

Beginning mainly in the eighteenth century, impatient reformers in Europe repudiated this traditional arrangement and assailed organized religion on the ground that it had become the principal bulwark of superstition and injustice. Liberals in the eighteenth century and socialists in the nineteenth century were mostly of this persuasion. As long as the old order of society encapsulated islands of urban privilege in a predominantly peasant sea, urban-based reformers could continue to attack ecclesiastical institutions and religious superstition with a clear conscience, believing that faith in the secular recipes for reform that they embraced could and should replace religious doctrine as a basis for social justice and equity.

But secular and anticlerical reform remained a minority faith, even when, as in France in 1791 and in Russia in 1917, advocates of such doctrines took power. Subsequent efforts to propagate the Cult of Reason in France and Marxist atheism in Russia failed to establish deep roots in popular consciousness. Meanwhile, in Europe and the rest of the world, religious responses remained important among the majority of persons affected by the necessity of actual adjustment to urban living. Multiform movements of religious revival in the nineteenth and twentieth centuries attest to this fact, and the piecemeal, practical reforms of the sort English and American liberals often adduce as proof of the superiority of democratic government drew much of their popular support from persons inspired by one or another form of religious commitment. Assuredly, from the abolition of slavery to the civil rights movement of the 1960s, practical efforts to reform American society drew inspiration from religious sources. Indeed it seems plausible to suggest that only when secular-minded reformers activated a background of religious support have they attained a clear majority for important legal changes in the United States. Those who explicitly reject organized religion and traditional faiths remain a minority. Even where outward signs of piety have decayed drastically, as is the case in western Europe, indifference and uncertainty rather than a definite commitment to secularism seems to prevail; for many unchurched persons, ideas and attitudes about social justice and political rights continue to be colored by their Christian heritage, even when they are unaware of it.

If, then, the appeal of secular, rationalistic doctrines is limited mainly to privileged and relatively comfortable persons, it seems safe to predict that among the majority of humankind, secularism will never rival the attractions of suitably remodeled forms of old-fashioned religion. A basic reason for this state of affairs is that even in affluent communities, most persons do face hardship and disappointment of one sort or another in the course of their lives and then need comfort and support of a kind that cold reason and individualistic pursuit of happiness cannot provide, while among the hundreds of millions of peasants and ex-peasants, whose inherited rural ways of life have become impractical or unacceptable, hardship and disappointment are and will remain the norm, at least for the immediate future. Their need for comfort and support is correspondingly acute and ever present.

Formulas for economic development, which constitute the U.S. government's official answer to Third World problems, simply do not address the felt needs of Third World peoples. Arguments about the advantages of free markets and exhortations to enrich oneself by shrewd exploitation of market opportunities ring hollow for nearly all who are caught in the toils of Third World urbanization. They need stronger medicine for body and soul, a practical substitute for the village solidarity and moral community which their parents both enjoyed and chafed at. Religious groups are best able to respond to such needs and seem likely to multiply accordingly.

The fact is that amending inequities, or what are perceived as inequities by newcomers to urban living, is far more difficult than secularly minded optimists once assumed. First of all, there is no short-run automatic balance between human numbers and remunerative jobs. Moreover, in urban contexts where a great variety of occupations and statuses exist in close proximity, there is no obviously just way to distribute income among different individuals and groups. The market, variously modulated by governmental regulations, may be the most efficient way to distribute income and allocate goods and services over the long run, but in the short run its operation is profoundly repugnant to almost all peasants and ex-peasants.

The reason is simple: from the point of view of subsistence cultivators, persons who buy cheap and sell dear are hard-hearted cheaters. To be sure, as economists never tire of pointing out, the increased wealth that efficient production and exchange may bring constitutes a powerful counter-attraction, but only over the long run. In 1776, Adam Smith explored and praised the implausible synergy of private selfishness and public advantage that a market economy could establish. But the increase in wealth that Adam Smith anatomized came only after centuries of exposure to market behavior had transformed British society profoundly. Popular tolerance of market relationships, and of inequalities between rich and poor that were generated by market exchanges, took centuries to establish in Great Britain—centuries during which merchants and bankers, initially Jews and then Italians, had operated in defiance of public opinion but protected by the monarchy, which drew a significant part of its income from them.

Obviously, it took a long time for public attitudes and daily habits to adjust to market relationships in Britain and in other west European countries. It is not surprising, therefore, that wherever subsistence agriculture was the norm of life within living memory, potential advantages of a market economy remain merely speculative and entirely imperceptible to millions and hundreds of millions of peasants and ex-peasants. They only see wicked middlemen growing rich at the expense of honest, hardworking people like themselves.

In a world where the wicked prosper while the upright suffer hardship and deprivation, even successful programs of economic development do little to assuage a popular sense of outrage at the injustices of the world. Half a century ago, Marxist and fascist revolutionaries seemed to have persuasive remedies that agreed in scornfully repudiating both liberal and religious ideas and ideals. But first fascists (after 1945) and then Marxists (after 1985) suffered demoralizing failure, leaving a rather limp and individualistic liberalism to compete with various and discrepant religious revivalisms at the task of improving human society and making it more nearly conform to popular hopes and expectations.

What distinguishes the current situation, therefore, is that all the modern secular faiths—liberal, communist, and fascist—that once claimed to have relegated religious worldviews and programs of social betterment to the dust bin of history are in disarray. This may turn out to be only a passing situation, but it is hard to imagine what would reverse the tide in any near future. Communist demoralization in Russia and eastern Europe is nearly total; the Marxist faith survives somewhat precariously among a governing gerontocracy in China and Vietnam and, perhaps, in Cuba. Oddly, both the most vigorous capitalist growth of the past fifty years and the surviving bastions of communism are rooted in societies where the Confucian heritage is very strong. Perhaps acquiescence in state management of economic relations and an uninhibited pursuit of private (read familial) advantage in the market place are both compatible with Confucianism. But in all the parts of the world where religious heritages feature the prophetic denunciation of worldly injustice, the contemporary collapse of secular communism, together with the inability of liberal individualism to supply a satisfactory guide for leading a good life to newly urbanized populations, certainly looks like an enormous strategic opening for religious reformation.

Yet it is still too soon to tell. Only in Iran have fundamentalists actually come to power. Most of the groups described in these pages are oppositionists, vigorous in criticizing things as they are in the wicked world, and far enough from the actual exercise of political power to be able to embrace extreme, unyielding positions without taking any account of differing points of view. Before such groups can leave sectarianism behind and become major contenders for the political direction of contemporary societies, far-reaching adjustments are sure to become necessary; it is not obvious which if any of them will in fact be willing to make such a transition.

The basic requirement for fundamentalists to come to power among the human majority is simple in principle and awkward in practice. What the peasants and ex-peasants of the world need is vivacious membership in local communities that are, nonetheless, fully compatible with effective participation in worldwide urban exchange nets. Peasant village communities existed until very recently with only marginal participation in those exchange nets. Rural folk maintained their moral community by distinguishing sharply between themselves and outsiders, treating fellow members of the village differently from the way they behaved toward others. But city environments require drastic modifications. In particular, learning to live by buying and selling goods and services makes it necessary to treat friends and neighbors as though they were strangers. Even for those who remain behind in the countryside, maximizing income by shrewd buying and selling requires betrayal of long-standing patterns of reciprocity among village families.

Effective adaptation to market behavior therefore weakens community ties and, especially in its initial stages, rewards the unjust and immoral while penalizing those who hold fast to older duties and obligations. Yet truly moral behavior, that is, backing away from the market and refusing to abandon tried and true methods of local subsistence agriculture, is plainly impossible when more young persons come of age than can find access to sufficient land for their support.

This is the bitter dilemma hundreds of millions of rural folk confront in Asia and Latin America, and soon will face in much of Africa as well. What is needed, surely, are new moral rules and a shared sense of community that does not inhibit the widening exchange of goods and services and eventual realization of the material benefits that economic development eventually may bring. But, as I pointed out above, the first, intuitive response of peasants and ex-peasants to their immersion in commercial networks is to feel cheated by those with whom they must deal. Anger and bewilderment result. In particular, poor peasants and ex-peasants abhor the injustice of allowing wholesale merchants to reap relatively enormous profits without doing any real work, whereas their own labors in the fields or in urban workshops produce only a meager and precarious living.

Marxist doctrines of class war fed on this indignation and may do so in the future, despite the recent discrediting of actual communist regimes. On the other hand, the prophetic tradition from the time of Amos has also been emphatic in denouncing the rich who profit from the sufferings of the poor. Religious fundamentalists seeking to preserve and revive community among the poor and dispossessed can obviously seize upon this strand in their religious heritage, and indeed practical success among the billions of suffering folk requires nothing less.

But religious fundamentalists differ from their Marxist rivals inasmuch as they expect God to right the wrongs they suffer from, either in an afterlife or by some sudden intervention in this world. As a result, the prophetic tradition in all of its major variants does not endorse any particular institutional recipe for the righting of wrong between rich and poor. Moral reformation of individuals and private, personal recognition of the duty of alms giving are about as far as the religious tradition goes in prescribing how human action should seek to improve society. The vague programs for economic and political reformation voiced by the groups described in these volumes reflect the lack of clearly defined scriptural authority for definite programs of social change, whether in the Christian, Muslim, or Buddhist tradition.

On the one hand, this defect may be regarded as a weakness. That was the way scornful Marxists and impatient liberals looked on old-fashioned religion in the recent past. Why rely on individuals and private moral reformation when it was social institutions and property rights that were at fault? But twentieth-century efforts to transform social institutions and to abolish or modify property rights so as to guarantee everyone the material basis for a good life have fallen far short of expectations. All too obviously, bureaucratic schemes for distribution and redistribution of goods have either created or been unable to prevent acute social ills. This casts considerable doubt on both liberal and communist programs for the reform of society. Perhaps, therefore, the slower, individualized, and from-the-bottom-up approach of religious reformation is preferable. Perhaps moral communities of fellow believers are necessary for social well-being. Perhaps only when such moral communities have come to terms with the dictates of market behavior can humanity at large expect to reap more fully the advantages of specialization and productive efficiency that economists so plausibly portray as the rational goal of economic development.

If so, the fundamentalists of the United States may well be in a strategic position to export their version of Christian teaching and economic individualism to the peasants and ex-peasants of Latin America and other parts of the earth. Something like this may already be happening in Guatemala, where missionary effort from the United States helped trigger the recent multiplication of Protestant churches. There and in other countries of Latin America the new-sprung evangelical churches are noticeably less hospitable to notions of class war than is the case among radical Roman Catholics. Protestant notions of individual morality, individual success in an exchange economy, and individual salvation are more or less mutually supportive. Combine such ideas with a vivacious congregational life, and Pentecostalists and others like them have what they need to survive in a difficult urbanizing world—that is, an emotionally supportive community which is fully compatible with effective participation in a market economy.

As is well known, Protestantism played a comparable role in early modern Europe. Despite recurrent yearnings for a truly righteous community and some influential efforts to build a community totally obedient to God and in accord with Scripture, mainline Protestant churches in fact reconciled themselves to preaching individualized morality. Eventually, they not only refrained from reprobating profitable buying and selling, as a populist strand in Roman Catholicism continued to do, but actually praised it. This accorded with the fact that Protestantism and capitalism tended to flourish together. Moreover, when new segments of the European population found it necessary to abandon old-fashioned subsistence agriculture and started to sell their labor instead, emotionally vibrant, sectarian versions of Protestantism often arose in response. The rise and spread of Methodism in Great Britain is the most obvious and important instance of this phenomenon, but Pietists in Holland and Germany played a similar role on the Continent until overtaken in the late nineteenth century by the rise of Marxism.

Perhaps, then, what is happening in Latin America today continues on new ground a process of religious adaptation to the breakdown of peasant life and the immersion of ex-peasants in urban, commercialized society that goes back to the Reformation of the sixteenth century. But in lands where Muslim, Buddhist, or Confucian heritages prevail, it seems unlikely that specifically Protestant Christian forms of religious fundamentalism can thrive. Instead their fundamentalisms seem far more closely aligned with nationalism and with popular reaction against what are felt to be foreign cultural and religious traditions.

This is especially clear among Muslims. More than anything else, reaffirmation of Islam, whatever its specific sectarian form, means the repudiation of European and American influence upon local society, politics, and morals. In Sri Lanka, the Buddhist monks who have become active in politics oppose Hindu Tamils instead, but their emphasis on solidarity against an outsider is otherwise similar. Energetic definition and propagation of a native identity may also be detected in Burma and Thailand, where religious revival, state building, nation building, and dislike of foreigners go hand in hand. No doubt the same may be said of Sikhs in India, of Lamaistic Buddhists in Tibet, and, mayhap, of Shintoists in Japan.

Development of a vivacious sense of national, ethnic identity is, in fact, another form of adaptation to the breakdown of village autonomy and local self-sufficiency. Instead of simply distinguishing fellow villagers from every kind of stranger, nationalists broaden fellowship to embrace a much larger population. This invites rural and urban, rich and poor to pursue common goals and cultivate a sense of commonality, despite the tensions attendant on the penetration of commercial relations into a countryside of peasants. And insofar as nationalism succeeds in establishing a sense of commonality up and down the social scale and among comparatively large populations, it also facilitates the continuing commercialization of everyday human relationships.

Perhaps for this reason, nationalism is the only secular faith of modern times whose appeal to Third World peoples is undiminished. Where liberalism and communism have faltered, it still rides high, even though in western Europe (and perhaps also in the United States) the vibrancy of attachment to the nation-state has noticeably dimmed since World War II. Painful experience of our century has made Europeans and Americans very much aware of the economic costs of national autarky and the political risks of war. But where populations are still emerging from rural isolation, the practical advantages of sharing in a nation-wide identity and the self-interest of governing officialdom coincide, thus sustaining rather vigorous assertions of nationhood.

National solidarity, of course, thrives on having an enemy, either within or outside state boundaries. How the enemy is identified and how the boundaries of the nation are drawn to include some and exclude others are always arbitrary, at least to begin with and before national institutions have had time to reshape popular consciousness. But the two most readily available markers of "us" as against "them," when once one leaves the limits of a primary face-to-face village community behind, are either a common language or a common religion. When linguistic and religious demarcations coincide, as is the case in Sri Lanka where Sinhalese Buddhists and Hindu Tamils confront one another, religious reformation (or merest affirmation) swiftly merges into political nationalism, and, in a crowded landscape, what begins as competition for land and for posts in government can escalate into bitter ethnic conflict and even civil war.

Rival religious and linguistic nationalisms, disputing the same ground, can be locally disastrous, as the history of Northern Ireland illustrates, and as recent events in Sri Lanka portend. More important for the world as a whole, however, is what will happen among Muslims whose religious heritage emphasizes the all-embracing community of the faithful despite sectarian differences and the enormous multiplicity of peoples who have become Muslim across the centuries. Islamic universalism obviously runs counter to local, territorial nationalisms. At the same time, sectarian identities interfere with the national homogeneity of existing states, save in rare instances, like Iran, where in the sixteenth century fanatical adherents of one version of Shi'ism seized power and enforced religious conformity as fiercely and effectively as the Hapsburgs were doing simultaneously in Spain.

Nationalism and religious reaffirmation therefore do not fit smoothly together within the realm of Islam. Religious fervor, however, separates Muslims from unbelievers and armors them against the overt influence of infidels—Christian, Jewish, or other. At the same time, new modes of mass communication have been used to propagate traditional religious doctrines in Iran and some other Muslim lands. Merely by bridging the age-old gap between town and country, the new mass communications are bound to affect social reality in far-reaching ways.

One possibility is that Muslim governments may be able to shepherd their peasant populations from rural isolation and subsistence living toward active participation in urban-based exchanges simply by reaffirming Qur'anic rules of personal conduct and public behavior and without trying to erase existing sectarian diversity. Islam was always urban and recognized buying and selling as fully compatible with a virtuous life. After all, Muhammad himself was a merchant before he became a prophet, thus legitimating bazaar trading beyond all cavil. Meticulous obedience to the precepts of Islam is difficult to reconcile with rural routines but fits smoothly into an urban existence. Accordingly, conscientious conformity to traditional religious rules can indeed provide newcomers to city life with a workable guide to personal and public behavior. Traditional Islam, therefore, enjoys full viability in an urbanizing, commercializing world; by pitting true believers against the rest of the world, some of the stresses associated with survival in urban contexts can, perhaps, be relieved by focusing hostile impulses against outsiders.

But solidarity that results in concentrating hostility upon outsiders is very dangerous in a world where weapons of mass annihilation make war far more destructive than before. And when fear and hatred clothe themselves in specifically religious dress, compromise and accommodation with infidels become especially difficult. The risk of catastrophic violence increases accordingly. This is the situation today between Jews and Arabs within Israel and across its borders; the American confrontation with Iraq has some of the same overtones, despite the secular character of both the American and Iraqi regimes.

Zionism and Islamic fundamentalism are simply irreconcilable. Some Jewish fundamentalists, however, adhere to principles that allowed peaceful coexistence of Jews and Muslims for many centuries, and it is not impossible that cities of the future will accommodate diverse ethnic and religious communities, living side by side but nonetheless separate, in much the same way that cities of the Islamic world traditionally have done. The reason for thinking this may occur is that unusual rates of demographic growth in the Third World since World War II have begun to coexist with incipient population decay in the rich countries of Europe and other industrialized lands, while modern communications and transport make migration across political and cultural boundaries easier than before.

Such circumstances have already brought millions of Muslims to western Europe and millions of Latinos to the United States. Merger of these newcomers into local society is fraught with difficulties. Differences of culture and of outward appearance tend to coincide; moreover, modern communications allow the newcomers to maintain regular connections with their homeland. Assimilation to the dominant nationality means abandonment of old ways and social connections, and this is always difficult. Simultaneously, host populations find it hard to accept newcomers who look and behave differently from themselves. Religious differences widen the gap. And because mosques and churches regularly induct children into the tenets of the faith, they allow the indefinite survival of separate collective identities even among groups living in the same place and exchanging goods and services on a daily basis.

Throughout their history, the great cities of Asia and eastern Europe adapted to this sort of permanent polyethnicity by allowing a series of religiously defined communities to exist side by side. Wherever Islamic governments prevailed, the Sacred law expressly enjoined toleration of Jews and Christians—People of the Book—on condition that they recognize Muslim political supremacy by paying taxes. But since Islamic law was only for Muslims, other religious communities had wide discretion in managing their own affairs. Even when local political authorities exacted taxes mercilessly, they relied on Jewish and Christian authorities—often clergy, sometimes merchants—to act as their agents. Chinese and Indian cities also accorded extensive autonomy to enclaves of foreigners as a matter of course; so did the medieval cities of western Europe as long as long-distance trade and large-scale financial transactions concentrated in foreign hands.

Because cities are places where strangers meet and trade with one another, complete ethnic and religious uniformity is inconceivable. The high level of ethnic uniformity that modern European nations took for granted was very unusual. It depended on the fact that the modern growth of European cities coincided with systematic population growth in their immediate hinterlands. Cities of western Europe therefore recruited immigrants from populations that shared a more or less common language and other traits with those preponderant among citizens. Assimilation to a common national norm was a feasible ideal under such circumstances, and modern European nations were, accordingly, created through educational and other administrative (mainly military) arrangements between the sixteenth and nineteenth centuries. When, however, cities recruit from afar and across cultural lines, as is now coming to be the case in all the richest countries of the world (except Japan), assimilation to a common norm becomes impractical. In such urban milieux, therefore, religiously defined communities seem very likely to become increasingly important, just as they were in olden times throughout Asia and eastern Europe.

This would surely bring Third World churches, mosques, and temples into the urban and industrial slums of Europe and the United States. In addition, religious syncretism can be expected to flourish, perhaps combining motifs from the American style of middle-class fundamentalism with traits imported from countries of origin. So far, there seems little evidence of fruitful interaction between the United States styles of evangelical piety and the religious life of poor immigrants to our cities. If it should develop, a connection between the needs of the ex-peasant world and the (mainly American) middle-class recipe for religious transcendence of urban anomie might have incalculable consequences for the long-range future. Only so could some sort of commonality between the life of the rich and prosperous in America and Europe and the struggling poor of Third World countries find effective institutional expression. Only so could nationalistic and other group hostilities be minimized. Only so, perhaps, could a worldwide exchange economy maximize wealth for humanity as a whole.

In closing it is wise to say again that, at this writing, the various fundamentalist groups described in the chapters of *Fundamentalisms and Society* and *Fundamentalisms and the State* remain marginal to their respective societies and, with the exception of Iran, only play sectarian, oppositionist roles. The mere fact that the majority of human beings are in social situations that make membership in religious communities attractive does not mean that any of these movements will actually be able to appeal to the hundreds of millions of souls in need of help and comfort. Nor does it mean that angry, secular ideologies may not overtake overtly religious programs of action. Moreover, religion itself may become angry and make group conflicts more irreconcilable than they would be otherwise. But in the long run, allowing for all the mistakes and retrograde currents that can prevail for a generation or more until their costs become unbearable, it seems reasonable to suggest that urban civilized existence, dependent on continual transactions with strangers, can only flourish when acting within a matrix of religiously defined local communities that give individual lives meaning and guidance, while also minimizing friction with outsiders, even, or especially, with those living immediately at hand.

If so, the importance of contemporary fundamentalist movements is considerable, for the seedbeds of future religious communities that might stabilize worldwide urban society can only emerge from their ranks. That, it seems to me, is the historic importance of these groups. The radical instability that prevails worldwide, as the human majority emerges painfully from rural isolation and struggles to accommodate itself to the dictates of an exchange economy, gives religious fundamentalists an extraordinary opportunity to channel mass responses either into an angry assault on aliens and infidels or toward peaceable symbiosis with strangers. Both paths are sure to be tried; which will work best and prevail in the long run is, perhaps, the capital question for the twenty-first century.

Notes

1. See Charles F. Keyes, "Buddhist Economics and Buddhist Fundamentalism in Burma and Thailand;" Said A. Arjomand, "Shi'ite Jurisprudence and Constitution-Making in the Islamic Republic of Iran;" and Robert Frykenberg, "The Impact of Hindu Fundamentalism," in Martin E. Marty and R. Scott Appleby, eds., *Fundamentalisms and the State: Remaking Politics, Economies, and Militance* (Chicago: University of Chicago Press, 1992).

2. Africa stands apart, for there landlords are seldom significant, and existing states are of recent origin and have correspondingly weak tax systems for extracting resources from the countryside. Nonetheless, rapid population growth and the communications revolution are putting strain on traditional modes of rural life in Africa, too, thanks to environmental degradation as well as to new-found forms for urban exploitation of the rural majority.

3. Hinduism is a partial exception, for it incorporated many rural elements into its mature form. Still, the organized cults of Shiva and Vishnu that dominate contemporary Hinduism probably took form in urban settings and continue to flourish in city and village alike.

CONTRIBUTORS

Shahla Haeri is a research fellow at the American Institute of Pakistan Studies in Lahore, Pakistan. An anthropologist who has taught at New York University, she has been a fellow at the Center for Middle Eastern Studies, Harvard University. Dr. Haeri is the author of *Law and Desire: Temporary Marriage in Shi'i Iran.*

Helen Hardacre is a historian of Japanese religions at Harvard University. She has also taught at Princeton University and Griffith University in Brisbane, Australia. Professor Hardacre is the author of *Shinto and the State, 1868–1988* and *Kurozumikyo and the New Religions.*

Krishna Kumar is professor of education at Delhi University, Delhi, India. He is the author of *The Social Character of Learning* and *The Political Agenda of Education: A Study of Colonialist and Nationalist Ideas.*

Jorge E. Maldonado is executive secretary for the Family Education Office of the World Council of Churches, Geneva, Switzerland. An ordained minister with the Evangelical Church of Ecuador, he is a sociologist and family therapist who has written numerous articles on family life in Latin America, as well as several textbooks for the training of family counselors.

William H. McNeill is the Robert A. Millikan Distinguished Service Professor of History, emeritus, at the University of Chicago. In 1964 he received the National Book Award for *The Rise of the West: A History of the Human Community.* His many other published works include *The Pursuit of Power: Technology, Armed Force, and Society since A.D. 1000* and *Mythistory and Other Essays.*

Everett Mendelsohn is professor of the history of science at Harvard University. He is the author or editor of a number of works, including *A Compassionate Peace: A Future for Israel, Palestine, and the Middle East* and *Science, Technology, and the Military.* Professor Mendelsohn is a fellow of the American Academy of Arts and Sciences.

James Moore is lecturer in history of science and technology at the Open University, Milton Keynes, England. His latest book, written with Adrian Desmond, is a comprehensive biography of Charles Darwin. He is also the author of *The Post-Darwinian Controversies*. Professor Moore is a member of the British Society for the History of Science and of the Conference on Faith and History.

D. Michael Quinn is a historian who has taught at Brigham Young University and served as a fellow of the National Endowment for the Humanities. He is currently a Dorothy Collins Brown fellow at the Huntington Library. Dr. Quinn is the author of *Early Mormonism and the Magic World View* and *The New Mormon History*.

Farhang Rajaee is an assistant professor of politics doing research on intellectual thought in Islam, particularly within the Iranian context. He is the author of *Islamic Values and Worldview*. Professor Rajaee lives in Iran and is an academic member of the Cultural Studies and Research Institute.

Susan Rose is associate professor of sociology at Dickinson College. She is the author of numerous works on the sociology of education, including *Keeping Them out of the Hands of Satan: Evangelical Schooling in America*.

Michael Rosenak is Mandel Professor of Jewish Education at the Hebrew University of Jerusalem. He is the author of *Commandments and Concerns: Jewish Religious Education in Secular Society* and *Teaching Jewish Values: A Conceptual Guide*.

Andrea B. Rugh is an anthropologist at the Institute of International Development at Harvard University and is currently doing research in Peshawar, Pakistan. She is the author of *Family in Contemporary Egypt* and *Reveal and Conceal: Dress in Contemporary Egypt*.

Quentin Schultze is professor of communication arts and sciences at Calvin College. He is the author of *Televangelism and American Culture: The Business of Popular Religion*, co-author of *Dancing in the Dark: Youth, Popular Culture, and the Electronic Media*, and editor of *American Evangelicals and the Mass Media*.

Majid Tehranian is professor of communication and director of the Spark M. Matsunaga Institute for Peace at the University of Hawaii. He has been a fellow at the Center for Middle Eastern Studies, Harvard University. Professor Tehranian is the author of *Technologies of Power: Information Machines and Democratic Prospects* and *Restructuring for Ethnic Peace*.

Bassam Tibi is professor of international relations at Georg-August University of Göttingen, Germany and has been a research associate at Harvard University since 1988. He has published many articles and books in English, German, and Arabic. Among Professor Tibi's books in English are *Arab Nationalism: A Critical Inquiry* and *Islam and the Cultural Accommodation of Social Change*.